An H. P. Lovecraft Encyclopedia

Howard P. Lovecraft, First Vice President U. A. P. A.

An H. P. Lovecraft Encyclopedia

S. T. Joshi and David E. Schultz

Hippocampus Press

New York

Published by Hippocampus Press
P.O. Box 641, New York, NY 10156.
http://www.hippocampuspress.com

Cover illustration by Gaile Ivaska.
Cover production by Barbara Briggs Silbert.
Hippocampus Press logo designed by Anastasia Damianakos.

First Paperback Edition
1 3 5 7 9 8 6 4 2

ISBN 0-9748789-1-X

To Dirk W. Mosig,

pioneer and friend

Contents

Preface   ix

Chronology   xiii

Abbreviations and Short Titles   xix

The Encyclopedia   1

General Bibliography   309

Index   313

Preface

During the past three decades, scholarly work on H. P. Lovecraft (1890–1937) has expanded exponentially in every phase of research. Building upon the early efforts of George T. Wetzel, Matthew H. Onderdonk, and Fritz Leiber, such scholars as Kenneth W. Faig, Jr., and R. Alain Everts revolutionized the understanding of Lovecraft's life, while Dirk W. Mosig, Donald R. Burleson, and many others examined his tales, poems, essays, and letters with perspicuity and precision. It was inevitable that these endeavors—resulting in numerous capable general studies of Lovecraft,[1] the first comprehensive Lovecraft bibliography,[2] the foundation of the journal *Lovecraft Studies* as a forum for scholarly research, the preparation of textually accurate editions of Lovecraft's stories, and, as a culmination, the publication of an exhaustive biography and an equally exhaustive collection of memoirs of Lovecraft[3]—would result in a marked rise in Lovecraft's literary recognition as a writer, thinker, and man of letters.

And yet, much of this research is scattered heterogeneously in small-press or academic publications, many out of print and inaccessible. It is in the hope that a gathering of widely dispersed information on Lovecraft will engender even more penetrating scholarship and also provide Lovecraft's many devotees with the tools for a more informed appreciation of his work that the present volume has been assembled.

In a compilation of this kind, the chief focus must be upon Lovecraft's literary work. For every such item, we have supplied (1) the word count; (2) the date of writing, as well as can be ascertained; and information on (3) its first publication; (4) its first appearance in a volume by Lovecraft; and (5) its appearance in textually corrected or annotated editions. Lovecraft is best known for his tales of horror and the supernatural; accordingly, the compilers have provided detailed plot synopses of every fictional work—stories, sketches, collaborative works, "revisions" or ghostwritten tales—written by Lovecraft from the age of seven until his death. Only brief critical commentary is supplied, since we feel it is not our place to enforce our own judgments or evaluations upon readers. Instead, we have devoted our commentary to relatively concrete matters: the literary or biographical sources for the tales, as frequently noted by Lovecraft himself in letters or other documents; relations between a given tale and others written earlier or later; particular features of a tale that require elucidation. At the end of every entry, we supply citations to books or articles (arranged chronologically) discussing the work in question. For books, only the year of publication is cited except in the case of small-press items, where we also supply the publisher. It should be noted that many general studies of Lovecraft treat individual tales, sometimes in considerable detail. The reader is referred to the bibliography at the end of the volume for such studies.

Other bodies of Lovecraft's work—essays, poetry, and letters—must perforce be treated less comprehensively than his fiction. Not all essays or poems have received separate entries, but only those that are of particular significance and have engendered discussion by scholars. As every poem by Lovecraft is now included in the recently published edition of *The Ancient Track: Complete Poetical Works* (2001), we have not cited this volume in any of the entries on Lovecraft's poems.

The entries on fictional characters in Lovecraft's tales are quite brief, since the story synopses provide a better means for discussing their actions and functions. Lovecraft deliberately downplayed the role of human characters in his tales. His "cosmic" perspective saw the human race as a tiny and insignificant element within the infinities of space and time; late in life he actually wrote, "the only 'heroes' I can write about are *phenomena*" (*SL* 5.19). This approach, however, produces difficulty in a reference volume of this kind, since the roles of many characters are quite minimal. Nevertheless, we have attempted to supply brief entries on these figures, with the exception of real individuals (e.g., Albert Einstein) mentioned in the stories. (This itself causes some difficulty with such a work as *The Case of Charles Dexter Ward,* a historical novel that utilizes real figures from history performing manifestly fictitious actions. None of these characters has been listed.) In some cases, members of a family are presented in a single omnibus entry, and their names appear in boldface. Life dates for a character are supplied whenever this information appears in the story. Many of Lovecraft's characters (including the first-person narrators of several important tales) are unnamed. Since their roles are often quite important and thus warrant discussion, we address them under the entry "Narrators, Unidentified," where they are grouped alphabetically by story title. Invented species (e.g., the fungi from Yuggoth in "The Whisperer in Darkness" or the multitude of bizarre creatures featured in *The Dream-Quest of Unknown Kadath*) are not listed; their roles can be ascertained in the story entries.

Lovecraft's colleagues, and the authors who influenced him, have been the subject of much diligent research on the part of scholars. We have written entries on many individuals who knew Lovecraft, even if only by correspondence; very obscure correspondents, about whom almost nothing is known, are excluded. Lovecraft apparently was influenced by a wide array of writers in the domain of supernatural fiction, but separate entries are provided only for such major figures as Edgar Allan Poe, Lord Dunsany, Arthur Machen, and Algernon

Blackwood. Mentions of other authors and works that influenced Lovecraft can be found in the entries on individual tales; see the index for references.

General topics relating to Lovecraft could theoretically be covered in an almost infinite range of entries, but we have limited our coverage to such things as Lovecraft's involvement with amateur journalism (specifically, the two leading amateur press associations of his time, the United Amateur Press Association and the National Amateur Press Association), his use of pseudonyms, his travels, and other major issues. No separate entry on Lovecraft's philosophical thought is included here, as the topic is too complex for succinct discussion.[4]

A bibliography listing important primary and secondary works on Lovecraft and a comprehensive index follow.

A word must now be said on what is *not* included in this volume.

One of the most popular aspects of Lovecraft's work is what has come to be known as the "Cthulhu Mythos" (a term Lovecraft himself never used). His literary pantheon (entities who, in many cases, prove merely to be extraterrestrials from the depths of space) has proved fascinating to readers and writers alike, to the extent that this "mythos" has taken on a life of its own and engendered innumerable imitations and purported sequels to Lovecraft's own work. We address none of this material in this volume. The "gods" themselves, with rare exceptions, do not figure as "characters" in any meaningful sense in the tales, so there are no entries on them. Similarly, we have provided no entries on writers who have attempted to follow in Lovecraft's footsteps, even though there is scarcely any writer of horror tales during the past seventy years who has not been influenced in one way or another by Lovecraft. Those interested in this entire subject are referred to Chris Jarocha-Ernst's *A Cthulhu Mythos Bibliography & Concordance* (1999).

Film, television, and other media adaptations of Lovecraft's work are similarly not covered here. Readers can find an abundance of information in Andrew Migliore and John Strysik's *The Lurker in the Lobby: A Guide to the Cinema of H. P. Lovecraft* (2000).

As noted, this volume cannot be considered in any sense a thorough proper name index to Lovecraft's work. For such an index, see S. T. Joshi's *An Index to the Fiction and Poetry of H. P. Lovecraft* (1992).

This volume had its origins in a work of substantially different nature planned many years ago but never completed. At that time, several colleagues wrote brief entries (chiefly on Lovecraft's family and colleagues) that have served as the nucleus for analogous articles included herein. We are grateful to Donald R. Burleson, Kenneth W. Faig, Jr., Will Murray, and Robert M. Price for allowing us to build upon their work. Other individuals, including Scott Connors, Daniel Harms, Donovan K. Loucks, and Christopher O'Brien, have supplied bits of valuable information.

NOTES

1. See Donald R. Burleson, *H. P. Lovecraft: A Critical Study* (1983); Peter Cannon, *H. P. Lovecraft* (1989); S. T. Joshi, *A Subtler Magick: The Writings and Philosophy of H. P. Lovecraft* (1996).

2. S. T. Joshi, *H. P. Lovecraft and Lovecraft Criticism: An Annotated Bibliography* (1981).

3. S. T. Joshi, *H. P. Lovecraft: A Life* (1996); Peter Cannon, ed., *Lovecraft Remembered* (1998).

4. For two very different discussions of this subject, see S. T. Joshi, *H. P. Lovecraft: The Decline of the West* (1990) and Timo Airaksinen, *The Philosophy of H. P. Lovecraft* (1999).

A Note on the Hippocampus Press Edition

For this edition, the authors have corrected a few errors and made numerous revisions to incorporate references to editions of works by Lovecraft and works of Lovecraft scholarship published since the first edition of this book.

—S. T. J., D. E. S.

Chronology

1890	August 20: Born at 454 Angell St. in Providence, R.I.
1890–93	Resides with parents at various locales in Massachusetts (Dorchester, 1890–92?; Dudley, summer 1892; Auburndale, 1892–93?) as father, Winfield Scott Lovecraft, pursues business interests.
1893	April 25: Winfield hospitalized at Butler Hospital in Providence; HPL and his mother, Sarah Susan Lovecraft, return to family home at 454 Angell St.
1897	First writings in fiction ("The Noble Eavesdropper") and poetry ("The Poem of Ulysses").
1898	Discovers Edgar Allan Poe. Voluminous writing of stories ("The Secret Cave," "The Mystery of the Grave-yard," "John the Detective"), some inspired by dime novels. Begins study of chemistry.
	July 19: Death of Winfield. HPL and his mother spend summer in Westminster, Mass.
1898–99, 1902–3	Attends Slater Avenue School.
1899	March 4: Begins handwritten journal, *The Scientific Gazette* (to 1905), largely devoted to chemistry.
1902	Winter: Discovers astronomy, largely from books in li-

brary of maternal grandmother. Writes tales inspired by Jules Verne (nonextant).

1903	August 2: Begins *The Rhode Island Journal of Astronomy* (to 1907). Much scientific work in chemistry, astronomy, geography, history, mythology.
1904	March 4: Death of HPL's maternal grandfather, Whipple Van Buren Phillips. Family's subsequent financial collapse causes move to 598 Angell St. in Providence.
1904–8	Intermittent attendance at Hope Street High School.
1905	Writes "The Beast in the Cave."
1906–8	Writes astronomy columns for *Pawtuxet Valley Gleaner* and [Providence] *Tribune.*
1908	Withdraws from high school because of nervous breakdown. Writes "The Alchemist."
1909–12	Takes correspondence courses in chemistry. Writes *A Brief Course in Inorganic Chemistry* (1910; nonextant).
1913	September: Literary controversy with John Russell in the letter column of *Argosy* leads to HPL's entry into amateur journalism (April 6, 1914).
1914–18	Writes astronomy column in [Providence] *Evening News.*
1914–23	Voluminous writing of essays, poetry, editorials, and reviews in the amateur press, mostly for the United Amateur Press Association (UAPA), but also later for the National Amateur Press Association (NAPA), which HPL joins in 1917. Early amateur colleagues include Maurice W. Moe, Rheinhart Kleiner, W. Paul Cook, and Samuel Loveman.
1915	April: Publishes first issue of amateur journal, *The Conservative* (to July 1923).
1917	May: Attempts enlistment in Rhode Island National Guard and later in the U.S. Army, but through his mother's influence is rejected.
	June: Writes "The Tomb," his first fictional work after a nine-year hiatus.
1917–18	Serves as president of the UAPA.

1919   March: HPL's mother hospitalized at Butler Hospital.

            Writes "Beyond the Wall of Sleep," "The White Ship,"
            "The Statement of Randolph Carter," and others.

            September: Discovers work of Lord Dunsany.

1920   Begins corresponding with Frank Belknap Long, Jr.
            Writes at least twelve stories, more than in any single year
            of his career, including "The Temple," "The Terrible Old
            Man," "Celephaïs," "From Beyond," "Nyarlathotep,"
            "The Picture in the House," and others.

1921   Writes "The Nameless City," "The Outsider," "The Music
            of Erich Zann," and others. Writes the "In Defence of
            Dagon" papers (January–October).

            May 24: Death of HPL's mother.

            July 4: Meets Sonia Haft Greene at the NAPA convention
            in Boston.

1921–22   Writes "Herbert West—Reanimator" to order for G. J.
            Houtain's *Home Brew* (first professional story appearance).

1922   April 6–12: First visit to New York City; meets Long,
            James F. Morton, and others.

            August: Begins corresponding with Clark Ashton Smith.

            August–September: Travels to Cleveland to meet Samuel
            Loveman and Alfred Galpin; stops in New York City on
            return trip. Writes "The Hound," "Hypnos," and "The
            Lurking Fear" (for *Home Brew*).

            December 17: Visits Marblehead, Mass., for the first time.

1923   Discovers Arthur Machen (then Algernon Blackwood and
            M. R. James the next year). Travels throughout New Eng-
            land (Marblehead, Salem, Newburyport, etc.). Writes "The
            Rats in the Walls," "The Festival," and others. Collaborates
            with C. M. Eddy, Jr. ("The Loved Dead" and others).

            October: Writes "Dagon" (1917) his first story published
            in *Weird Tales*.

1924   March 3: Marries Sonia H. Greene and moves to Brooklyn,
            N.Y. Refuses editorship of *Weird Tales*. Ghostwrites "Un-

der the Pyramids" for Harry Houdini (published as "Imprisoned with the Pharaohs"). Writes "The Shunned House."

1925	January 1: Sonia takes job in Cleveland. HPL moves to single-room apartment in Brooklyn Heights. Attempts futilely to secure employment. Writes "The Horror at Red Hook" (August 1–2), "He" (August 18), and "In the Vault" (September 18).
1925–27	Writes "Supernatural Horror in Literature" for W. Paul Cook's *The Recluse* (1927).
1926	April 17: Returns to Providence (10 Barnes St.), essentially ending marriage (divorce proceedings not undertaken until 1929). Writes "The Call of Cthulhu," "Pickman's Model," "The Silver Key," and others. Begins corresponding with August Derleth.
1926–27	Writes *The Dream-Quest of Unknown Kadath*.
1927	Writes *The Case of Charles Dexter Ward,* "The Colour out of Space." Begins corresponding with Donald Wandrei.
	August: Travels to Vermont, Maine, and elsewhere in New England.
1928	May–July: Spends summer in Brooklyn with Sonia as she tries to set up hat shop. Travels extensively (Brattleboro, Vt.; Athol and Wilbraham, Mass.; Endless Caverns, Va.). Writes "The Dunwich Horror."
1929	April–May: Travels extensively (Yonkers, N.Y.; Norfolk, Williamsburg, Richmond, Va.; New York City; New Paltz and Hurley, N.Y.).
1929–30	Ghostwrites "The Mound" for Zealia Bishop. Writes *Fungi from Yuggoth.*
1930	April–June: Travels (New York City; Charleston, S.C.; Richmond, Va.; Kingston and West Shokan, N.Y.; Athol and Worcester, Mass.). Begins corresponding with Henry S. Whitehead and Robert E. Howard. Writes "The Whisperer in Darkness." Ghostwrites "Medusa's Coil" for Zealia Bishop.
	August: Three-day excursion to Quebec. Writes lengthiest nonfiction work, *A Description of the Town of Quebeck* (October–January 1931).

1931	May–June: Travels (St. Augustine, Dunedin, Key West, Fla.; Savannah, Ga.; Charleston; Richmond; New York City). Writes *At the Mountains of Madness* and "The Shadow over Innsmouth."
1932	May–July: Travels (New York City; Shenandoah Valley; Knoxville and Chattanooga, Tenn.; Natchez and New Orleans, La. [meets E. Hoffmann Price]). Writes "The Dreams in the Witch House." Revises stories for Hazel Heald ("Out of the Æons" and others).
	July 3: Death of HPL's elder aunt Lillian D. Clark.
1932–33	Writes "Through the Gates of the Silver Key" (with E. Hoffmann Price).
1933	April: Begins corresponding with Robert Bloch.
	May 15: Moves to 66 College St. with younger aunt, Annie E. P. Gamwell. Later, writes "The Thing on the Doorstep." Revises "Supernatural Horror in Literature" for incomplete serialization in *The Fantasy Fan* (October 1933–February 1935).
1934	April–July: Travels (Charleston; Savannah; St Augustine; Fredericksburg, Va.; spends May–June with R. H. Barlow in De Land, Fla.).
1934–35	Writes "The Shadow out of Time."
1935	June–September: Travels (Fredericksburg; Charleston; New York City; spends June–August with Barlow in De Land, Fla.).
	November: Writes "The Haunter of the Dark."
1936	Corresponds briefly with Willis Conover, Fritz Leiber, and James Blish. Barlow visits HPL in Providence (July–September). Revises *Well-Bred Speech* for Anne Tillery Renshaw.
1937	March 15: Dies at Jane Brown Memorial Hospital in Providence. Barlow appointed literary executor.
1939	Arkham House (August Derleth and Donald Wandrei) publishes *The Outsider and Others.*

Abbreviations and Short Titles

AHT	Arkham House transcipts of H. P. Lovecraft's letters
AMS	autograph manuscript
An1	*The Annotated H. P. Lovecraft* (1997)
An2	*More Annotated H. P. Lovecraft* (1999)
AT	*The Ancient Track: Complete Poetical Works* (2001)
BWS	*Beyond the Wall of Sleep* (1943)
Cats	*Something about Cats and Other Pieces* (1949)
CC	*The Call of Cthulhu and Other Weird Stories* (1999)
CE	*Collected Essays* (2004–06; 5 vols.)
Crypt	*Crypt of Cthulhu* (magazine)
D	*Dagon and Other Macabre Tales* (rev. ed. 1986)
DB	*The Dark Brotherhood and Other Pieces* (1966)
DH	*The Dunwich Horror and Others* (rev. ed. 1984)
DWH	*The Dreams in the Witch House and Other Weird Stories* (2004)
ET	Schultz and Joshi, *An Epicure in the Terrible* (1991)
FDOC	Joshi, *H. P. Lovecraft: Four Decades of Criticism* (1991)
HM	*The Horror in the Museum and Other Revisions* (rev. ed. 1989)
HPL	H. P. Lovecraft
JHL	John Hay Library, Brown University, Providence, R.I.
LR	Cannon, *Lovecraft Remembered* (1998)
LS	*Lovecraft Studies* (magazine)
Marginalia	*Marginalia* (1944)
MM	*At the Mountains of Madness and Other Novels* (rev. ed. 1985)
MW	*Miscellaneous Writings* (1995)
NAPA	National Amateur Press Association
O	*The Outsider and Others* (1939)

PZ	*From the Pest Zone: The New York Stories* (2002)
SHSW	State Historical Society of Wisconsin, Madison
SL	*Selected Letters* (1965–76; 5 vols.)
SR	*The Shuttered Room and Other Pieces* (1959)
TD	*The Thing on the Doorstep and Other Weird Stories* (2001)
UAPA	United Amateur Press Association
WT	*Weird Tales* (magazine)

A

"Account of Charleston, An." Essay (20,700 words); probably written in the fall of 1930. First published in *MW;* rpt. *CE*4.

HPL's most exhaustive travelogue of Charleston, written in a flawless re-creation of eighteenth-century English. It supplies a comprehensive history of the city from its settlement in 1652 to 1930, followed by a discussion of Charleston architecture and a detailed walking tour. Also included are HPL's drawings of selected Charleston dwellings and a printed map of Charleston on which HPL has traced his recommended itinerary in red pencil. HPL evidently did not distribute the essay, even among his colleagues (the AMS survives at JHL). In 1936, when H. C. Koenig wished to explore Charleston, HPL condensed and modernized the essay in a letter to Koenig (subsequently revised and published by Koenig as *Charleston* [1936]; rpt. *Marginalia*).

Ackerman, Forrest J (b. 1916). American agent, author, editor. Ackerman has been a science fiction fan since the late '20s; he corresponded sporadically with HPL from around 1931 onward. (One letter to him by HPL, dated December 24, 1935, was published in the fanzine *Imagination* [January 1938].) He insti-gated a controversy in "The Boiling Point" column (*Fantasy Fan,* September 1933f.) when he criticized Clark Ashton Smith's "The Dweller in Martian Depths" (*Wonder Stories,* March 1933); HPL and his colleagues wrote numer-ous responses sharply criticizing Ackerman. All responses are reprinted in *The Boiling Point* (Necronomicon Press, 1985). HPL poked fun at Ackerman in "The Battle That Ended the Century" (1934; with R. H. Barlow), referring to him as "the Effjay of Akkamin," and "In the Walls of Eryx" (1936; with Ken-neth Sterling), where mention is made of "wriggling akmans" and "efjeh-weeds." He was later editor of *Famous Monsters of Filmland* magazine (1958–

80), which was instrumental in maintaining fan interest in weird fiction (and specifically horror films) during an otherwise lean period for the horror genre.

Ad Criticos. Poem in four books (46, 48, 46, and 34 lines); first published in the *Argosy* (January 1914 [first book] and February 1914 [second book]); last two books first published in *Saturnalia and Other Poems* (1984). These satirical poems attack HPL's epistolary enemies in the *Argosy*'s letter column, who had attacked him after he had criticized the romance writer Fred Jackson. The last two "books" did not appear in the *Argosy* as had the first two.

Akeley, Henry Wentworth. In "The Whisperer in Darkness," the reclusive farmer in Townshend, Vt., who notifies Albert Wilmarth (the narrator) of his encounters with the alien beings from the planet Yuggoth. Akeley's mind is eventually stored in a mechanical apparatus by the aliens, one of whom (possibly Nyarlathotep himself), masquerading as Akeley, lures Wilmarth to Akeley's farmhouse to destroy him. The character was inspired in part by the rustic Bert G. Akley, whom HPL met during his trip to Vermont in 1927. Henry's son, **George Goodenough Akeley,** residing in San Diego, is named partly for the amateur poet Arthur Goodenough, whose rustic abode partly suggested the Akeley farmhouse.

"Alchemist, The." Juvenile story (3,700 words); written 1908. First published in the *United Amateur* (November 1916); first collected in *SR*; corrected text in *D.*

Antoine, last of the Comtes de C——, tells the tale of his life and ancestry. This ancient aristocratic line has occupied a lofty castle in France surrounded by a dense forest, but a deadly curse seems to weigh upon it. Antoine finally learns the apparent cause when he comes of age and reads a manuscript passed down through the generations. In the thirteenth century an ancient man, Michel ("usually designated by the surname of Mauvais, the Evil, on account of his sinister reputation"), dwelt on the estate together with his son Charles, nicknamed Le Sorcier. These two practiced the black arts, and it was rumored they sought the elixir of life. Many disappearances of children were attributed to them. When Godfrey, the young son of Henri the Comte, is missing, Henri accosts Michel and kills him in a rage; just then Godfrey is found, and Charles, who learns of the deed, pronounces a curse:

> May ne'er a noble of thy murd'rous line
> Survive to reach a greater age than thine!

He thrusts a vial in the face of Henri, who dies instantly. From that time on no comte of the line lives beyond the age of thirty-two, Henri's age when he died. This curse continues for hundreds of years, and Antoine is compelled to believe that he will suffer a similar fate. Wandering in his deserted castle, he finds a hidden cellar and encounters a hideous looking man "clad in a skull-cap and long mediaeval tunic of dark colour." The man tells how Charles Le Sorcier killed Henri and also Godfrey when the latter reached Henri's age; but Antoine wonders how the curse could have been continued thereafter, "when Charles Le Sorcier must in the course of Nature have died." As the man attacks Antoine, the latter hurls a torch at him, setting him afire. Just before he expires, however, he reveals the truth: he himself is Charles Le Sorcier, having lived for 600 years to continue his revenge against the family that killed his father.

This is the first extant tale by HPL to be avowedly supernatural. It was first published at the urging of W. Paul Cook, who read it in manuscript and found it indicative of great promise; largely at Cook's urging, HPL resumed the writing of fiction in 1917.

Alfredo; a Tragedy. Verse drama (411 lines); dated September 14, 1918, as by "Beaumont and Fletcher" (i.e., John Fletcher [1579–1625] and Francis Beaumont [c. 1585–1616], the Jacobean dramatists). First published in *DB*.

The play is a send-up of Alfred Galpin's high school romances, written in the form of an Elizabethan tragedy. Alfredo (Galpin), the Prince Regent, yearns for Margarita (Margaret Abraham), but she claims to find him too studious for her "airy will"; nevertheless, she becomes jealous when she sees him spending much time studying with Hypatia. She and Hecatissa (an unattractive woman previously scorned by Alfredo) plot together to gain revenge. During the presentation of a play in which Alfredo and Hypatia, now engaged, act in the presence of King Rinarto (Rheinhart Kleiner), Alfredo and Hypatia drink from a goblet that has been poisoned by Hecatissa; they lie dying. In a rage, Gonzago perceives the trickery and kills Hecatissa; her father, Olero, kills Gonzago; Teobaldo (HPL), Alfredo's tutor, kills Olero; Margarita kills Teobaldo; Alfredo, in his death throes, manages to stab and kill Margarita; Rinarto, in grief, drinks from the goblet and dies, leaving Mauricio (Maurice W. Moe), a Cardinal, to lament the tragedy and count his beads.

Allen, Zadok (1831–1927). In "The Shadow over Innsmouth," the alcoholic nonagenarian of Innsmouth who, when plied with liquor by Robert Olmstead, babbles the town's horrible secrets and then disappears mysteriously. It is from Allen that Olmstead first learns that he has the "Marsh eyes"—hinting at his kinship with Old Man Marsh. Allen shares the life dates of, and bears a strong resemblance to, the amateur poet Jonathan E. Hoag, with whom HPL had been acquainted since 1918. Allen may also have been suggested by the character Humphrey Lathrop, the elderly doctor in Herbert Gorman's *The Place Called Dagon* (1927).

Alos. In "Polaris," the narrator's friend, commander of the last forces of the Lomarians against the Inutos.

Altberg-Ehrenstein, Karl Heinrich, Graf von. The narrator of "The Temple." The Lieutenant-Commander of the German submarine U-29, he is the last surviving crew member when his stricken vessel sinks to the bottom of the Atlantic Ocean, where he apparently finds the ruins of Atlantis. He leaves behind his written account on August 20, 1917—HPL's twenty-seventh birthday.

Amateur Journalism. The amateur journalism movement consisted of various groups of writers belonging to the two leading amateur organizations of the period, the National Amateur Press Association (NAPA), founded in 1876, and the United Amateur Press Association (UAPA), founded in 1895. HPL's pamphlet *United Amateur Press Association: Exponent of Amateur Journalism* (1915; rpt. *MW* and *CE*1) explains the principles of amateurdom. Members could publish their own journals or contribute to those edited by others (HPL did both). Those who issued journals mailed them to members of their choice (addresses of members were supplied in the "official organs," the *United Amateur* and the *National Amateur*). No minimum publishing requirement was imposed; so long as members paid yearly dues, they were members in good standing. The NAPA held its annual convention in early July; the UAPA held its annual convention in late July. At those times elections were held for the offices of President, Vice-President, Treasurer, Official Editor, and others; other positions (such as the Department of Public Criticism in the UAPA and the Bureau of Critics in the NAPA) were appointed by the President. The Official Editor was responsible for editing the official organ.

HPL joined the UAPA in April 1914 at the invitation of Edward F. Daas, who noticed HPL's contributions to the letter column of the *Argosy*. During his first year HPL contributed a few pieces in prose and verse, but his activity blossomed in 1915 when he was chosen to replace Ada P. Campbell as Chairman of the Department of Public Criticism (HPL's first article was published in the *United Amateur,* January 1915); in April he published the first of thirteen issues of his journal, *The Conservative.* From 1914 to 1921 he contributed voluminously to a wide variety of periodicals. Although a loyal "United man," HPL joined the NAPA in 1917 in the hope that it might lead to harmony between the organizations.

HPL held several offices in the UAPA: Chairman of the Department of Public Criticism (1915–17, 1918–19), First Vice-President (1915–16), President (1917–18), Official Editor (July 1917, 1920–22, 1924–25). He was interim President of the NAPA (November 1922–July 1923), taking over for William J. Dowdell, who had resigned. HPL's amateur activity lagged after the collapse of the UAPA in 1926 but resumed in 1931 when he became a member of the Bureau of Critics (corresponding to the UAPA's Department of Public Criticism); he wrote numerous critical articles (mostly on poetry) for the *National Amateur* from 1931 to 1936. Aside from editing *The Conservative,* HPL was a coeditor, assistant editor, or associate editor of *The Badger* (June 1915), *The Credential* (April 1920), *The Inspiration* (Tribute Number, April 1917), and *The United Cooperative* (December 1918, June 1919, April 1921). He also assisted members of the Providence Amateur Press Club in editing two issues of *The Providence Amateur* (June 1915 and February 1916). In the first he is listed as "Literary Director" and in the second as "Official Editor."

HPL also wrote voluminously about amateurdom. *United Amateur Press Association: Exponent of Amateur Journalism* is a recruiting pamphlet published in late 1915, when he was First Vice-President of the UAPA; it is his second separate publication (following *The Crime of Crimes* [1915]). *Looking Backward* (1920) is an examination of amateur journals of the 1885–95 period. *Further Criticism of Poetry* (1932), a criticism of amateur verse written on April 18, 1932, appeared separately because it was too lengthy to be published in the *Na-*

tional Amateur. Some Current Motives and Practices (1936) is a forceful defense of NAPA President Hyman Bradofsky against other members' vicious attacks upon him. HPL's first autobiographical article, "The Brief Autobiography of an Inconsequential Scribbler" (*Silver Clarion,* April 1919), focuses on his amateur activity. Other important essays are "The Dignity of Journalism" (*Dowdell's Bearcat,* July 1915), "For What Does the United Stand?" (*United Amateur,* May 1920), "What Amateurdom and I Have Done for Each Other" (1921; *Boys' Herald,* August 1937), "Lucubrations Lovecraftian" (*United Co-operative,* April 1921), and "A Matter of Uniteds" (*Bacon's Essays,* Summer 1927). All appear in *Collected Essays* (Vol. 1).

HPL attended only two national amateur conventions, both for NAPA, in July 1921 (when he read his humorous speech "Within the Gates" [in *MW*] and first met his future wife, Sonia H. Greene), and in July 1930. Both were held in Boston. He attended regional amateur gatherings in Boston in 1920–21 and in Brooklyn (Blue Pencil Club) in 1924–25. In amateurdom HPL met many of his closest and most enduring friends and colleagues, including Frank Belknap Long, Maurice W. Moe, Rheinhart Kleiner, James F. Morton, Alfred Galpin, Samuel Loveman, and Wilfred B. Talman.

On the whole, amateur journalism appealed to HPL because it echoed his stated literary goal of writing as nonremunerative "self-expression," because it provided him with a forum where his literary and critical skills could be exhibited and because it supplied him with a network of friends with whom he could correspond on various topics and thereby hone his philosophical, aesthetic, and literary views. HPL is still regarded a giant in the amateur world, and articles on him continue to appear in *The Fossil,* the organ of amateur alumni.

"Americanism." Essay (1,120 words); probably written in the summer of 1919. First published in the *United Amateur* (July 1919); rpt. *MW* and *CE5.*

Americanism is "expanded Anglo-Saxonism"; therefore, the "melting-pot" idea is dangerous and pernicious. America should build upon the values fostered by the English colonists.

"Amissa Minerva." Poem (92 lines); probably written in early 1919. First published in *Toledo Amateur* (May 1919).

A pungent satire lampooning the freakishness of modern poetry, mentioning several poets by name (Amy Lowell, Edgar Lee Masters, Carl Sandburg, etc.).

See Steven J. Mariconda, "On Lovecraft's 'Amissa Minerva,'" *Etchings and Odysseys* No. 9 [1986]: 97–103.

"Ancient Track, The." Poem (44 lines); written on November 26, 1929. First published in *WT* (March 1930).

Brooding poem in which the narrator comes upon a milestone ("Two miles to Dunwich") on a lonely road and subsequently encounters nameless horrors. This is the only other mention of Dunwich in HPL's fiction and poetry aside from "The Dunwich Horror" (1928).

See Donald R. Burleson, "On Lovecraft's 'The Ancient Track,'" *LS* No. 28 (Spring 1993): 17–20.

Andrews, Marshall. In "The Disinterment," a disreputable physician who claims to have concocted a bizarre scheme to treat his friend's case of leprosy by first simulating the man's death and then giving him a new identity. In fact, he drugs the man and transplants the man's head on to the body of an African American. Andrews is later killed by his friend.

Angell, George Gammell. In "The Call of Cthulhu," Angell is a professor of Semitic languages at Brown University. In 1908, at a meeting of the American Archaeological Society, Angell first learns of the Cthulhu Cult when he is approached by inspector John R. Legrasse with a sculpture of a strange idol. Seventeen years later, when the artist Henry Anthony Wilcox shows him a bizarre bas-relief that he has just fashioned from something he dreamt of, Angell embarks anew on research into the strange cult—an act that ultimately results in his untimely death.

Angell's last name is derived from Angell Street, one of the leading thoroughfares in Providence (itself named for Thomas Angell, a companion of Roger Williams and one of the original settlers of the city). The middle name is an echo of HPL's aunt, Annie E. Phillips Gamwell (in Providence speech, "Gamwell" and "Gammell" would be pronounced in an approximately similar manner).

Anger, William Frederick (b. 1921). Correspondent of HPL (1934–36). With Louis C. Smith, Anger planned an index to *WT* and an edition of HPL's *Fungi from Yuggoth* (both unfinished). He was the author (with Smith) of "An Interview with E. Hoffman [*sic*] Price" (*Fantasy Fan,* December 1934).

Arkham. Fictitious city in Massachusetts invented by HPL. The city is first cited in "The Picture in the House" (1920); other tales that feature Arkham are "Herbert West—Reanimator" (1921–22), "The Unnamable" (1923), "The Colour out of Space" (1927), "The Dunwich Horror" (1928), "The Shadow over Innsmouth" (1931), "The Dreams in the Witch House" (1932), "Through the Gates of the Silver Key" (1932–33), "The Thing on the Doorstep" (1933), and "The Shadow out of Time" (1934–35). It is the home of Miskatonic University (first cited in "Herbert West—Reanimator"); there is also an Arkham Historical Society (in "The Shadow over Innsmouth") and an Arkham Sanitarium (in "The Thing on the Doorstep"). It had a newspaper in the 1880s, the *Arkham Gazette* (in "The Colour out of Space"); a more recent paper, presumably dating to the 1920s, is the *Arkham Advertiser* (in "The Dunwich Horror" and other stories). In *At the Mountains of Madness,* one of the expeditionary ships to Antarctica is named *Arkham.* HPL drew a map of the city on at least three occasions; one is reproduced as "Map of the Principal Parts of Arkham, Massachusetts" (*Acolyte,* Fall 1942), another in *Marginalia* (facing p. 279), and another (from a letter to Robert Bloch, [April 1936]) as the frontispiece to *Letters to Robert Bloch* (Necronomicon Press, 1993).

Will Murray has conjectured that Arkham was at first situated in central Massachusetts and that its name and possibly its location were derived from the tiny hamlet Oakham. Research by Robert D. Marten makes this theory extremely unlikely. Marten maintains that Arkham was always located on the North Shore and (as HPL repeatedly declares) was a fictional analogue of Salem. HPL definitively states: "My mental picture of Arkham is of a town something like Salem in atmosphere & style of houses, but more hilly (Salem is flat except for Gallows Hill, which is outside the town proper) & with a college (which Salem hasn't). The street layout is nothing like Salem's. As to the location of Arkham—I fancy I place the town & the imaginary Miskatonic somewhere north of Salem—perhaps near Manchester. My idea of the place is slightly in from the sea, but with a deep water channel making it a port" (HPL to F. Lee Baldwin, April 29, 1934; ms., JHL). Marten conjectures that the name Arkham was based upon Arkwright, a town in R.I. now consolidated into the community of Fiskville. HPL remarked that "The Dunwich Horror" "belongs to the Arkham cycle" (*SL* 2.246), but the significance of this phrase is unclear. Possibly he was referring to the fact that several of his recent tales had involved not merely a pseudomythological backdrop but also an imaginary New England topography.

See Will Murray, "In Search of Arkham Country," *LS* No. 13 (Fall 1986): 54–67; Will Murray, "In Search of Arkham Country Revisited," *LS* Nos. 19/20 (Fall 1989): 65–69; Robert D. Marten, "Arkham Country: In Rescue of the Lost Searchers," *LS* No. 39 (Summer 1998): 1–20.

Armitage, Henry. In "The Dunwich Horror," the librarian of Miskatonic University (A. M. Miskatonic, Ph.D. Princeton, Litt. D. Johns Hopkins). He encounters Wilbur Whateley in the library, but refuses to let him take home a copy of the *Necronomicon,* sensing that it could lead to cataclysmic results. He later sees Whateley die in the library while trying to steal the book. With great effort, he deciphers Whateley's encrypted diary and realizes the threat that the Whateley family (specifically, Whateley's monstrous twin brother) poses to the world, and he leads the expedition to exterminate it.

Arruda, Capt. Manuel. In *The Case of Charles Dexter Ward,* the captain of a ship, the *Fortaleza,* of Barcelona, bound from Cairo to Providence. In 1770 it is stopped by authorities and found to contain large numbers of Egyptian mummies, scheduled for delivery to "Sailor A. B. C." (i.e., Joseph Curwen). HPL derived the name from a Manuel Arruda who was a door-to-door fruit seller in Providence in the 1920s.

Asbury, Herbert (1891–1963). American journalist and author of *The Gangs of New York* (1928) whose horror anthology *Not at Night!* (Macy-Macius/The Vanguard Press, 1932) contains HPL's "The Horror at Red Hook." The volume proved to be pirated from several anthologies edited by Christine Campbell Thomson. For a time *WT* (from which most of the stories derived) threatened to sue the publisher (HPL gave his support to the suit provided it would involve no financial expenditure on his part; see *SL* 2.260–61), but the publisher eventually withdrew the book from circulation.

Asellius, Sex[tus]. In "The Very Old Folk," the military tribune of the fifth cohort of the XIIth legion in the Roman province of Hispania Citerior (Spain), who is ordered to investigate reports of peculiar events in the hills above Tarraco.

"Ashes." Short story (3,220 words); written in collaboration with C. M. Eddy, Jr., probably in the fall of 1923. First published in *WT* (March 1924); first collected in *HM* (rev. ed. 1989 only).

A scientist, Arthur Van Allister, has discovered a chemical compound that will reduce any substance to fine white ashes. He hires an assistant, Malcolm Bruce, who quickly falls in love with Van Allister's secretary, Marjorie Purdy. Sometime later Bruce is alarmed that Marjorie seems to have disappeared. He enters Van Allister's laboratory and sees a glass jar filled with white ashes. Horrified at the thought that the scientist has tried out his experiment on his secretary, Bruce tussles with Van Allister, in the course of which he lowers the scientist into the vat containing his formula. Later it is discovered that Marjorie had merely been locked in a closet; but since Van Allister had been planning to destroy Marjorie with his formula, his death is presumably justified.

No one would know that HPL had had any hand in this story (which, aside from the general triteness of the plot, features a conventional romance element very foreign to his own manner) if HPL had not said so (see *SL* 1.257). It is the first of HPL's revisions of tales by C. M. Eddy; he presumably touched up a draft by Eddy rather than writing from notes or a synopsis.

Aspinwall, Ernest B. (b. 1873). Randolph Carter's older cousin, Aspinwall is mentioned briefly in "The Silver Key." In "Through the Gates of the Silver Key," he represents Carter's heirs as one of the men who attempt to settle Carter's estate following his disappearance. An "L. Aspinwall" was Treasurer and a Director with Whipple V. Phillips (HPL's grandfather) of Phillips's Snake River Company.

Astrology, Articles on. Six articles written in late 1914 for the [Providence] *Evening News* to combat the astrological articles of J. F. Hartmann. All articles (including those by Hartmann) rpt. *Science vs. Charlatanry: Essays on Astrology* (Strange Co., 1979) and *CE*3. They are: Letter to the editor (September 9; as "Science Versus Charlatanry"); Letter to the editor (October 10; as "The Falsity of Astrology"); Letter to the editor (October 13; as "Astrlogh [*sic*] and the Future" [by "Isaac Bickerstaffe, Jr."]); "Delavan's Comet and Astrology" (October 26 [by "Isaac Bickerstaffe, Jr."]); Letter to the editor (December 17; as "The Fall of Astrology"); Letter to the editor (December 21 [by "Isaac Bickerstaffe, Jr."]).

HPL was irked when the local astrologer Joachim Friedrich Hartmann (1848–1930) published an article in the *Evening News,* "Astrology and the European War" (September 9), in the exact location (the top of the last page) where HPL's astronomy columns typically appeared. HPL replied with two hostile and intemperate letters, to the first of which Hartmann replied with a letter of his own (published October 7). HPL then employed the satirical method of Jonathan Swift, who in his "Isaac Bickerstaffe" articles predicted the death of the astrologer Partridge and then wrote a convincing account of Partridge's death, whereupon Partridge had a difficult time proving he was still alive; HPL's pieces merely parody astrological technique by making vague and absurd predictions of the distant future. Hartmann feebly rejoined with two further pieces—"The Science of Astrology" (October 22) and "A Defense of Astrology" (December 14)—in which he ridiculed the Bickerstaffe pieces, unaware that HPL had written them.

Astronomy, Articles on. See "Mysteries of the Heavens Revealed by Astronomy"; *Pawtuxet Valley Gleaner,* Astronomy Articles for; [Providence] *Evening News,* Astronomy Articles for; [Providence] *Tribune,* Astronomy Articles for.

Astronomy/The Monthly Almanack. Two juvenile scientific journals (eventually combined) written by HPL, 1903–4. The first five issues bear the title *Astronomy* as follows: 1, No. 1 (August 1903); 1, No. 2 (September 1903); 1, No. 3 (October 1903); 1, No. 4 (November 1903) (combined with *The Monthly Almanack;* includes *An Annual of Astronomy for the Year 1903: First Edition: Novr. 25, 1903*); 1, No. 5 (December 1905). The next issue is titled *The New Monthly Almanack for December, 1903.* The next appears as *Astronomy: January 1904: Combined with the Monthly Almanack.* The final issue bears the title *The Monthly Almanack: Combined with "Astronomy": Feb'y, 1904.*

The publications consist largely of technical charts of the solar system and constellations, data on the moon's phases, planetary aspects, and the like.

"Astrophobos." Poem (42 lines in 7 stanzas); written in mid-November 1917. First published in the *United Amateur* (January 1918). The title means "[one who] fears stars," and tells of a person who looks to the stars for beauty and tranquillity but finds in them only horror and sadness.

At the Mountains of Madness. Short novel (41,500 words); written February 24–March 22, 1931. First published in *Astounding Stories* (February, March, and April 1936); first collected in *O;* corrected text in *MM;* annotated version in *AnI* and *TD.*

The Miskatonic Antarctic Expedition of 1930–31, led by William Dyer (his full name is given only in "The Shadow out of Time"), begins promisingly but ends in tragedy and horror. Employing a new boring device invented by engineer Frank H. Pabodie, the expedition makes great progress at sites on the shore of McMurdo Sound (across the Ross Ice Shelf from where Admiral Byrd's expedition had only recently camped). But the biologist Lake, struck by some peculiar markings on soapstone fragments he has found, feels the need to conduct a subexpedition far to the northwest. There he makes a spectacular discovery: not only the world's tallest mountains ("Everest out of the running," he laconically radios the camp), but then the frozen remains—some damaged, some intact—of monstrous winged, barrel-shaped creatures that cannot be reconciled with the known fauna of this planet. They seem half-animal and half-vegetable, with tremendous brain capacity and, apparently, with more senses than we have. Lake, who has read the *Necronomicon,* jocosely thinks they may be the Elder Things or Old Ones spoken of in that book and elsewhere, who are "supposed to have created all earth-life as jest or mistake."

Later Lake's subexpedition loses radio contact with the main party, apparently because of the high winds in that region. Dyer feels he must come to Lake's aid and takes a small group of men in some airplanes to see what has gone amiss. To their horror, they find the camp devastated—by the winds or the sled dogs or some other nameless forces—but discover no trace of the intact specimens of the Old Ones. When they come upon damaged specimens "insanely" buried in the snow, they are forced to conclude that it is the work of the one missing human, Gedney. Dyer and the graduate student Danforth decide to take a trip by themselves beyond the titanic mountain plateau to see if they can find any explanation for the tragedy.

As they scale the plateau, they find to their amazement an enormous stone city, fifty to one hundred miles in extent, clearly built millions of years ago, long before any humans could have evolved from apes. Exploring some of the interiors, they are forced to conclude that the city was built by the Old Ones. Because the buildings contain, as wall decorations, many bas-reliefs supplying the history of the Old Ones' civilization, they learn that the Old Ones came from space some fifty million years ago, settling in Antarctica and eventually branching out to other areas of the earth. They built their huge cities with the aid of shoggoths—amorphous, fifteen-foot masses of protoplasm that they controlled by hypnotic suggestion. Over time the shoggoths gained a semi-stable brain and began to develop a will of their own, forcing the Old Ones to conduct several campaigns of resubjugation. Later, other extraterrestrial races—including the fungi from Yuggoth and the Cthulhu spawn—came to the earth and engaged in battles over territory with the Old Ones, and eventually the latter were forced back to their original Antarctic settlement. They had also lost the ability to fly through space. The reasons for their abandonment of the city, and for their extinction, are unfathomable.

Dyer and Danforth then stumble upon signs that someone dragging a sled had passed by, and they follow it, finding first some huge albino penguins, then the sled with the remains of Gedney and a dog, then a group of decapitated Old Ones, restored from suspended animation by being thawed in Lake's camp. Then they hear an anomalous sound—a musical piping over a wide range. Could it be some other Old Ones? They flee madly, but they simultaneously turn their flashlights upon the thing for an instant and find that it is a shoggoth: "It was a terrible, indescribable thing vaster than any subway train—a shapeless congeries of protoplasmic bubbles, faintly self-luminous, and with myriads of temporary eyes forming and unforming as pustules of greenish light all over the tunnel-filling front that bore down upon us, crushing the frantic penguins and slithering over the glistening floor that it and its kind had swept so evilly free of all litter." As they fly back to camp, Danforth shrieks in horror: he has seen something that unhinges his mind, but he refuses to tell Dyer what it is. All he can do is make the eldritch cry, *"Tekeli-li! Tekeli-li!"*

The novel is the culmination of HPL's lifelong fascination with the Antarctic, beginning when as a boy he had written treatises on *Wilkes's Explorations* and *The Voyages of Capt. Ross, R.N.,* and had followed with avidity reports of the explorations of Borchgrevink, Scott, Amundsen, and others early in the century. As Jason C. Eckhardt has demonstrated, the early parts of the novel show the influence of Admiral Byrd's expedition of 1928–30, as well as other contemporary expeditions. HPL may also have found a few hints on points of style and imagery in the early pages of M. P. Shiel's novel *The Purple Cloud* (1901; reissued 1930), which relates an expedition to the Arctic.

It is possible to conjecture what led HPL to write the novel when he did. The lead story in the November 1930 *WT* was a poorly written and unimaginative tale by Katharine Metcalf Roof, "A Million Years After," that dealt with the hatching of ancient dinosaur eggs. HPL fumed when he read it, not only because it won the cover design but also because he had been badgering Frank Belknap Long for years to write a story on this idea; Long had balked because he felt that H. G. Wells's "Æpyornis Island" had anticipated the idea. In mid-October, after seeing the Roof tale in print, HPL wrote: "Why, damn it, boy, I've half a mind to write an egg story myself right now—though I fancy my primal ovoid would hatch out something infinitely more palaeogean and unrecognisable than the relatively commonplace dinosaur" (*SL* 3.186–87). HPL may have felt that the use of a viable dinosaur egg was impossible, so that the only solution would be the freezing of ancient living entities in the Arctic or Antarctic regions. Note that entry #169 in his commonplace book (dating to around 1930) reads "What hatches from primordial egg." However, the novel is more in the spirit of entry #31 (c. 1919): "Prehistoric man preserved in Siberian ice."

HPL was also inspired by the paintings of the Himalayas by Nicholai Roerich (1874–1947), seen the previous year at the Roerich Museum when it opened in New York. Roerich is mentioned six times in the novel. HPL probably did not set the tale in the Himalayas both because they were fairly well known and because he wanted to create the sense of awe implicit in mountains taller than any yet discovered. Only the relatively uncharted Antarctic continent could fulfill both functions.

The Old Ones are the real focus of the novel. HPL gradually transforms them from objects of terror to symbols for the best in humanity; as Dyer declares: "Poor devils! After all, they were not evil things of their kind. They were the men of another age and another order of being. Nature had played a hellish jest on them . . . and this was their tragic homecoming. . . . Scientists to the last—what had they done that we would not have done in their place? God, what intelligence and persistence! What a facing of the incredible, just as those carven kinsmen and forbears had faced things only a little less incredible! Radiates, vegetables, monstrosities, star-spawn—whatever they had been, they were men!"

The most significant way the Old Ones are identified with human beings is in Dyer's historical digression, specifically in regard to the Old Ones' social and economic organization. In many ways they represent a utopia toward which HPL hoped humanity could aspire. The sentence "Government was evidently complex and probably socialistic" establishes that HPL had himself by this time converted to moderate socialism. The Old Ones' civilization is founded upon slavery of a sort, and there is some suggestion that the condition of the shoggoths might, in part, resemble that of African Americans. The exhaustive history of the Old Ones on this planet, portraying their rise and fall, suggests HPL's absorption of Oswald Spengler's *The Decline of the West,* with its similar emphasis on the inexorable rise and fall of successive civilizations.

In terms of HPL's work, the novel makes explicit what has been evident all along—most of the "gods" of his mythology are merely extraterrestrials and that their followers (including the authors of the books of occult lore to which reference is so frequently made by HPL and others) are mistaken as to their true nature. Robert M. Price, who first noted this "demythologizing" feature in HPL, has pointed out that *At the Mountains of Madness* does not make any radical break in this pattern, but it does emphasize the point more clearly than elsewhere.

The novel has been called a "sequel" to Poe's *Narrative of Arthur Gordon Pym;* but, at least in terms of plot, it cannot be considered such: it picks up on very little of Poe's enigmatic work except for the cry "Tekeli-li!," as unexplained in Poe as in HPL, and the allusion to Mt. Erebus as *Yaanek* from "Ulalume." It is not clear that *Pym* even influenced the work in any significant way. Jules Zanger has observed that the novel is "no completion [of *Pym*] at all: it might be better described as a parallel text, the two tales coexisting in a shared context of allusion" ("Poe's Endless Voyage: *The Narrative of Arthur Gordon Pym,*" *Papers on Language and Literature* 22, No. 3 [Summer 1986]: 282).

HPL declared that the short novel was "capable of a major serial division in the exact middle" (HPL to August Derleth, March 24, [1931]; ms., SHSW), suggesting that, at least subconsciously, he envisioned the work as a two-part serial in *WT*. But Farnsworth Wright rejected it in July 1931. HPL reacted bitterly (see *SL* 3.395) and let the novel sit for years. Then, in the fall of 1935, the young Julius Schwartz, acting as agent, took it to F. Orlin Tremaine, editor of *Astounding Stories,* who accepted it at once, apparently without reading it (see Will Murray, "Julius Schwartz on Lovecraft," *Crypt* No. 76 [Hallowmas 1990]: 14–18). It was published, however, with severe editorial tampering: HPL's long paragraphs were split up, punctuation was altered, and (toward the end) several passages, amounting to about 1,000 words, were omitted. HPL fumed at the alterations, calling Tremaine "that god-damn'd dung of a hyaena" (HPL to R. H. Barlow, June 4, 1936; ms., JHL). He corrected by hand his three sets of *Astounding,* but in the end did not correct many alterations (e.g., the Americanization of his British spellings). These corrected copies were used as the basis of the first Arkham House edition, but even so the text contained nearly 1,500 errors, mostly in spelling and punctuation, but also in the omission of two small passages toward the beginning. The text was restored (based upon the surviving typescript except for passages where HPL made demonstrable revisions on scientific points) in *MM* (1985 edition).

See Robert M. Price, "Demythologizing Cthulhu," *LS* No. 8 (Spring 1984): 3–9, 24; Bert Atsma, "An Autopsy of the Old Ones," *Crypt* No. 32 (St. John's Eve 1985): 3–7; Ben P. Indick, "Lovecraft's POElar Adventure," *Crypt* No. 32 (St. John's Eve 1985): 25–31; Peter Cannon, "*At the Mountains of Madness* as a Sequel to *Arthur Gordon Pym,*" *Crypt* No. 32 (St. John's Eve 1985): 33–34; Will Murray, "The Trouble with Shoggoths," *Crypt* No. 32 (St. John's Eve 1985): 35–38, 41; Jason C. Eckhardt, "Behind the Mountains of Madness," *LS* No. 14 (Spring 1987): 31–38; Marc A. Cerasini, "Thematic Links in *Arthur Gordon Pym, At the Mountains of Madness,* and *Moby Dick,*" *Crypt* No. 49 (Lammas 1987): 3–20; S. T. Joshi, "Lovecraft's Alien Civilisations: A Political Interpretation," in *Primal Sources: Essays on H. P. Lovecraft* (Hippocamput Press, 2003); S. T. Joshi, "Textual Problems in *At the Mountains of Madness,*" *Crypt* No. 75 (Michaelmas 1990): 16–21; Robert M. Price, "Patterns in the Snow: A New Reading of *At the Mountains of Madness,*" *Crypt* No. 81 (St. John's Eve 1992): 48–51; Peter Cannon, Jason C. Eckhardt, Steven J. Mariconda, and Hubert Van Calenbergh, "On *At the Mountains of Madness:* A Panel Discussion," *LS* No. 34 (Spring

1996): 2–10; David A. Oakes, "A Warning to the World: The Deliberative Argument of *At the Mountains of Madness,*" *LS* No. 39 (Summer 1998): 21–25; S. T. Joshi, "Some Sources for 'The Mound' and *At the Mountains of Madness,*" in *Primal Sources: Essays on H. P. Lovecraft* (Hippocampus Press, 2003).

Atal. Briefly noted as an innkeeper's son in "The Cats of Ulthar," Atal is, in "The Other Gods," the priest who accompanies Barzai the Wise in his quest up Hatheg-Kla to find the gods of earth. He then becomes, in *The Dream-Quest of Unknown Kadath,* an ancient patriarch who advises Randolph Carter in his quest for the gods.

Atwood, Professor. In *At the Mountains of Madness,* a professor of physics and a member of the Miskatonic Antarctic Expedition of 1930–31.

Aylesbury. Fictitious town in Massachusetts, invented by HPL for "The Dunwich Horror" (1928), where it is presumably near Dunwich. The name is perhaps derived from Amesbury, a town in the far northeastern corner of the state, near Haverhill and Newburyport, and the late home of John Greenleaf Whittier. HPL passed through Amesbury on several occasions, including in August 1927. There is a real town in England called Aylesbury.

"Azathoth." Projected novel (480 words extant); written June 1922. First published in *Leaves* (1938); first collected in *Marginalia;* corrected text in *D.* The surviving text notes that "When age fell upon the world, and wonder went out of the minds of men," a man "travelled out of life on a quest into the spaces whither the world's dreams had fled." The man dwelt in a city "of high walls where sterile twilight reigned," and as a reaction from this environment he began dreaming "the dreams that men have lost."

HPL describes the work as a "weird Vathek-like novel" (*SL* 1.185), referring to the Arabian novel *Vathek* (1786) by William Beckford, which HPL first read in July 1921. HPL perhaps means that *Azathoth* is an attempt both to capture *Vathek*'s air of dreamlike fantasy and to imitate its continuous flow of narrative and absence of chapter divisions (as with *The Dream-Quest of Unknown Kadath*). As early as October 1921 he had been thinking of writing "a weird Eastern tale in the 18th century manner" (HPL to Winifred Jackson, October 7, 1921; ms., JHL). After beginning the work, HPL commented: "The rest—for which this introduction prepares the reader, will be material of the *Arabian Nights* type. I shall defer to no modern critical canon, but shall frankly slip back through the centuries and become a myth-maker with that childish sincerity which no one but the earlier Dunsany has tried to achieve nowadays. I shall go out of the world when I write, with a mind centred not in literary usage, but in the dreams I dreamed when I was six years old or less—the dreams which followed my first knowledge of *Sinbad*, of *Agib*, of *Baba-Abdallah,* and of *Sidi-Nonman*" (HPL to Frank Belknap Long, June 9, 1922; AHT).

See Will Murray, "On 'Azathoth,'" *Crypt* No. 53 (Candlemas 1988): 8–9; Donald R. Burleson, "On Lovecraft's Fragment 'Azathoth,'" *LS* Nos. 22/23 (Fall 1990): 10–12, 23.

B

Babson, Eunice. In "The Thing on the Doorstep," a servant of Edward and Asenath Derby who, after being dismissed by Edward, appears to exact some kind of blackmail from him.

Baird, Edwin (1886–1957). First editor of *WT* (March 1923–April 1924). Baird was a writer for the popular magazines during the early decades of the century (HPL presumably read some of his stories in the Munsey magazines). Owner J. C. Henneberger picked Baird to edit *WT,* even though he seemed to have no particular expertise in weird fiction. Baird accepted five of HPL's stories when they were submitted in May 1923 (see *SL* 1.227) but insisted that HPL resubmit them double-spaced; HPL grudgingly did so. Although ousted as editor of *WT,* Baird continued to edit Henneberger's *Detective Tales* and in that capacity rejected, in July 1925, HPL's "The Shunned House."

Balbutius, Cn[aeus]. In "The Very Old Folk," the legatus of the Roman province of Hispania Citerior (Spain), who does not wish to investigate reports of peculiar events in the hills above Tarraco but is ordered to do so by the proconsul, P. Scribonius Libo.

Baldwin, F[ranklin] Lee (1913–1987). Weird fiction fan and correspondent of HPL (1933–36). Baldwin first wrote HPL in the fall of 1933 proposing to issue "The Colour out of Space" as a booklet. HPL revised the tale slightly for the prospective publication, but the plan never materialized. In early 1934 HPL put Baldwin in touch with Duane W. Rimel, who by coincidence lived in the same small town (Asotin, Washington). The two took turns reading HPL's letters to each of them. Baldwin wrote two columns of news notes for the *Fantasy Fan:* "Side Glances" (April, May, September 1934) and "Within the Circle" (June, July, August, October, November 1934, January, February 1935), much of the information

for which was derived from HPL's letters to him, as was the significant early article, "H. P. Lovecraft: A Biographical Sketch," originally scheduled to appear in
the *Fantasy Fan* but, following that magazine's demise, published in *Fantasy
Magazine* (April 1935). Baldwin later revised the article as "Some Lovecraft Sidelights" (*Fantasy Commentator,* Spring 1948). Excerpts of one letter (now at JHL)
were published as "Lovecraft as an Illustrator" (*Acolyte,* Summer 1943).

See Kenneth W. Faig, Jr., ed., *Within the Circle: In Memoriam F. Lee Baldwin* (Moshassuck Press, 1988).

**"Ballade of Patrick von Flynn; or, The Hibernio-German-American Eng-
land-Hater, Ye."** Poem (60 lines); written no later than April 23, 1915. First
published in the *Conservative* (April 1916).

A crude satire in which a group of anti-English Irishmen meet with some
Germans, begin drinking, and threaten to join forces to slander England. HPL
tactlessly sent the poem to the Irish-American John T. Dunn, whose reaction can
be gauged by HPL's comment: "I . . . am scarcely surprised that the 'von Flynn'
ballad proved less than pleasing" (HPL to John T. Dunn, June 28, 1916; *Books
at Brown* 38–39 [1991–92]: 182). The poem is oddly prescient, as it was published at the very time of the Easter Rebellion in Dublin, when some Irish rebels
joined forces with the Germans to overthrow British rule in Ireland. HPL continued to rant about the menace of unpatriotic Irish-Americans in "Lucubrations
Lovecraftian" (1921).

Barlow, Robert H[ayward] (1918–1951). Short-story writer, poet, artist, sculptor, publisher, collector, scholar, and HPL's literary executor. When Barlow began
corresponding with HPL in 1931, he concealed from HPL the fact that he was only
thirteen. Among his early fantasy writings are "Annals of the Jinns" (*Fantasy Fan,*
October 1933–February 1935), "The Slaying of the Monster" (1933), and "The
Hoard of the Wizard-Beast" (1933). Other tales appeared in various magazines of
the NAPA, which Barlow joined at HPL's suggestion; "Eyes of the God" (*Sea
Gull,* May 1933) won the story laureateship for that year. Barlow attempted to
bind and distribute HPL's *The Shunned House* (1928), but bound only a few copies (HPL's was in leather). He invited HPL to visit him at his home in De Land,
Fla., in the summer of 1934, and HPL stayed from May 2 to June 21. At that time
the two wrote the spoof "The Battle That Ended the Century" and two poems under the general title "Bouts Rimés," and HPL drew his celebrated portrait of
Cthulhu. HPL revised Barlow's "'Till A' the Seas'" (*Californian,* 1935) in January 1935, when Barlow was visiting colleagues in New York. Barlow again invited HPL to Florida in the summer of 1935, and HPL remained from June 9 to
August 18. At that time they wrote an unfinished parody, "Collapsing Cosmoses,"
and set type for Frank Belknap Long's poetry collection, *The Goblin Tower,*
which Barlow issued from his Dragon-Fly Press. Barlow also typed HPL's "The
Shadow out of Time." He wrote a superb HPL-influenced tale, "A Dim-
Remembered Story" (*Californian,* Summer 1936; rpt. Necronomicon Press, 1980),
apparently without HPL's assistance. He visited HPL in Providence in the summer
of 1936; shortly thereafter they collaborated on "The Night Ocean" (*Californian,*
Winter 1936), although the recently discovered typescript of the story shows that

the bulk of the tale is Barlow's. In the mid-1930s he brimmed with ideas for literary projects: an edition of Henry S. Whitehead's letters, to be entitled *Caneviniana;* a collection of C. L. Moore's tales; a volume of Clark Ashton Smith's poetry, *Incantations;* and booklets of HPL's *Fungi from Yuggoth* and collected poetry. Although some of these projects were begun, none was completed; but in conjunction with *Fungi from Yuggoth* (which Barlow partially typeset), the sonnet-cycle finally achieved its canonical form in the summer of 1936, with the addition of "Recapture" at Barlow's suggestion. Barlow published two issues of an amateur magazine, *The Dragon Fly* (October 15, 1935, May 15, 1936), although neither contained work by HPL. For Christmas 1935 Barlow published HPL's *The Cats of Ulthar* in an edition of forty-two copies.

Barlow aided significantly in the preservation of HPL's manuscripts by typing texts in exchange for autograph manuscripts. HPL named him his literary executor in "Instructions in Case of Decease" (1936); Annie E. P. Gamwell formalized the relationship in a document drawn up on March 26, 1937. Barlow came to Providence to sort through HPL's papers, taking some away (in accordance with the "Instructions") and donating others to the John Hay Library of Brown University. He assisted August Derleth and Donald Wandrei in preparing *O,* but they ostracized him from the field, particularly Wandrei, who believed Barlow had stolen HPL's papers. (HPL perhaps was more patient than Wandrei and Derleth with Barlow's persistent requests for their manuscripts.) Barlow edited HPL's *Notes & Commonplace Book* (1938), contributed to the *Acolyte,* and lent assistance to the first bibliography of HPL, by Francis T. Laney and William H. Evans (1943). He also edited two outstanding issues of the mimeographed fanzine *Leaves* (Summer 1937, 1938), containing rare works by HPL, A. Merritt, and other weird writers. He moved to Mexico around 1943, where he taught at several colleges, later becoming a professor of anthropology at Mexico City College and a distinguished anthropologist of Indian culture and poet (*Poems for a Competition* [1942], *A View from a Hill* [1947]). He wrote a poignant memoir of HPL, "The Wind That Is in the Grass" (in *Marginalia;* rpt. *LR*). He committed suicide on January 1, 1951, in Mexico City, when threatened with exposure of his homosexuality. See *Eyes of the God,* ed. S. T. Joshi, David E. Schultz, and Douglas A. Anderson (Hippocampus Press, 2002), containing Barlow's collected weird fiction and poetry, and *On Lovecraft and Life* (containing his journal of HPL's 1934 visit and his 1940s autobiography), ed. S. T. Joshi (Necronomicon Press, 1992).

See Lawrence Hart, "A Note on Robert Barlow," *Poetry* 78 (May 1951): 115–16; George T. Smisor, "R. H. Barlow and *Tlalocan,*" *Tlalocan* 3, No. 2 (1952): 97–102; Clare Mooser, "A Study of Robert Barlow: The T. E. Lawrence of Mexico," *Mexico Quarterly Review* 3, No. 2 (1968): 5–12; George T. Wetzel, "Lovecraft's Literary Executor," *Fantasy Commentator* 4, No. 1 (Winter 1978–79): 34–43; Kenneth W. Faig, Jr., "R. H. Barlow," *Journal of the H. P. Lovecraft Society* No. 2 (1979): [7–36]; Kenneth W. Faig, Jr., "Robert H. Barlow as H. P. Lovecraft's Literary Executor: An Appreciation," *Crypt* No. 60 (Hallowmas 1988): 52–62; S. T. Joshi, "R. H. Barlow and the Recognition of Lovecraft," *Crypt* No. 60 (Hallowmas 1988): 45–51, 32; S. T. Joshi, "Introduction" to Barlow's *On Lovecraft and Life* (Necronomicon Press, 1992); Steven J. Jordan, "H. P. Lovecraft in Florida," *LS* No. 42 (Summer 2001): 34–48.

Barry, Denys. In "The Moon-Bog," an American who buys and restores his ancestral castle in Kilderry, Ireland. When he attempts to drain the nearby bog, the spirits that dwell there exact their vengeance on him. Like Barry, HPL always hoped (unrealistically) to buy back his ancestral home.

Barzai the Wise. In "The Other Gods," the learned scholar who "knew so much of the gods . . . that he was deemed half a god himself." He attempts to scale Hatheg-Kla to glimpse the elusive gods of earth, thinking his great knowledge of them will protect him from their wrath. He thinks he finds them, but instead he encounters "the other gods," and, for his hubris, he is swept into the sky.

Bates, Harry [Hiram Gilmore], III (1900–1981), American author and editor. Bates was the first editor of the Clayton *Astounding Stories of Super-Science* (now *Analog*) and *Strange Tales of Mystery and Terror* (1931–33). He rejected at least five stories submitted by HPL to *Strange Tales* ("The Doom That Came to Sarnath," "The Nameless City," "Beyond the Wall of Sleep," and "Polaris" in April 1931; "In the Vault" in May 1931). HPL did have an uncredited contribution to *Strange Tales* when Henry S. Whitehead's "The Trap" (at least half of which was written by HPL) appeared in March 1932. Bates was the author of the Hawk Carse stories (as by Anthony Gilmore) and of "Farewell to the Master" (*Astounding Stories,* October 1940), adapted as *The Day the Earth Stood Still* (1951).

See Will Murray, "Lovecraft and *Strange Tales,*" *Crypt* No. 74 (Lammas 1990): 3–11.

Batta. In "Winged Death," the houseboy of Dr. Thomas Slauenwite, whom Slauenwite deliberately causes to be bitten by a strange insect to see if the untreated bite is fatal. It proves to be so.

"Battle That Ended the Century, The." Short story (1,200 words); written in collaboration with R. H. Barlow, June 1934. First published as a mimeographed flyer (June 1934); rpt. *Acolyte* (Fall 1944); first collected in *Cats*; corrected text in *Eyes of the God* (Hippocampus Press, 2002).

On the eve of the year 2001, a great heavyweight fight is held between Two-Gun Bob, the Terror of the Plains, and Knockout Bernie, the Wild Wolf of West Shokan. After several rounds, Two-Gun Bob is declared the winner, but the World Court reverses the verdict and the Wild Wolf is declared the true victor.

The squib was conceived when HPL was visiting Barlow in Florida in the summer of 1934. Barlow was clearly the originator, as typescripts prepared by him survive, one with extensive revisions in pen by HPL. The idea was to mention as many mutual colleagues as possible, in various comical contexts relating to their actual literary work or personality. Barlow had initially cited them by their actual names, but HPL felt that this was not very interesting, so he devised parodic or punning names for them: Frank Belknap Long is alluded to as Frank Chimesleep Short, HPL as Horse-Power Hateart.

Barlow and HPL then circulated the whimsy, but in such a way that its authorship would not be immediately evident. The plan was this: Barlow would mimeograph the item (copies exist in two 8½″ × 14″ sheets, each with text on one side only) and then have the copies mailed from a location that could not be traced to either HPL or Barlow. It appears that fifty duplicated copies were prepared toward the middle of June and were sent to Washington, D.C., where they would be mailed (possibly by Elizabeth Toldridge, a colleague of both HPL's and Barlow's but not associated with the weird fiction circle). This seems to have been done just before HPL left De Land and began heading north, so that the items would be in the hands of associates by the time HPL reached Washington.

In correspondence, the two authors talk in conspiratorial tones about its reception by colleagues: "Note the signature—Chimesleep Short—which indicates that our spoof has gone out & that he [Long] at least thinks I've seen the thing. Remember that if you didn't know anything about it, you'd consider it merely a whimsical trick of his own—& that if you'd merely seen the circular, you wouldn't think it worth commenting on. I'm ignoring the matter in my reply" (HPL to R. H. Barlow, June 29, 1934; ms., JHL). Some colleagues were amused, but others were less so. HPL notes: "Wandrei wasn't exactly in a rage, but (according to Belknap) sent the folder on to Desmond Hall with the languid comment, 'Here's something that may interest you—it doesn't interest me'" (HPL to R. H. Barlow, July 21, 1934; ms., JHL).

Bayboro. Fictitious town in Maine invented either by HPL or by C. M. Eddy; mentioned in "The Loved Dead" (1923) and "Deaf, Dumb, and Blind" (1924).

"Beast in the Cave, The." Juvenile story (2,500 words); first draft written in the spring of 1904; final draft completed April 21, 1905. First published in *Vagrant* (June 1918); first collected in *Marginalia;* corrected text in *D.*

A man slowly realizes that he is lost in Mammoth Cave and may never be found. He wavers between resignation at his fate and a desire for self-preservation; but when he begins shouting to call attention to himself, he summons not the guide who had led his tour group but a shambling beast whom he cannot see in the blackness of the cave but can only hear. In attempting to protect himself from the creature he hurls rocks at it and appears to have fatally injured it. Fleeing from the scene, he comes upon the guide and leads him back to the site of his encounter with the beast. The "beast" turns out to be a man who has been lost in the cave for years.

HPL notes that he spent "days of boning at the library" (i.e., the Providence Public Library) in researching the locale of the tale, Mammoth Cave in Kentucky. It is perhaps a kind of mirror-image of Poe's "The Murders in the Rue Morgue": in that story, what are taken to be the actions of a man turn out to have been performed by an ape, whereas here what is taken for an ape proves to be a man. The last page of the autograph manuscript bears the notation

> Tales of Terror
>   I. The Beast in the Cave
> By H. P. Lovecraft
>   (Period—Modern)

We do not know what other tales were to make up this volume.

Bennett, George. In "The Lurking Fear," he and William Tobey accompany the narrator to the Martense mansion in search of the entity that haunts it. They spend the night, but Bennett and Tobey mysteriously disappear.

"Beyond the Wall of Sleep." Short story (4,360 words); written Spring 1919. First published in *Pine Cones* (October 1919), an amateur journal edited by John Clinton Pryor; rpt. *Fantasy Fan* (October 1934) and *WT* (March 1938); first collected in *BWS;* corrected text in *D;* annotated version in *TD.*

Joe Slater (or Slaader), a denizen of the Catskill Mountains, is interned in a mental institution in 1900 because of the horrible murder of another man. Slater seems clearly mad, filled with strange cosmic visions that he, in his "debased patois," is unable to articulate coherently. The narrator, an intern at the asylum, takes a special interest in Slater because he feels that there is something beyond his comprehension in Slater's wild dreams and fancies. He contrives a "cosmic 'radio'" with which he hopes to establish mental communication with Slater. After many fruitless attempts, communication finally occurs, preceded by weird music and visions of spectacular beauty: Slater's body has in fact been occupied all his life by an extraterrestrial entity that for some reason has a burning desire for revenge against the star Algol (the Daemon-Star). With the impending death of Slater, the entity will be free to exact the vengeance it has always desired. Then reports come on February 22, 1901, of a nova near Algol.

HPL notes that the story was inspired by a passing mention of Catskill Mountain denizens in an article on the New York State Constabulary in the *New York Tribune*—"How Our State Police Have Spurred Their Way to Fame," by F. F. Van de Water (April 27, 1919). The story presumably was written shortly thereafter. The article actually mentions a family named the Slaters or Slahters as representative of the decadent squalor of the mountaineers. HPL concludes the story with an account of the nova taken verbatim from his copy of Garrett P. Serviss's *Astronomy with the Naked Eye* (1908).

Some have claimed that the story was influenced by Ambrose Bierce's "Beyond the Wall" (in the revised edition of *Can Such Things Be?* [1909]). HPL had first read Bierce in 1919, but there is no similarity between the two stories except in their titles, as Bierce's tale is a conventional ghost story that bears no resemblance to HPL's. There may be an influence from Jack London's *Before Adam* (1906), although there is no evidence that HPL read it. The novel is an account of hereditary memory, in which a man from the modern age has dreams of the life of his remote ancestor in primitive times. At the very outset of the novel London's character remarks: "Nor . . . did any of my human kind ever break through the wall of my sleep." Other passages seem to be echoed in HPL's story. In effect, HPL presents a mirror-image of *Before Adam:* whereas London's narrator is a modern (civilized) man who has visions of a primitive past, Joe Slater is a primitive human being whose visions, as HPL declares, are such as "only a superior or even exceptional brain could conceive."

Bierce, Ambrose [Gwinnett] (1842–c. 1914). American short story writer and journalist. His best tales are collected in *Tales of Soldiers and Civilians* [*In the Midst of Life*] (1891) and *Can Such Things Be?* (1893), the former containing his Civil War tales (many filled with moments of terror and grue) and tales of psychological horror, the latter his weird fiction. HPL first read Bierce (at the instigation of Samuel Loveman) in 1919. HPL discusses Bierce's work in "Supernatural Horror in Literature," where he quotes from Loveman's preface to Bierce's *Twenty-one Letters of Ambrose Bierce* (1922), published by HPL's friend George Kirk. The invisible monster in "The Damned Thing" is a likely influence on "The Dunwich Horror." Clark Ashton Smith felt that "In the Vault" had "the realistic grimness of Bierce" (letter to HPL, March 11, 1930; ms., JHL). HPL discusses the authorship of *The Monk and the Hangman's Daughter* (cotranslated with Adolphe de Castro [later a client of HPL] from the German of Richard Voss) in *SL* 1.203–7. Frank Belknap Long revised de Castro's *Portrait of Ambrose Bierce* (1929) after HPL declined.

See Carey McWilliams, *Ambrose Bierce: A Biography* (A. & C. Boni, 1929); M. E. Grenander, *Ambrose Bierce* (Twayne, 1971); Roy Morris, Jr., *Ambrose Bierce: Alone in Bad Company* (Crown, 1995).

Birch, George. The undertaker of Peck Valley (state unknown), who is the subject of "In the Vault." His carelessness and unprofessionalism not only cause him to be imprisoned in the local cemetery's receiving tomb but also exact the revenge of one of the corpses temporarily stored there.

Bishop, Mamie. In "The Dunwich Horror," the "common-law wife" of Earl Sawyer, who is one of the first to see Wilbur Whateley after he is born. She is the confidante of Wilbur's mother, Lavinia. Mamie's relationship to **Seth Bishop** is unspecified. Seth's cattle suffer bizarre wounds from Wilbur's twin brother. **Silas Bishop** is merely said to be "of the undecayed Bishops."

Bishop, Zealia Brown Reed (1897–1968). Revision client and correspondent of HPL. Samuel Loveman introduced her to HPL around 1928. She wished to write romantic fiction, but HPL attempted to steer her toward weird or serious mainstream work. HPL ghostwrote "The Curse of Yig" (*WT*, November 1929) in 1928 from a plot synopsis and a questionnaire pertaining to the Oklahoma setting for the story; "The Mound" (December 1929–January 1930) and "Medusa's Coil" (May 1930) were written from brief plot-germs (HPL's synopsis for the latter survives in AHT). *WT* rejected "The Mound" when it was submitted by Frank Belknap Long, who was acting as Bishop's agent; Long then abridged the text, but it was again rejected. The stories, having been rewritten by August Derleth, appeared in *WT* ("The Mound" in November 1940; "Medusa's Coil" in January 1939). The corrected texts were not published until *HM*. The three stories were published in *The Curse of Yig* (Arkham House, 1953), for which Bishop wrote an error-filled memoir, "H. P. Lovecraft: A Pupil's View" (rpt. *LR*).

Blackwood, Algernon [Henry] (1869–1951). British author whose work HPL praised highly: he considered "The Willows" (in *The Listener and Other Stories* [1907]) the best weird tale in all literature. "The Wendigo" (in *The Lost Valley and Other Stories* [1910]) probably influenced "The Dunwich Horror" in its use of anomalous footprints to indicate the presence of a supernatural entity. Oddly enough, HPL did not care for Blackwood when he first read him in 1920 (see HPL to the Gallomo, [January] 1920; AHT); but when HPL read "The Willows" in an anthology in late 1924, he was convinced that, despite his unevenness, Blackwood was among the leading authors of supernatural fiction, particularly in his suggestions of cosmicism. Blackwood was a mystic with a fascination for Eastern thought; his novel *The Centaur* (1911) is his spiritual autobiography. *John Silence—Physician Extraordinary* (1908) popularized the use of the "psychic detective"; it was imitated by William Hope Hodgson and others. Blackwood also wrote fantasies for and about children, including *Jimbo: A Fantasy* (1909) and *The Education of Uncle Paul* (1909). HPL praised *Incredible Adventures* (1914), a collection of four long stories, in "Supernatural Horror in Literature" and elsewhere (see, e.g., *SL* 5.160). Late in life Blackwood became popular on BBC radio and television. See *Selected Tales* (1938), *Tales of the Uncanny and Supernatural* (1949), *Tales of the Mysterious and Macabre* (1967), and his autobiography *Episodes Before Thirty* (1923).

See Mike Ashley, "Lovecraft and Blackwood: A Surveillance," *Crypt* No. 51 (Hallowmas 1987): 3–8, 14; Mike Ashley, "The Cosmic Connection," *Crypt* No. 57 (St. John's Eve 1988): 3–9; Mike Ashley, *Algernon Blackwood: A Bio-Bibliography* (Greenwood Press, 1987); S. T. Joshi, "Algernon Blackwood: The Expansion of Consciousness," in Joshi's *The Weird Tale* (University of Texas Press, 1990); Mike Ashley, *Algernon Blackwood: An Extraordinary Life* (2001).

Blake, Richard. In "Deaf, Dumb, and Blind," the author-poet from Boston who rents a country cottage near Fenham, thinking it will provide imaginative stimulus for his work. While there, he becomes aware of an unseen presence and later is found dead.

Blake, Robert. In "The Haunter of the Dark," the writer of weird tales from Milwaukee, Wis., who moves to Providence, R.I., for inspiration. He keeps a diary of his investigations of the Free-Will Church, which he had first observed from his window but then sought out across town. He unwittingly disturbs the unseen presence residing in the abandoned church and, in the end, dies from his encounter with the avatar of Nyarlathotep.

Blake is loosely based on Robert Bloch, to whom the story is dedicated. (Blake's Milwaukee address was Bloch's real address at the time the story was written.) However, he also embodies attributes of HPL himself. The view from Blake's room in Providence is exactly that which HPL saw. The titles of the stories attributed to Blake are parodies of HPL's and Bloch's own stories.

Blandot. In "The Music of Erich Zann," the "paralytic" landlord of the boarding house on the Rue d'Auseil where Zann and the narrator reside.

Blish, James (1921–1975). Pioneering American science fiction writer who corresponded briefly with HPL (1936). Blish and his friend William Miller planned to issue a fanzine, *The Planeteer,* and in the spring of 1936 asked HPL for contributions. HPL sent them the poem "The Wood," which was to appear in September 1936; although the pages containing the poem were printed, the issue was never completed. HPL continued to correspond with Blish and Miller (apparently writing to them jointly) until the summer. Three of his letters to them were published in the fanzine *Phantastique/Science Fiction Critic* (March 1938); rpt. HPL's *Uncollected Letters* (Necronomicon Press, 1986). Blish went on to become a distinguished science fiction writer, with such landmark novels as *A Case of Conscience* (1958), *Black Easter* (1968), and *Doctor Mirabilis* (1964; rev. 1971).

See David Ketterer, *Imprisoned in a Tesseract: The Life and Work of James Blish* (1987).

Bloch, Robert (1917–1994). American novelist and short story writer. He first encountered HPL's work in *WT* in 1927; he corresponded with HPL (1933–37); see *Letters to Robert Bloch,* ed. David E. Schultz and S. T. Joshi (Necronomicon Press, 1993; supplement, 1993). Bloch invented an analogue to HPL's *Necronomicon,* Ludvig Prinn's *Mysteries of the Worm,* in "The Secret in the Tomb" (*WT,* May 1935); HPL coined the Latin title, *De Vermis Mysteriis.* Bloch also created *Cultes des Goules* (often misattributed to August Derleth because the *fictional* author is the "Comte d'Erlette"), *The Cabala of Saboth,* and the *Black Rites* of the mad priest Luveh-Keraph. He wrote a playful trilogy with HPL, comprising Bloch's "The Shambler from the Stars" (*WT,* September 1935), HPL's "The Haunter of the Dark" (written November 1935; *WT,* December 1936), and Bloch's "The Shadow from the Steeple" (*WT,* September 1950). HPL lent advice on Bloch's early tale "Satan's Servants" (written in early 1935; first published in *Cats*), but does not appear to have written any prose in the story. Most of Bloch's Lovecraftian tales are collected in *Mysteries of the Worm,* ed. Lin Carter (1981; rev. ed. [by Robert M. Price] Chaosium, 1993). Bloch later turned to the genres of mystery and suspense, writing such notable novels as *The Scarf* (1947), *Psycho* (1959), *The Dead Beat* (1960), and many others. *Strange Eons* (1978) is a Lovecraftian pastiche. See his autobiography, *Once Around the Bloch* (1993).

See Randall Larson, *Robert Bloch* (Starmont House, 1986); Randall Larson, *The Complete Robert Bloch: An Illustrated International Bibliography* (Fandom Unlimited, 1986); S. T. Joshi, "A Literary Tutelage: Robert Bloch and H. P. Lovecraft," *Studies in Weird Fiction* No. 16 (Winter 1995): 13–25.

"Bolshevism." Essay (500 words); probably written in the summer of 1919. First published in the *Conservative* (July 1919); rpt. *MW* and *CE5.* A warning not to listen to "long-haired anarchists" who preach social upheaval and a condemnation of the "almost sub-human Russian rabble" who caused the Russian revolution in 1917.

Bolton. Actual town in east-central Massachusetts, cited by HPL in "Herbert West—Reanimator" (1921–22), "The Rats in the Walls" (1923), and "The Colour out of Space" (1927). The earlier story cites a Bolton Worsted Mills, but that mention is puzzling because in HPL's day Bolton was a tiny agricultural hamlet with no industries of significance. This led Robert D. Marten (see entry on "Arkham") to conjecture that HPL coined the name Bolton, unaware of the real town of that name. Its location appears to be near Arkham (Salem), as the real Bolton is not. HPL mentioned passing through Bolton in October 1934, so he may have known of it earlier.

Bonner, Marion F. (1883–1952). Neighbor and correspondent of HPL (1936–37). Several of HPL's letters to her (the originals of which at JHL contain hand-colored illustrations of letterhead for HPL's imaginary feline fraternity, the Kappa Alpha Tau) are included in *SL* 5. See her article, "Miscellaneous Impressions of H.P.L." (1945; in *LR*).

"Book, The" (title supplied by R. H. Barlow). Story fragment (1,200 words); probably written c. October 1933. First published in *Leaves* (1938); first collected in *Marginalia;* corrected text in *D.*

The unnamed first-person narrator, whose "memories are very confused," tells of coming upon a "worm-riddled book" in an obscure bookstall near the river. Recognizing it, in spite of the absence of its opening pages, as a rare and forbidden work, he wishes to purchase it; but the old man tending the bookstall merely "leered and tittered," refusing payment for it. The narrator hurries through the narrow streets to his home, sensing vague and disturbing presences around him. As he reaches home and begins examining the book in his attic study, he hears a faint scratching at the window—evidently a creature he had summoned by uttering an incantation in the book. After that time his perceptions are seriously affected: "Mixed with the present scene was always a little of the past and a little of the future. . . ." Further bizarre events occur as the narrator continues to chant the formulae in the book. At this point the fragment ends.

R. H. Barlow dated the fragment to 1934, but in a letter of October 1933 HPL writes: "I am at a sort of standstill in writing—disgusted at much of my older work, & uncertain as to avenues of improvement. In recent weeks I have done a tremendous amount of experimenting in different styles & perspectives, but have destroyed *most* [emphasis added] of the results" (*SL* 4.289). The fragment appears to be an attempt to recast *Fungi from Yuggoth* in prose. The existing text narrates the events outlined in the first three poems of the sonnet-cycle (which indeed present a connected narrative); the fact that the text terminates at this point may suggest that HPL had no idea how to write the rest of the cycle as a coherent story.

See S. T. Joshi, "On 'The Book,'" *Nyctalops* 3, No. 4 (April 1983): 9–13; rpt. *Crypt* No. 53 (Candlemas 1988): 3–7; Michael Cisco, "The Book of 'The Book,'" *LS* No. 42 (Summer 2001): 5–21.

Bor, Dam. In "Collapsing Cosmoses," an operator of a "cosmoscope" who sees a dangerous enemy approaching the planet from outer space.

Borellus. Author of an unnamed work cited as an epigraph to *The Case of Charles Dexter Ward* (1927). HPL found the name and the passage in his copy of Cotton Mather's *Magnalia Christi Americana* (1702). Borellus is the seventeenth-century alchemist Pierre Borel (c. 1620–1689), not (as Roger Bryant conjectured) the Italian scientist Giovanni Borelli (1608–1679).

See Roger Bryant, "The Alchemist and the Scientist: Borellus and the Lovecraftian Imagination," *Nyctalops* 2, No. 3 (January–February 1975): 26–29, 43; Barton L. St. Armand, "The Source for Lovecraft's Knowledge of Borellus in *The Case of Charles Dexter Ward*," *Nyctalops* 2, No. 6 (May 1977): 16–17.

"Bouts Rimés." Two poems: "Beyond Zimbabwe" (8 lines) and "The White Elephant" (8 lines); cowritten with R. H. Barlow on May 23, 1934. First published in *Saturnalia and Other Poems* (1984). Barlow selected the end rhymes, then HPL composed the text.

Bowen, Hannah. In "The Shunned House," a woman who is hired by William Harris to be a servant at the house but who dies a few months later.

Boyle, Dr. E. M. In "The Shadow out of Time," an Australian (possibly a psychologist) who brings Nathaniel Wingate Peaslee's papers relating to his bizarre "dreams" to the attention of Robert B. F. Mackenzie, and who then accompanies Peaslee and Mackenzie on an expedition to the Great Sandy Desert.

Bradofsky, Hyman (b. 1906). Correspondent of HPL (1934–37). He was president of the NAPA in 1935–36 and came under vicious attack by other members (in part, perhaps, because he was Jewish); HPL defended him in the essay "Some Current Motives and Practices" (1936), which R. H. Barlow mimeographed and distributed. As editor of the amateur journal *The Californian* (1933f.), he offered unprecedented space for lengthy contributions of fiction, essays, and poetry. The Summer 1937 memorial issue is devoted to HPL, containing fine memoirs (including Bradofsky's own poignant brief recollection in the column, "Amateur Affairs") and hitherto unpublished writings by HPL.

Briden, William. In "The Call of Cthulhu," a sailor on the crew of the *Emma* who, seeing Cthulhu, goes mad and later dies.

Brinton, William. In "The Rats in the Walls," the archaeologist who leads the exploration party into the crypt discovered beneath Exham Priory.

Brobst, Harry K[ern] (b. 1909). Friend of HPL (1932–37). Born in Wilmington, Del., Brobst came with his family to Allentown, Pa., around 1921, befriending the young Carl F. Strauch, with whom he shared an interest in weird fiction and *WT*. Brobst particularly liked the work of HPL, Clark Ashton Smith, and other *WT* writers. Securing HPL's address from Farnsworth Wright, Brobst wrote to HPL, probably in the autumn of 1931, receiving a cordial reply. In early 1932, Brobst entered a program in psychiatric nursing at Butler Hospital in Providence, and from that time till HPL's death he was a frequent visitor at HPL's home and companion on his local travels, including Bristol and Warren, R.I., in March 1932 (*SL* 4.29) and a tour of Butler Hospital sometime in 1932 (*SL* 4.191). In July 1933 Brobst joined HPL in welcoming E. Hoffmann Price; it was on this occasion that the three of them spent an entire night dissecting a story by Strauch. Brobst has confirmed that HPL worked briefly as a ticket agent in a movie theater in downtown Providence and has also noted that in 1936 HPL was horrified at the stories of Nazi atrocities as related to him by an acquaintance (a Mrs. Shepherd) who had visited Germany. Brobst visited HPL frequently in Butler Hospital during the latter's terminal illness. He wrote letters to R. H. Barlow on March 2 and March 13, 1937, describing HPL's condition, and saw HPL two days before his death, asking him how he felt; HPL replied, "Sometimes the pain is unbearable." Brobst and his wife attended HPL's funeral service and burial on March 18, 1937. Subsequently Brobst gained a B.A. in psychology from Brown University and an M.A. and Ph.D. from the University of Pennsylvania. He spent many years teaching at Oklahoma State University. His extensive recollections of HPL are recorded in "An Interview with Harry K. Brobst" (*LS* Nos. 22/23 [Fall 1990]: 24–42; abridged version in *LR* as "Autumn in Providence: Harry K. Brobst on Lovecraft").

Brown, Luther. In "The Dunwich Horror," a hired boy at George Corey's farm who sees the huge footprints of Wilbur Whateley's monstrous twin brother in the vicinity of Cold Spring Glen.

Brown, Walter. In "The Whisperer in Darkness," the "surly farmer" whose dealings with the aliens from Yuggoth result in his mysterious disappearance.

Bruce, Malcolm. In "Ashes," the assistant of the scientist Arthur Van Allister. Bruce mistakenly thinks Van Allister has used his secretary in an experiment to test his newly discovered chemical compound, and after a struggle he subjects the scientist to the same formula.

Bullen, John Ravenor (1886–1927). Canadian poet and amateur journalist. He possibly introduced HPL to the Transatlantic Circulator (an Anglo-American correspondence group) in 1921. Some of his poetry later appeared in HPL's *Conservative.* When Bullen died, his mother asked HPL to prepare an edition of Bullen's poetry, and HPL did so. The Recluse Press (W. Paul Cook) published *White Fire* in 1927 (a second edition was printed in 1929 but never bound). HPL's preface is a revised version of his essay "The Poetry of John Ravenor Bullen" (*United Amateur,* September 1925).

"Bureau of Critics." Series of articles in the *National Amateur* (1923–36), reviewing contributions by amateur journalists of the NAPA. The articles appeared as follows: "Bureau of Critics" (March 1923); "Bureau of Critics" (December 1931); "Critics Submit First Report" (December 1932); "Report of Bureau of Critics" (March 1933); "Report of Bureau of Critics" (June 1933); "Bureau of Critics Comment on Verse, Typography, Prose" (December 1933); "Chairman of the Bureau of Critics Reports on Poetry" (September 5, 1934); "Report of the Bureau of Critics" (December 1934); "Report of the Bureau of Critics" (March 1935); "Lovecraft Offers Verse Criticism" (June 1935); "Some Current Amateur Verse" (December 1935); rpt. *CE1.*

The articles are similar to the "Department of Public Criticism" pieces HPL wrote for the UAPA. Here, however, he generally focused on amateur verse; he usually managed to persuade other critics (e.g., Helm C. Spink, Edward H. Cole, Rheinhart Kleiner) to write sections on prose, typography, and other subjects.

Bush, David Van (1882–1959). Itinerant lecturer, would-be poet, and popular psychologist; revision client of HPL. He joined the UAPA in 1916; he first came in touch with HPL through the Symphony Literary Service (a revision service operated by HPL, Anne Tillery Renshaw, and others) in early 1917. Bush was at the time the author of several poetry volumes (not revised by HPL), including *Peace Poems and Sausages* (1915) and *Soul Poems and Love Lyrics* (1916). HPL revised many poetry volumes and psychology manuals during the period 1920–25, including *Grit and Gumption* (1921), *Inspirational Poems* (1921), *Applied Psychology and Scientific Living* (1922; HPL admits to writing two or three chapters; other chapters were written by Bush's staff), *Poems of Mastery and Love Verse* (1922), *Practical Psychology and Sex Life* (1922), etc. HPL met Bush in Boston in the summer of 1922 (see *SL* 1.185–88); he wrote the essay "East and West Harvard Conservatism" (an account of Bush's lecture in Cambridge) for Bush's magazine *Mind Power Plus* (c. 1922). (No issues are known to exist; only a clipping of HPL's essay survives in JHL.) Bush provided HPL with a steady income through the mid-1920s, as HPL charged $1 for 8 lines of poetry revised.

C

C———, **Antoine, Comte de.** In "The Alchemist," the last of a long line of comtes, each of whom suffers a mysterious death prior to the age of thirty-two—the age of **Henri, Comte de C———,** when, in the thirteenth century, he blamed Michel Mauvais, a wizard residing on his estates, for the disappearance of his son **Godfrey.** Later Godfrey is found alive, but in the meantime Henri has killed Michel. Michel's son, Charles Le Sorcier, pronounces a curse that appears to affect all the Comtes de C———, including Godfrey's son **Robert** and Robert's son **Louis.**

"Call of Cthulhu, The." Short story (12,000 words); written probably in August or September 1926. First published in *WT* (February 1928); first collected in *O;* corrected text in *DH;* annotated version in *An2* and *CC.*

The narrator (identified, only in the subtitle [omitted in many editions], as "the late Francis Wayland Thurston, of Boston") gives an account of the strange facts he has assembled, both from the papers of his recently deceased granduncle, George Gammell Angell, and from personal investigation. Angell, a professor of Semitic languages at Brown University, had collected several peculiar pieces of data. First, he had taken extensive notes of the dreams and artwork of a young sculptor, Henry Anthony Wilcox, who had come to him with a bas-relief he had fashioned in his sleep on the night of March 1, 1925. The sculpture is of a hideous-looking alien entity, and Wilcox had reported that, in the dream that had inspired it, he had repeatedly heard the words *"Cthulhu fhtagn."* It was this that had piqued Angell's interest, for he had encountered these words or sounds years before, at a meeting of the American Archaeological Society, in which a police inspector from New Orleans named John Raymond Legrasse had brought in a sculpture very much like Wilcox's and claimed that it had been worshipped in the Louisiana bayou by a degraded cult that had chanted the phrase *"Ph'nglui mglw'nafh Cthulhu R'lyeh wgah'nagl fhtagn."* One cult member translated this outlandish utterance thus: "In his house at R'lyeh dead Cthulhu waits dreaming." A mestizo named Castro told Legrasse that Cthulhu was a vast being that had come from the stars when the earth was young, along with another set of entities named the Great Old Ones. He was entombed in the sunken city of R'lyeh and would emerge when the "stars were ready" to reclaim control of the earth. The cult "would always be waiting to liberate him." Castro points out that these matters are spoken of in the *Necronomicon* of the mad Arab Abdul Alhazred.

Scarcely knowing what to make of this bizarre material, Thurston stumbles on a newspaper clipping telling of strange events aboard a ship in the Pacific Ocean; accompanying the article is a picture of a bas-relief very similar to those of Wilcox and Legrasse. Thurston goes to Oslo to talk with the Norwegian sailor, Gustaf Johansen, who had been on board the ship, but finds that he is dead. Johansen had, however, left an account of his experience showing that he had encountered Cthulhu when the city of R'lyeh rose from the sea-bottom as the result of an earthquake; but, presumably because the stars were not "ready," the city sinks again, returning Cthulhu to the bottom of the ocean. But the mere existence of this titanic entity is an unending source of profound unease to Thurston because it shows how tenuous is mankind's vaunted supremacy upon this planet.

The story had been plotted a full year earlier, as recorded in HPL's diary entry for August 12–13, 1925: "Write out story plot—'The Call of Cthulhu.'" But the origin of the tale goes back even further, to an entry in his commonplace book (#25) that must date to late 1919 or January 1920:

Man visits museum of antiquities—asks that it accept a bas-relief *he has* just made—*old* & learned curator laughs & says he cannot accept anything so modern. Man says that

"dreams are older than brooding Egypt or the contemplative Sphinx or garden-girdled Babylonia"

& that he had fashioned the sculpture in his dreams. Curator bids him shew his product, & when he does so curator shews horror, asks who the man may be. He tells modern name. "No—*before that*" says curator. Man does not remember except in dreams. Then curator offers high price, but man fears he means to destroy sculpture. Asks fabulous price—curator will consult directors. ¶ Add good development & describe nature of bas-relief.

This is the fairly literal encapsulation of a dream HPL had, which he describes at length in two letters of the period (*Dreams and Fancies* [Arkham House, 1962], pp. 49–50; *SL* 1.114–15).

There are two dominant literary influences on the tale. One is Guy de Maupassant's "The Horla," which HPL probably read subsequent to the dream of 1920; it was contained in Julian Hawthorne's *The Lock and Key Library* (1909), which HPL purchased in 1922. In "Supernatural Horror in Literature" HPL writes of it: "Relating the advent to France of an invisible being who lives on water and milk, sways the minds of others, and seems to be the vanguard of a horde of extra-terrestrial organisms arrived on earth to subjugate and overwhelm mankind, this tense narrative is perhaps without a peer in its particular department. . . ." The other influence is Arthur Machen's "Novel of the Black Seal" (an episode of *The Three Impostors* [1895]), which features just the kind of "piecing together of dissociated knowledge" contained in HPL's story; there is even a newspaper clipping that plays a role in the coincidental assembling of

information leading Machen's protagonist, Professor Gregg, to confirm his suspicions of the existence of the "Little People" in Wales; the difficult-to-
pronounce name *Ixaxar* suggests HPL's *Cthulhu;* and the Sixtystone itself suggests the bas-relief of Cthulhu.

Another influence on the tale is theosophy. HPL cites a theosophical work,
W. Scott-Elliot's *The Story of Atlantis and the Lost Lemuria* (1925), in the story;
the theosophists are themselves mentioned in the second paragraph. Castro's
wild tale of the Great Old Ones makes allusions to cryptic secrets that "deathless
Chinamen" told him—a nod to the theosophists' accounts of Shamballah, the
Tibetan holy city (the prototype of Shangri-La) whence the doctrines of theosophy are supposed to have originated. Still another influence is A. Merritt's "The
Moon Pool" (1918), which takes place on or near the island of Ponape in the
Carolines. Merritt's mention of a "moon-door" that, when tilted, leads the characters into a lower region of wonder and horror, seems similar to the huge door
whose inadvertent opening by the sailors causes Cthulhu to emerge from R'lyeh.

The story contains are several autobiographical elements. The name of the
narrator, Francis Wayland Thurston, is clearly derived from Francis Wayland
(1796–1865), president of Brown University from 1827 to 1855. Gammell is a
legitimate variant of Gamwell (a reference to HPL's aunt Annie E. P. Gamwell),
while Angell is both the name of one of the principal thoroughfares in Providence (HPL had resided in two different houses on Angell Street) and one of the
most distinguished families in the city. Wilcox is a name from HPL's ancestry.
Mention of "a learned friend in Paterson, New Jersey; the curator of a local museum and a mineralogist of note" is a clear allusion to James F. Morton. (The
name Castro is, however, not derived from HPL's colleague Adolphe Danziger
de Castro, as HPL did not become acquainted with him until late 1927.) The
earthquake cited in the story actually occurred.

The Fleur-de-Lys building at 7 Thomas Street, residence of Wilcox, is a real
structure, still standing. Bertrand K. Hart, literary editor of the *Providence Journal* and author of a regular column, "The Sideshow," read the story in an anthology (see below) and was astounded to find that Wilcox's residence and his were
one and the same. Feigning offense, he vowed in his column of November 30,
1929, to send a ghost to HPL's home at 3 A.M. to scare him; HPL promptly
wrote the poem "The Messenger" at 3:07 A.M. that night. Hart published the
poem in his column of December 3.

"The Call of Cthulhu" is manifestly an exhaustive reworking of "Dagon"
(1917). In that tale we have many nuclei of the later work—an earthquake that
causes an undersea land mass to emerge to the surface; the notion of a titanic
monster dwelling under the sea; and—although this is barely hinted in
"Dagon"—the fact that an entire civilization, hostile or at best indifferent to
mankind, is lurking on the underside of our world.

On the pronunciation of *Cthulhu* HPL gives somewhat different accounts in
various letters; his most exhaustive discussion occurs in 1934: ". . . the word is
supposed to represent a fumbling human attempt to catch the phonetics of an
absolutely non-human word. The name of the hellish entity was invented by
beings whose vocal organs were not like man's, hence it has no relation to the
human speech equipment. The syllables were determined by a physiological

equipment wholly unlike ours, *hence could never be uttered perfectly by human throats.* . . . The actual sound—as nearly as human organs could imitate it or human letters record it—may be taken as something like *Khlûl'-hloo,* with the first syllable pronounced gutturally and very thickly. The *u* is about like that in *full;* and the first syllable is not unlike *klul* in sound, hence the *h* represents the guttural thickness" (HPL to Duane W. Rimel, July 23, 1934; *SL* 5.10–11). Various colleagues give very different, and clearly inaccurate, reports of HPL's pronunciation of the word in their presence. In any case, it is not pronounced "Kathoo-loo," as commonly assumed.

Farnsworth Wright of *WT* rejected "The Call of Cthulhu" in October 1926. In May 1927 it was rejected by the obscure pulp magazine *Mystery Stories,* edited by Robert Sampson. The next month Donald Wandrei, who was visiting Wright in Chicago while hitchhiking from St. Paul to Providence, urged Wright to reconsider the story (just as HPL had asked Wright to reconsider Wandrei's "The Red Brain"), slyly suggesting that HPL was planning to submit it to other magazines and thereby begin developing other markets for his work. In early July Wright asked to see the tale again and accepted it. It appeared in T. Everett Harré's *Beware After Dark!* (1929), thereby constituting one of the earliest appearances of HPL's stories in hardcover.

See Robert M. Price, "HPL and HPB: Lovecraft's Use of Theosophy," *Crypt* No. 5 (Roodmas 1982): 3–9; Steven J. Mariconda, "On the Emergence of 'Cthulhu,'" *LS* No. 15 (Fall 1987): 54–58 (rpt. in Mariconda's *On the Emergence of "Cthulhu" and Other Observations* [Necronomicon Press, 1995]); Peter Cannon, "The Late Francis Wayland Thurston, of Boston: Lovecraft's Last Dilettante," *LS* Nos. 19/20 (Fall 1989): 32, 39; Robert M. Price, "Correlated Contents," *Crypt* No. 82 (Hallowmas 1992): 11–16; Stefan Dziemianowicz, "On 'The Call of Cthulhu,'" *LS* No. 33 (Fall 1995): 30–35; Michael Garrett, "Death Takes a Dive: 'The City in the Sea' and Lovecraft's 'The Call of Cthulhu,'" *LS* No. 35 (Fall 1996): 22–24.

Campbell, George. In "The Challenge from Beyond," a geologist who encounters a curious crystalline cube while on vacation in the Canadian woods and becomes mentally drawn into it. He eventually realizes that the cube is a mind-exchange device launched by an interstellar civilization—"a mighty race of worm-like beings."

Campbell, Paul J[onas] (1884–1945), amateur journalist and editor of *Invictus* and *The Liberal,* for which HPL wrote "A Confession of Unfaith" (published in February 1922). He corresponded sporadically with HPL (c. 1915–37). HPL discusses him in the section "Campbell's Plan" in the essay "Finale" (*Badger,* June 1915).

Canevin, Gerald. In "The Trap," a teacher at an academy in Connecticut whose pupil, Robert Grandison, becomes trapped in a magic mirror that Canevin had brought back with him from the Virgin Islands. Canevin is a frequently recurring character in Henry S. Whitehead's tales, especially those set in the Virgin Islands. In his introduction to *Jumbee and Other Uncanny Tales* (1944), R. H.

Barlow notes: "The character 'Gerald Canevin' is Whitehead himself, a harking back to Caer n'-Avon. 'I use the form "Canevin" because it is easily pronounced and is made up of "cane" and "vin," that is, cane-wine—RUM, the typical product of the West Indies. . . .'"

Carroll, ⸺. In *At the Mountains of Madness,* a graduate student and a member of the Miskatonic Antarctic Expedition of 1930–31. He accompanies Lake on his subexpedition and is killed by the Old Ones.

Carter, Christopher. In "The Silver Key," Randolph Carter's great-uncle, who raised Randolph on a farm near Arkham and Kingsport. He lives there with his wife **Martha.** Randolph returns to the farm when he finds the silver key and becomes a boy again. Christopher is mentioned in passing in "Through the Gates of the Silver Key."

Carter, Randolph W. (b. 1873). HPL introduced the recurring character Randolph Carter in "The Statement of Randolph Carter," in which Carter is modeled after HPL from an actual dream. In "The Unnamable," Carter, who narrates the story, is briefly identified (by last name only) as a writer of weird fiction, like HPL. *The Dream-Quest of Unknown Kadath* is a picaresque narrative of Carter's adventures in his search for the sunset city of his dreams. In "The Silver Key" (written before *Dream-Quest*), Carter, a disillusioned man past middle age, is not so much a character as a fictional exponent of HPL's philosophical outlook. As an elderly man, Carter finds he has "lost the key to the gate of dreams." In a dream, his deceased grandfather (unnamed) tells him of an ancestral "silver key," which Carter finds in the attic upon waking. Having found the key, Carter then disappears. In "Through the Gates of the Silver Key," Carter is presumed dead, and others step in to settle his estate. The Swami Chandraputra tells of what happened to Carter following his disappearance. The Swami is revealed to be Carter himself, but residing in the body of Zkauba the Wizard from the planet Yaddith.

The W. in Carter's name appears only in the "stationery" that HPL and R. H. Barlow designed for HPL in June 1935. Although HPL clearly identified with Carter on many different levels, Carter is not as autobiographical a character as many others in HPL's fiction; he is, instead, a construct representing various of HPL's philosophical and aesthetic views.

Case of Charles Dexter Ward, The. Short novel (51,500 words); written late January–March 1, 1927. First published (abridged) in *WT* (May and July 1941); first collected in *BWS;* corrected text in *MM;* annotated version in *TD.*

Joseph Curwen, a learned scholar and man of affairs, leaves Salem for Providence in 1692, eventually building a succession of elegant homes in the oldest residential section of the city. Curwen attracts attention because he does not seem to age much, even after the passing of fifty or more years. He also acquires very peculiar substances from all around the world for apparent chemical—that is, alchemical—experiments; his haunting of graveyards does not help his reputation. When Dr. John Merritt visits Curwen, he is both impressed and disturbed by the number of alchemical and cabbalistic books on his shelves; in particular, he sees a copy of Borellus with one key passage—concerning the use of the "essential Saltes" of humans or animals for purposes of resurrection—heavily underscored.

In an effort to restore his reputation, Curwen arranges a marriage for himself with the well-born Eliza Tillinghast, the daughter of a ship-captain under Curwen's control. This so enrages Ezra Weeden, who had hoped to marry Eliza himself, that he begins an exhaustive investigation of Curwen's affairs. After several more anomalous incidents, the elders of the city—among them the four Brown brothers; Rev. James Manning, president of the recently established college (later to be known as Brown University); Stephen Hopkins, former governor of the colony; and others—decide that something must be done. A raid on Curwen's property in 1771, however, produces death, destruction, and psychological trauma among the participants well beyond what might have been expected of a venture of this sort. Curwen is evidently killed, and his body is returned to his wife for burial. He is never spoken of again, and as many records concerning him as can be found are destroyed.

A century and a half pass, and in 1918 Charles Dexter Ward—Curwen's direct descendant by way of his daughter Ann—accidentally discovers his relation to the old wizard and seeks to learn all he can about him. Although always fascinated by the past, Ward had previously exhibited no especial interest in the *outré;* but as he unearths more and more information about Curwen—whose exact physical double he proves to be—he strives more and more to duplicate his ancestor's cabbalistic and alchemical feats. He undertakes a long voyage overseas to visit the presumable descendants of individuals with whom Curwen had been in touch in the eighteenth century. He finds Curwen's remains and, by the proper manipulation of his "essential Saltes," resurrects him. But something begins to go astray. He writes a harried letter to Dr. Marinus Bicknell Willett, the family doctor, with the following disturbing message: "Instead of triumph I have found terror, and my talk with you will not be a boast of victory but a plea for help and advice in saving both myself and the world from a horror beyond all human conception or calculation. . . . Upon us depends more than can be put into words—all civilisation, all natural law, perhaps even the fate of the solar system and the universe. I have brought to light a monstrous abnormality, but I did it for the sake of knowledge. Now for the sake of all life and Nature you must help me thrust it back into the dark again."

But, perversely, Ward does not stay for the appointed meeting with Willett. Willett tracks him down, but something astounding has occurred: although still of youthful appearance, his talk is eccentric and old-fashioned, and his stock of memories of his own life seems to have been bizarrely depleted. Willett undertakes a harrowing exploration of Curwen's old Pawtuxet bungalow, which Ward had restored for conducting experiments; he finds, among other anomalies, all manner of half-formed creatures at the bottom of deep pits. He confronts Ward—who he now realizes is no other than Curwen—in the madhouse where he has been committed; Curwen attempts an incantation against him, but Willett counters with one of his own, reducing Curwen to a "thin coating of fine bluish-grey dust."

While living in Brooklyn, HPL was contemplating a "novelette of Salem horrors which I may be able to cast in a sufficiently 'detectivish' mould to sell to

Edwin Baird for *Detective Tales*—which rejected 'The Shunned House'" (HPL to L. D. Clark, July 27, 1925; ms., JHL); but then, in September, he read Gertrude Selwyn Kimball's *Providence in Colonial Times* (1912) at the New York Public Library, and this rather dry historical work fired his imagination. He was, however, still talking of the Salem idea in late January 1927 (see *SL* 2.99). Perhaps the Kimball book—as well as his return to Providence—led to a uniting of the Salem idea with a work about his hometown. It was from this book that the anecdotes about John Merritt, Dr. Checkley, and other points mentioned early in the novel derive.

The genesis of the work goes back beyond August 1925. The quotation from Borellus—Pierre Borel (c. 1620–1689), the French physician and chemist—is a translation or paraphrase by Cotton Mather in *Magnalia Christi Americana* (1702), which HPL owned. Since the epigraph from Lactantius that heads "The Festival" (1923) also comes from the *Magnalia,* HPL may have found the Borellus passage at that time also. It is entry #87 in his commonplace book, which dates roughly to April 1923.

In late August 1925 HPL's aunt Lillian related to him an anecdote about his hometown. HPL replied: "So the Halsey house is haunted! Ugh! That's where Wild Tom Halsey kept live terrapins in the cellar—maybe it's their ghosts. Anyway, it's a magnificent old mansion, & a credit to a magnificent old town!" (HPL to Lillian D. Clark, August 24, 1925; ms., JHL). The Thomas Lloyd Halsey house at 140 Prospect Street is the model for Charles Dexter Ward's residence, which HPL deliberately renumbers 100 Prospect Street. Now broken into apartments, it is still a superb late Georgian structure (c. 1800) fully deserving the encomium HPL gives it in his novel.

One significant literary influence may be Walter de la Mare's novel *The Return* (1910). HPL had first read de la Mare in the summer of 1926; of *The Return* he remarks in "Supernatural Horror in Literature": "we see the soul of a dead man reach out of its grave of two centuries and fasten itself upon the flesh of the living, so that even the face of the victim becomes that which had long ago returned to dust." In de la Mare's novel, actual psychic possession is involved, as there is not in *Charles Dexter Ward,* and, although the focus in *The Return* is on the afflicted man's personal trauma rather than the unnaturalness of his condition, HPL has manifestly adapted the general scenario in his own work.

Although there are many autobiographical touches in the portraiture of Ward, many surface details appear to be taken from a person actually living in the Halsey mansion at this time, William Lippitt Mauran (b. 1910). HPL was probably not acquainted with Mauran, but it is highly likely that he observed Mauran on the street and knew of him. Mauran was a sickly child who spent much of his youth as an invalid, being wheeled through the streets in a carriage by a nurse. Indeed, a mention early in the novel that Ward as a young boy was "wheeled . . . in a carriage" in front of the "lovely classic porch of the double-bayed brick building" that was his home may reflect an actual glimpse HPL had of Mauran in the early 1920s, before he went to New York. Moreover, the Mauran family owned a farmhouse in Pawtuxet, exactly as Curwen is said to have done. Other details of Ward's character fit Mauran more closely than HPL. One other amusing in-joke is a mention of Manuel Arruda, captain of a Spanish vessel, the

Fortaleza, which delivers a nameless cargo to Curwen in 1770. Manuel Arruda was actually a Portuguese door-to-door fruit merchant operating on College Hill in the later 1920s.

The novel does not appear to involve psychic possession in the obvious sense: in the latter stages of the novel the resurrected Curwen actually kills Ward and pretends to be him. But psychic possession of a subtler sort may nevertheless come into play. Curwen marries not only because he wishes to repair his reputation, but because he needs a descendant. He seems to know that he will one day die and require resurrection by the recovery of his "essential Saltes," so he makes careful arrangements to this effect: he prepares a notebook for "One Who Shal Come After" and leaves sufficient clues toward the location of his remains. It appears, then, that Curwen exercises psychic possession on Ward so that the latter finds first his effects, then his body, and brings him back to life.

In many ways the novel is a refinement of "The Horror at Red Hook": Curwen's alchemy parallels Suydam's cabbalistic activities; Curwen's attempt to repair his standing in the community with an advantageous marriage echoes Suydam's marriage with Cornelia Gerritsen; Willett as the valiant counterweight to Curwen matches Malone as the adversary of Suydam. HPL again dipped into his relatively small store of basic plot elements and again retold a mediocre tale in masterful fashion.

HPL, however, felt that the novel was an inferior piece of work, a "cumbrous, creaking bit of self-conscious antiquarianism" (HPL to R. H. Barlow, [March 19, 1934]; ms., JHL). He therefore made no effort to prepare it for publication, even though publishers throughout the 1930s professed greater interest in a weird novel than a collection of stories. R. H. Barlow began preparing a typescript in late 1934, and in 1936 was still typing it, but he typed only twenty-three pages. Barlow did not deposit the manuscript at JHL until around 1940, by which time a full transcript (full of errors, however) had been made by Derleth and Wandrei for its abridged appearance in *WT* and its complete appearance in *BWS.* It was published separately by Victor Gollancz (London, 1951) and subsequently reprinted in this form by Panther, Belmont, and Ballantine.

See Barton L. St. Armand, "Facts in the Case of H. P. Lovecraft," *Rhode Island History* 31, No. 1 (February 1972): 3–10 (rpt. *FDOC*); April Selley, "Terror and Horror in *The Case of Charles Dexter Ward,*" *Nyctalops* 3, No. 1 (January 1980): 8, 10–14; M. Eileen McNamara and S. T. Joshi, "Who Was the Real Charles Dexter Ward?" *LS* Nos. 19/20 (Fall 1989): 40–41, 48; David Vilaseca, "Nostalgia for the Origin: Notes on Reading and Melodrama in H. P. Lovecraft's *The Case of Charles Dexter Ward,*" *Neophilologus* 75, No. 4 (October 1991): 481–95; Richard Ward, "In Search of the Dread Ancestor: M. R. James' 'Count Magnus' and Lovecraft's *The Case of Charles Dexter Ward,*" *LS* No. 36 (Spring 1997): 14–17.

Casey. In "The Shadow over Innsmouth," a factory inspector who overheard strange sounds in the Gilman House, the Innsmouth hotel where he was staying. When inspecting the Marsh Refinery, he found the books in total disorder and with no indication of where it obtained the gold it refined.

HPL discovered in 1928 that he had Caseys in his Rhode Island ancestry (see *SL* 2.236–37).

Castro. In "The Call of Cthulhu," the aged mestizo who tells Inspector John R. Legrasse the story of the Great Old Ones following a raid of the Cthulhu cult in Louisiana. (He is not named for HPL's colleague Adolphe de Castro, whom HPL encountered a year or so after writing the story.)

"Cats and Dogs." Essay (6,050 words); written on November 23, 1926. First published in *Leaves* (Summer 1937); rpt. *Cats* (as "Something about Cats"); rpt. *MW* and *CE5*.

This delightful essay was written for a Blue Pencil Club meeting in New York—which HPL, having returned to Providence that spring, was unable to attend—at which the relative merits of cats and dogs would be debated. HPL, vastly preferring felines, sees in cats a symbol of aristocracy, unemotionalism, and pride ("The dog is a peasant and the cat is a gentleman"). He maintains that cats are much superior in intellect than dogs, are not dependent upon human beings, and are far more aesthetically beautiful than dogs. In the first appearance of the essay, some of HPL's more outrageously oligarchical statements (e.g., "whether the forces of disintegration are already too powerful for even the fascist sentiment to check, none may yet say") were expunged by R. H. Barlow; his editing was copied by August Derleth (who also retitled the essay) in *Cats*. The unexpurgated text was first presented in *MW*.

"Cats of Ulthar, The." Short story (1,350 words); written on June 15, 1920. First published in *Tryout* (November 1920); rpt. *WT* (February 1926) and *WT* (February 1933); published as separate booklet (Cassia, FL: Dragon-Fly Press, 1935); first collected in *O;* corrected text in *D;* annotated version in *DWH*.

The narrator proposes to explain how the town of Ulthar passed its "remarkable law" that no man may kill a cat. There was once a very evil couple who hated cats and who brutally murdered any that strayed on their property. One day a caravan of "dark wanderers" comes to Ulthar, among which is the little boy Menes, owner of a tiny black kitten. When the kitten disappears, the heartbroken boy, learning of the propensities of the cat-hating couple, "prayed in a tongue no villager could understand." That night all the cats in the town vanish, and when they return in the morning they refuse for two entire days to touch any food or drink. Later it is noticed that the couple has not been seen for days; when at last the villagers enter their house, they find two clean-picked skeletons.

There are several superficial borrowings from Dunsany: the name of the boy Menes (possibly derived from King Argimenes of the play *King Argimenes and the Unknown Warrior,* in *Five Plays* [1914]); the "dark wanderers" (perhaps an echo of the "Wanderers . . . a weird, dark tribe" mentioned toward the end of "Idle Days on the Yann," in *A Dreamer's Tales* [1910]). The entire scenario is probably inspired by the many similar tales of elementary revenge in *The Book of Wonder* (1912).

See Jason C. Eckhardt, "Something about the Cats of Ulthar," *Crypt* No. 15 (Lammas 1983): 28–29.

Cave, Hugh B[arnett] (b. 1910). American pulp writer and correspondent of HPL in the 1930s. Cave contributed voluminously to the weird and science fiction pulps from 1929 onward and became a prototypical "professional" writer. In the 1930s, Cave resided in Pawtuxet, R.I., but he and HPL never met. The two engaged in a heated exchange of correspondence (nonextant) regarding the ethics and aesthetics of writing for the pulps. Some of Cave's pulp writing is collected in *Murgunstrumm and Others* (Carcosa House, 1977) and *Death Stalks the Night* (Fedogan & Bremer, 1995). He has recently written several horror novels for paperback publishers as well as a memoir, *Magazines I Remember* (Chicago: Tattered Pages Press, 1994).

See Audrey Parente, *Pulp Man's Odyssey: The Hugh B. Cave Story* (1988).

"Celephaïs." Short story (2,550 words); written in early November 1920. First published in Sonia Greene's amateur journal, the *Rainbow* (May 1922); rpt. *Marvel Tales* (May 1934) and *WT* (June–July 1939); first collected in *O;* corrected text in *D;* annotated version in *CC.*

Kuranes (who has a different name in waking life) escapes the prosy world of London by dream and drugs. In this state he comes upon the city of Celephaïs, in the Valley of Ooth-Nargai. It is a city of which he had dreamed as a child, and there "his spirit had dwelt all the eternity of an hour one summer afternoon very long ago, when he had slipt away from his nurse and let the warm sea-breeze lull him to sleep as he watched the clouds from the cliff near the village." But Kuranes awakes in his London garret and finds that he can return to Celephaïs no more. He dreams of other wondrous lands, but his sought-for city continues to elude him. He increases his use of drugs, runs out of money, and is turned out of his flat. Then, as he wanders aimlessly through the streets, he comes upon a cortege of knights who "rode majestically through the downs of Surrey," seeming to gallop back in time as they do so. They leap off a precipice and drift softly down to Celephaïs, and Kuranes knows that he will be its king forever. Meanwhile, in the waking world, the tide at Innsmouth washes up the corpse of a tramp, while a "notably fat and offensive millionaire brewer" purchases Kuranes's ancestral mansion and "enjoys the purchased atmosphere of extinct nobility."

HPL notes that the story was based upon an entry in his commonplace book (#10) reading simply: "Dream of flying over city." Another entry (#20) was perhaps also an inspiration: "Man journeys into the past—or imaginative realm—leaving bodily shell behind." The story is strikingly similar in conception to Dunsany's "The Coronation of Mr. Thomas Shap" (in *The Book of Wonder*, 1912). There a businessman imagines himself the King of Larkar, and as he continues to dwell obsessively on (and in) this imaginary realm his work in the real world suffers, until finally he is placed in a madhouse. The image of horses drifting dreamily over a cliff may echo the conclusion of Ambrose Bierce's "A Horseman in the Sky" (in *Tales of Soldiers and Civilians*, 1891), where a man seems to see a horse flying through the air after he has shot the rider—who proves to be his own father.

Kuranes returns for a very different purpose in *The Dream-Quest of Unknown Kadath* (1926–27). Likewise, the city of Innsmouth, here set in England, later becomes a decaying seaport in Massachusetts.

"Challenge from Beyond, The." Round-robin short story (6,100 words; HPL's part, 2,640 words); HPL's part written in late August 1935. First published in *Fantasy Magazine* (September 1935); first collected in *BWS;* corrected text (HPL's part only) in *MW.*

[C. L. Moore:] George Campbell, camping in the Canadian woods, hears the shriek of an animal outside his tent. Reaching for an object to hurl at the creature, he grasps what he takes to be a stone; it proves to be a curious crystal cube. Some shape seems embedded in the center of the cube—a disk with characters incised upon it. [A. Merritt:] Campbell ponders the cube, seeing its interior alternately glow and fade. He hears music, then feels himself being sucked into the cube. [HPL:] Campbell seems to be hurtling through space at an incredible speed. At length he feels himself lying upon a hard, flat surface. He remembers reading in the Eltdown Shards about a mighty race of wormlike creatures on a distant planet who sent out crystal cubes that would exercise fascination upon any intelligent entity who encountered them. The mind of that individual would be sucked into the cube and made to inhabit the wormlike body of the alien race, while the mind of the alien race inhabited the other's body and learned all it could about the civilization in question. After a time a reversal would be effected. The cone-shaped beings who had inhabited Australia millions of years ago had learned of the nature of these cubes and sought to destroy them, thereby earning the wrath of the wormlike creatures. As Campbell ponders this bizarre tale, he realizes that he is now in the body of the wormlike creature. [Robert E. Howard:] Awaking from his faint, Campbell snatches a sharp-pointed metal shard and approaches the god of the creatures, intent on killing it. [Frank Belknap Long:] On the alien planet, George Campbell, in the body of a wormlike creature, kills the god and becomes a god of the worm people himself, while on earth the creature occupying the body of Campbell dies a raving madman.

The story was the brainchild of Julius Schwartz, who wanted two round-robin stories of the same title, one weird and one science fiction, for the third anniversary issue of *Fantasy Magazine.* He signed Moore, Long, Merritt, HPL, and a fifth undecided writer for the weird version, and Stanley G. Weinbaum, Donald Wandrei, E. E. "Doc" Smith, Harl Vincent, and Murray Leinster for the science fiction version. It was something of a feat to have harnessed all these writers—especially the resolutely professional A. Merritt—for such a venture, in which each author would write a section building upon what his or her predecessor had done; but the weird tale did not go quite according to plan.

Moore initiated the story with a rather lackluster account of George Campbell. Long then wrote what HPL calls "a rather clever development" (*SL* 5.500); but this left Merritt in the position of actually developing the story. Merritt balked, saying that Long had somehow deviated from the subject matter suggested by the title, and refused to participate unless Long's section was dropped and Merritt allowed to write one of his own. Schwartz, not wanting to lose such a big name, weakly went along with the plan. Merritt's own version fails to move the story along in any meaningful way. HPL realized that he would have to take the story in hand and actually make it go somewhere.

Notes to HPL's segment survive (published in *LS* No. 9 [Fall 1984]: 72–73) and contain drawings of the alien entities he introduces into the tale (giant worm- or centipede-like creatures). His segment is clearly an adaptation of the central conception of "The Shadow out of Time"—mind-exchange. Accordingly, the idea got into print months before its much better utilization in the latter story. HPL's segment is three to four times as long as that of any other writer's, or nearly half the story.

Robert E. Howard was persuaded to take the fourth installment, while Long—whom HPL talked into returning to the project after he had abandoned it when Schwartz dropped his initial installment—concludes the story.

The complete weird and science fiction versions appear in *The Challenge from Beyond* (Necronomicon Press, 1990).

Chambers, Robert W[illiam] (1865–1933). American author. HPL discovered his early fantastic writing—*The King in Yellow* (1895), *The Maker of Moons* (1896), *In Search of the Unknown* (1904); also the later novel *The Slayer of Souls* (1920)—in early 1927, and he hastily updated "Supernatural Horror in Literature" just prior to publication to include a discussion of this work. Other weird works (not, apparently, read by HPL) include *The Mystery of Choice* (1897), *The Tracer of Lost Persons* (1906), *The Tree of Heaven* (1907), and *The Talkers* (1923). Chambers borrowed mythical names—Hastur, Carcosa, etc.—from Bierce; some of these (along with such of Chambers's own inventions as Yian) were in turn borrowed by HPL. "The Harbor-Master" (a separate short story later incorporated as the opening chapters of the episodic novel *In Search of the Unknown*) may have influenced "The Shadow over Innsmouth." Chambers later became a best-selling writer of sentimental romances.

See Lee Weinstein, "Chambers and *The King in Yellow*," *Romantist* No. 3 (1979): 51–57; S. T. Joshi, "Robert W. Chambers," *Crypt* No. 22 (Roodmas 1984): 26–33, 17.

Chandraputra, Swami. In "Through the Gates of the Silver Key," he attends the meeting to divide Randolph Carter's estate, purportedly with information about what happened to Carter following Carter's disappearance. The Swami is actually a disguise for Zkauba the Wizard from the planet Yaddith, whom Carter became after he passed through the Gate of Dreams. The Swami is also mentioned briefly in "Out of the Æons."

Charging Buffalo. In "The Mound," a young buck who in 1541 guides Panfilo de Zamacona to the entrance of a mound in what is now Oklahoma, but refuses to accompany Zamacona within. Some time earlier he had tentatively explored the mound, and he tells Zamacona tales of the Old Ones living within.

Choynski, Paul. In "The Dreams in the Witch House," an occupant of the Witch House in Arkham during the period of Walter Gilman's bizarre dreams and sleepwalking.

"City, The." Poem (45 lines in 9 stanzas); probably written in the fall of 1919. First published in *Vagrant* (October 1919); rpt. *WT* (July 1950).

The narrator finds himself in a strange but splendid city and strives to remember when and how he had known it before; finally a revelation comes to him and he "flew from the knowledge of terrors forgotten and dead."

See Dirk W. Mosig, "Poet of the Unconscious," *Platte Valley Review* 6, No. 1 (April 1978): 60–66.

Clapham-Lee, Major Sir Eric Moreland, D.S.O. In "Herbert West—Reanimator," a surgeon who dies when his plane is shot down as it is approaching a base in Flanders where Herbert West is stationed with a Canadian regiment. As Clapham-Lee is nearly decapitated in the plane crash, West perversely reanimates the head and the body separately. Later Clapham-Lee exacts his vengeance on West.

Clarendon, Dr. Alfred Schuyler. In "The Last Test," a physician who is appointed medical director of the San Quentin Penitentiary by the governor but is later removed because of his handling of the case of a prisoner stricken with black fever, whose death prompts fear of an epidemic in San Francisco. Clarendon is in fact not trying to find a cure for black fever at all, but—under the evil influence of the mysterious Surama, who acts as his assistant—is attempting to produce a serum that will induce a disease that will kill all humankind. He tries to inject his sister, **Georgina,** with the serum; prevented from doing so, he injects himself instead. Fearing the outcome, he destroys himself and his clinic by fire.

Clark, Franklin Chase, M.D. (1847–1915). Husband of HPL's elder aunt Lillian Delora Phillips Clark. He attended high school in Warren, R.I., and received an A.B. from Brown University (1869). He studied literature and attended special classes given by Oliver Wendell Holmes, Sr., and received a medical degree from the College of Physicians and Surgeons in New York City (1872). Returning to Providence as an intern at Rhode Island Hospital, Clark served as surgeon in the outpatient department (1876–83). He conducted a private medical practice from 1872 to 1915 and also served as physician for Providence Dispensary and for the Home for Aged Women (1883–84) and as acting police surgeon for the City of Providence (1896). He was a prolific writer of articles on medicine, natural history, and genealogy; collections of his magazine articles and of his manuscripts are held in the University Archives at Brown. He married Lillian Delora Phillips on April 10, 1902; they had no children. In 1904, with HPL's father and grandfather both dead, Clark became the leading male adult figure in HPL's life; HPL testifies that his early prose and verse were much improved by Clark's assistance (see *SL* 1.38). Clark died on April 16, 1915, of cerebral hemorrhage and chronic Bright's disease; HPL wrote a poetic tribute, "An Elegy on Franklin Chase Clark, M.D." ([Providence] *Evening News,* April 29, 1915). Dr. Elihu Whipple in "The Shunned House" (1924), Dr. George Gammell Angell in "The Call of Cthulhu" (1926), and Dr. Marinus Bicknell Willett in *The Case of Charles Dexter Ward* (1927) are probably based in part on Clark; perhaps also Dr. Henry Armitage in "The Dunwich Horror" (1928) and Dr. Nathaniel Wingate Peaslee in "The Shadow out of Time" (1934–35).

Clark, Lillian D[elora Phillips] **(1856–1932).** First child of Whipple V. Phillips and Robie Alzada Place Phillips; elder sister of Sarah Susan Phillips Lovecraft, HPL's mother. She spent two academic years at the Wheaton Seminary in Norton, Mass. (1871–73), and completed her education at the Rhode Island Normal School. She was a schoolteacher prior to her marriage to Dr. Franklin Chase Clark, M.D., on April 10, 1902; they had no children. After Dr. Clark's death, she lived in various rented rooms in Providence, including 135 Benefit Street (the locale for "The Shunned House" [1924]) in 1919–20. She was the principal housekeeper for HPL at 598 Angell Street during 1919–24, after the hospitalization and death of HPL's mother. HPL wrote an enormous number of letters (now at JHL) to her during his New York period (1924–26); in spite of her chronic poor health, she came to Brooklyn in December 1924 to assist HPL in moving to 169 Clinton Street. Upon HPL's return to Providence in April 1926, Lillian took rooms immediately above his at 10 Barnes Street. She was a gifted painter in oils who exhibited at the Providence Art Club. She died on July 3, 1932.

Clay, Ed. In "The Mound," the elder of two brothers in the Oklahoma Territory who explore the mound region in 1920. He comes back three months later with his hair turned white and a strange scar branded on his forehead. He claims that his brother **Walker** had died after being captured by Indians. Later Ed commits suicide after writing a note urging that the mound region be left alone.

Club of the Seven Dreamers, The. A "hideous novel" conceived by HPL in March 1920 (see *SL* 1.110); probably never begun. Possibly it was not intended to be a genuine novel but rather a series of short stories with different narrators—these being the "seven dreamers" of the title. If so, the conception would be somewhat similar to Poe's plans for *Tales of the Folio Club;* in his preface to this volume (first printed in James A. Harrison's collected edition of Poe [1902]), Poe declares that "The number of the club is limited to eleven." One may also suspect the influence of John Osborne Austin's *More Seven Club Tales* (1900), a book that HPL owned about strange happenings in Rhode Island. This slim volume contains seven stories, each narrated by a different individual, mostly figures from seventeenth-century Rhode Island. Only a few of the tales are genuinely weird, and even they are rather innocuous ghost stories; but HPL may have found the format suggestive.

Coates, Walter J[ohn] **(1880–1941).** Amateur journalist in North Montpelier, Vt., who issued the little magazine *Driftwind,* which contained much poetry by HPL as well as "The Materialist Today" (initially a letter to Coates, c. May 1926; published in *Driftwind* for October 1926 and also as a separate brochure [Driftwind Press, 1926] in fifteen copies). Coates contributed a lengthy essay on Vermont poetry to W. Paul Cook's *Recluse* (1927). He was the author and editor of many volumes of poetry, including *Mood Songs: Voices within Myself* (Hartford, Vt.: Solitarian Press, 1921), *Vermont in Heart and Song* (editor) (North Montpelier, Vt., 1926), *Vermont Verse: An Anthology* (editor) (Brattleboro, Vt.: Stephen Daye Press, 1931), *Harvest: A Sheaf of Poems from* Driftwind (editor) (North Montpelier, Vt.: Driftwind Press, 1933). He corresponded sporadically with HPL to the end of the latter's life, and wrote an obituary of HPL for *Drift-wind*, April 1937.

Cole, Edward H[arold] (1892–1966). Massachusetts amateur journalist; editor of *The Olympian*. He came in touch with HPL in late 1914, when he advised HPL to assist the Providence Amateur Press Club; he met HPL in December 1914. Their correspondence continued until HPL's death. He married Helene E. Hoffman (1893–1919), who gave birth to a son, E[dward] Sherman Cole (b. 1918), to whom HPL wrote a few whimsical letters in early 1919. Upon Helene Hoffman Cole's death, HPL wrote a poetic tribute, "Helene Hoffman Cole: 1893–1919: The Club's Tribute" (*Bonnet*, June 1919), as well as a prose article, "Helene Hoffman Cole—Litterateur" (*United Amateur*, May 1919). HPL frequently visited Cole in the Boston area in the 1920s and 1930s. After HPL's death, Cole edited a special issue of *The Olympian* (Autumn 1940) devoted to HPL, for which he wrote a lengthy memoir, "Ave atque Vale!" (rpt. *LR*).

Cole, Ira A[lbert] (1883–?). Kansas amateur journalist and editor of *The Plainsman*, for which HPL wrote "On the Cowboys of the West" (December 1915). He became a member of the round-robin correspondence group, the Klei-comolo (1915–19?), with HPL, Rheinhart Kleiner, and Maurice W. Moe. HPL published some of Cole's poems in *The Conservative* ("The Dream of a Golden Age," July 1915; "In Vita Elysium," July 1917). Cole later converted to Pentacostalism. He wrote a brief memoir of HPL, "A Tribute from the Past" (*O-Wash-Ta-Nong*, 1937; rpt. *LR*).

"Collapsing Cosmoses." Short story fragment (640 words); written in collaboration with R. H. Barlow. First published in *Leaves* (1938); first collected in *MW*.

Dam Bor looks through his cosmoscope and sees an enemy fleet advancing through space. He and the narrator go to the Great Council Chamber to alert delegates from other galaxies. Hak Ni, a commander, is asked by Oll Stof, the president of the chamber, to battle the fleet. He does so. The fragment ends at this point.

The idea was for each author to write alternating paragraphs, although HPL sometimes wrote only a few words before yielding the pen to his younger colleague, so that considerably more than half the piece is Barlow's, as are a fair number of the better jokes. As a satire on the space operas popularized by Edmond Hamilton, E. E. "Doc" Smith, and others, the story is fairly effective.

"Colour out of Space, The." Short story (12,300 words); written in March 1927. First published in *Amazing Stories* (September 1927); first collected in *O;* corrected text in *DH;* annotated version in *AnI* and *CC*.

A surveyor for the new reservoir to be built "west of Arkham" encounters a bleak terrain where nothing will grow; the locals call it the "blasted heath." The surveyor, seeking an explanation for the term and for the cause of the devastation, finally finds an old man, Ammi Pierce, living near the area, who tells him an incredible tale of events that occurred in 1882. A meteorite had landed on the property of Nahum Gardner and his family. Scientists from Miskatonic University who examine the object find that its properties are very bizarre: the substance refuses to cool, displays shining spectroscopic bands never seen before, and fails to react to conventional solvents. Within the meteorite is a "large coloured globule": "The colour . . . was almost impossible to describe; and it was only by analogy that they called it colour at all." When tapped with a hammer, it bursts. The meteorite itself, continuing anomalously to shrink, finally disappears.

Henceforth increasingly odd things occur. Nahum's harvest yields apples and pears unprecedentedly huge in size, but they prove unfit to eat; plants and animals undergo peculiar mutations; Nahum's cows start to give bad milk. Then Nahum's wife Nabby goes mad, "screaming about things in the air which she could not describe"; she is locked in an upstairs room. Soon all the vegetation starts to crumble to a grayish powder. Nahum's son Thaddeus goes mad after a visit to the well, and his sons Merwin and Zenas also break down. Then there is a period of days when Nahum is not seen or heard from. Ammi finally summons the courage to visit his farm and finds that the worst has happened: Nahum himself has gone insane, babbling only in fragments; but that is not all: "That which spoke could speak no more because it had completely caved in." Ammi brings policemen, a coroner, and other officials to the place, and after a series of bizarre events they see a column of the unknown color shoot into the sky from the well; but Ammi sees a small fragment of it return to earth. The gray expanse of the "blasted heath" grows by an inch per year, and no one can say when it will end.

The reservoir in the tale is the Quabbin Reservoir, plans for which were announced in 1926, although it was not completed until 1939. And yet, HPL declares in a late letter that it was the Scituate Reservoir in Rhode Island (built in 1926) that caused him to use the reservoir element in the story (HPL to Richard Ely Morse, October 13, 1935; ms., JHL). He saw the reservoir when he passed through the west-central part of the state on the way to Foster in late October 1926. But HPL surely was also thinking of the Quabbin, which is located exactly in the area of central Massachusetts where the tale takes place, and which involved the abandonment and submersion of entire towns in the region. Also, Clara Hess's statement that HPL's mother once told her about "weird and fantastic creatures that rushed out from behind buildings and from corners at dark" reminds one of Nabby Gardner's madness.

HPL felt the story was more an "atmospheric study" (*SL* 2.114) than an orthodox narrative. The lack of clear answers to many of the central issues in the tale—specifically, the nature of the meteorite (is it—or the colored globule inside it—animate in any sense that we can recognize? Does it house a single entity or many entities? What are their physical properties? What are their aims, goals, and motives?)—is not a failing but a virtue. As HPL said of Machen's "The White People," "the *lack of anything concrete* is the *great asset* of the story" (*SL* 3.429). It is precisely because we cannot define the nature—either physical or psychological—of the entities in "The Colour out of Space" (or even know whether they are entities or living creatures as we understand them) that produces a sense of horror. In this story HPL most closely achieves his goal of avoiding the depiction of "the human form—and the local human passions and conditions and standards—. . . as native to other worlds or other universes" (*SL* 2.150).

The story is the first of HPL's major tales to effect the union of horror and science fiction that became the hallmark of his later work. It is therefore not surprising that *Amazing Stories* (the first science fiction pulp magazine) readily accepted it upon submittal, early in the summer of 1927. But *Amazing Stories* became a closed market to HPL when editor Hugo Gernsback paid him only $25 for the story—a mere ⅕¢ per word—and then only after three dunning letters. Although in later years HPL briefly considered requests from Gernsback or from his associate editor, C. A. Brandt, for further submissions, he never again sent a tale to *Amazing Stories.* He always remembered Gernsback as "Hugo the Rat."

Sam Moskowitz's assertion that HPL submitted the story first to *WT,* and then to *Argosy,* is unwarranted; see HPL to Clark Ashton Smith, July 15, 1927 (ms., JHL): "As for 'The Colour Out of Space'—Wandrei tells me that *Amazing Stories* doesn't pay well, so that I'm sorry I didn't try *WT* first."

See Will Murray, "Sources for 'The Colour out of Space,'" *Crypt* No. 28 (Yuletide 1984): 3–5; Steven J. Mariconda, "The Subversion of Sense in 'The Colour out of Space,'" *LS* Nos. 19/20 (Fall 1989): 20–22; Donald R. Burleson, "Prismatic Heroes: The Colour out of Dunwich," *LS* No. 25 (Fall 1991): 13–18; Robert M. Price, "A Biblical Antecedent for 'The Colour out of Space,'" *LS* No. 25 (Fall 1991): 23–25; Donald R. Burleson, "Lovecraft's 'The Colour out of Space,'" *Crypt* No. 93 (Lammas 1996): 19–20.

"Commercial Blurbs." Series of five advertising articles written in 1925 (general title coined by R. H. Barlow). First published in *LS* (Spring 1988); rpt. *MW, CE5.*

The five articles are as follows: "Beauty in Crystal" (on the Corning Glass Works, Corning, N.Y.); "The Charm of Fine Woodwork" (on the Curtis Companies, Clifton, IA); "Personality in Clocks" (on the Colonial Manufacturing Company, Zealand, MI); "A Real Colonial Heritage" (on the Erskine-Danforth Corporation, New York, N.Y.); and "A True Home of Literature" (on the Alexander Hamilton Book Shop, Paterson, N.J.). The articles were written in early 1925 for a trade magazine conceived by one Yesley (a friend of Arthur Leeds): authors would write the advertising copy (based on press notices or advertising matter supplied by the company) and have it published in the magazine; salesmen would then take the issue to the companies in question and urge them to buy a quantity of the magazines for advertising purposes, whereupon the author would get 10% of the net sales. But the venture never materialized, so far as can be ascertained, and HPL's articles apparently were never published. HPL clearly sought out "high-toned" establishments to write about, and his articles—seemingly stiff and formal—are presumably meant to suggest the aristocratic quality of the products manufactured or sold by the companies about which he is writing.

Commonplace Book. Notes (5,000 words); written between late 1919/early 1920 and 1935. First published in *The Notes & Commonplace Book* (Futile Press, 1938); rpt. *BWS, SR, MW* and *CE5.* Annotated version in *Commonplace Book* (1987).

No "book" at all, HPL's commonplace book was merely a sheaf of long, narrow, folded sheets of paper, on which he jotted ideas for stories. In January 1920, he wrote to Rheinhart Kleiner, "I have lately . . . been collecting ideas and images for subsequent use in fiction. For the first time in my life, I am keeping a 'commonplace-book'—if that term can be applied to a repository of gruesome and fantastick thought" (*SL* 1.106). In May 1934, after a decade and a half of keeping and using the book, HPL described it as follows, in a note jotted on the manuscript for presentation to a young friend: "This book consists of ideas, images & quotations hastily jotted down for possible future use in weird fiction. Very few are actually developed plots—for the most part they are merely suggestions or random impressions designed to set the memory or imagination working. Their sources are various—dreams, things read, casual incidents, idle conceptions, & so on."

Few entries in the book are story plots per se; most are merely notes to jog the memory or spur the imagination. Consider these sample entries from c. 1920: "Transposition of identity." "Man followed by invisible *thing.*" "Fisherman casts his net into the sea by moonlight—what he finds." The first entry is the shortest possible description of an idea developed at length in two late stories: "The Thing on the Doorstep" and "The Shadow out of Time." The next contains an early scene from *Fungi from Yuggoth,* and also scenes from "The Dunwich Horror" and "The Shadow out of Time." The last finds its way into "The Haunter of the Dark" in a throwaway passage about a fisherman finding the Shining Trapezohedron in his net. In the manuscript, HPL noted the use of only a handful of items. However, many of the recorded images find their way into many of his works—perhaps not as complete story ideas, but as elements of stories; others are not used exactly as written, but modified to suit a particular need.

In 1938, the Futile Press published HPL's notebook, derived from a manuscript in the possession of R. H. Barlow and augmented by later notes HPL kept on a typed copy made for him by Barlow. See "Notes on Weird Fiction" concerning the related material published with these notes. In *BWS* and *SR,* the commonplace book entries were conflated with the supplemental material, mistakenly identifying all the notes as part of HPL's commonplace book; also, the text was based not on Barlow's Futile Press Edition, but on the truncated typescript that Barlow had made for HPL. The annotated edition of 1987 restores all notes (including rejected items) to their proper sequence.

Comptons. In "The Curse of Yig" and "The Mound," **Sally ("Grandma"),** married to **Joe,** mother of **Clyde,** is a first-generation pioneer, "a veritable mine of anecdote and folklore." She is the source of the story about their neighbors, the Davises, in "The Curse of Yig," and it is she who discovers Walker Davis's body.

"Confession of Unfaith, A." Essay (2,170 words); probably written in late 1921. First published in the *Liberal* (February 1922); rpt. *MW* and *CE5.*

One of HPL's most significant personal and philosophical essays, tracing the development of his rejection of orthodox Christianity from boyhood (when, under the influence of classical mythology, he actually thought he saw dryads and satyrs in the woods near his home) to maturity. HPL copied much of the essay in his autobiographical letter to Edwin Baird, February 3, 1924 (*SL* 1.299–302).

Conover, Willis (1920–1996). Weird fiction fan who corresponded with HPL (1936–37). Conover wished to start a fan magazine, the *Science-Fantasy Correspondent,* and asked HPL to contribute; HPL sent him "Homecoming" (a sonnet from *Fungi from Yuggoth*), which appeared in the first issue (November–December 1936). The poem "In a Sequestered Providence Churchyard Where Once Poe Walked" appeared in the March–April 1937 issue. Late in 1936 Conover expressed his intention to resume the serialization of "Supernatural Horror in Literature" from the point at which it had ceased in the *Fantasy Fan;* accordingly, HPL prepared a synopsis of the earlier segments (Conover later published this as a booklet, *Supernatural Horror in Literature as Revised in 1936* [Carrollton-Clark, 1974]). But Conover never ran "Supernatural Horror in Literature," nor the celebrated portrait of HPL as an eighteenth-century gentleman, which he commissioned Virgil Finlay to draw; the latter appeared on the cover of the April 1937 issue of *Amateur Correspondent,* Corwin F. Stickney's successor to *Science-Fantasy Correspondent.* In part as a result of HPL's death, Conover lost his interest in weird fiction for many years. For much of his career he worked with the Voice of America. In 1975 he published his exquisitely printed memoir, *Lovecraft at Last* (Carrollton-Clark; rpt. Cooper Square Press, 2002), containing extracts of his letters from HPL and much other interesting matter. He recommenced the *Science-Fantasy Correspondent,* but only for one issue (1975); that issue did, however, contain Kenneth Sterling's fine memoir, "Caverns Measureless to Man," along with additional letters by HPL.

See obituary, *New York Times,* May 19, 1996, Sec. I, p. 35.

Conservative, The. Amateur magazine edited by HPL (1915–23). Rpt. (unabridged) as *The Conservative: Complete* (Necronomicon Press, 1976, 1977); selections as *The Conservative,* ed. S. T. Joshi (Necronomicon Press, 1990).

The magazine consists of 13 issues: 1, No. 1 (April 1915), 8 pp.; 1, No. 2 (July 1915), 12 pp.; 1, No. 3 (October 1915), 16 pp.; 1, No. 4 (January 1916), 4 pp.; 2, No. 1 (April 1916), 4 pp.; 2, No. 2 (July 1916), 4 pp.; 2, No. 3 (October 1916), 12 pp.; 2, No. 4 (January 1917), 4 pp.; 3, No. 1 (July 1917), 4 pp.; 4, No. 1 (July 1918), 8 pp.; 5, No. 1 (July 1919), 12 pp.; No. 12 (March 1923), 8 pp.; No. 13 (July 1923), 28 pp. [For complete table of contents, see S. T. Joshi, *H. P. Lovecraft and Lovecraft Criticism: An Annotated Bibliography* (1981), pp. 173–77.]

The first issue was printed by an unidentified Providence printer. The next five issues were printed by The Lincoln Press (Albert A. Sandusky), Cambridge, Mass. The next three were printed locally, and W. Paul Cook printed the final four. HPL wrote most of the first three issues himself, but subsequently opened the magazine to prose and poetic contributions by his associates, including Rheinhart Kleiner, Winifred Virginia Jackson, Anne Tillery Renshaw, Alfred Galpin, Samuel Loveman, and others. The issue for July 1916 consists entirely of Henry Clapham McGavack's essay "The American Proletariat versus England." Beginning with the October 1916 issue, HPL instituted an editorial column entitled "In the Editor's Study," containing some of his most controversial political, social, and literary musings.

Rheinhart Kleiner reports on the effect of reading the first issue: ". . . many were immediately aware that a brilliant new talent had made itself known. The entire contents of the issue, both prose and verse, were the work of the editor, who obviously knew exactly what he wished to say, and no less exactly how to say it. *The Conservative* took a unique place among the valuable publications of its time, and held that place with ease through the period of seven or eight years during which it made occasional pronouncements. Its critical pronouncements were relished by some and resented by others, but there was no doubt of the respect in which they were held by all" ("Howard Phillips Lovecraft," *Californian* 5, No. 1 [Summer 1937]: 5). But HPL's contributions to the issues of 1915–19 are on the whole dogmatic, narrow, and intolerant; he was taken heavily to task for his reactionary racial and literary views by such amateurs as Charles D. Isaacson and James F. Morton. The last two issues reveal a significant broadening of intellectual horizons and a more sophisticated appreciation of cultural change, and thereby foreshadow the development of HPL's aesthetic and moral thought in his last decade.

Cook, W[illiam] Paul (1881–1948). Printer, publisher, and amateur press editor residing in Athol, Mass.; he published under the pseudonym Willis Tete Crossman. Cook served as Official Editor (1918–19) and President of the NAPA (1919–20); he was also appointed Official Editor of the UAPA in 1907, but resigned before the end of his term. He edited and published several amateur magazines, including *The Monadnock Monthly, The Vagrant, The Recluse,* and *The Ghost.* He met HPL in 1917 through amateur journalism, Cook agreeing to print HPL's *Conservative.* His encouragement was instrumental in HPL's resumption of fiction writing in 1917. Cook wrote a brief article, "Howard P. Lovecraft's Fiction" (*The Vagrant,* November 1919) as a preface to "Dagon"— the first critical article on HPL's stories. He published many of HPL's early weird tales and poems in *The Vagrant.* In late 1925 he enlisted HPL to write "Supernatural Horror in Literature" for *The Recluse* (1927); in 1928 he printed HPL's story "The Shunned House" (rejected by Farnsworth Wright for *WT*) as a small book; his subsequent financial and nervous breakdown, brought on by the death of his wife in 1930, prevented the binding of the book. A small number of sheets of the 300-copy edition were bound by R. H. Barlow; the remainder were bound by Arkham House in 1959–61. In visiting Cook at his home in Athol in the summer of 1928, HPL absorbed many details of local history and lore reflected in his fiction, notably "The Dunwich Horror." In 1940, Cook wrote *In Memoriam: Howard Phillips Lovecraft* (Driftwind Press, 1941), which he typeset himself; it is still perhaps the best memoir of HPL. His "A Plea for Lovecraft" (*The Ghost,* May 1945) warned against a distorted image of HPL beginning to emerge, largely because of the publications from Arkham House.

See R. Alain Everts, "The Man Who Was W. Paul Cook," *Nyctalops* 3, No. 2 (March 1981): 10–12.

"Cool Air." Short story (3,440 words); written probably in February 1926. First published in *Tales of Magic and Mystery* (March 1928); rpt. *WT* (September 1939); first collected in *O;* corrected text in *DH;* annotated version in *An2, CC,* and *PZ.*

The narrator, having "secured some dreary and unprofitable magazine work" in the spring of 1923, finds himself in a run-down boarding-house whose landlady is a "slatternly, almost bearded Spanish woman named Herrero" and occupied generally by low-life except for one Dr. Muñoz, a cultivated and intelligent retired medical man who is continually experimenting with chemicals and indulges in the eccentricity of keeping his room at a temperature of about 55° by means of an ammonia cooling system. Muñoz suffers from the effects of a horrible malady that struck him eighteen years ago. He is obliged to keep his room increasingly cooler, as low as 28°. When, in the heat of summer, his ammonia cooling system fails, the narrator undertakes a frantic effort to fix it, enlisting "a seedy-looking loafer" to keep the doctor supplied with the ice that he repeatedly demands in ever larger amounts. But it is to no avail: when the narrator returns from his quest for air-conditioner repairmen, he finds the boarding-house in turmoil; the loafer, faced with some nameless horror, had quickly abandoned his task of supplying ice. When the narrator enters Muñoz's room, he sees a "kind of dark, slimy trail [that] led from the open bathroom to the hall door" and "ended unutterably." In fact, Muñoz died eighteen years before and had kept himself functioning by artificial preservation.

There are several autobiographical touches in the story. The setting is the brownstone at 317 West 14th Street (between Eighth and Ninth Avenues) in Manhattan, occupied in August–October 1925 by George Kirk, both as a residence and as the site of his Chelsea Book Shop. HPL describes it in a letter: "It is a typical Victorian home of New York's 'Age of Innocence', with tiled hall, carved marble mantels, vast pier glasses & mantel mirrors with massive gilt frames, incredibly high ceilings covered with stucco ornamentation, round arched doorways with elaborate rococo pediments, & all the other earmarks of New York's age of vast wealth & impossible taste. Kirk's rooms are the great ground-floor parlours, connected by an open arch, & having windows only in the front room. These two windows open to the south on 14th St., & have the disadvantage of admitting all the babel & clangour of that great crosstown thoroughfare with its teeming traffick & ceaseless street-cars" (HPL to Lillian D. Clark, August 19–23, 1925; ms., JHL). Dr. Muñoz may have been suggested by HPL's neighbor across the street, "the fairly celebrated Dr. Love, State Senator and sponsor of the famous 'Clean Books bill' at Albany . . . evidently immune or unconscious of the decay" (HPL to B. A. Dwyer, March 26, 1927; AHT). Even the ammonia cooling system has an autobiographical source. In August 1925 HPL's aunt Lillian had told him of a visit to a theatre in Providence, to which he replied: "Glad you have kept up with the Albee Co., though surprised to hear that the theatre is *hot*. They have a fine ammonia cooling system installed, & if they do not use it it can only be through a niggardly sense of economy" (HPL to Lillian D. Clark, August 7, 1925; ms., JHL).

HPL stated that the inspiration for the tale was not, as one might expect, Poe's "Facts in the Case of M. Valdemar" but Machen's "Novel of the White Powder" (HPL to Henry Kuttner, July 29, 1936; *Letters to Henry Kuttner* [Necronomicon Press, 1990], p. 21), in which a hapless student unwittingly takes a drug that reduces him to "a dark and putrid mass, seething with corruption and hideous rottenness, neither liquid nor solid, but melting and changing before our eyes, and bubbling with unctuous oily bubbles like boiling pitch."

WT rejected "Cool Air" in March 1926, possibly because its gruesome conclusion would invite censorship, as in the case of "The Loved Dead." It was one of eight stories that HPL submitted in late 1927 to the poor paying and short-lived *Tales of Magic and Mystery;* HPL received $18.50 for it.

See Bert Atsma, "Living on Borrowed Time: A Biologist Looks at 'M. Valdemar' and 'Cool Air,'" *Crypt* No. 4 (Eastertide 1981): 11–13; Will Murray, "A Note on 'Cool Air,'" *Crypt* No. 28 (Yuletide 1984): 20–21.

Corey, Benijah. In "The Silver Key," the hired man of the young Randolph Carter's Uncle Christopher. When Carter, having found the silver key, returns bodily to his childhood, "Benijy" chides "Randy" for being late for supper.

Corey, George. In "The Dunwich Horror," the owner of a farm near Cold Spring Glen. His wife is not named. His relationship to **Wesley Corey,** one of the party that exterminates Wilbur Whateley's twin brother, is not specified.

Crane, [Harold] Hart (1899–1932). American poet. HPL (through his friend Samuel Loveman) met Crane in Cleveland in August 1922 and saw him again in New York in 1924–26, when he was working on *The Bridge* (1930). HPL parodied Crane's "Pastorale" (*Dial*, October 1921) in "Plaster-All" (1922?; *LS* No. 27 [Fall 1992]: 30–31), in which Crane is apparently the first-person narrator of the poem. Crane speaks of HPL in his letters, referring to him as "piping-voiced" and "that queer Lovecraft person." HPL saw Crane one last time in late 1930, as the ravages of alcoholism were taking effect. HPL admired Crane's poetry, despite its modernism: he referred to *The Bridge* as "a thing of astonishing merit" (*SL* 3.152).

See Thomas Horton, *Hart Crane: The Life of an American Poet* (1937); Susan Jenkins Brown, *Robber Rocks: Letters and Memories of Hart Crane, 1923–1932* (1969); John Unterecker, *Voyager: A Life of Hart Crane* (1969); Thomas S. W. Lewis, ed., *Letters of Hart Crane and His Family* (1974); Paul Mariani, *The Broken Tower: A Life of Hart Crane* (1999); Steven J. Mariconda, "H. P. Lovecraft: Reluctant American Modernist," *LS* No. 42 (Summer 2001): 22–34.

Crawford, William L. (1911–1984). Semi-professional publisher in Everett, Pa. In the fall of 1933, Crawford proposed to start a nonpaying weird magazine, *Unusual Stories.* For this he commissioned HPL's autobiographical sketch "Some Notes on a Nonentity," although it never ran in the magazine. Although he accepted HPL's "Celephaïs" and "The Doom That Came to Sarnath" for *Unusual Stories,* neither appeared there; instead, they appeared in Crawford's *Marvel Tales* (May 1934 and March–April 1935, respectively). Around July 1934 HPL wrote "Some Notes on Interplanetary Fiction" for one of Crawford's magazines, but the essay was published in the *Californian* (Winter 1935). In the spring of 1935 Crawford contemplated reviving the defunct *Fantasy Fan,* with HPL as editor; but the plan never materialized. He also thought of issuing either *At the Mountains of Madness* or "The Shadow over Innsmouth" as a booklet, or both together in one volume; he considered submitting the latter story to *Astounding Stories* after hearing of the acceptance there of *At the Mountains of Madness* and "The Shadow out of Time," but it is not clear whether he did so. Then, in late 1935, he focused on the issuance of "The Shadow over Innsmouth" as a book. The project came to fruition in November 1936 (although the copyright page declares the date of publication as April 1936), but the book was so riddled with typographical errors that HPL insisted on an errata sheet (which, alas, was also faulty). *The Shadow over Innsmouth,* issued under the imprint of the Visionary Publishing Company, was the only book of HPL's fiction to be published and distributed in his lifetime. Crawford printed 400 copies but bound only 200; the others were later destroyed. The book features a dust jacket and four interior illustrations by Frank Utpatel. Crawford wrote of the venture in "Lovecraft's First Book" (in *SR;* rpt. *LR*).

"Crawling Chaos, The." Short story (3,020 words); written in collaboration with Winifred Virginia Jackson, probably in December 1920. First published (as by "Elizabeth Berkeley and Lewis Theobald, Jun.") in the *United Co-operative* (April 1921), a cooperative amateur journal edited by HPL, Jackson, and others; first collected in *BWS;* corrected text in *HM.*

The narrator tells of his one experience with opium, when a doctor unwittingly gave him an overdose to ease his pain. After experiencing a sensation of falling, "curiously dissociated from the idea of gravity or direction," he finds himself in a "strange and beautiful room lighted by many windows." A sense of fear comes over him, and he realizes that it is inspired by a monotonous pounding that seems to come from below the house in which he finds himself. Looking out a window, he sees that the pounding is caused by titanic waves that are rapidly washing away the piece of land on which the house stands, transforming the land into an ever-narrowing peninsula. Fleeing through the back door of the house, the narrator finds himself walking along a sandy path and rests under a palm tree. Suddenly a child of radiant beauty drops from the branches of the tree, and presently two other individuals—"a god and goddess they must have been"—appear. They waft the narrator into the air and are joined by a singing chorus of other heavenly individuals who wish to lead the narrator to the wondrous land of Teloe. But the pounding of the sea disrupts this throng, and the narrator appears to witness the destruction of the world.

The story was written shortly after the prose poem "Nyarlathotep" (whose opening phrase is "Nyarlathotep . . . the crawling chaos . . ."). HPL remarks in a letter: "I took the title C. C. from my Nyarlathotep sketch . . . because I liked the sound of it" (HPL to R. H. Barlow, [December 1, 1934]; ms., JHL). HPL appears to allude to the genesis of the story in a letter of May 1920, in which he notes the previous collaboration with Jackson, "The Green Meadow": "I will enclose—subject to return—an account of a Jacksonian dream which occurred in the early part of 1919, and which I am some time going to weave into a horror story . . ." (*SL* 1.116). It is not certain whether this dream was the nucleus of "The Crawling Chaos," but since there are no other story collaborations with Jackson, the conjecture seems likely.

Various points in the account carry the implication that the narrator is not actually dreaming or hallucinating but envisioning the far future of the world—a point clumsily made by his conceiving of Rudyard Kipling as an "ancient" author. It is manifest that the entire tale was written by HPL; as with "The Green Meadow," Jackson's only contribution must have been the dream whose imagery probably laid the foundations for the opening segments.

Alfred Galpin ("Department of Public Criticism," *United Amateur,* November 1921) wrote charitably of the tale: "The narrative power, vivid imagination and poetic merit of this story are such as to elevate it above certain minor but aggravating faults of organisation and composition."

"Crime of the Century, The." Essay (970 words); probably written in early 1915. First published in the *Conservative* (April 1915); rpt. *Trail* (January 1916), *MW,* and *CE5.*
HPL asserts that the British and the Germans are committing a kind of racial suicide, since they are "blood brothers" belonging to the same Teutonic race—a race that is "the summit of evolution" and destined to rule all other races in the world.

Crofts, Anna Helen. Amateur writer and collaborator with HPL. Crofts lived in North Adams, Mass., in the far northwestern corner of the state. She collaborated with HPL on the story "Poetry and the Gods" (*United Amateur,* September 1920), published as by "Anna Helen Crofts and Henry Paget-Lowe." Nothing further is known of Crofts; she appeared sporadically in the amateur press, and may have been introduced to HPL by Winifred Jackson. The degree of her involvement in "Poetry and the Gods" is also unknown: HPL never mentions the tale in any extant correspondence.

Cthulhu Mythos. Term devised by August Derleth to denote the pseudomythology underlying some of HPL's tales, chiefly the "cosmic" stories of his last decade of writing.
It is difficult to know how seriously HPL himself regarded his invented pantheon or his invented New England topography (which has also been regarded by later critics as an important component of the Mythos). That pantheon developed from his very earliest work—"Dagon" (1917)—to his last, and it was in a state of constant flux, as HPL never felt bound to present a rigidly consistent theogony from one tale to the next. His own references to his pseudomythology are vague and inconsistent, suggesting that, even though he employed it often enough, it was merely for coloration, not the primary theme of his fiction. One of HPL's first comments on the matter is briefly stated in a letter to James. F. Morton (April 1, 1927; AHT), when he remarks that he has written an "atmospheric episode of the Arkham cycle" (i.e., "The Colour out of Space"). He next noted that "The Dunwich Horror" (1928) "belongs to the Arkham cycle" (*SL* 2.246). In 1934 he told a correspondent, "I'm not working on the actual text of any story just now, but am planning a novelette of the Arkham cycle [never written]—about what happened when somebody inherited a queer old house on the top of Frenchman's Hill & obeyed an irresistible urge to dig in a certain queer, abandoned graveyard on Hangman's Hill at the other edge of the town. This story will probably not involve the actual supernatural—being more of the 'Colour out of Space' type . . . . . greatly-stretched 'scientifiction'" (HPL to F. Lee Baldwin, March 27, 1934; ms. JHL). He never elucidates this expression "Arkham cycle," which appears to suggest that his invented topography (Arkham, Innsmouth, Kingsport, Dunwich) is a central component of certain loosely linked tales.

Writing to Clark Ashton Smith ([November 11, 1930]; ms. in private hands), HPL mentioned Yog-Sothoth as one of several "ingredients of the Miskatonic Valley myth-cycle." In early 1931, HPL wrote to Frank Belknap Long: "I really agree that 'Yog-Sothoth' is a basically immature conception, & unfitted for really serious literature. . . . But I consider the use of actual folk-myths as even more childish than the use of new artificial myths, since in employing the former one is forced to retain many blatant puerilities and contradictions of experience which could be subtilised or smoothed over if the supernaturalism were modelled to order for the given case. The only permanently artistic use of Yog-Sothothery, I think, is in symbolic or associative phantasy of the frankly poetic type; in which fixed dream-patterns of the natural organism are given an embodiment & crystallisation. . . . But there is another phase of cosmic phantasy (which may or may not include frank Yog-Sothothery) whose foundations appear to me as better grounded than those of ordinary oneiroscopy; personal limitation regarding the *sense of outsideness*" (*SL* 3.293–94). HPL's comment shows that his "pseudo-mythology" is not so much a "false" or made-up mythology, but an anti-mythology—the only kind of mythology that could be possible in this day and age. It is not a mythology of the kind invented or believed in by previous cultures—lore or legend intended to explain or account for the history of humankind, the history of the universe, the exploits of heroes, and so on. In fact, the careful reader of his stories will realize that it is no mythology at all, but a cycle of events intended to be perceived by only the more primitive or impressionable characters as *real* in the context of the fiction. Again, HPL's use of the term "Yog-Sothothery" is unclear, but it appears to denote his more "cosmic" narratives (the letter was written during his writing of *At the Mountains of Madness*). The context in which HPL used "Yog-Sothothery" (which resembles such terms as *tomfoolery* and *chicanery*) suggests that HPL took his pseudomythology none too seriously.

HPL emphasized that *all* his tales—whether they used his pseudomythology or his invented topography or not—were linked philosophically. His canonical utterance on the subject occurs in a letter to Farnsworth Wright (July 5, 1927), accompanying the resubmittal of "The Call of Cthulhu" to *WT* and at a time by which he had written the majority of his tales, but only a few of what most proponents refer to as his "mythos" fiction: "Now all my tales are based on the fundamental premise that common human laws and interests and emotions have no validity or significance in the vast cosmos-at-large. . . . To achieve the essence of real externality, whether of time or space or dimension, one must forget that such things as organic life, good and evil, love and hate, and all such local attributes of a negligible and temporary race called mankind, have any existence at all" (*SL* 2.150).

As early as the fall of 1927, when Frank Belknap Long wrote "The Space-Eaters," HPL's associates were "adding" components to various elements of his tales—in this case, his ever-growing library of mythical volumes of occult lore (Long invented John Dee's translation of the *Necronomicon*, citing it as an epigraph to his tale, although the epigraph was omitted in its first appearance in *WT,* July 1928). HPL cited Long's invention in "History of the *Necronomicon*" (1927). In late 1929 Clark Ashton Smith wrote "The Tale of Satampra Zeiros," which invented the toad-god Tsathoggua. Whether Smith was inspired by HPL's example is debatable; in fact, it was HPL who borrowed from Smith, citing Tsathoggua in his revision of Zealia Bishop's "The Mound" (1929–30), on which he was then working, and also in "The Whisperer in Darkness" (1930). Smith himself later wrote, in reference to several citations by other authors of elements he had invented: "It would seem that I am starting a mythology" (Smith to August Derleth, January 4, 1933; ms., SHSW).

In 1930 N. J. O'Neail wrote a letter to *WT* (March 1930) inquiring whether "Kathulos" cited in Robert E. Howard's "Skull-Face" (1929) was related to or derived from Cthulhu. Howard in turn queried HPL as to the reality of the various mythological elements cited in HPL's tales, to which HPL replied: "Regarding the solemnly cited myth-cycle of Cthulhu, Yog-Sothoth, R'lyeh, Nyarlathotep, Nug, Yeb, Shub-Niggurath, etc. etc.—let me confess that this is all a synthetic concoction of my own" (*SL* 3.166), going on to say that he dropped references to this myth-cycle in his ghostwritten tales purely for fun. Howard himself thereupon began dropping references to HPL's myth-cycle in his tales, although neither he nor Smith nor Donald Wandrei nor even younger disciples such as Robert Bloch ever actually wrote stories *about* HPL's mythic conceptions—they merely dropped references to HPL's entities in the course of their tales, for the sake of cryptic allusiveness and verisimilitude. It is an exaggeration to say that HPL "encouraged" these imitations or elaborations of his myth-cycle; in most cases, the writers simply made additions of their own accord, and HPL (usually out of courtesy) praised the results.

August Derleth, however, appears to have become obsessed with the Mythos, from as early as 1931, when he wrote the first draft of "The Return of Hastur" (*WT,* March 1939). At that time he suggested to HPL that the myth-cycle be given a name; he offered the Mythology of Hastur. HPL replied: "It's not a bad idea to call this Cthulhuism & Yog-Sothothery of mine 'The Mythology of Hastur'—although it was really from Machen & Chambers & others rather than through the Bierce-Chambers line, that I picked up my gradually developing hash of theogony—or daimonogeny" (HPL to August Derleth, May 16, 1931; ms., SHSW). (HPL refers to his derivation of the term Hastur from Robert W. Chambers's *The King in Yellow* [1895]; Chambers himself derived it from various tales of Ambrose Bierce. In "Some Notes on a Nonentity" [1933] HPL stated that it was from Lord Dunsany that HPL "got the idea of the artificial pantheon and myth-background represented by 'Cthulhu', 'Yog-Sothoth', 'Yuggoth', etc.," suggesting that HPL was adapting the imaginary pantheon found in Dunsany's early volumes of tales, *The Gods of Pegāna* [1905] and *Time and the Gods* [1906].) He also wrote to Robert Bloch (late May 1933): "As for the synthetic myth-cycle—I suppose I got the idea from Poe's allusions to fabulous lands of his own dreaming, from Dunsany's artificial pantheon, & from Machen's portentous references to 'Aklo letters', 'Voorish domes', &c." (*Letters to Robert Bloch*, p. 11). HPL went on to say in another letter to Derleth: "The more these synthetic daemons are written up by different authors, the better they become as general background-material! I *like* to have others use my Azathoths & Nyarlathoteps—& in return I shall use Klarkash-Ton's [Clark Ashton Smith] Tsathoggua, your monk Clithanus, & Howard's Bran" (HPL to August Derleth, August 3, 1931;

ms., SHSW). Derleth used that last sentence as a license to continue writing tales using HPL's pseudomythology, although even before HPL's death he warned at least one writer (Henry Kuttner) to avoid using HPL's pseudomythological elements in his own work as doing so could hamper HPL's ability to earn income from his own ideas. Ultimately Derleth himself departed from the tradition of HPL's own colleagues by writing stories entirely *about* HPL's mythic conceptions, rather than using them as "general background-material."

In 1932 the composer Harold S. Farnese engaged HPL in an epistolary discussion of HPL's theory and practice of weird fiction. Farnese seems to have misunderstood much of what HPL said to him, and after HPL's final move to 66 College Street, the two lost touch with each other. Then, after HPL's death, when August Derleth asked Farnese to lend him HPL's correspondence for use in *SL,* Farnese replied (April 11, 1937; ms., SHSW) that he could not at the moment find all his letters from HPL, but he supplied what he had, as well as what he claimed was a direct quotation from one missing letter: "Upon congratulating HPL upon his work, he answered, '*You will, of course, realize that all my stories, unconnected as they may be, are based on one fundamental lore or legend: that this world was inhabited at one time by another race, who in practicing black magic, lost their foothold and were expelled, yet love on outside ever ready to take possession of this earth again.*' 'The Elders,' as he called them" (emphasis by Farnese). This quotation does not appear in any surviving letter by HPL to Farnese or anyone else. Derleth, however, found the quotation useful in his own interpretation of the Mythos, which differed radically from what HPL himself conceived. (Derleth was unable to recall where he had obtained the quotation and, very late in life, became angry when Richard L. Tierney asked him to verify its source.) This interpretation featured several key notions:

1. *The Old Ones* (a term HPL used in several stories to denote several different entities, most notably the barrel-shaped extraterrestrials in *At the Mountains of Madness*) *are "evil" or "malignant" and are opposed by the "Elder Gods" as forces of good.* But HPL never mentions any such entities as "Elder Gods"; "Elder Ones" are cited in "The Strange High House in the Mist" and some other tales, but their exact denotation is unclear. HPL did not regard his Old Ones as evil or malignant, although in some cases they presented a physical danger to humanity.

2. *The major gods of HPL's mythology were "elementals": Cthulhu a water elemental, Nyarlathotep an earth elemental, and Hastur an air elemental.* Since HPL purportedly failed to provide a fire elemental, Derleth obligingly supplied Cthugha. HPL, however, did not conceive of his "gods" as elementals; the fact that Cthulhu is an extraterrestrial *imprisoned* (not enthroned) in the underwater city of R'lyeh makes it highly illogical that it should be considered a water elemental. The glancing citation of Hastur in "The Whisperer in Darkness" does not make it clear that it is even an entity (in Bierce, Hastur is the god of shepherds; in Chambers, a star or constellation).

3. *HPL's mythology parallels the "expulsion of Satan from Eden and Satan's lasting power of evil" in Christian mythology* (Derleth, "Introduction" to HPL's *The Dunwich Horror and Others* [Arkham House, 1963], p. xiii). This interpretation appealed to the Roman Catholic Derleth but is absurd when attributed to the atheist HPL.

4. *There is a rigid distinction to be made between those of HPL's tales that "belonged" to the "Cthulhu Mythos" and those that did not.* Much subsequent criticism (by Francis T. Laney, Lin Carter, and others) was involved in debating which stories did or did not "belong" to the Mythos, but most critics failed to note that HPL scat-

tered references to his pseudomythology, his imaginary topography, and his mythical books across many stories, making the exercise of segregating them into mutually exclusive categories a futile endeavor.

5. *HPL consciously developed his mythology, but died before he could accomplish all he intended to do.* But HPL had no such intention; only Derleth seems to have arrived at this conclusion. See, for example, his statement concerning his "posthumous collaboration" with HPL, "The Shuttered Room," that it is a "wedding of the Innsmouth and Dunwich themes, as manifestly HPL intended to do, judging by his scant notes" (Derleth to Felix Stefanile, August 11, 1958; ms., SHSW). There is no evidence in HPL of an Innsmouth theme, or a Dunwich theme, or that he intended to join them.

Derleth began expounding his view of the Mythos—and attributing it to HPL— as early as the article "H. P. Lovecraft, Outsider" (*River,* June 1937), in which he first mentioned the "Cthulhu mythology" and first cited the spurious "All my stories" quotation. He continued to disseminate this view in books, articles, and introductions to HPL's stories for the rest of his life. He also wrote numerous "posthumous collaborations" with HPL, taking plot germs from HPL's commonplace book (most of which had no connection with his pseudomythology), making "Cthulhu Mythos" tales of them, and affixing HPL's name to them. He also wrote numerous "Cthulhu Mythos" tales of his own (e.g., *The Mask of Cthulhu* [1958], *The Trail of Cthulhu* [1962]). In some cases he urged other writers (such as Ramsey Campbell and Brian Lumley) to "add" to the "Cthulhu Mythos"; in other cases he threatened legal action against others who sought to do so (e.g., in regard to the pulp writer C. Hall Thompson) when their work did not conform to his interpretation. What is most difficult to comprehend is that Derleth published HPL's statement to Farnsworth Wright (cited above) in *Marginalia* (in "Two Comments," pp. 305–6), as though it were an important statement about HPL's work; and yet, even though it was diametrically opposed to the conception Derleth had devised, Derleth nevertheless continued to emphasize the less tenable statement—the "black magic" quotation provided by Farnese.

Despite research in the 1970s by Richard L. Tierney, Dirk W. Mosig, and others exposing the errors of Derleth's interpretation, numerous writers continued to write their own takeoffs of the Mythos, a phenomenon that gathered considerable steam in the 1990s with many anthologies of "Cthulhu Mythos" stories assembled by Robert M. Price. Few scholars today, however, regard HPL's pseudomythology as significant in itself; rather, they see it as one of several ways through which HPL expressed his distinctive cosmic vision.

See Matthew H. Onderdonk, "The Lord of R'lyeh," *Fantasy Commentator* 1, No. 6 (Spring 1945): 103–14 (rpt. *LS* No. 7 [Fall 1982]: 8–17); George T. Wetzel, "The Cthulhu Mythos: A Study," in *HPL,* ed. Meade and Penny Frierson (1972) (rpt. *FDOC*); Richard L. Tierney, "The Derleth Mythos," in *HPL,* ed. Meade and Penny Frierson (1972); Dirk W. Mosig, "H. P. Lovecraft: Myth-Maker," *Whispers* 3, No. 1 (December 1976): 48–55 (revised version in *FDOC*); Robert M. Price, "Demythologizing Cthulhu," *LS* No. 8 (Spring 1984): 3–9; Will Murray, "The Dunwich Chimera and Others," *LS* No. 8 (Spring 1984): 10–24; Will Murray, "An Uncompromising Look at the Cthulhu Mythos," *LS* No. 12 (Spring 1986): 26–31; David E. Schultz, "Who Needs the 'Cthulhu Mythos'?" *LS* No. 13 (Fall 1986): 43–53; Thekla Zachrau, *Mythos und Phantastik: Funktion und Struk-*

tur der Cthulhu-Mythologie in den phantastischen Erzäahlungen H. P. Lovecrafts (Peter Lang, 1986); Donald R. Burleson, S. T. Joshi, Will Murray, Robert M. Price, and David E. Schultz, "What Is the Cthulhu Mythos?" (panel discussion), *LS* No. 14 (Spring 1987): 3–30; David E. Schultz, "The Origin of Lovecraft's 'Black Magic' Quote," *Crypt* No. 48 (St. John's Eve 1987): 9–13 (revised version in *The Horror of It All,* ed. Robert M. Price [Starmont House, 1990]); Robert M. Price, *H. P. Lovecraft and the Cthulhu Mythos* (Starmont House, 1990); Steven J. Mariconda, "Toward a Reader-Response Approach to the Lovecraft Mythos," in Mariconda's *On the Emergence of "Cthulhu" and Other Observations* (Necronomicon Press, 1995); David E. Schultz, comp., "Notes Toward a History of the Cthulhu Mythos," *Crypt* No. 92 (Eastertide 1996): 15–33; Chris Jarocha-Ernst, *A Cthulhu Mythos Bibliography & Concordance* (Armitage House, 1999).

"Curse of Yig, The." Short story (7,030 words); ghostwritten for Zealia Brown Reed Bishop, in the spring of 1928. First published in *WT* (November 1929); rpt. *WT* (April 1939); first collected in *BWS;* corrected text in *HM.*

Dr. McNeill, who runs an insane asylum in Guthrie, Oklahoma, tells the narrator (a researcher investigating snake lore) of the legend of Yig, "the half-human father of serpents," specifically in relation to the story of two settlers, Walker and Audrey Davis, who had come to the Oklahoma Territory in 1889. Walker has an exceptional fear of snakes, and has heard tales of Yig ("the snake-god of the central plains tribes—presumably the primal source of the more southerly Quetzalcoatl or Kukulcan . . . an odd, half-anthropomorphic devil of highly arbitrary and capricious nature") and of how the god avenges any harm that may come to snakes; so he is particularly horrified when his wife kills a brood of rattlers near their home. Late one night, the couple sees the entire floor of their bedroom covered with snakes; Walker gets up to stamp them out but falls down, extinguishing the lantern he is carrying. Audrey, now petrified with terror, soon hears a hideous popping noise—it must be Walker's body, so puffed with snake-venom that the skin has burst. Then she sees an anthropoid shape silhouetted in the window. Thinking it to be Yig, she takes an axe and hacks it to pieces when it enters the room. In the morning the truth is known: the body that burst was their old dog, bitten by countless snakes, while the figure that has been hacked to pieces is Walker. In a final twist, Dr. McNeill shows the narrator a loathsome half-snake, half-human entity kept in his asylum: it is not Audrey herself, but the entity to which she gave birth three-quarters of a year later.

HPL wrote: "this story is about 75% mine. All I had to work on was a synopsis describing a couple of pioneers in a cabin with a nest of rattlesnakes beneath, the killing of the husband by snakes, the bursting of the corpse, & the madness of the wife, who was an eye-witness to the horror. There was no plot or motivation—no prologue or aftermath to the incident—so that one might say the story, as a story, is wholly my own. I invented the snake-god & the curse, the tragic wielding of the axe by the wife, the matter of the snake-victim's identity, & the asylum epilogue. Also, I worked up the geographic & other incidental colour—getting some data from the alleged authoress, who knows Oklahoma, but more from books" (HPL to August Derleth, October 6, [1929]; ms., SHSW). HPL sent the completed tale to Bishop in early March 1928, making it clear in his letter to her that even the title is his. He adds: "I took a great deal of care with this tale, and was especially anxious to get the beginning smoothly adjusted. . . . For geographical atmosphere and colour I had of course to rely wholly on your answers to my questionnaire, plus such printed descriptions of Oklahoma as I could find." HPL charged Bishop $17.50 for the tale. She sold the story to *WT* for $45.

Curwen, Joseph (1662/3–1771; 1928). In *The Case of Charles Dexter Ward,* Curwen arrives in Providence from Salem in 1692 seeking asylum. As a result of his alchemical studies, he lives a preternaturally long life but also attracts unwanted attention. He marries Eliza Tillinghast, the daughter of one of his ship-captains, in an attempt to improve his standing in society. A wealthy man, he ingratiates himself among the townspeople of Providence by donating books to the library and money to various civic undertakings. Ezra Weeden, a jealous suitor of Eliza, investigates Curwen's furtive doings and organizes the raid on the Curwen bungalow in Pawtuxet, which results in Curwen's apparent death. The people of Providence seek to expunge all references to Curwen from the public record and nearly succeed. However, Curwen's great-great-great-grandson, Charles Dexter Ward, accidentally learns of his unknown and feared ancestor, eventually unearthing Curwen's papers and using the occult information they contain to resurrect Curwen from his "essential Saltes." Curwen (now restored to life but masquerading as a "Dr. Allen"), Ward, and their cohorts around the world continue the task of securing the "essential Saltes" of all the great geniuses of the human race so as to gain some kind of control over the world or even the universe. But when Ward becomes "squeamish" in carrying out this plan, Curwen kills him and attempts to take his place (the two bear a strong physical resemblance). Curwen's secret is discovered by Ward's physician, Marius Bicknell Willett, who ultimately destroys him.

"Cycle of Verse, A." Poem cycle consisting of three poems, "Oceanus" (16 lines), "Clouds" (22 lines), and "Mother Earth" (40 lines); written in November and December 1918. First two poems first published in the *National Enquirer* (March 20, 1919); third poem first published in the *National Enquirer* (March 27, 1919); all three poems published under the general title in *Tryout* (July 1919).

The poems tell of the weirdness to be found in the ocean, the sky, and the earth ("from whence all horrors have their birth").

Czanek, Joe. In "The Terrible Old Man," a thief (of Polish ancestry) who meets a bad end when he attempts to rob an old sea captain of his reputed hoard of Spanish gold and silver.

D

Daas, Edward F. (1879–1962). Amateur journalist in Milwaukee, Wis., who read HPL's letters and poems in the letter column of the *Argosy* and, in early 1914, invited HPL to join the UAPA. Daas was then Official Editor of the UAPA; he held the office again in 1915–16, but resigned before completing his term; in 1919–20 he was First Vice-President. On June 21–22, 1920, he visited HPL in Providence.

Daemon of the Valley. In "Memory," a supernatural entity who, as "Memory, . . . wise in lore of the past," informs a Genie of the former existence and current extinction of the human race.

"Dagon." Short story (2,240 words); written July 1917. First published in *Vagrant* (November 1919); rpt. *WT* (October 1923); rpt. *WT* (January 1936); first collected in *O;* corrected text in *D;* annotated version in *CC.*

The unnamed narrator is about to kill himself after writing his account because he has no more money for the morphine that prevents him from thinking of what he has experienced. A supercargo on a vessel during the Great War, this individual is captured by a German sea-raider but manages to escape five days later in a boat. He drifts in the sea, encountering no land or other ship. One night he falls asleep, awaking to find himself half-sucked in "a slimy expanse of hellish black mire which extended about me in monotonous undulations as far as I could see"; evidently there had been an upheaval of some subterranean land mass while he slept. In a few days the mud dries, permitting the narrator to walk along its vast expanse. He aims for a hummock far in the distance, and when finally attaining it finds himself looking down into "an immeasurable pit or canyon." Descending the side of the canyon, he notices a "vast and singular object" in the distance: it is a gigantic monolith "whose massive bulk had known the workmanship and perhaps the worship of living and thinking creatures."

Stunned by the awareness that such a civilization existed unknown to human science, the narrator explores the monolith, finding repellent marine bas-reliefs and inscriptions on it. But a still greater shock is coming to the narrator, for now a living creature emerges from the waves. He flees, and later finds himself in a San Francisco hospital, having been rescued by an American ship. But his life is shattered; he cannot forget what he has seen, and morphine is only a temporary palliative. His narrative concludes when he writes: "God, *that hand!* The window! The window!"

"Dagon" was in part inspired by a dream. In responding to a criticism regarding the narrator's actions, HPL writes: ". . . the hero-victim *is* half-sucked into the mire, yet he *does* crawl! He pulls himself along in the detestable ooze, tenaciously though it cling to him. I know, for I dreamed that whole hideous crawl, and can yet feel the ooze sucking me down!" (*In Defence of Dagon* [1921]; *MW* 150). William Fulwiler senses the general influence of Irvin S. Cobb's "Fishhead," a tale of a fishlike human being who haunts an isolated lake, and a tale that HPL praised in a letter to the editor when it appeared in the *Argosy* on January 11, 1913. HPL exhaustively rewrote "Dagon," in various ways, in both "The Call of Cthulhu" (1926) and "The Shadow over Innsmouth" (1931).

Some critics have believed that the monster actually appears at the end of the story; but the notion of a hideous creature shambling down the streets of San Francisco is preposterous, and we are surely to believe that the narrator's growing mania has induced a hallucination. HPL remarked, shortly after writing the story, that "Both ['The Tomb' and 'Dagon'] are analyses of strange monomania, involving hallucinations of the most hideous sort" (HPL to Rheinhart Kleiner, August 27, 1917; "By Post from Providence").

See Will Murray, "Dagon in Puritan Massachusetts," *LS* No. 11 (Fall 1985): 66–70; William Fulwiler, "'The Tomb' and 'Dagon': A Double Dissection," *Crypt* No. 38 (Eastertide 1986): 8–14.

Dalton, James. In "The Last Test," the governor of California who is in love with Dr. Alfred Clarendon's sister, Georgina. Dalton prevents Clarendon from conducting a medical experiment on her.

Danforth, ———. In *At the Mountains of Madness,* the graduate student who accompanies William Dyer in his explorations of the ruins of the Old Ones' city in the Antarctic. Before the two leave, Danforth witnesses something so horrifying that he suffers a nervous breakdown.

Davenport, Eli. In "The Whisperer in Darkness," the author of an "exceedingly rare monograph" recording material obtained orally prior to 1839 from old Vermont denizens concerning the possible existence of a hidden race of alien entities in the mountains.

Davis, Dr. In "In the Vault," George Birch's original personal physician, who is summed to Birch's side when the latter crawls out of the receiving tomb in which he had been trapped. Davis, recognizing the nature and cause of Birch's injuries, berates his patient for his carelessness and callousness.

Davis, [Francis] Graeme (1882–1938). Early amateur journalist who, as Official Editor of the NAPA (1917–18), violently attacked both HPL and the UAPA in two articles in his journal, *The Lingerer:* "With Consideration for the Conservative" (Summer 1917) and "Mere Musings" (Winter 1917). HPL responded to the former with "A Reply to *The Lingerer*" (*Tryout,* June 1917).

Davis, Sonia H[aft Greene Lovecraft] (1883–1972). HPL's wife (1924–29). Born Sonia Haft Shafirkin in Ichnya (near Kiev), in the Ukraine, she came to Liverpool with her mother and brother around 1890; her mother, Racille, went on to New York and married Solomon H——— (last name unknown) in 1892. Sonia joined her mother later that year. She married Samuel Seckendorff in 1899; a son, born in 1900, died after three months, and a daughter, Florence, was born on March 19, 1902. Seckendorff later adopted the name Greene from a friend in Boston. The marriage was turbulent, and Samuel Greene died in 1916, apparently by his own hand.

In 1917 Sonia became acquainted with James F. Morton, who introduced her to amateur journalism. She was by this time a highly paid executive at a clothing store in Manhattan, Ferle Heller's, and had a salary of $10,000. She resided at 259 Parkside Avenue in the fashionable Flatbush section of Brooklyn. She came to the NAPA convention in Boston in early July 1921; Rheinhart Kleiner introduced her to HPL. Shortly thereafter she contributed $50 to the UAPA (see *SL* 1.143). A correspondence with HPL ensued, and over the next two and a half years she visited Providence as frequently as her business schedule (which indeed entailed considerable traveling) allowed. She published, at considerable expense, two lavish issues of the amateur journal *The Rainbow* (October 1921, May 1922); the first contained HPL's "Nietzscheism and Realism" (a series of aphorisms derived from two of his letters to Sonia) and his revision of Sonia's poem "Mors Omnibus Communis," the second his story "Celephaïs."

In the spring of 1922 Sonia persuaded HPL to come to New York to meet his friends, notably Samuel Loveman; HPL stayed in Sonia's apartment (April 6–12) while she stayed with a neighbor. She then persuaded HPL to spend more than a week with her in Gloucester and Magnolia, Mass. (June 26–July 5)—evidently the first time HPL had spent time alone with a woman to whom he was not related. At this time Sonia conceived the idea for the story "The Horror at Martin's Beach," which HPL later revised for her (published in *WT* [November 1923] as "The Invisible Monster"). The story "Four O'Clock" (first published in *HM* [1970 ed.]) may also have been conceived then, but Sonia later testified that HPL merely suggested that she write it, and did not contribute any prose to the story (see Sonia H. Davis to Winfield Townley Scott, December 11, 1948; ms., JHL). In late July, HPL came to New York again—both to see Sonia and to continue on to Cleveland, where he spent time with Loveman and Alfred Galpin (July 30–August 15). Returning to New York, he stayed with Sonia until mid-October.

By the spring of 1924 it was clear that HPL and Sonia were seriously involved. The impetus to marry probably came from her, but HPL agreed to it apparently without reluctance. He did not, however, inform his aunts of his decision; instead, he boarded a train to New York on March 2 and married Sonia the next day at St. Paul's Cathedral in Manhattan. They left for a honeymoon in Philadelphia on March 4, but they spent much of the time retyping "Under the Pyramids," a story ghostwritten for Harry Houdini, the typescript of which HPL had left in the Providence train station. They settled in Sonia's apartment in Flatbush. (Her daughter Florence moved out around this time; evidence suggests that Florence did not approve of Sonia's marriage to HPL.) Shortly thereafter Sonia either lost her position at Ferle Heller's or resigned in order to begin her own independent hat shop; this venture was a failure, and by July HPL himself had to consider finding employment; his efforts were notably unsuccessful. From May 1924 to July 1925 Sonia was President of the UAPA and HPL Official Editor; they managed to publish a few issues of the *United Amateur,* largely containing contributions by themselves and their colleagues.

In October 1924 Sonia was stricken with a gastric attack and had to spend several days in a hospital. By the end of December she managed to secure employment at Mabley & Carew's, a department store in Cincinnati; she left on December 31. Sonia's health continued to be poor. She twice spent time in a private hospital in Cincinnati, and by late February 1925 had lost her position and returned to Brooklyn. She spent most of the period from late March to early June in the home of a woman physician in Saratoga Springs, N.Y. After staying in Brooklyn for most of June and July, she secured a job at Halle's, the leading department store in Cleveland, and worked there for just under a year. The result was that, during the period 1925–26 (when HPL moved into a single-room apartment at 169 Clinton Street in Brooklyn), she was with HPL for a total of only three months, mostly for a few days at a time at widely scattered intervals.

By the spring of 1926 Sonia acquiesced in the wishes of HPL's aunts that HPL return to Providence. She came with him to assist him in the relocation on April 17, spending about a week with him before returning to Brooklyn (she had by this time left Halle's). At some point, either at this time or some months later, Sonia proposed opening a hat shop in Providence; but HPL's aunts refused the offer, feeling it shameful for their nephew to have a wife working as a tradeswoman in their native city, where they were still part of the informal social aristocracy. For the next two years their relationship was conducted almost solely by correspondence, although HPL did return to New York on September 13–19, 1926, presumably because Sonia (who now had a position in Chicago) was on a purchasing trip to New York and asked HPL to come. In the spring of 1928 Sonia asked HPL to come to Brooklyn again, as she was setting up another hat shop. HPL stayed at her apartment (395 East 16th Street) from April 24 to June 7 while helping her set up the shop.

By the end of 1928 Sonia must have begun to press for divorce, since she was no longer satisfied with a marriage by correspondence. HPL repeatedly refused to grant the divorce, claiming that a "gentleman did not divorce his wife without cause," but he finally relented. Because of the restrictive divorce laws in New York State, the divorce was initiated in Rhode Island, under the charade that Sonia had deserted HPL. The final decree must have been issued in March or April 1929, but HPL did not sign it; therefore, he was never technically divorced from Sonia, and Sonia's subsequent marriage was legally bigamous.

The last time Sonia saw HPL was in mid-March 1933, when she had come to Hartford, Conn., for a visit and asked HPL to join her. (In correspondence HPL mentions the trip but not that he was meeting Sonia.) Later that year Sonia left for California; prior to her departure she destroyed HPL's letters to her (only a few postcards survive). In 1936 she married Dr. Nathaniel Davis. She did not hear of HPL's death until 1945. Three years later her memoir "Howard Phillips Lovecraft as His Wife Remembers Him" appeared in the *Providence Sunday Journal* (August 22, 1948), heavily edited by Winfield Townley Scott, the *Journal's* literary editor. Further edited by August Derleth, it appeared in *Cats* as "Lovecraft as I Knew Him" (rpt. *LR*). The original version, which survives at JHL, was published uncut bearing her original title: *The Private Life of H. P. Lovecraft* (Necronomicon Press, 1985, 1992). Additional recollections were published as "Memories of Lovecraft: I" (*Arkham Collector,* Winter 1969; rpt. *LR*). Some letters by her to August Derleth in the 1940s were published in Gerry de la Ree's article, "When Sonia Sizzled" (in Wilfred B. Talman, et al., *The Normal Lovecraft* [Gerry de la Ree, 1973]).

See R. Alain Everts, "Mrs. Howard Phillips Lovecraft," *Nyctalops* 2, No. 1 (April 1973): 45.

Davis, Walker and Audrey. In "The Curse of Yig," they are settlers in the Oklahoma Territory in 1889. Walker, who has a tremendous fear of snakes, is inadvertantly killed by Audrey when she mistakes him for Yig, the legendary snake god. She herself gives birth to three half-human, half-snake offspring, of which only one survives.

"Deaf, Dumb, and Blind." Short story (4,720 words); written in collaboration with C. M. Eddy, c. February 1924. First published in *WT* (April 1925); first collected in *DB;* corrected text in *HM.*

A deaf, dumb, and blind man, Richard Blake, "the author-poet from Boston," rents a lonely cottage—the Tanner place, on the outskirts of Fenton—because he thinks its "weird traditions and shuddering hints" might be an imaginative stimulus. The hermit Simeon Tanner had been found dead in the house in 1819, and something about the expression on his face led the townspeople to burn the body and the books and papers in the house. Blake moves into the place with his manservant, Dobbs. But after some anomalous incident Dobbs flees, babbling incoherently. Blake is left to himself, and he records his impressions in a diary he is preparing on his typewriter. This diary shows that Blake had become aware of some nameless presence in the house, and presently he somehow *hears* bizarre sounds, then a blast of cold air, and finally icy fingers "that draw me down into a cesspool of eternal iniquity." Blake is found dead, and Dr. Arlo Morehouse, who comes to investigate, becomes certain that the final bit of writing found in the machine was not typed by Blake.

In a letter to August Derleth (in *DB*), Eddy reports: "[HPL] was unhappy with my handling of the note found in the typewriter at the very end of the protagonist's account of his eerie experiences, the final paragraph that seemed to have been typed by one of his persecutors. After several conferences over it, and an equal number of attempts on my part to do it justice, he finally agreed to rewrite the last paragraph." This seems to suggest—although perhaps not by design—that HPL revised only the last paragraph; in truth, the entire tale was probably revised, although Eddy presumably wrote the first draft.

The tale's conclusion bears some analogy with "The Statement of Randolph Carter": in that story, the monstrous entity makes its presence known by speech (through a telephone); here, the entity reveals itself by writing. There is also a foreshadowing of "The Dunwich Horror," in that Simeon Tanner is said to have "bricked up the windows of the southeast room, whose east wall gave on the swamp," suggesting that he had kept some creature imprisoned within the room, just as Old Man Whateley attempted to contain Wilbur Whateley's twin.

[Death Diary.] Written January 1–March 11, 1937.

HPL's so-called death diary is mentioned in his obituary in the *New York Times:* "As he neared the end of his life, he turned his scholarly interest to a study of his own physical condition and daily wrote minutely of his case for his physician's assistance. His clinical notes ended only when he could no longer hold a pencil." The diary does not survive—R. H. Barlow probably kept it after he had gone through HPL's papers—but Barlow transcribed numerous entries from it in his letter to August Derleth of March 31, 1937 (ms., SHSW). These entries have been published as an appendix to R. Alain Everts, *The Death of a Gentleman: The Last Days of Howard Phillips Lovecraft* (Strange Co., 1987); rpt. *CE5.*

de Castro, Adolphe (1859–1959). Correspondent and revision client of HPL. He was born Gustav Adolphe Danziger in a German-speaking Russian territory along the Baltic Sea, and studied at the University of Bonn. He moved to the United States in 1886, was employed at one time or another at tasks as diverse as dentist and American consul in Madrid. He became acquainted with Ambrose Bierce and did the basic translation from German into English of *Der Mönch des Berchtesgarten* (1890) by Richard Voss (1851–1918), which Bierce then revised and polished; it was published as *The Monk and the Hangman's Daughter* (serialized 1891; book form 1892). He adopted the name de Castro (from a remote Spanish ancestor) in 1921. His *Portrait of Ambrose Bierce* (revised by Frank Belknap Long, who also wrote a preface, after HPL turned down the job) was published in 1929; it tells of his efforts to find Bierce in Mexico in early 1920s. De Castro also wrote several treatises (e.g., *Jewish Forerunners of Christianity* [E. P. Dutton, 1903]), novels, and volumes of poetry. He published a short story collection, *In the Confessional and the Following* (1893); in 1927, seeking to capitalize upon his relations with Bierce, he came in touch with HPL (through Samuel Loveman) and asked HPL to rewrite some stories for republication. HPL stated that he managed to "land" at least three with magazines, but only two are known: "The Last Test" (*WT,* November 1928; originally "A Sacrifice for Science") and "The Electric Executioner" (*WT,* August 1930; originally "The Automatic Executioner"). De Castro's originals were reprinted in *Crypt* No. 10 (1982). In 1934–35 HPL considered revising de Castro's social-political treatise *The New Way,* but ultimately declined. During a visit to Providence in August 1936, de Castro, HPL, and R. H. Barlow composed acrostic poems on Edgar Allan Poe in St. John's churchyard. De Castro's was later published in *WT* (May 1937).

See Chris Powell, "The Revised Adolphe Danziger de Castro," *LS* No. 36 (Spring 1997): 18–25.

de la Mare, Walter [John] (1873–1956). British author whose weird work (a small segment of his *oeuvre*) HPL admired. HPL first read de la Mare in the summer of 1926 (see *SL* 2.57) and accordingly added a substantial paragraph about him to "Supernatural Horror in Literature," singling out stories in *The Riddle and Other Stories* (1923) and *The Connoisseur and Other Stories* (1926), notably "Seaton's Aunt" (in the former volume), de la Mare's best-known weird tale. HPL also spoke highly of the novel *The Return* (1910; rev. 1922), which, in its depiction of a man possessed by the spirit of an eighteenth-century criminal, was surely an influence on HPL's *The Case of Charles Dexter Ward* (1927). HPL also had praise for de la Mare's weird poem "The Listeners" (in *The Listeners and Other Poems,* 1912). De la Mare is today probably better known for his writings for children, but his weird tales still attract a devoted following.

See Diana Ross McCrosson, *Walter de la Mare* (1966); Theresa Whistler, *Imagination of the Heart: The Life of Walter de la Mare* (1993).

Delapore, ———. The narrator of "The Rats in the Walls," whose decision to restore Exham Priory, the home of his ancestors in England, ultimately leads to his downfall and his confinement in an insane asylum. **Gilbert de la Poer,** first Baron Exham, was granted the site of Exham Priory in 1261. **Walter de la Poer,** eleventh Baron Exham, fled to Virginia, probably in the seventeenth century, and founded the family later known as Delapore. **Randolph Delapore** is the cousin of the narrator of "The Rats in the Walls," who "became a voodoo priest after he returned from the Mexican War." **Alfred Delapore** is the narrator's son. In 1917, he served overseas as an aviation officer, becoming friendly with Capt. Edward Norrys. He was injured and died two years later. His name is probably a nod toward HPL's friend, Alfred Galpin.

"Department of Public Criticism." Column criticizing amateur publications appearing in the *United Amateur;* rpt. *CE*1.

HPL wrote the columns for: January 1915; March 1915; May 1915; September 1915; December 1915; April 1916; June 1916; August 1916 (subtitled "First Annual Report, 1915–1916"); September 1916; March 1917; May 1917; July 1917; January 1918; March 1918; May 1918; September 1918 (in part); November 1918 (in part); January 1919 (in part); March 1919; May 1919 (in part).

HPL notes ("What Amateurdom and I Have Done for Each Other") that he had been appointed chairman of the Department of Public Criticism in the fall of 1914, taking over for Ada P. Campbell; HPL was then reappointed to the post for the 1915–16 and 1916–17 terms. Rheinhart Kleiner was appointed chairman for 1917–18, but HPL notes (letter to Arthur Harris, January 12, 1918; ms., JHL) that Kleiner was unable to serve, so that HPL ended up writing some of the articles for that official year. He was reappointed for the 1918–19 year.

The articles are, on the whole, rather mundane criticisms of the prose and verse appearing in the amateur journals of the period, largely concerned with pointing out grammatical errors in prose and errors in meter and scansion in poetry; occasionally HPL reveals his own prejudices by contesting the authors' opinions on literary, social, and political topics. The column was largely designed for an educational purpose, as a means of assisting amateurs to improve their writing skills. Some of HPL's articles are of great length—the column for September 1915 is 7,225 words long.

Derby, Edward Pickman. In "The Thing on the Doorstep," the weak-willed husband of Asenath Waite, who forces him to exchange his personality with hers. As a youth, Derby was a boy genius, who published the volume of poetry, *Azathoth and Other Horrors.* After undergoing several horrible experiences in the company of his wife, including participation in various gatherings of the witch-cult, he summons up the nerve to kill Asenath, burying her in the basement of their house in Arkham. But Asenath's personality survives, and she thrusts Derby's personality into her decaying corpse while she occupies his own body. With incredible effort, Derby unearths himself from his makeshift grave and brings a message to his longtime friend Daniel Upton, urging Dan to kill the individual occupying his own body.

Derby appears to be a synthesis of HPL's various protégés—chiefly Frank Belknap Long and Alfred Galpin—and perhaps Clark Ashton Smith. Like HPL, Derby marries a strong-willed woman somewhat late in life, although the woman HPL married was several years older than him whereas Asenath is fifteen years younger than Edward.

Derleth, August [William] (1909–1971). Novelist, poet, biographer, anthologist, correspondent of HPL (1926–37), and later his publisher. Derleth published stories in *WT* from 1926 onward; he began work on serious regional writing and character studies around 1929 with *The Early Years* (later published as *Evening in Spring* [1941]). He graduated from the University of Wisconsin in 1930, writing an honor's thesis, "The Weird Tale in English Since 1890," influenced heavily by HPL's "Supernatural Horror in Literature" (it was published in the *Ghost,* May 1945). He began writing "Solar Pons" detective stories in 1929; later he wrote Judge Peck detective novels (read by HPL) published by Loring & Mussey. His first serious mainstream work to be published was *Place of Hawks* (Loring & Mussey, 1935), consisting of four novelettes, all read in manuscript by HPL. Derleth collaborated with Mark Schorer on numerous horror tales, including "Lair of the Star-Spawn" (*WT,* August 1932; title suggested by HPL), which introduced the Tcho-Tcho people (mentioned by HPL in "The Shadow out of Time"). He became fascinated with HPL's mythos around 1931; at that time he urged HPL to name it "The Mythology of Hastur." A resolute professional writer, he urged HPL to market his work more vigorously. In 1933, without HPL's permission, he submitted to *WT* "The Shadow over Innsmouth," which was rejected, and "The Dreams in the Witch House," which was accepted. He also tried to interest Loring & Mussey in a collection of HPL's work in early 1935, but the stories HPL submitted were rejected.

Stunned by HPL's death in 1937, Derleth began immediately with Donald Wandrei (to whom HPL had introduced him in 1927) to compile HPL's writings into three volumes (fiction, essays and miscellany, and letters). Scribner's and

Simon & Schuster turned down *The Outsider and Others,* so Derleth and Wandrei published it themselves in 1939 under the imprint of Arkham House. Arkham House published many later volumes by HPL, all compiled by Derleth, including *BWS, Marginalia* (1944), *Cats* (1949), *SR* (1959), *Dreams and Fancies* (1962), *Collected Poems* (1963), and *DB* (1966), some of which contain valuable memoirs by HPL's colleagues, commissioned by Derleth. He compiled HPL's *Best Supernatural Stories* for World Pub. Co. (1945) and later disseminated HPL's work in England (Victor Gollancz) and in foreign languages (see his article, "H. P. Lovecraft: The Making of a Literary Reputation, 1937–1971," *Books at Brown* 25 [1977]: 13–25). From 1937 onward he arranged for the transcription of HPL's letters for the project that was eventually published, with many delays, as *Selected Letters* (1965–76; 5 vols.), although Donald Wandrei performed most of the actual editing.

Derleth veritably controlled all HPL activity from 1937 to 1971. He wrote many tales of the "Cthulhu Mythos," veering far from HPL's original conception, including "The Return of Hastur" (first draft 1931; rewritten 1937; *WT,* March 1939), *The Mask of Cthulhu* (Arkham House, 1958), and *The Trail of Cthulhu* (Arkham House, 1962). He also wrote sixteen "posthumous collaborations" with HPL, most of which were based on brief entries in HPL's commonplace book (the short novel *The Lurker at the Threshold* [Arkham House, 1945] contains a small amount of actual prose by HPL); they are gathered in *The Watchers out of Time and Others* (Arkham House, 1974). He encouraged some writers to contribute to the mythos but discouraged others (e.g., C. Hall Thompson). He compiled *Tales of the Cthulhu Mythos* (Arkham House, 1969). Derleth wrote many articles attributing his views of the mythos to HPL, among them "H. P. Lovecraft, Outsider" (*River,* June 1937; later revised as the introduction to *The Outsider and Others*), which coined the term "Cthulhu mythology." He wrote a brief biocritical study, *H. P. L.: A Memoir* (1945); decades later he did considerable work on an expanded edition, *H. P. Lovecraft: Notes toward a Biography,* but did not complete it (the manuscript survives in SHSW, where the bulk of Derleth's papers and HPL's letters to him reside). He also compiled many anthologies of weird and science fiction (many including stories by HPL) and wrote numerous mainstream novels, short stories, poetry, biographies, etc.

See *100 Books by August Derleth* (Arkham House, 1962); Robert M. Price, "The Lovecraft-Derleth Connection," *LS* No. 7 (Fall 1982): 18–23; Alison M. Wilson, *August Derleth: A Bibliography* (Scarecrow Press, 1983).

de Russy, Antoine. In "Medusa's Coil," a Louisiana planter whose decaying mansion is visited by the narrator, who spends the night there. De Russy's tale about his son and his mysterious wife, whom he buried in the cellar of his house, constitute the story's narrative.

de Russy, Denis. In "Medusa's Coil," a young man who visits Paris and there falls in love with and marries the mysterious Marceline Bedard, whom he brings to Missouri to live with him. His friend Frank Marsh is captivated by Marceline, and he desires to paint her portrait. De Russy suspects his wife of infidelity with

Marsh, but later he realizes that Marsh has been trying to inform him of his wife's tainted background, and he kills her. He is strangled by Marceline's animate hair.

de Russy, Marceline (Bedard). In "Medusa's Coil," an alluring young woman in Paris who claims to be the illegitimate daughter of the Marquis de Chameaux, but who, after she marries Denis de Russy and returns with him to his estate in Missouri, is revealed to be not only an ancient entity endowed with animate hair, but also "a negress."

"Descendant, The" (title supplied by R. H. Barlow). Fragmentary story (1,500 words); probably written in early 1927. First published in *Leaves* (1938); first collected in *Marginalia;* corrected text in *D.*

Lord Northam is thought "harmlessly mad" by the people who know him; he lives with a cat in Gray's Inn, London, and "all he seeks from life is not to think." A man of great learning, Northam has been scarred by some harrowing incident in the past. One day a young man named Williams brings Lord Northam a copy of the *Necronomicon,* at the mere sight of which Northam faints. He then tells Williams the story of his life: he is a member of a family that extends very far back in history, perhaps to one Cnaeus Gabinius Capito, a military tribune in Roman Britain who had supposedly come upon "strange folk ... [who] made the Elder Sign in the dark." Northam himself, in his youth, had sought to penetrate the mysteries of Satanism and occultism, filled with "the tantalising faith that somewhere an easy gate existed, which if one found would admit him freely to those outer deeps whose echoes rattled so dimly at the back of his memory." (At this point the fragment ends.)

It is difficult to ascertain HPL's plans for this item. In April 1927 he speaks of "making a very careful study of *London* ... in order to get background for tales involving richer antiquities than America can furnish" (HPL to August Derleth, [April 15, 1927]; ms., SHSW), leading one to believe that the fragment was written around this time (not in 1926, as commonly assumed). Some external features of Lord Northam bring Arthur Machen and Lord Dunsany to mind, although in a superficial way. Northam lives at Gray's Inn, where Machen lived for many years; and Northam is the "nineteenth Baron of a line whose beginnings went uncomfortably far back into the past," just as Dunsany was the eighteenth Baron in a line founded in the twelfth century. Northam, like Randolph Carter in "The Silver Key," undertakes a wide-ranging sampling of various religious and aesthetic ideals, allowing us perhaps to believe that the fragment was written after "The Silver Key."

See S. T. Joshi, "On 'The Descendant,'" *Crypt* No. 53 (Candlemas 1988): 10–11.

Description of the Town of Quebeck, A. Essay (78,000 words); written September 1930–January 14, 1931. First published in HPL's *To Quebec and the Stars* (1976), ed. L. Sprague de Camp; rpt. *CE4.*

HPL's single longest literary work—an exhaustive history of Quebec and a detailed travelogue of the city and neighboring regions, based upon his first ecstatic visit to the region in late summer of 1930. HPL relied largely on published histories and guidebooks for much of his historical account, but the travelogue section is manifestly based upon first-hand experience. The entire text is written in exquisite eighteenth-century English and reflects a British attitude in recording the defeat of the French by the English in the course of the eighteenth century. The text is filled with HPL's drawings of typical Quebec architecture, and there is an appendix providing French and English names of prominent landmarks and the origins of place-names and street-names. HPL never prepared the text for publication, nor even a typescript to circulate among colleagues; hence it long remained unpublished. De Camp's edition contains many mistranscriptions and also fails to correct several instances of HPL's erroneous French.

"Despair." Poem (40 lines in 5 stanzas); written c. February 19, 1919. First published in *Pine Cones* (June 1919).

A brooding, pessimistic poem speaking of "Sweet Oblivion" to be found "beyond the groans and grating / Of abhorrent Life." HPL notes (*SL* 1.79) that the poem was written in response to the illness of his mother, who had suffered a nervous breakdown and would soon be transferred to Butler Hospital, where she would die two years later.

Desrochers, ———. In "The Dreams in the Witch House," a French Canadian who lives in the room directly below Walter Gilman's in the Witch House in Arkham, and who sees and hears numerous odd things during the time of Gilman's dreams and sleepwalking.

Dexter, Mercy. In "The Shunned House," the maiden sister of Rhoby (Dexter) Harris, who moves into the Shunned House in 1768 to tend to Rhoby, who had lapsed into insanity after the death of her husband and several of her children. Her health begins to fail from the moment she occupies the house, and she dies in 1782.

[Diary: 1925.] Diary (ms., JHL); in *CE5*.

A small pocket diary in which HPL wrote very compressed records of his activities during 1925, when he was living alone at 169 Clinton Street. A sample entry: [March 1] "Up noon—call on GK [George Kirk]—SH [Sonia] get dinner here—eggs—pot. chips—crackers—cheese GW coffee—read papers—write Sonny [Frank Belknap Long] telephone—SL [Samuel Loveman] GK RK [Rheinhart Kleiner] call & go out to dinner—Wrote LDC [Lillian D. Clark]////Boys return—Session at Kirk's—out to Scotch Bakery—GK & HP return to talk till dawn—retire."

"Diary of Alonzo Typer, The." Short story (8,260 words); ghostwritten for William Lumley, October 1935. First published in *WT* (February 1938); first collected in *BWS;* corrected text in *HM*.

In a spectral house in upstate New York, strange forces were summoned by a Dutch family, the van der Heyls, that had resided there. Alonzo Typer, an occult explorer, attempts to fathom the mysteries of the place. He senses several strange presences in the house, especially in the cellar. He realizes that he will probably not be allowed to leave and that some great cataclysm is to occur around Walpurgisnacht (May Eve). At length he discovers that an "ancient for-gotten One" is lurking beneath the house who will show Typer "the gateway I would enter, and give me the lost signs and words I shall need." At the climactic moment, Typer realizes that he himself is related to the van der Heyls and that he has been called here for the fulfilling of some hideous purpose. Typer contin-ues writing in his diary to the last: "Too late—cannot help self—black paws materialise—am dragged away toward the cellar. . . ."

The story was based upon a nearly illiterate draft produced by Lumley (pub-lished in *Crypt* No. 10 [1982]: 21–25). HPL, while preserving such as he could of the draft—including such of Lumley's inventions as the *Book of Forbidden Things,* "the seven lost signs of terror," the mysterious city Yian-Ho, and the like—has at least made some coherent sense of the plot. The preposterous con-clusion, however, is HPL's own.

HPL revised the story for no pay, thinking that it would encourage Lumley's efforts at writing. Lumley promptly submitted the story to *WT,* where it was accepted in December 1935 for $70, but for some reason there was a long delay in its magazine publication.

"Disinterment, The." Short story (4,600 words); written in collaboration with Duane W. Rimel, September 1935. First published in *WT* (January 1937); cor-rected text in *HM.*

The unnamed narrator awakes to find himself in a hospital bed in a private clinic—a "veritable medieval fortress." He then remembers that he had con-tracted leprosy while in the Orient and had appealed to his friend, Marshall An-drews, for help. Andrews, a surgeon of dubious reputation, persuades the narrator to spend nearly a year in his castle undergoing treatment. Then An-drews goes to the West Indies to study "native" medical methods. Returning, Andrews claims that he has found a drug in Haiti that could simulate death, even to temporary rigor mortis. The plan is to inject the narrator with the drug, have him declared dead, interred in a grave, and then resurrected. In this way the nar-rator could assume another identity without the stigma of leprosy. As the narra-tor wakes, he feels the lingering effects of the drug, and he seems paralyzed. Gradually the paralysis passes, but movement of arms and legs is still painful and jerky. There seems to be some kind of alienation between the narrator's head and the rest of his body. Tormented by dreams and suspecting that some nameless experiment has been made upon him, he staggers out of bed, finds Andrews sleeping in a chair, and kills him with a candelabrum. He later kills Andrews' butler, Simes. Going outside, he approaches his manor house and en-ters the family cemetery. He comes to his own tombstone, begins to dig up the grave, and finds to his horror his own headless body: Andrews had transplanted his head upon the body of an African American from Haiti.

HPL discusses the story in a letter to Rimel of September 28, 1935: "First of all, let me congratulate you on the story. Really, it's *splendid*—one of your best so far! The suspense & atmosphere of dread are admirable, & the scenes are very vividly managed. . . . I've gone over the MS. very carefully with a view to improving the smoothness of the prose style—& I hope you'll find the slight verbal changes acceptable" (ms., JHL). The critical issue is what to make of this statement (the manuscript or typescript, with HPL's putative corrections, does not survive). The fact that HPL refers to "slight verbal changes" should not lead us to minimize his role in the tale, since this may simply be an instance of his customary modesty. Rimel maintains that HPL performed only slight revisions on the story; but if so, then Rimel never came so close to imitating HPL's style and idiom. The tale bears some resemblance to HPL's early tales of the macabre, notably "The Outsider."

See Will Murray, "Facts in the Case of 'The Disinterment,'" *LS* No. 17 (Fall 1988): 30–33.

"Does Vulcan Exist?" Essay, purportedly by HPL, dating to 1906. Printed by August Derleth in *H.P.L.: A Memoir* (1945); rpt. *CE3*.

Derleth claimed that this item was part of or an entire astronomy column published in the *Providence Journal;* but HPL had no column in the *Journal.* It is more likely that this is an unpublished juvenile manuscript that Derleth had come upon when going through HPL's papers and that he assumed it had appeared in the *Journal* (probably the only Providence newspaper of which he was aware). From internal evidence, the text seems to be by HPL and probably does date to around 1906.

Dombrowski, Mr. and Mrs. In "The Dreams in the Witch House," the landlords of the Witch House in Arkham at the time when Walter Gilman experiences his bizarre dreams and sleepwalking.

"Doom That Came to Sarnath, The." Short story (2,740 words); written on December 3, 1919. First published in the *Scot* (June 1920), a Scottish amateur journal edited by Gavin T. McColl; rpt. *Marvel Tales* (March–April 1935) and *WT* (June 1938); first collected in *BWS;* corrected text in *D;* annotated version in *DWH.*

Ten thousand years ago, in the land of Mnar, stood the stone city of Ib near a vast still lake. Ib was inhabited by "beings not pleasing to behold": they were "in hue as green as the lake and the mists that rise above it . . . they had bulging eyes, pouting, flabby lips, and curious ears, and were without voice." Many eons later new folk came to Mnar and founded the city of Sarnath; these were the first human beings of the region, "dark shepherd folk with their fleecy flocks." They loathed the creatures of Ib and destroyed both the town and its inhabitants, preserving only the "sea-green stone idol chiselled in the likeness of Bokrug, the water-lizard." After this Sarnath flourished greatly. Every year a festival is held commemorating the destruction of Ib, and the thousandth year of this festival was to be of exceptional lavishness. But during the feasting and celebrating Sarnath is overrun by "a horde of indescribable green voiceless things with bulging eyes, pouting, flabby lips, and curious ears." Sarnath is destroyed.

Many features in the story betray borrowings from Dunsany, but all in externals. HPL thought he had come by the name Sarnath independently, but maintained that he later found it in a story by Dunsany; this is not, however, the case. Sarnath is also a real city in India (purportedly the place where Buddha first taught), but HPL may not have known this. The green idol Bokrug is reminiscent of the green jade gods of Dunsany's play *The Gods of the Mountain* (in *Five Plays*, 1914). Mention of a throne "wrought of one piece of ivory, though no man lives who knows whence so vast a piece could have come" echoes a celebrated passage (noted by HPL in "Supernatural Horror in Literature") in "Idle Days on the Yann" (in *A Dreamer's Tales*, 1910) of an ivory gate "carved out of one solid piece!" The style of the tale is also superficially Dunsanian.

Douglas, Capt. J. B. In *At the Mountains of Madness,* the captain of the brig *Arkham,* one of the supply ships for the Miskatonic Antarctic Expedition of 1930–31.

Dow, Johnny. In "The Horror in the Burying-Ground," a friend of Tom Sprague who goes mad after witnessing the apparent deaths of Sprague and his enemy, Henry Thorndike.

Dowdell, William J. (1898–1953). Amateur writer in Cleveland. Dowdell edited several amateur journals, including *Dowdell's Bearcat,* which printed several works by HPL, including the essay "The Dignity of Journalism" (July 1915) and the poems "To Samuel Loveman, Esquire . . ." (December 1915) and "An American to Mother England" (November 1916). HPL criticized Dowdell's *Cleveland Sun* (coedited with Anthony F. Moitoret and Edwin D. Harkins) for its excessive imitation of cheap newspaper standards, especially its inclusion of "The Best Sport Page in Amateurdom" (see "Department of Public Criticism," *United Amateur,* September 1916). In 1919 Dowdell led a campaign criticizing HPL's purportedly high-handed centralization of authority in the UAPA (see "For Official Editor—Anne Tillery Renshaw," *Conservative,* July 1919); in 1922 HPL lost his battle, being ousted as Official Editor of the UAPA. At this time Dowdell was himself President of the NAPA, but resigned late in the year (HPL later remarked that Dowdell "ran off with a chorus girl": HPL to Lillian D. Clark, July 27, 1925; ms., JHL); the NAPA's Executive Judges appointed HPL interim President for 1922–23. No more is heard of Dowdell either in amateur circles or in professional journalism.

Dream-Quest of Unknown Kadath, The. Short novel (43,100 words); written October 1926–January 22, 1927. First published in *BWS;* rpt. *Arkham Sampler* (Winter 1948–Autumn 1948); corrected text in *MM;* annotated version in *DWH.*

Randolph Carter engages in a quest through dreamland in search of the "sunset city" of his dreams, which he can no longer attain. The city is described as follows: "All golden and lovely it blazed in the sunset, with walls, temples, colonnades, and arched bridges of veined marble, silver-basined fountains of prismatic spray in broad squares and perfumed gardens, and wide streets marching between delicate trees and blossom-laden urns and ivory statues in gleaming rows; while on steep northward slopes climbed tiers of red roofs and old peaked gables harbouring little lanes of grassy cobbles." He believes that his only recourse is to plead his case before the "hidden gods of dream that brood capricious above the clouds on unknown Kadath." No one in dreamland knows where Kadath is, and the journey appears to be fraught with dangers, but Carter undertakes the quest nonetheless.

He first visits the land of the zoogs, "furtive and secretive" creatures who live in burrows or in the trunks of trees. They do not know where Kadath is, but one elderly zoog has heard that a copy of the "inconceivably old Pnakotic Manuscripts" is at Ulthar and that it tells much about the gods. So Carter makes his way to Ulthar, beyond the river Skai, where the friendly cats cluster about him. Carter seeks the patriarch Atal, who long ago had ascended Mt. Hatheg-Kla in the company of Barzai the Wise, in order to look upon the gods; only Atal had come down. Carter drugs Atal with the zoogs' moon-wine, so that Atal becomes talkative: he tells Carter of a great image of the gods (called the Great Ones or the gods of earth) carved on Mt. Ngranek, on the isle of Oriab; if Carter were to see this image, and then look for similar images among the races of dreamland, he would probably find the gods. The gods, after all, were fond of marrying the daughters of men and producing offspring who had divine blood in their veins and divine features on their countenances.

At Atal's urging, Carter joins a caravan bound for Dylath-Leen, a great city on the Southern Sea. Arriving there, he hears that ships from Baharna, a city on Oriab, came occasionally to trade at Dylath-Leen. These ships had an unsavory reputation, for they would merely exchange enormous rubies for hordes of black slaves. Presently such a ship comes into the harbor, and Carter speaks to one of the merchants on it; but the merchant plies Carter with drugged wine, and he is taken aboard the ship as a prisoner. Carter suspects that the ship is in league with the Other Gods, who under the aegis of the crawling chaos Nyarlathotep protect the mild gods of earth. The ship sails between the Basalt Pillars of the West, and then leaps into the air and lands on the moon, eventually docking at a peculiar city on a "leprous-looking coast"; on the shore are huge grayish-white toadlike creatures moving cargo and slaves off the ships. Other creatures, turbaned and approximately human in outline, are also seen. Two of the toad-creatures seize Carter and take him to a dungeon, and later he is led in a procession, surrounded by both the toads and the almost-human entities. Suddenly Carter hears the yell of a cat, and he realizes that the moon is where all cats come at night. Carter, knowing the cats' language, utters a cry for help; and there ensues a battle between the cats on one side and the toad-creatures and almost-humans on the other side. The cats prevail and then make a gigantic leap back to earth, Carter safely carried along in their midst.

Carter finds himself back at Dylath-Leen and this time boards a ship for the isle of Oriab. Reaching the port of Baharna, Carter undertakes the arduous ascent of Mt. Ngranek; finally attaining the farther side of it, he is astounded at the enormous face carved thereon. But mingled with his awe is recognition, for Carter knows that he has seen likenesses of that face in the taverns of the seaport Celephaïs, ruled by King Kuranes. Carter knows he must head there, but before he can climb down the mountain he is plucked by hideous winged creatures with no faces—the night-gaunts. They bear him beyond the Peaks of Thok and leave him in the vale of Pnath, "where crawl and burrow the enormous bholes." Carter is, however, aware that bholes are terrified of ghouls, and he has had dealings in the past with ghouls—specifically with one ghoul named Richard Upton Pickman, who used to be a man. Carter summons the ghouls, who lower an enormous rope ladder up which he climbs to the top of a crag. The ghouls take

Carter to Pickman, who "had become a ghoul of some prominence in abysses nearer the waking world." Carter outlines his plan to get to the enchanted wood and thence to Celephaïs, but Pickman tells him that to do so he will have to pass through the kingdom of the gugs, "hairy and gigantic," and their enemies, the ghasts. Pickman gives Carter a handful of ghouls to accompany him to the gugs' kingdom and has Carter disguise himself as a ghoul.

Carter and the ghouls reach the kingdom of the gugs. They seek to ascend a cliff to the enchanted wood, but encounter an enormous gug, fifteen feet high and with a mouth that opens vertically. At that moment, however, the gug is attacked by a swarm of ghasts, and this allows Carter and his escorts to go forth and reach an enormous tower with huge stone steps leading up. After "aeons of climbing" they reach the summit, going through a stone trapdoor just before a gug can capture them. At this point the ghouls leave Carter to return to their own realm. As he is making his way through the enchanted wood, he overhears zoogs planning a war of revenge upon the cats, who had killed several zoogs when Carter was at Ulthar. Carter realizes that he must foil the plan, so he summons the cats and informs them of the zoogs' scheme.

Carter follows the river Oukranos to Kiran and Thran, and there boards a galleon to Celephaïs. He describes to the mariners the face on Mt. Ngranek, and the mariners tell him that people matching that description are found in a far-away twilight land called Inganok, close to Leng. After passing by Hlanith, Carter comes to Celephaïs, where he meets his old friend Kuranes. But Kuranes, although now a king, longs for his old home, Trevor Towers, in England, and suggests that Carter's "sunset city" may not be as satisfying as he thinks.

At length a ship from Inganok docks at the harbor, and Carter is thrilled to see "living faces so like the godlike features on Ngranek." Carter takes passage on their ship and eventually comes to the onyx city of Inganok. He is unnerved to see again the slant-eyed merchant who had drugged him in Dylath-Leen, but the latter disappears before Carter can speak to him. Carter wishes to talk with the onyx-miners in the north, so he hires a yak for the purpose and makes his way to the quarries. Ascending the black cliffs higher and higher, Carter reaches the crest and sees, far in the distance, what appears to be an enormous range of black mountains, but is in fact a series of gigantic onyx figures, "their right hands raised in menace against mankind." From their laps Carter sees arising a black cloud of shantak-birds. In front of him he sees the slant-eyed merchant astride a yak and leading a horde of shantaks. The merchant compels Carter to mount one of the birds, and they fly through space to the doorway of a windowless stone monastery in Leng. Carter is led before a "lumpish figure robed in yellow silk . . . and having a yellow silken mask over its face," whom Carter realizes as the "high-priest not to be described, of which legend whispers such fiendish and abnormal possibilities." At one point the priest's mask slips, and the brief glimpse of the face impels Carter to flee madly through the labyrinthine corridors of the monastery. Without warning he slides down an almost vertical burrow and, seemingly miles below, finds himself in a ruined city that he recognizes is Sarkomand.

Carter sees a glow ahead, and approaching carefully he sees that it is a campfire near the seashore, where a black galley from the moon is docked; around the campfire Carter sees a group of the toadlike moon-beasts, who have captured his erstwhile ghoul escorts. Carter realizes that he must summon help, so he goes down an immense set of spiral staircases; but as he is slipping down the steps, he is caught up by night-gaunts. Now aware that the night-gaunts are in league with the ghouls, Carter utters a ghoul-cry and tells the night-gaunt to take him back to Pickman and his cohorts. Explaining the situation to the ghouls, he sees them arraying themselves for battle, each ghoul jumping astride a night-gaunt and flying toward the seashore where the captured ghouls are being held. Another battle ensues, with the ghouls and night-gaunts eventually victorious. The ghouls decide to exterminate the garrison of the toadlike creatures, and they board a captured galley with the night-gaunts and defeat the moon-beasts and their al-most-human slaves in a titanic struggle.

In gratitude for Carter's assistance, the entire army of ghouls and night-gaunts agrees to accompany Carter in approaching the Great Ones in their castle and making a plea for his sunset city. Flying over Leng and Inganok, they see Kadath looming in front of them—a mountain of almost inconceivable height, with the Great Ones' castle on top. They begin an ascent, but after a time Carter notices that the night-gaunts are no longer flapping their wings: a "force not of earth" has seized the army and is bearing it up to the castle. Swept into the castle, Carter finds to his amazement that the place is entirely empty and dark, except for one small light that glowed from a tower room.

Then a "daemon trumpet" blasts three times, and Carter notices that he is now alone—the ghouls and night-gaunts have disappeared. Accompanied by an array of "giant black slaves," a "tall, slim figure with the young face of an antique Pharaoh" approaches him. It is Nyarlathotep, "messenger of the Other Gods," and he speaks at length to Carter. The Great Ones, the gods of earth, have deserted their castle to dwell amidst Carter's own sunset city, and this is why he himself is denied it in his dreams. But what is that sunset city? Nyarlathotep tells him:

> "For know you, that your gold and marble city of wonder is only the sum of what you have seen and loved in youth. It is the glory of Boston's hillside roofs and western windows aflame with sunset; of the flower-fragrant Common and the great dome on the hill and the tangle of gables and chimneys in the violet valley where the many-bridged Charles flows drowsily. These things you saw, Randolph Carter, when your nurse first wheeled you out in the springtime, and they will be the last things you will ever see with eyes of memory and of love. . . .
>
> ". . . These, Randolph Carter, are your city; for they are yourself. New-England bore you, and into your soul she poured a liquid loveliness which cannot die. This loveliness, moulded, crystallised, and polished by years of memory and dreaming, is your terraced wonder of elusive sunsets; and to find that marble parapet with curious urns and carven rail, and descend at last those endless balustraded steps to the city of broad squares and prismatic fountains, you need only to turn back to the thoughts and visions of your wistful boyhood."

What Carter must do is to go back to his sunset city and urge the Great Ones to return to their castle. Nyarlathotep provides Carter with a shantak to take him back, and they fly off. But Carter becomes aware that it is all a trick: the shantak plunges him "through shoals of shapeless lurkers and caperers in darkness" and is heading toward the great throne of Azathoth in "those inconceivable, unlighted chambers beyond Time." It then occurs to Carter that all he has to do is wake up in his Boston room, leave dreamland behind, and take cognizance of the beauty to be found on his doorstep. He does so, and Nyarlathotep's plan to destroy Carter and deprive him of his sunset city is foiled.

While writing the story, HPL expressed considerable doubts about its merits: "I . . . am very fearful that Randolph Carter's adventures may have reached the point of palling on the reader; or that the very plethora of weird imagery may have destroyed the power of any one image to produce the desired impression of strangeness" (*SL* 2.94). And elsewhere: "Actually, it isn't much good; but forms useful practice for later and more authentic attempts in the novel form" (*SL* 2.95). The novel has, indeed, inspired highly contradictory judgments, some HPL enthusiasts finding it almost unreadable and others, like L. Sprague de Camp (*Lovecraft: A Biography* [Doubleday, 1975], p. 280), comparing it to the *Alice* books and the fantasies of George MacDonald.

If there is any dominant literary influence on the novel, it is probably William Beckford's *Vathek* (1786), which is similarly an exotic fantasy written without chapter divisions. Several other features of plot and diction bring Beckford's Arabian fantasy to mind. One other possible influence is John Uri Lloyd's curious novel of underworld adventure, *Etidorhpa* (1895), which HPL read in 1918 (see *SL* 1.54–55). This strange work, full of windy philosophy and science defending the idea of a hollow earth, nevertheless contains some spectacularly bizarre and cosmic imagery of the narrator's seemingly endless underworld adventures, although no specific passage seems to be echoed in HPL's work. Nevertheless, HPL's dreamworld creates the impression of being somehow underground (as in Carter's descent of the 700 steps to the gate of deeper slumber), so perhaps he was thinking of how Lloyd's narrator purportedly plunges beneath the actual surface of the earth on his peregrinations. (Some have believed that the episode involving the high-priest with the yellow silken mask is an allusion to Robert W. Chambers's *The King in Yellow* [1895], but HPL would not read this work until two months after completing the *Dream-Quest.*)

The novel seeks to unite most of HPL's previous "Dunsanian" tales, making explicit references to features and characters in such tales as "Celephaïs," "The Cats of Ulthar," "The Other Gods," "The White Ship," and others (not to mention the "real-world" story "Pickman's Model"); but in doing so it creates considerable confusion. In particular, it suddenly transfers the settings of these tales into the dreamworld, whereas those tales themselves had manifestly been set in the dim prehistory of the real world.

It has frequently been conjectured that the tale carries out HPL's old novel idea "Azathoth" (1922); but while this may be true superficially in the sense that both works seem to center around protagonists venturing on a quest for some wondrous land, in reality the novel of 1926 presents a thematic reversal of the novel idea of 1922. In the earlier work—conceived at the height of HPL's Decadent phase—the unnamed narrator "travelled out of life on a quest into the spaces whither the world's dreams had fled"; but he does this because "age fell upon the world, and wonder went out of the minds of men." In other words, the narrator's only refuge from prosy reality is the world of dream. Carter thinks that this is the case for him, but at the end he finds more value and beauty in that reality—transmuted by his dreams and memories—than he believed. (Carter's realization is prefigured in the episode involving Kuranes.)

In this sense, the resurrection of the Dunsanian idiom—not used since "The Other Gods" (1921)—is meant not so much as a homage as a repudiation of Dunsany, at least of what HPL at this moment took Dunsany to be. Just as, when he wrote "Lord Dunsany and His Work" in 1922, he felt that the only escape from modern disillusion would be to "worship afresh the music and colour of divine language, and take an Epicurean delight in those combinations of ideas and fancies which we know to be artificial," so in 1926—after two years spent away from the New England soil that he now realized was his one true anchor against chaos and meaninglessness—he felt the need to reject these decorative artificialities.

See Peter Cannon, "The Influence of *Vathek* on H. P. Lovecraft's *The Dream-Quest of Unknown Kadath*" (in *FDOC*); L. D. Blackmore, "Middle-Earth, Narnia and Lovecraft's Dream World: Comparative World-Views in Fantasy," *Crypt* No. 13 (Roodmas 1983): 6–15, 22; S. T. Joshi, "The Dream World and the Real World in Lovecraft," *Crypt* No. 15 (Lammas 1983): 4–15; S. T. Joshi, "Lovecraft and *The Dream-Quest of Unknown Kadath*," *Crypt* No. 37 (Candlemas 1986): 25–34, 59; Giuseppe Lippi, "Lovecraft's Dream-World Revisited," *LS* No. 26 (Spring 1992): 23–25.

"Dreams in the Witch House, The." Short story (14,940 words); written in February 1932. First published in *WT* (July 1933); first collected in *O;* corrected text in *MM;* annotated version in *DWH.*

A mathematics student at Miskatonic University named Walter Gilman who lives in a peculiarly angled room in the old Witch House in Arkham begins having bizarre dreams filled with sights, sounds, and shapes of an utterly indescribable cast; other dreams, much more realistic in nature, reveal a huge rat with human hands named Brown Jenkin, apparently the familiar of the witch Keziah Mason, who once dwelt in the Witch House. Meanwhile Gilman, in his classwork, begins to display a remarkable intuitive grasp of hyperspace, or the fourth dimension. But then his dreams take an even weirder turn, and there are indications that he is sleepwalking. Keziah seems to be urging him on in some nameless errand ("He must meet the Black Man, and go with them all to the throne of Azathoth at the centre of ultimate Chaos"). Then in one very clear dream he sees himself "half lying on a high, fantastically balustraded terrace above a boundless jungle of outlandish, incredible peaks, balanced planes, domes, minarets, horizontal discs poisoned on pinnacles, and numberless forms of still greater wildness." The balustrade is decorated with designs representing ridged, barrel-shaped entities (i.e., the Old Ones from *At the Mountains of Madness*); but Gilman wakes screaming when he sees the living barrel-shaped entities coming toward him. The next morning the barrel-shaped ornament—which he had broken off the balustrade *in the dream*—is found in his bed.

Things seem rapidly to be reaching some hideous culmination. A baby is kidnapped and cannot be found. Then, in a dream, Gilman finds himself in a strangely angled room with Keziah, Brown Jenkin, and the baby. Keziah is going to sacrifice the child, but Gilman knocks the knife from her hand. He and Keziah engage in a fight, and he manages to frighten her momentarily by displaying a crucifix given to him by a fellow tenant; when Brown Jenkin comes to her aid, he kicks the familiar down an abyss, but not before it has made some sort of sacrificial offering with the baby's blood. The next night Gilman's friend Frank Elwood sees a ratlike creature eat its way through Gilman's body to his heart. The Witch House is rented no more, and years later, when it is razed, an enormous pile of human bones going back centuries is discovered, along with the bones of a huge ratlike entity.

The working title for the story was "The Dreams of Walter Gilman." HPL states that it was typed by a revision client as payment for revisory work (HPL to August Derleth, May 14, [1932]; ms., SHSW). This may be Hazel Heald, who claimed to have typed the story. The existing manuscript (at JHL) may, however, be one that August Derleth "copied" (i.e., retyped) about a year later, as HPL suggests (*SL* 4.146). This typescript is remarkably accurate, and the typist seems to have had a fair ability to read HPL's handwriting. HPL was so uncertain about the merits of his work that he elicited his colleagues' opinions on the story before he submitted it anywhere, and so he circulated both the original and the carbon among his correspondents. Several seemed to like the story, but August Derleth's reaction was very much the contrary, as HPL's response suggests: ". . . your reaction to my poor 'Dreams in the Witch House' is, in kind, about what I expected—although I hardly thought the miserable mess was *quite* as bad as you found it. . . . The whole incident shews me that my fictional days are probably over" (HPL to August Derleth, June 6, 1932; ms., SHSW). Elsewhere he elaborates on Derleth's verdict: ". . . Derleth didn't say it was *unsalable;* in fact, he rather thought it *would* sell. He said it was a *poor story,* which is an entirely different and much more lamentably important thing" (*SL* 4.91). In other words, in Derleth's opinion the story was just like most of the work appearing in *WT,* on which HPL regularly heaped abuse. Accordingly, HPL refused to submit the tale anywhere and merely let it gather dust. A year or so later Derleth asked to see the story again and surreptitiously submitted it to Farnsworth Wright, who accepted it readily and paid HPL $140 for it.

While the tale contains vividly cosmic vistas of hyperspace, HPL does not appear to have thought out the details of the plot satisfactorily. What is the significance of the Old Ones in the story? To what purpose is the baby kidnapped and sacrificed? How can HPL the atheist allow Keziah to be frightened by the sight of a crucifix? Why does Nyarlathotep appear in the conventional figure of the Black Man? What is the purpose of the abyss aside from providing a convenient place down which to hurl Brown Jenkin? How does Brown Jenkin subsequently emerge from the abyss to devour Gilman's heart? It seems as if HPL were aiming merely for a succession of startling images without bothering to fuse them into a logical sequence.

The story is HPL's ultimate modernization of a conventional myth (witchcraft) by means of modern science. Fritz Leiber notes that it is "Lovecraft's most carefully worked out story of hyperspace-travel. Here (1) a rational foundation for such travel is set up; (2) hyperspace is visualized; and (3) a trigger for such travel is devised." Leiber elaborates on these points, noting that the absence of any mechanical device for such travel is vital to the tale, for otherwise it would be impossible to imagine how a "witch" of the seventeenth century could have managed the feat; in effect, Keziah simply applied advanced mathematics and "thought" herself into hyperspace.

See Fritz Leiber, "Through Hyperspace with Brown Jenkin" (in *DB;* rpt. *FDOC*); Ronald Shearer, "The Witches in 'The Witch House,'" *Crypt* No. 5 (Roodmas 1982): 26–27; Will Murray, "Was There a Real Brown Jenkin?" *Crypt* No. 7 (Lammas 1982): 24–26.

Drogman, Abdul Reis el. In "Under the Pyramids," a guide who leads Harry Houdini to the top of the Great Pyramid to witness a boxing match between two other Arabs—an incident that proves to be a trap whereby el Drogman binds Houdini and thrusts him down an immense hole in the Great Pyramid. Later, Houdini wonders at the anomalous resemblance of el Drogman to the ancient pharaoh, King Khephren.

Dudley, Jervas. In "The Tomb," the "dreamer and visionary" who develops a monomaniacal obsession with the Hyde family vault on his own family's estate.

Dunn, John T[homas] (1889–1983). Irish-American living in North Providence who came in touch with HPL in late 1914 in the Providence Amateur Press Club and corresponded with him for the period 1915–17. (HPL's letters to him, edited by S. T. Joshi and David E. Schultz, were published in *Books at Brown* 28–29 [1991–92]: 157–223.) He assisted HPL in editing two issues of the *Providence Amateur* (June 1915, February 1916); for the first issue HPL wrote a poem, "To the United Amateur Press Association from the Providence Amateur Press Club," discussing Dunn and other members. HPL also wrote "Lines on Graduation from the R.I. Hospital's School of Nurses" for Dunn to recite; it was published under Dunn's name (*Tryout,* February 1917). Dunn and HPL argued over the Irish question and World War I; Dunn refused to register for the draft and was sentenced to a long prison term, but was released shortly after the war and became a Catholic priest. He was interviewed late in life by L. Sprague de Camp (see "Young Man Lovecraft," *Xenophile,* October 1975; rpt. *LR*).

Dunsany, Lord (Edward John Moreton Drax Plunkett, 18th Baron Dunsany) (1878–1957). Irish author of fantasy tales. Author of many stories of imaginary-world fantasy, including *The Gods of Pegāna* (1905), *Time and the Gods* (1906), *The Sword of Welleran* (1908), *A Dreamer's Tales* (1910), *The Book of Wonder* (1912), *Fifty-one Tales* (1915), *The Last Book of Wonder* (1916), and *Tales of Three Hemispheres* (1919); also plays, including *Five Plays* (1914) and *Plays of Gods and Men* (1917). HPL first read *A Dreamer's Tales* in late 1919 from a recommendation by amateur journalist Alice Hamlet; he attended a lecture given by Dunsany in Boston on October 20, 1919 (see *SL* 1.91–93). Many of HPL's early tales—"The Doom That Came to Sarnath" (1919), "The White Ship" (1919), "The Cats of Ulthar" (1920), "Celephaïs" (1920), "The Quest of Iranon" (1921), "The Tree" (1921), "The Other Gods" (1921)—are clear imitations of Dunsany. Later stories such as "The Silver Key" (1926) and "The Strange High House in the Mist" (1926) refine the Dunsanian influence. *The Dream-Quest of Unknown Kadath* (1926–27) appears to be a tribute to Dunsany, but may be a kind of repudiation of him in Randolph Carter's abandonment of otherworldly fantasy for memories of his youth. See entries on these stories for discussions of works by Dunsany that may have influenced them.

In "Some Notes on a Nonentity" (1933) HPL states that he "got the idea of the artificial pantheon and myth-background represented by 'Cthulhu', 'Yog-Sothoth', 'Yuggoth', etc." from Dunsany, who in *The Gods of Pegāna* and *Time and the Gods* (and in those volumes alone) wrote a linked series of tales involving an invented pantheon in the imaginary realm of Pegāna. HPL wrote a lecture read before an amateur journalists' group, "Lord Dunsany and His Work" (1922); Dunsany is also discussed in "Supernatural Horror in Literature" (1927). HPL did not seem to care for Dunsany's later work, even though much of it—beginning with *The Curse of the Wise Woman* (1933)—parallels HPL's in its use of topographical realism.

Late in life Dunsany came across HPL's stories and noted that "in the few tales of his I have read I found that he was writing in my style, entirely originally & without in any way borrowing from me, & yet with my style & largely my material" (letter to August Derleth, March 28, 1952; quoted in *LS* No. 14 [Spring 1987]: 38).

See T. E. D. Klein, "Some Notes on the Fantasy Tales of H. P. Lovecraft and Lord Dunsany," Honors thesis: Brown University, 1969; Mark Amory, *Biography of Lord Dunsany* (Collins, 1972); Darrell Schweitzer, "Lovecraft and Lord Dunsany," in *Essays Lovecraftian,* ed. Darrell Schweitzer (1976; rev. ed. as *Discovering H. P. Lovecraft* [Starmont House, 1987]); Robert M. Price, "Dunsanian Influence on Lovecraft Outside His 'Dunsanian' Tales," *Crypt* No. 76 (Hallowmas 1990): 3–5; S. T. Joshi and Darrell Schweitzer, *Lord Dunsany: A Bibliography* (Scarecrow Press, 1993); S. T. Joshi, *Lord Dunsany: Master of the Anglo-Irish Imagination* (Greenwood Press, 1995).

Dunwich. Fictitious city in Massachusetts invented by HPL.

Dunwich was created for "The Dunwich Horror" (1928) and is cited only in that tale and in the poem "The Ancient Track" (1929). It was based roughly upon the area in south-central Massachusetts around the towns of Wilbraham, Monson, and Hampden (see *SL* 3.432–33), which HPL had seen in the two weeks he had spent with Edith Miniter in Wilbraham just prior to writing the story in the summer of 1928. Some parts of the locale were, however, imported from north-central Massachusetts, specifically the area around Athol (Sentinel Hill in the story seems derived, at least in name, from a Sentinel Elm Farm in Athol), including the Bear's Den, a wooded ravine that HPL's friend H. Warner Munn showed him.

HPL presumably derived the name Dunwich from the decaying town on the southeast coast of England. The town is the basis of a poem by Algernon Charles Swinburne, "By the North Sea" (although Dunwich is not mentioned in the poem); Dunwich is also mentioned in Arthur Machen's short novel *The Terror* (1917), which HPL is known to have read (see *SL* 1.304, 310). Oddly enough, the English Dunwich seems more similar in character to HPL's Innsmouth. For the English town see Rowland Parker, *Men of Dunwich* (1978).

"Dunwich Horror, The." Novelette (17,590 words); written in August 1928. First published in *WT* (April 1929); first collected in *O;* corrected text in *DH;* annotated version in *An1* and *TD.*

In the seedy area of Dunwich in "north central Massachusetts" live a number of backwoods farmers. One family, the Whateleys, has been the source of particular suspicion ever since the birth, on Candlemas 1913, of Wilbur Whateley, the offspring of an albino woman and an unknown father. Lavinia's father, Old Whateley, shortly after the birth makes an ominous prediction: *"some day yew folks'll hear a child o' Lavinny's a-callin' its father's name on the top o' Sentinel Hill!"* Wilbur grows anomalously fast, and by age thirteen is nearly seven feet tall. He is intellectually precocious, having been educated by the books in Old Whateley's shabby library. In 1924 Old Whateley dies, but manages to instruct his grandson to consult "page 751 *of the complete edition*" of some book so that he can "open up the gates to Yog-Sothoth." Two years later Lavinia disappears and is never seen again. In the winter of 1927 Wilbur makes his first trip out of Dunwich, to consult the Latin edition of the *Necronomicon* at the Miskatonic University Library; but when he asks to borrow the volume, he is denied by the old librarian Henry Armitage. He tries to do the same at Harvard but is similarly rebuffed. Then, in the late spring of 1928, Wilbur breaks into the Miskatonic library to steal the book, but is killed by the vicious guard-dog. His death is very repulsive: ". . . it is permissible to say that, aside from the external appearance of face and hands, the really human element in Wilbur Whateley must have been very small. When the medical examiner came, there was only a sticky whitish mass on the painted boards, and the monstrous odour had nearly disappeared. Apparently Whateley had no skull or bony skeleton; at least, in any true or stable sense. He had taken somewhat after his unknown father."

Meanwhile bizarre things are happening elsewhere. The monstrous entity the Whateleys had evidently been raising bursts forth, having no one to feed or tend to it. It creates havoc throughout the town, crushing houses as if they were matchsticks. Worst of all, it is completely invisible, leaving only huge footprints to indicate its presence. It descends into a ravine called the Bear's Den, then later emerges and causes hideous devastation. Armitage has in the meantime been decoding the diary in cipher that Wilbur had kept and finally learns the true state of affairs: "His [Armitage's] wilder wanderings were very startling indeed, including . . . fantastic references to some plan for the extirpation of the entire human race and all animal and vegetable life from the earth by some terrible elder race of beings from another dimension." Armitage knows how to stop it, and he and two colleagues ascend a small hill facing Sentinel Hill, where the monster appears to be heading. They are armed with an incantation to send the creature back to the dimension it came from, as well as a sprayer containing a powder that will make it visible for an instant. The incantation and powder both work as planned, and the entity is seen to be a huge, ropy, tentacled monstrosity that shouts, "HELP! HELP! . . . *ff—ff—ff*—FATHER! FATHER! YOG-SOTHOTH!" and is completely obliterated. It was Wilbur Whateley's twin brother.

There are several significant literary influences on the tale. The central premise—the sexual union of a "god" or monster (in this case Yog-Sothoth, the entity first cited rather nebulously in *The Case of Charles Dexter Ward*) with a human woman—is taken from Arthur Machen's "The Great God Pan"; HPL makes no secret of it, having Armitage say of the Dunwich people at one point, "Great God, what simpletons! Shew them Arthur Machen's Great God Pan and they'll think it a common Dunwich scandal!" The use of bizarre footsteps to indicate the presence of an otherwise undetectable entity is borrowed from Algernon Blackwood's "The Wendigo." HPL knew well the celebrated tales featuring invisible monsters—Maupassant's "The Horla" (certain features of which he had adapted for "The Call of Cthulhu"); Fitz-James O'Brien's "What Was It?"; Bierce's "The Damned Thing"—and derived hints from each of them in his own creation. A less well-known tale, Anthony M. Rud's "Ooze" (*WT*, March 1923; rpt. *The Moon Terror and Stories* by A. G. Birch et al. [1927]), also deals with an invisible monster that eventually bursts forth from the house in which it is trapped. A still more obscure work, Harper Williams's *The Thing in the Woods* (1924)—read by HPL in the fall of 1924—involves a pair of twins, one of whom (a werewolf) is locked in a shed. In addition, the story may derive from an entry (#162) in HPL's commonplace book: "Ultimate horror—grandfather returns from strange trip—mystery in house—wind & darkness—grandf. & mother engulfed—questions   forbidden—somnolence—investigation—cataclysm—screams overheard—." It was shortly after writing "The Curse of Yig" for Zealia Bishop that HPL wrote "The Dunwich Horror," a somewhat more satisfying story of his own devising about a "god" mating with humans.

HPL acknowledged (see *SL* 3.432–33) that Dunwich was in the Wilbraham area, and it is clear that the topography and some of the folklore (whippoorwills as psychopomps of the dead) were derived from eight days (June 29–July 7, 1928) spent with Edith Miniter in Wilbraham. But, if Wilbraham is roughly the setting for Dunwich, why does HPL declare in the story that the town is located in *north* central Massachusetts? Some parts of the locale are taken from that region, specifically the Bear's Den, an actual locale near Athol to which HPL was taken by his friend H. Warner Munn on June 28. HPL describes the site vividly in a letter to his aunt: "There is a deep forest gorge there; approached dramatically from a rising path ending in a cleft boulder, & containing a magnificent terraced waterfall over the sheer bed-rock. Above the tumbling stream rise high rock precipices crusted with strange lichens & honeycombed with alluring caves. Of the latter several extend far into the hillside, though too narrowly to admit a human being beyond a few yards" (HPL to Lillian D. Clark, July 1, 1928; ms., JHL). The name Sentinel Hill is taken from a Sentinel Elm Farm in Athol.

Although very popular with readers, the story has been criticized for being an obvious good-vs.-evil tale with Armitage representing the forces of good and the Whateley family representing the forces of evil. Donald R. Burleson suggests that the tale be read as a satire or parody, pointing out that it is the Whateley twins (regarded as a single entity) who, in mythic terms, fulfill the traditional role of the "hero" much more than Armitage does (e.g., the mythic hero's descent to the underworld is paralleled by the twin's descent into the Bear's Den), and pointing out also that the passage from the *Necronomicon* cited in the tale— "Man rules now where They [the Old Ones] ruled once; They shall soon rule where man rules now"—makes Armitage's "defeat" of the Whateleys merely a temporary staving off of the inevitable. These points are well taken, but HPL offers no evidence that the tale was meant parodically (i.e., as a satire on immature readers of the pulp magazines) or that the figure of Armitage is meant anything but seriously. He suggests the reverse when he writes: "[I] found myself psychologically identifying with one of the characters (an aged scholar who finally combats the menace) toward the end" (HPL to August Derleth, [September 1928]; ms., SHSW). Armitage is clearly modeled upon Marinus Bicknell Willett of *The Case of Charles Dexter Ward:* he defeats the "villains" by incantations, and he is susceptible to the same flaws—pomposity, arrogance, self-importance—that can be seen in Willett.

The popularity of the tale can be seen both in its wide reprinting in anthologies (most notably in Herbert A. Wise and Phyllis Fraser's *Great Tales of Terror and the Supernatural* [Random House/Modern Library, 1944]) and in a film adaptation of 1970.

See Donald R. Burleson, "Humour Beneath Horror: Some Sources for 'The Dunwich Horror' and 'The Whisperer in Darkness,'" *LS* No. 2 (Spring 1980): 5–15; Robert M. Price, "The Pine Barrens Horror," *Crypt* No. 7 (Lammas 1982): 27–30; Donald R. Burleson, "The Mythic Hero Archetype in 'The Dunwich Horror,'" *LS* No. 4 (Spring 1981): 3–9; Will Murray, "The Dunwich Chimera and Others," *LS* No. 8 (Spring 1984): 10–24; Peter H. Cannon, "Call Me Wizard Whateley: Echoes of *Moby Dick* in 'The Dunwich Horror,'" *Crypt* No. 49 (Lammas 1987): 21–23; Donald R. Burleson, "Lovecraft and the World as Cryptogram," *LS* No. 16 (Spring 1988): 14–18; Robert M. Price, "Not in the Spaces We Know but Between Them: 'The Dunwich Horror' as an Allegory of Reading," *Crypt* No. 83 (Eastertide 1993): 22–24; Donald R. Burleson, "A Note on Metaphor vs. Metonymy in 'The Dunwich Horror,'" *LS* No. 38 (Spring 1998): 16–17.

Dwight, Frederick N. In "In the Walls of Eryx," an employee of the Venus Crystal Company whose decaying corpse the narrator, Kenton J. Stanfield, finds in the invisible maze in which he himself becomes entrapped.

Dwight, Walter C. In *The Case of Charles Dexter Ward,* a professional painter in Providence who restores the painting of Joseph Curwen found by Charles Dexter Ward in the house on Olney Court.

Dwyer, Bernard Austin (1897–1943). Correspondent of HPL, residing in West Shokan and Kingston, N.Y. Dwyer reached HPL through *WT* in early 1927 and continued to correspond with him to the end of HPL's life. He published one poem in *WT* ("Ol' Black Sarah," October 1928), but otherwise wrote little; he also devoted himself to pictorial art. HPL visited him in Kingston in May 1929 in the course of examining the colonial antiquities in nearby Hurley and New Paltz; again for a few days in June 1930, at which time Dwyer evidently made several substantial suggestions for the revision of HPL's work in progress, "The Whisperer in Darkness." Dwyer was one of the leading protagonists ("Knockout Bernie, the Wild Wolf of West Shokan") of the spoof, "The Battle That Ended the Century" (1934). After HPL's death, Dwyer excerpted a letter to him from HPL, written probably in the fall of 1933, and sent it to *WT,* where it was published as "The Wicked Clergyman" (later "The Evil Clergyman").

Dyer, William. In *At the Mountains of Madness,* the professor of geology at Miskatonic University who leads the Miskatonic Antarctic Expedition of 1930–31 and who narrates the novel. Dyer also leads the subexpedition in search of Lake's party, only to find it wiped out. With the graduate student Danforth, he explores and reports at length on the ancient city and civilization of the Old Ones. Dyer's last name only is supplied in *At the Mountains of Madness;* his first name is given in "The Shadow out of Time," in which is accompanies Nathaniel Wingate Peaslee on his expedition to Australia.

E

"East and West Harvard Conservatism." Essay (1,110 words); probably written in the summer of 1922. First published in *Mind Power Plus* (date unknown; probably 1922); rpt. *CE5*.

The article is on David Van Bush's New England lecture campaign and the success of his popular psychology in staid Massachusetts. Probably commissioned by Bush, the article appeared in his magazine, *Mind Power Plus,* which HPL mentions as "newly-founded" in June 1922 (see *SL* 1.186). No copies of the magazine have been located; only a tearsheet of the article from the magazine (where it occupies pp. 55–56) is extant at JHL.

"East India Brick Row, The." Poem (48 lines in quatrains); written early to mid-December 1929. First published in the *Providence Journal* (January 8, 1930).

The poem was written in a futile attempt to prevent the destruction of early nineteenth-century warehouses on South Water Street in Providence, which HPL admired for their humble beauty but which had become so decrepit that it would have been difficult to restore them. HPL notes (letter to August Derleth, [January 1930]; ms., SHSW) that the poem received such a favorable response from readers in the newspaper that he received a cordial letter from the editor about it.

See Joseph Payne Brennan, "Lovecraft's 'Brick Row,'" *Macabre* No. 5 (Summer 1959): 21–22.

Eddy, Clifford M[artin], Jr. (1896–1971). Author and correspondent of HPL. A native of Providence, R I., Eddy was a precocious reader and writer, interested in mythology and the occult. His first published tale, "Sign of the Dragon" (*Mystery Magazine,* 1919), was a detective story. Various tales of mystery, ghosts, and song-writing (he himself later wrote songs, including "When We Met by the Blue Lagoon" and "In My Wonderful Temple of Love") continued to appear through 1922 in various magazines. He came in touch with HPL in 1923 (see letter to Frank Belknap Long, October 7, 1923 [*SL* 1.254], where HPL refers to Eddy as "the new Providence amateur"). (His wife Muriel in *The Gentleman from Angell Street* [1961] claims that they had met HPL and his mother as early as 1918, but this seems to be a fabrication.) HPL frequently visited the Eddys' home in East Providence. Eddy and HPL took scenic walks, one to the Old Stone Mill in Newport, R.I. (August Derleth later incorporated notes taken by HPL on this occasion into *The Lurker at the Threshold* [1945]), another to Dark Swamp (see *SL* 1.264–67). Though they never found the swamp, the legendry surrounding the place seems to have influenced the opening of "The Colour out of Space" (1927); in 1967 Eddy began an unfinished fictionalized account of the trip entitled "Black Noon" (published in *Exit into Eternity*). HPL revised four stories for Eddy: "Ashes" (*WT,* March 1924), "The Ghost-Eater" (*WT,* April 1924), "The Loved Dead" (*WT,* May–June–July 1924), and "Deaf, Dumb, and Blind" (*WT,* April 1925). The two collaborated on *The Cancer of Superstition,* ghostwritten for Harry Houdini, but the escape artist's death in October 1926 curtailed the project. (Notes and surviving fragments were published in *DB.*) See Eddy's collections *Exit to Eternity* (Oxford Press, 1973), *Erased from Exile* (Stygian Isle Press, 1976), and *The Terror out of Time* (Dyer-Eddy, 1976). He wrote a brief memoir, "Walks with H. P. Lovecraft" (in *DB*).

See George Popkins, "He Wrote of the Supernatural," *Providence Evening Bulletin* (November 25, 1963): 37.

Eddy, Muriel E[lizabeth] (Gammons) (1896–1978). Wife of C. M. Eddy and friend of HPL. In *A Gentleman from Angell Street* (1961; rpt. *LR*), Mrs. Eddy maintains that her husband's mother (Mrs. Grace Eddy) had come to know HPL's mother at a woman suffrage meeting in 1918 and that at this time the two discovered that their sons were both enthusiasts of the weird. HPL purportedly invited the Eddys to join the UAPA, and Mrs. Eddy also claims that she and her husband contributed to C. W. Smith's amateur magazine, *The Tryout.* Then there was a hiatus in relations, but HPL got back in touch shortly after the death of his mother in May 1921. This entire account is, however, missing from Mrs. Eddy's first memoir, "Howard Phillips Lovecraft" (in *Rhode Island on Lovecraft,* ed. Donald M. Grant and Thomas P. Hadley [1945]), and it appears to be a late fabrication intended to magnify the Eddys' role in HPL's life. The Eddys do not appear on any membership lists of the UAPA; none of their work appeared in the *Tryout;* and there is no evidence that Mrs. Lovecraft was interested in woman suffrage. It appears that HPL came to know the Eddys only in the fall of 1923. Mrs. Eddy wrote numerous memoirs of HPL, all saying much the same things as her 1945 account; among them are "Memories of H.P.L." (*Magazine of Horror,* Winter 1965–66), "Howard Phillips Lovecraft's Marriage and Divorce" (*Haunted,* June 1968), *Howard Phillips Lovecraft: The Man and the Image* (1969), "H. P. Lovecraft among the Demons" (*The Rhode Islander* [*Providence Sunday Journal* Magazine], March 8, 1970), *H. P. Lovecraft Esquire: Gentleman* (n.d.), and *The Howard Phillips Lovecraft We Knew* (n.d.). She had two daughters, Ruth Eddy and Faye (Eddy) Dyer; the former wrote a brief memoir of HPL, "The Man Who Came at Midnight" (*Fantasy Commentator,* Summer–Fall 1949).

"Editorial." Published in the *Conservative* (April 1915, July 1915, October 1915); rpt. *The Conservative: Complete* (1976; rev. ed. 1977) and *CE1*.

These items contain general remarks on the nature and purpose of his amateur journal; later articles contain rebuttals of criticisms he has received in other amateur papers.

"Editorial." Published in the *United Amateur* (July 1917 [as "Editorially"], November 1920, September 1921, January 1922, May 1924, July 1925); rpt. *CE1*.

HPL wrote these editorials in his capacity as Official Editor of the UAPA and Editor of the *United Amateur* (HPL was guest editor of the July 1917 issue, taking over for Official Editor Andrew F. Lockhart, who had resigned). They cover events of importance in the amateur community. The articles of 1920–22 attempt to deflect criticism from some members that HPL was concentrating too much authority upon himself and his close associates; but HPL and his party lost the election of July 1922 over this very issue. HPL's party (now including Sonia H. Greene as president) was voted back into office in July 1923, but the outgoing official board withheld funds so that no *United Amateur* could be issued until May 1924. HPL's last two editorials are, accordingly, both bitter and melancholy in their lament for the decline of the UAPA, which collapsed in 1926.

Edkins, Ernest A[rthur] (1867–1946). Amateur writer and correspondent of HPL (1932–37). Edkins was one of the leading writers of the "halcyon days" (c. 1885–1895) of amateur journalism. In his account of this period, "Looking Backward" (1920), written long before he knew Edkins, HPL speaks of Edkins's poem "The Suicide" as "a supremely artistic bit of weird genius . . . a bit of night-black poetical fancy so arresting in its sombre power that we cannot refrain from reproducing it here in full. . . ." Edkins later left amateurdom and repudiated much of his literary work, becoming instead a businessman in Highland Park, Ill. (later Coral Gables, Fla.). HPL, getting in touch with him in 1932, eventually lured him back into amateur activity. Edkins produced several issues of the amateur journal *Causerie* in 1936; that for February 1936 contained the first appearance of "Continuity" (from *Fungi from Yuggoth*). In this same issue Edkins also wrote a brief review of *The Cats of Ulthar* (1935). HPL preserved all Edkins's letters to him, but in his eloquent memoir "Idiosyncrasies of HPL" (*Olympian,* Autumn 1940; in *LR*) Edkins notes that he lost most or all of HPL's letters to him.

See Rheinhart Kleiner, *Ernest A. Edkins: A Memoir* (Newtonville, Mass.: Oakwood Press, 1947).

"Eidolon, The." Poem (98 lines); probably written in the fall of 1918. First published in *Tryout* (October 1918).

Using the trimeter line favored by Poe, HPL tells of an eidolon (image) called "Life" that proves to be "laden" with "foul horrors."

"Electric Executioner, The." Short story (8,050 words); ghostwritten for Adolphe de Castro, in July 1929. First published in *WT* (August 1930); first collected in *Cats*; corrected text in *HM*.

The unnamed narrator is asked by the president of his company to track down a man named Feldon who has disappeared with some papers in Mexico. Boarding a train, the man later finds he is alone in a car with one other occupant, who seems to be a dangerous maniac. This person apparently has devised a hoodlike instrument for performing executions and wishes the narrator to be the first experimental victim. Realizing he cannot overwhelm the man by force, the narrator seeks to delay the experiment until the train reaches the next station, Mexico City. He first asks to be allowed to write a letter disposing of his effects; then he asserts that he has newspaper friends in Sacramento who would be interested in publicizing the invention; and finally he says that he would like to make a sketch of the thing in operation—why doesn't the man put it on his own head so that it can be drawn? The madman does so; but then the narrator, having earlier perceived that the lunatic has a taste for Aztec mythology, pretends to be possessed by religious fervor and begins shouting Aztec and other names at random as a further stalling tactic. The madman begins shouting also, and in the process his device pulls taut over his neck and executes him; the narrator faints. When revived, the narrator finds the madman no longer in the car, although a crowd of people is there; he is informed no one was ever in the car. Later Feldon is discovered dead in a remote cave—with certain objects unquestionably belonging to the narrator in his pockets.

The story is a radically revised version of a tale called "The Automatic Executioner," published in de Castro's collection, *In the Confessional and the Following* (1893). Part of the characterization of the madman is drawn from a somewhat more harmless person HPL met on the train ride from New York to Washington on a recent journey—a German who kept repeating "Efferythingk iss luffly!" "I vass shoost leddingk my light shine!" and other random utterances (see "Travels in the Provinces of America" [1929]). The madman in "The Electric Executioner" does in fact say at one point, "I shall let my light shine, as it were." Later, in the course of uttering the names of various Aztec gods, the narrator cries out: "Ya-R'lyeh! Ya-R'lyeh! . . . Cthulhutl fhtaghn! Niguratl-Yig! Yog-Sototl—." The spelling variants are intentional, as HPL wished to give an Aztec cast to the names so as to suggest they were part of that culture's theology. Otherwise, HPL has followed de Castro's plot even more faithfully than in "The Last Test"—retaining character names, the basic sequence of incidents, and even the final supernatural twist (although sensibly suggesting that it was Feldon's astral body, not the narrator's, that was in the car). HPL was paid only $16 for his work, but de Castro sold the story for $175.

Eliot, ——. The auditor to whom the events of "Pickman's Model" are addressed.

Eliot, Matt. In "The Shadow over Innsmouth," the first mate on one of Capt. Obed Marsh's ships. While in the South Seas, he hears reports of an island where the inhabitants can procure all the fish they want and also seem to have unlimited quantities of gold. He later realizes that this bounty is the result of the natives' mating with loathsome sea-creatures, and he urges Obed to have nothing to do with the place. He later disappears from Innsmouth.

Elton, Basil. In "The White Ship," the keeper of the North Point lighthouse, who tells of his adventures aboard the White Ship.

Elwood, Frank. In "The Dreams in the Witch House," a student at Miskatonic University and friend of Walter Gilman who attempts to help control Gilman's sleepwalking and determine the source of Gilman's strange dreams. He witnesses Gilman's horrible death at the hands of Brown Jenkin.

Eshbach, Lloyd Arthur (1910–2003). Science fiction writer and publisher from Reading, Pa., and correspondent of HPL (1935–37?). Since 1931 Eshbach had published several stories in the science fiction pulps, but in early 1935 he was beginning a general magazine called *The Galleon* and asked HPL to contribute. HPL sent a story and two sonnets from *Fungi from Yuggoth,* but only "Background" (May–June 1935) and "The Quest of Iranon" (July–August 1935) were published before the magazine changed focus and became a regional Pennsylvania magazine; accordingly, Eshbach returned "Harbour Whistles," which he had also accepted. After World War II Eshbach successively founded two small presses in the fantasy field, Fantasy Press and Polaris Press. He also published a collection of his science fiction stories (*The Tyrant of Time,* 1955) and an anthology of essays on science fiction writing (*Of Worlds Beyond,* 1964).

"Evil Clergyman, The." Letter excerpt (1,720 words); probably written in the fall of 1933. First published (as "The Wicked Clergyman") in *WT* (April 1939); first collected in *BWS*; corrected text in *D.*

The unnamed narrator explains how he is ushered into an attic chamber by a "grave, intelligent-looking man" who tells about someone referred to only as *"he,"* who used to live in the place. The man sternly adjures the narrator not to stay after dark nor to touch the object on the table, which looks like a matchbox. Then the man leaves the narrator alone. Examining his surroundings, the narrator finds it filled with old books of magic and alchemy. At length, he props the matchbox-like object against a book and shines his flashlight—which emits a peculiar violet light—upon it. The narrator senses another person in the room—a man attired in the "clerical garb of the Anglican church" who appears subtly evil-looking. This person begins throwing the books into the fireplace. Then others in clerical outfits appear; they seem to be passing some judgment upon the evil-looking clergyman. After they depart, the clergyman takes up a coil of rope, mounts a chair, and with a strange look of *triumph* hangs himself. The narrator then lurches backward down the stairwell. Shortly thereafter a group of people come into the room, including the man who had first led the narrator into the place. He at once realizes that the narrator has fiddled with the box, for the narrator, in outward appearance, now bears the countenance of the clergyman.

The "story" is an account of a dream described in a letter to Bernard Austin Dwyer. HPL remarks in a letter to Clark Ashton Smith (October 22, 1933) that "Some months ago I had a dream of an evil clergyman in a garret full of forbidden books" (*SL* 4.289–90), and it is likely that the dream was recounted to Dwyer at this time or slightly earlier. Some of the imagery and atmosphere are reminiscent of "The Festival," although the dream takes place in England.

Unlike "The Thing on the Doorstep" and other tales, this dream-fragment does not involve *mind*-transference but transference of a very physical sort: because the protagonist unwisely handled the small box that he had specifically been told not to touch, he summoned the "evil clergyman" and somehow effected an exchange of external features with him, while yet retaining his mind and personality. It is difficult to say how HPL would have developed this conventional supernatural scenario.

"Ex Oblivione." Prose poem (715 words); probably written in late 1920 or early 1921. First published (as by "Ward Phillips") in the *United Amateur* (March 1921); rpt. *Phantagraph* (July 1937); first collected in *BWS;* corrected text in *MW.*

A depressed and embittered narrator seeks various exotic worlds in dream as an antidote to the grinding prosiness of daily life; later, when "the days of waking became less and less bearable from their greyness and sameness," he begins to take drugs to augment his nightly visions. In the "dream-city of Zakarion" he comes upon a papyrus containing the thoughts of the dream-sages who once dwelt there, he reads of a "high wall pierced by a little bronze gate," which may or may not be the entrance to untold wonders. Realizing that "no new horror can be more terrible than the daily torture of the commonplace," the narrator takes more and more drugs in an effort to find this gate. Finally he seems to come upon it—the door is ajar. As he enters, he finds to his ecstasy that the realm he is entering is nothing other than "native infinity of crystal oblivion from which the daemon Life had called me for one brief and desolate hour."

The story reiterates the topos ("Life is more horrible than death") that was the apparent theme of the lost story "Life and Death"; the notion is probably derived from HPL's reading of Schopenhauer at this time. Compare, for example, *In Defence of Dagon:* "There is nothing better than oblivion, since in oblivion there is no wish unfulfilled" (*MW* 166).

See Paul Montelone, "'Ex Oblivione': The Contemplative Lovecraft," *LS* No. 33 (Fall 1995): 2–14

F

"Facts Concerning the Late Arthur Jermyn and His Family." Short story (3,720 words); probably written in the fall of 1920. First published in the *Wolverine* (March and June 1921); rpt. *WT* (April 1924) and *WT* (May 1935); first collected in *O;* corrected text in *D;* annotated version in *CC*.

Sir Arthur Jermyn was of a venerable but eccentric family. In the eighteenth century, Sir Wade Jermyn "was one of the earliest explorers of the Congo region," but was placed in a madhouse after speaking wildly of "a prehistoric white Congolese civilisation." He had brought back from the Congo a wife—reportedly the daughter of a Portuguese trader—who was never seen. The offspring of the union were very peculiar in both physiognomy and mentality. In the middle of the nineteenth century, a Sir Robert Jermyn killed nearly his entire family as well as a fellow African explorer who had brought back strange tales (and perhaps other things) from the area of Sir Wade's explorations. Arthur Jermyn seeks to redeem the family name by continuing Sir Wade's researches and perhaps vindicating him. Pursuing reports of a white ape who became a goddess in the prehistoric African civilization, he comes upon the remains of the site in 1912 but finds little confirmation of the story of the white ape. This confirmation is supplied by a Belgian explorer who ships the object to Jermyn House. The hideous rotting thing is found to be wearing a locket containing the Jermyn coat of arms; what remains of its face bears an uncanny resemblance to that of Arthur Jermyn. When he sees this object, Jermyn douses himself in oil and sets himself aflame.

The story is somewhat more complex than it appears on the surface. We are apparently to believe that there is more going on than merely a single case of miscegenation. The narrator's opening comment ("Science, already oppressive with its shocking revelations, will perhaps be the ultimate exterminator of our human species—if separate species we be—for its reserve of unguessed horrors could never be borne by mortal brains if loosed upon the world"), in particular the clause "if separate species we be," is a generalized statement that does not logically follow if we are to assume that it is only the Jermyn line that has been tainted by a white ape in its ancestry; instead, the implication appears to be that the Congolese city discovered by Sir Wade Jermyn is the source for all white civilization. To a racist like HPL, this would have been the acme of horror.

HPL makes a suggestive comment on the literary source for the tale:

[The] origin [of "Arthur Jermyn"] is rather curious—and far removed from the atmosphere it suggests. Somebody had been harassing me into reading some work of the iconoclastic moderns—these young chaps why pry behind exteriors and unveil nasty hidden motives and secret stigmata—and I had nearly fallen asleep over the tame backstairs gossip of Anderson's *Winesburg, Ohio*. The sainted Sherwood, as you know, laid bare the dark area which many whited village lives concealed, and it occurred to me that I, in my weirder medium, could probably devise some secret behind a man's ancestry which would make the worst of Anderson's disclosures sound like the annual report of a Sabbath school. Hence Arthur Jermyn. (HPL to Edwin Baird, [c. October 1923]; *WT,* March 1924)

In its first *WT* appearance the story appeared under the title "The White Ape," much to HPL's disgust. Later appearances use the title "Arthur Jermyn"; HPL's original and full title (used in the *Wolverine* appearance) was not restored until the corrected edition of 1986.

Alfred Galpin, writing under the house name Zoilus, remarked of the tale: "It is perfect in execution, restrained in manner, complete, and marked by Mr. Lovecraft's uniquely effective handling of introductory and concluding portions. The legend is not so powerful as many of Mr. Lovecraft's dreamings have been, but it is unquestionably original and does not derive from Poe, Dunsany, or any other of Mr. Lovecraft's favorites and predecessors" (*Wolverine,* November 1921). Samuel Loveman also discusses the story at length in the column "Official Criticism: Bureau of Critics," *National Amateur* 44, No. 2 (November 1921): 29, 33.

See S. T. Joshi, "What Happens in 'Arthur Jermyn'?" *Crypt* No. 75 (Michaelmas 1990): 27–28; Bennett Lovett-Graff, "'Life Is a Hideous Thing': Primate-Geniture in H. P. Lovecraft's 'Arthur Jermyn,'" *Journal of the Fantastic in the Arts* 8, No. 3 (1997): 370–88.

Fantasy Fan, The. Fan magazine edited by Charles D. Hornig; typeset and printed by Conrad Ruppert (September 1933–February 1935).

The Fantasy Fan was the first fan magazine in the weird fiction field. Charles D. Hornig of Elizabeth, N.J., at the age of seventeen, founded it and managed to keep it going for eighteen monthly issues, even though the circulation was never very large (its print run probably did not exceed 300, and it had only sixty subscribers). Right from the start, however, Hornig sought to secure the most prestigious weird and science fiction authors he could, and HPL not only sent Hornig numerous contributions of his own but encouraged his colleagues—Clark Ashton Smith, Robert E. Howard, even the resolutely professional August Derleth—to submit to the magazine stories and articles that had been rejected elsewhere. *The Fantasy Fan* was, accordingly, an interesting mix of news, articles, stories, poems, and miscellany. Hornig, however, made an error in initiating a column of controversy entitled "The Boiling Point," which quickly led to acrimonious letter exchanges between HPL, Forrest J. Ackerman, Clark Ashton Smith, and numerous others; the column was terminated with the February 1934 issue.

Perhaps Hornig's greatest accomplishment was the serialization of the revised version of HPL's "Supernatural Horror in Literature" (October 1933–February 1935). However, the serialization proceeded at such a slow place that it reached only the middle of Chapter VIII before the magazine folded. *The Fantasy Fan* also saw the first publication of HPL's stories, "The Other Gods" (November 1933) and "From Beyond" (June 1934), as well as reprints (from amateur papers) of "Polaris" (February 1934) and "Beyond the Wall of Sleep" (October 1934); it also published "The Book" (October 1934), "Pursuit" (October 1934), "The Key" (January 1935), and "Homecoming" (January 1935) from *Fungi from Yuggoth*. Brief excerpts of HPL's letters to Hornig appeared regularly in the magazine's letter column. The October 1934 issue was dedicated to HPL.

After the demise of *The Fantasy Fan,* numerous attempts were made to revive or succeed it, but no magazine truly filled its place as a news organ, a forum for the expression of fans' views, and a venue for work by distinguished writers in the field.

Farnese, Harold S. (1885–1945). Musical composer and correspondent of HPL (1932–33). In July 1932, Farnese (assistant director of the Institute of Musical Art, Ltd. in Los Angeles) asked HPL's permission to set to music two sonnets from *Fungi from Yuggoth*. HPL granted permission, and by September Farnese had written and performed music for "Mirage" and "The Elder Pharos." HPL never heard or saw the pieces, and it was not until HPL died that Farnese had the sheet music printed and circulated (a page from "The Elder Pharos" is printed in *SL* 4, facing p. 159). Farnese tried to enlist HPL's help in writing a libretto for a planned opera entitled *Yurregarth and Yannimaid* (later *Fen River*), but HPL declined, suggesting Clark Ashton Smith as librettist. After HPL moved in 1933, the two fell out of touch.

Farnese became the unwitting source of the spurious "Black Magic" quotation attributed by August Derleth to HPL, and thus generating a long misunderstanding of the nature of HPL's work. See entry on Cthulhu Mythos for details.

See Kenneth W. Faig, Jr., "A Note Regarding the Harold Farnese Musical Pieces," *Dark Brotherhood Journal* 1, No. 1 (June 1971): 12–14; David E. Schultz, "The Origin of Lovecraft's 'Black Magic' Quote," *Crypt* No. 48 (St. John's Eve 1987): 9–13 (revised version in *The Horror of It All,* ed. Robert M. Price [Starmont House, 1990]).

Farr, Fred. In "The Dunwich Horror," one of the party that exterminates Wilbur Whateley's monstrous twin brother.

Feldon, Arthur. In "The Electric Executioner," the "furtive" assistant superintendent with the Tlaxcala Mining Company, who absconds with important company papers. He is pursued by the narrator of the story and is accidentally killed by the hoodlike execution device he has invented.

Fenham. Fictitious town in Maine invented either by HPL or by C. M. Eddy and cited in "The Loved Dead" (1923) and "Deaf, Dumb, and Blind" (1924).

Fenner, Matthew. In "In the Vault," a man for whom George Birch builds a new coffin, when he recognizes that his first effort was somewhat shoddy for the person intended. Birch uses the rejected casket for someone he did not like very well, with disastrous results.

Fenton, Dr. In "Beyond the Wall of Sleep," a physician at a psychopathic institution in upstate New York and the boss of the narrator, an intern there.

"Festival." Poem (20 lines in 4 stanzas); written around Christmas 1925. First published in *WT* (December 1926) (as "Yule Horror").

A poem to Farnsworth Wright, editor of *WT,* speaking of Wright as an "abbot and priest" at a "devil-wrought feast." Wright, taken with the work, published it but dropped its last stanza, which alluded directly to him.

"Festival, The." Short story (3,700 words); probably written in October 1923. First published in *WT* (January 1925); rpt. *WT* (October 1933); first collected in *O;* corrected text in *D;* annotated version in *CC.*

The first-person narrator finds himself in Kingsport, Mass., on the Yuletide "that men call Christmas though they know in their hearts it is older than Bethlehem and Babylon, older than Memphis and mankind." He follows a course along the old town that can be traversed to this day. He passes by the old cemetery on the hill, where "black gravestones stuck ghoulishly through the snow like the decayed fingernails of a gigantic corpse," and makes his way to a house with an overhanging second story and full of antique furnishings. Eventually he is led from the house by its occupants, including a man whose face seems to be a cunningly made waxen mask. He and the other townspeople make their way to a church in the center of town; entering it, they all descend robotically down a "trap-door of the vaults which yawned loathsomely open just before the pulpit," where the celebrants worship a sickly green flame next to an oily river and then ride off on the backs of hybrid winged creatures. The narrator resists ascending the creature reserved for him, and in doing so he jostles his companion's waxen mask; horrified at some nameless sight, he plunges into the river and eventually finds himself in St. Mary's hospital in Arkham. He asks for a copy of the *Necronomicon* of Abdul Alhazred, and therein reads a passage that appears to confirm the events he has experienced, specifically in relation to entities that "have learned to walk that ought to crawl."

The story is based upon HPL's several trips to Marblehead, Mass., beginning in December 1922. Of his first trip there HPL later wrote that it was "the most powerful single emotional climax experienced during my nearly forty years of existence. In a flash all the past of New England—all the past of Old England—all the past of Anglo-Saxondom and the Western World—swept over me and identified me with the stupendous totality of all things in such a way as it never did before and never will again. That was the high tide of my life" (*SL* 3.126–27). The course of the narrator's journey through the town corresponds to an actual route that leads to the center of Marblehead; the house with the overhanging second story is probably to be identified with an actual house at 1 Mugford Street. The church where the climactic incidents occur has long been thought to be St.

Michael's Episcopal Church in Frog Lane, but this identification appears to be incorrect: St. Michael's has no steeple, and allusions to it in this story and later tales make it clear that it is on a hill and that it is a Congregational church. In all likelihood, HPL was probably referring to one of two now-destroyed Congregational churches in the city. The old cemetery on the hill is clearly Old Burial Hill, where many ancient graves are to be found.

In 1933 HPL stated in reference to the tale: "In intimating an alien race I had in mind the survival of some clan of pre-Aryan sorcerers who preserved primitive rites like those of the witch-cult—I had just been reading Miss Murray's *The Witch-Cult in Western Europe*" (*SL* 4.297). This controversial work of anthropology by Margaret A. Murray, published in 1921, made the claim (regarded by modern scholars as highly unlikely) that the witch-cult in both Europe and America had its origin in a pre-Aryan race that was driven underground but continued to lurk in the hidden corners of the earth. HPL had just read a similar fictional exposition of the idea in Arthur Machen's stories of the "Little People" and was accordingly much taken with this conception; he would allude to it in many subsequent references to the Salem witches in his tales, and as late as 1930 he was presenting the theory seriously (see *SL* 3.182–83). The epigraph, from Lactantius, appears to derive from HPL's ancestral copy of Cotton Mather's *Magnalia Christi Americana*.

See Donovan K. Loucks, "Antique Dreams: Marblehead and Lovecraft's Kingsport." *LS* No. 42 (Summer 2001): 48–55.

Finlay, Virgil [Warden] (1914–1971), American artist; perhaps the most accomplished artist to appear in the pulp magazines. Finlay came in touch with HPL in September 1936 and corresponded with HPL until the latter's death. Finlay actually offered to illustrate HPL's tales for a potential book of his work, even though HPL had no prospects for any such book publication at the time. HPL was prodigiously impressed with Finlay's art, and in late November 1936 he wrote a sonnet ("To Mr. Finlay, upon His Drawing for Mr. Bloch's Tale, 'The Faceless God'"; *Phantagraph,* May 1937), based upon Finlay's illustration of Robert Bloch's "The Faceless God" (*WT,* May 1936). Finlay himself illustrated HPL's "The Haunter of the Dark" (*WT,* December 1936) and "The Thing on the Doorstep" (*WT,* January 1937). Prior to HPL's death Finlay executed his celebrated portrait of HPL as an eighteenth-century gentleman, although there is no evidence that HPL ever saw it; it was scheduled to appear in Willis Conover's *Science-Fantasy Correspondent,* but it appeared in April 1937 as the cover of that magazine's successor, *Amateur Correspondent.* Finlay went on to prepare dust-jacket illustrations for HPL's *O* and *Marginalia.* HPL's letters to him were excerpted in "Letters to Virgil Finlay" (*Fantasy Collector's Annual,* 1974).

See Virgil Finlay, *Virgil Finlay* (Donald M. Grant, 1971), with lengthy contributions by Sam Moskowitz and Gerry de la Ree; Gerry de la Ree, *Virgil Finlay Remembered* (Gerry de la Ree, 1981).

"For What Does the United Stand?" Essay (535 words); probably written in the spring of 1920. First published in the *United Amateur* (May 1920); rpt. *MW* and *CE*1.

Brief article on the importance of the UAPA in fostering education and the literary development of amateur writers.

Foster, Abel. In "Two Black Bottles," the sexton of a church in Daalbergen, N.J., who studies the occult books amassed by the church's first pastor, Guilliam Slott. It is Foster who imprisons the soul of the current pastor, Vanderhoof, in a bottle. As in the case of Vanderhoof, his own soul is trapped in a similar bottle that, when broken, causes Foster to crumble to dust.

Foxfield. Fictitious town in Massachusetts invented by HPL, although never cited in any story. A "Plan of Foxfield—for possible fictional use" in HPL's handwriting survives in AHT; it indicates that Foxfield is east of Aylesbury and Dunwich and northwest of Arkham.

See Will Murray, "Where Was Foxfield?" *LS* No. 33 (Fall 1995): 18–23 (the back cover prints a reconstruction of HPL's map).

"From Beyond." Short story (3,030 words); written on November 16, 1920. First published in the *Fantasy Fan* (June 1934); rpt. *WT* (February 1938); first collected in *BWS;* corrected text in *D;* annotated version in *DWH.*

Crawford Tillinghast is a scientist who has devised a machine that will "break down the barriers" that limit our perception of phenomena to what our five senses perceive. He shows to his friend, the narrator, "a pale, outré colour or blend of colours" that he maintains is ultraviolet, ordinarily invisible to the human eye. As the experiment continues, the narrator begins to perceive amorphous, jellylike objects drifting through what he previously thought was empty air; he even sees them "brushing past me and occasionally *walking or drifting through my supposedly solid body.*" Later, as the experiment becomes increasingly peculiar and as Tillinghast begins shouting madly about the creatures he controls through his machine, the narrator suddenly fires a shot from a pistol, destroying the machine. Tillinghast is found dead of apoplexy.

The story appears to be a fictionalization of some conceptions that HPL found in Hugh Elliot's *Modern Science and Materialism* (1919), a book that significantly influenced his early philosophical thought (see *SL* 1.134, 158). In particular, Elliot exhaustively discusses the limitations of our sense-perceptions (specifically citing ultraviolet rays) and goes on to note that most solid matter is largely empty space. Several entries in HPL's commonplace book written around this time (see #34–#36) appear to derive from Elliot's book. Some of the characterization and imagery derive from HPL's Civil War dream of early 1920 (see *SL* 1.100–102).

In the original draft (revised much later for its first appearance), the scientist was named Henry Annesley. Both "Crawford" and "Tillinghast" are two old and wealthy families of colonial Providence (both are mentioned in *The Case of Charles Dexter Ward*). The story was submitted to several pulp magazines in the 1920s, including *WT* and *Ghost Stories,* but uniformly rejected.

See S. T. Joshi, "The Sources for 'From Beyond,'" *Crypt* No. 38 (Eastertide 1986): 15–19; Peter Dendle, "Patristic Demonology and Lovecraft's 'From Beyond,'" *Journal of the Fantastic in the Arts* 8, No. 3 (1997): 281–93.

Frome, Nils [Helmer] (1918–1962). Swedish-born fan of weird and science fiction and late correspondent of HPL (1936–37). Residing for much of his life in Fraser Mills, Canada (a suburb of Vancouver), Frome early became interested in science fiction and solicited from HPL a contribution to his fan magazine, *Supramundane Stories.* HPL sent him the prose poem "Nyarlathotep" and "Notes on Writing Weird Fiction," both of which appeared in the second and last issue of *Supramundane Stories* (Spring 1938). Frome appeared to exhibit an interest in fortune-telling, reincarnation, and other such things, and HPL's letters to him forcefully argue against their validity. The letters were published (along with those to James Blish and William Miller, Jr.) in *Phantastique/Science Fiction Critic* (March 1938); rpt. HPL's *Uncollected Letters* (Necronomicon Press, 1986).

See Sam Moskowitz, ed., *Howard Phillips Lovecraft and Nils Helmer Frome* (Moshassuck Press, 1989).

Frye Family. In "The Dunwich Horror," a family (comprising **Elmer** and his wife **Selina**) dwelling on the eastern edge of Cold Spring Glen. They and their farmhouse are "erased" by Wilbur Whateley's twin brother.

Fungi from Yuggoth. Series of thirty-five sonnets initially, dated December 27, 1929–January 4, 1930 (ms., JHL). The complete cycle of thirty-six poems was not published in its entirety until *BWS;* the separate appearance *Fungi from Yuggoth* ([Washington, D.C.:] Bill Evans, June 1943) lacks the final three sonnets.

In the first three sonnets, the unnamed narrator obtains a mysterious tome—a "book that told the hidden way / Across the void and through the space-hung screens"—from an ancient bookseller and is followed home by an unseen pursuer. The remaining poems, which HPL considered suitable for publication independent of the introductory poems, are discontinuous vignettes concerning a variety of unrelated weird themes, told in the first person and (apparently) third person. The cumulative effect is that of a series of shifting dream images.

The poem was written following a burst of versifying, after a long hiatus, that occurred in late 1929, the other poems being "Recapture," The East India Brick Row," "The Outpost," and "The Messenger." HPL referred to the *Fungi* as "pseudo-sonnets," not out of modesty but because he recognized that most were a hybrid form combining elements of the classic Petrarchan and Shakespearean sonnet forms, contrived to provide an element of surprise in the final line. He lent the poem to Elizabeth Toldridge in mid-January, writing: "There are 33 here, but I shall probably grind out a dozen or so more before I consider the sequence concluded" (*SL* 3.116). To date HPL had written thirty-five, leaving aside the two concluding poems in the event that he did indeed "grind out" others. He did not. His typescript of the cycle long consisted of only thirty-three poems (Clark Ashton Smith had one such copy). When R. H. Barlow prepared a new typescript (in September 1934), "Evening Star" and "Continuity" finally were included (numbered XXXIV and XXXV as when HPL first composed them). It was not until 1936, when Barlow planned an edition of the complete cycle, that *Fungi from Yuggoth* achieved its present form, with "Recapture" (mid-November 1929) inserted as the third to last poem and "Evening Star" and "Continuity" renumbered to accommodate it.

HPL published five of the poems in the *Providence Journal* in 1930. *WT* selected another ten, publishing them under the heading "Fungi from Yuggoth" but renumbering the poems to coincide with the shortened selection. Over the next six years, HPL gave others to amateur or fan publications, including *Causerie, Driftwind, Fantasy Fan, Galleon, Interesting Items, Phantagraph, Pioneer, Science-Fantasy Correspondent, Science Fiction Barb,* and *Silver Fern.* Poems accepted by *Fantasy Magazine, Fantaisiste's Mirror, Recluse,* and *Ripples from Lake Champlain* never appeared. Many poems appeared more than once in magazines during HPL's lifetime; two appeared in books: "The Canal" in *Harvest: A Sheaf of Poems from* Driftwind (1933) and "Harbour Whistles" in *Threads in Tapestry* (1936). Only "Expectancy" (XXVIII) was never published periodically.

For the name Yuggoth, see entry on "The Whisperer in Darkness."

See Winfield Townley Scott, "A Parenthesis on Lovecraft as a Poet" (*FDOC* 211–16); R. Boerem, "The Continuity of the *Fungi from Yuggoth*" (*FDOC* 222–25); David E. Schultz, "H. P. Lovecraft's *Fungi from Yuggoth,*" *Crypt* No. 20 (Eastertide 1984): 3–7; Ralph E. Vaughan, "The Story in *Fungi from Yuggoth,*" *Crypt* No. 20 (Eastertide 1984): 9–11; David E. Schultz, "The Lack of Continuity in *Fungi from Yuggoth,*" *Crypt* No. 20 (Eastertide 1984): 12–16; Donald R. Burleson, "Scansion Problems in Lovecraft's 'Mirage,'" *LS* No. 24 (Spring 1991): 18–19, 21; Robert H. Waugh, "The Structural and Thematic Unity of *Fungi from Yuggoth,*" *LS* No. 26 (Spring 1992): 2–14; Dan Clore, "Metonyms of Alterity: A Semiotic Interpretation of *Fungi from Yuggoth,*" *LS* No. 30 (Spring 1994): 21–32.

G

Galpin, Alfred (1901–1983). Amateur writer, composer, and correspondent of HPL (1917–37). Galpin, one of Maurice W. Moe's students in Appleton (Wis.) High School, was appointed Fourth Vice-President of the UAPA for the 1917–18 term, and HPL came in touch with him in late 1917. Galpin (who in the amateur press sometimes appeared under the pseudonym Consul Hasting) went on to hold several other positions in the UAPA—including First Vice-President (1918–1919), President (1920–21), and chairman of the Department of Public Criticism (1919–22)—but published only one issue of his own amateur periodical, *The Philosopher* (December 1920), which contained the first appearance of HPL's "Polaris" and Galpin's own weird vignette, "Marsh-Mad: A Nightmare." HPL held off writing "The Tree" (which he had conceived no later than the summer of 1918) for several years because he felt that "Marsh-Mad" (which he had read in ms.) anticipated the "living tree" idea. HPL reports that his philosophical thought was strongly influenced by Galpin's (see *SL* 1.128); it was possibly at Galpin's suggestion that HPL first read Nietzsche in late 1918 (see Galpin's essay, "Nietzsche as a Practical Prophet," *The Rainbow,* October 1921). HPL not only wrote several birthday and other tributes in verse to Galpin—"To Alfred Galpin, Esq." (1920), "To a Youth" (1921), "To Mr. Galpin" (1921)—but also numerous poems relating to Galpin's high-school romances, envisioning Galpin as an ancient Greek shepherd pursuing, or pursued by, a nymph. Among them are "Damon and Delia, a Pastoral" (1918), "To Delia, Avoiding Damon" (1918), "Damon—a Monody" (1919), "Hylas and Myrrha" (1919), and "Myrrha and Strephen" (1919). HPL's poems "To the Eighth of November" (1918) and "Birthday Lines to Margfred Albraham" (1919) are jointly dedicated to Galpin and Margaret Abraham, who shared the same birthday. HPL's short play *Alfredo* (1918) features Galpin as its title character and Abraham as the character Margarita. Galpin himself wrote a homage/parody of HPL's "Nemesis," titled "Selenaio-Phantasma" (*Conservative,* July 1918), and at an unspecified date (probably before 1920) collaborated with HPL on the poem

"Nathicana," published (*Vagrant,* Spring 1927) under the pseudonym Albert Frederick Willie (the first two names echo Galpin's first name; "Willie" alludes to Galpin's mother's maiden name, Willy). By late 1919 Galpin had become, with Maurice W. Moe, a member of HPL's correspondence cycle, the Gallomo, although it did not seem to last much more than a year.

On July 29, 1922, HPL boarded a train in New York for Cleveland, arriving the next day. He was met by Galpin, who resided at 9231 Birchdale Avenue. HPL stayed until August 15. At that time Galpin gave HPL a copy of Clark Ashton Smith's *The Star-Treader and Other Poems* (1912), prompting HPL to write to Smith. On August 18–20, 1925, when he was living in Brooklyn, HPL met Galpin's wife, a Frenchwoman who had arrived from Paris and would then move on to Cleveland. Galpin later moved to Italy and became a professional pianist and composer. Upon HPL's death he composed a "Lament for H.P.L." for solo piano (the score is reproduced in full in *Marginalia*) and later wrote a poignant memoir, "Memories of a Friendship" (1959; in *LR*). After the 1920s HPL and Galpin had little contact, and Galpin lost or destroyed most of his letters from HPL; only twenty-seven now survive at JHL.

See H. P. Lovecraft, *Letters to Alfred Galpin,* ed. David E. Schultz and S. T. Joshi (Hippocampus Press, 2003).

Galpin, Alfred (Old Bugs). In "Old Bugs," a once-successful writer who took to drink and thereby alienated the woman he loved, Eleanor Wing. He dies in the attempt to prevent Wing's son, Alfred Trever, from imbibing alcohol at a tavern.

Gamba. In "Winged Death," a factor's messenger whom Dr. Thomas Slauenwite deliberately causes to be bitten by a strange insect. Slauenwite cures him, but allows another bitten African, Batta, to die.

Gamwell, Annie E[meline] Phillips (1866–1941). Fifth and last child of Whipple V. Phillips and Robie Alzada Place Phillips; youngest sister of Sarah Susan Phillips Lovecraft, HPL's mother. Gamwell was educated in Providence and married Edward Francis Gamwell on June 3, 1897; they had two children, a son, Phillips Gamwell, and a daughter, Marion Roby Gamwell, who lived only five days in February 1900. She separated from her husband some time prior to the death of her son in Colorado at the end of 1916. During part of the period 1919–24, she assisted her sister Lillian Clark in keeping house for HPL at 598 Angell Street; however, in a letter to her dated August 27, 1921 (*SL* 1.148), HPL writes of her recently taking up residence in New Hampshire. She visited ancestral sites in western Rhode Island with HPL in 1926 and 1929. On May 15, 1933, she took up housekeeping with HPL in a second-story flat at 66 College Street, but broke her ankle soon after moving in; she also underwent an operation to remove a cancerous breast early in 1936 (in his letters HPL discreetly referred to the cause of her hospitalization as "grippe"). She was shocked to find her nephew's "Instructions in Case of Decease" (*LS* No. 11 [Fall 1985]: 71–73) in the fall of 1936 and was unable to care for him effectively when he became gravely ill in the early months of 1937 because of her own illness. R. H. Barlow came to Providence shortly after HPL's death and with her permission deposited most of

HPL's literary papers in the John Hay Library of Brown University during the period 1937–42. August Derleth and Donald Wandrei also visited her in Providence in 1938. They dedicated to her the first hardcover collection of HPL's stories, *O*. She died of cancer in early 1941.

Gamwell, Edward F[rancis] (1869–1936). Married HPL's aunt Annie Emeline Phillips on June 3, 1897. He received the A.B. from Brown University in 1894. Gamwell was city editor of the Cambridge (Mass.) *Chronicle* (1896–1901), editor and proprietor of the Cambridge *Tribune* (1901–12), and editor of the *Budget* and *American Cultivator,* both published from Boston (1913–15); thereafter, he engaged in independent commercial writing and advertising. He was the editor of *An Historic Guide to Cambridge* (1907). Gamwell separated from his wife sometime before the end of 1916. He removed from Cambridge to Boston about 1931. HPL notes that it was Gamwell's journalistic work that inspired him to begin the *Rhode Island Journal of Astronomy* in 1903 (see *SL* 1.39).

See Kenneth W. Faig, Jr., *Edward Francis Gamwell and His Family* (Moshassuck Press, 1991).

Gamwell, Phillips (1898–1916). Son of Annie E. Phillips Gamwell and Edward F. Gamwell. He was the only other member of HPL's generation in descent from Whipple V. Phillips and his wife Robie A. Place Phillips. He lived most of his short life with parents in Cambridge, Mass. He began corresponding with HPL around 1910. HPL donated his boyhood stamp collection to him. HPL later attributed his fondness for letter-writing to the extensive correspondence he had with Gamwell from 1912 to 1916 (see *SL* 3.370). In October 1916 Gamwell and his mother traveled to Roswell, Col., where Phillips's paternal grandmother Victoria Clarissa Maxwell had relatives, in an attempt to regain his failing health. He died there on December 31, 1916, of tuberculosis. HPL wrote a poetic tribute, "An Elegy on Phillips Gamwell, Esq." (Providence *Evening News,* January 5, 1917).

Gardner. In "The Colour out of Space," the family on whose farm the strange meteorite lands. **Nahum** is the patriarch, the last survivor of the blight that overtakes his farm. When his wife **Nabby** (short for Abigail) goes mad, he locks her in the attic, where she becomes a "terrible thing [that] very slowly and perceptibly moved as it continued to crumble" and ultimately "does not reappear in [Ammi Pierce's] tale as a moving object." **Zenas** is their oldest son, followed by **Thaddeus** (1866–1883) and **Merwin** (sometimes affectionately called Mernie). Thaddeus goes mad, and Merwin and Zenas disappear into the poisoned well.

Gedney, ———. In *At the Mountains of Madness,* a graduate student and a member of the Miskatonic Antarctic Expedition of 1930–31. He accompanies Lake on his subexpedition and is subsequently discovered, dead, by Dyer and Danforth deep within the Old Ones' city.

Genie. In "Memory," a supernatural entity who asks the Daemon of the Valley of the deeds and identity of the creatures (i.e., human beings) in a deserted valley.

Gerritsen, Cornelia. In "The Horror at Red Hook," a society woman from Bayside, Queens, whom Robert Suydam marries to deflect attention from his bizarre activities and improve his social standing. She and her husband die mysteriously on their wedding day.

"Ghost-Eater, The." Short story (3,880 words); written in collaboration with C. M. Eddy, Jr., in October 1923. First published in *WT* (April 1924); first collected in *DB;* corrected text in *HM.*

The first-person narrator needs to get from Mayfair to Glendale (two cities in Maine) but can find no one to take him. So he goes by himself on foot, stopping at night in a deserted wood. After sleeping for a time, he awakens in the night and realizes that it will shortly begin raining. Entering a clearing, he sees on the farther side of it a building—a "neat and tasteful house of two stories." Knocking at the place, he is invited in by a "strikingly handsome" man who, with a faint trace of a foreign accent, invites him to stay for the night. Retiring to an upstairs bedroom, the traveler (who is carrying a large amount of money on his person) decides to exercise caution: he arranges the bedclothes to make it appear as if he is sleeping there, and prepares to settle down in a chair for the duration of the night. Shortly thereafter he hears footsteps ascending the stairs. The door opens and a man whom he had never seen before ("indubitably a foreigner") enters the room. This man disrobes, gets into the vacant bed, and appears to go to sleep. The narrator is unclear whether the scene he has witnessed is real or merely a dream, so he reaches over the recumbent figure and seeks to grasp the man's shoulder; but *"my clutching fingers had passed directly through the sleeping form, and seized only the sheet below!"* Horrified and confused, the narrator now hears the sound of additional footsteps on the stairs; his room is now entered by a "great gray wolf" whose eyes *"were the gray phosphorescent eyes of my host as they had peered at me through the darkness of the kitchen."* The wolf howls and springs at the sleeping figure on the bed, apparently tearing out the man's throat. The traveler empties his revolver in the direction of the wolf, but every shot hits the wall without apparently harming the wolf in any way. Somehow the traveler staggers to Glendale, where he learns the story of Vasili Oukranikov, who came from Russia sixty years before and built a house in the woods. Oukranikov had the reputation of being a "werewolf and eater of men." One day he invited Count Feodore Tchernevsky (who lived in Mayfair) to his home; that evening the count was found in a mangled state, with a gray wolf hovering over the body. The wolf was killed and buried in the house, and the house was then burned down. But at every full moon the wolf is seen to roam the area again.

A conventional ghost/werewolf story, the impetus for its writing clearly came from Eddy. HPL wrote to Eddy's wife, Muriel, on 20 October 1923: "Here, at last, is the amended 'Ghost-Eater', whose appearance I trust Mr. Eddy will find satisfactory. I made two or three minor revisions in my own revised version, so that as it stands, it ought to be fairly acceptable to an editor" (quoted in *DB,* p. 97). The suggestion is that Eddy wrote the initial draft, HPL exhaustively revised it, and then slightly revised this draft.

Gifford, Jonathan. In "The Lurking Fear," a friend of Jan Martense who, worried over the lack of correspondence from Jan, comes to the Martense mansion in the fall of 1763, only to be told that Jan is dead.

Gilman, Walter. In "The Dreams in the Witch House," the student of advanced mathematics and physics at Miskatonic University who resides at the old Witch House in Arkham. In his strange dreams and bouts of sleepwalking (induced by the strangely angled room in which lives), he observes bizarre landscapes and encounters the witch Keziah Mason, who formerly inhabited his room. Gilman is ultimately killed by Brown Jenkin, the witch's familiar.

Glendale. Fictitious town in Maine invented either by HPL or by C. M. Eddy and cited in "The Ghost-Eater" (1923).

Gll'-Hthaa-Ynn. In "The Mound," the leader of a cavalcade of men and beasts who comes upon Panfilo de Zamacona in a temple in the underworld realm beneath the mound and leads him back to the great city of Tsath.

Goodenough, Arthur [Henry] (1871–1936). American poet and amateur journalist from Brattleboro, Vt. He was the author of several small, privately printed volumes of poetry, including *"Blossoms of Yesterday"* (1896), *My Lady's Shoes and Other Poems* (1911), *Songs of Four Decades* (1927), and *Grass of Parnasses* (ed. Walter John Coates) (1937). His poem "Lovecraft—an Appreciation" (included in his "Further Recollections of Amateur Journalism," *Vagrant,* Spring 1927) was in parts so effusive that HPL thought it a parody, but Goodenough's friend W. Paul Cook convinced him it was genuine. HPL accordingly responded with his own poetic tribute, "To Arthur Goodenough, Esq." (*Tryout,* September 1918). HPL visited Goodenough in Brattleboro in August 1927 and also in June 1928; this latter visit, in which several other local writers participated, was written up in the *Brattleboro Reformer* (June 18, 1928) under the title "Literary Persons Meet in Guilford." Goodenough's home seems to be a partial inspiration for Akeley's home in "The Whisperer in Darkness" (1930).

Grandison, Robert. In "The Trap," a student who becomes entrapped in the magic mirror at the house of Gerald Canevin.

"Green Meadow, The." Short story (2,330 words); written in collaboration with Winifred Virginia Jackson, c. 1918 or 1919. First published in *Vagrant* (Spring 1927) (as "Translated by Elizabeth Neville Berkeley and Lewis Theobald, Jun."); first collected in *BWS;* corrected text in *HM.*

An introductory note states that the following narrative was found in a notebook embedded in a meteorite that landed in the sea near the coast of Maine. This notebook was made of some unearthly substance and the text was *"Greek of the purest classical quality."* The narrative itself tells of a person who finds himself (or, conceivably, herself) on a peninsula near a rushing stream, not knowing who he is and how he got there. The peninsula breaks off its land mass and floats down the river, which is gradually wearing away the soil of the newly created island. The narrator sees in the distance a green meadow. His island is approaching it, and gradually he hears a weird singing on it; but as he approaches close enough to see "the *source* of the chanting," he suddenly experiences a cataclysmic revelation: "therein was revealed the hideous solution of all which had puzzled me." But after a few hints the text becomes illegible.

HPL admits that the story was based upon a dream that Jackson had, probably in late 1918, and that this dream "was exceptionally singular in that I had one exactly like it myself—save that mine did not extend so far. It was only when I had related my dream that Miss J. related the similar and more fully developed one" (*SL* 1.116). Elsewhere HPL states that he added the "quasi-realistic ... introduction from my own imagination" (HPL to the Gallomo, [January] 1920; AHT). The fact of the document being in Greek is intended to suggest that it is the "narrative of an ancient Greek philosopher who had escaped from the earth and landed on some other planet" (*SL* 1.136), although it is difficult to arrive at this conclusion from the text alone.

See Stefan Dziemianowicz, "'The Green Meadow' and 'The Willows': Lovecraft, Blackwood, and a Peculiar Coincidence," *LS* Nos. 19/20 (Fall 1989): 33–39.

Gresham, Mr. In "The Loved Dead," the owner of the Gresham Corporation, a company that maintains the largest funeral parlors in the city of Fenham, who finds the narrator making love to a corpse and dismisses him from his service. Later Gresham dies in "the influenza epidemic" (i.e., of 1918–19).

Grey Eagle, Chief. In "The Curse of Yig" and "The Mound," an American Indian, nearly 150 years old. It is he who corroborates much of the folklore constituting the narrative of "The Mound."

Guiney, Louise Imogen (1861–1920). Massachusetts poet and critic. HPL states that he and his parents boarded with Guiney and her mother in Auburndale, Mass., in the winter of 1892–93 (see *SL* 2.207), but independent confirmation of this stay has not been found. HPL, however, had clear recollections of the Guiney residence, including its numerous dogs. It was formerly thought that some unpublished Guiney letters (to F. H. Day) written in the summer of 1892 contain allusions to the Lovecrafts, but in fact they refer to some German houseguests. HPL claimed that his mother was acquainted with Guiney; the latter, a Catholic, had attended the Academy of the Sacred Heart in Providence (1872–79), but there is no record of Sarah Susan Phillips having gone there. HPL also stated that he was dandled on the knee of the aged Oliver Wendell Holmes at the Guiney residence; Holmes was indeed a friend of Guiney, so this memory is likely to be genuine. Guiney wrote many books of poetry (*Songs at the Start* [1884]; verse collected in *Happy Ending* [1909; rev. 1927]) and criticism (*Goose-Quill Papers* [1885]). HPL owned her cowritten book, *Three Heroines of New England Romance* (1895). Her selected letters (containing no mention of HPL's family) were published in 1920 (2 vols.).

H

Haines, Mark. In "Two Black Bottles," the proprietor of a grocery store in Daalbergen, N.J., who tells the narrator of the strange events surrounding the death of the narrator's uncle, Johannes Vanderhoof.

"Hallowe'en in a Suburb." Poem (35 lines in 7 stanzas); probably written in early 1926. First published in the *National Amateur* (March 1926) (as "In a Suburb"); rpt. *Phantagraph* (June 1937); rpt. *WT* (September 1952).
     An evocation of the wonders and terrors of Halloween.

Halsey, Allan. In "Herbert West—Reanimator," the dean of the medical school of Miskatonic University. He opposes Herbert West's experiments in reanimation, but when he succumbs to typhoid, West resuscitates him with only partial success.

Hammett, [Samuel] Dashiell (1894–1961). Pioneering American writer of "hard-boiled" detective fiction who compiled the horror anthology *Creeps by Night* (1931), containing HPL's "The Music of Erich Zann." HPL, August Derleth, and other colleagues made numerous suggestions to Hammett regarding stories for inclusion in the volume. The anthology was reprinted in the UK as *Modern Tales of Horror* (1932).

Hardman, 'Squire. In "Sweet Ermengarde," the owner of the mortgage on the home of Hiram Stubbs, whose daughter, Ermengarde, he hopes to marry. After a succession of adventures, he does so.

Harré, T[homas] Everett (1884–1948). American journalist who assembled the horror anthology *Beware After Dark!* (1929), containing HPL's "The Call of Cthulhu," of which he stated in his introduction: ". . . in its cumulative awesomeness and building of effect to its appalling finale, [it] is reminiscent of

Poe." HPL met Harré when he visited New York in January 1934 (see *SL* 4.341). Harré published several novels as well as two further anthologies, *The Bedside Treasury of Love* (1945) and *Treasures of the Kingdom* (1947).

Harris, Arthur (1893–1966). Amateur journalist in Wales and correspondent of HPL (1915–37). Harris, living in Llandudno, published one of the longest-running amateur journals, *Interesting Items,* which ran from 1904 (as *Llandudno's Weekly*) to 1956, each issue usually consisting only of four to eight small pages. Harris published HPL's poems "1914" (March 1915), "The Crime of Crimes" (July 1915), and two sonnets of *Fungi from Yuggoth.* Harris published "The Crime of Crimes" as a pamphlet; it thereby became HPL's first separate publication. Copies are exceptionally scarce: three are known to be in existence. HPL continued to correspond with Harris for the entirety of his life, although as early as 1918 his letters numbered no more than one or two a year.

Harris, William (d. 1764). In "The Shunned House," a merchant and seaman, the first inhabitant of the Shunned House, along with his wife **Rhoby (Dexter) Harris** and their children **Elkanah** (1755–1766), **Abigail** (1757–1763), **William, Jr.** (1759–1797), and **Ruth** (1761–1763). Most of the family and their servants die while living in the house. Rhoby goes mad, and although William, Jr., becomes quite sickly, he survives, enlists in the army, and returns to the house. He marries **Phoebe (Hetfield) Harris** of Elizabethtown, N.J., in 1780, but after she gives birth to a stillborn daughter, he moves out of the house and shuts it down. In 1785 his wife bears a son, **Dutee Harris,** and after his parents die in the yellow fever epidemic of 1797, he is raised by his cousin, **Rathbone Harris,** son of William's cousin **Peleg Harris.** Later descendants are Dutee's son **Welcome Harris** (d. 1862), Welcome's son **Archer Harris** (d. 1916), and Archer's son **Carrington Harris,** the current (i.e., as of 1924) owner of the Shunned House.

Harris, Woodburn (1888–1988). Correspondent of HPL, living in Vermont. He came in touch with HPL around 1929, probably through the mediation of Walter J. Coates. HPL revised some of Harris's tracts against Prohibition, although these do not appear to have been published. Only three of HPL's letters to him survive, but one of these was a handwritten letter of seventy pages (see *SL* 3.58).

Hart, Bertrand K[elton] (1892–1941). Literary editor of the *Providence Journal* who briefly corresponded with HPL. In his column in the *Journal,* "The Sideshow," in mid-November 1929, Hart printed a list of what a colleague had recommended as the ten greatest horror stories ever written. HPL found the list so tame that he submitted his own list, published in Hart's column for November 23; Hart called the list "a little masterpiece of comparative criticism." Other lists, by August Derleth and Frank Belknap Long, were published in the column for November 25. Hart then stumbled upon HPL's "The Call of Cthulhu" in Harré's *Beware After Dark!,* and professed to be outraged at the fact that the artist Wilcox's home was given as 7 Thomas Street, where Hart himself had once resided. In the column for November 30 he threatened to send a ghost to

HPL's doorstep at 3 A.M. that night. At 3:07 A.M. HPL wrote the sonnet "The Messenger" and sent it to Hart, who published it in his column for December 3. Hart printed a letter by HPL in his column for March 18, 1930. Some of Hart's columns discussing HPL were gathered in *The Sideshow of B. K. Hart*, ed. Philomela Hart (1941). Although Hart repeatedly expressed a wish to meet HPL, he never did so; possibly HPL, with his typically exaggerated modesty, felt himself too insignificant to meet so recognized a figure in local journalism.

Hartmann, J|oachim| F|riedrich| (1848–1930). Astrologer who incurred HPL's ire when he wrote the article "Astrology and the European War" in the Providence *Evening News* for September 4, 1914. HPL and Hartmann exchanged several polemics in the *Evening News*—the former with "Science versus Charlatanry" (September 9) and "The Falsity of Astrology" (October 10); the latter with a letter to the editor (October 7) and "The Science of Astrology" (October 22)—until HPL finally silenced him with satires written under pseudonym Isaac Bickerstaffe, Jr. (derived from Jonathan Swift's Isaac Bickerstaffe pieces satirizing the astrologer Partridge): "Astrology and the Future" (October 13) and "Delavan's Comet and Astrology" (October 26). After Hartmann's last article ("A Defense of Astrology," December 14), HPL concluded with an article under his own name ("The Fall of Astrology," December 17) and one final Bickerstaffe article (letter to the editor, December 21). Articles on both sides are collected in *Science vs. Charlatanry* (1979).

Hartwell, Dr. In "The Dunwich Horror," Henry Armitage's personal physician.

"Haunter of the Dark, The." Short story (9,350 words); written November 5–9, 1935. First published in *WT* (December 1936); first collected in *O;* corrected text in *DH;* annotated version in *CC* and *An2*.

Robert Blake, a young writer of weird fiction, comes to Providence for a period of writing. Looking through his study window down College Hill and across to the far-away and vaguely sinister Italian district known as Federal Hill, Blake becomes fascinated by an abandoned church "in a state of great decrepitude." Eventually he gains the courage actually to go to the place and enter it, and he finds many anomalous things within. There are strange and forbidden books; there is, in a large square room, an object resting upon a pillar—a metal box containing a curious gem or mineral—that exercises an unholy fascination upon Blake; and there is the decaying skeleton of a newspaper reporter whose notes Blake reads. The notes speak of the ill-regarded Starry Wisdom church, whose congregation gained in numbers throughout the nineteenth century and was suspected of satanic practices of a very bizarre sort, until the city finally shut the church in 1877. The notes also mention a "Shining Trapezohedron" and a "Haunter of the Dark" that cannot exist in light. Blake concludes that the object on the pillar is the Shining Trapezohedron, and in an "access of gnawing, indeterminate panic fear" he closes the lid of the object and flees the place.

Later he hears strange stories of some object lumbering within the belfry of the church, stuffing pillows in all the windows so that no light can come in. A tremendous electrical storm on August 8–9 causes a blackout for several hours.

A group of superstitious Italians gathers around the church with candles, and they sense an enormous dark object emerging from the belfry. Blake's diary tells the rest of the tale. He feels that he is somehow losing control of his sense of self ("My name is Blake—Robert Harrison Blake of 620 East Knapp Street, Milwaukee, Wisconsin. . . . I am on this planet"; and still later: "I am it and it is I"); his perspective is all confused; finally he sees some nameless object approaching him. The next morning he is found dead—of electrocution, even though his window was closed and fastened.

What, in fact, has happened to Blake? The poignant but seemingly cryptic entry "Roderick Usher" in his diary tells the whole story. Just as in "Supernatural Horror in Literature" HPL analyzed Poe's "The Fall of the House of Usher" as a tale that "displays an abnormally linked trinity of entities at the end of a long and isolated family history—a brother, his twin sister, and their incredibly ancient house all sharing a single soul and meeting one common dissolution at the same moment," so in "The Haunter of the Dark" we are to believe that the entity in the church—the Haunter of the Dark, described as an avatar of Nyarlathotep—has possessed Blake's mind but, at the moment of doing so, is struck by lightning and killed, and Blake dies as well.

The story came about almost as a whim. Robert Bloch had written "The Shambler from the Stars" in the spring of 1935, in which a character—never named, but clearly meant to be HPL—is killed. HPL was taken with the story, and when it was published in *WT* (September 1935), a reader, B. M. Reynolds, praised it and had a suggestion to make: "Contrary to previous criticism, Robert Bloch deserves plenty of praise for *The Shambler from the Stars.* Now why doesn't Mr. Lovecraft return the compliment, and dedicate a story to the author?" (*WT* 36, No. 5 [November 1935]: 652). At the time HPL read this, he had just learned of the acceptances by *Astounding Stories* of *At the Mountains of Madness* and "The Shadow out of Time." Bolstered by the news, he took up Reynolds's suggestion, and the resulting story tells of one Robert Blake (a very transparent allusion to Robert Bloch, to whom HPL dedicated the story) who dies a glassy-eyed corpse staring out his study window.

Several of the surface details of the plot were taken directly from Hanns Heinz Ewers's "The Spider," which HPL read in Dashiell Hammett's *Creeps by Night* (1931). This story involves a man who becomes fascinated with a strange woman he sees through his window in a building across from his own, until finally he seems to lose hold of his own personality. The entire story is told in the form of the man's diary, and at the end he writes: "My name—Richard Bracquemont, Richard Bracquemont, Richard—oh, I can't get any farther. . . ."

Many landmarks described in the story are manifestly based upon actual sites. The view from Blake's study is a poignant description of what HPL saw from his own study at 66 College Street. The same view can be seen today from such a vantage point as Prospect Terrace on the brow of College Hill. Blake's address, as given in the story, was Bloch's actual address in Milwaukee. The church that figures so prominently in the tale was St. John's Catholic Church on Atwell's Avenue in Federal Hill (torn down in 1992). This church was situated on a raised plot of ground, as in the story, although there was (at least in recent years) no metal fence around it. It was, in HPL's day, the principal Catholic church in the area. The description of the interior and belfry of the church is quite accurate. HPL heard that the steeple had been destroyed by lightning in late June of 1935 (he was not there at the time, being in Florida visiting R. H. Barlow); instead of rebuilding the steeple, the church authorities simply put a cap on the brick tower (see HPL to Richard F. Searight, December 24, 1935; *Letters to Richard F. Searight* [Necronomicon Press, 1992], p. 70).

See Steven J. Mariconda, "Some Antecedents of the Shining Trapezohedron," *Etchings and Odysseys* No. 3 [1983]: 15–20 (rpt. in Mariconda's *On the Emergence of "Cthulhu" and Other Observations* [Necronomicon Press, 1995]).

Hawthorne, Nathaniel (1804–1864). American novelist and short story writer. Hawthorne was a central figure in early Gothic literature in America and a major influence on HPL, who at the age of six first developed a fascination with Graeco-Roman mythology by reading Hawthorne's rewritings of Greek myths, *A Wonder Book* (1852) and *Tanglewood Tales* (1853). *The House of the Seven Gables* (1851)—which HPL in "Supernatural Horror in Literature" deemed "New England's greatest contribution to weird literature"—probably influenced HPL's "The Picture in the House" (1920), "The Shunned House" (1924), and *The Case of Charles Dexter Ward* (1927). "The Outsider" (1921) may in part have been inspired by Hawthorne's "Fragments from the Journal of a Solitary Man." HPL's *The Dream-Quest of Unknown Kadath* (1926–27) shows the influence of both Hawthorne's *The Marble Faun* (1860) and his short story "The Great Stone Face" (in *The Snow Image, and Other Twice-told Tales* [1852]); "The Dreams in the Witch House" (1932) was heavily influenced by Hawthorne's unfinished novel *Septimius Felton,* as "The Unnamable" (1923) was by *Dr. Grimshawe's Secret* (1883).

See Dirk W. Mosig, "Poe, Hawthorne and Lovecraft: Variations on a Theme of Panic," *Romantist* Nos. 4–5 (1980–81): 43–45; Donald R. Burleson, "H. P. Lovecraft: The Hawthorne Influence," *Extrapolation* 22, No. 3 (Fall 1981): 262–69.

Hayden, Ben. In "The Man of Stone," a friend of the narrator who takes the narrator with him to investigate the uncannily lifelike sculptures of Arthur Wheeler.

"He." Short story (4,310 words); written on August 11, 1925. First published in *WT* (September 1926); first collected in *O;* corrected text in *D;* annotated version in *CC* and *PZ.*

The narrator ruefully announces: "My coming to New York had been a mistake. . . ." He had hoped to find literary inspiration in the "teeming labyrinths" of the city, but instead finds only "a sense of horror and oppression which threatened to master, paralyse, and annihilate me." The narrator confesses that the gleaming towers of New York had captivated him at first, but later he came to realize that "this city of stone and stridor is not a sentient perpetuation of Old New York as London is of Old London and Paris of Old Paris, but that it is in fact quite dead, its sprawling body imperfectly embalmed and infested with queer animate things which have nothing to do with it as it was in life." He seeks out Greenwich Village as the one area in the city where antiquity can still be found; it is here, at 2:00 one August morning, that he meets "the man." This person has an archaic manner of speaking and is wearing similarly archaic attire, and the narrator takes him for a harmless eccentric; but the latter immediately senses a fellow antiquarian. The man leads him on a circuitous tour of old alleys and courtyards, finally coming to "the ivy-clad wall of a private estate," where the man lives. In the manor house the man begins to relate an account of his "ancestor," who practiced some sort of sorcery, in part from knowledge gained from the Indians in the area; later he conveniently killed them with bad rum, so that he alone now had the secret information he had extracted from them. What is the nature of this knowledge? The man leads the narrator to a window and, parting the curtains, reveals an idyllic rural landscape—it can only be the Greenwich of the eighteenth century, brought magically before his eyes. The narrator, stunned, asks harriedly, "Can you—dare you—go *far?*" In scorn the man parts the curtains again and this time shows him an apocalyptic sight of the future ("I saw the heavens verminous with strange flying things, and beneath them a hellish black city of giant stone terraces with impious pyramids flung savagely to the moon, and devil-lights burning from unnumbered windows"). The narrator screams in horror, inadvertently summoning the spirits of the murdered Indians, who manifest themselves in the form of a black slime, burst in on the pair, and make off with the archaic man (who is himself the "ancestor"), while the narrator falls through successive floors of the building and then crawls out to Perry Street. Later we learn that the narrator has now returned to his native New England.

The story was written in the course of an all-night tour of the antiquities of the New York metropolitan area. By 7 A.M. on August 11, HPL had reached Elizabeth, N.J., by ferry. There he purchased a 10¢ composition book at a shop, went to Scott Park, and wrote the story. The actual location of the story is Greenwich Village; specifically, a courtyard off Perry Street that HPL had explored the previous August in response to an article on it (in a regular column, "Little Sketches about Town") in the *New York Evening Post* (August 29, 1924). His description of the courtyard is quite accurate. Moreover, HPL probably knew that the area had been heavily settled by Indians (they had named it Sapohanican) and that a sumptuous mansion was built in the block bounded by Perry, Charles, Bleecker, and West Fourth Streets sometime between 1726 and 1744, being the residence of a succession of wealthy citizens until it was razed in 1865. This is clearly the manor house of the archaic gentleman. The vision of past and future New York as seen in the window of the house may have been derived from Lord Dunsany's picaresque novel *The Chronicles of Rodriguez* (1922), in which Rodriguez and a companion make an arduous climb of a mountain to the house of a wizard, who in alternate windows unveils vistas of wars past and to come.

See S. T. Joshi, "Lovecraft and Dunsany's *Chronicles of Rodriguez*," *Crypt* No. 82 (Hallowmas 1992): 3–6; Kenneth W. Faig, Jr., "Lovecraft's 'He,'" *LS* No. 37 (Fall 1997): 17–25.

Heald, Hazel (1896–1961). Revision client of HPL, residing in Somerville, Mass. According to Muriel E. Eddy (*The Gentleman from Angell Street* [1961]),

Heald was a member of a New England writers' club that Mrs. Eddy had begun; sometime in 1932 Mrs. Eddy introduced Heald to HPL, having read "The Man of Stone," which she found poorly written but with an interesting plot. Although other parts of Mrs. Eddy's memoir appear falsified or erroneous, nothing in HPL's letters contradicts this account; HPL, in fact, never mentions how he first came to know Heald. HPL eventually revised five stories for her—"The Man of Stone," "Winged Death," "The Horror in the Museum," "Out of the Aeons," and "The Horror in the Burying-Ground"—most of them in 1932–33. (See entries on individual stories for details of publication and other particulars.) Four of the stories feature an element in common: a human being who is either dead or immobilized but whose brain is alive ("Winged Death" features a man whose brain or personality ends up in the body of an insect). Mrs. Eddy suggests that Heald, a divorcée, was romantically attracted to HPL and that she once invited him to a candlelight dinner in Somerville; in his memoir W. Paul Cook notes that after his trip to Quebec in the summer of 1932, HPL stopped to visit him in Athol, Mass., and that "he was going to take a midnight bus to Providence after dinner in Somerville" (Cook does not mention Heald in his account). HPL himself does not seem to have been particularly attracted to Heald. Heald did not keep her letters from HPL.

Heaton, ———. In "The Mound," a young man who in 1891 goes to the mound region in Oklahoma looking for treasure but returns with his mind shattered by something he has seen. He dies eight years later in an epileptic fit.

Henneberger, J[acob] C[lark] (1890–1969). Magazine publisher who, with J. M. Lansinger, founded Rural Publications, Inc., in 1922, to publish a variety of popular magazines. Henneberger achieved great success with the magazine *College Humor* (begun in 1922), and now envisioned founding a line of varied periodicals in the detective and horror fields. Having received assurances from such established writers as Hamlin Garland and Ben Hecht that they would be willing to contribute stories of an "unconventional" sort to a new magazine, Henneberger started *WT* in March 1923; but in the end these and other well-known authors did not submit to the magazine, leaving its early issues open to many tyros and amateurs. Henneberger installed Edwin Baird as his first editor, and the latter accepted all five of the stories HPL submitted to him in May 1923. Henneberger commissioned HPL to ghostwrite "Under the Pyramids" for Harry Houdini, paying him $100 upon receipt of the manuscript in early March 1924. By this time, however, the magazine was in serious financial trouble; it and its companion, *Detective Tales,* were now $40,000 in debt. For this and other reasons, HPL turned down Henneberger's offer to be the new editor of the magazine; specifically, HPL, newly married and settled in Brooklyn, did not wish to pull up stakes and move to Chicago to edit the magazine, as would have been required. Henneberger then sold off his share of *Detective Tales* to Lansinger, appointed Farnsworth Wright as editor of *WT,* and came to an agreement with B. Cornelius, the printer of the magazine, whereby Cornelius would be the chief stockholder with an agreement that if the $40,000 owed him was ever repaid by profits from the magazine, the stock would be returned to Henneberger. This never happened. In the fall of 1924 Henneberger provisionally hired HPL to edit a new humor magazine that he was planning (possibly titled the *Magazine of Fun*) at $40 per week; HPL spent the next several weeks preparing jokes for the magazine, but it never got off the ground. Henneberger gave HPL a credit of $60 at the Scribner Book Shop; although HPL attempted to have the credit converted to cash, he was unable to do so, and so he and Frank Belknap Long selected a large number of books (see *SL* 1.355–56). Henneberger sporadically communicated with HPL over the next few years, but to no particular effect. See Henneberger's late memoir, "Out of Space, Out of Time," *Deeper Than You Think* 1, No. 2 (July 1968): 3–5.

"Herbert West—Reanimator." Short story (12,100 words); written from early October 1921 to mid-June 1922. First published as a serial (under the title "Grewsome Tales") in *Home Brew* (February, March, April, May, June, and July 1922); rpt. *WT* (March, July, September, November 1942, September, November 1943); first collected in *BWS;* corrected text in *D;* annotated version in *An2* and *CC.*

The story is narrated by a friend and colleague of Dr. Herbert West; both he and West attended the Miskatonic University Medical School in Arkham and later went on to experience various adventures as practicing physicians. It was in medical school that West derived his peculiar theories about the possibility of reanimating the dead. These views "hinged on the essentially mechanistic nature of life; and concerned means for operating the organic machinery of mankind by calculated chemical action after the failure of natural processes. . . . my friend believed that artificial reanimation of the dead can depend only on the condition of the tissues; and that unless actual decomposition has set in, a corpse fully equipped with organs may with suitable measures be set going again in the peculiar fashion known as life." The six episodes of the story show West producing more and more hideous instances of reanimation. In the first, West injects a serum into a corpse, but it seems to produce no results; the two doctors bury the corpse in the potter's field, only to learn later that it came to life after all. In the second, West reanimates Dr. Allan Halsey, who as head of the medical school had vigorously opposed West's experiments and had died in the typhoid epidemic that raged through Arkham. Halsey creates havoc throughout the city before he is caught and locked up in Sefton Asylum. In the third, West and the narrator have set up practice in the small Massachusetts town of Bolton and attempt to resurrect an African American—an amateur boxer named Buck Robinson, "The Harlem Smoke"—but seem to find that the serum "prepared from experience with white specimens only" will not work on him; later they learn otherwise. In the fourth episode the narrator, returning from a vacation with his parents in Illinois, finds West in a state of unusual excitement. He has designed an embalming fluid that will preserve a corpse in a state of freshness indefinitely and claims that a traveling salesman who had come to visit West had died unexpectedly and would therefore serve as a perfect specimen because of the freshness of the corpse. When it is reanimated, the narrator finds that West's account of the matter is not wholly accurate. The fifth episode takes us to the horrors of the Great War, where West and the narrator have enlisted in a Canadian regiment in 1915. West now seeks to put into practice still more eccentric views on the reanimation of the dead and does so in a loathsome manner. The sixth episode finds the two doctors in Boston after the war, and it ends with the various reanimated bodies returning to tear West to pieces and bear off the fragments of his corpse through ancient underground tunnels leading to a cemetery.

George Julian Houtain, an amateur colleague of HPL, commissioned "Herbert West—Reanimator" for the early issues of his professional humor magazine, *Home Brew*. As such, it is difficult to deny that the tale is—or in the course of writing became—a parody, not only of itself but also of lurid supernatural fiction. HPL complained of his reduction to a Grub Street hack by writing a "manifestly inartistic" (*SL* 1.158) serial story, but he seems to have enjoyed the task. Some commentators state that HPL was not fully paid the $5 per episode promised by Houtain, but letters confirm that he received complete payment.

It has commonly been assumed that the obvious influence upon the story is Mary Shelley's *Frankenstein* (1818); but the method of West's reanimation of the dead (whole bodies that have died only recently) is very different from that of Victor Frankenstein (the assembling of a huge composite body from disparate parts of bodies), and only the most general influence can be detected. The core of the story is so elementary a weird conception that no literary source need be postulated.

The story is the first to mention Miskatonic University, although the name Miskatonic had been used in "The Picture in the House" (1920). Five of the six segments are set in New England. Bolton, the setting for the third episode, is the name of a real town in east-central Massachusetts; but it was not a "factory town" as HPL describes it, but rather a tiny agricultural community. This has led Robert D. Marten to assume that HPL did not then know of the existence of the real Bolton and coined the name independently. In the first segment the mention of the "deserted Chapman farmhouse beyond Meadow Hill" probably alludes to "the large Chapman house" (*SL* 1.108) in Providence, which burned down in February 1920.

See Robert D. Marten, "Arkham Country: In Rescue of the Lost Searchers," *LS* No. 39 (Summer 1998): 1–20.

Herrero, Mrs. In "Cool Air," the slatternly landlady of the brownstone on West 14th Street in New York City where Dr. Muñoz lives. Her son **Esteban** brings food, laundry, medicine, and other necessities to Dr. Muñoz, but when the latter's condition worsens, his mother refuses to permit Esteban to run errands for him.

Hiram. In "The Tomb," Jervas Dudley's faithful servant, who promises Dudley that he will be interred in the Hyde family vault.

"History of the *Necronomicon*." Sketch (715 words); written in the fall of 1927 (see *SL* 2.201). First published as a pamphlet (Oakman, Ala.: Rebel Press, [1938]) by Wilson Shepherd; rpt. *MW*.

A tongue-in-cheek "history" of the sinister book and its equally sinister author, Abdul Alhazred. HPL traces the book's history from its writing in the eighth century to its translation into Greek, Latin, and other languages, stressing the rarity of surviving copies of any edition of the book. HPL drew up the history largely in order to be consistent in subsequent references to the tome in fiction.

Hoadley, Abijah. In "The Dunwich Horror," a Congregational minister who in 1747 delivers a sermon on "the close presence of Satan and his imps" in Dunwich.

Hoag, Jonathan E[than] (1831–1927). Poet living in and around Troy, N.Y., who entered amateur journalism late in life. HPL wrote birthday poems to him from 1918 to 1927; they presumably corresponded, but no letters have surfaced. Hoag's descriptions of the Catskill Mountains may have contributed to the topographical atmosphere of "Beyond the Wall of Sleep" and "The Lurking Fear," set there. HPL compiled and wrote an introduction to Hoag's *Poetical Works* (privately printed, 1923); it constituted the first appearance of a work by HPL in hardcover. HPL, Samuel Loveman, and James F. Morton revised some of Hoag's poetry in the process of editing the volume. The book was funded by Hoag (not by HPL, as has sometimes been asserted). The poems "Death" (*Silver Clarion,* November 1918) and "To the American Flag" are included in the book; they were later attributed to HPL (first by Rheinhart Kleiner, who reprinted the poems in the *Californian,* Summer 1937), but seem clearly to be Hoag's; possibly HPL revised them. HPL wrote an elegy, "Ave atque Vale" (*Tryout,* December 1927), at Hoag's death. Hoag may have been a partial inspiration for the character Zadok Allen in "The Shadow over Innsmouth," whose life-dates exactly match Hoag's.

Hodgson, William Hope (1877–1918). Weird novelist and short story writer who died in Belgium during World War I. He wrote four novels—*The Boats of the "Glen Carrig"* (1907), *The House on the Borderland* (1908), *The Ghost Pirates* (1909), and *The Night Land* (1912)—all written around 1902–5, probably published in reverse order (see Gafford). There is also a story collection, *Carnacki, the Ghost-Finder* (1913), imitating Blackwood's "psychic detective," John Silence. HPL read Hodgson in 1934 at the urging of bibliophile Herman C. Koenig, who was circulating his Hodgson volumes among HPL's circle. HPL wrote an enthusiastic article, "The Weird Work of William Hope Hodgson" (*Phantagraph,* February 1937), and added a section on him for a putative revised version of "Supernatural Horror in Literature" (this revised version was not published until its appearance in *O*). The cosmic terror of *The House on the Borderland* and *The Night Land* may have influenced "The Shadow out of Time." Much of Hodgson's work was collected and published posthumously. HPL's enthusiasm for Hodgson's work no doubt influenced August Derleth's decision to republish much of it through Arkham House.

See Sam Moskowitz, "William Hope Hodgson," in Hodgson's *Out of the Storm* (1975); *William Hope Hodgson: Voyages and Visions,* ed. Ian Bell (1987); Sam Gafford, "Writing Backwards: The Novels of William Hope Hodgson," *Studies in Weird Fiction* No. 11 (Spring 1992): 12–15.

Holm, Axel (1612–1687). In "The Trap," a Danish scholar expert in both glass working and magic who designs a mirror that can draw human beings and other objects into a strange fourth-dimensional world within itself. He achieves a kind of immortality in this manner (so long as the mirror itself is intact), but finds existence to be extremely tiresome, enlivened only by drawing other people into the mirror-world.

Holt, Ebenezer. In "The Picture in the House," the eighteenth-century merchant from Salem who trades to the aged cannibal of the story a copy of Pigafetta's *Regnum Congo.*

"Homes and Shrines of Poe." Essay (2,010 words); written in July 1934. First published in the *Californian* (Winter 1934); rpt. *Acolyte* (Fall 1943), *MW,* and *CE4.*
   A brief survey of Poe's residences in Philadelphia, Richmond, Charlottesville, Baltimore, New York, and Fordham, all of which HPL had personally visited.

Hornig, Charles D[erwin] (1916–1999), youthful editor of *The Fantasy Fan* (September 1933–February 1935), the first important fanzine in weird fiction. Hornig, residing in Elizabeth, N.J., accepted HPL's offer to serialize a revised version of "Supernatural Horror in Literature" there, but the serialization had progressed only to the middle of Chapter 8 by the time of magazine's folding. Over much of the period he was editing *The Fantasy Fan,* Horning was also managing editor of *Wonder Stories* (1933–36). On May 25, 1935 (his nineteenth birthday), he met HPL in Providence. He edited *Science Fiction* (1939–41), *Future Fiction* (1939–40), and *Science Fiction Quarterly* (1940–41) but abandoned them all by 1941.

"Horror at Martin's Beach, The." Short story (2,410 words); written in collaboration with Sonia H. Greene, probably in June 1922. First published (as "The Invisible Monster") in *WT* (November 1923); first collected in *Cats;* corrected text in *HM.*
   The crew of a fishing smack kills a sea creature "fifty feet in length, of roughly cylindrical shape, and about ten feet in diameter" at Martin's Beach (an unspecified and imaginary locale, but presumably near Gloucester, Mass., which is mentioned several times). Scientists prove the creature to be a mere infant, hatched only a few days previously and probably originating from the deep sea; the day after it is placed on exhibition, it and the vessel that caught it disappear without a trace. Some days later a terrified cry for help emerges from the sea, and the lifeguards throw out a life-preserver to assist the stricken individual; but the life-preserver, attached to a long rope, appears to have been grasped by some nameless entity that pulls it out to sea, and when the lifeguards and other individuals attempt to reel it in, they not only find themselves unable to do so, but also find that they cannot release the rope. They are inexorably dragged to their deaths in the sea. The idea is that the parent of the infant creature has not only grasped the life-preserver but also hypnotized the rescuers so that their wills no longer function. (This is why Prof. Alton's article "Are Hypnotic Powers Confined to Recognized Humanity?" is cited early in the text.) The tale bears a striking (but accidental) similarity to the British horror film *Gorgo* (1961).

"Horror at Red Hook, The." Short story (8,400 words); written on August 1–2, 1925. First published in *WT* (January 1927); first collected in *BWS;* corrected text in *D;* annotated version in *An2, PZ,* and *DWH.*

Thomas Malone, an Irish police detective working from the Borough Hall station in Brooklyn (near the racially heterogeneous slum known as Red Hook), becomes interested in the case of Robert Suydam, a wealthy man of ancient Dutch ancestry who lives in Flatbush. Suydam first attracts notice by "loitering on the benches around Borough Hall in conversation with groups of swarthy, evil-looking strangers." He realizes that his clandestine activities must be masked by a façade of propriety; he foils the attempts of relatives to deem him legally incompetent by ceasing to be seen with the foreigners and marries Cornelia Gerritsen, "a young woman of excellent position" whose wedding attracts "a solid page from the Social Register." The wedding celebration held aboard a steamer at the Cunard Pier ends in horror as the couple is found horribly murdered and completely bloodless. Incredibly, officials follow the instructions written on a sheet of paper, signed by Suydam, and turn his body over to a suspicious group of men headed by "an Arab with a hatefully negroid mouth."

The scene shifts to a dilapidated church in Red Hook that has been turned into a dance-hall, in the basement of which loathsome monstrosities perform horrible rites to Lilith. Suydam's corpse, miraculously revivified, resists being sacrificed to Lilith and somehow manages to overturn the pedestal on which she rests (with the result that the corpse sends "its noisome bulk floundering to the floor in a state of jellyish dissolution"), thereby somehow ending the horror. All this time detective Malone merely watches from a convenient vantage point, although the sight so traumatizes him that he must spend many months recuperating in a small village in Rhode Island.

HPL notes in a letter to Frank Belknap Long that the story "deals with hideous cult-practices behind the gangs of noisy young loafers whose essential mystery has impressed me so much. The tale is rather long and rambling, and I don't think it is very good; but it represents at least an attempt to extract horror from an atmosphere to which you deny any qualities save vulgar commonplaceness" (*SL* 2.20). HPL records in his 1925 diary that he visited Red Hook on March 8, 1925. Sonia H. Greene in her memoir claims to supply the inspiration for the tale: "It was on an evening while he, and I think Morton, Sam Loveman and Rheinhart Kleiner were dining in a restaurant somewhere in Columbia Heights that a few rough, rowdyish men entered. He was so annoyed by their churlish behavior that out of this circumstance he wove 'The Horror at Red Hook'" (*The Private Life of H. P. Lovecraft* [Necronomicon Press, 1992], p. 12). Whether it was any single incident, or the cumulative effect of HPL's New York experience, that led to the writing of the story remains in doubt.

There is much local color in the story, derived from HPL's growing familiarity with Brooklyn. The dance-hall church is very likely modeled on a church (now destroyed) near the waterfront in Red Hook. This church was, evidently, actually once used as a dance hall. Suydam's residence is said to be in Martense Street (very close to 259 Parkside) and near the Dutch Reformed Church (on which "The Hound" was based); probably no specific house is intended, and there does not seem to be any on Martense Street that might correspond to it.

Another piquant reference, not relating to topography, is to the fact that some of the evil denizens of Red Hook are of a Mongoloid stock originating in Kurdistan—"and Malone could not help recalling that Kurdistan is the land of the Yezidis, last survivors of the Persian devil-worshippers." This appears to be a borrowing from E. Hoffmann Price's fine tale "The Stranger from Kurdistan," published in *WT* (July 1925), where mention is made of the devil-worshipping Yezidis. HPL would, however, not become personally acquainted with Price for another seven years.

Much of the magical mumbo-jumbo in the story was copied directly from the articles on "Magic" and "Demonology" (both by E. B. Tylor, celebrated author of the landmark anthropological work, *Primitive Culture* [1871]) from the 9th edition of the *Encyclopaedia Britannica,* which HPL owned. Specifically, these borrowings involve the Latin quotation from the medieval writer Antoine Delrio (or Del Rio), *An sint unquam daemones incubi et succubae, et an ex tali congressu proles nasci queat?* ("Have there ever been demons, incubi, and succubi, and from such a union can offspring be born?") from the entry on "Demonology"; and, from the entry on "Magic," the invocation uttered at the beginning and end of the story ("O friend and companion of night . . .") and the strange Graeco-Hebraic incantation that Malone finds on the wall of the dance-hall church. In a later letter (see "The Incantation from Red Hook," in *The Occult Lovecraft* [1975]) HPL attempts to supply a translation of the formula, but commits several errors in the process (the encyclopedia entry provided no translation).

The character of Malone may also have something to do with the genesis—or, rather, the particular form—of the story. Sometime before writing "The Horror at Red Hook" HPL had submitted "The Shunned House" to *Detective Tales,* the magazine that had been founded together with *WT* and of which Edwin Baird was the editor. But Baird rejected the story. HPL seems to have sought to make "The Horror at Red Hook" a kind of detective story by including the figure of a police detective, even though the actual narrative is supernatural. In early August 1925, HPL planned to send "The Horror at Red Hook" to *Detective Tales* (HPL to Lillian D. Clark, August 8, 1925; ms., JHL); whether he did so is unclear, but if so, the tale was rejected. HPL later remarked that the story was consciously written with *WT* in mind (HPL to August Derleth, November 26, 1926; ms., SHSW).

See Robert M. Price, "The Humor at Red Hook," *Crypt* No. 28 (Yuletide 1984): 6–9.

"Horror in the Burying-Ground, The." Short story (5,810 words); ghostwritten for Hazel Heald, c. 1933 or 1934. First published in *WT* (May 1937); first collected in *Cats;* corrected text in *HM.*

In the rustic town of Stillwater, the village undertaker, Henry Thorndike, has devised a peculiar chemical compound that, when injected into a living person, will simulate death even though the person is alive and conscious. Thorndike attempts to dispose of an enemy, Tom Sprague (of whose sister Sophie he is fond), in this fashion, but in the course of embalming the body he is himself injected with the substance. Although Thorndike, before he lapses into immobility, pleads not to be entombed, he is pronounced dead and buried alive.

HPL never mentions the story in any extant correspondence, so its date of composition is difficult to specify; but he seems not to have had much to do with Heald after 1934, and this is evidently the last of the tales he ghostwrote for her. Much of the story is narrated in a backwoods patois reminiscent—and perhaps a parody—of that used in "The Dunwich Horror." The use of the names Akeley (from "The Whisperer in Darkness"), Zenas (from "The Colour out of Space"), Atwood (from *At the Mountains of Madness*), and Goodenough (referring to HPL's amateur colleague Arthur Goodenough) suggest that the story is meant, if not as an actual parody, at least as an instance of graveyard humor.

"Horror in the Museum, The." Short story (11,440 words); ghostwritten for Hazel Heald, probably in October 1932. First published in *WT* (July 1933); first collected in *BWS;* corrected text in *HM.*

The curator of a waxworks museum in London, George Rogers, claims to have captured the deity Rhan-Tegoth on an expedition to Alaska. Rogers shows his skeptical friend Stephen Jones a photograph of the entity, and then shows him the corpse of a dog that has been sucked dry of blood, with puncture wounds all over its body; he claims that he had fed the dog to Rhan-Tegoth, who is kept locked in a crate in the basement of the museum. Irked by Jones's disbelief of his tale, Rogers challenges Jones to spend the night alone in the museum. Jones agrees, and in the course of the night he seems to hear curious noises in the basement; but it proves to be Rogers himself, who appears to have gone mad and wishes to sacrifice Jones to his deity. Jones manages to overpower Rogers and tie him up; but then both of them hear another noise, and Jones is horrified to see *"a black paw ending in a crab-like claw. . . ."* He flees. Coming back a week later, he sees what appears to be a wax statue of Rogers, drained of blood and with numerous puncture wounds on his body; his horror is augmented by noting a scratch on Rogers's cheek—one that had been made during their tussle.

HPL says of the story: "My latest revisory job comes so near to pure fictional ghost-writing that I am up against all the plot-devising problems of my bygone auctorial days" (HPL to E. Hoffmann Price, October 20, 1932; ms., JHL). Elsewhere HPL says: "'The Horror in the Museum'—a piece which I 'ghost-wrote' for a client from a synopsis so poor that I well-nigh discarded it—is virtually my own work" (*SL* 4.229). One would like to think the story a self-parody of HPL's own mythos: the description of Rhan-Tegoth brings Cthulhu to mind, but in this case we have not merely a representation of Cthulhu but the actual god himself, trapped in the basement of a museum. The sight of the "black paw" is reminiscent of the conclusion of "Under the Pyramids."

Houdini, Harry (pseudonym of Ehrich Weiss, 1874–1926), magician and debunker of spiritualism. In early 1924 J. C. Henneberger, owner of *WT,* in an attempt to salvage the magazine, hired Houdini—then at the height of his celebrity—as a regular columnist. The column "Ask Houdini" appeared in the issues for March, April, and May–June–July 1924. Houdini also appeared as the author of the short stories "The Hoax of the Spirit Lover" (April 1924) and "The Spirit Fakers of Hermannstadt" (March and April 1924), possibly ghostwritten by Walter Gibson. Henneberger commissioned HPL to write an account of an adventure that Houdini purportedly had in Egypt; but as HPL investigated the details of the incident (told to him in correspondence with Henneberger), he found that it was almost entirely mythical. HPL therefore asked Henneberger for as much imaginative latitude as possible in writing the story. The result was "Under the Pyramids" (published in the May–June–July issue as "Imprisoned with the Pharaohs"). Henneberger was going to print a joint byline to the story, but because HPL had written it in the first person (as if narrated by Houdini), he felt obliged to omit HPL's name. Houdini, reading the story in manuscript, expressed great approbation of it (see *SL* 1.328). In the fall of 1924, when HPL, now in New York, was having difficulty finding employment, Houdini asked HPL to visit him at his apartment at 278 West 113th Street in Manhattan, as he would put HPL in touch with "someone worth-while" (*SL*1.354). At the meeting, in early October, Houdini gave HPL an introduction to Brett Page, the head of a newspaper syndicate; HPL met Page on October 14, but no job resulted from it. In the fall of 1926 Houdini came in touch with HPL again. He first asked HPL to write an article attacking astrology, for which he paid $75 (see *SL* 2.76, 79). (This article apparently does not survive.) Then he commissioned HPL and C. M. Eddy (who may have done revision work for him at an earlier date) jointly to ghostwrite a full-scale book on superstition, but his sudden death on October 31 put an end to the plans, as Houdini's widow did not wish to pursue the project. A synopsis of the book, along with the text of one chapter, survive in HPL's papers under the title *The Cancer of Superstition* (in *DB*). Houdini gave HPL a copy of his own debunking of spiritualism, *A Magician among the Spirits* (1924), with the inscription: "To my friend Howard P. Lovecraft, / Best Wishes, / Houdini. / 'My brain is the key that sets me free.'"

See Ruth Brandon, *The Life and Many Deaths of Harry Houdini* (1993); Kenneth Silverman, *Houdini!!!* (1996).

Houghton, Dr. In "The Dunwich Horror," a physician who is summoned by Wilbur Whateley during Old Whateley's terminal illness.

"Hound, The." Short story (3,000 words); written c. October 1922; first published in *WT* (February 1924); rpt. *WT* (September 1939); first collected in *O;* corrected text in *D;* annotated version in *An2* and *CC*.

The story involves the escapades of the narrator and his friend St. John in that "hideous extremity of human outrage, the abhorred practice of grave-robbing." The two "neurotic virtuosi," who are "wearied with the commonplaces of a prosaic world," can find in this loathsome activity the only respite from their "devastating ennui." One day they seek the grave in Holland of "one buried for five centuries, who had himself been a ghoul in his time and had stolen a potent thing from a mighty sepulchre." When they unearth this grave, they find "much— amazingly much" left of the object despite the lapse of half a millennium. They find an amulet depicting a crouching winged hound and take this prize for their unholy museum of charnel objects in England.

Upon their return, strange things begin to happen. Their home seems besieged by a nameless whirring or flapping, and over the moors they hear the "faint, distant baying" as of a gigantic hound. One night, as St. John is walking home alone from the station, he is torn to ribbons by some "frightful carnivorous thing." As he lies dying, he manages to utter, "The amulet—that damned thing—." The narrator realizes that he must return the amulet to the Holland grave, but one night in Rotterdam thieves take it. Later the city is shocked by a "red death" in a squalid part of town. The narrator, driven by some fatality, returns to the churchyard and digs up the old grave. As he uncovers it, he finds "the bony thing my friend and I had robbed; not clean and placid as we had seen it then, but covered with caked blood and shreds of alien flesh and hair, and leering sentiently at me with phosphorescent sockets and sharp ensanguined fangs yawning twistedly in mockery of my inevitable doom." The narrator, after telling his tale, proposes to "seek with my revolver the oblivion which is my only refuge from the unnamed and unnamable."

The story was written sometime after HPL and his friend Rheinhart Kleiner visited the churchyard of the Dutch Reformed Church (1796) in Brooklyn on September 16, 1922. HPL remarks: "From one of the crumbling gravestones— dated 1747—I chipped a small piece to carry away. It lies before me as I write— & ought to suggest some sort of a horror-story. I must some night place it beneath my pillow as I sleep . . . who can say what *thing* might not come out of the centuried earth to exact vengeance for his desecrated tomb?" (*SL* 1.198). The character St. John is a clear nod to Kleiner, whom HPL referred to in correspondence as Randolph St. John, as if he were a relative of Henry St. John, Viscount Bolingbroke.

"The Hound" has been criticized for being overwritten, but it appears to be a self-parody, as becomes increasingly evident from the obvious literary allusions (St. John's "that damned thing" echoing the celebrated tale by Ambrose Bierce; the "red death" and the indefinite manner of dating ["On the night of September 24, 19—"], meant as playful nods to Poe; the baying of the hound clearly meant to recall Doyle's *The Hound of the Baskervilles;* and, as Steven J. Mariconda has demonstrated, many nods to Joris-Karl Huysmans, particularly *A Rebours*).

Some autobiographical touches in the story are noteworthy. While St. John is clearly meant to be Kleiner, the connection rests only in the name, as there is not much description of his character. The museum of tomb-loot collected by the protagonists may be a reference to Samuel Loveman's impressive collection of *objets d'art* (*not* taken from tombs): HPL first saw the collection in September 1922 and was much impressed by it. The original typescript of the story includes a reference to a new colleague: "A locked portfolio, bound in tanned human skin, held the unknown and unnamable drawings of Clark Ashton Smith." HPL revised this passage (on the advice of C. M. Eddy, Jr. [see *SL* 1.292–93]) before submitting it to *WT.*

In terms of HPL's developing pseudomythology, "The Hound" is important in that it contains the first explicit mention of the *Necronomicon* and attributes it to Abdul Alhazred.

See Steven J. Mariconda, "'The Hound'—A Dead Dog?" *Crypt* No. 38 (Eastertide 1986): 3–7; rpt. in Mariconda's *On the Emergence of "Cthulhu" and Other Observations* (Necronomicon Press, 1995); James Anderson, "A Structural Analysis of H. P. Lovecraft's 'The Hound,'" *Crypt* No. 88 (Hallowmas 1994): 3–5.

"House, The." Poem (36 lines in 4 stanzas); written c. July 16, 1919. First published in the *National Enquirer* (December 11, 1919); rpt. *Philosopher* (December 1920).

HPL notes (*SL* 1.357) that the poem was inspired by the same house (at 135 Benefit St.) in Providence that would later serve as the setting for "The Shunned House" (1924).

Houtain, George Julian (1884–1945), amateur journalist (President of the NAPA, 1915–17) who edited *The Zenith* and wrote a brief article, "20 Webster Street: Lovecraft," in the January 1921 issue (rpt. *LR*) after meeting HPL at an amateur convention in Boston in July 1920. They met again at another amateur convention in Boston on February 22, 1921. Houtain married E. Dorothy MacLaughlin; with her, he established the humor magazine, *Home Brew,* with elements of mild sexual titillation, for which he commissioned HPL to write a series of six "Grewsome Tales" for $5 each. HPL complied with "Herbert West—Reanimator" (serialized February–July 1922), his first professional fiction sale. HPL later wrote a four-part serial, "The Lurking Fear," for *Home Brew* (published January–April 1923). *Home Brew* later became *High Life* and folded sometime in 1924. HPL referred to it as a "vile rag" (*SL* 4.170).

Howard, Robert E[rvin] (1906–1936), pulp writer from Cross Plains, Tex., best known as the author of "sword and sorcery" tales of Conan, King Kull, Bran Mak Morn, and Solomon Kane, in which the supernatural, historical fiction, and adventure are mingled. When HPL's "The Rats in the Walls" was reprinted in *WT* (June 1930), Howard detected in the story what he believed to be an unconventional theory regarding the early settlement of Britain; he accordingly wrote to editor Farnsworth Wright, who passed the letter on to HPL. Their correspondence lasted until the end of Howard's life and was tremendously voluminous (an estimated 430,000 words—279,000 by Howard—survive). Much of it was devoted to lengthy, even acrimonious, disputes over the relative merits of civilization and barbarism (Howard, scion of one of the pioneer settlers of Texas, Dr. I. M. Howard, saw in barbarism a freedom and vigor lacking in modern life), and the relative merits of intellectual and physical activity. Howard's side survives largely intact, but HPL's letters were inadvertently destroyed by Dr. Howard some years after Howard's death; they now exist, only partially, in extensive transcripts prepared by Arkham House. Howard's *Selected Letters* (Necronomicon Press, 1989–91; 2 vols.) includes many of his letters to HPL.

Some of Howard's horror stories are indebted to HPL; notable among them are "The Black Stone" (*WT,* November 1931), "Worms of the Earth" (*WT,* November 1932), and "The Fire of Asshurbanipal" (*WT,* December 1936). Various items of Lovecraftian lore are mentioned in several stories. Most of Howard's Lovecraftian tales are collected in *Cthulhu* (1987). HPL mentioned the serpent-men of Valusia (from Howard's "The Shadow Kingdom" [*WT,* August 1929]) and one of Conan's forebears, the Cimmerian chieftain Crom-Ya, in "The Shadow out of Time" (1934–35). Howard invented an analogue to the *Necronomicon: Nameless Cults* (or the Black Book) by von Juntz (HPL supplied the author's first names, Friedrich Wilhelm). August Derleth then coined the putative

German title, *Unaussprechlichen Kulten.* Howard is one of the central characters in the spoof "The Battle That Ended the Century" (1934). HPL was shaken by Howard's suicide in June 1936, and he wrote a poignant tribute, "In Memoriam: Robert Ervin Howard" (*Fantasy Magazine,* September 1936); a shorter version, "Robert Ervin Howard: 1906–1936," appeared in the *Phantagraph,* August 1936.

See Glenn Lord, *The Last Celt: A Bio-bibliography of Robert Ervin Howard* (1976); L. Sprague de Camp, Catherine Crook de Camp, and Jane Whittington Griffin, *Dark Valley Destiny: The Life of Robert E. Howard* (1983); Don Herron, ed., *The Dark Barbarian: The Writings of Robert E. Howard: A Critical Anthology* (Greenwood Press, 1984); Marc A. Cerasini and Charles Hoffman, *Robert E. Howard* (1987); Robert M. Price, "Robert E. Howard and the Cthulhu Mythos," *LS* No. 18 (Spring 1989): 10–13, 29

Hutchins Family. In "The Dunwich Horror," neighbors of Wilbur Whateley. Wilbur shoots **Elam Hutchins's** dog Jack. Elam's relationship to "old" **Sam Hutchins** and **Will Hutchins,** who assist in exterminating Wilbur's twin brother, is unspecified.

Hutchinson, Edward. In *The Case of Charles Dexter Ward,* one of Joseph Curwen's colleagues in the pursuit of the "essential Saltes" by which human beings can be resuscitated after death. He lived in Salem-Village (i.e., Danvers) in the seventeenth and eighteenth centuries and has survived into the 1920s: Charles Dexter Ward visits him in Transylvania, where Hutchinson has a castle and goes by the name Baron Ferenczy. Dr. Willett takes measures to destroy him.

Hyde. In "The Tomb," the family whose ancestral vault is haunted by Jervas Dudley. Dudley becomes convinced that he is a Hyde when he finds an old porcelain miniature with his likeness and the initials J. H., for "Jervase Hyde."

"Hypnos." Short story (2,840 words); written c. March 1922. First published in *National Amateur* (May 1923); rpt. *WT* (May–June–July 1924) and *WT* (November 1937); first collected in *O;* corrected text in *D;* annotated version in *DWH.*

The narrator, a sculptor, encounters a man at a railway station. This person had fallen unconscious, and the narrator, struck with the man's appearance ("the face [was] . . . oval and actually *beautiful.* . . . I said to myself, with all the ardour of a sculptor, that this man was a faun's statue out of antique Hellas"), takes it upon himself to rescue the man, who becomes the sculptor's only friend. The two engage in "studies" of some nameless sort—studies "of that vaster and more appalling universe of dim entity and consciousness which lies deeper than matter, time, and space, and whose existence we suspect only in certain forms of sleep—those rare dreams beyond dreams which never come to common men, and but once or twice in the lifetime of imaginative men." The sensations they experience in dream are almost inexpressible, but the narrator's teacher is always "vastly in advance" in the exploration of these realms of quasi-entity. But at some point the teacher encounters some awesome horror that causes him to shriek into wakefulness. Previously they had augmented their dream-visions with drugs; now they take drugs in a desperate effort to keep awake. They reverse their previous reclusiveness (they had dwelt in an "old manor-house in hoary Kent") and seek as many "assemblies of the young and the gay" as they can, but it is all for naught. One night the teacher cannot stay awake for all the efforts of his sculptor friend, something happens, and all that is left of the teacher is an exquisitely sculpted bust of "a godlike head of such marble as only old Hellas could yield," with the word HYPNOS at the base. People maintain that the narrator never had a friend, but that "art, philosophy, and insanity had filled all my tragic life."

There is an ambiguity maintained to the end of the tale as to whether the narrator's friend actually existed or was merely a product of his imagination; but this point may not affect the analysis appreciably. The tale is, as with "The Other Gods," one of hubris, although more subtly suggested. At one point the narrator states: "I will hint—only hint—that he had designs which involved the rulership of the visible universe and more; designs whereby the earth and the stars would move at his command, and the destinies of all living things be his." If the friend really existed, then he is merely endowed with overweening pride and his doom—at the hands of the Greek god of sleep, Hypnos—is merited. On a psychological interpretation, the friend becomes merely an aspect of the narrator's own personality; note how, after the above statement, he adds harriedly, "I affirm—I swear—that I had no share in these extreme aspirations"—a clear instance of the conscious mind shirking responsibility for its subconscious fantasies. Like "Beyond the Wall of Sleep," the story features the notion that certain "dreams" provide access to other realms of entity beyond that of the five senses or the waking world.

An early entry in HPL's commonplace book (#23) provides the plot-germ for the story: "The man who would not sleep—dares not sleep—takes drugs to keep himself awake. Finally falls asleep—& *something* happens—" A recently discovered typescript of the tale bears the dedication "To S[amuel] L[oveman]," probably in recognition of his interest in Greek antiquity, evinced in much of his verse.

See Steven J. Mariconda, "H. P. Lovecraft: Art, Artifact, and Reality," *LS* No. 29 (Fall 1993): 2–12.

I

"Ibid." Short story (1,720 words); written probably in the summer of 1928. First published in *O-Wash-Ta-Nong* (January 1938); rpt. *Phantagraph* (June 1940); first collected in *Uncollected Prose and Poetry II* (1980); corrected text in *MW*.

In this "biography" of the celebrated Ibidus, the author is careful to point out that his masterpiece was not, as is sometimes believed, the *Lives of the Poets* but in fact the famous "*Op. Cit.* wherein all the significant undercurrents of Graeco-Roman expression were crystallised once for all." Ibid was born in 486 and taught rhetoric in Rome. His fortunes were mixed during the succession of barbarian invasions in Italy, and by 541 he had moved to Constantinople. He died in 587, but his remains later were exhumed and his skull began a long series of peregrinations and ended up—by way of Charlemagne, Alcuin, William the Conqueror, Oliver Cromwell, and others—in the New World, specifically in Salem, Mass., then in Providence, and finally in Milwaukee, where it rolled down into the burrow of a prairie-dog, only to be brought back to earth by a convulsion of Nature.

HPL on one occasion dated this sketch to 1927 (see HPL to Maurice W. Moe, January 19, [1931]; AHT), but the first mention of it is in a letter by Moe to HPL dated August 3, 1928, so a date of 1928 seems more probable. The story was either included in a letter to Moe or was a separate enclosure in a letter to him; its epigraph ("'. . . As Ibid says in his famous *Lives of the Poets.*'—From a student theme") may refer to an actual statement from a paper by one of Moe's students. HPL uses this real or fabricated piece of fatuity as the springboard for an exquisite tongue-in-cheek squib with numerous in-jokes (particularly in relation to HPL's residence in Providence and Moe's in Milwaukee).

The target of the satire in "Ibid" is not so much the follies of students as the pomposity of academic scholarship. It is full of learned but preposterous footnotes and owlish references to real and fabricated historical events. Moe considered submitting the sketch to the *American Mercury* or some such journal and asked

HPL to revise it slightly; but later he and HPL concluded that revision for a commercial magazine was not possible and that the work "would have to be content with private circulation" (Maurice W. Moe to HPL, January 29, 1931; ms., JHL).

"Idealism and Materialism—A Reflection." Essay (4,310 words); written in 1919/20/21. First published in the *National Amateur* ("July 1919"); rpt. *MW* and *CE5*.

Forceful essay presenting an anthropology of religion (derived largely from Nietzsche and from John Fiske's *Myths and Myth-Makers* [1872]), asserting that religious belief is a holdover from primitive times in which human beings invented gods as a means of explaining natural phenomena, the causes of which they did not understand. HPL mentions his "seeing" a dryad in the woods near his home at the age of seven or eight, an anecdote repeated in "A Confession of Unfaith" (1922). Its date of composition is unknown: the July 1919 *National Amateur* was long delayed and did not appear until the summer of 1921; as the issue also contained HPL's "The Picture in the House" (December 1920), the essay could have been written in 1920 or early 1921.

"In a Major Key." Essay (1,050 words); probably written in the summer of 1915. First published in the *Conservative* (July 1915); rpt. *MW* and *CE1*..

A response to Charles D. Isaacson's *In a Minor Key* that seeks to refute Isaacson's claims that Walt Whitman is a great American thinker and poet, that race prejudice is an unmitigated evil, and that pacifism is a morally upright stance to take in the face of the European war. The essay contains an untitled poem (18 lines), which in a letter HPL titled "Fragment on Whitman" (*SL* 1.57), condemning the sexual elements in Whitman's poetry.

"In a Sequester'd Providence Churchyard Where Once Poe Walk'd." Acrostic poem (13 lines); written on August 8, 1936. First published in *Four Acrostic Sonnets on Edgar Allan Poe* (1936); rpt. *Science-Fantasy Correspondent* (March–April 1937; as "In a Sequestered Churchyard Where Once Poe Walked"); *HPL* (Bellville, N.J.: Corwin F. Stickney, 1937); *WT* (May 1938) (as "Where Poe Once Walked").

The poem was written in St. John's Churchyard in Providence, where HPL and his guests R. H. Barlow and Adolphe de Castro wrote acrostic "sonnets" (they lack one line for a true sonnet) to Poe. De Castro promptly send his to *WT,* where it was accepted; HPL's and Barlow's were rejected, as Farnsworth Wright only wished one such poem. Maurice W. Moe hectographed the three poems, along with one of his own, in *Four Acrostic Sonnets on Edgar Allan Poe*. Later Henry Kuttner wrote another.

See David E. Schultz, "In a Sequester'd Churchyard," *Crypt* No. 57 (St. John's Eve 1988): 26–29, which reprints all five poems.

In Defence of Dagon. Collective title for a series of three essays: "The Defence Reopens!" (3,820 words; January 1921); "The Defence Remains Open!" (5,980 words; April 1921); and "Final Words" (2,100 words; September 1921). First published in its entirety in *In Defence of Dagon* (Necronomicon Press, 1985); rpt. *CE5*. Brief excerpts from the first two essays appeared as "In Defense of Dagon," *Leaves* (1938).

The essays were written in response to comments on HPL's poems and stories submitted to the Transatlantic Circulator, an Anglo-American organization of amateur journalists who circulated their work in manuscript and commented on it. The essays present a strong defense of HPL's brand of weird fiction (the weird writer is "the poet of twilight visions and childhood memories, but sings only for the sensitive"), calling upon Oscar Wilde's critical theories to combat the notion that weird art (or any art) can be "morbid" or "unhealthy." HPL also vigorously defends his atheistic materialism (first expressed in a letter or essay that does not now survive), maintaining that religion has been largely disproven by the sciences of physics and biology and that anthropology has accounted for the origin of religious belief. Many comments by other members of the Circulator (which included John Ravenor Bullen, who was perhaps responsible for HPL's entry into the group) survive at JHL.

"In Memoriam: Robert Ervin Howard." Essay (1,580 words); written in June or July 1936. First published in *Fantasy Magazine* (September 1936); rpt. *MW* and *CE5*.

Poignant overview of Howard's life and work, written shortly after his suicide. The essay is based largely on a letter to E. Hoffmann Price (July 5, 1936). A shorter version (probably written first) appeared as "Robert Ervin Howard: 1906–1936" (*Phantagraph,* August 1936). HPL also wrote a letter to *WT* on Howard's death (published in the letter column in October 1936).

"In the Editor's Study." A regular column of commentary in issues of the *Conservative* (1916–23); rpt. *The Conservative: Complete* (Necronomicon Press, 1976, 1977) and *CE1*.

The column appeared in seven issues of the paper. In October 1916 there were three subsections: "The Proposed Author's Union" (a satirical squib on unionization of authors); "Revolutionary Mythology" (on extravagant praise of the heroes of the American Revolution); and "The Symphonic Ideal" (on the need to remain "childlike and contented" in the modern age). In January 1917 there were two subsections: "The Vers Libre Epidemic" (an attack on free verse) and "Amateur Standards" (on a political feud in the UAPA). In July 1917 there was one subsection: "A Remarkable Document" (on a temperance article by Booth Tarkington). In July 1918 there were six subsections: "Anglo-Saxondom" (on the need for America and Great Britain to unite against immigrants); "Amateur Criticism" (on the criticism of amateur writing; specifically directed at Prof. Philip B. McDonald); "The United 1917–1918" (on the accomplishments of the UAPA during the past year); "The Amateur Press Club" (on a new international organization of amateur journalists); "Ward Phillips Replies" (a paragraph prefacing HPL's poem "Grace," responding to a poem written by Rheinhart Kleiner); and *"Les Mouches Fantastiques"* (on a literarily radical amateur journal edited by Elsa Gidlow and Roswell George Mills). In July 1919 there was one subsection: "The League" (a jaundiced look at the inability of the League of Nations to stop war). In March 1923 there were two subsections: "Rursus Adsumus" (on HPL's revival of the *Conservative*) and "Rudis Indigestaque Moles" (a condemnation of the literary radicalism of T. S. Eliot's *The Waste Land*). In

July 1923 the column appeared without any subsections, discussing the need to take cognizance of recent developments in art and philosophy.

"In the Vault." Short story (3,430 words); written on September 18, 1925. First published in *Tryout* (November 1925); rpt. *WT* (April 1932); first collected in *O;* corrected text in *DH;* annotated version in *PZ* and *DWH.*

George Birch is the careless and thick-skinned undertaker of Peck Valley, somewhere in New England. He finds himself trapped in the cemetery's receiving tomb where eight coffins are being stored for the winter by the slamming of the door in the wind and the breaking of the neglected latch. Birch realizes that the only way to escape the tomb is to pile the coffins like a pyramid and squeeze through the transom. Although working in the dark, he is confident that he has stacked the coffins in the sturdiest manner possible; in particular, he believes that he has placed the well-made coffin of the diminutive Matthew Fenner on the very top, rather than the flimsy coffin initially built for Fenner but later used for the tall Asaph Sawyer, a vindictive man whom he had not liked in life. Ascending his "miniature Tower of Babel," Birch finds that he has to knock out some of the bricks around the transom in order for his large body to escape. As he does so, his feet fall through the top coffin into the decaying contents within. He feels horrible pains in his ankles—as from splinters or loose nails—but manages to crawl out the window and drop to the ground. He cannot walk—his Achilles tendons have been cut—but drags himself to the cemetery lodge where he is rescued. Later Dr. Davis examines his wounds and finds them very unnerving. Going to the receiving-tomb, he learns the truth: Asaph Sawyer was too big to fit Fenner's coffin, so Birch had phlegmatically cut off Sawyer's feet at the ankles to make the body fit; but he had not reckoned on Sawyer's inhuman vengeance. The top coffin was not Fenner's but Sawyer's, and the wounds in Birch's ankles are teeth marks.

The plot of the story was suggested to HPL sometime in August 1925 by C. W. Smith, editor of *Tryout.* It is spelled out in a letter: ". . . an undertaker imprisoned in a village vault where he was removing winter coffins for spring burial, & his escape by enlarging a transom reached by the piling-up of the coffins" (*SL* 2.26). HPL has, of course, added a supernatural element. But the story remains a commonplace tale of supernatural vengeance. As in "Pickman's Model," HPL attempts unsuccessfully to write in a more homespun, colloquial vein.

HPL dedicated the story to C. W. Smith, "from whose suggestion the central situation is taken." HPL submitted it to Farnsworth Wright of *WT,* but it was rejected in November 1925; Wright gave as a reason the fact that (in HPL's words) "its extreme gruesomeness would not pass the Indiana censorship" (HPL to Lillian D. Clark, December 2, 1925; ms., JHL). The reference is to the banning of C. M. Eddy's "The Loved Dead." HPL then sent it to the *Tryout,* where it appeared in the issue for November 1925 (the issue was published in early December). Later, in August 1926, the story was submitted to *Ghost Stories,* a very crude pulp magazine that specialized in purportedly "true" confession-style stories involving the supernatural; possibly HPL felt that the plain style of the tale would pass muster with the editors, but it was rejected. Finally, in late 1931, after August Derleth prepared a new typescript to replace HPL's tattered original, HPL resubmitted the story to *WT* at Derleth's urging. It was accepted, and HPL was paid $55.

"In the Walls of Eryx." Short story (12,000 words); written in collaboration with Kenneth J. Sterling, January 1936. First published in *WT* (October 1939); first collected in *BWS;* corrected text in *D*.

Kenton J. Stanfield, of the Venus Crystal Company, is exploring for the valuable crystals—used for power both on Venus and back on earth—near the company's post of Terra Nova when he sees an immense crystal sitting in a field on the plateau (the "Erycinian Highland") of Eryx. (In Greek mythology, Eryx is the son of Aphrodite [Venus].) Approaching the object at a run, Stanfield is startled to encounter an invisible obstruction. He gradually realizes that the object is an invisible maze, made of some glasslike substance that is preternaturally hard. He finds an entrance and begins to approach the crystal, which appears to be in the very center of the maze. He continually seems to make progress but is always halted by an unexpected barrier. Stanfield begins to crack under the strain and is half convinced there is something supernatural about the maze. Then the "man-lizards" native to Venus surround the maze and seem to mock Stanfield by waving their feelers at him. Days pass; Stanfield's supply of oxygen and food dwindle; every attempt to find the right passageway to the crystal fails, nor can Stanfield find his way out of the maze. Finally he collapses and dies. His body, and the diary he had kept, is found by another operative of the Venus Crystal Company, who realizes that Stanfield could easily have emerged from the maze by proceeding through the opening *behind* him.

Sterling has stated that the idea of the invisible maze was his and that this core idea was adapted from Edmond Hamilton's story (which HPL liked), "The Monster-God of Mamurth" (*WT,* August 1926), which concerns an invisible building in the Sahara Desert. Sterling wrote a draft of 6,000 to 8,000 words; HPL rewrote the story ("in very short order," Sterling declares) on a small pad of lined paper, making it considerably longer in the process (see Sterling, "Caverns Measureless to Man" [1976]; in *LR*, pp. 375–78). Sterling's account suggests that the version as we have it is entirely HPL's prose, and indeed it reads as such; but one suspects (Sterling's original draft is not extant) that, as with the collaborated tales with Price and Lumley, HPL tried to preserve as much of Sterling's own prose, and certainly his ideas, as possible.

The authors have made the tale amusing with in-jokes on certain mutual colleagues: Kenton J. Stanfield's initials are those of Sterling; sificlighs = Science Fiction League, to which Sterling belonged; farnoth-flies = editor Farnsworth Wright of *WT;* ugrats = Hugo the Rat, HPL's name for editor Hugo Gernsback of *Wonder Stories;* effjay weeds and wriggling akmans = Forrest J. Ackerman; tuckahs = Bob Tucker; darohs = Jack Darrow, these latter three being well-known fans. Some jokes are probably HPL's, since they resemble the punning names he devised for "The Battle That Ended the Century."

The hackneyed use of Venus as a setting for the tale is perhaps its one significant drawback. The notion of a human being walking without difficulty (albeit with an oxygen mask and protective suit) on the surface of Venus was not preposterous in its day. There was much speculation as to the surface conditions of the planet, some astronomers believing it to be steamy and swampy like our own Palaeozoic age, others that it is a barren desert blown by dust storms; still others thought the planet covered with huge oceans of carbonated water or even with hot oil. It was only in 1956 that radio waves showed the surface temperature to be a minimum of 570° F, while in 1968 radar and radio observations at last confirmed the temperature to be 900° F and the surface atmospheric pressure to be at least ninety times that of the earth.

HPL's handwritten draft was presumably typed by Sterling, since the existing typescript is in an unrecognizable typewriter face. The byline reads (surely at HPL's insistence) "By Kenneth Sterling and H. P. Lovecraft." Sterling reports that the story was submitted to *WT* shortly after it was written but was rejected. It apparently was then submitted to *Astounding Stories, Blue Book, Argosy, Wonder Stories,* and perhaps *Amazing Stories* (all these names, except the last, are crossed out on a sheet prefacing the typescript). Finally it was resubmitted to *WT* and accepted. Sterling received $120, half of which he gave to HPL's surviving aunt, Annie E. P. Gamwell.

Innsmouth. Fictitious city invented by HPL. Innsmouth was first mentioned in "Celephaïs" (1920), but clearly set in England. It was revived for two sonnets ("The Port" [VIII] and "The Bells" [XIX]) of *Fungi from Yuggoth* (1929–30), where the setting is unspecified, although New England seems likely. In "The Shadow over Innsmouth" (1931) it is unequivocally set on the North Shore of Massachusetts. HPL states in letters that it was inspired by his revisiting of the decaying town of Newburyport (see *SL* 3.435), although that city has now been much restored as a haven for tourists. Innsmouth is briefly cited again in "The Dreams in the Witch House" (1932) and "The Thing on the Doorstep" (1933).

Iranon. In "The Quest of Iranon," the bard who seeks his far-off home of Aira where he is a prince. In Teloth, the inhabitants have no use for his "profession," and they force him to work as a cobbler. Iranon does not age. He later sets out on a voyage, with a young friend, Romnod, to seek Aira. After many years he learns that he is no prince at all, but only a beggar's son. He dies an old man.

Isaacson, Charles D[avid] (1891–1936). Amateur journalist who edited *In a Minor Key,* the first issue of which (undated, but published in early 1915) advocated pacifism, condemned prejudice against African Americans and Jews, and praised Walt Whitman; HPL responded with a hostile attack, "In a Major Key" (*Conservative,* July 1915). Isaacson shot back with "Concerning the Conservative" (*In a Minor Key* No. 2 [1915]), as did James F. Morton in another article in the same issue. HPL promised to write a devastating rebuttal, but aside from a poetical squib, "Gems from 'In a Minor Key'" (*Conservative,* October 1915), he published nothing; later in the year he wrote a long satirical poem, "The Isaacsonio-Mortoniad," attacking both Isaacson and Morton, but did not publish it. Isaacson visited HPL briefly when passing through Providence on July 1, 1916. He later wrote several books on music: *Face to Face with Great Musicians* (1918–21; 2 vols.) and *The Simple Story of Music* (1928).

"Isaacsonio-Mortoniad, The." Poem (136 lines); written no later than September 14, 1915. First published in *Saturnalia and Other Poems* (1984).

Part of HPL's feud with Charles D. Isaacson and James F. Morton, who had responded to HPL's attacks on Isaacson's amateur paper, *In a Minor Key* (see HPL's "In a Major Key," *Conservative,* July 1915) with attacks of their own in the second issue of *In a Minor Key* (undated, but probably dating to September 1915). The pungent satire claims to reveal the absurdities and inconsistencies in Isaacson's defense of Walt Whitman and his appeals for racial tolerance, and Morton's evangelical atheism. HPL apparently decided against publishing the poem in the amateur press.

Iwanicki, Father. In "The Dreams in the Witch House," a Catholic priest at St. Stanislaus' Church in Arkham who gives a crucifix to one of Walter Gilman's friends, Joe Mazurewicz, who then gives it to Gilman to protect him from Keziah Mason. Iwanicki had first been cited in the so-called "discarded draft" of "The Shadow over Innsmouth" (written in late 1931, a few months before "The Dreams in the Witch House"), but was excised from the final draft. See *MW* 65.

J

Jack. The narrator of "The Man of Stone," who accompanies Ben Hayden on a trip to see the celebrated sculptures of Arthur Wheeler.

Jackson, Henry. In "The Man of Stone," a man who is treated for tuberculosis near Lake Placid, N.Y., where he hears of the tale that constitutes the narrative of the story and which he passes on to his friend, Ben Hayden, who then goes to investigate the story.

Jackson, Winifred Virginia (1876–1959). Amateur poet living in the Boston area and friend of HPL. HPL was extensively involved with Jackson in amateur journalism during the period 1918–21. He wrote a brief biographical sketch of her, "Winifred Virginia Jordan: Associate Editor" (*Silver Clarion,* April 1919; as by "El Imparcial"), followed by a lengthy critical analysis, "Winifred Virginia Jackson: A 'Different' Poetess" (*United Amateur,* March 1921); he published several of her poems in his amateur journal, *The Conservative;* he contributed a poem on Jonathan E. Hoag to her amateur journal, *Eurus* (February 1918); he served as Official Critic for another journal edited by Jackson, *The Bonnet,* for whose only known issue (June 1919) he contributed a poem ("Helene Hoffman Cole: 1893–1919: The Club's Tribute") and an unsigned editorial ("Trimmings"); he joined her in editing *The United Co-operative,* three issues of which were published (December 1918, June 1919, April 1921). On a more personal level, he wrote a poem to her ("On Receiving a Portraiture of Mrs. Berkeley, ye Poetess") on Christmas Day 1920, after receiving her photograph; the title refers to the pseudonym (Elizabeth Berkeley) under which she widely appeared in the amateur press. The poem was evidently not published at the time. By this time HPL had collaborated with her on a story, "The Green Meadow," based upon a dream by Jackson; later, probably in 1921, they collaborated on "The Crawling Chaos"; both were published as by "Elizabeth Berkeley and Lewis Theobald, Jun."

Their relations may have been somewhat more personal. According to research by George T. Wetzel and R. Alain Everts, HPL and Jackson were widely regarded in amateur circles as being romantically involved. Evidence for this assertion is somewhat indirect, the strongest coming from HPL's wife Sonia, who purportedly stated, "I stole HPL away from Winifred Jackson." There is also a photograph of HPL and Jackson at the seaside (probably in Massachusetts). But since HPL stated to Sonia in the summer of 1922 that he had not been kissed since he was a boy, the "romance" must have been somewhat lacking in passion. Also, Wetzel and Everts claim that Jackson married an African American, Horace Jackson, in 1915 (hence her appearance in earlier amateur journals as Winifred Virginia Jordan); she had divorced him by early 1919 and then carried on a longtime affair with the African American poet and critic William Stanley Braithwaite (1878–1962). If HPL had known of either involvement, he presumably—given his severe prejudice against African Americans—would have ceased all relations with Jackson. HPL met Jackson on several occasions, but always at amateur gatherings in the company of others: July 4–5 and September 5, 1920, in Allston, Mass., and (probably) at the NAPA convention in early July 1921 (the same convention at which he first met Sonia). There is no evidence that HPL met or corresponded with her after July 1921.

Jackson's poem "Insomnia" (*Conservative*, October 1916) may have influenced the opening quatrains of HPL's "Psychopompos" (1917–18). That issue contained "The Unknown," as by "Elizabeth Berkeley"; the poem is actually by HPL. He later stated that this poem and another ("The Peace Advocate," *Tryout*, July 1917) had appeared under Jackson's pseudonym "in an effort to mystify the [amateur] public by having widely dissimilar work from the same nominal hand" (HPL to the Gallomo, September 12, 1921; AHT). Jackson published only two books of poetry, *Backroads: Maine Narratives, with Lyrics* (1927) and *Selected Poems* (1944).

See George T. Wetzel and R. Alain Everts, *Winifred Virginia Jackson—Lovecraft's Lost Romance* (Strange Co., 1976).

Jacobi, Carl (1908–1997). Minnesota author of over 100 stories in pulp magazines including *WT, Terror Tales, Amazing Stories, Short Stories, Galaxy, Fantastic Universe, Mike Shayne Mystery Magazine, Thrilling Adventures,* and *Thrilling Mystery.* HPL enjoyed Jacobi's "Mive" (originally a prize-winning story in Fall 1928 issue of *Minnesota Quarterly,* the student magazine of the University of Minnesota) in *WT* (January 1932) and wrote to Jacobi about it (see *SL* 4.24–25). Two stories show Lovecraftian influence: "The Tomb from Beyond" (*Wonder Stories,* November 1933) and "The Aquarium" (in August Derleth's *Dark Mind, Dark Heart* [1962]). Jacobi published three collections with Arkham House: *Revelations in Black* (1947), *Portraits in Moonlight* (1964), *Disclosures in Scarlet* (1972); a final collection of tales, *Smoke of the Snake,* appeared in 1994.

See R. Dixon Smith, *Lost in the Rentharpian Hills: Spanning the Decades with Carl Jacobi* (1985).

James, M[ontague] R[hodes] (1862–1936). British author of four celebrated volumes of ghost stories—*Ghost-Stories of an Antiquary* (1904), *More Ghost*

Stories of an Antiquary (1911), *A Thin Ghost and Others* (1919), and *A Warning to the Curious* (1925)—all of which HPL owned and spoke of enthusiastically in "Supernatural Horror in Literature." (James also wrote a children's fantasy, *The Five Jars* [1922], which HPL read but did not own.) HPL came upon James at the New York Public Library in December 1925, when he began research for his essay. At that time he ranked James as one of the four "modern masters" (along with Machen, Blackwood, and Dunsany), but in later years he complained that James had no sense of the "cosmic," and by 1932 he referred to him as "the earthiest member of the 'big four'" (*SL* 4.15). Nevertheless, James's structural complexity may have influenced HPL, especially in his longer tales. Richard Ward has made a good case for the influence of James's "Count Magnus" upon HPL's *The Case of Charles Dexter Ward*. James's ghost stories were collected in the much-reprinted volume, *The Collected Ghost Stories of M. R. James* (1931). In his own day, James was better known as an authority on medieval manuscripts and a Biblical scholar. His edition of the *Apocryphal New Testament* (1924) long remained standard.

See S. G. Lubbock, *A Memoir of Montague Rhodes James* (1939); Jack Sullivan, *Elegant Nightmares: The English Ghost Story from LeFanu to Blackwood* (1978); Richard William Pfaff, *Montague Rhodes James* (1980); Michael Cox, *M. R. James: An Informal Portrait* (1983); Richard Ward, "In Search of the Dread Ancestor: M. R. James' 'Count Magnus' and Lovecraft's *The Case of Charles Dexter Ward*," *LS* No. 36 (Spring 1997): 14–17.

Jermyn, Arthur. In "Facts Concerning the Late Arthur Jermyn and His Family," a poet and scholar who sets fire to himself after examining a boxed object from Africa. The entire Jermyn line is marked by a strange history. In the eighteenth century, **Sir Wade Jermyn,** Arthur's great-great-great-grandfather, explored the Congo, bringing back with him a mysterious wife. **Sir Philip Jermyn,** Wade's son and Arthur's great-great-grandfather, though a baronet, joins the navy as a common sailor and disappears one night as his ship lay off the coast of the Congo. **Sir Robert Jermyn,** Arthur's great-grandfather, kills his entire family except for a two-year old grandson, when he learns certain information about his past. Philip's second son, **Nevil,** marries a commoner and sires a son, **Sir Alfred Jermyn,** who is Arthur's father. He joins the Barnum & Bailey circus (never explicitly named, but alluded to as "The Greatest Show on Earth") but is killed by a gorilla with whom he was conducting a boxing match.

Johansen, Gustav. In "The Call of Cthulhu," the Norwegian second mate of the schooner *Emma*. He is the sole survivor of the ship's crew and is rescued, on board the *Alert,* which his crew had boarded after their own vessel was sunk in a melee with that ship's crew. Thurston, the narrator, learns of his experience in a chance newspaper article, and when Thurston seeks him in Oslo, he finds that, like Prof. Angell, he has died under mysterious circumstances. Johansen's diary describes his crew's encounter with Cthulhu.

Johnson, Dr. Richard H. (d. 1933). In "Out of the Æons," the curator of the Cabot Museum of Archaeology in Boston. The story is a manuscript prepared by him before his mysterious death by heart failure. It is he who obtains the strange living mummy for the museum.

Jones, Algernon Reginald. In "Sweet Ermengarde," a "city chap" who seeks to seduce Ermengarde Stubbs but is rejected.

Jones, Dr. In "The Last Test," the jealous assistant of Dr. Alfred Clarendon at San Quentin Penitentiary, who contrives to have Clarendon removed from his post and himself appointed in his place.

Jones, Stephen. In "The Horror in the Museum," the doubting friend of George Rogers, who spends a night in Rogers's Museum. When he glimpses a monstrous creature there, he flees; upon returning a week later, he finds that Rogers has been destroyed by the creature.

Juvenile Works: Fiction. Aside from HPL's surviving juvenile fiction—"The Little Glass Bottle," "The Secret Cave," "The Mystery of the Grave-yard," "The Mysterious Ship," "The Beast in the Cave," and "The Alchemist" (see entries on these tales)—we know of several other nonextant tales written prior to 1908.

HPL's first work of fiction was "The Noble Eavesdropper" (1897), which concerned "a boy who overheard some horrible conclave of subterranean beings in a cave" (HPL to J. Vernon Shea, July 19–31, 1931; ms., JHL). It may have been inspired by the *Arabian Nights,* with its frequent citation of caves. Other stories written prior to 1902 were "The Haunted House" and "John, the Detective." The latter presumably focused on HPL's dime-novel detective, King John (featured in "The Mystery of the Grave-yard"). HPL also cites a tale called "The Secret of the Grave," but this may be the same as "The Mystery of the Grave-yard." In 1905 he wrote a tale called "Gone—but Whither?" Late in life he discovered the composition book containing the title of the story and remarked: "I'll bet it was a hell-raiser! The title expresses the fate of the tale itself" (*SL* 5.140).

HPL also notes writing "several yarns" about Antarctica around 1899, inspired by W. Clark Russell's *The Frozen Pirate* (1887). HPL was also devoted to Jules Verne, noting that "many of my tales showed the literary influence of the immortal Jules"; he goes on to describe one of them: "I wrote one story about that side of the moon which is forever turned way from us—using, for fictional purposes, the Hansen theory that air and water still exist there as the result of an abnormal centre of gravity in the moon. I hardly need add that the theory is really exploded—I was even aware of that fact at the time—but I desired to compose a 'thriller'" (*SL* 1.19).

HPL also claimed to have written detective stories "very often, the works of A. Conan Doyle being my model so far as plot was concerned." In describing one he writes: "One long-destroyed tale was of twin brothers—one murders the other, but conceals the body, and tries to *live the life of both*—appearing in one place as himself, and elsewhere as his victim. (Resemblance had been remarkable.) He meets sudden death (lightning) when posing as the dead man—is identified by a scar, and the secret is finally revealed in his diary. This, I think, antedates my 11th year" (*SL* 1.20). As late as September 1934, he still contemplated developing a story along similar lines (*SL* 5.33–34).

HPL's fascination with ancient Rome led to the writing of at least one tale: "The idea of a Roman settlement in America is something which occurred to me years ago—in fact, I began a story with that theme (only it was about Central America & not U.S.) in 1906 or 1907, tho' I never finish'd it" (HPL to Lillian D. Clark, November 14–19, 1925; ms., JHL).

Of "The Picture" (1907) HPL remarks: "I had a man in a Paris garret paint a mysterious canvas embodying the quintessential essence of all horror. He is found clawed & mangled one morning before his easel. The picture is destroyed, as in a titanic struggle—but in one corner of the frame a bit of canvas remains ... & on it the coroner finds to his horror the painted counterpart of the sort of claw which evidently killed the artist" (*Letters to Robert Bloch* [Necronomicon Press, 1993], p. 15). The story seems to anticipate "Pickman's Model" (1926).

Juvenile Works: Poetry. HPL's earliest surviving work is a poem: "The Poem of Ulysses: Written for Young People." The extant manuscript is labeled a "second edition" and dated to November 8, 1897; the first edition presumably dates prior to August 20, 1897, since HPL states that the work was initially written at the age of six ("A Confession of Unfaith" [1922]). It is a retelling of the basic plot of the *Odyssey* in 88 lines, based upon HPL's readings in Bulfinch's *Age of Fable,* Pope's translation of the *Odyssey,* and a work that HPL refers to as "Harpers Half Hour Series" (presumably a paraphrase of the *Odyssey* for juveniles). The meter is derived from HPL's early favorite, Coleridge's *Rime of the Ancient Mariner.* It was first published in *Juvenilia: 1897–1905* (1984).

There are four other surviving juvenile poetical works. "Ovid's Metamorphoses" is a fairly literal verse translation of the first 88 lines of Ovid's poem (HPL's version takes 116 lines) and shows that HPL had learned Latin well enough by this time to perform the task. It probably dates to around 1900, as it is listed in a catalogue of works found at the back of *Poemata Minora, Volume 2* (September 1902). "H. Lovecraft's Attempted Journey betwixt Providence & Fall River on the N.Y.N.H.H.&H.R.R." (1901) is a comic poem that speaks of HPL's first ride on a trolley car through Providence and adjoining suburbs. "C.S.A.: 1861–1865" (1902) is a work supporting the South (Confederate States of America) during the Civil War. HPL notes (letter to Rheinhart Kleiner, November 16, 1916; AHT) that he placed it on the desk of Abbie E. Hathaway (principal of the Slater Avenue School), whose father was a Union soldier. *Poemata Minora, Volume 2* consists of five short poems: "Ode to Selene or Diana," "To the Old Pagan Religion," "On the Ruin of Rome," "To Pan," and "On the Vanity of Human Ambition." The text is profusely illustrated by HPL's drawings. HPL published three of the poems (under pseudonyms) in the *Tryout,* April 1919: the first as "To Selene," the second as "The Last Pagan Speaks," and the fourth as "Pan." *Poemata Minora* as a whole was first published in *Juvenilia: 1897–1905.* There is no indication of the contents of Volume 1, which apparently dates to 1901.

We know of several other nonextant poetical works: "The Iliad" and "The Aeneid" (presumably paraphrases of the ancient epics), "The Hermit," and "The

Argonauts" (presumably a retelling of the voyage of the *Argo* as recounted by Apollonius Rhodius and other writers).

One last surviving poem is "De Triumpho Naturae: The Triumph of Ignorance over Northern Ignorance" (July 1905). This viciously racist work is based upon (and dedicated to) William Benjamin Smith, author of the tract *The Color Line: A Brief in Behalf of the Unborn* (1905), which asserted, among other things, that freed African Americans will eventually die out because of their inherent biological inferiority and their physiological and psychological weaknesses. HPL's poem is a poetical encapsulation of the idea.

All extant works are included in *AT.*

Juvenile Works: Science. Aside from *The Scientific Gazette, The Rhode Island Journal of Astronomy,* and *Astronomy/The Monthly Almanack,* HPL wrote numerous other periodicals and treatises on chemistry, astronomy, and other subjects prior to 1908.

Of chemical treatises, four survive: *Chemistry, Chemistry, Magic & Electricity* (presumably *Chemistry II*), *Chemistry III,* and *Chemistry IV.* In a catalogue of his works at the back of *Poemata Minora, Volume 2* (1902), HPL noted a series of chemistry books in six volumes; these are presumably the first four. There are also two separate treatises, *The Art of Fusion Melting Pudling & Casting* and *A Good Anaesthetic.* Nonextant treatises include: *Iron Working; Acids; Explosives;* and *Static Electricity.*

Of astronomical treatises, there is one issue of *The Planet* (1, No. 1, August 29, 1903); *My Opinion as to the lunar canals* (dated 1903); *Annals of the Providence Observatory, Vol. 1: Observations of a General Character During 1903* (1904); and *Providence Observatory: Forecast for Providence & Vicinity Next 24h* (a forecast for April 4–5, 1904). There are three surviving volumes of a series of monographs under the general title "The Science Library": 1. *Naked Eye Selenography;* 2. *The Telescope;* 5. *On Saturn and His Ring.* The six missing volumes are: 3. *Life of Galileo;* 4. *Life of Herschel (revised);* 6. *Selections from Author's "Astronomy";* 7. *The Moon, Part I;* 8. *The Moon, Part II;* 9. *On Optics.*

Several early treatises (nonextant) testify to HPL's devotion to geography, specifically his fascination with Antarctica: *Antarctic Atlas, Voyages of Capt. Ross, R.N.,* and *Wilkes's Explorations.* The last treatise was extant as late as 1936, as HPL sent it to C. L. Moore, who returned it to HPL after seeing it (see *SL* 5.237).

Of miscellaneous treatises there is extant one issue of *The Railroad Review* (1, No. 1, December 1901). Nonextant are such works as *Mythology for the Young* (possibly a condensation of Bulfinch's *Age of Fable,* which HPL read around the age of five), *Egyptian Myths,* and two historical treatises: *Early Rhode Island* and *An Historical Account of Last Year's War with SPAIN* (1899).

In 1905 HPL produced one of his most substantial juvenile works: *A Manual of Roman Antiquities.* In the *Rhode Island Journal of Astronomy* (July 30, 1905) HPL gives an outline of the work, stating that it will also contain "biographies of certain great Romans"; but a notice in the *Rhode Island Journal* of August 13, 1905, states that the volume is ready but that the biographies could not be included. The work does not survive.

Also nonextant is *A Brief Course in Astronomy—Descriptive, Practical, and Observational; for Beginners and General Readers* (1906), of which HPL states: "it got as far as the typed and hand-illustrated stage (circa one hundred and fifty pages)" (*SL* 5.141). One part of the work appears to be extant in AHT, under the title *Celestial Objects for All*. Its preface declares that "The greater part of this work is also printed in 'A Brief Course in Astronomy' by the same author."

HPL's juvenile scientific work culminates in *A Brief Course in Inorganic Chemistry* (1910), written during his "recluse" phase of 1908–13, when he was taking correspondence courses in chemistry. HPL only describes it as a "bulky manuscript" (*SL* 1.75), and we know nothing more about it.

K

Kalem Club. Informal band of friends in New York City, of which HPL was the central figure. According to Rheinhart Kleiner, the club existed in a rudimentary form prior to HPL's advent to New York in March 1924, its original members including Rheinhart Kleiner, Everett McNeil, and perhaps James F. Morton. When HPL arrived, he introduced several more members, notably Frank Belknap Long, George Kirk, and Arthur Leeds. The club initially met on Thursday nights, but later shifted to Wednesdays because Long attended night classes at New York University. Still later there were separate "McNeil" and "Leeds" meetings because of a dispute between these two members over a small loan that the former had made to the latter; many members did not go to the McNeil meetings (held at Everett McNeil's apartment in Hell's Kitchen) because they found McNeil tiresome. HPL always attended both meetings. The club was not named until February 1925; Kirk provides an account of the event: "Because all of the last names of the permanent members of our club begin with K, L or M, we plan to call it the KALEM KLYBB" (George Kirk to Lucile Dvorak, February 1925; quoted in Hart, "Walkers in the City" [see under George Kirk]). HPL, however, never refers to it under this name in his correspondence, making mention only of "the gang" or "The Boys." The club achieved its heyday in 1925, especially with HPL largely unemployed and living by himself. HPL took pride in being a solicitous host for the meetings held at his apartment, purchasing an aluminum pail for 49¢ to fetch coffee from the neighboring delicatessen; he would serve it and various desserts on his best china. In late 1925 Wilfred B. Talman and Vrest Orton were enrolled as members, but it was decided that the name would not be changed; these two were very sporadic participants in any event. By the spring of 1928, however (two years after HPL's departure from New York), HPL notes that the club had "almost dissolved" (HPL to Lillian D. Clark, April 29–30, 1928; ms., JHL), leading one to suspect that he had been the driving force behind it.

See Rheinhart Kleiner, "After a Decade and the Kalem Club," *Californian* 4, No. 2 (Fall 1936): 45–47; rpt. *LS* No. 28 (Spring 1993): 34–35.

Kalos. In "The Tree," the sculptor, erstwhile friend of Musides, who competes with him in creating a sculpture of Tyché for the Tyrant of Syracuse. Musides poisons Kalos that he may take the prize, but Kalos exacts revenge from beyond the grave. The name means "fair" or "beautiful" in Greek.

Kingsport. Fictitious city in Massachusetts invented by HPL. Kingsport first appeared in "The Terrible Old Man" (1920) but was not then based upon any specific site; only in "The Festival" (1923) was it identified with Marblehead, a living museum of colonialism, which HPL visited in December 1922. It is cited briefly in "The Silver Key" (1926), used extensively in "The Strange High House in the Mist" (1926), and mentioned glancingly in *The Dream-Quest of Unknown Kadath* (1926–27), *The Case of Charles Dexter Ward* (1927), "The Shadow over Innsmouth" (1931), "Through the Gates of the Silver Key" (1932–33), and "The Thing on the Doorstep" (1933). A Kingsport Head (presumably a headland near the town) is cited in *At the Mountains of Madness* (1931) and "The Shadow over Innsmouth."

Kirk, George Willard (1898–1962). Bookseller, publisher, and friend of HPL. Born in Akron, Ohio, he entered the book trade at an early age. He spent the years 1920–22 in California, where he became acquainted with Clark Ashton Smith. In early 1922 he published his only book: Samuel Loveman's edition of *Twenty-one Letters of Ambrose Bierce.* He met HPL when the latter came to Cleveland in August 1922; at that time Kirk gave HPL a copy of Smith's *Odes and Sonnets* (1918), thereby encouraging HPL to get in touch with Smith. In August 1924 Kirk came to New York to establish a bookshop. By this time he was engaged to Lucile Dvorak but did not have enough money to support her. His numerous letters to her provide vivid descriptions of HPL and his friends in New York. He participated in numerous all-night walks around New York with HPL and other members of the Kalem Club. In early 1925 Kirk moved into the same apartment house at 169 Clinton Street, Brooklyn, where HPL was residing (prompting HPL's poem, "To George Kirk, Esq., Upon His Entertaining a Company in His New-Decorated Chambers, 18th January 1925"), but stayed only a few months. On April 11–12, 1925, Kirk and HPL undertook a whirlwind excursion to Washington, D.C., seeing all the sights in a few hours (with assistance from amateur colleague Anne Tillery Renshaw, who had a car). From August to October 1925 Kirk resided at 317 West 17th Street in Manhattan; HPL in fact helped him move both his personal possessions and his books for his bookshop. HPL later used the building as the setting for "Cool Air" (1926). HPL wrote a birthday poem to Kirk on the occasion of his twenty-seventh birthday, November 25, 1925 ("To George Willard Kirk, Gent., of Chelsea-Village, in New York, Upon His Birthday"; published in the *National Amateur,* May 1927, as "George Willard Kirk"). HPL occasionally helped Kirk address envelopes for catalogue mailings, and in exchange for this help Kirk gave HPL an enormous quantity of envelopes with the obsolete return address of Kirk's bookshop; HPL used them until they finally ran out in the mid-1930s. During HPL's visit to New York in September 1926, Kirk introduced HPL to Howard Wolf, a reporter for the *Akron Beacon Journal;* sometime during the following year Wolf wrote an article on HPL in his column, "Variety" (exact date not known, as only the clipping survives; rpt. *LR*). Kirk married Lucile Dvorak on March 5, 1927, setting up the Chelsea Bookshop at 58 West 8th Street (which is not in fact in Chelsea), remaining there for more than a decade. He and his wife visited HPL in Providence in early September 1929. HPL continued to meet Kirk on his visits to New York in the 1930s, but otherwise their contact appears to have been slight.

See Mara Kirk Hart, "Walkers in the City: George Willard Kirk and Howard Phillips Lovecraft in New York City, 1924–1926," *LS* No. 28 (Spring 1993): 2–17 (abridged version in *LR*).

Kleiner, Rheinhart (1892–1949). Poet, amateur journalist, and one of HPL's oldest associates. He came in touch with HPL in early 1915, when he received the first issue of HPL's *Conservative* (April 1915). With Maurice Moe and Ira A. Cole, they formed the round-robin correspondence circle, the Kleicomolo (Kleiner was probably the author of an unsigned article, "The Kleicomolo," in the *United Amateur,* March 1919). He frequently commented upon HPL's activities in his amateur journal, *The Piper;* HPL's "The Allowable Rhyme" (*Conservative,* October 1915) is a defense of his views against Kleiner. HPL's poem "The Bookstall" (*United Official Quarterly,* January 1916) is dedicated to Kleiner. The two poets frequently wrote poems to each other, including Kleiner's "To Mary of the Movies" (*Piper,* September 1915) and HPL's "To Charlie of the Comics" (*Providence Amateur,* February 1916), on Mary Pickford and Charlie Chaplin, respectively; Kleiner's "John Oldham: 1653–1683" and HPL's "John Oldham: A Defence" (both in the *United Co-operative,* June 1919); Kleiner's "To a Movie Star" and HPL's "To Mistress Sophia Simple, Queen of the Cinema" (both in the *United Amateur,* November 1919); Kleiner's "Ethel: Cashier in a Broad Street Buffet" and HPL's "Cindy: Scrub Lady in a State Street Skyscraper" (both in *Tryout,* June 1920). In October 1919 HPL and Kleiner jointly wrote several short squibs on fellow amateurs, collectively titled "On Collaboration."

Kleiner wrote the first analysis of HPL's poetry, "A Note on Howard P. Lovecraft's Verse" (*United Amateur,* March 1919). He first met HPL on July 1, 1916, while passing through Providence; he returned for visits in 1917, 1918 (after which he wrote a poem, "At Providence in 1918," *Conservative,* July 1919) and 1920. HPL met him when he came to New York on two occasions in 1922; during the latter visit, on September 16, HPL and Kleiner visited the churchyard of the Dutch Reformed Church in Brooklyn, inspiring HPL to write "The Hound" the next month. Kleiner appears in the story as "St. John," referring to HPL's nickname for him, "Randolph St. John" (a purported descendant of Henry St. John, Viscount Bolingbroke). HPL and Kleiner met frequently during HPL's years in New York (1924–26), as members of the Kalem Club. During this time Kleiner worked for the Fairbanks Scales Co. Kleiner wrote several memoirs of HPL after the latter's death, including "Howard Phillips Lovecraft" (*Californian,* Summer 1937) and "A Memoir of Lovecraft" (in HPL's *Cats*). He edited a series of extracts of HPL's letters to him, concentrating on amateur affairs, titled "By Post from Providence" (*Californian,* Summer 1937). After HPL left New York in 1926, he lost touch with Kleiner for nearly a decade, but they resumed correspondence in 1936–37. Although a prolific poet, Kleiner published only a small number of his poems in book form, mostly in scarce small-press editions: *Metrical Moments* (1937), *Nine Sonnets* (1940), *Pegasus in Pasture* (1943), and so on.

Klenze, Lieutenant. In "The Temple," the next to last surviving crew member of the disabled German submarine U-29. In his confinement, he believes he is being summoned by the dead man from whom he confiscated an ivory amulet and then exits the stricken vessel to his death.

Knockout Bernie. In "The Battle That Ended the Century," one of two antagonists who engage in a boxing match in the year 2001. The character (nicknamed "the Wild Wolf of West Shokan") is a parody of HPL's friend Bernard Austin Dwyer, of West Shokan, N.Y.

Koenig, H[erman] C[harles] (1893–1959). Bibliophile and late associate of HPL. Koenig, employed in the Electrical Testing Laboratories in New York, came in touch with HPL in the fall of 1933 when he asked HPL how to procure the *Necronomicon.* In the summer of 1934 Koenig began circulating books by William Hope Hodgson among HPL's circle, leading to HPL's enthusiastic article "The Weird Work of William Hope Hodgson" (*Phantagraph,* February 1937). HPL met Koenig on several occasions during his visits to New York in the Christmas seasons of 1934 and 1935; on January 2, 1935, HPL, R. H. Barlow, and Frank Belknap Long visited the Electrical Testing Laboratories, a place where electrical appliances were tested. In early 1936 Koenig was planning a trip to Charleston and, knowing that HPL had visited it, asked him for some tips on the sights there. HPL dusted off his unpublished 1930 essay, "An Account of Charleston," and revised and abridged it in a letter to Koenig. Koenig was so taken with the account that he ran off about twenty-five mimeographed copies in March, titling it *Charleston.* Koenig had made several mistranscriptions of HPL's handwriting, and he also asked HPL to rewrite the beginning so that it read as an essay; HPL complied, and Koenig ran off about thirty to fifty copies of the revised version, enclosing it in a paper folder and reproducing as photostats some of HPL's drawings of Charleston sites. After HPL's death Koenig edited the small-press magazine *The Reader and Collector,* reprinting HPL's Hodgson essay (June 1944) and publishing a lengthy article, "Modern Mythological Fiction" by Robert Butman (October 1945, January 1946, and April 1946), which discussed HPL in part (Fritz Leiber's response, "Butman's Essay," appeared in October 1946). Koenig worked with August Derleth to reprint Hodgson's four novels with Arkham House (*The House on the Borderland and Other and Other Novels,* 1946).

Kranon. In "The Cats of Ulthar," a burgomaster in Ulthar.

Kuntz, Eugene B[asil] (1865–1944). Prussian-born poet, Presbyterian minister, and amateur journalist. HPL edited Kuntz's slim collection of poems, *Thoughts* *and Pictures* (Haverhill, Mass.: "Cooperatively published by H. P. Loveracft [*sic*] and C. W. Smith," 1932), probably revising the poems in the process. Later he wrote a plug for the volume, "Dr. Eugene B. Kunz [*sic*]" (*Hodge Podge,* September 1935).

Kuranes. In "Celephaïs," the dream identity of an unidentified but once-wealthy person in the waking world. His "real" self, through dreams and drugs, escapes his mundane existence as a writer in London to find the city of Celephaïs, of which he had dreamt as a child. When he awakens, he cannot return to Celephaïs, although he dreams of other wondrous realms; but finally he is able to return forever as its king, although his body is later found washed up on the shore. In *The Dream-Quest of Unknown Kadath,* Kuranes greets Randolph Carter, who has voyaged in dream to Celephaïs. It now appears that Kuranes, although a king in dreamland, longs to return to his real life in Cornwall. He warns Carter that his "sunset city" may not be as wondrous as he imagines it to be.

Kuttner, Henry (1915–1958). Science fiction writer from Los Angeles and correspondent of HPL. Early in his career Kuttner wrote in various genres of pulp fiction, including horror; see "The Graveyard Rats" (*WT,* March 1936), which some of HPL's colleagues thought he had written or ghostwritten. Kuttner, however, came in touch with HPL only after the story had been accepted for publication. The correspondence lasted from February 1936 to February 1937 (see *Letters to Henry Kuttner,* ed. David E. Schultz and S. T. Joshi [Necronomicon Press, 1990]). HPL assisted on the topographical background for "The Salem Horror" (*WT,* May 1937), a story clearly influenced by "The Dreams in the Witch House." Other Lovecraftian tales by Kuttner have now been reprinted in *The Book of Iod,* ed. Robert M. Price (Chaosium, 1995). Kuttner created numerous additions to HPL's myth-cycle. In late 1936 Kuttner wrote an acrostic poem on Poe ("Where He Walked") after he learned that HPL and his colleagues had done so earlier in the year. In May 1936 HPL asked Kuttner to pass on some photographs to C. L. Moore, thereby introducing the two authors to each other. They married in 1940 and collaboratively wrote some of the most imaginative work in the "Golden Age" of science fiction. See *The Best of Henry Kuttner* (1975).

See Shawn Ramsey, "Henry Kuttner's Cthulhu Mythos Tales: An Overview," *Crypt* No. 51 (Hallowmas 1987): 21–23, 14; Gordon R. Benson, Jr., and Virgil S. Utter, *C. L. Moore and Henry Kuttner: A Marriage of Souls and Talent: A Working Bibliography* (Albuquerque, N.M.: Galactic Central, 1989).

L

Lake, ———. In *At the Mountains of Madness,* a professor of biology on the Miskatonic Antarctic Expedition who leads an exploration party that is destroyed by the Old Ones, whom his group unwittingly resuscitates from suspended animation.

"Last Test, The." Novelette (19,330 words); ghostwritten for Adolphe de Castro, in October–November 1927. First published in *WT* (November 1928); first collected in *Cats;* corrected text in *HM.*

Dr. Alfred Clarendon, a renowned physician and medical researcher, is appointed to the post of medical director of the California State Penitentiary at San Quentin by his old friend, Governor James Dalton. (Dalton's father had been ruined on Wall Street by Clarendon's father, but the younger Dalton held no grudge.) Clarendon's home in San Francisco is run by his sister Georgina, with whom Dalton has long been in love. Clarendon is working on an antitoxin for black fever. In the course of his work he has had to travel to exotic places, and he has brought back a band of Tibetan servants, over whom Clarendon has placed an enigmatic figure named Surama.

Shortly after Clarendon's arrival at San Quentin, one of the inmates comes down with black fever; Clarendon places the man in a separate ward so that he can study the case himself, thereby enraging his assistant, Dr. Jones, who wishes to assist. The inmate dies, and later several other prisoners contract the disease. News of the epidemic spreads throughout San Francisco, causing a panic that drives many citizens from the city. Eventually the panic subsides, but Clarendon is criticized for his handling of the matter; he pays no attention, however, to the bad press he receives. Governor Dalton continues to defend Clarendon, in spite of the latter's curt refusal to allow him to marry Georgina.

Dr. Jones then contrives to change the manner of institutional appointments, with the result that Clarendon is fired from his position and Jones installed in his place. Clarendon lapses into depression and rarely stirs from his home. With Surama, he continues experiments of various sorts in his own laboratory, but Georgina is horrified when she overhears a conversation between the two men that suggests their intention to use human patients for their experiments. She asks Dalton's help in a situation that seems to be growing increasingly tense, especially after she overhears further bizarre conversations that cause her to fall in a faint. Clarendon revives her, and in the process contemplates using her in some nameless experiment. But before he can do so, Dalton arrives and demands an explanation. Clarendon collapses, injecting himself with the serum he was planning to give his sister. He then confesses the truth: he was not even on the track of an antitoxin for black fever but was under the spell of Surama, an evil Atlantean mage who has developed a disease that "isn't of this earth" to overwhelm mankind. Clarendon urges Dalton to burn the clinic and everything in it, including Surama. Presently Dalton sees the clinic going up in flames: apparently Clarendon had set the fire himself, destroying Surama before he himself succumbed to his self-inflicted disease.

The story is a radical revision of a tale entitled "A Sacrifice to Science" in de Castro's book, *In the Confessional and the Following* (1893); in his letters HPL refers to it as "Clarendon's Last Test." He received $16 for this work, while de Castro received $175 from *WT*. It should be pointed out that de Castro's original tale is not at all supernatural. It is merely a long drawn-out melodrama or adventure story in which a scientist seeks a cure for a new type of fever (never described in detail) and, having run out of patients because of the bad reputation he has gained as a man who cares only for science and not for human life, seeks to convince his own sister to be a "sacrifice to science" in the furtherance of his quest. HPL has turned the whole scenario into a supernatural tale while preserving the basic framework—the California setting, the characters (although the names of some have been changed), the search for a cure to a new type of fever, and (although this now becomes only a minor part of the climax) Clarendon's attempt to persuade his sister to sacrifice herself. But—aside from replacing the nebulously depicted assistant of Dr. Clarendon ("Dr. Clinton" in de Castro) named Mort with the much more redoubtable Surama—he has added much better motivation for the characters and the story as a whole. HPL made the tale about half again as long as de Castro's original; although he remarked of the latter that "I nearly exploded over the dragging monotony of [the] silly thing" (*SL* 2.107), his version is not without monotony and prolixity of its own. For his own amusement, HPL has added glancing references to his own developing myth-cycle, including, oddly enough, the first mention of Shub-Niggurath, Nug, and Yeb in his work.

Lawton, Captain George E. In "The Mound," a pioneer who had come to the Oklahoma Territory in 1889 and in 1916 investigates the mound region; he comes back a week later with his feet neatly cut off at the ankles and strangely *younger* in appearance.

Lazare, Edward (1904–1991). Brief associate of HPL. The two first met in Cleveland in August 1922, when Lazare was a member of Hart Crane's literary circle. They met again in September 1924, at Samuel Loveman's apartment in

Columbia Heights; at that time HPL thought that Lazare would become a "fitting accession to our select circle of The Boys [i.e., the Kalem Club]" (HPL to Lillian D. Clark, September 29–30, 1924; ms., JHL), but Lazare dropped out shortly thereafter. He later became the editor of *American Book-Prices Current* (1940–65).

Leavitt, Robert. In "Herbert West—Reanimator," a traveling salesman from St. Louis whom Herbert West kills in order to test a revivifying solution he has invented.

Leeds, Arthur (1882–1952?). Friend of HPL in New York. Leeds was something of a rolling stone, having been with a traveling circus as a boy and performing odd jobs throughout his career; during the time HPL knew him in New York (1924–26) he was a columnist for *Writer's Digest* and an occasional contributor to the pulp magazines (he had one story, "The Return of the Undead," in *WT,* November 1925). He became a member of the Kalem Club, although his dispute with Everett McNeil over a small amount of money the latter had lent him led to separate "Leeds" and "McNeil" meetings. In the spring of 1925 Leeds urged HPL to do freelance work for a man named Yesley in writing advertising copy; HPL wrote several pieces (R. H. Barlow gave them the collective name "Commercial Blurbs"), but the venture did not pan out. HPL appears to have continued to keep in sporadic touch with Leeds after he left New York, but few letters have surfaced. In March 1932 Leeds recommended to an editor at Vanguard that he consider a collection of HPL's tales, but the editor wished a novel; nevertheless, the editor looked at some of HPL's stories, but eventually turned down the collection.

Legrasse, John Raymond. In "The Call of Cthulhu," Inspector of Police for the city of New Orleans. In 1908, he visits with George Gammell Angell at the annual meeting of the American Archaeological Society, in St. Louis, to discuss his findings concerning the Cthulhu cult.

Leiber, Fritz [Reuter] (1910–1992). Writer, editor, actor, and teacher. He first discovered HPL when he read "The Colour out of Space" in *Amazing Stories* (September 1927). He and his wife Jonquil corresponded with HPL during the last six months of his life. HPL read a draft of Leiber's "Adept's Gambit" (the first Fafhrd and Gray Mouser story), and in a lengthy letter of December 19, 1936, suggested numerous alterations. The story originally contained Cthulhu Mythos elements, but Leiber excised them before publication. It was first published in *Night's Black Agents* (1947), which contains several stories influenced by HPL. HPL also read Leiber's poem cycle, "Demons of the Upper Air" (first published as a booklet, 1969). Leiber began a full-fledged Mythos tale, "The Terror from the Depths," in 1937; it was completed in 1975 and published in Edward P. Berglund's *Disciples of Cthulhu* (1976) and in the revised edition (1990) of *Tales of the Cthulhu Mythos.* Another novella written at this time, *The Dealings of Daniel Kesserich* (published 1997), has strong Lovecraftian elements. *Conjure Wife* (1953) was perhaps inspired in part by "The Dreams in the Witch House." "To Arkham and the Stars" (in HPL's *DB*) is a kind of parody-homage to HPL. Leiber was the author of many articles on HPL, including "A

Literary Copernicus" (in *Cats*; rpt. *FDOC* and *LR*), "My Correspondence with Lovecraft" (*Fresco,* Spring 1958; rpt. *LR*), "The 'Whisperer' Re-examined" (*Haunted,* December 1964), "Through Hyperspace with Brown Jenkin" (in *DB;* rpt. *FDOC* and *LR*), "The Cthulhu Mythos: Wondrous and Terrible" (*Fantastic,* June 1975), and "Lovecraft in My Life" (*Journal of the H. P. Lovecraft Society,* 1976). Leiber wrote some of the most distinguished science fiction, fantasy, and horror literature of the century and is perhaps the only one of HPL's colleagues who can rival him in literary substance. *Fritz Leiber and H. P. Lovecraft: Writers of the Dark* (Holicong, Pa.: Wildside Press, 2003) contains Lovecraft's letters to Leiber and Leiber's fiction with Lovecraft's influence.

See Stefan Dziemianowicz, "Dead Ringers: The Leiber-Lovecraft Connection," *Crypt* No. 76 (Hallowmas 1990): 8–13; Bruce Byfield, *Witches of the Mind: A Critical Study of Fritz Leiber* (Necronomicon Press, 1991); Nicholaus Clements, "Lovecraft and the Early Leiber," *LS* No. 41 (Spring 1999): 23–24; S. T. Joshi, "Passing the Torch: H. P. Lovecraft's Influence on Fritz Leiber," *Studies in Weird Fiction* No. 24 (Winter 1999): 17–25.

Letters, Lovecraft's. Shortly after his death, HPL's longtime friend Maurice W. Moe wrote: "If there is ever a survey to determine the greatest letter-writer in history, the claims of Lovecraft deserve close investigation" ("Howard Phillips Lovecraft: The Sage of Providence," *O-Wash-Ta-Nong,* [1937]). While it is unlikely that HPL will soon attain celebrity solely or largely on the basis of his letters, it is now abundantly clear that his correspondence ranks among the pinnacles of his literary achievement.

The number of letters written by HPL has been a matter of debate. L. Sprague de Camp (*Lovecraft: A Biography* [1975]) casually estimated a figure of 100,000, but this is probably too high. HPL stated in 1936 that he wrote 5 to 10 letters per day (*SL* 5.369); if we assume that he maintained this ratio over his literary career (1914–36), we arrive at 42,000 to 84,000 letters. Given that HPL was probably not considering the vast numbers of postcards he wrote during his travels, the total figure is probably closer to the higher than the lower amount. But mere numbers do not tell the whole story. What makes HPL's letters remarkable, beyond their sheer quantity and size, is their extraordinary candor; their abundance of wit, humor, satire, and persiflage; and their exhaustive and penetrating discussions of a wide range of topics including philosophy, literature and literary theory, history, art and architecture (especially of colonial America), and the contemporary political, economic, cultural, and social trends of the nation and the world. His letters are, in this regard, far more interesting and perspicacious than many of his essays on the same subjects.

HPL remarked that "Not until I was twenty years old did I write any letters worthy of the name." He attributed his enthusiasm for letter-writing at this time to his cousin Phillips Gamwell, who, although only twelve, "blossomed out as a piquant letter-writer eager to discuss the various literary and scientific topics broached during our occasional personal conversations" (*SL* 3.370). HPL gained his initial celebrity (or, rather, notoriety) by the letters in prose and verse to the *Argosy* attacking the sentimental fiction of Fred Jackson, which aroused a storm of protest on the part of Jackson's supporters. It was, however, when HPL joined the amateur journalism movement in 1914 that he first began writing letters regularly and voluminously. No doubt many of these letters concerned routine matters of amateur business and were correspondingly short; few of these have survived. The letters that do survive are those to his earliest colleagues in amateur journalism—Maurice W. Moe (1914f.), Edward H. Cole (1914f.), Rheinhart Kleiner (1915f.), and Alfred Galpin (1918f.). No letters to W. Paul Cook, who was instrumental in HPL's resumption of fiction-writing in 1917, survive. HPL came in touch with Samuel Loveman in 1917, but very few letters to him are extant, most of them being of much later date. There is a small batch of letters to John T. Dunn (a member of the Providence Amateur Press Club) of 1915–17, mingling amateur affairs and controversial political topics (especially the Irish question); they have been published in *Books at Brown* (38–39 [1991–92]: 157–223). Some letters to Winifred Virginia Jackson of 1918–21 survive, but they do not settle the question of whether HPL and Jackson were romantically involved. Early letters to Anne Tillery Renshaw supply hints of HPL's employment in the Symphony Literary Service. In 1920 HPL came into epistolary contact with Frank Belknap Long, who had just joined the amateur movement. Long was a lifelong friend of HPL, but HPL's letters to him after the spring of 1931 have been lost. Only two letters to HPL's mother (1920–21) survive; they were both written while she was confined in Butler Hospital. No letters to other members of HPL's family, with the exception of a few letters to his aunt Annie Gamwell, survive prior to 1924, although a few letters by HPL's grandfather Whipple Van Buren Phillips to HPL, dating to as early as 1894, survive at JHL and in private hands.

Two distinctive groups of letters are the round-robin cycles, the Kleicomolo and the Gallomo. In these cycles, the various members (Kleiner, Ira A. Cole, Moe, and HPL in the first; Galpin, HPL, and Moe in the second) would sequentially write letters discussing one or more controversial topics; as the batches of letters circulated to each member, he would remove his previous contribution and write a fresh letter, commenting on the letters of the others. In an unsigned article (probably by Kleiner), "The Kleicomolo" (*United Amateur,* March 1919), it was noted that "One of the members [Moe?] was desirous of keeping a complete copy of the correspondence, and began by copying the letters as they went through his hands. This task soon became so great as to be impracticable, and the rest elected him librarian and promised to send him carbon copies of their instalments." But only the letters by HPL survive, and not many of these: only three to the Kleicomolo (1916–17) and four to the Gallomo (1919–21).

HPL's involvement with his future wife, Sonia H. Greene, could presumably be traced in the many letters he wrote to her from 1921 to their marriage in 1924; Sonia herself reports that for two years HPL wrote letters to her almost daily, "sometimes filling 30, 40 and even 50 pages of finely written script" (*The Private Life of H. P. Lovecraft* [Necronomicon Press, 1985 (rev. ed. 1992)], p. 18). But around 1935, two years after their last meeting, Sonia went out into a field and burned all the letters, so that only a few postcards now survive in private hands. In 1922 HPL came in touch with Clark Ashton Smith, to whom he would write 160 letters and 60 postcards. James F. Morton also became a close if argumentative colleague in 1922, and HPL's letters to him are among the most remarkable he ever wrote for their breadth of subject and pungency of style.

HPL's solitary letter to the first editor of *Weird Tales,* Edwin Baird (February 3, 1924), and many letters to his successor, Farnsworth Wright, allow glimpses of HPL's conflicted involvement with that pulp magazine.

HPL's two years in New York (1924–26) are exhaustively chronicled in letters to his aunts Lillian Clark and Annie Gamwell; the letters to Lillian alone for this period total about 200,000 words. (See *Letters from New York* (2004.) They allow nearly a day-to-day record of HPL's activities and fluctuating temperament during this critical period in his life. Few letters to members of the "Kalem Club" (James F. Morton, Everett McNeil, Arthur Leeds, Long, George Kirk, Wilfred B. Talman, and others) survive for this period, since HPL saw them frequently in person. Letters to Talman are abundant for a later period. Upon his return to Providence, HPL came into contact with August Derleth and Donald Wandrei; his correspondence with these two writers survives almost intact. His letters to Derleth—more than 380—may represent the greatest number of letters to any of his correspondents. In 1930 HPL received a letter from pulp writer Robert E. Howard, and there began a sporadic but extremely voluminous correspondence that lasted until Howard's suicide in 1936; the letters total roughly 200,000 words by HPL and 300,000 by Howard. HPL's single longest surviving letter—70 handwritten pages (35 pages written on both sides) and totaling 33,500 words—was written to the little-known Vermonter Woodburn Harris in 1929.

HPL's work as revisionist caused him to come into contact with would-be writers, but only letters to Zealia Bishop (1928–30) and Richard F. Searight (1933–37) survive in any quantity. The letters to Adolphe de Castro (1928–36) are very scattered, and there are none to David Van Bush or Hazel Heald.

By the 1930s HPL had become a fixture in the worlds of pulp fiction and fantasy fandom, and he accordingly began corresponding with a great many fellow writers (notably E. Hoffmann Price [1932–37] and Henry S. Whitehead [1931–32]) and disciples (R. H. Barlow [1931–37], Robert Bloch [1933–37], Duane W. Rimel [1934–37], F. Lee Baldwin [1934–35], Donald A. Wollheim [1936–37], Wilson Shepherd [1936–37], C. L. Moore [1936–37], Fritz Leiber [1936–37], and Willis Conover [1936–37]). The letters to Whitehead were, however, evidently destroyed.

HPL preserved relatively few letters he received over a lifetime of correspondence; not only because of restricted space in his usually cramped quarters, but because most of these letters probably did not seem to him of enduring interest. Exceptions are the early letters of Donald Wandrei (later ones were kept only sporadically) and the letters from Robert E. Howard, E. Hoffmann Price, C. L. Moore, and the amateur writer Ernest A. Edkins (1932–37). None of HPL's letters to Edkins survive. Frank Belknap Long's and James F. Morton's letters survive in fair numbers but with many gaps and omissions; there are few letters by August Derleth. A fair number of Clark Ashton Smith's letters are extant; substantial extracts have been published as *Letters to H. P. Lovecraft* (Necronomicon Press, 1987).

Late in life HPL admitted that he had 97 regular correspondents (HPL to R. H. Barlow, January 3, 1937 [ms., JHL]). On the purpose of maintaining such a far-flung correspondence HPL wrote: "As a person of very retired life, I met very few different sorts of people in youth—and was therefore exceedingly narrow and provincial. Later on, when literary activities brought me into touch with widely diverse types by mail—Texans like Robert E. Howard, men in Australia, New Zealand, &c., Westerners, Southerners, Canadians, people in old England, and assorted kinds of folk nearer at hand—I found myself opened up to dozens of points of view which would otherwise never have occurred to me. My understanding and sympathies were enlarged, and many of my social, political, and economic views were modified as a consequence of increased knowledge. Only correspondence could have effected this broadening; for it would have been impossible to have visited all the regions and met all the various types involved, while books can never talk back or discuss" (*SL* 4.389). It can thus be seen that, aside from all questions of courtesy and gentlemanliness, HPL's correspondence was vital to his intellectual and aesthetic development, putting the lie to those critics who assert that he "wasted" his time writing so many letters.

The publication of HPL's letters was a high priority with Derleth and Wandrei as they were founding Arkham House to preserve HPL's work in book form. Wandrei in particular was determined to preserve HPL's correspondence, and Derleth wasted little time in contacting HPL's colleagues and urging them either to transcribe the letters themselves or to send the letters to him so that his secretary, Alice Conger, could transcribe them. In this way Derleth and Wandrei produced the so-called Arkham House Transcripts—nearly 50 volumes of single-spaced typescripts of letters (each volume averaging about 100 pages) upon which the long-delayed *Selected Letters* (published in 5 volumes in 1965–76, and largely edited by Wandrei) were based. These transcripts contain texts of many letters that may no longer survive in manuscript, as well as full (or, at any rate, more extensive) versions of letters published in abridged form in the *Selected Letters* or not published at all. Otherwise, most of HPL's letters now survive at JHL; the letters to Derleth are at the State Historical Society of Wisconsin, and a few other letters are scattered in other institutions or in the hands of collectors. The letters in the *Selected Letters* are in almost every instance abridged, and occasionally the abridgements result in incoherence or a misleading impression of HPL's meaning. Numerous typographical errors also mar the edition, as well as the absence of an index. S. T. Joshi has supplied the latter (Necronomicon Press, 1980 [rev. ed. 1991]). Joshi and David E. Schultz have prepared annotated editions of unabridged letters to individual correspondents—*Letters to Henry Kuttner* (1990); *Letters to Richard F. Searight* (1992); *Letters to Robert Bloch* (1993); *Letters to Samuel Loveman and Vincent Starrett* (1994) (published by Necronomicon Press) and *Letters to Alfred Galpin* (Hippocampus Press, 2003)—and the joint correspondence of Lovecraft and Donald Wandrei, *Mysteries of Time and Spirit* (Night Shade Books, 2002). Also of note is *Lord of a Visible World: An Autobiography in Letters* (Ohio University Press, 2000), in which Joshi and Schultz have arranged published and unpublished letters in the form of an autobiography, covering many aspects of HPL's life, work, and thought.

See S. T. Joshi, "A Look at Lovecraft's Letters," in *Primal Sources: Essays on H. P. Lovecraft* (Hippocampus Press, 2003).

Libo, P[ublius] Scribonius. In "The Very Old Folk," the proconsul of the Roman province of Hispania Citerior (Spain) who orders a cohort to investigate reports of peculiar events in the hills above Tarraco.

Liddeason, Eli. In "The Shunned House," a man who is hired by William Harris to be a servant at the house, but who dies about a year later, after marrying another servant, Mehitabel Pierce.

"Life and Death." Short story or prose poem; evidently published in an amateur journal (c. 1920), but text not currently available.

This is one of the few authentically "lost" stories by HPL, but its existence and whereabouts remain in doubt. In his commonplace book (entry #27) HPL records the title and plot germ of the story: "Death—its desolation & horror—bleak spaces—sea-bottom—dead cities. But Life—the greater horror! Vast unheard-of reptiles & leviathans—hideous beasts of prehistoric jungle—rank slimy vegetation—evil instincts of primal man—Life is more horrible than death." The entry probably dates to early 1920; in contrast to other used entries, HPL has not crossed out this entry or otherwise indicated that it was used. He never mentions or alludes to the story in any extant correspondence.

After HPL's death, R. H. Barlow wrote to August Derleth that he thought he once saw "Life and Death" (Barlow to Derleth, June 14, 1944; ms., SHSW). Around this time W. Paul Cook told Derleth that he thought the story had appeared in the *United Amateur,* but this is not the case. George T. Wetzel, in describing the research for his bibliography of HPL, stated that he saw the story as published in an amateur journal, but he subsequently lost the reference and was unable to locate it (see "The Research of a Biblio," in *Howard Phillips Lovecraft: Memoirs, Critiques and Bibliographies* [1955]). Wetzel's research on HPL's amateur publications was conducted largely at the Fossil Collection of Amateur Journalism, then at the Franklin Institute in Philadelphia; but the collection was subsequently vandalized, as many published works by HPL were cut out of the journals with a razor. Examination of many other amateur journalism collections by several scholars has failed to turn up the item.

One wonders, then, whether HPL actually wrote and published "Life and Death." The plot germ above could in fact refer to the prose poem "Ex Oblivione" (*United Amateur,* March 1921), and the rather vague recollections of Barlow, Cook, and Wetzel may refer to it or to some other work altogether.

"Life for Humanity's Sake." Essay (710 words); probably written in the summer of 1920. First published in *American Amateur* (September 1920); rpt. *MW* and *CE5.*

The essay is a plea to reject both hedonism and theism in the face of the probable meaninglessness and inconsequence of the human race within the boundless cosmos. HPL asserts that a "real ethical philosophy can be founded only on practicalities" and urges that "the goal of mental evolution and the subordination of pain stands so conspicuously before us."

Lillibridge, Edwin M. In "The Haunter of the Dark," the inquisitive reporter for the *Providence Telegram* (a real newspaper) who disappears in 1893—as it turns out, inside the Free-Will Church, where the Starry Wisdom sect holds its services. His remains are discovered by Robert Blake when he investigates the abandoned building.

Little, Myrta Alice (1888–1967), friend and correspondent of HPL (1921) residing in Hampstead, N.H. Little joined the UAPA in the spring of 1921, and HPL planned to visit her in late May, but the death of HPL's mother postponed the plans, and he visited her only on June 8–9; the two of them also went to see "Tryout" Smith in Haverhill. HPL returned to New Hampshire in August 25–26, exploring the Haverhill Historical Society with Little. HPL describes her as a former college professor who was attempting to become a professional writer, but her only known published work is a Christmas pageant for children, *Sweet Christmas Time* (1929), published under her married name, Myrta Little Davies. HPL's one surviving letter to her was published in *LS* No. 26 (Spring 1992): 26–30.

"Little Glass Bottle, The." Juvenile story (460 words); written c. 1898–99. First published in *SR;* corrected text in *Juvenilia: 1897–1905* (1985) and *MW.*

A ship commanded by a Captain William Jones comes upon a bottle with a message in it (probably suggested by Poe's "MS. Found in a Bottle"). This note—written in a very wild and hasty hand on HPL's autograph manuscript—announces the writer as John Jones (no relation to the captain, one imagines) and says that there is a treasure to be found on the spot marked with an asterisk on the reverse of the note (here we find a crude map of the Indian Ocean, with a nebulous land mass labeled "Austrailia" [*sic*] at the bottom left). This note is dated January 1, 1864.

Captain Jones decides that "it would pay to go" to the spot, and the crew do so. There they find another note from John Jones: "Dear Searcher excuse me for the practical joke I have played on you but it serves you right to find nothing for your foolish act . . ." But John kindly defrays their expenses with an iron box containing "$25.0.00," whatever that is. After reading this note (inexplicably dated December 3, 1880) Captain Jones delivers the one funny line in the entire story: "I'd like to kick his head off."

The story is an early attempt at humor. For later tales of this sort, see "Ibid," "A Reminiscence of Dr. Samuel Johnson," and "Sweet Ermengarde."

"Living Heritage: Roman Architecture in Today's America, A." Essay (12,760 words); written in December 1934. First published in this form in *CE5.*

The essay was written at the request of Maurice W. Moe, who asked HPL to write an essay of his choice for an amateur magazine being produced by his students. HPL wrote a rather routine account of traces of Roman architectural principles in American cities (much of it based upon first-hand observation of sites in New York City and elsewhere). HPL sent Moe the essay without typing it; he later thought Moe had lost the manuscript (the student magazine never materialized). The essay, however, survives in AHT. HPL apparently retained the prefatory section of the essay, which appeared as "Heritage or Modernism: Common Sense in Art Forms" in the *Californian* (Summer 1935). This article lambastes modern art and architecture for being consciously theoretical and too radically divergent from the artistic traditions of the past.

Lockhart, Andrew F[rancis] (1890–1964), amateur journalist from Milbank, South Dakota, and author of the first article on HPL, "Little Journeys to the Homes of Prominent Amateurs" (*United Amateur,* September 1915), a biographical sketch; the information for it was surely derived exclusively from correspondence with HPL. HPL responded with a biographical sketch of Lockhart in the series, "Little Journeys to the Homes of Prominent Amateurs" (*United Amateur,* October 1915), written under the pseudonym "El Impartial." Lockhart edited the professional temperance journal *Chain Lightning,* which HPL wrote about in "More *Chain Lightning*" (*United Official Quarterly,* October 1915). HPL also wrote the poem, "To Mr. Lockhart, On His Poetry" (*Tryout,* March 1917); its appearance in a South Dakota newspaper has not been located.

Long, Frank Belknap, Jr. (1901–1994). American short story writer, novelist, and poet, and one of HPL's closest friends. Long, a lifelong New Yorker, was not quite nineteen when he first came in touch with HPL in early 1920; he was about to enter New York University to study journalism but would later transfer to Columbia, leaving without a degree. His father was a prosperous dentist, and the family resided at 823 West End Avenue in Manhattan. Long developed an interest in the weird by reading the Oz books, Jules Verne, and H. G. Wells in youth, and he exercised his talents both in prose and in poetry. He discovered amateur journalism when he won a prize from *The Boy's World* and received an invitation to join the UAPA; he seems to have done so around the end of 1919. His first published tale was "Dr. Whitlock's Price" (*United Amateur,* March 1920), a mediocre mad scientist story. It was followed by a powerful prose-poetic tale, "The Eye Above the Mantel" (*United Amateur,* March 1921). HPL found Long a stimulating correspondent, especially in regard to his aesthetic tastes, focusing on the Italian Renaissance and French literature. HPL published some of Long's work in his *Conservative* (e.g., "Felis: A Prose Poem" [July 1923], about Long's pet cat) and paid tribute to Long in a flattering article, "The Work of Frank Belknap Long, Jun.," published anonymously in the *United Amateur* (May 1924) but clearly by HPL. HPL also wrote a birthday poem to Long: "To Endymion" (*Tryout,* September 1923). (HPL wrongly believed that Long was born in 1902; Long himself in later years gave his birth year as 1903, but Peter Cannon's consultation of New York City birth records confirm that his year of birth was 1901.) They first met when HPL visited New York in April 1922. In the summer of 1923 Long did HPL the great favor of introducing him to the work of Arthur Machen, which profoundly influenced HPL's later tales. He may have been a significant influence in HPL's adoption of a "Decadent" aesthetic in the early 1920s, which represented a major shift in his previous classicist aesthetic. The two authors met with great frequency during HPL's stay in Brooklyn (1924–26), at which time they were the chief members of the Kalem Club. Long contributed to stories to early issues of *WT,* notably "Death Waters" (December 1924) and "The Ocean Leech" (January 1925), both of which convey Long's fascination with the sea.

Perceiving the depression and despair HPL was feeling in New York, Long apparently wrote to HPL's aunts in Providence in early 1926, recommending that they invite HPL to return home. (Long has supplied varying accounts of this incident; in one version he states that he himself wrote the letter, in another he claims that his mother did so.) In 1926 W. Paul Cook published Long's first book of poetry, *A Man from Genoa*. In 1927 Long wrote the story, "The Space-Eaters," in which HPL is featured as a character (referred to only as "Howard"; the other major character is named "Frank"). The story contains, as an epigraph, a quotation from the *Necronomicon* as translated by Dr. John Dee (the epigraph was omitted in the story's first appearance in *WT,* July 1928); it constitutes the first "addition" to HPL's pseudomythology. A year later Long (whose family had moved to 230 West 97th Street) wrote "The Hounds of Tindalos" (*WT,* March 1929), an explicit imitation of HPL and a brief preface to the stillborn edition of HPL's *The Shunned House* (1928). HPL, in turn, ghostwrote for Long the preface to Mrs. William B. Symmes's *Old World Footprints* (W. Paul Cook/The Recluse Press, 1928), a slim poetry collection by Long's aunt.

In 1929 Long wrote the short novel, *The Horror from the Hills* (*WT,* January and February–March 1931; published in book form 1963), which incorporates verbatim a letter by HPL recounting his great "Roman dream" of Halloween 1927. At this time Long—who had teamed with HPL in a revision service (an advertisement for this service appeared in *WT,* August 1928)—was working with Zealia Bishop and also Adolphe de Castro, whose memoir *Portrait of Ambrose Bierce* (Century Co., 1929) Long revised after HPL refused to do so; it contains a preface, signed "Belknap Long." Long's parents frequently brought HPL on various motor trips: to various spots in upstate New York and Connecticut in April 1928; to Kingston, New York, in May 1929; to Cape Cod in August 1929, August 1930, and July 1933; and to Asbury Park, N.J., in July 1930. The Longs' spacious apartment also served as HPL's base of operations during his Christmas visits to New York in 1932–33, 1933–34, 1934–35, and 1935–36.

By the early 1930s Long had turned to science fiction or science fantasy, writing voluminously for *Astounding Stories* and other pulps. HPL began to feel that Long had sold himself out (see *SL* 5.400). At this same time, paradoxically, Long was espousing Bolshevism, engendering vigorous debates in their letters. His most notable story, "Second Night Out" (originally published as "The Black, Dead Thing"), appeared in *WT* (October 1933). In 1935 HPL participated in the round-robin story "The Challenge from Beyond," persuading Long to write the final segment after he had left the project. When visiting R. H. Barlow that summer in Florida, HPL helped set type for Long's second poetry collection, *The Goblin Tower* (Dragonfly Press, 1935), correcting some of Long's faulty meter in the process. HPL's letters to Long are among the richest and most wide-ranging of all his correspondence; however, the letters after April 1931 have been lost, and even the letters up to that date exist primarily in transcriptions prepared by Arkham House.

Long learned of HPL's death when he read the brief obituary in the *New York Times* on March 16, 1937. He wrote only three times about HPL, aside from brief letters published in magazines: "Random Memories of H.P.L." (in *Marginalia;* rpt. *LR*), "H. P. L. in Red Hook" (in *The Occult Lovecraft,* ed. Anthony Raven [1975]), and *Howard Phillips Lovecraft: Dreamer on the Nightside* (Arkham House, 1975). The book-length memoir was written in considerable haste as a direct result of Long's reading of the manuscript of L. Sprague de Camp's

Lovecraft: A Biography (1975), which Long felt to be a biased portrait of HPL; it was exhaustively revised by Arkham House's editor, James Turner. Long also wrote a brief preface to a collection of HPL's tales, *The Colour out of Space* (Jove, 1978 [inadvertently omitted from the first printing]). His introduction to *The Early Long* (Doubleday, 1975), a collection of his best stories, provides illumination on his own life and work, as does his brief *Autobiographical Memoir* (Necronomicon Press, 1985). In his later years he lived in great poverty with his wife, Lyda, in an apartment in the Chelsea district of Manhattan.

Long wrote prolifically in the fields of horror and science fiction. His best tales are collected in two Arkham House volumes, *The Hounds of Tindalos* (1946) and *The Rim of the Unknown* (1972). Among his science fiction tales, the most notable are *John Carstairs, Space Detective* (1949) and *Mars Is My Destination* (1949). *Odd Science Fiction* (1964) contains *The Horror from the Hills* and two other tales. The best of his poetry, as selected by himself, was gathered in *In Mayan Splendor* (Arkham House, 1977); his uncollected poetry has been assembled by Perry M. Grayson in *The Darkling Tide* (Tsathoggua Press, 1995).

See Tom Collins, "Frank Belknap Long on Literature, Lovecraft, and the Golden Age of 'Weird Tales,'" *Twilight Zone* 1, No. 10 (January 1982): 13–19; Ben P. Indick, "In Memoriam: Frank Belknap Long," *LS* No. 30 (Spring 1994): 3–4; Peter Cannon, *Long Memories: Recollections of Frank Belknap Long* (British Fantasy Society, 1997); S. T. Joshi, "Things from the Sea: The Early Weird Fiction of Frank Belknap Long," *Studies in Weird Fiction* No. 25 (Summer 2001): 33–40.

"Looking Backward." Essay (7,680 words); probably written in late 1919 or early 1920. First published in the *Tryout* (February, March, April, May, and June 1920); rpt. as a booklet (Haverhill, Mass.: C. W. Smith, [1920]); rpt. *Aonian* (Autumn and Winter 1944); rpt. as a booklet (Necronomicon Press, 1980); rpt. *CE1*.

This discursive essay on the "halcyon days" of amateur journalism (1885–95) was based on a sheaf of amateur journals given to HPL by C. W. Smith, editor of the *Tryout*. HPL remarks on the general naïveté and unsophistication of many of the contributions; notes that the amateurs of the period generally divide into three categories, "the literati, the plodders, and the politicians"; and discusses contributions by several amateurs, including Joseph Dana Miller, Brainerd Emery, Finlay Aaron Grant, Thomas G. Harrison, and Ernest A. Edkins (later a colleague of HPL).

"Lord Dunsany and His Work." Essay (3,910 words); delivered as lecture to an amateur journalists' group in Boston, December 1922. First published in *Marginalia;* rpt. *MW* and *CE2*.

This somewhat superficial survey of Dunsany's work concludes with HPL's declaration that modern science has destroyed traditional moral and aesthetic responses and that the "Dresden-china Arcadia" of Dunsany, and the creation of a deliberately artificial world of the imagination, may be a solution to the problem of art in the modern world. As such, the essay represents a significant stage in HPL's evolution from classicism through Decadence to his final stage of cosmic regionalism.

Lovecraft Family. HPL records an elaborate family history for his paternal ancestors, most of it deriving from records copied from his great-aunt Sarah Allgood (d. 1908) in 1905. The Lovecraft family line in England as given by HPL in his letter to Frank Belknap Long (*SL* 2.182) is unproven, even to the extent of identifying his alleged great-great-grandfather, Thomas Lovecraft (1745–1826), who HPL claimed was forced to sell his seat at Minster Hall near Newton-Abbot in Devonshire in 1823 to pay off a debt, resulting in the scattering of his family. His great-grandparents, Joseph S. Lovecraft (1775–1850) and Mary Fulford Lovecraft (1782–1864), emigrated from Devonshire to New York state, together with six children (John, William, Joseph, Aaron, George, and Mary), arriving in Rochester, N.Y., in 1831. (The difficulty in locating immigration records concerning the Lovecraft family at probable ports of entry in the United States suggests that there may be some validity to the tradition preserved by HPL that the emigrants first settled in Ontario, Canada, in 1827.) Although HPL stated that his great-grandfather died on an experimental farm in upstate New York shortly after emigrating, Joseph S. Lovecraft, the patriarch of the American Lovecraft line, actually survived to die in Rochester in 1850 at an advanced age. In the 1850 census of Rochester, all Joseph and Mary's sons, with the exception of Aaron, may be found listed as tradesmen; HPL's grandfather, George Lovecraft (c. 1818–1895), for example, is listed as a harness-maker. However, the brothers were listed as property owners and fairly prosperous. George Lovecraft and his wife Helen Allgood (1821–1881) removed from Rochester to Mt. Vernon, N.Y., in the 1860s; they had three children who survived to adulthood: Emma Jane Lovecraft Hill (1847–1925), Winfield Scott Lovecraft (1853–1898), and Mary Louise Lovecraft Mellon (1855–1916). HPL appears to have had very little contact with his aunts Emma and Mary. He was almost certainly the last of the male Lovecraft line on the North American continent, although there are still living descendants of Joseph S. Lovecraft and Mary Fulford Lovecraft in the female line.

See R. Alain Everts, "The Lovecraft Family in America," *Xenophile* 2, No. 6 (October 1975): 7, 16; Kenneth W. Faig, Jr., "Lovecraft's Ancestors," *Crypt* No. 57 (St. John's Eve 1988): 19–25; Richard D. Squires, *Stern Fathers 'Neath the Mould: The Lovecraft Family in Rochester* (Necronomicon Press, 1995).

Lovecraft, Sarah Susan Phillips (1857–1921). Mother of HPL; second daughter of Whipple V. Phillips and Robie A. Place Phillips, born in the Place-Battey house on Moosup Valley Road in Foster, R.I. She spent one academic year at the Wheaton Seminary (Norton, Mass.) in 1871–72; she was otherwise educated in Providence, where she presumably met her friend, the poet Louise Imogen Guiney. It is not known how she met her future husband, Winfield Scott Lovecraft. They married on June 12, 1889, at St. Paul's Church (Episcopal) in Boston. The couple resided initially in Dorchester, Mass., but Sarah returned to her father's home in Providence to give birth to HPL on August 20, 1890. According to Sonia H. Davis ("Memories of Lovecraft: I" [1971]; in *LR*), Sarah had wanted a girl and had started a hope-chest for that eventuality; she dressed HPL in frocks until he was about four, and kept him in long, golden curls until he demanded at the age of six that they be cut. The family apparently lived in various Boston suburbs, renting quarters in the Auburndale home of Louise Imogen Guiney and her mother during the winter of 1892–93 (according to HPL's testimony); they also spent a vacation in Dudley, Mass., in the summer of 1892. They purchased a home lot in Auburndale, but Winfield's illness in 1893 forced the sale of the lot and the return of Sarah and her son to her father's home in Providence. She indulged HPL in many of his youthful interests, purchasing books and toys for him (she gave him Andrew Lang's translation of the *Arabian Nights* for Christmas 1898), as well as a chemistry set when he became interested in that science in 1898. She vacationed with HPL in Foster at the home of Whipple Phillips's brother James Wheaton Phillips in 1896 (probably as a relief from the death of HPL's grandmother earlier that year) and in Westminster, Mass., in 1899. By necessity, she and HPL moved from 454 Angell Street to smaller quarters at 598 Angell Street in 1904 after the death of Whipple Phillips and the subsequent mismanagement of his estate. Sarah and HPL lived alone in this house from 1904 to 1919. A neighbor, Clara L. Hess, in comments written to August Derleth (see Derleth, "Lovecraft's Sensitivity" [1949]; rpt. *LR*), says that the house had a "strange and shut-up air" and that Sarah said HPL had a "hideous face." This is likely to have been around 1908. Sonia H. Davis states that HPL once admitted that his mother's attitude toward him had been "devastating" (see "Memories of Lovecraft: I"). Appalled by HPL's attempt to enlist in the R.I. National Guard in May 1917, she pulled strings with the family doctor to have HPL declared unfit to serve. The death of her brother, Edwin E. Phillips, in November 1918 probably increased her feelings of insecurity. Hess reports that Sarah once told her about "weird and fantastic creatures that rushed out from behind buildings and from corners at dark" and that once when riding a trolley Sarah did not seem to know where she was. This was probably shortly before her nervous breakdown during the winter of 1918–19; she was removed to Butler Hospital on March 13, 1919. HPL was initially stunned by her absence from home but eventually grew accustomed to it. He wrote her a few letters (those dating to February 24 and March 17, 1921, survive), as well as short poems on Christmas and on her birthday. It was only during her hospital stay that HPL began traveling modestly, attending amateur gatherings in Boston and elsewhere. Sarah died unexpectedly on May 24,1921, after undergoing a gall bladder operation. HPL's initial reaction was shock and even incipient inclinations toward suicide (see *SL* 1.133), but he rapidly recovered his spirits. HPL's feelings about his mother can be inferred from the opening pages of "The Thing on the Doorstep" (1933), in which the young Edward Derby is said to have been prevented from playing unconstrainedly with other children and was "kept closely chained" to his parents' side. When he is thirty-four, Derby's mother dies: "for months he was incapacitated with some odd psychological malady. . . . Afterward he seemed to feel a sort of grotesque exhilaration, as if of partial escape from some unseen bondage." True enough, HPL's emergence from hermitry—as well as his association with Sonia—only began after his mother's death. HPL frequently made remarks such as "My health improved vastly and rapidly, though without any ascertainable cause, about 1920–21" (*SL* 3.370), not acknowledging (publicly, at any rate) that his mother's death was a key to his subsequent emotional maturation.

See Kenneth W. Faig, Jr, *The Parents of Howard Phillips Lovecraft* (Necronomicon Press, 1990).

Lovecraft, Winfield Scott (1853–1898). Father of HPL; the only son to survive to adulthood of George Lovecraft (c. 1818–1895) and Helen Allgood (1821–1881), of Rochester, N.Y. HPL states that his father attended a military school and made modern languages his specialty, but the identity of the school is unknown. Richard D. Squires has discovered that Winfield worked as a blacksmith from 1871 to 1873; thereafter he disappears from the record for more than fifteen years. He married Sarah Susan Phillips in Boston on June 12, 1889. He was apparently employed (as was his father for a time) as a "commercial traveler" (i.e., selling to the trade, not door-to-door), probably for Gorham & Co. (Silversmiths) of Providence. The only testimony for this employment comes from Sonia H. Davis's 1948 memoir (in *LR*); presumably it was told to her by HPL. Winfield lived in the Boston metropolitan area in 1889–92. He made a business trip to Chicago in the spring of 1893 but had to be returned to Providence under restraint following an incident in his hotel room in which (as noted in his medical records) he claimed that the chambermaid had insulted him and that "certain men were outraging his wife" (who was back in Providence). He was admitted to Butler Hospital on April 25, 1893, remaining there for five years, until his death on July 19, 1898. Some scholars have conjectured that HPL visited his father in the hospital, but HPL repeatedly denies that he did so. He states that Winfield was "never conscious" (*SL* 1.6) during his hospital stay, but that clearly was not so; possibly this was the reason HPL was given by his family to explain why he could not visit his father in the hospital. His death certificate lists "general paresis" as cause of death; he probably died of tertiary neurosyphilis, which he had probably been contracted as early as 1871 but no later than 1881, years before he met Sarah. (The negative result of the Wassermann test performed on HPL during his final illness at Rhode Island Hospital in 1937 makes it extremely unlikely that HPL suffered from congenital syphilis, as was once conjectured by David H. Keller.) Winfield left an estate of approximately $10,000. A family portrait, dating to 1892 (printed as the frontispiece to *SR*), is the only known photograph of Winfield. HPL had few memories of his father: he remembered slapping his father on the knee and saying, "Papa, you look just like a young man!" (*SL* 4.355) and said that his father warned him not to "fall into Americanisms of speech" (*SL* 3.362). HPL notes some of Winfield's clothing—"his immaculate black morning-coat and vest, ascot tie, and striped grey trousers" (ibid.) and says that he wore some of the ascots and wing collars himself (the photograph of HPL on the cover of the September 1915 *United Amateur* shows him wearing these items). A family friend, Ella Sweeney, once called Winfield a "pompous Englishman."

See Kenneth W. Faig, Jr, *The Parents of Howard Phillips Lovecraft* (Necronomicon Press, 1990); M. Eileen McNamara, M.D., "Winfield Scott Lovecraft's Final Illness," *LS* No. 24 (Spring 1991): 14; "Medical Record of Winfield Scott Lovecraft," *LS* No. 24 (Spring 1991): 15–17; Richard D. Squires, *Stern Fathers 'Neath the Mould: The Lovecraft Family in Rochester* (Necronomicon Press, 1995).

"Loved Dead, The." Short story (4,000 words); written in collaboration with C. M. Eddy, Jr., probably in October 1923. First published in *WT* (May–June–July 1924); rpt. *Arkham Sampler* (Summer 1948); first collected in *DB;* corrected text in *HM.*

A man living in the rural village of Fenham becomes, as a result of a repressive upbringing, a necrophile; accordingly, he works for one undertaking establishment after another so as to achieve the desired intimacy with corpses. He then begins to commit murders, after which he secures "an ecstatic hour of pleasure, pernicious and unalloyed." On one occasion, however, an employer catches him embracing a corpse and dismisses him. He then enlists in the army during World War I as an opportunity to be near corpses. Returning to Fenham, now a city of some size, he again works for an undertaker and again begins committing murders. At length he arouses the suspicions of the police, and they begin tracking him down as he flees from one hiding place to another. Ending up in a cemetery, he writes an account of his crimes before committing suicide.

The story reads as if HPL had written it from beginning to end, although it clearly was based on a draft by Eddy. The tale is manifestly a self-parody and in its florid language brings to mind "The Hound." Some passages are remarkably explicit for their day: "One morning Mr. Gresham came much earlier than usual—came to find me stretched out upon a cold slab deep in ghoulish slumber, my arms wrapped about the stark, stiff, naked body of a foetid corpse! He roused me from my salacious dreams, his eyes filled with mingled detestation and pity."

When the tale was published in *WT,* it elicited a protest from authorities in Indiana, who sought to have the issue banned. Subsequently, editor Farnsworth Wright became hesitant to accept any stories from HPL that featured explicitly gruesome passages of the kind found in "The Loved Dead," and as a result several of HPL's later tales were rejected.

See David E. Schultz, "On 'The Loved Dead,'" *Crypt* No. 17 (Hallowmas 1983): 25–28.

Loveman, Samuel (1887–1976), poet, playwright, and longtime friend of HPL. Loveman, a native of Cleveland, joined amateur journalism around 1905 and published much of his verse—most of it of a classicist, *fin-de-siècle* cast—in the amateur press and, later, in little magazines. He wrote to Ambrose Bierce in 1908 and later sent him his first book, the slim self-published volume *Poems* (1911). He published Bierce's letters to him as *Twenty-one Letters of Ambrose Bierce* (Cleveland: George Kirk, 1922), with a preface that HPL quoted extensively in "Supernatural Horror in Literature." He later got in touch with George Sterling (1869–1926) and Clark Ashton Smith. HPL had been reading Loveman's poetry in old amateur papers since at least 1915; at that time he wrote the poem, "To Samuel Loveman, Esq., on His Poetry and Drama, Writ in the Elizabethan Style" (*Dowdell's Bearcat,* December 1915). In 1917 HPL wrote to Loveman (then stationed in Fort Gordon, Georgia) expressing admiration for his verse. At HPL's urging Loveman began contributing again to the amateur press, publishing three issues of his own little magazine, *The Saturnian* (June–July 1921, August–September 1921, March 1922), containing his own poems as well as his translations from Heine, Baudelaire, and Verlaine. In December 1919 HPL had a dream involving himself and Loveman, which he wrote almost verbatim into the story "The Statement of Randolph Carter" (1919). About a year later Loveman figured in another dream, which HPL wrote as the prose poem "Nyarlathotep" (1920). HPL first met Loveman in April 1922 in New York. In August 1922 HPL visited him and Alfred Galpin in Cleveland; by this time Loveman had become a close friend of the young Hart Crane, and he introduced HPL to Crane's friends, including William Sommer, William Lescaze, Edward Lazare, and Gordon Hatfield, whose homosexuality offended HPL. The manuscript of HPL's "Hypnos" (1922) bears a dedication "To S. L." In 1922–23 Loveman assisted HPL in editing *The Poetical Works of Jonathan E. Hoag* (1923). Loveman appeared occasionally in later issues of HPL's *Conservative,* notably with the controversial poem "To Satan," printed on the front page of the July 1923 issue. HPL had anonymously praised Loveman's poetry effusively in the "Bureau of Critics" column of the *National Amateur* (March 1922); this review served as the springboard for an attack on Loveman himself by the amateur critic Michael Oscar White in an installment of his series "Poets of Amateur Journalism" (*Oracle,* December 1922). In turn, White was attacked and Loveman defended by Frank Belknap Long ("An Amateur Humorist," *Conservative,* March 1923) and Alfred Galpin ("A Critic of Poetry," *Oracle,* August 1923). HPL himself responded to White in the "In the Editor's Study" column of the *Conservative,* July 1923.

In September 1924 Loveman came to New York, following Hart Crane and settling at 78 Columbia Heights in Brooklyn Heights. For the next year and a half he and HPL were closely in touch as members of the Kalem Club. They met Hart Crane on several occasions in late 1924. By September 1925 Loveman had secured a job at Dauber & Pine bookshop (Fifth Avenue and 12th Street) and worked there for the next several years. In March 1926 he arranged for HPL to be paid to address envelopes for three weeks, one of the few remunerative positions HPL secured during his New York stay. Loveman later made the spectacular claim (unsupported by documentary evidence) that HPL was so depressed during the latter stages of his New York stay that he carried poison on his person so that he could commit suicide if he felt unduly depressed (see Joshi, *H. P. Lovecraft: A Life,* pp. 388–89). In 1926 W. Paul Cook published Loveman's long neo-Grecian poem, *The Hermaphrodite,* which HPL had read and admired years earlier. The July 1926 *United Amateur* included a poem by Loveman about HPL, "To Mr. Theobald."

After HPL returned to Providence, he and Loveman communicated chiefly by correspondence; but Loveman did come to Providence in January 1929, after which the two of them visited Boston, Salem, and Marblehead for a few days. Loveman advised Adolphe de Castro and Zealia Bishop to approach HPL for revision work. On December 31, 1933, HPL attended a New Year's Eve party at Loveman's apartment in Brooklyn Heights, at which time he met Hart Crane's mother. On this occasion Loveman alleges that his friend Patrick McGrath spiked HPL's punch, so that HPL began speaking very volubly (see "Lovecraft as a Conversationalist"). HPL gives no indication of such a thing and probably would have detected alcohol in his drink. Loveman and HPL spent two days in Boston in October 1935. In 1936 the Caxton Press issued Loveman's *The Hermaphrodite and Other Poems*, the only substantial volume of his poetry published in his lifetime. See now *Out of the Immortal Night* (Hippocampus Press, 2004).

After HPL's death Loveman wrote two memoirs, "Howard Phillips Lovecraft" (in *Cats*) and "Lovecraft as a Conversationalist" (*Fresco*, Spring 1958); both are in *LR*. Gradually—in part perhaps because of correspondence with Sonia H. Davis around 1947, when she revealed to him the depth of HPL's anti-Semitism—Loveman began turning against HPL. In a vicious article, "Of Gold and Sawdust" (in *The Occult Lovecraft*, ed. Anthony Raven [1975]), Loveman accuses HPL of being a racist and a hypocrite. It appears that Loveman destroyed his letters from HPL, as almost none survive (in "Lovecraft as a Conversationalist" he claims to possess 500 pages of HPL's letters). The few that do survive were published in HPL's *Letters to Samuel Loveman and Vincent Starrett* (Necronomicon Press, 1994). Loveman is now perhaps best known as a friend of Hart Crane. He wrote numerous articles about Crane and assisted in Brom Weber's *Hart Crane: A Biographical and Critical Study* (1948); an interview with him about Crane was published as a pamphlet, *Hart Crane: A Conversation with Samuel Loveman* (New York: Interim Books, 1964). His play *The Sphinx* (which HPL read and admired) was published by W. Paul Cook in 1944.

Lowndes, Robert A[ugustine] W[ard] (1916–1998). Author, editor, and late correspondent of HPL. HPL wrote Lowndes two letters, dated January 20 and February 20, 1937 (published in *Crypt* No. 62 [Candlemas 1989]: 39–47), encouraging Lowndes in his early literary ventures. Lowndes became very active in science fiction fandom in the 1940s, writing numerous science fiction tales as well as stories of many other types. He edited *Future Fiction* (1941–60), *Science Fiction* (1943, 1953–60), and other magazines but became best known as the editor of the magazines of the Health Knowledge chain: *Magazine of Horror* (1963–71), *Startling Mystery Stories* (1966–71), *Weird Terror Tales* (1969–70), *Bizarre Fantasy Tales* (1970–71), and others; they contained numerous reprints of HPL's work.

"Lucubrations Lovecraftian." Essay (4,570 words); probably written in early 1921. First published in the *United Co-operative* (April 1921); rpt. *MW* and *CE*1.

The essay is divided into four parts. "The Loyal Coalition" concerns an organization in Boston designed to counteract anti-English propaganda sponsored by Irish-Americans; "Criticism Again!" deals with criticisms directed toward him by John Clinton Pryor and W. Paul Cook about HPL's opinionated reviews of amateur journals in the Department of Public Criticism; "Lest We Forget" is a brief diatribe on the need for military preparedness against foreign aggression; and "A Conjecture" is a very short but pungent attack on Elsa Gidlow, who had written derisively of HPL in an unspecified amateur journal. The essay as a whole contains some of HPL's most forceful—and, on occasion, unrestrained—polemical writing.

Lumley, William (1880–1960). Eccentric friend of HPL, born in New York City but residing most of his life in Buffalo, N.Y. In late 1935 HPL revised his

"The Diary of Alonzo Typer" from a draft prepared by Lumley (the original draft was published in *Crypt* No. 10 [1982]: 21–25). HPL also revised Lumley's "occasional bits of verse," perhaps including "The Elder Thing" (*Fantasy Fan*, January 1935). Lumley, a nearly illiterate would-be author, was occupied as a watchman for the Agrico Chemical Company in Buffalo for most of his career. An occultist, he claimed to have voyaged to various mysterious lands such as China and Nepal, and asserted that the myth-cycle written by HPL and his colleagues was based upon the truth. "We may *think* we're writing fiction, and may even (absurd thought!) disbelieve what we write, but at bottom we are telling the truth in spite of ourselves" (*SL* 4.271). He came in touch with HPL around 1931, and they seemed to remain in contact to the end of HPL's life, but only a few of HPL's letters to him survive.

"Lurking Fear, The." Short story (8,170 words); written in mid- to late November 1922. First published in *Home Brew* (January, February, March, and April 1923); rpt. *WT* (June 1928); first collected in *O;* corrected text in *D;* annotated version in *DWH.*

In the first episode, the narrator is searching for the unknown entity that had wreaked havoc among the squatters of the Catskills near the Martense mansion. He is convinced that the haunted mansion must be the locus of the horror, and he takes two colleagues, George Bennett and William Tobey, with him to the place one night. They all sleep in the same bed in one room of the mansion, having provided exits either through the door of the room or the window. Although one of the three is to stay awake while the others rest, a strange drowsiness affects all three. The narrator wakes and finds that the thing has snatched both Bennett and Tobey, who were sleeping on either side of him. Why was he spared?

The second episode finds the narrator coming upon another associate, Arthur Munroe, to assist him in his endeavors. They know that the lurking fear customarily roams abroad during thunderstorms, and during one such storm they stop in a hamlet to wait it out. Munroe, who has been looking out the window, seems anomalously fascinated by something outside and does not respond to a summons. When the narrator shakes his shoulder, he finds that "Arthur Munroe was dead. And on what remained of his chewed and gouged head there was no longer a face."

In the third episode the narrator realizes that he must explore the history of the mansion to come to terms with its lurking horror. The mansion had been built in 1670 by Gerrit Martense, a wealthy Dutchman who hated the English; his descendants similarly shunned the people around them and took to intermarrying with the "numerous menial class about the estate." One descendant, Jan Martense, seeks to escape this unhealthy reclusiveness and is killed for his pains. The episode ends with a cataclysmic sight of a "nameless thing" in a subterranean tunnel he stumbles upon as he digs in Jan Martense's grave.

In the final episode the truth is finally learned: there is not one monster but a whole legion of them. The entire mountain is honeycombed with underground passageways housing loathsome creatures, half apes and half moles. They are the "ultimate product of mammalian degeneration; the frightful outcome of isolated spawning, multiplication, and cannibal nutrition above and below the ground; the embodiment of all the snarling chaos and grinning fear that lurk behind life." In other words, they are the degenerate descendants of the house of Martense.

The story was, like "Herbert West—Reanimator," commissioned for *Home Brew* by George Julian Houtain; but in this case, Houtain provided synopses of the previous segments at the head of the final three episodes, so that HPL need not summarize them in the text itself. At HPL's request, Clark Ashton Smith was commissioned to illustrate the text. Smith had a bit of fun by drawing trees and vegetation obviously in the shape of genitalia, but he may not have been paid for his work. (The *Home Brew* text was reprinted in facsimile by Necronomicon Press in 1977.)

The tale continues the theme of hereditary degeneration found in "Facts Concerning the Late Arthur Jermyn and His Family" and continuing through "The Rats in the Walls" and "The Shadow over Innsmouth"; indeed, "The Lurking Fear" could be thought of as a trial run for "The Shadow over Innsmouth."

There are some minor autobiographical touches in the story. Arthur Munroe's name is probably borrowed from HPL's boyhood friends, the Munroe brothers. The name Jan Martense may have been taken from the Jan Martense Schenck house (1656) in Flatbush, the oldest existing house in New York City. HPL did not see this house during either of his 1922 New York visits and may not, in fact, have learned of it until after writing "The Lurking Fear"; there is, however, a Martense Street very near Sonia Greene's apartment at 259 Parkside Avenue in Brooklyn, and this may be the origin of the name.

See Bennett Lovett-Graff, "Lovecraft: Reproduction and Its Discontents," *Paradoxa* 1, No. 3 (1995): 325–41.

Lyman, Dr. In *The Case of Charles Dexter Ward,* a Boston physician who is one of several experts brought in to assess Charles Dexter Ward's mental condition.

M

Macauley, George W[illiam] (1885–1969). Amateur journalist and colleague of HPL. Macauley coedited *The New Member* (a magazine for recent recruits to the UAPA) when HPL first joined amateur journalism and accordingly accepted HPL's earliest amateur contribution, the essay "A Task for Amateur Journalists" (July 1914). He received his first letter from HPL on October 23, 1914, and continued to correspond regularly until about 1920, after which their correspondence was reduced to Christmas cards; but it revived in 1932. In 1915 HPL wrote to him: "I wish that I could write fiction, but it seems almost an impossibility." After HPL's death Macauley published several works by and about HPL in his amateur journal, *The O-Wash-Ta-Nong,* including "Perverted Poesie or Modern Metre" (December 1937), "Ibid" (January 1938), and "Extracts from H. P. Lovecraft's Letters to G. W. Macauley" (Spring 1938; rpt. *LS* No. 3 [Fall 1980]: 11–16).

Machen, Arthur [Llewellyn Jones] (1863–1947). Welsh author of horror stories, journalist, autobiographer. Machen gained early notoriety for "The Great God Pan" (1890; collected in *The Great God Pan and The Inmost Light* [1894]), *The Three Impostors* (1895), and other works that were accused of being the outpourings of a diseased and licentious imagination. HPL discovered Machen in late spring 1923, evidently at the urging of Frank Belknap Long (see *SL* 1.250); at that time HPL actually considered Machen "the greatest living author" (*SL* 1.234). Machen was temperamentally very different from HPL: an Anglo-Catholic and mystic, he bitterly resented the increasing authority of science over human affairs. HPL's "The Dunwich Horror" seems clearly a borrowing of the central idea of "The Great God Pan" (a god impregnating a human being), while that of "Cool Air" is (by HPL's own admission) derived in part from "Novel of the White Powder" (a segment in *The Three Impostors*). "The Call of Cthulhu" and "The Whisperer in Darkness" owe something to "Novel of the Black Seal" in the same volume, which conveys horror by the "documentary approach" of slow and meticulous accumulation of physical evidence. HPL also appreciated the sensitive aesthetic novel *The Hill of Dreams* (1907) and the short horror novel *The Terror* (1917), as well as Machen's autobiographies, *Far Off Things* (1922), *Things Near and Far* (1923), and *The London Adventure* (1924), which speak poignantly of his impoverished life in London and his walks around that city. "The Unnamable" (1923) may reflect Machen's critical theories as expressed in *Hieroglyphics: A Note upon Ecstasy in Literature* (1902). HPL also read Machen's late novel, *The Green Round* (1933), but found it disappointingly vague and unfocused. Machen's best short tales are collected in *The House of Souls* (1906), which contains "The White People," considered by HPL the second greatest weird tale in all literature; see also *Tales of Horror and the Supernatural* (1948).

See Wesley D. Sweetser, *Arthur Machen* (1964); S. T. Joshi, "Arthur Machen: The Mystery of the Universe," in *The Weird Tale* (1990); Mark Valentine, *Arthur Machen* (1995).

Mackenzie, Robert B. F. In "The Shadow out of Time," the mining engineer who points out to Nathaniel Wingate Peaslee that the scenes Peaslee describes from his disturbing dreams match exactly those found in the Great Sandy Desert in Australia. Mackenzie meets Peaslee in Arkham to plan an expedition to explore the Australian ruins.

Malkowski, Dr. In "The Dreams in the Witch House," a physician in Arkham who attends to Walter Gilman during the latter's final days.

Malone, Thomas F. In "The Horror at Red Hook," a New York police detective who follows the case of Robert Suydam. The case proves so unsettling that he must take a leave of absence in Pascoag, R.I.

"Man of Stone, The." Short story (6,460 words); ghostwritten for Hazel Heald, probably in summer 1932. First published in *Wonder Stories* (October 1932); first collected in *Marginalia;* corrected text in *HM.*

Daniel "Mad Dan" Morris finds in his ancestral copy of the *Book of Eibon* a formula to turn any living creature into a stone statue. Morris admits that the formula "depends more on plain chemistry than on the Outer Powers" and that "What it amounts to is a kind of petrification infinitely speeded up." He successfully turns the trick on Arthur Wheeler, a sculptor who he believes had been making overtures to his wife Rose. He then attempts the same procedure on Rose herself, locking her in the attic and feeding her large amounts of salty meat along with water containing the solution; but she secretly manages to catch rain water from the window and does not drink the water. When Morris is asleep, Rose forces the lock on her door, ties up her husband in his chair (using the same whip with which he had repeatedly beaten her), and, with a funnel, forces him to drink his own solution. He is turned into stone. Rose, weakened and depressed over Wheeler's death, then takes the solution herself. Morris's diary, with a final entry by Rose, is found later by two visitors to the remote cabin.

In a letter to August Derleth (September 30, 1944), Heald wrote: "Lovecraft helped me on this story as much as on the others, and did actually rewrite paragraphs. He would criticize paragraph after paragraph and pencil remarks beside them, and then make me write them until they pleased him" (note in *The Horror in the Museum and Other Revisions* [1970 ed.], p. 27). This would seem to suggest that HPL revised a draft by Heald, but the evidence indicates that he wrote the entire text himself, presumably from her plot outline. The story appears to be the first of the five Heald revisions.

Manly, Jack. In "Sweet Ermengarde," a handsome but impoverished young man who hopes to marry Ermengarde Stubbs. He seeks a fortune in the city, but in the end his quest for Ermengarde's hand is unsuccessful.

Manton, Joel. In "The Unnamable," the principal of East High School and a believer in "old wives' superstitions" although skeptical of the existence of anything so horrible as to be "unnamable." At the end of the tale he learns differently. Manton is based on HPL's colleague, the high school teacher and amateur journalist Maurice W. Moe.

Marcia. In "Poetry and the Gods," a dreamy young woman who writes free verse and later encounters the Greek gods and the shades of several of the great poets of the world.

Marigny, Etienne-Laurent de. In "Through the Gates of the Silver Key," the "distinguished Creole student" of Eastern antiquities, who served with Randolph Carter in the French Foreign Legion and is one of the four individuals who attempt to settle Carter's estate. Carter had named de Marigny his executor. De Marigny is also mentioned as the author of a scholarly article published in *The Occult Review* in "Out of the Æons" (Heald) concerning the hieroglyphics on the mysterious cylinder. He is loosely modeled after HPL's collaborator on the story, E. Hoffmann Price.

Marsh, Barnabas (Old Man) (b. 1862). In "The Shadow over Innsmouth," the owner of the Marsh refinery in Innsmouth. He is grandson of **Capt. Obed Marsh** (1790–1878), who, in the 1840s, brought back to Innsmouth from his travels in the South Seas a wife who was in fact a monstrous amphibian hybrid, in exchange for treasure. **Onesiphorus Marsh** was Old Man Marsh's father; his wife was a woman (actually a hybrid monster) never seen in public.

Marsh, Frank. In "Medusa's Coil," a painter and friend of Denis de Russy, who tries to warn de Russy of the true background of his wife. Marsh begins to paint Marceline's portrait, but de Russy suspects them of having an affair. (Marceline does, in fact, attempt to seduce Marsh, but he resists.) When Antoine de Russy finds Marceline slain, he suspects Marsh. However, Denis de Russy has killed her and cut off her sinister hair.

Martense, Jan. In "The Lurking Fear," a member of a Dutch family that built the Martense mansion atop Tempest Mountain. The mansion was built in 1670 by **Gerrit Martense**, a wealthy New Amsterdam merchant. Jan, returning to the mansion in 1760 after several years in the army, is later killed, probably by his own family, because he has discovered the family's horrible secret: their unwholesome inbreeding has caused them to decline on the evolutionary ladder.

Mason, Keziah. In "The Dreams in the Witch House," the witch who once lived in the old Witch House in Arkham during the celebrated witch hunts in Essex County, occupying the room now inhabited by the student Walter Gilman. The witch plagues Gilman's troubled dreams, and her ratlike familiar kills him.

"Materialist Today, The." Essay (1,210 words); probably written in the summer of 1926. First published in *Driftwind* (October 1926); also as a separate pamphlet (Driftwind Press, 1926); rpt. *MW* and *CE5*.
    A brief exposition of materialist metaphysics and ethics, the essay asserts that "*mind* seems very clearly not a *thing,* but a *mode of motion* or *form of energy*" and that "all matter is in a state of balance betwixt formation and disintegration." HPL states that the "essay" was part of a letter to Walter J. Coates, editor of *Driftwind,* prepared for publication at Coates's insistence (HPL to August Derleth, October 19, 1926; ms., SHSW).

"Matter of Uniteds, A." Essay (1,720 words); probably written in the spring of 1927. First published in *Bacon's Essays* (Summer 1927); rpt. *MW* and *CE1*.
    This substantial essay discusses the split in the UAPA following the disputed election of 1912, leading to the formation of the United Amateur Press Association of America, a group based in Seattle and led by F. Roy Erford, and the UAPA. HPL also wrote of this matter in an unsigned editorial, "The Pseudo-United" (*United Amateur,* May 1920). In both articles, HPL suggests that the UAPA of A was the "rebel" organization, but historians generally conclude that HPL's UAPA was largely responsible for the split.

Mauvais, Michel. In "The Alchemist," a wizard who is killed by Henri, comte de C———, who suspects him of making away with his son Godfrey. Michel's son, Charles le Sorcier, exacts vengeance on the subsequent comtes de C——— for the next 600 years.

Mazurewicz, Joe. In "The Dreams in the Witch House," a loomfixer who resides in the Witch House in Arkham and attempts to help Walter Gilman cope with his bizarre dreams and sleepwalking. At one point he gives Gilman a crucifix, which assists in temporarily warding off the witch Keziah Mason during one of Gilman's dreams.

McNeil, [Henry] Everett (1862–1929). Author of sixteen boys' books and friend of HPL. He first met HPL in New York in September 1922; he was a member of the Kalem Club during 1924–26. McNeil was one of the first to urge HPL to contribute to the newly founded *WT* (see HPL to James F. Morton, March 29, 1923; AHT). He was the author of *Dickon Bend the Bow and Other Wonder Tales* (1903), *The Lost Treasure Cave; or, Adventures with the Cowboys of Colorado* (1905), *In Texas with Davy Crockett: A Story of the Texas*

War of Independence (1908; rpt. 1937), *The Cave of Gold: A Tale of California in '49* (1911), *Tonty of the Iron Hand* (1925), *Daniel Du Luth; or, Adventuring on the Great Lakes* (1926), *The Shores of Adventure; or, Exploring in the New World with Jacques Cartier* (1929), and others, many of them published by E. P. Dutton (HPL believed that Dutton's stingy contracts contributed to McNeil's poverty). He lived mostly in poor parts of New York City, notably Hell's Kitchen; because of this, and because of a feud within the Kalem Club that caused separate "McNeil" and "Leeds" meetings, many members avoided coming to McNeil's apartment, but HPL always came. He appreciated McNeil's childlike naïveté; George Kirk described him as "an oldster—lovely purely white hair, writes books for boys and does not need to write down to them, he is quite equal mentally" (the comment was not meant derogatorily). Late in life, suffering from poor health, he moved to Tacoma, Washington, to live with his sister but died shortly after arriving there. HPL wrote an unaffected tribute to him in a letter to James F. Morton (*SL* 3.92–94; see also 3.112–15). "The Pigeon-Flyers" of *Fungi from Yuggoth* was inspired by McNeil's death.

McNeill, Dr. In "The Curse of Yig," the curator of an insane asylum in Guthrie, Oklahoma. He informs the narrator of the story of the legend of Yig, the snake-god. His asylum houses the half-human, half-snake offspring of Audrey Davis and Yig.

McTighe, ———. In *At the Mountains of Madness,* a radio operator on the Miskatonic Antarctic Expedition of 1930–31 who takes down shorthand accounts of the discoveries of Lake's subexpedition and relays them to the operator on board the brig *Arkham.*

"Medusa's Coil." Novelette (16,950 words); ghostwritten for Zealia Brown Reed Bishop, May–August 1930. First published in *WT* (January 1939); first collected in *Marginalia;* corrected text in *HM.*

A traveler in Missouri finds himself in a deserted region with night coming on. He then spots a decaying mansion set back from the road and approaches it, hoping to find shelter for the night. The place is occupied by an old man, Antoine de Russy, who expresses alarm at the prospect of the traveler spending the night at his place. He finally agrees to house the traveler, and in the course of the evening he tells his tale:

His son, Denis de Russy, had gone to Paris and had fallen in love with a mysterious Frenchwoman, Marceline Bedard. Without his father's permission or knowledge, Denis marries Marceline and brings her back to Missouri to live. In Paris, Marceline had practiced what seemed to be relatively innocuous occultist rituals for the apparent purpose of increasing her tantalizing allure, but when she comes to Missouri she is looked upon with awe and terror by the black servants, especially one "very old Zulu woman" named Sophonisba.

Then, in the summer of 1916, Denis's longtime friend Frank Marsh, a painter, comes to visit the de Russys. He wishes to paint Marceline, thinking that her exoticism will revive him from the aesthetic rut in which he finds himself. He begins the portrait, but tensions rise as Denis believes that Marsh and Marceline are having an affair behind his back. To relieve the situation, Antoine contrives to send Denis to New York to attend his business affairs; but he is disturbed when he overhears Marceline clearly trying to seduce Marsh, who resists her advances.

At last Marsh's painting is done, but horror is in the offing. Antoine awakes one day to find Marceline in a pool of her own blood, her long, luxurious hair hacked off. Marsh must be the culprit; but when Antoine follows a bloody trail to an upstairs room, he finds Marsh dead, with his son Denis crouching next to him, "a tousled, wild-eyed thing." Denis maintains that he killed Marceline because "she was the devil—the summit and high-priestess of all evil." He had come back home because he continued to suspect that Marsh and Marceline were lovers; but as he saw Frank's painting, he realized that Marsh was trying to warn him about his wife, conveying by means of his painting that she was a "leopardess, or gorgon, or lamia." After he had killed Marceline, her hair continued to exhibit signs of animation, and as he hacked off her hair it wrapped itself around Marsh and choked him to death. After telling his tale to his father, Denis dies.

Antoine buries the bodies of Marsh (with Marceline's coils still around him), Marceline, and his son in the cellar. He has, however, preserved Marsh's painting, and reluctantly he takes the traveler up to the room where it is kept. As the two are looking at it, the strands of hair begin to lift themselves from the painting and seem about to strike Antoine. The traveler draws out his automatic and shoots the painting, but Antoine curses at the traveler: the painting has to be kept intact, otherwise Marceline and her coils will revive and come out of their grave. Sounds from the basement seem to confirm that this is happening, so the two men flee; the house in any event is ablaze from a candle that Antoine had dropped in the studio. The traveler makes it to his car, but he sees Antoine overtaken by a "bald, naked figure," and also dimly perceives some large snakelike form among the tall weeds and bushes. As he drives to the nearest town, he learns that the de Russy mansion had in fact burned down five or six years ago. The traveler then informs us of the ultimate horror of the matter: Marceline was, "though in deceitfully slight proportion," a negress.

Notes for the story survive (in AHT), including both a plot outline and a "Manner of Narration" (a synopsis of events in order of narration); here too it is made clear that the final racist revelation—"woman revealed as vampire, lamia, &c. &c.—& unmistakably (surprise to reader as in original tale) a negress"—is meant to be the culminating horror of the tale. The mention here of an "original tale" may suggest that there was a draft of some kind by Bishop, but if so, it does not survive.

WT rejected the story. Later in 1930 HPL discussed with Frank Belknap Long (Bishop's agent) the possibility of sending it to Ghost Stories (HPL to Frank Belknap Long, [November 1930]; AHT), but if it was sent there, it was again rejected. As with "The Mound," the tale was heavily altered and rewritten by August Derleth for its magazine appearance, and he continued to reprint the adulterated texts in book form until the corrected text appeared in 1989.

See Marc A. Cerasini, "Dark Passion: 'Medusa's Coil' and 'Black Canaan,'" Crypt No. 11 (Candlemas 1983): 33–36.

"Memory." Prose poem (350 words); probably written in the spring of 1919. First published in the *United Co-operative* (June 1919), an amateur journal co-edited by HPL, Winifred Jackson, and others. First collected in *BWS;* corrected text in *MW.*

A Daemon of the Valley holds a colloquy with "the Genie that haunts the moonbeams" about the previous inhabitants of the valley of Nis, through which the river Than flows. The Genie has forgotten these creatures, but the Daemon declares: "I am Memory, and am wise in lore of the past, but I too am old. These beings were like the waters of the river Than, not to be understood. Their deeds I recall not, for they were but of the moment. Their aspect I recall dimly, for it was like to that of the little apes in the trees. Their name I recall clearly, for it rhymed with that of the river. These beings of yesterday were called Man."

Poe's influence dominates this very short work: there is a Demon in Poe's "Silence—a Fable"; "the valley Nis" is mentioned in Poe's "The Valley of Unrest" (whose original title was "The Valley Nis," although HPL may not have been aware of the fact); and "The Conversation of Eiros and Charmion," which features a dialogue like that of HPL's tale, speaks of the destruction of all earth life by means of a fire caused by a comet passing near the earth.

See Lance Arney, "The Extinction of Mankind in the Prose Poem 'Memory,'" *LS* No. 21 (Spring 1990): 38–39.

Menes. In "The Cats of Ulthar," the little boy whose kitten disappears following the arrival of "dark wanderers" in Ulthar. He elicits supernatural intervention in exacting vengeance for the loss of his kitten.

Merritt, A[braham] (1884–1943). American author and longtime editor of *American Weekly* (the magazine supplement to the Hearst papers). HPL considered the novelette "The Moon Pool" (*Argosy,* June 22, 1918) one of the ten best weird tales in literature; he disliked the later novel version (*The Moon Pool,* 1919), and came to believe that Merritt sold himself out to the pulps when he could have been the equal of Machen and Blackwood as a weird writer. Some images in "The Moon Pool," as well as the setting on Ponape, may have influenced "The Call of Cthulhu" (1926). *The Dwellers in the Mirage* (1932) may be a homage to HPL in its use of extra-dimensional octopus demon Khalk'ru (an analogue to Cthulhu?). Other novels: *The Metal Monster* (serialized 1920; book form 1946), *The Ship of Ishtar* (serialized 1924; book form 1926), *Seven Footprints to Satan* (serialized 1927; book form 1928), *The Face in the Abyss* (1931), *Burn, Witch, Burn!* (serialized 1932; book form 1933), *Creep, Shadow!* (1934). *The Fox Woman* (1949) is a short story collection. HPL met Merritt in New York on January 8, 1934, when Merritt took HPL to dinner at the Players Club in Gramercy Park. At that time HPL noted: "He knows all about my work, & praises it encouragingly" (HPL to Annie E. P. Gamwell, [January 8, 1934]; ms., JHL). They collaborated (with C. L. Moore, Robert E. Howard, and Frank Belknap Long) on "The Challenge from Beyond" (*Fantasy Magazine,* September 1935).

See T. G. L. Cockcroft, "Random Notes on Merritt and Lovecraft," *Telepath* 1, No. 2 (October 1954): 2–4; Sam Moskowitz, *A. Merritt: Reflections in the Moon Pool: A Biography* (Philadelphia: Oswald Train, 1985).

"Messenger, The." Poem (sonnet); written at 3:07 A.M., November 30, 1929. First published in the *Providence Journal* (December 3, 1929), in B. K. Hart's column "The Sideshow"; rpt. *WT* (July 1938).

Hart had read "The Call of Cthulhu" and expressed mock outrage at the fact that HPL had set the tale in part in a boarding-house at 7 Thomas Street in Providence, where Hart himself had once lived. He threatened (in a "Sideshow" column of November 30, 1929) to send a "large and abiding ghost" to HPL's residence at 3 A.M. HPL accordingly wrote the poem shortly after the designated time of the ghost's arrival. Winfield Townley Scott ("A Parenthesis on Lovecraft as Poet" [1945]; rpt. *FDOC*) believed the poem to be "perhaps as wholly satisfactory as any poem [HPL] ever wrote."

See Donald R. Burleson, "On Lovecraft's 'The Messenger,'" *Crypt* No. 57 (St. John's Eve 1988): 15–18.

Mevana. In "Winged Death," an African from Uganda who, when he develops an unusual illness after being bitten by an insect, is brought to Dr. Thomas Slauenwite to be healed. Slauenwite cures him with antitoxin, whereupon Mevana leads Slauenwite to the lake where he was bitten so that the latter can capture the insects that caused the strange malady.

Miller, Wesley P. In "In the Walls of Eryx," the superintendent of Group A of the Venus Crystal Company. He writes the report about the discovery of the body of Kenton J. Stanfield in the invisible maze.

Miniter, Edith [May Dowe] (1867–1934). Novelist, poet, and amateur journalist residing in central Massachusetts. She was the daughter of amateur writer Jennie E. T. Dowe (about whom HPL wrote an elegy, "In Memoriam: J. E. T. D.," *Tryout,* March 1919). She was the editor of *The Muffin Man* (April 1921), which contained a parody of HPL, "Falco Ossifracus: By Mr. Goodguile"; also of *Aftermath* (a paper issued after amateur conventions). She published one novel professionally, *Our Natupski Neighbors* (Henry Holt, 1916)—about Polish immigrants in Massachusetts—and short stories for professional magazines. HPL claimed that Miniter turned down the job of revising Bram Stoker's *Dracula* for publication. Miniter first met HPL at an amateur convention held at her home at 20 Webster Street in Allston (a suburb of Boston) in July 1920, and again at amateur conventions in Allston on March 10, 1921, and in Malden (another suburb of Boston) on April 12, 1923. She invited HPL to spend two weeks with her and her cousin Evanore Beebe in Wilbraham, Mass., at which time she told HPL about the local legendry (including the story of whippoorwills used in "The Dunwich Horror"). See HPL's memoir, "Mrs. Miniter—Estimates and Recollections" (1934; first published in the *Californian,* Spring 1938). HPL also wrote an elegy, "Edith Miniter" (*Tryout,* August 1934). In 1934–35 HPL was assembling material for a memorial volume on Miniter to be published by W. Paul Cook, but it never materialized; but he ended up with many of her papers and manuscripts (now at JHL). One, a letter written in 1853 by her great-uncle George Washington Tupper, a forty-niner, inspired the minor character named Tupper in "The Shadow out of Time" (1934–35). Much of Miniter's work in the amateur press has now been collected in *Going Home and Other Amateur Writings* (Moshassuck Press, 1995) and *The Coast of Bohemia and Other Writings* (Moshassuck Press, 2000)

Mladdna. In "'Till A' the Seas,'" an old woman who, in the distant future, is (along with a young man named Ull) the last surviving member of the human race. When she dies, Ull is left alone.

Moe, Maurice W[inter] (1882–1940). Teacher, amateur journalist, and long-time friend and correspondent of HPL. Moe taught English at Appleton High School (Appleton, Wis.) and later at West Division High School in Milwaukee. He came in touch with HPL no later than the end of 1914 and maintained a substantial correspondence from that time until HPL's death; it was at Moe's suggestion, in the summer of 1916, that he, HPL, Rheinhart Kleiner, and Ira A. Cole begin a round-robin correspondence cycle, the Kleicomolo. Later, in 1919–21, Moe, HPL, and Alfred Galpin formed the Gallomo correspondence group. For a time Moe made copies of all the correspondents' contributions, but these copies do not appear to survive. A devout theist, Moe argued repeatedly with HPL on religion, but their discussions—at times heated but never acrimonious—appear not to have altered either individual's viewpoints significantly. In one of these argumentative letters (May 15, 1918; *SL* 1.60–66) HPL recounted a dream that later served as the basis for "Polaris" (1918). Moe contributed frequently to the amateur press (and also to scholarly journals on education: see "Amateur Journalism and the English Teacher," *English Journal,* February 1915) but never edited a paper of his own. He did, however, establish the Appleton High School Press Club for his students; they issued a paper, *The Pippin.* HPL wrote two poems commemorating two issues of the paper (those for December 1918 and May 1919), although neither poem was published at the time. Through this press club HPL became acquainted, in late 1917, with Alfred Galpin, then a student at Appleton High School. In 1917 HPL also wrote a brief poem, "To M. W. M." (in "News Notes," *United Amateur,* July 1917); HPL's play *Alfredo* (1918) includes Moe as a character under the guise of Cardinal Maurizio; still later HPL wrote the poem "On the Return of Maurice Winter Moe, Esq., to the Pedagogical Profession" (*Wolverine,* June 1921), commemorating Moe's move to Milwaukee. HPL's "The Unnamable" (1923) features, in Joel Manton, a character clearly based upon Moe. HPL met Moe for the first time on August 10, 1923, when Moe came to Providence; they later went by bus to Boston, where they met Moe's wife and two small boys, Donald and Robert. The next day HPL took Moe, Albert A. Sandusky, and Edward H. Cole on a walking trip to Marblehead, but after trudging for hours the latter three protested and refused to go any further; HPL, still spry, grudgingly relented.

For the next thirteen years their relations consisted solely of correspondence. HPL got into the habit of typing long letters to Moe recounting his various travels (the essays "Observations on Several Parts of America" [1928] and "Travels in the Provinces of America" [1929] are two such items), which Moe was to read and then pass on to other colleagues. In 1927 or 1928 HPL wrote a satirical biography of Ibid, which Moe thought of submitting to the *American Mercury;*

but it was later decided that the piece was too specialized for a general readership, so it remained unpublished until it appeared in the *O-Wash-Ta-Nong* (January 1938). By this time HPL was assisting Moe extensively in the revision of his treatise on the appreciation of poetry, *Doorways to Poetry,* of which HPL thought very highly. One result of the work was HPL's "Sonnet Study" (1929?), consisting of one Petrarchan and one Shakespearean sonnet. HPL also wrote several dozen sonnets, including *Fungi from Yuggoth,* and other poems after a long hiatus. *Doorways* was never published, and the manuscript does not seem to survive. A small pamphlet, *Imagery Aids* (Wauwatosa, Wis.: Kenyon Press, 1931), may be all that is left of this treatise. In late 1934 Moe asked HPL to contribute an article of his choice for an amateur magazine being produced by his students; HPL wrote an essay on traces of Roman architecture in America and sent it to Moe. It never appeared in the magazine, and HPL later believed it to be lost; but a transcript survives in AHT. HPL wrote the essay "Heritage or Modernism: Common Sense in Art Forms" (*Californian,* Summer 1935) as an introduction to the Roman architecture piece.

Moe visited HPL for the second and final time on July 18–19, 1936, as he and his son Robert (who was working in Bridgeport, Conn.) came to Providence. HPL had been corresponding regularly with Robert since 1934. Since they had a car, they managed to visit several of the surrounding towns—Pawtuxet, Warren, and Bristol. At that time Moe and HPL participated in a final correspondence group, the Coryciani, although only two letters by HPL survive. After HPL, R. H. Barlow, and Adolphe de Castro wrote their acrostic poems on Poe on August 8, 1936, Moe himself wrote one of his own and then hectographed all four as *Four Acrostic Sonnets on Edgar Allan Poe* (1936). August Derleth reprinted Moe's poem in his anthology, *Poetry out of Wisconsin* (1937). After HPL's death Moe wrote the brief but poignant memoir, "Howard Phillips Lovecraft: The Sage of Providence" (*O-Wash-Ta-Nong,* [1937]; rpt. *LR*).

"Moon-Bog, The." Short story (3,430 words); written shortly before March 10, 1921. First published in *WT* (June 1926); first collected in *BWS;* corrected text in *D;* annotated version in *DWH.*

Denys Barry, who comes from America to reclaim an ancestral estate in Kilderry, Ireland, decides to empty the bog on his land: "For all his love of Ireland, America had not left him untouched, and he hated the beautiful wasted space where peat might be cut and land opened up." The peasants refuse to assist him for fear of disturbing the spirits of the bog. Barry calls in outside workers and the project continues apace, even though the workers confess suffering from strange and troublesome dreams. One night the narrator, Barry's friend, awakes and hears a piping in the distance: "wild, weird airs that made me think of some dance of fauns on distant Maenalus" (a curious nod to "The Tree"). Then he sees the laborers dancing as if under some form of hypnosis, along with "strange airy beings in white, half indeterminate in nature, but suggesting pale wistful naiads from the haunted fountains of the bog." But the next morning the workers seem to remember nothing of the night's events. The next night things reach a climax: the piping is heard again, and the narrator again sees the "white-clad bog-wraiths" drifting toward the deeper waters of the bog, followed by the mesmerised laborers. Then a shaft of moonlight appears, and "upward along that pallid path my fevered fancy pictured a thin shadow slowly writhing; a vague contorted shadow struggling as if drawn by unseen daemons." It is Denys Barry, who is spirited off and never seen again.

The story was written for a St. Patrick's Day gathering of amateurs in Boston (although the meeting took place on March 10, a week before St. Patrick's Day). The tale is one of the most conventionally supernatural in HPL's oeuvre. It bears an accidental similarity of plot to Lord Dunsany's novel *The Curse of the Wise Woman* (1933).

Moore, C|atherine| L|ucile| (1911–1987). Author of weird and science fiction tales, living in Indianapolis, Indiana, and late correspondent of HPL (1934–37). HPL enjoyed her early tales, especially "Shambleau" (*WT,* November 1933) and "Black Thirst" (*WT,* April 1934); he came in touch with her in 1934 when R. H. Barlow wished to publish some of her tales and asked HPL to write to her about it. HPL introduced her to Henry Kuttner in 1936; they married in 1940 and collaborated on most of their works thereafter. HPL's letters to her survive only in fragments, but he kept hers. In his letters HPL keenly discusses the current political and economic situation and the interplay of economics and artistic creation; he repeatedly advised Moore not to buckle down to hackwork for the pulps. She collaborated with HPL (along with A. Merritt, Robert E. Howard, and Frank Belknap Long) on "The Challenge from Beyond" (*Fantasy Magazine,* September 1935). Moore went on to write many important works of fantasy and science fiction, including "Judgment Night" (1943) and "Vintage Season" (1946).

See Susan Gubar, "C. L. Moore and the Conventions of Women's Science Fiction," *Science-Fiction Studies* 7 (March 1980): 16–27; Gordon R. Benson, Jr., and Virgil S. Utter, *C. L. Moore and Henry Kuttner: A Marriage of Souls and Talent: A Working Bibliography* (Albuquerque, N.M.: Galactic Central, 1989).

Moore, Dr. Henry Sargent. In "Winged Death," a Professor of Invertebrate Biology at Columbia University, author of *Diptera of Central and Southern Africa,* who is killed by his rival, Dr. Thomas Slauenwite.

Morehouse, Dr. Arlo. In "Deaf, Dumb, and Blind," a physician who finds the body of the author Richard Blake in a country cottage, along with the strange message that he (or some other entity) had left in Blake's typewriter.

Morgan, Dr. Francis. In "The Dunwich Horror," a man (whether a medical doctor or a professor is unclear) who, with Henry Armitage and Warren Rice, leads the party that exterminates Wilbur Whateley's monstrous twin brother.

Morris, Daniel ("Mad Dan"). In "The Man of Stone," the occupant of a cabin in the town of Mountain Top (in upstate New York) whose diary constitutes the bulk of the narrative. He learns of a technique perfected by his ancestor, Bareut Picterse Van Kauran, for turning living creatures into stone, and he uses it on a man whom he suspects of having designs on his wife, **Rose.** He also attempts to use it on her, but she thwarts him and successfully turns the tables on him.

Morse, Richard Ely (1909–1986). Poet and correspondent of HPL. Morse, a graduate of Amherst College and residing in Princeton, N.J., was introduced to HPL by Samuel Loveman in May 1932 when HPL was passing through New York; a brisk correspondence thereupon ensued. At the time Morse was a librarian at Princeton University, but in 1933 he moved to Washington, D.C., to do research for his uncle at the Library of Congress. He published one book of poetry, *Winter Garden* (Amherst, Mass.: Poetry Society of Amherst College, 1931). His copy for HPL bears the inscription: "For Howard Lovecraft, Magnus Magister, in return for all his gracious kindness and friendship and for all the shuddering pleasure of his tales and verse with admiration and gratitude from Richard Ely Morse." Morse also published "Some Modern Book Illustrations" (*Californian* 4, No. 4 [Spring 1937]).

Morton, James Ferdinand, Jr. (1870–1941), pamphleteer, amateur journalist, and friend of HPL. Morton received a simultaneous B.A. and M.A. from Harvard in 1892. In 1896–97 he was president of the NAPA; in later years he would become president of the Thomas Paine Natural History Association and vice president of the Esperanto Association of North America. He wrote numerous pamphlets supporting free speech, free love, and the single tax and attacking religion and race prejudice; among his publications are *The Rights of Periodicals* (1905?), *The Curse of Race Prejudice* (1906?), *Sex Morality, Past, Present and Future* (with William J. Robinson and others) (1912), *The Case of Billy Sunday* (with others) (1915), *Exempting the Churches* (1916), and others. Early in life he was an evangelical atheist, but later he converted to Bahaism. Morton first crossed swords with HPL when he defended Charles D. Isaacson against HPL's attack ("In a Major Key") in "'Conservatism' Gone Mad" (*In a Minor Key* No. 2 [1915]); HPL responded with a poem (unpublished at the time), "The Isaacsonio-Mortoniad" (1915). At the time the two were not acquainted. They met unexpectedly at an amateur gathering in Boston on September 5, 1920. Although HPL was immediately taken with Morton, they only became regular correspondents after HPL met Morton again in his two visits to New York in April and September 1922. Morton assisted HPL in revising Jonathan E. Hoag's poems for *The Poetical Works of Jonathan E. Hoag* (1923). He visited HPL in Providence in September 1923, and HPL showed him around Marblehead, Mass., as well as the remote villages of Chepachet and Pascoag, in northwestern Rhode Island. Morton returned to Providence on December 27, 1923. He appears to have been one of the original members of the Kalem Club and met frequently with HPL at its meetings and at other times during the latter's New York stay (1924–26). In 1924 HPL and Morton formed the Crafton Revision Service (an ad for it appeared in *L'Alouette*, September 1924), but evidently it did not do much business. In February 1925 Morton became curator of the Paterson (N.J.) Museum, serving there for the remainder of his life. For a time he hoped to hire HPL as an assistant, but the prospect never materialized. HPL visited Paterson on August 30, 1925, finding the city itself dismal but the nearby Buttermilk Falls picturesque. A year later HPL commemorated the visit in "The Call of Cthulhu" (1926), when the narrator finds an important newspaper clipping while "visiting a learned friend in Paterson, New Jersey; the curator of a local museum and a mineralogist of note."

On July 19, 1927, Morton visited HPL (now back in Providence) along with Frank Belknap Long and Donald Wandrei; on the 23rd he, HPL, and Wandrei staged their ice cream eating contest at Maxfield's in Warren, R.I., each of them sampling twenty-eight different flavors of ice cream. HPL also assisted Morton in securing rock specimens for his museum. On May 12, 1928, HPL visited Morton in Paterson; Morton repaid the favor by passing through Providence in June 1929 and again on July 31–August 2, 1933. Morton came to Rhode Island again on August 4–7, 1934, visiting the town of Buttonwoods in quest of genealogical data. Otherwise HPL's and Morton's friendship was conducted by correspondence, and HPL's side of it is among the most scintillating and wide ranging of any of his letters. The whereabouts of most of these letters are, however, unknown, and to current knowledge they survive only in extensive extracts in AHT. After HPL's death Morton wrote a brief memoir, "A Few Memories" (*Olympian*, Autumn 1940; in *LR*).

Moulton, ———. In *At the Mountains of Madness,* a pilot on the Miskatonic Antarctic Expedition of 1930–31. He accompanies Lake on his subexpedition and is killed by the Old Ones.

"Mound, The." Novelette (29,560 words); ghostwritten for Zealia Brown Reed Bishop, December 1929–January 1930. First published (abridged) in *WT* (November 1940); first collected in *BWS;* corrected text in *HM.*

A member of Coronado's expedition of 1541, Panfilo de Zamacona y Nuñez, leaves the main group and conducts a solitary expedition to the mound region of what is now Oklahoma. There he hears tales of an underground realm of fabulous antiquity and (more to his interest) great wealth and finds an Indian who will lead him to one of the few remaining entrances to this realm, although the Indian refuses to accompany him on the actual journey. Zamacona comes upon the civilization of Xinaian (which he pronounces "K'n-yan"), established by quasi-human creatures who came from outer space. These inhabitants have developed remarkable mental abilities, including telepathy and the power of dematerialization—the process of dissolving themselves and selected objects around them into their component atoms and recombining them at some other location. Zamacona initially expresses wonder at this civilization but gradually finds that it has declined both intellectually and morally from a much higher level and has now become corrupt and decadent. He attempts to escape but suffers a horrible fate. His written record of his adventures is unearthed in modern times by an archeologist, who paraphrases his incredible tale.

Bishop's original plot-germ for the story (as recorded by R. H. Barlow on the surviving typescript) was of the most skeletal sort: "There is an Indian mound near here, which is haunted by a headless ghost. Sometimes it is a woman." HPL found this idea "insufferably tame & flat" (*SL* 3.97) and fabricated a lengthy novelette of underground horror, incorporating many conceptions of his evolving myth-cycle, including Cthulhu (under the variant form Tulu).

The story is the first of HPL's tales to utilize an alien civilization as a transparent metaphor for certain phases of human (and, more specifically, Western) civilization. Initially, K'n-yan seems a Lovecraftian utopia: the people have conquered old age, have no poverty because of their relatively few numbers and their thorough mastery of technology, use religion only as an aesthetic ornament, practice selective breeding to ensure the vigor of the "ruling type," and pass the day largely in aesthetic and intellectual activity. But as Zamacona continues to observe the people, he begins to notice disturbing signs of decadence. Science is "falling into decay"; history is "more and more neglected"; and gradually religion is becoming less an aesthetic ritual and more a degraded superstition. The narrator concludes: "It is evident that K'n-yan was far along in its decadence—reacting with mixed apathy and hysteria against the standardised and time-tabled life of stultifying regularity which machinery had brought it during its middle period." This comment mirrors HPL's ruminations regarding the current state of Western civilization (see, e.g., *SL* 2.309).

The story was far longer a work than HPL needed to write for this purpose, and its length bode ill for prospects of publication. *WT* was on increasingly shaky ground, and Farnsworth Wright had to be careful what he accepted; accordingly, he rejected the story in early 1930 because it was too long and not capable of convenient division as a serial. HPL had, apparently, already been paid by Bishop for his work, but he no doubt would have liked to see the story in print.

The belief that Frank Belknap Long had some hand in the writing of the story—derived from Zealia Bishop's declaration that "Long ... advised and worked with me on that short novel" ("H. P. Lovecraft: A Pupil's View" [1953]; in *LR*)—is countered by Long's own declaration that "I had nothing whatever to do with the writing of *The Mound.* That brooding, somber, and magnificently atmospheric story is Lovecraftian from the first page to the last" (*Howard Phillips Lovecraft: Dreamer on the Nightside* [Arkham House, 1975], pp. xiii–xiv). Long was at this time acting as Bishop's agent. He had apparently typed HPL's manuscript of the tale, for the typescript seems to come from Long's typewriter. After *WT* rejected the story, Bishop evidently felt that the text should be abridged in order to make it more salable. Long did this by reducing the initial typescript's eighty-two pages to sixty-nine—not by retyping, but by merely omitting some sheets and scratching out parts of others with a pen. The carbon was kept intact. Long apparently attempted to market the shortened version, but without success. After HPL's death, August Derleth prepared a radically adulterated and abridged text for publication in *WT,* which was reprinted in Arkham House editions until the unadulterated text was published in 1989.

See W. E. Beardson, "The Mound of Yig?" *Etchings and Odysseys* No. 1 (1973): 10–13; S. T. Joshi, "Who Wrote 'The Mound'?" *Nyctalops* No. 14 (March 1978): 41–42 (revised in *Crypt* No. 11 [Candlemas 1983]: 27–29, 38); Peter H. Cannon, "'The Mound': An Appreciation," *Crypt* No. 11 (Candlemas 1983): 30–32, 51; Michael DiGregorio, "'Yig,' 'The Mound' and American Indian Lore," *Crypt* No. 11 (Candlemas 1983): 25–26, 38; S. T. Joshi, "Lovecraft's Alien Civilisations: A Political Interpretation" and "Some Sources for 'The Mound' and *At the Mountains of Madness,"* in *Primal Sources: Essays on H. P. Lovecraft* (Hippocampus Press, 2003).

"Mrs. Miniter—Estimates and Recollections." Essay (5,210 words); written on October 16, 1934. First published in the *Californian* (Spring 1938); rpt. *MW* and *CE1.*

This poignant essay traces the amateur career of the recently deceased Edith Miniter, with a discussion of her household (including her cousin Evanore Beebe and numerous pets) at a rural home, Maplehurst, outside of Wilbraham, Mass., which HPL visited in 1928. The essay was intended for a booklet devoted to Miniter, to be published by W. Paul Cook, for which HPL had gathered numerous other articles, but the project came to naught. HPL also wrote an elegy, "Edith Miniter" (*Tryout,* August 1934).

Müller, ———. In "The Temple," the boatswain on the German submarine U-29 who apparently commits suicide to escape the horrors he thinks are besetting the vessel.

Munn, H[arold] Warner (1903–1981). American writer of fantasy and horror tales, and friend of HPL. His first story, "The Werewolf of Ponkert" (*WT,* July 1925), was based on a remark in HPL's letter to *WT* (March 1924): "Take a werewolf story, for instance—who ever wrote a story from the point of view of the wolf, and sympathising strongly with the devil to whom he has sold himself?" But it appears that Munn misunderstood the import of HPL's remark, for he has the werewolf regret his condition. Munn wrote several more werewolf stories under the generic title "Tales of the Werewolf Clan"; some were gathered as *The Werewolf of Ponkert* (1958). He was introduced to HPL by W. Paul Cook in the summer of 1927; HPL visited him in Athol, Mass., in the summer of 1928, at which time (on June 28) Munn took HPL to the Bear's Den, a remarkable forest gorge later cited in "The Dunwich Horror" (1928). Cook and Munn visited HPL in Providence in June 1929; HPL returned the favor by visiting Cook and Munn in Athol the next June. HPL and Munn seemed to communicate only sporadically in the 1930s. Munn went on to write many stories for the pulps as well as fantasy and historical novels, including *Merlin's Ring* (1974) and *The Lost Legion* (1980). Late in life he wrote a brief memoir, "H.P.L.: A Remembrance" (*Whispers,* December 1976; in *LR*).

Muñoz, Dr. In "Cool Air," the doctor who treats the narrator when he has a heart attack. Since Muñoz had died eighteen years previously, he keeps his apartment refrigerated to increasingly cooler temperatures to maintain his artificially preserved body. He appears to have been based in part on a Dr. Love (see entry on "Cool Air").

Munroe, Arthur. In "The Lurking Fear," he accompanies the narrator to the haunted Martense mansion, after two other searchers disappear, only to meet a loathsome fate.

Munroe, Chester Pierce (1889–1943). Boyhood friend of HPL, residing at 66 Patterson Avenue in Providence, about four blocks away from HPL's residence at 454 Angell Street. HPL and Munroe became acquainted around 1902, when they attended the Slater Avenue School. HPL remarks that "Chester Pierce Munroe & I claimed the proud joint distinction of being the worst boys in Slater Ave. School. . . . We were not so actively destructive as merely antinomian in an arrogant & sardonic way—the protest of individuality against capricious, arbitrary, & excessively detailed authority" (HPL to Helen Sully, December 4, 1935; ms., JHL). At that time they and other friends formed the Providence Detective Agency and the Blackstone Military Band. It is not clear whether Chester attended Hope Street High School with HPL, but Chester did, in 1905, follow HPL's lead in operating a hectographed paper, the *East Side News,* similar to HPL's *Rhode Island Journal of Astronomy;* in 1905–06 they revived the Providence Detective Agency and Blackstone Military Band, which had apparently been in abeyance for some time, and also formed the Providence Astronomical Society and the East Side Historical Club. Chester also presumably assisted in building the Great Meadow Country Clubhouse in Rehoboth, Mass. (see Munroe, Harold Bateman). On August 12, 1912, Chester was a witness to HPL's will. By 1915 Chester had established himself at the Grove Park Inn in Asheville, North Carolina, although his occupation is unknown. HPL had persuaded him to join amateur journalism, and HPL wrote the article "Introducing Mr. Chester Pierce Munroe" (*Conservative,* April 1915) welcoming him to the organization. In return, Chester apparently arranged for HPL to write the astronomy series "Mysteries of the Heavens" in the *Asheville Gazette-News* (February 16–May 17, 1915).

Munroe, Harold Bateman (1891–1966). Brother of Chester P. Munroe and boyhood friend of HPL. Like his brother, Harold was a member of the various gangs or boyhood groups in which HPL was involved, such as the Providence Detective Agency and the Blackstone Military Band. HPL reports that he and Harold were "Confederates in sympathy, & used to act out all the battles of the War in Blackstone Park" (HPL to Lillian D. Clark, [May 2, 1929]; ms., JHL). Not much is heard of Harold until August 8, 1921, when Harold, now a businessman as well as a deputy sheriff, peremptorily summoned HPL to revisit the Great Meadow Country Clubhouse, just across the state line in Rehoboth, Mass., which HPL and his friends had built around 1907, with the assistance of a Civil War veteran named James Kay. Harold and HPL resolved to resume holding monthly meetings at the clubhouse, along with other boyhood friends such as Ronald Upham and Stuart Coleman, but the plan was quickly forgotten. Munroe is not to be confused with Harold W. Munro, a classmate of HPL's at Hope Street High School and author of the memoir "Lovecraft, My Childhood Friend" (1983; in *LR*).

"Music of Erich Zann, The." Short story (3,480 words); probably written in December 1921. First published in the *National Amateur* (March 1922); rpt. *WT* (May 1925) and *WT* (November 1934); first collected in *O;* corrected text in *DH;* annotated version in *TD.*
    The narrator has "examined maps of the city with the greatest of care," but he cannot find the Rue d'Auseil, where he once dwelt as an "impoverished student of metaphysics" and heard the music of Erich Zann. Zann is a mute viol-player who played in a cheap theatre orchestra and dwelt in the garret apartment of a boarding-house run by "the paralytic Blandot"; the narrator, occupying a room on the fifth floor, occasionally hears Zann playing wild tunes featuring harmo-

nies that seem to have no relation to any known style of music. One night he meets Zann in the hallway and asks to listen in while he plays; Zann accedes, but plays only ordinary music, although it is nevertheless affecting and apparently of his own composition. When the narrator asks Zann to play some of his weirder numbers, and even begins to whistle one of them, Zann reacts with horror and covers the narrator's mouth with his hand. When the narrator attempts to look out the curtained window of the apartment, Zann prevents him from doing so. Later Zann has the narrator move to a lower floor so that he can no longer hear the music. One night, as the narrator comes to Zann's door, he hears "the shrieking viol swell into a chaotic babel of sound" and later hears an "awful, inarticulate cry which only the mute can utter, and which rises only in moments of the most terrible fear or anguish." Demanding entry, he is let in by a harried Zann, who manages to calm himself and writes a scribbled note saying that he will prepare "a full account in German of all the marvels and terrors which beset him." An hour passes while Zann writes; then a strange sound seems to come from the curtained window: ". . . it was not a horrible sound, but rather an exquisitely low and infinitely distant musical note. . . ." Zann immediately stops writing, picks up his viol, and commences to play with demoniac fury: "He was trying to make a noise; to ward something off or drown something out. . . ." The glass of the window breaks, blowing out the candle and plunging the room into darkness; a sudden gust of wind catches up the manuscript and bears it out the window. As the narrator attempts to save it, he gains his first and last look out that lofty window, but sees "only the blackness of space illimitable; unimagined space alive with motion and music, and having no semblance to anything on earth." The narrator runs into Zann in an effort to flee, encountering the mad player still playing mechanically even though he seems to be dead. Rushing from the building, he finds the outside world seemingly normal. But he has, from that time, been unable to find the Rue d'Auseil.

HPL always considered the tale among his best, although in later years noted that it had a sort of negative value: it lacked the flaws—notably overexplicitness and overwriting—that marred some of his other works, both before and after. It might, however, be said that HPL erred on the side of *under*explicitness in the very nebulous horror to be seen through Zann's garret window.

In referring to Zann's instrument throughout the story as a "viol," HPL appears to mean the stringed instrument played between the legs and shaped like a cello; the term is not a poeticism for violin. HPL confirms this when he refers to Zann as a "'cellist" (HPL to Elizabeth Toldridge, [October 31, 1931?; ms., JHL]; that is, violoncellist.

The story appears to be set in Paris. The French critic Jacques Bergier claimed to have corresponded with HPL late in the latter's life and purportedly asked him how and when he had ever seen Paris in order to derive so convincing an atmosphere for the tale; HPL is said to have replied, "In a dream, with Poe" (Jacques Bergier, "Lovecraft, ce grand génie venu d'ailleurs," *Planète* No. 1 [October–November 1961]: 43–46). This story is probably apocryphal, as there is no evidence that Bergier corresponded with HPL. HPL himself stated, shortly after writing the story, "It is not, as a whole, a dream, though I have dreamt of steep streets like the Rue d'Auseil" (HPL to Frank Belknap Long, February 8,

1922; *SL* 1.166–7). The word *Auseil* does not exist in French (nor does *Zann* exist in German), but it has plausibly been asserted that the place name is meant to suggest the phrase *au seuil* ("at the threshold")—that is, that both Zann's room and his music are at the threshold between the real and the unreal. HPL knew only a smattering of French, but he could have come up with such an elementary coinage.

The story was among the most frequently reprinted in HPL's lifetime. Aside from the appearances listed above, it was included in Dashiell Hammett's celebrated anthology, *Creeps by Night* (1931) and its various reprints (e.g., *Modern Tales of Horror* [1932]); it was reprinted in the *Evening Standard* (London) (24 October 1932), occupying a full page of the newspaper. It was to have appeared in an anthology from the Denis Archer firm, but HPL's permission came too late to allow its inclusion. It was one of the first of HPL's tales to be included in a textbook: James B. Hall and Joseph Langland's *The Short Story* (1956).

See John Strysik, "The Movie of Erich Zann and Others," *LS* No. 5 (Fall 1981): 29–32; Donald R. Burleson, "'The Music of Erich Zann' as Fugue," *LS* No. 6 (Spring 1982): 14–17; Robert M. Price, "Erich Zann and the Rue d'Auseil," *LS* Nos. 22/23 (Fall 1990): 13–14; Carl Buchanan, "'The Music of Erich Zann': A Psychological Interpretation (or Two)," *LS* No. 27 (Fall 1992): 10–13.

Musides. In "The Tree," the sculptor who poisons his friend Kalos in order that he might win the competition they are engaged in to create a statue of Tyché for the Tyrant of Syracuse. He is killed and his sculpture destroyed by a limb from the tree at Kalos' tomb that breaks off in a storm. The name means "son of the Muses" in Greek.

Mwanu. In "Facts Concerning the Late Arthur Jermyn and His Family," he is the chief of the Kaliri tribe in the Congo. It is he who confirms to Arthur Jermyn the legends that Arthur has heard about his ancestry.

"My Favourite Character." Poem (36 lines in 6 stanzas); written on January 31, 1925. First published in the *Brooklynite* (January 1926).

This comic poem—in which HPL examines numerous characters in classic and contemporary works of literature, but then decides that, in regard to determining his favorite, "I'll frankly give myself the nomination"—was written for a Blue Pencil Club meeting, in which amateurs were asked to prepare literary contributions on a stated topic.

"Mysteries of the Heavens Revealed by Astronomy." Series of astronomy columns for the *Asheville* [N.C.] *Gazette-News* (February 16–May 17, 1915); rpt. *CE3*.

The series, as published, consists of thirteen sections, some subdivided into two parts: I. "The Sky and Its Contents" (February 16); II. "The Solar System" (February 20); III. "The Sun" (February 23); IV. "The Inferior Planets" (February 27); V. "Eclipses" (March 2); VI. "The Earth and Its Moon" (March 6); VII. "Mars and the Asteroids" (March 9); VIII. "The Outer Planets" (March 13 and 27); IX. "Comets and Meteors" (March 16 and 30); X. "The Stars" (March 20 and 23); XI. "Clusters and Nebulae" (April 13 and 16); XII. "The Constellations" (April 27 and May 1); XIII. "Telescopes and Observatories" (May 11 and 17). However, the first installment announced the series as consisting of fourteen sections, so it appears that section XIV and, probably, the final segment of XIII are lost. Librarians at the Asheville Public Library report that several issues following May 17 are missing, and it is likely that the missing segments appeared here. In the first installment HPL describes the series as "designed for persons having no previous knowledge of astronomy. Only the simplest and most interesting parts of the subject have here been included." HPL's boyhood friend Chester P. Munroe (at this time working in Asheville) probably arranged to have HPL write the articles for the local paper, although there is no documentary evidence to support this assertion. Late in life HPL unearthed the articles and remarked: ". . . their obsoleteness completely bowled me over. The progress of the science in the last twenty or thirty years had left me utterly behind . . ." (*SL* 5.422).

"Mysterious Ship, The." Juvenile story (460 words); written 1902. First published in *SR;* corrected text in *Juvenilia: 1897–1905* (1985) and *MW.*

A "strange brig" docks at various ports, with the result that various individuals are found to have disappeared. The ship goes all over the world and deposits its kidnapped individuals at the North Pole. At this point HPL relates a "geographical fact" that "At the N. Pole there exists a vast continent composed of volcanic soil, a portion of which is open to explorers. It is called 'No-Mans Land.'" Some unnamed individuals find the kidnapped individuals, who then go to their respective homes and are showered with honors.

HPL has prepared this story as a twelve-page booklet, with the imprint: "The Royal Press. 1902." He is clearly aiming for dramatic concision: some of the nine chapters of the story are no more than twenty-five words in length. A revised or elaborated version of the story has recently been found in the HPL materials collected by August Derleth at Arkham House. This version (still unpublished) fleshes out each chapter to about seventy-five to one hundred words each, so that the total comes to 780 words, almost twice the length of the original.

"Mystery of Murdon Grange, The." Round-robin serial tale; apparently "published" in a typewritten manuscript magazine, *Hesperia,* circulated by HPL in 1918–21. Apparently nonextant.

HPL first describes the item in a letter dated June 27, 1918: "My *Hesperia* will be critical & educational in object, though I am 'sugar-coating' the first number by 'printing' a conclusion of the serial *The Mystery of Murdon Grange.* . . . It is outwardly done on the patchwork plan as before—each chapter bears one of my different *aliases*—Ward Phillips—Ames Dorrance Rowley— L. Theobald, &c." (*SL* 1.68). This would seem to suggest that the serial— evidently a parody of a dime-novel mystery—was written entirely by HPL, each chapter or segment affixed with a different pseudonym; but the one segment that has actually been located suggests otherwise. This segment appeared in the amateur journal *Spindrift* 5, No. 1 (Christmas 1917): 26–27, and contains the end of chapter 2 and the beginning of chapter 3; it is signed "B[enjamin] Winskill," an amateur journalist living in Buxted, Sussex, UK. The journal was edited by Ernest Lionel McKeag of Newcastle-upon-Tyne. What this suggests is that the story was a round-robin serial, with several different amateurs writing various segments; at best, HPL wrote one or more subsequent chapters in *Hesperia*, perhaps issuing them as continuations of the serial presumably begun in *Spindrift*. HPL never mentions "The Mystery of Murdon Grange" in any other extant correspondence, but mentions *Hesperia* in June 1921 as an ongoing enterprise (*SL* 1.136). HPL would type several carbon copies of the paper and send each copy on a designated round of circulation to amateurs; HPL appears to allude to it in "Amateur Journalism: Its Possible Needs and Betterment" (a lecture delivered on September 5, 1920): "I myself attempted to circulate [a manuscript magazine] two years ago, yet it disappeared before it could leave New England" (*MW* 449). No issues of *Hesperia* have been found.

"Mystery of the Grave-yard; or, 'A Dead Man's Revenge': A Detective Story, The." Juvenile story (1,310 words); written c. 1898–99. First published in *SR;* corrected text in *Juvenilia: 1897–1905* (1985) and *MW*.

Joseph Burns has died. Burns's will instructs the rector, Mr. Dobson, to drop a ball in his tomb at a spot marked "A." He does so and disappears. A man named Bell announces himself at the residence of Dobson's daughter, saying that he will restore her father for the sum of £10,000. The daughter, thinking fast, calls the police and cries, "Send King John!" King John, arriving in a flash, finds that Bell has jumped out the window. He chases Bell to the train station, but Bell gets on a train as it is pulling out of the station. There is no telegraph service between the town of Mainville, where the action is taking place, and the "large city" of Kent, where the train is headed. King John rushes to a hackney cab office and says to a black hackman that he will give him two dollars (even though pounds were mentioned before) if he can get him to Kent in fifteen minutes. Bell arrives in Kent, meets with his band of desperadoes (which includes a woman named Lindy), and is about to depart with them on a ship when King John dramatically arrives, declaring: "John Bell, I arrest you in the Queen's name!" At the trial, it is revealed that Dobson had fallen down a trapdoor at the spot marked "A" and had been kept in a "brilliantly lighted, and palatial apartment" until he rescues himself by making a wax impression of the key to the door and makes a dramatic entrance at the trial. Bell is sent to prison for life; Miss Dobson has become Mrs. King John.

The story is clearly influenced by the dime novel, a form of popular fiction widely read by unsophisticated readers from 1860 to the early twentieth century. HPL himself admitted reading several series of adventure stories in dime-novel format, including those focusing on such "heroes" as Nick Carter, Old King Brady, and Prince John. Possibly HPL's King John is a fusion (at least in name) of Old King Brady and Prince John. (King John is presumably the hero of another lost HPL story written around this time, "John, the Detective.") Many dime novels suggested the supernatural but explained it away at the end, as HPL's story does, and many had frenetic, action-packed plots. HPL also attempts a rudimentary form of dialect in the speech of the hackman.

N

"**Nameless City, The.**" Short story (5,070 words); probably written in mid- to late January 1921. First published in the *Wolverine* (November 1921); rpt. *Fanciful Tales* (Fall 1936) and *WT* (November 1938); first collected in *O;* corrected text in *D;* annotated version in *DWH.*

An archaeologist seeks to explore the nameless city, which lies "remote in the desert of Araby." It was of this place that Abdul Alhazred "the mad poet" dreamed the night before he wrote his "unexplainable couplet":

> That is not dead which can eternal lie,
> And with strange aeons even death may die.

The narrator burrows into the sand-choked apertures that lead into some of the larger structures of the city. He is disturbed by the odd proportions of a temple into which he crawls, for the ceiling is very low to the ground and he can scarcely kneel upright in it. He descends an immense staircase that leads down into the bowels of the earth, where he finds a large but still very low-built hall with odd cases lining the walls and frescoes covering the walls and ceiling. The creatures in the cases are very peculiar—apparently reptilian, but in size approximating a small man. Even though it is these anomalous entities who are portrayed in the frescoes, the narrator convinces himself that they are mere totem-animals for the human beings who must have built the city and that the historical tableaux depicted in the frescoes are metaphors for the actual (human) history of the place. But this delusion is shattered when the narrator perceives a gust of cold wind emerging from the end of the hallway, where a great bronze gate lies open and from which a strange phosphorescence emerges. He then sees in the luminous abyss the entities themselves rushing in a stream before him. Somehow he manages to escape and tell his story.

HPL admits (*SL* 1.122) that it was largely inspired by a dream, which in turn was triggered by a suggestive phrase in Dunsany's *Book of Wonder,* "The unreverberate blackness of the abyss" (the last line of "The Probable Adventure of the Three Literary Men"). A more concrete source is the entry on "Arabia" in the 9th edition of the *Encyclopaedia Britannica,* which HPL owned. He copied down part of this entry in his commonplace book (#47), especially the part about "Irem, the City of Pillars . . . supposed to have been erected by Shedad, the latest despot of Ad, in the regions of Hadramaut, and which yet, after the annihilation of its tenants, remains entire, so Arabs say, invisible to ordinary eyes, but occasionally, and at rare intervals, revealed to some heaven-favoured traveller." HPL mentions Irem in passing in his tale, suggesting that the nameless city was an even older city. A later entry in the commonplace book (#59) is clearly an account of the dream that inspired the story: "Man in strange subterranean chamber—seeks to force door of bronze—overwhelmed by influx of waters."

Although the tale remained among HPL's favorites, he said it was "rejected by all the paying editors" (HPL to Duane W. Rimel, February 14, 1934; ms, JHL). *WT* rejected it twice. In early 1932 the story was accepted by Carl Swanson for a new magazine, *Galaxy,* but it never got off the ground. *The Fantasy Fan* accepted it but also failed before it could be published. Julius Schwartz's *Fantasy Magazine* rejected it, and *The Galleon* may also have done so. It finally appeared in the semi-professional magazine *Fanciful Tales,* edited by Wilson Shepherd and Donald A. Wollheim, with "59 bad misprints" (*SL* 5.368).

Abdul Alhazred makes his first appearance in HPL's work in this story, although he is not yet declared to be the author of the *Necronomicon.* The basic scenario of the tale was utilized, with vast expansion of depth and detail, in *At the Mountains of Madness.*

See Dan Clore, "Overdetermination and Enigma in Alhazred's Cryptic Couplet," *LS* No. 34 (Spring 1996): 11–13.

Narrators, Unidentified. Many of HPL's tales are narrated by individuals who, although not identified by name, either play an integral part in the story or serve merely as the conduit through which the events of the story are conveyed. They are described briefly below:

"The Beast in the Cave": The narrator becomes lost exploring the Mammoth Cave. In trying to escape, he encounters and kills a denizen of the cave, who turns out to be not a beast but a man.

"Beyond the Wall of Sleep": The narrator is an intern at the state (New York) psychopathic institution. It is he who cares for Joe Slater and who devises a "cosmic radio" to communicate with the "dream-soul" (actually an extraterrestrial entity) who temporarily inhabits Slater's body.

"The Book": The narrator of the fragment obtains an ancient handwritten volume—presumably from a book dealer. He perceives that he is followed home, "for he who passes the gateways [to which the book is a "key"] always wins a shadow, and never again can he be alone." Upon reading the book, he finds he can no longer "see the world as I had known it."

"The Colour out of Space": The narrator is a surveyor, working on the outskirts of Arkham where a new reservoir is to be built. He finds that those living there consider the area of the former Nahum Gardner farm to be "evil," but no one will divulge any information as to why, except the aged Ammi Pierce. The narrator serves as a mouthpiece for Pierce's story.

"The Crawling Chaos": The narrator, who is accidentally administered an overdose of opium, tells the ensuing drug-induced vision, ending in his witnessing the destruction of the world.

"The Curse of Yig": The narrator is researching snake lore in Oklahoma, investigating the legend of Yig. The curator of an insane asylum reveals to him the only surviving half-human, half-snake offspring of Yig and a human female.

"Dagon": The narrator, a supercargo on an unspecified sailing vessel, is captured in the Pacific Ocean by a German man-of-war. He escapes in a small boat and, after several days of drifting, finds himself run aground. He encounters first a Cyclopean monolith bearing strange marine carvings, then a hideous monster of the kind depicted on the monolith. He escapes and ultimately finds himself confined in a hospital in San Francisco. He later comes to believe that he is still pursued by the creature.

"The Disinterment": The narrator awakens in a hospital bed to find that he was stricken with leprosy and treated for it by his friend Marshall Andrews. He learns that Andrews has unorthodoxly "cured" him of the disease by transplanting his head to the body of an African American.

"The Electric Executioner": The narrator is an auditor with the Tlaxcala Mining Company of San Francisco. He is tasked with finding one Arthur Feldon, who disappeared in Mexico with important company papers. He finds himself on a train in the company of a dangerous maniac, who claims to have devised a hoodlike instrument for performing executions. The narrator tricks the madman into donning the device, and the man is accidentally killed by it. The narrator faints, but is later informed that he was alone in the train car.

"The Evil Clergyman": The narrator investigates the attic chamber of an absent clergyman, whose library contains not only theological and classical books, but also treatises on magic. Somehow, the narrator invokes the clergyman, who alters the appearance of the narrator to resemble his own. Since this is not a story, but an account of an actual dream from a letter to Bernard Austin Dwyer, the "narrator" is HPL himself.

"Ex Oblivione": The narrator, weary with the "ugly trifles of existence," begins dreaming of a gate in a "golden valley," later discovering that the gate leads to oblivion.

"The Festival": The narrator visits his ancestral (seventeenth century) home in Kingsport because his ancestors are bidden to "keep festival . . . once every century, that the memory of primal secrets not be forgotten." When the identity of the old man he encounters there—"the true deputy of my fathers"—is accidentally revealed to him, he leaps into the underground river beneath the house and is found the next day half frozen in the harbor. Those who tend to him at the hospital dismiss his account of his experiences as a "psychosis," although he is convinced his experience was real.

"From Beyond": The narrator is the "best friend" of the crazed inventor and philosopher Crawford Tillinghast. Tillinghast demonstrates for him a weird device that reveals the existence of creatures that cannot be perceived by the five senses. In terror, the narrator fires his revolver at Tillinghast's machine and destroys it, and thus is unable to prove what Tillinghast has shown him.

"The Ghost-Eater": Traveling on foot, the narrator encounters a house in a deserted wood, where he stays for the evening, to encounter what he later learns may have been a werewolf.

"The Green Meadow": The narrator (writing in classical Greek) tells of how he finds himself near a stream on a peninsula that breaks off and floats away. He approaches an island and experiences a revelation, which is not revealed, as the concluding text of his narrative is illegible.

"The Haunter of the Dark": The narrator, perhaps a detective, is probably the most distant observer of any story by HPL—his presence hinted at only by the invitation, "let us summarise the dark chain of events from the expressed point of view of [Robert Blake,] their chief actor."

"He": Increasingly disillusioned by his residence in New York City, the narrator seeks out the few remaining havens of antiquity in the city. He encounters an elderly man—a kindred spirit—who leads him to an out-of-the-way place where he is shown pandemoniac visions of a New York of both the past and the future. The narrator is found on the street, badly battered and unable to retrace his way back to the old man's place. He ultimately returns "home to the pure New England lanes." Though developed only rudimentarily, the narrator is perhaps the most autobiographical of HPL's characters in spirit.

"Herbert West—Reanimator": The narrator is a friend and colleague of Herbert West, first as fellow medical student, then later a partner in practice. He observes the outcome of all West's experiments and witnesses West's demise at the hands of West's partially successful experiments in reanimation—a fate he himself escapes because he was merely West's assistant.

"The Hound": The narrator and his colleague, St. John, are graverobbers and "neurotic virtuosi," who amass a museum of charnel trophies. After St. John is destroyed by the creature from whom they steal an ancient amulet, the narrator vows to take his own life to escape the fate that befell his friend.

"Hypnos": The narrator, a sculptor, claims to have had a friend who led him on various dream voyages, and who perished after offending Hypnos, "lord of sleep," leaving him a perfectly sculptured bust of marble. Quite naturally, the narrator is considered mad, the bust being thought to be his own handiwork.

"In the Vault": The narrator is the personal physician and confidant of George Birch, the careless undertaker to whom the events of the story are told.

"The Loved Dead": The reclusive narrator tells of the onset and progression of his necrophilia, before taking his own life as he is about to be apprehended by the police.

"The Lurking Fear": Accompanied by two friends, the narrator seeks "the lurking fear" in the deserted Martense mansion on Tempest Mountain. His investigation reveals the presence of a race of apelike entities—the degenerate offspring of the Martense family—living in a network of tunnels beneath the house.

"Medusa's Coil": The narrator is a traveler in Missouri who seeks lodging as night approaches. He comes to the dilapidated home of Antoine de Russy, who reluctantly allows him to spend the night. The narrator hears from de Russy the tale of his son, Denis, and his strange wife, Marceline, both dead now and both buried in the cellar by de Russy. Later, as the two observe the painting of the wife, the narrator senses that the painting is animated, and in terror he shoots it with his pistol, thereby revivifying her corpse in the cellar. As de Russy and the narrator flee, the house is accidentally set afire. In town, the narrator is informed that the house had burned down some years ago.

"The Moon-Bog": Denys Barry invites his friend, the narrator, to visit him at his new home—his ancestral estate—in Kilderry, Ireland. The narrator witnesses Barry's demise at the hands of the vengeful spirits that inhabit the bog that Barry drains.

"The Mound": The narrator goes to Oklahoma to investigate and corroborate a ghost-tale he had heard among the white settlers and Indians. He discovers the magnetic cylinder containing the narrative of Panfilo de Zamacona y Nuñez, concerning the subterranean realm of K'n-yan.

"The Music of Erich Zann": The narrator, a student of metaphysics, takes up residence in an ancient building on the Rue d'Auseil. There he hears the unearthly music of Erich Zann, whom he tries to meet so that he may hear more of Zann's music. One night he visits Zann, when he hears Zann call out as if in terror. Zann begins playing maniacally, and when they hear strange rattlings at Zann's garret window, the narrator looks through it, but sees only "the blackness of space illimitable." He flees the house, and when he tries to find it again he cannot.

"The Nameless City": In the desert of Araby, the narrator discovers an ancient "nameless city," which he explores only to find that it was not fashioned by men but by strange, reptilian creatures.

"The Night Ocean": The narrator, an artist, tells of the nebulous, unseen presences he senses on the beach or in the ocean during his vacation to a tourist area during the off season.

"Nyarlathotep": The narrator confusedly recalls the coming of a mysterious Pharaoh-like individual named Nyarlathotep, who appears to be the harbinger of the collapse of the universe.

"The Outsider": The narrator knows nothing of his ancestry or origins— indeed, little at all about himself. He thinks that he lives in a castle, but when he ascends to its tower to look at the surrounding landscape, he emerges at ground level—suggesting that his dwelling had been far underground. He goes exploring and finds a home in which much revelry is taking place. Just as he attempts to meet the inhabitants, they flee in terror from a hideous creature that has entered the home simultaneously with the narrator. The narrator is shocked to learn that the creature is merely his reflection in a mirror.

"The Picture in the House": The narrator, who is bicycling through the Miskatonic Valley seeking genealogical data, is caught in a rainstorm and seeks shelter in a ramshackle house, where he encounters a preternaturally old man who turns out to be a cannibal.

"Polaris": In dream, the narrator is tasked with manning the watch-tower of Thapnen, to warn against a siege by the city's foes, the Inutos. Unfortunately, the Pole Star casts a spell on him, and he falls asleep at his post. He awakens to real life, but believes he still dreams and vainly tries to "awaken" so that he can warn his fellow Lomarians of imminent attack by the Inutos.

"The Shadow over Innsmouth": See Olmstead, Robert (whose name is provided only in HPL's notes for that story).

"The Shunned House": The narrator is the nephew of Dr. Elihu Whipple; his own profession is not specified. As a youth, the narrator heard much about the mysterious "shunned house," about which Whipple had conducted considerable research. His interest piqued by his uncle's findings, he visits the house with increasing frequency, until he stays there overnight and observes "the thin, yellowish, shimmering exhalation" that he had seen there in his youth. He and Whipple attempt to eradicate the entity, but during their vigil the entity overtakes Whipple and the narrator is compelled to kill his uncle to release the old man from the grip of the entity. Finally, he pours carboys of acid into the earth to destroy the thing.

"The Silver Key": See Phillips, Ward (who is identified as the narrator only in "Through the Gates of the Silver Key").

"The Transition of Juan Romero": The narrator is a laborer in the Norton Mine, in the American Southwest. He and Romero investigate a strange throbbing sound emanating from the mine. Romero becomes separated from the narrator and disappears into the cave. The narrator sees something he cannot describe, nor can he be certain whether he has seen anything or merely dreamt it, but somehow he escapes the mysterious fate that befalls Romero.

"What the Moon Brings": The narrator admits to being terrified of the moon and moonlight, because they seem to transform the known landscape into something unfamiliar and hideous.

"Nathicana." Poem (99 lines); probably written no later than 1920, apparently in conjunction with Alfred Galpin. First published in the *Vagrant* ([Spring 1927]).

A poem speaking in Poe-like accents of the mysterious woman Nathicana. It was meant as "a parody on those stylistic excesses which really have no basic meaning" (HPL to Donald Wandrei, [August 2, 1927]; ms., JHL). Apparently Galpin was somehow involved in the composition, as the pseudonym under which the poem was published ("Albert Frederick Willie") alludes in its first two names to Galpin and in its last name to his mother's maiden name, Willy.

Necronomicon. Mythical book of occult lore invented by HPL.

The work is first cited by name in "The Hound" (1922), although its purported author, Abdul Alhazred, was cited as the author of an "unexplainable couplet" in "The Nameless City" (1921). HPL states that the name Abdul Alhazred was supplied to him at the age of five by "a family elder—the family lawyer [Albert A. Baker], as it happens—but I can't remember whether I asked him to make up an Arabic name for me, or whether I merely asked him to criticise a choice I had otherwise made" (HPL to Robert E. Howard, January 16, 1932; AHT). The coinage was somewhat unfortunate, as it contains a reduplicated article (Abd*ul Al*hazred). A more idiomatic coinage would have been Abd el-Hazred.

HPL cited his book so frequently in his tales that by late 1927 he felt the need to write a "History of the *Necronomicon*" to keep his references consistent. At that time he noted that the work had been written by Alhazred around 700 C.E. and titled by him *Al Azif* (a term HPL lifted from Samuel Henley's notes to William Beckford's *Vathek,* referring to the nocturnal buzzing of insects). It was translated into Greek in 950 by Theodorus Philetas but subsequently banned by the patriarch Michael. HPL then attributes a Latin translation of 1228 to Olaus Wormius, mistakenly believing that this seventeenth-century Danish scholar lived in the thirteenth century (see "Regner Lodbrog's Epicedium"). HPL notes an English translation by John Dee—a detail Frank Belknap Long provided in "The Space-Eaters" (*WT,* July 1928), written earlier in 1927 and read by HPL in manuscript (see *SL* 2.171–72). In a late letter (*SL* 5.418) HPL attempts a derivation of the Greek title: "*nekros,* corpse; *nomos,* law; *eikon,* image = An Image [or Picture] of the Law of the Dead." Unfortunately, HPL is almost entirely wrong. By the laws of Greek etymology, the word would derive from *nekros, nemo* (to divide, hence to examine or classify), and *-ikon* (neuter adjectival suffix) = "An examination or classification of the dead."

How HPL came up with the idea of the *Necronomicon* is unclear. His first mythical book was the Pnakotic Manuscripts, cited in "Polaris" (1918); an unnamed book is mentioned in "The Statement of Randolph Carter" (1919). Donald R. Burleson ("Lovecraft: The Hawthorne Influence," *Extrapolation* 22 [Fall 1981]: 267) notes that an "old volume in a large library,—every one to be afraid to unclasp and open it, because it was said to be a book of magic" cited in one of Nathaniel Hawthorne's notebooks, which HPL is known to have read around 1920; but recall that among the "infinite array of stage properties" that HPL in "Supernatural Horror in Literature" identifies in the standard Gothic novel were "mouldy hidden manuscripts." Poe's tales are also full of allusions to real and imaginary books. Probably no single source is to be identified in HPL's use of the mythical book.

HPL's longest quotations from the *Necronomicon* occur in "The Festival" (1923) and "The Dunwich Horror" (1928). Indeed, the book is rarely quoted elsewhere; instead, its contents are merely alluded to. Robert M. Price ("Genres in the Lovecraftian Library," *Crypt* No. 3 [Candlemas 1982]: 14–17) identifies a shift in HPL's use of the book, from a demonology (guide to heretical beliefs) to a grimoire (a book of spells and incantations). Still later, as HPL "demythologized" his imaginary pantheon of "gods" and revealed them to be merely extraterrestrial aliens, the *Necronomicon* is shown to be considerably in error in regard to the true nature of these entities: in *At the Mountains of Madness* the narrator notes that the Old Ones of Antarctica were "the originals of the fiendish elder myths which things like the Pnakotic Manuscripts and the *Necronomicon* affrightedly hint about."

When asked late in life by James Blish why he did not write the *Necronomicon* himself, HPL noted that in "The Dunwich Horror" he had cited from page 751 of the work, making the writing of such a book a very extensive undertaking. He wisely added: ". . . one can never *produce* anything even a tenth as terrible and impressive as one can awesomely *hint* about. If anyone were to try to *write* the *Necronomicon,* it would disappoint all those who have shuddered at cryptic references to it." This has not stopped several individuals over the past twenty-five years from producing books bearing the title *Necronomicon,* some of which are indeed clever hoaxes but surely very far from HPL's own conception of the work.

See August Derleth, "The Making of a Hoax" (in *DB*); Mark Owings, *The Necronomicon: A Study* (Baltimore: Mirage Associates, 1967); Robert M. Price, "Higher Criticism and the *Necronomicon*," *LS* No. 6 (Spring 1982): 3–13; Dan Clore, "The Lurker at the Threshold of Interpretation: Hoax *Necronomicons* and Paratextual Noise," *LS* No. 42 (Summer 2001): 64–74.

"Nemesis." Poem (55 lines in 11 stanzas); written on November 1, 1917. First published in *Vagrant* (June 1918); rpt. *WT* (April 1924).

Using the meter of Swinburne's *Hertha*, HPL notes that the poem "presents the conception, tenable to the orthodox mind, that nightmares are the punishments meted out to the soul for sins committed in previous incarnations—perhaps millions of years ago!" (*SL* 1.51). HPL parodies the poem in "A Brumalian Wish" (among his Christmas greetings). Alfred Galpin wrote an imitation of it in "Selenaio-Phantasma" (*Conservative*, July 1918). HPL used ll. 8–10 as the epigraph to "The Haunter of the Dark" (1935).

See Donald R. Burleson, "On Lovecraft's 'Nemesis,'" *LS* No. 21 (Spring 1990): 40–42.

"News Notes." Column in the *United Amateur,* customarily written by the Official Editor of the UAPA. HPL wrote the columns for July 1917; September 1918 (in part); September, November 1920; January, March, May, July, September, November 1921; January, March, May 1922; May 1924; July 1925; rpt. *CE1*.

The articles deal with the activities of various amateurs; HPL makes sure to note several of his own colleagues, including W. Paul Cook, Maurice W. Moe, George Julian Houtain, Alfred Galpin, Winifred Virginia Jackson, Myrta Alice Little, Sonia H. Greene (discussed extensively in the columns for September 1921 and May 1924), Samuel Loveman, Clark Ashton Smith, and Frank Belknap Long.

Ni, Hak. In "Collapsing Cosmoses," a military commander in the "intradimensional city of Kastor-Ya" who takes steps to combat the interstellar menace approaching the planet.

"Nietzscheism and Realism." Essay (1,680 words); probably written in the summer of 1921. First published in the *Rainbow* (October 1921; as "Nietscheism and Realism"); rpt. *MW* and *CE5*.

The text is a series of excerpts from two letters written to Sonia H. Greene (HPL to the Gallomo, August 21, 1921; AHT). HPL offers cynical reflections on politics and society, many of them inspired (in spite of the title) not from Nietzsche but from Schopenhauer. In politics, HPL recommends an aristocracy "because I deem it the only agency for the creation of those refinements which make life endurable for the human animal of high organisation." Democracy and ochlocracy (rule of the mob), on the other hand, merely squanders "the aesthetic and intellectual resources which aristocracy bequeathed them and which they could never have created for themselves." HPL considerably refined these views in his later political philosophy but never wholly abandoned them.

"Night Ocean, The." Short story (9,840 words); written in collaboration with R. H. Barlow, summer 1936. First published in the *Californian* (Winter 1936); first collected in *HM*, corrected text in *Eyes of the God* (Hippocampus Press, 2002.

The narrator, a painter, comes to a sea resort named Ellston Beach to rest from the grueling task of completing a painting for a competition. He rents a bungalow far from the town, facing directly onto the beach and the ocean. Initially, as he wanders the beach and swims in the ocean, he appears to derive benefit from the tranquil atmosphere; but gradually he begins to feel uneasy. He hears that a few tourists had drowned inexplicably. Then he comes upon an object on the beach that looks like a rotted hand that may have been gnawed upon by some sea creature. At length, as his loneliness and unease continue, he seems to see—in the course of a furious rainstorm—a strange figure ("a dog, a human being, or something more strange") emerging from the water, carrying something across its shoulder. For a moment the narrator thinks this creature is approaching his bungalow, but it veers away at the last minute. The narrator is left pondering the mysteries of the night ocean.

The manuscript of this story has recently been discovered (it had been microfilmed by Barlow's literary executor, George T. Smisor), and it shows that all the plotting and most of the prose is Barlow's, with HPL revising the language throughout but contributing perhaps less than 10% to the overall story. HPL himself told Hyman Bradofsky (editor of the *Californian*) that he "ripped the text to pieces in spots" (HPL to Hyman Bradofsky, November 4, 1936; ms., JHL); but in letters to others he commends the story highly, something he is not likely to have done if he had had a great deal to do with it.

The story is a finely atmospheric weird tale. It comes very close—closer, perhaps, than any of HPL's own works with the exception of "The Colour out of Space"—to capturing the essential spirit of the weird, as HPL wrote of some of Blackwood's works in "Supernatural Horror in Literature": "Here art and restraint in narrative reach their very highest development, and an impression of lasting poignancy is produced without a single strained passage or a single false note. . . . Plot is everywhere negligible, and atmosphere reigns untrammelled."

See Brian Humphreys, "'The Night Ocean' and the Subtleties of Cosmicism," *LS* No. 30 (Spring 1994): 14–21.

"Nightmare Lake, The." Poem (66 lines); probably written in the fall of 1919. First published in *Vagrant* (December 1919).

In "distant Zan" there is an ominous lake filled with dreadful creatures—lizards, snakes, ravens, vampires, necrophagi—but the final horror comes when the narrator realizes that the lake covers over a sunken city that contains still greater monstrosities.

Nith. In "The Cats of Ulthar," a "lean" notary in Ulthar.

Norrys, Capt. Edward. In "The Rats in the Walls," he is a former member of the Royal Flying Corps and friend of Alfred Delapore. Norrys assists Alfred's father (the narrator of the story) in the restoration of Exham Priory and helps him attempt to find the source of the mysterious sound of rats heard throughout the castle. Ultimately the senior Delapore kills and partially devours him.

Northam, Lord. In "The Descendant," an eccentric, aged scholar, of a family whose ancestral line reaches back to Roman Britain, who, as a younger man, had explored both formal religions and occult sciences (much like Randolph Carter in "The Silver Key"). When Williams, a young friend, brings him a copy of the *Necronomicon,* Northam first reacts with horror and then tells a tale of horrors in Roman Britain.

Notes on Weird Fiction. Written c. summer and fall 1933. First published (b, c, and d only) in *The Notes & Commonplace Book* (Futile Press, 1938); rpt. *CE2.* Erroneously published as part of HPL's "commonplace book" in *BWS* and *SR.*

In 1933, HPL began to keep notes in a pocket calendar from his concentrated rereading of the classic works of weird fiction, in an attempt to reinvigorate himself for fiction-writing. The notebook contains four items: (a) "Weird Story Plots" (unpublished) consists of brief plot summaries primarily of the works of Poe, Blackwood, Machen, and M. R. James. From those summaries he compiled (b) "A list of certain basic underlying horrors effectively used in weird fiction" and (c) "List of primary ideas motivating possible weird tales," a further distillation, giving likely motives for weird occurrences. He then composed the rough draft of (d) "Suggestions for writing weird story (the *idea* and plot being tentatively decided on)" and "Elements of a Weird Story & Types of Weird Story," an instructional piece for turning plot ideas into effective stories. HPL eventually polished (d) into "Notes on Writing Weird Fiction."

"Notes on Writing Weird Fiction." Essay (1,490 words); probably written in 1933. First published in *Amateur Correspondent* (May–June 1937); also in *Supramundane Stories* (Spring 1938) and in *Marginalia;* rpt. *MW* and *CE2.*

Presumably written during HPL's revaluation of the weird classics in the summer and fall of 1933, the essay propounds HPL's evolved theory of weird fiction as the attempt to "achieve, momentarily, the illusion of some strange suspension or violation of the galling limitations of time, space, and natural law." It also presents a summary of HPL's own methods for writing stories, in which he advises the creation of two synopses, one listing events in order of absolute occurrence, the other in order of their narration in the story. The first three publications of the essay derive from three slightly differing manuscripts; the first appearance is probably preferable.

Noyes, ———. In "The Whisperer in Darkness," he is sent to the railroad station to retrieve Albert Wilmarth to the Akeley farmhouse. His is the "cultivated male human voice" heard on the recordings Akeley sent to Wilmarth. Unknown to Wilmarth, he is an agent of the aliens from Yuggoth.

"Nyarlathotep." Prose poem (1,150 words); probably written in November or December 1920. First published in the *United Amateur* (dated November 1920, but issued at least two months later); rpt. *National Amateur* (July 1926); first collected in *BWS;* corrected text in *MW;* annotated version in *CC.*

In a "season of political and social upheaval," the people "whispered warnings and prophecies which no one dared consciously repeat." It was then that Nyarlathotep emerged out of Egypt. He begins giving strange exhibitions featuring peculiar instruments of glass and metal and evidently involving anomalous uses of electricity. In one of these exhibitions the narrator sees, on a kind of movie screen, "the world battling against blackness; against the waves of destruction from ultimate space; whirling, churning; struggling around the dimming, cooling sun." The world seems to be falling apart: buildings are found in ruins, people begin gathering in queues, each of them proceeding in different directions, apparently to their deaths. Finally the universe itself seems to be on the brink of extinction.

HPL notes that the piece not only was based largely on a dream, but also that the first paragraph (presumably following the very brief opening paragraph) was written while he was still half-asleep (*SL* 1.160). As with "The Statement of Randolph Carter," the dream involved Samuel Loveman, who wrote HPL the following note: "Don't fail to see Nyarlathotep if he comes to Providence. He is horrible—horrible beyond anything you can imagine—but wonderful. He haunts one for hours afterward. I am still shuddering at what he showed." HPL states that the peculiar name Nyarlathotep came to him in this dream, but one can conjecture at least a partial influence in the name of Dunsany's minor god Mynarthitep (mentioned fleetingly in "The Sorrow of Search," in *Time and the Gods*) or of the prophet Alhireth-Hotep (mentioned in *The Gods of Pegāna*). -*Hotep* is of course an Egyptian root, befitting Nyarlathotep's Egyptian origin. The fact that Nyarlathotep "had risen up out of the blackness of twenty-seven centuries" places him in the 22nd Dynasty of Egypt (940–730 B.C.E.).

Will Murray has plausibly conjectured that Nyarlathotep (described in the prose poem as an "itinerant showman") was based upon Nicola Tesla (1856–1943), the eccentric scientist and inventor who created a sensation at the turn of the century for his strange electrical experiments. Nyarlathotep recurs throughout HPL's later fiction and becomes one of the chief "gods" in his invented pantheon. But he appears in such widely divergent forms that it may not be possible to establish a single or coherent symbolism for him; to say merely, as some critics have done, that he is a "shape-shifter" (something HPL never genuinely suggests) is only to admit that even his physical form is not consistent from story to story, much less his thematic significance.

See Will Murray, "Behind the Mask of Nyarlathotep," *LS* No. 25 (Fall 1991): 25–29.

O

O'Brien, Edward J[oseph Harrington] (1890–1941). Anthologist and literary critic. HPL admired his annual series, *The Best Short Stories . . .* (1915f.), believing it to be superior to another series, Blanche Colton Williams's *O. Henry Memorial Award Prize Stories* (1919f.), which HPL felt reflected commercial rather than literary values. O'Brien cited HPL in the volumes for 1924 ("The Picture in the House" [one star]), 1928 ("The Colour out of Space" [three stars]), and 1929 ("The Dunwich Horror" [three stars], "The Silver Key" [one star]); he published HPL's "Biographical Notice" in the 1928 volume (it was not repeated in 1929, as such biographies were published only for first-time recipients of three-star ratings). HPL admired O'Brien's *The Dance of the Machines: The American Short Story and the Industrial Age* (1929), which HPL deemed "a splendid exposé of the vulgar shallowness, insincerity, and worthlessness of American commercial fiction under the false-standarded conditions of the present" (*SL* 4.91).

O'Brien, "Kid." In "Herbert West—Reanimator," a semi-professional boxer (presumably Irish but with "a most un-Hibernian hooked nose," suggesting that he may actually be Jewish) who inadvertently kills Buck Robinson, an African American, in an informal bout in Bolton, Mass.

"Observations on Several Parts of America." Essay (9,700 words); probably written in the fall of 1928. First published in *Marginalia* (as "Observations on Several Parts of North America"); rpt. *MW* and *CE4*.

The first of HPL's several travelogues, which cover his annual spring and summer voyages; written in the form of an open letter to Maurice W. Moe and meant to be circulated to HPL's other colleagues (hence it exists as a typescript rather than as an autograph ms.). It deals with HPL's arrival in Brooklyn in the spring of 1928, progressing through his travels to the Hudson River region, Tarrytown and Sleepy Hollow, Vt. (Vrest Orton's home near Brattleboro), Athol (W.

Paul Cook) and Wilbraham (Edith Miniter), Mass., Baltimore, Annapolis, Alexandria and Mt. Vernon (home of George Washington), Washington, D.C., and the Endless Caverns near New Market, Va. Moe excerpted the section on Sleepy Hollow as "Sleepy Hollow To-day" and published it as a signed article in *Junior Literature: Book Two,* ed. Sterling Leonard and Harold Y. Moffett (New York: Macmillan, 1930). (Moe had served as an assistant editor.)

"Old Bugs." Short story (3,010 words); probably written just prior to July 1919. First published in *SR;* rpt. *MW.*

In the year 1950 an old derelict, Old Bugs, haunts Sheehan's Pool Room in Chicago. Although a drunkard, he exhibits traces of refinement and intelligence; no one can figure out why he carries an old picture of a lovely and elegant woman on his person at all times. One day a young man named Alfred Trever enters the place in order to "see life as it really is." Trever is the son of Karl Trever, an attorney, and a woman who writes poetry under the name Eleanor Wing. Eleanor had once been married to a man named Alfred Galpin, a brilliant scholar but one imbued with "evil habits, dating from a first drink taken years before in woodland seclusion." These habits had caused the termination of the marriage; Galpin had gained fleeting fame as an author but eventually dropped from sight. Meanwhile Old Bugs, listening to Alfred Trever tell of his background, suddenly leaps up and dashes the uplifted glass from Trever's lips, shattering several bottles in the process. Old Bugs dies of overexertion, but Trever is sufficiently repulsed at the whole turn of events that his curiosity for liquor is permanently quenched. When the picture of the woman found on Old Bugs is passed around, Trever realizes that it is of his own mother: Old Bugs is the erstwhile Alfred Galpin.

The story was written to dissuade Galpin—who wished to sample alcohol just prior to its being made illegal in July 1919—from engaging in such an activity. It is not nearly as ponderous as it sounds, and is in fact a little masterpiece of comic deflation and self-parody. The name Eleanor Wing is that of a girl in the Appleton High School Press Club; possibly Galpin was attracted to her. Galpin, in a brief introductory note to the first publication, states that at the end of the piece HPL had written: *"Now* will you be good?!"

"Old Christmas." Poem (322 lines); written in late 1917. First published in the *Tryout* (December 1918); rpt. *National Enquirer* (December 25, 1919).

HPL's single longest poem, telling of the genial pleasures of an old English Christmas. HPL sent the poem through the Transatlantic Circulator, a group of Anglo-American amateur journalists; John Ravenor Bullen spoke highly of it: ". . . the ever-growing charm of eloquence (to which assonance, alliteration, onomatopoeic sound and rhythm, and tone colour contribute their entrancing effect) displayed in the poem under analysis, proclaims Mr. Lovecraft a genuine poet, and 'Old Christmas' an example of poetical architecture well-equipped to stand the test of time."

"Old England and the 'Hyphen.'" Essay (1,140 words); probably written in the fall of 1916. First published in the *Conservative* (October 1916); rpt. *MW* and *CE5.*

England should not be regarded as a foreign country to the "genuine native stock" of America, so that it is right that Americans should support the English in the European war.

Olmstead, Robert (b. 1906). In "The Shadow over Innsmouth," the young man who, on a sight-seeing and genealogical excursion to Newburyport, takes a detour in search of antiquarian sights to the shunned town of Innsmouth. While there, he learns the town's blighted history, but having learned too much, he barely escapes with his life. In the aftermath of his harrowing experience, he finds through further genealogical study that he shares the ancestry of the hated citizens of Innsmouth; but he decides not to kill himself as others in his family had done when they learned the dreaded secret, but to accept and embrace his fate as one of the hybrid amphibian-people. His great-grandmother is Alice Marsh (not named specifically in the story), daughter of Capt. Obed Marsh and the sea-thing, Pth-thya-l'hi. She married Joshua Orne of Arkham; their daughter Eliza Orne married James Williamson of Cleveland, and their daughter, Mary Williamson, married Henry Olmstead of Akron (neither parent is named specifically in the story). Robert Olmstead is their son. This genealogy is explicitly spelled out only in HPL's notes to the story (published in *Cats* [1949]).

Like Olmstead, HPL was an antiquarian and amateur genealogist, inclined to frugality. HPL well recognized the strong influence of heredity in his own life. Photographs of his family show a striking resemblance between HPL and ancestors of generations past. Olmstead was eight years old when his uncle Douglas Williamson committed suicide upon discovering his tainted ancestry. HPL surely was mindful of the madness of his own parents—he was eight years old when his father died in a madhouse.

Olney, Thomas. In "The Strange High House in the Mist," a philosopher who "taught ponderous things in a college by Narragansett Bay" (Brown University?), who comes with his family to Kingsport, ascends to meet an unnamed bearded man at his house perched atop a lofty cliff, and comes down curiously changed.

"Omnipresent Philistine, The." Essay (890 words); probably written in the spring of 1924. First published in the *Oracle* (May 1924); rpt. *MW* and *CE2*.

Largely a response to fellow amateur Paul Livingston Keil, the essay maintains that art should be judged only by aesthetic, not moral, standards, and that the censorship of art is more dangerous than the potential moral or social problems caused by radical art. HPL declares, rather surprisingly, that James Branch Cabell's *Jurgen* and James Joyce's *Ulysses* are "significant contributions to contemporary art" (although he later confessed that he never actually attempted to read *Ulysses*).

Orabona. In "The Horror in the Museum," the mysterious assistant of George Rogers in Rogers's Museum in London who helps Rogers capture a god or monster in Alaska and bring it back to the museum. Later it appears that Orabona has allowed the god to feed upon Rogers, with the result that Rogers has been turned into a wax statue.

Orne, Benjamin. In "The Shadow over Innsmouth," the husband of Alice Marsh and the father of **Eliza Orne,** the maternal grandmother of the narrator, Robert Olmstead.

Orne, Capt. James P. In "The Horror at Martin's Beach," the captain of the fishing smack *Alma,* whose crew captures and kills an enormous sea creature, but is in turn overwhelmed by the creature's much larger parent.

Orne, Simon/Jedediah. In *The Case of Charles Dexter Ward,* one of Joseph Curwen's colleagues in the pursuit of the "essential Saltes" by which human beings can be resuscitated after death. Living in Salem, he leaves the town in 1720 after attracting suspicion by failing to grow visibly old. Thirty years later a person named Jedediah Orne, claiming to be his son, returns to Salem and claims his property. Dr. Willett later discovers that Simon and Jedediah are the same person and that Charles Dexter Ward very likely visited him (now living in Prague) as late as 1924. Willett takes measures to destroy Orne.

Orton, [Kenneth] Vrest [Teachout] (1897–1986). Man of letters and friend of HPL. W. Paul Cook introduced HPL to Orton in late 1925. At this time he worked in the advertising department of the *American Mercury;* later he became an editor of the *Saturday Review.* He first met HPL on December 22, 1925, and became a member of the Kalem Club, although his attendance was very sporadic. In June 1928 Orton, living outside Brattleboro, Vt., invited HPL to visit for an extended period; HPL stayed from June 10 to June 24. Numerous individuals whom he met during this time were later adapted for use in "The Whisperer in Darkness" (1930), including Orton's neighbors, the Lees (whose name was used for "Lee's Swamp" in the story); Charles Crane, who ran "The Pendrifter," a column in the *Brattleboro Daily Reformer;* and Bert G. Akley, a self-taught painter and photographer whose name (and, in part, personality) was used for the character Henry Wentworth Akeley. Orton contributed an article on HPL to "The Pendrifter," entitled "A Weird Writer Is in Our Midst" (June 16, 1928; rpt. *LR*). HPL visited Orton and his family (then residing in Yonkers) for a short time in April 1929. In late 1931 Orton, now operating the Stephen Daye Press in Brattleboro, arranged for HPL to copyedit and proofread Leon Burr Richardson's *History of Dartmouth College* (1932). HPL hoped to do more work for the Stephen Daye Press, but apparently no more assignments were offered to him. Orton published the first bibliography of Theodore Dreiser, *Dreiseriana: A Book about His Books* (New York: Stratford Press, 1929); among his other works are *And So Goes Vermont: A Picture Book of Vermont as It Is* (editor) (Weston, Vt.: Countryman Press; New York: Farrar & Rinehart, 1937) and *Goudy, Master of Letters* (Chicago: Black Cat Press, 1939). He became celebrated as the founder of the Vermont Country Store. Late in life he wrote a brief memoir, "Recollections of H. P. Lovecraft" (*Whispers,* March 1982; in *LR*).

Osborn, Joe. In "The Dunwich Horror," one of the party that exterminates Wilbur Whateley's twin brother. It is likely that he runs Osborn's General Store, although HPL does not state this explicitly in the story.

"Other Gods, The." Short story (2,020 words); written on August 14, 1921. First published in the *Fantasy Fan* (November 1933); rpt. *WT* (October 1938); first collected in *BWS;* corrected text in *D;* annotated version in *DWH.*

The "gods of earth" have forsaken their beloved mountain Hatheg-Kla and have betaken themselves to "unknown Kadath in the cold waste where no man treads"; they have done this ever since a human being from Ulthar, Barzai the Wise, attempted to scale Hatheg-Kla and catch a glimpse of them. Barzai was much learned in the "seven cryptical books of Hsan" and the "Pnakotic Manuscripts of distant and frozen Lomar," and knew so much of the gods that he wished to see them dancing on. Hatheg-Kla. He undertakes this bold journey with his friend, Atal the priest. For days they climb the rugged mountain, and as they approach the cloud-hung summit Barzai thinks he hears the gods; he redoubles his efforts, leaving Atal far behind. But his eagerness turns to horror. He thinks he actually sees the gods of earth, but instead they are "'The *other* gods! The *other* gods! The gods of the outer hells that guard the feeble gods of earth!'" Barzai is swept up ("'Merciful gods of earth, *I am falling into the sky!*'") and is never seen again.

The story is a textbook example of hubris, similar to many written by Dunsany (see, e.g., "The Revolt of the Home Gods," in *The Gods of Pegāna,* 1905). The seven cryptical books of Hsan are mentioned again in *The Dream-Quest of Unknown Kadath;* in the first appearance of this story, "Hsan" was erroneously rendered as "Earth."

See Robert M. Price, "'The Other Gods' and the Four Who Erected Paradise," *Crypt* No. 15 (Lammas 1983): 19–20.

Oukranikov, Vasili. In "The Ghost-Eater," a Russian who had built a house in the woods between Mayfair and Glendale who is discovered to be a "werewolf and eater of men." After a Russian count is found with his body mangled, the townspeople kill the wolf; but his ghost returns every May Eve to reenact the murder.

"Out of the Æons." Short story (10,310 words); ghostwritten for Hazel Heald, probably in August 1933. First published in *WT* (April 1935); first collected in *BWS;* corrected text in *HM.*

An ancient mummy is housed in the Cabot Museum of Archaeology in Boston, with an accompanying scroll in indecipherable characters. The mummy and scroll remind the narrator—the curator of the museum—of a wild tale found in the *Black Book* or *Nameless Cults* of von Junzt, which tells of the god Ghatanothoa, "whom no living thing could behold . . . without suffering a change more horrible than death itself. Sight of the god, or its image . . . meant paralysis and petrification of a singularly shocking sort, in which the victim was turned to stone and leather on the outside, while the brain within remained perpetually alive." Von Junzt goes on to speak of an individual named T'yog who, 175,000 years ago, attempted to scale Mount Yaddith-Gho on the lost continent of Mu, where Ghatanothoa resided, and to "deliver mankind from its brooding menace"; he was protected from Ghatanothoa's glance by a magic formula, but at the last minute the priests of Ghatanothoa stole the parchment on which the formula was written and substituted another one for it. The antediluvian mummy in the museum, therefore, is T'yog, petrified for millennia by Ghatanothoa.

HPL was working on the story in early August 1933 (see *SL* 4.222). Heald's contribution is indicated in a letter: "'Out of the Æons' may be regarded as a story of my own. The only thing supplied by the alleged authoress is the idea of an ancient mummy found to have a living brain" (HPL to R. H. Barlow, April 20, 1935; ms., JHL). Elsewhere he says: "Regarding the scheduled 'Out of the Æons'—I should say *I did* have a hand in it . . . I *wrote* the damn thing!" (*SL* 5.130). The story—probably the best of those ghostwritten for Heald—unites the atmosphere of HPL's early "Dunsanian" tales with that of his later "Mythos" tales: T'yog's ascent of Yaddith-Gho bears thematic and stylistic similarities with Barzai the Wise's scaling of Hatheg-Kla in "The Other Gods," and the entire subnarrative about Mu is narrated in a style analogous to that of Dunsany's tales and plays of gods and men.

See William Fulwiler, "Mu in 'Bothon' and 'Out of the Eons,'" *Crypt* No. 11 (Candlemas 1983): 20–24.

"Outpost, The." Poem (52 lines in quatrains); written on November 26, 1929. First published in *Bacon's Essays* (Spring 1930); rpt *Fantasy Magazine* (May 1934).

The subject of the poem is a king of Zimbabwe who "fears to dream." *WT* rejected the poem because of its length. HPL probably derived some of the plot and imagery from accounts of Zimbabwe told to him by Edward L. Sechrist, who had actually explored the ruins of the African city.

"Outsider, The." Short story (2,620 words); probably written in spring or summer 1921. First published in *WT* (April 1926); rpt. *WT* (June–July 1931); first collected in *O;* corrected text in *DH;* annotated version in *CC*.

A mysterious individual has spent his entire life virtually alone except for some aged person who seems to take care of him. He resides in an ancient castle that has no mirrors. At length he decides to forsake the castle and seek the light by climbing the tallest tower of the edifice. With great effort he manages to ascend the tower and experiences "the purest ecstasy I have ever known: for shining tranquilly through an ornate grating of iron . . . was the radiant full moon, which I had never before seen save in dreams and in vague visions I dared not call memories." But horror follows this spectacle, for he now observes that he is not at some lofty height but has merely reached *"the solid ground."* Stunned by this revelation, he walks dazedly through a wooded park where a "venerable ivied castle" stands. This castle is "maddeningly familiar, yet full of perplexing strangeness to me"; but he detects the sights and sounds of joyous revelry within. He steps through a window of the castle to join the merry band, but at that instant "there occurred one of the most terrifying demonstrations I had ever conceived": the partygoers flee madly from some hideous sight, and the protagonist appears to be alone with the monster who has seemingly driven the crowd away in frenzy. He thinks he sees this creature "beyond the golden-arched doorway leading to another and somewhat similar room" and finally does catch a clear glimpse of it. It proves to be a loathsome monstrosity—"a compound of all that is unclean, uncanny, unwelcome, abnormal, and detestable. It was the ghoulish shade of decay, antiquity, and desolation; the putrid, dripping eidolon of unwholesome revelation; the awful baring of that which the merciful earth should always hide." He seeks to escape the monster, but inadvertently falls forward instead of retreating; at that instant he touches *"the rotting outstretched paw of the monster beneath the golden arch."* It is only then that he realizes that that arch contains *"a cold and unyielding surface of polished glass."*

On the level of plot, "The Outsider" makes little sense and in fact reads as if a transcription of a dream. It appears, from the Outsider's various remarks regarding his puzzlement at the present shape of the ivied castle he enters, that he is some long-dead ancestor of the current occupants of the castle. His emergence in the topmost tower of his underground castle places him in a room containing "vast shelves of marble, bearing odious oblong boxes of disturbing size"— clearly the mausoleum of the castle on the surface. Even if the Outsider is some centuried ancestor, there is no explanation for how he has managed to survive— or rise from the dead—after all this time. Whether that castle exists in reality (in which case it is difficult to imagine how it could have an "endless forest" surrounding it) or is merely a product of the Outsider's imagination is left unclear.

Many commentators have attempted to speculate on a literary influence for the concluding image of the Outsider's touching the mirror and seeing himself. Colin Wilson (*The Strength to Dream,* 1961) has suggested both Poe's classic story of a double, "William Wilson," and also Wilde's fairy tale "The Birthday of the Infanta," in which a twelve-year-old princess is initially described as "the most graceful of all and the most tastefully attired" but proves to be "a monster, the most grotesque monster he had ever beheld. Not properly shaped as all other people were, but hunchbacked, and crooked-limbed, with huge lolling head and a mane of black hair." George T. Wetzel ("The Cthulhu Mythos: A Study," in *FDOC*) has put forth Hawthorne's curious sketch, "Fragments from the Journal of a Solitary Man," in which a man dreams that he is walking down Broadway in a shroud, only discovering the fact by seeing himself in a shop window. There is also a celebrated passage in Mary Shelley's *Frankenstein* (1818) in which the monster sees his own reflection for the first time in a pool of water. This influence seems more likely in view of the fact that the earlier scene, where the Outsider disturbs the party by stepping through the window, may also have been derived from *Frankenstein:* "'One of the best of [the cottages] I entered, but I had hardly placed my foot within the door before the children shrieked, and one of the women fainted.'"

Preeminently, however, the story is a homage to Poe. August Derleth maintained that "The Outsider" could pass as a lost tale of Poe's; but HPL's own later judgment, expressed in a 1931 letter to J. Vernon Shea, seems more accurate: "Others . . . agree with you in liking 'The Outsider', but I can't say that I share this opinion. To my mind this tale—written a decade ago—is too glibly *mechanical* in its climactic effect, & almost comic in the bombastic pomposity of its language. As I re-read it, I can hardly understand how I could have let myself be tangled up in such baroque & windy rhetoric as recently as ten years ago. It represents my literal though unconscious imitation of Poe at its very height" (*SL* 3.379). Specifically, the tale's opening paragraphs closely echo the opening of "Berenice," while the scene in the brilliantly lit castle brings to mind the lavish party scene in "The Masque of the Red Death."

In 1934 HPL provided an interesting sidelight into the composition of the story. As recollected by R. H. Barlow, HPL stated: "'The Outsider' [is] a series of climaxes—originally intended to cease with the graveyard episode; then he wondered what would happen if people would see the ghoul; and so included the second climax; finally he decided to have the Thing see itself!"

The autobiographical implications of the story have perhaps been overstressed by critics. The Outsider's concluding remark—"I know always that I am an outsider; a stranger in this century and among those who are still men"—has been thought to be prototypical of HPL's entire life, but this is clearly a considerable exaggeration. The Outsider's early reflections on his childhood—"Unhappy is he to whom the memories of childhood bring only fear and sadness"—manifestly contradict HPL's own accounts of his generally happy and carefree childhood. In a very general way "The Outsider" may possibly be indicative of HPL's own self-image, particularly the image of one who always thought himself ugly and whose mother told at least one individual about her son's "hideous" face.

See David J. Brown, "The Search for Lovecraft's 'Outsider,'" *Nyctalops* 2, No. 1 (April 1973): 46–47; Dirk W. Mosig, "The Four Faces of 'The Outsider,'" *Nyctalops* 2, No. 2 (July 1974): 3–10 (rpt. with revisions in Mosig's *Mosig at Last* [West Warwick, R.I.: Necronomicon Press, 1997]); William Fulwiler, "Reflections on 'The Outsider,'" *LS* No. 2 (Spring 1980): 3–4; Robert M. Price, "Homosexual Panic in 'The Outsider,'" *Crypt* No. 8 (Michaelmas 1982): 11–13; Mollie L. Burleson, "The Outsider: A Woman?" *LS* Nos. 22/23 (Fall 1990): 22–23; Donald R. Burleson, "On Lovecraft's Themes: Touching the Glass" (in *ET*); Mollie L. Burleson, "Mirror, Mirror: Sylvia Plath's 'Mirror' and Lovecraft's 'The Outsider,'" *LS* No. 31 (Fall 1994): 10–12; Carl Buchanan, "'The Outsider' as an Homage to Poe," *LS* No. 31 (Fall 1994): 12–17; Robert H. Waugh, "'The Outsider,' the Terminal Climax, and Other Conclusions," *LS* No. 34 (Spring 1996): 13–24; Paul Montelone, "The Inner Significance of 'The Outsider,'" *LS* No. 35 (Fall 1996): 9–21; Robert H. Waugh, "Lovecraft and Keats Confront the 'Awful Rainbow,'" *LS* No. 35 (Fall 1996): 24–36; No. 36 (Spring 1997): 26–39; Robert H. Waugh, "The Outsider, the Autodidact, and Other Professions," *LS* No. 37 (Fall 1997): 4–15; No. 38 (Spring 1998): 18–33.

P

Pabodie, Frank H. In *At the Mountains of Madness,* the professor of engineering who devises the special drill used to conduct geologic borings on the Miskatonic Antarctic Expedition.

***Pawtuxet Valley Gleaner,* Astronomy Articles for.** Seventeen known articles, published in 1906; rpt. *First Writings: Pawtuxet Valley Gleaner* (Necronomicon Press, 1976; rev. ed. 1986) and *CE3.*

The articles appeared as follows: "The Heavens for August" (July 27); "The Skies of September" (August 31); "Is Mars an Inhabited World?" (September 7); "Is There Life on the Moon?" (September 14); "An Interesting Phenomenon" (September 21); "October Heavens" (September 28); "Are There Undiscovered Planets?" (October 5); "Can the Moon Be Reached by Man?" (October 12); "The Moon" (October 19); [untitled] (October 26); "The Sun" (November 2); "The Leonids" (November 9); "Comets" (November 16); "December Skies" (November 30); "The Fixed Stars" (December 7); "Clusters-Nebulae" (December 21); "January Heavens" (December 28).

These are—aside from HPL's letter to the editor of the *Providence Sunday Journal* (June 3, 1906)—the earliest published works by HPL, although contemporaneous with the astronomy articles for the [Providence] *Tribune* (1906–08), which commenced only a few days after the first of the *Gleaner* articles. The paper was a rural weekly published in the village of Phenix, R.I. (a community now incorporated into the town of West Warwick); HPL remarks of it: "The name 'Phillips' is a magic word in Western Rhode Island, & the *Gleaner* was more than willing to print & feature anything from Whipple V. Phillips' grandson" (*SL* 1.40). The articles range from surveys of the celestial phenomena for the coming month to discussions of provocative questions regarding the heavens: HPL here maintains that Percival Lowell's belief in the artificiality of the Martian "canals" is "not only possible, but probable," although in later columns he heaped ridicule upon the idea; he claims that the most plausible way to get to the moon would be to send off a projectile by electrical repulsion. Some of the columns are revised versions of articles first "published" in HPL's hectographed paper, *The Rhode Island Journal of Astronomy.*

HPL remarks (*SL* 1.40) that the articles continued through 1907 and 1908; but no issues of the paper have been found after December 28, 1906. Evidence suggests, however, that the paper continued until at least the end of 1907 and probably into 1908, so that a whole series of articles by HPL may be lost.

Peabody, E. Lapham. In "The Shadow over Innsmouth," the curator of the Arkham Historical Society, who assists Robert Olmstead in his genealogical research, pointing out that Olmstead's uncle Douglas Williamson had preceded him on a similar quest.

Peaslee, Nathaniel Wingate. He is a professor of political economy at Miskatonic University and the narrator and protagonist of "The Shadow out of Time." He is married to **Alice Keezar** and father of **Robert K.** (b. 1898), **Wingate** (b. 1900), and **Hannah** (b. 1903). On May 14, 1908, Peaslee suffers a breakdown while lecturing, appearing to be stricken with amnesia until his memory suddenly returns on September 27, 1913. His restored self has no memory of the five-year period of amnesia. Even as he attempts to determine his activities over that period, he is plagued by dreams (which seem vividly like actual memories) and "pseudo-memories" of bizarre creatures in an equally bizarre setting. He thinks the dreams and pseudo-memories are related to the studies he engaged in during his amnesia, but the accounts he publishes in a psychological journal are corroborated by a mining engineer, who says the scenes he described in fact exist in the Great Sandy Desert of Australia. Peaslee accompanies the engineer to the site to investigate it. The creatures no longer exist, but the ruins there are astonishingly familiar to him. In his dreams, he believed himself to have been the victim of mind-exchange with an incredibly alien creature living in the earth's ancient past; while the alien occupied his own body, he himself had been tasked with writing a history of the era to which he had belonged. Peaslee finally wends his way through the ruins of an ancient library, seeking the evidence that would prove his dreams to be actual memories. He finds, but loses, the proof he desires and fears—a document in his own handwriting that could not be less than 150,000,000 years old.

Peaslee may be the most thoroughly developed of HPL's characters. His demeanor and attitude are much like HPL's. HPL's period of reclusiveness in 1908–13, following his abrupt departure from high school without a diploma, coincides with the duration of Peaslee's amnesia. HPL's description of Peaslee's reemergence in the present is remarkably similar to his famous account of his emergence from his "New York exile" of 1924–26. And yet Peaslee himself seems to be modeled somewhat on HPL's father, Winfield Scott Lovecraft. Peaslee's eccentric behavior during his amnesia resembles Winfield's own during the period of his madness, both of which last five years. Of course, Winfield never did recover, but Peaslee did. Eight-year-old Wingate "held fast to a faith that [Peaslee's] proper self would return," as one might imagine young HPL felt about his father's condition. The revelation about Peaslee's past occurs on July 17–18; HPL's father died July 19.

Peaslee, Wingate (b. 1900). In "The Shadow out of Time," the son of the story's narrator, Nathaniel Wingate Peaslee, and the only one of Peaslee's children to return to him after his "amnesia" of 1908–13. Wingate becomes a professor of psychology and accompanies his father on his fateful expedition to the Great Sandy Desert in Australia.

Petaja, Emil (1915–2000). Science fiction fan and writer of Finnish ancestry residing in Montana, and correspondent of HPL. Petaja came in touch with HPL in late 1934. The next year he proposed teaming with Duane W. Rimel to form a fan magazine, *The Fantaisiste's Mirror,* that would resume serializing HPL's "Supernatural Horror in Literature" from the point it had left off in the defunct *Fantasy Fan,* but the magazine never materialized. He and HPL continued corresponding until the latter's death. In later years Petaja contributed to *Amazing Stories* and *WT,* and wrote several science fiction and fantasy novels, some based upon Finnish legendry.

Phillips, Edwin E[verett] (1864–1918). HPL's maternal uncle; the only son of Whipple V. Phillips and Robie A. Place Phillips. He was associated with Whipple in the Snake River Co. and the Owyhee Land and Irrigation Co. in the 1890s. He married Martha Helen Mathews on July 30, 1894, divorced her, and remarried her on March 23, 1903. He was variously employed as rent collector, real estate agent, operator of the Edwin E. Phillips Refrigeration Co., etc. According to HPL, he "lost a lot of dough for my mother and me in 1911" (*SL* 3.367). HPL never mentions his uncle's death in any surviving correspondence, leading one to suspect that he was not close to him.

Phillips Family. HPL was descended from Asaph Phillips (1764–1829) and his wife Esther Phillips (1767–1842). HPL visited the site of their homestead on Howard Hill in Foster, R.I., in 1929. Asaph's descent from Michael Phillips (d. 1686), Newport freeman of 1668, is not proven but is given by Henry Byron Phillips in his Phillips genealogy at the California State Genealogical Society. HPL's late claim that Michael was the youngest son of the Rev. George Phillips (d. 1644), a 1630 emigrant who became minister of Watertown, Mass., is unsupported by any authority and almost certainly specious. Asaph and Esther had eight children, the youngest of whom was Captain Jeremiah Phillips (1800–1848), who married Robie Rathbun (1797–1848) in 1823. During the 1820s Jeremiah served in the militia. His political persuasions can be inferred not only from his profession and background but from the fact that he gave his son Whipple (1833–1904) the middle name Van Buren in honor of Martin Van Buren, who had been inaugurated as Andrew Jackson's vice president on March 4, 1833. Jeremiah purchased the Isaac Blanchard grist mill on the Moosup River in 1833 and was tragically crushed to death when his long coat accidentally got caught in its gearing. Their mother Robie having died the previous July, the four surviving children (two sons and two daughters) were left as orphans. One of these, Whipple V. Phillips, was HPL's grandfather. HPL also had some contact with his grand-uncle, James Wheaton Phillips (1830–1901).

See Kenneth W. Faig, Jr., *Some of the Descendants of Asaph Phillips and Esther Whipple of Foster, Rhode Island* (Glendale, Ill.: Moshassuck Press, 1993).

Phillips, James Wheaton (1830–1901). HPL's grand-uncle; elder brother of Whipple V. Phillips. He married Jane Ann Place on November 6, 1853. He owned a farm on Johnson Road in Foster, R.I., where HPL and his mother stayed for two weeks in 1896 and again in 1908. HPL and Annie Gamwell visited the site in October 1926.

Phillips, Robie Alzada (1827–1896). HPL's maternal grandmother; wife of Whipple V. Phillips, whom she married on January 27, 1856. They had five children (see entry for Whipple Van Buren Phillips below). Her death and subsequent mourning by the family terrified young HPL and inspired dreams of "night-gaunts," which he would much later use in fiction (e.g., *The Dream-Quest of Unknown Kadath* [1926–27], the "Night-Gaunts" sonnet of *Fungi from Yuggoth* [1929–30], etc.). Her collection of astronomy books served as the nucleus of HPL's own collection after he became interested in the science in late 1902. HPL spells her name as "Rhoby," but her tombstone (at Swan Point Cemetery in Providence) gives her name as "Robie."

Phillips, Ward. In "Through the Gates of the Silver Key," an old man from Providence, R.I., and a correspondent of Randolph Carter who argues against the dispersal of Carter's estate because he believes him to be still alive. Although not so identified in "The Silver Key," he is the first-person narrator of that story. "Ward Phillips" was a pseudonym that HPL used for various of his poems as published in amateur journals.

Phillips, Whipple Van Buren (1833–1904). HPL's maternal grandfather; son of Capt. Jeremiah Phillips (1800–1848) and Robie Rathbun (1797–1848). He was educated in Foster, R.I., and the East Greenwich Academy. He spent 1852–53 in Delavan, Ill. (a temperance town), on the farm of his uncle, James Phillips (1794–1878). He married Robie Alzada Place on January 27, 1856. They had five children: Lillian Delora (Phillips) Clark, Sarah Susan Phillips Lovecraft, Emeline Estella (1859–1866), Edwin Everett, and Annie Emeline (Phillips) Gamwell. Whipple moved the family to Coffin's Corner, R.I., around 1859; he quickly made a fortune from real estate and other business and was able to purchase all the land in the town, which he named Greene after the Rhode Island Revolutionary War hero Nathanael Greene. He served as postmaster at Greene (1860–66) and as representative for Coventry in the Rhode Island General Assembly (1870–72). He joined the Masonic order and built a Masonic hall in Greene. Whipple suffered a financial collapse in 1870, but recovered sufficiently to move to Providence in 1874; after residing for some years at 276 Broadway on the West Side, he built a large house at 194 (later numbered 454) Angell Street in 1881. He went to the Paris Exposition in 1878 and traveled widely around the Continent, especially to Italy. In 1884 he formed the Snake River Company to pursue land interests in Idaho; he also named the town of Grand View, building a large Grand View hotel there. In 1889 he formed the Owyhee Land and Irrigation Company. Its chief object was the building of a dam over the Bruneau River (not the Snake River, as HPL notes in his letters), but it was washed away in 1890; although later rebuilt, the expense of building and maintaining the dam and other properties contributed to the collapse of the company in 1901. An irrigation ditch was washed out in 1904; a few days later, Whipple suffered a cerebral hemorrhage and died on March 28. Subsequent mismanagement of his estate caused HPL and his mother to move from 454 Angell Street to 598 Angell Street. His estate was valued at $25,000, of which $5,000 went to Sarah Susan and $2,500 to HPL. Whipple Phillips wrote to HPL sporadically from Idaho and told him oral weird tales in the Gothic mode. He proved to be an admirable replacement for HPL's stricken father. His death, and the removal from 454 Angell Street, impelled HPL to give serious consideration to suicide (see *SL* 4.358–59).

See Kenneth W. Faig, Jr., "Whipple V. Phillips and the Owyhee Land and Irrigation Company," *Owyhee Outpost* No. 19 (May 1988): 21–30.

Pickman, Richard Upton. In "Pickman's Model," a painter, of Salem ancestry, whose paintings of outré subjects are assumed to be the fruits of a keen imagination, but are ultimately found to be from real life and from first-hand knowledge of forbidden subjects. He is compared to Gustave Doré, Sidney Sime, and Anthony Angarola. He disappears mysteriously, after emptying his pistol at an unseen monster lurking in the basement of his studio in the North End of Boston during a visit by the narrator of the story. In *The Dream-Quest of Unknown Kadath,* Pickman becomes a ghoul, like the subject of many of his paintings in "Pickman's Model."

HPL describes Pickman not as a fantaisiste, but as a realist—a term HPL came to feel best described himself following his shift toward cosmic fictional themes around 1926.

"Pickman's Model." Short story (5,570 words); probably written in early September 1926. First published in *WT* (October 1927); rpt. *WT* (November 1936); first collected in *O;* corrected text in *DH;* annotated version in *An2* and *TD.*

The narrator, Thurber, tells why he ceased association with the painter Richard Upton Pickman of Boston, who has recently disappeared. He had maintained relations with Pickman long after his other acquaintances had dropped him because of the grotesqueness of his paintings, and so on one occasion he was taken to Pickman's secret cellar studio in the decaying North End of Boston, near the ancient Copp's Hill Burying Ground. Here were some of Pickman's most spectacularly demonic paintings; one in particular depicts a "colossal and nameless blasphemy with glaring red eyes" nibbling at a man's head as a child chews a stick of candy. When a strange noise is heard, Pickman maintains it must be rats clambering through the underground tunnels honeycombing the area. Pickman, in another room, fires all six chambers of his revolver—a rather odd way to kill rats. After leaving, Thurber finds that he had inadvertently taken a photograph affixed to the canvas; thinking it a mere shot of scenic background, he is horrified to find that it is a picture of the monster itself—"*it was a photograph from life.*"

HPL portrayed the North End setting quite faithfully, right down to many of the street names; but, less than a year after writing the story, he was disappointed to find that much of the area had been razed to make way for new development. HPL's comment at the time (when he took Donald Wandrei to the scene) is of interest: "the actual alley & house of the tale [had been] utterly demolished; a whole crooked line of buildings having been torn down" (HPL to Lillian D. Clark, [July 17, 1927]; ms., JHL). This suggests that HPL had an actual house in mind for Pickman's North End studio. The tunnels mentioned in the story are also real: they probably date from the colonial period and may have been used for smuggling.

The story is noteworthy in that it expresses many of the aesthetic principles on weird fiction that HPL had just outlined in "Supernatural Horror in Literature." Thurber notes: ". . . only the real artist knows the actual anatomy of the terrible or the physiology of fear—the exact sort of lines and proportions that connect up with latent instincts or hereditary memories of fright, and the proper colour contrasts and lighting effects to stir the dormant sense of strangeness." This statement is HPL's ideal of weird literature as well. And when Thurber confesses that "Pickman was in every sense—in conception and in execution—a thorough, painstaking, and almost scientific *realist,*" one thinks of HPL's allusion to his recent abandonment of the Dunsanian prose-poetic technique for the "prose realism" (*SL* 3.96) that would be the hallmark of his later work. The colloquial style of the story (as with "In the Vault") is unconvincing; Thurber, although supposedly a "tough" guy who had been through the world war, expresses implausible horror and shock at Pickman's paintings: his reactions seem strained and hysterical. Pickman recurs as a minor character in *The Dream-Quest of Unknown Kadath.*

"Pickman's Model," perhaps because it is relatively conventional, has proved popular with readers. It was anthologized in HPL's lifetime, in Christine Campbell Thomson's *By Daylight Only* (1929) and again in Thomson's *Not at Night Omnibus* (1937).

See Will Murray, "In Pickman's Footsteps," *Crypt* No. 28 (Yuletide 1984): 27–32; James Anderson, "'Pickman's Model': Lovecraft's Model of Terror," *LS* Nos. 22/23 (Fall 1990): 15–21; K. Setiya, "Aesthetics and the Artist in 'Pickman's Model'" (one of "Two Notes on Lovecraft"), *LS* No. 26 (Spring 1992): 15–16.

"Picture, The." Nonextant juvenile story; written in 1907. Described in HPL's commonplace book as concerning a "painting of ultimate horror." In a letter to Robert Bloch (June 1, 1933) he says of it: "I had a man in a Paris garret paint a mysterious canvas embodying the quintessential essence of all horror. He is found clawed & mangled one morning before his easel. The picture is destroyed, as in a titanic struggle—but in one corner of the frame a bit of canvas remains . . . & on it the coroner finds to his horror the painted counterpart of the sort of claw which evidently killed the artist" (*Letters to Robert Bloch* [Necronomicon Press, 1993], p. 15). The story was possibly influenced by Poe's "The Oval Portrait," in which a painter, in painting a portrait of his wife, insidiously sucks the life from the woman and transfers it into the portrait.

"Picture in the House, The." Short story (3,350 words); written on December 12, 1920. First published in the *National Amateur* ("July 1919" [not released until summer 1921]); rpt. *WT* (January 1924) and *WT* (March 1937); first collected in *O;* corrected text in *DH;* annotated version in *An2* and *CC.*

The narrator, "in quest of certain genealogical data," is traveling by bicycle throughout New England. One day a heavy downpour forces him to take shelter at a decrepit farmhouse in the "Miskatonic Valley." When his knocks fail to summon an occupant, he believes the house to be uninhabited and enters; but shortly the occupant, who had been asleep upstairs, makes an appearance. The man seems very old, but also quite ruddy of face and muscular of build. His clothes are slovenly, and he seems to have just awoken from a nap. The old man, seemingly a harmless backwoods farmer speaking in "an extreme form of Yankee dialect I had thought long extinct" ("'Ketched in the rain, be ye?'"), notes that his visitor had been examining a very old book on a bookcase, Pigafetta's *Regnum Congo,* "printed in Frankfort in 1598." This book continually turns, as if from frequent consultation, to plate XII, depicting "in gruesome detail a butcher's shop of the cannibal Anziques." The old man avers that he obtained the book from a sailor from Salem years ago, and as he babbles in his increasingly loathsome patois he begins to make vile confessions of the effects of that plate: "'Killin' sheep was kinder more fun—but d'ye know, 'twan't quite *satisfyin'.* Queer haow a *cravin'* gits a holt on ye—As ye love the Almighty, young man, don't tell nobody, but I swar ter Gawd thet picter begun ta make me *hungry fer victuals I couldn't raise nor buy—.'"* At that point a drop of liquid falls from the ceiling directly upon the plate. The narrator thinks at first it is rain but then observes that it is a drop of blood. A thunderbolt conveniently destroys the house and its tenant, but the narrator somehow survives.

The tale contains the first mention of the term "Miskatonic" and the fictional city of Arkham. The location of Arkham has been the source of considerable debate. Will Murray conjectured that the Arkham of "The Picture in the House" was situated in central Massachusetts, but Robert D. Marten concludes that HPL had always conceived of Arkham (as he did explicitly in later tales) to be an approximate analogue of Salem, hence on the eastern coast of Massachusetts. The name Arkham may (as Marten speculates) have been coined from Arkwright, a former village (now incorporated into the town of Fiskville) in Rhode Island. "Miskatonic" (which Murray, studying its Algonguin roots, translates approximately to "red-mountain-place") appears to be derived by analogy from Housatonic, a well-known river running from central Massachusetts through Connecticut.

HPL makes numerous errors in his description of Pigafetta's *Regnum Congo,* since he derived his information secondhand from an appendix to Thomas Henry Huxley's essay "On the History of the Man-like Apes," in *Man's Place in Nature and Other Anthropological Essays* (1894).

The story is the first to make exhaustive use of a backwoods New England dialect that HPL would employ in several later tales for purposes of verisimilitude. Jason C. Eckhardt has plausibly conjectured that its use here derives largely from James Russell Lowell's *Biglow Papers* (1848–62), where a slightly different version of the dialect is used. Eckhardt notes that Lowell himself declares the dialect to be long extinct in New England; its use by HPL thereby enhances the suggestion of the old man's preternatural age.

HPL's brooding opening reflections on the unnatural repressiveness of early New England life and the neuroses it produced are echoed in his analysis of Nathaniel Hawthorne in "Supernatural Horror in Literature" (see also *SL* 3.175).

HPL revised the tale somewhat for later appearances; one alteration was particularly significant. At the conclusion of his initial portrayal of the old man, HPL had written: "On a beard which might have been patriarchal were unsightly stains, some of them disgustingly suggestive of blood." This catastrophically telegraphs the ending, and he wisely omitted it for subsequent appearances.

See Peter Cannon, "Parallel Passages in 'The Adventure of the Copper Beeches' and 'The Picture in the House,'" *LS* No. 1 (Fall 1979): 3–6; S. T. Joshi, "Lovecraft and the *Regnum Congo*," *Crypt* No. 28 (Yuletide 1984): 13–17; Will Murray, "In Search of Arkham Country," *LS* No. 13 (Fall 1986): 54–67; Jason C. Eckhardt, "The Cosmic Yankee" (in *ET*); Robert H. Waugh, "'The Picture in the House': Images of Complicity," *LS* No. 32 (Spring 1995): 2–8; Robert D. Marten, "Arkham Country: In Rescue of the Lost Searchers," *LS* No. 39 (Summer 1998): 1–20; Scott Connors, "Pictures at an Exhibition," *LS* No. 41 (Spring 1999): 2–9; J. C. Owens, "The Mirror in the House: Looking at the Horror of Looking at the Horror," *LS* No. 42 (Summer 2001): 74–79.

Pierce, Ammi (born c. 1842, as was Ambrose Bierce, whose name his own resembles). In "The Colour out of Space," he is the only person who will tell the narrator of the events that befell his neighbors, the Nahum Gardner family, which he witnessed largely at first hand.

Poe, Edgar Allan (1809–1849), American author and predominant literary influence on HPL, who read him beginning at the age of eight. Poe pioneered the short story, the short horror tale, and the detective story; he was also an important poet, critic, and reviewer. In 1916 HPL referred to Poe as "my God of Fiction" (*SL* 1.20); only the subsequent influence of Lord Dunsany and Arthur Machen diluted the Poe influence on HPL's early work. As late as 1929 HPL was lamenting: "There are my 'Poe' pieces & my 'Dunsany' pieces—but alas—where are any 'Lovecraft' pieces?" (*SL* 2.315, where "any" is misprinted as "my"). HPL's "The Outsider" draws on "Berenice" and "The Masque of the Red Death"; "The Hound" is very Poesque in style; "The Rats in the Walls" shows the influence of "The Fall of the House of Usher"; "Cool Air" was perhaps influenced by "Facts in the Case of M. Valdemar," although HPL believed Machen's "Novel of the White Powder" to be a more central influence. *At the Mountains of Madness* draws slightly upon *The Narrative of Arthur Gordon Pym of Nantucket* (1838). Poe's poetry also influenced HPL (mostly in terms of metrical schemes) in such poems as "Nemesis," "The City," "The House," "The Eidolon," "The Nightmare Lake," "Despair," "Nathicana," and others. HPL echoes Poe's doctrine of the unity of effect in "Supernatural Horror in Literature" and exemplifies it in his tales.

HPL saw Poe as the central figure in the development of horror fiction, modifying the moribund Gothic conventions so that they became capable of revealing psychological realities; accordingly, he devoted a substantial chapter to Poe in

"Supernatural Horror in Literature." HPL also wrote "Homes and Shrines of Poe," a discursive survey of Poe's residences in Virginia, Philadelphia, New York, and elsewhere (nearly all of which he had visited in person), for Hyman Bradofsky's *Californian* (Winter 1934). In August 1936, he wrote an acrostic "sonnet" on Poe's name, titling it (in the original ms.) "In a Sequester'd Providence Churchyard Where Once Poe Walk'd" (first published in *Science-Fantasy Correspondent*, March–April 1937).

See T. O. Mabbott, "Lovecraft as a Student of Poe," *Fresco* 8, No. 3 (Spring 1958): 37–39; Robert Bloch, "Poe and Lovecraft" (1973; rpt. *FDOC*); Dirk W. Mosig, "Poe, Hawthorne and Lovecraft: Variations on a Theme of Panic," *Romantist* Nos. 4–5 (1980–81): 43–45; Robert M. Price, "Lovecraft and 'Ligeia,'" *LS* No. 31 (Fall 1994): 15–17.

"Poe-et's Nightmare, The." Poem (303 lines); written in 1916 (see *SL* 1.59). First published in the *Vagrant* (July 1918); rpt. *WT* (July 1952) (central section only; titled "Aletheia Phrikodes").

One of HPL's longest poems, and perhaps his most ambitious single weird poem. It recounts (in rhyming couplets) how Lucullus Languish, a "student of the skies" but also a "connoisseur of rarebits and mince pies," overate and had the nightmare related in the central section of the poem, written—unusually for HPL—in Miltonic blank verse (whose Greek title, "Aletheia Phrikodes," means "the frightful truth"). Here Lucullus is taken by a nameless guide on a voyage through the universe and shown the insignificance of humanity within the boundless reaches of space and time. Horrified, Languish wakes up and (in a resumption of the rhyming couplets) resolves never to mix food and poetry again.

The work is perhaps HPL's first enunciation of cosmicism, predating even his early stories (e.g., "Dagon"). In later years HPL found the rhymed framework dissatisfying, thinking that it detracted from the seriousness of the cosmic message; accordingly, when R. H. Barlow was contemplating issuing HPL's collected verse, HPL instructed Barlow to omit that part. HPL revised a small part of the blank verse section ("Alone in space, I view'd a feeble fleck . . . .") and included it in "May Skies" ([Providence] *Evening News*, May 1, 1917).

See R. Boerem, "A Lovecraftian Nightmare" (in *FDOC*).

"Poetry and the Gods." Short story (2,540 words); written in collaboration with Anna Helen Crofts, probably in the summer of 1920. First published in the *United Amateur* (September 1920) (as by "Anna Helen Crofts and Henry Paget-Lowe"); first collected in *The Lovecraft Collectors Library*, Volume 1 (1952); corrected text in *D*.

Marcia is a young woman who, though "outwardly a typical product of modern civilisation," feels strangely out of tune with her time. She picks up a magazine and reads a piece of free verse, finding it so evocative that she lapses into a languid dream in which Hermes comes to her and wafts her to Parnassus where Zeus is holding court. She is shown six individuals sitting before the Corycian cave; they are Homer, Dante, Shakespeare, Milton, Goethe, and Keats. "These were those messengers whom the Gods had sent to tell men that Pan had passed not away, but only slept; for it is in poetry that Gods speak to men." Zeus tells

Marcia that she will meet a man who is "our latest-born messenger," a man whose poetry will somehow bring order to the chaos of the modern age. She later meets this person, "the young poet of poets at whose feet sits all the world," and he thrills her with his poetry.

Nothing is known about the origin of this story (which HPL never mentions in any extant correspondence) nor about HPL's coauthor, aside from the fact that she resided at 343 West Main Street in North Adams, Mass., in the far northwestern corner of the state. Probably the impetus for writing the story came from Crofts; she may also have written the tidbits of free verse in the story, since HPL despised free verse (and actually comments in the story that "It was only a bit of *vers libre,* that pitiful compromise of the poet who overleaps prose yet falls short of the divine melody of numbers . . ."). The prose of the rest of the story appears to be HPL's.

Poetry, Lovecraft's. HPL wrote more than 250 poems from 1897 to 1936. The great majority of these were written in imitation of the occasional verse of Dryden and Pope, with extensive use of the heroic couplet. In 1914 HPL, responding to Maurice W. Moe's urging to vary his metrical style, wrote: "Take the form away, and nothing remains. I have no real poetic ability, and all that saves my verse from utter worthlessness is the care which I bestow on its metrical construction" (*SL* 1.3–4). HPL's devotion to verse may perhaps have been augmented by his mother, who reportedly considered him a "poet of the highest order" (*LR* 16). Accordingly, for at least the first seven years of his mature literary period (1914–21), HPL attempted to achieve mastery in verse.

HPL's surviving juvenile poetry consists largely of imitations or translations of Greek and Latin epics, although one specimen, "H. Lovecraft's Attempted Journey betwixt Providence & Fall River . . ." (1901), is a delightful comic poem on a modern theme—his initial ride on an electric trolley. Other early work is marred by racist sentiments ("De Triumpho Naturae" [1905]; "New-England Fallen" [1912]; "On the Creation of Niggers" [1912]). His first published poem, "Providence in 2000 A.D." ([Providence] *Evening Bulletin,* March 4, 1912), is a satire directed against Italian-American residents in his native city.

HPL's entry into amateur journalism in 1914 was triggered by his writing of several pungent satires in the Augustan mode published in the *Argosy* (1913–14). In the amateur press, he found ready venues for a great quantity of his verse. The poems fall roughly into a variety of nonexclusive categories: occasional verse, seasonal and topographical poems, poems on amateur affairs, political poems, satires, and (beginning in 1916) weird poetry. On the whole, only the last two categories reveal consistent competence. Some of the satires are themselves on political subjects (e.g., "To General Villa" [*Blarney Stone,* November–December 1914]) or on amateur affairs (e.g., "On a Modern Lothario" [*Blarney-Stone,* July–August 1914]). His first separately published work was the poem *The Crime of Crimes* (1915), on the sinking of the *Lusitania.*

HPL wrote poetry with great facility. He noted that the ten-line poem "On Receiving a Picture of Swans" took about ten minutes to compose (*SL* 1.13). "A Mississippi Autumn" (*Ole Miss',* December 1915) was signed "Howard Phillips Lovecraft, Metrical Mechanic." HPL had no illusions as to the quality of much of his verse. In 1918, after making an exhaustive list of his published poems, he noted: "What a mess of mediocre & miserable junk. He hath sharp eyes indeed, who can discover any trace of merit in so worthless an array of bad verse" (*SL* 1.60).

HPL's weird verse does, however, deserve some special attention, if only because it comprises an interesting appendage to his weird fiction. "The Poe-et's Nightmare" (1916) is one of the earliest expressions of his distinctive brand of cosmicism, speaking apocalyptically in blank verse: "Alone in space, I view'd a feeble fleck / Of silvern light, marking the narrow ken / Which mortals call the boundless universe." Many other poems are metrical and stylistic imitations of Poe's verse: "The Rutted Road" (1917); "Nemesis" (1917); "The Eidolon" (1918); "Despair" (1919); "The House" (1919); "The City" (1919). "Psycho-pompos: A Tale in Rhyme" (1917–18) is a long poem on the werewolf theme; HPL curiously included it in several lists of his prose tales. Later verse begins to show greater distinctiveness and originality, such as the pungent "The Cats" (1925) and the pensive "Primavera" (1925) and "The Wood" (1929). In late 1929, after several years in which he wrote relatively little verse, HPL experienced a remarkable outburst of poetic inspiration, producing "The Outpost," "The Ancient Track," the flawless sonnet "The Messenger," and the sonnet cycle *Fungi from Yuggoth* (1929–30) in short order. After several more years of quiescence, HPL produced finely crafted sonnets to Virgil Finlay and Clark Ashton Smith in late 1936.

Of the satires, "Gryphus in Asinum Mutatus" (1915) is an amusing take-off of Ovid's *Metamorphoses;* "Ye Ballade of Patrick von Flynn" (1915) is a skewering of Irish-Americans' support of Germany during World War I; "The Isaacsonio-Mortoniad" (1915) is a long and piquant send-up of Charles D. Isaacson and James F. Morton, who had attacked HPL in the amateur press; and "The Dead Bookworm" (1917) and "On the Death of a Rhyming Critic" (1917) are delightful parodies of himself. In a letter to Alfred Galpin (August 21, 1918) HPL wrote several satires of love poetry, as he had done earlier with "Laeta; a Lament" (1915). "Amissa Minerva" (1919) is a sharp attack on modern poetry, with several poets cited by name. HPL's most unrestrained satire is "Medusa: A Portrait" (1921), a vicious lampoon of Ida C. Haughton, an amateur writer with whom HPL was feuding. But his greatest satire departs as completely as possible from the Augustan mode: "Waste Paper: A Poem of Profound Insignificance" (1922?), a parody of T. S. Eliot's *The Waste Land,* written entirely in free verse. His satiric poetry was the theme of the first critical article on HPL's verse, Rheinhart Kleiner's "A Note on Howard P. Lovecraft's Verse" (*United Amateur,* March 1919).

Not much can be said of other aspects of HPL's poetry. T. O. Mabbott remarked that "his poetry seems to me mostly written 'with his left hand'" ("H. P. Lovecraft: An Appreciation" [1944], *FDOC* 43), while Winfield Townley Scott delivered the most severe indictment, referring to the bulk of HPL's verse as "eighteenth-century rubbish" ("Lovecraft as a Poet" [1945]), although speaking kindly of "The Messenger" and *Fungi from Yuggoth.* HPL's poetry still receives relatively little critical scrutiny, although the *Fungi* has been analyzed from numerous perspectives. As HPL's complete verse has now been gathered in *The*

Ancient Track: Complete Poetical Works (2001), one may hope that this body of his work will now be the subject of further study.

See Winfield Townley Scott, "Lovecraft as a Poet," in *Rhode Island on Lovecraft,* ed. Donald M. Grant and Thomas P. Hadley (rev. ed. as "A Parenthesis on Lovecraft as Poet" in Scott's *Exiles and Fabrications* [1961] and in *FDOC*); S. T. Joshi, "A Look at Lovecraft's Fantastic Poetry," *Aklo,* Summer 1991, pp. 20–30.

"Polaris." Short story (1,530 words); probably written in late spring or summer 1918. First published in the *Philosopher* (December 1920), an amateur paper edited by Alfred Galpin; rpt. *National Amateur* (May 1926), *Fantasy Fan* (February 1934), and *WT* (December 1937); first collected in *O;* corrected text in *D;* annotated version in *DWH.*

The narrator appears to have a dream in which he is initially a disembodied spirit contemplating some seemingly mythical realm, the land of Lomar, whose principal city Olathoë is threatened with attack from the Inutos, "squat, hellish, yellow fiends." In a subsequent "dream" the narrator learns that he has a body, and is one of the Lomarians. He is "feeble and given to strange faintings when subjected to stress and hardships," so is denied a place in the actual army of defenders; but he is given the important task of manning the watch-tower of Thapnen, since "my eyes were the keenest of the city." Unfortunately, at the critical moment Polaris, the Pole Star, winks down at him and casts a spell so that he falls asleep; he strives to wake up and finds that when he does so he is in a room through whose window he sees "the horrible swaying trees of a dream-swamp" (i.e., his "waking" life). He convinces himself that "I am still dreaming," and vainly tries to wake up, but is unable to do so.

The story is not a dream-fantasy but rather—like "The Tomb"—a case of psychic possession by a distant ancestor, as indicated by the poem inserted in the tale, which the narrator fancies the Pole Star speaks to him: "Slumber, watcher, till the spheres / Six and twenty thousand years / Have revolv'd, and I return / To the spot where now I burn." This alludes to the fact that Polaris's position is not fixed above the North Pole, and that, as the earth wobbles on its axis, it takes twenty-six thousand years for Polaris to return to its position above the Pole. (When the Pyramids of Egypt were built, Alpha Draconis was the Pole Star; in thirteen thousand years, Vega will be.) In other words, the man's spirit has gone back twenty-six thousand years and identified with the spirit of his ancestor.

"Polaris" was in part the result of a controversy over religion between HPL and Maurice W. Moe. In a long letter to Moe (May 15, 1918; *SL* 1.62) HPL notes that "Several nights ago I had a strange dream of a strange city—a city of many palaces and gilded domes, lying in a hollow betwixt ranges of grey, horrible hills. . . . I was, as I said, aware of this city visually. I was in it and around it. But certainly I had no corporeal existence." (HPL cites the dream in the course of discussing the importance of distinguishing between dream and reality.) The story was presumably written shortly after this date.

HPL himself frequently remarked on the story's apparent stylistic similarity to the work of Lord Dunsany, which HPL would read only a year or so later; but possibly the style of the tale was derived from Poe's prose poems, which themselves partly influenced Dunsany's style.

See S. T. Joshi, "On 'Polaris,'" *Crypt* No. 15 (Lammas 1983): 22–25; Ralph E. Vaughan, "The Horror of 'Polaris,'" *Crypt* No. 15 (Lammas 1983): 26–27.

"Power of Wine: A Satire, The." Poem (80 lines); written in late 1914. First published in the [Providence] *Evening News* (January 13, 1915); rpt. *Tryout* (April 1916); rpt. *National Enquirer* (March 28, 1918).

HPL satirizes the ill effects of liquor and intoxication. For other poems on this theme, see "Temperance Song" (*Dixie Booster,* Spring 1916), "Monody on the Late King Alcohol" (*Tryout,* August 1919), and other untitled poems included in *AT.* See also the humorous story "Old Bugs" (1919).

Pratt, Dr. In "The Horror in the Burying-Ground," an old physician who, summoned to the Sprague house after Tom Sprague has suffered some kind of fit, pronounces Sprague dead and hands the body over to Henry Thorndike, the undertaker. Later Pratt is disturbed by suspicions that Sprague is not in fact dead. Shortly thereafter he declares Thorndike dead after the latter suddenly takes ill at Sprague's funeral.

"President's Message." Published in the *United Amateur* (September 1917, November 1917, January 1918, March 1918, May 1918, July 1918); rpt. *CE1.*

Routine reports of amateur activity written by HPL during his presidency of the UAPA.

"President's Message." Published in the *National Amateur* (November [1922]-January 1923, March 1923, May 1923, July 1923, September 1923 [as "The President's Annual Report"]); rpt. *CE1.*

Reports on amateur activity issued by HPL upon his taking over the presidency of the NAPA after the resignation of William J. Dowdell.

Price, E[dgar] Hoffmann (1898–1988), pulp writer and correspondent of HPL (1932–37). HPL may have been influenced by Price's work years before he ever met him: "The Horror at Red Hook" (1925) makes reference to a devil-worshipping sect, the Yezidis, which was probably borrowed from Price's "The Stranger from Kurdistan" (*WT,* July 1925). HPL's first encounter (indirect) with Price was unfavorable: "after due deliberation & grave consultation with E. Hoffmann Price, [Farnsworth] Wright has very properly rejected my 'Strange High House in the Mist,' as not sufficiently clear for the acute minds of his highly intelligent readers" (HPL to Donald Wandrei, [August 2, 1927]; ms. JHL). HPL first met Price in New Orleans on June 12, 1932, when Robert E. Howard telegraphed Price of HPL's presence there. HPL spent at least another week in New Orleans, much of it in Price's company. (A curious myth has emerged that Price took HPL to a brothel, whereupon HPL was purportedly amused to discover that several of the women were readers of his stories in *WT.* This story—apocryphal or not—applies to Seabury Quinn.) An extensive correspondence, mostly dealing with pulp fiction, ensued. Price, having lost a regular job in May 1932, was compelled to write all manner of work for the pulps and defended the practice against HPL's condemnation of pulp fiction as formulaic hackwork. HPL thought enough of Price's letters to preserve them in full (they are now at JHL). In late August 1932 Price wrote a sequel to "The Silver Key," entitled "The Lord of Illusion" (first published in *Crypt* No. 10 [1982]: 47–56), hoping that HPL would revise it and allow it to be published as a collaboration. HPL was reluctant to undertake the task, but finally, in April 1933, completed his extensive revision of it, retitling it "Through the Gates of the Silver Key." In a letter to Price (October 3, 1932; *SL* 4.74–75) HPL spoke of the need to revise the story radically to bring it in line with the original "Silver Key," but in the end he kept as many of Price's conceptions as possible, as well as some of his language. The story was initially rejected by *WT* but later accepted, appearing in July 1934. Price visited HPL in Providence in June–July 1933; it was on this occasion that Price and Harry Brobst brought a six-pack of beer, prompting HPL to query, "And what are you going to do with so *much* of it?" Price went on to write many stories for the pulps; late in life he wrote several novels. His best tales were collected in *Strange Gateways* (Arkham House, 1967); another selection of his tales is found in *Far Lands, Other Days* (Carcosa, 1975). Price wrote a substantial memoir, "The Man Who Was Lovecraft" (in *Cats*; rpt. *LR*), along with several slighter pieces, including "The Sage of College Street" (*Amateur Correspondent,* May–June 1937), "H. P. Lovecraft the Man" (*Diversifier,* May 1976), and several astrological analyses of HPL.

"Primavera." Poem (72 lines in 9 stanzas); written on March 27, 1925. First published in the *Brooklynite* (April 1925).

The springtime causes the narrator to reflect on the mystic realms he has known in the past; he has been "haunted by recollections / Of lands that were not of earth." As with most of the poems of 1924–26, "Primavera" was written for a meeting of the Blue Pencil Club, an amateur organization in Brooklyn whose meetings HPL grudgingly attended to please his wife.

"Professional Incubus, The." Essay (1,210 words); probably written in early 1924. First published in the *National Amateur* (March 1924); rpt. *MW* and *CE2*.

HPL avers that the lack of good fiction in amateurdom is a result of the amateurs' quest to ape the false standards of professional popular fiction.

"Providence." Poem (52 lines in quatrains); written on September 26, 1924. First published in the *Brooklynite* (November 1924); rpt. *Brooklynite* (May 1927); rpt. *Californian* (Summer 1937).

The poem was written for a meeting of the Blue Pencil Club on the topic "The Old Home Town"; HPL took occasion to speak longingly, from Brooklyn, of his devotion to the scenic and historic beauties of his hometown. HPL notes (letter to Lillian D. Clark, November 17–18, 1924; ms., JHL) that the poem was also published in the [Providence] *Evening Bulletin* in early to mid-November, but this appearance has not been found. The appearance in *Collected Poems* (1963) omits three stanzas.

[Providence] *Evening News,* **Astronomy Articles for.** Series of fifty-three astronomy articles (1914–18).

The articles appeared as follows: "The January Sky" (January 1, 1914); "The February Sky" (January 31, 1914); "The March Sky" (March 2, 1914); "The April Sky" (March 31, 1914); "May Sky" (May 1, 1914); "The June Sky" (May 29, 1914); "The July Sky" (June 30, 1914); "The August Sky" (August 1, 1914); "The September Sky" (September 1, 1914); "The October Sky" (September 30, 1914); "The November Sky" (October 31, 1914); "The December Sky" (November 30, 1914); "The January Sky" (December 31, 1914); "The February Sky" (January 30, 1915); "The March Sky" (February 27, 1915); "April Skies" (April 1, 1915); "The May Sky" (April 30, 1915); "The June Skies" (June 1, 1915); "The July Skies" (June 30, 1915); "The August Skies" (July 31, 1915); "September Skies" (September 1, 1915); "October Skies" (October 1, 1915); "November Skies" (November 1, 1915); "December Skies" (November 30, 1915); "January Skies" (December 31, 1915); "The February Skies" (February 1, 1916); "March Skies" (March 1, 1916); "April Skies" (April 1, 1916); "May Skies" (May 3, 1916); "June Skies" (June 1, 1916); "July Skies" (July 1, 1916); "August Skies" (August 1, 1916); "September Skies" (September 1, 1916); "October Skies" (October 2, 1916); "November Skies" (October 31, 1916); "December Skies" (December 1, 1916); "January Skies" (January 2, 1917); "February Skies" (February 1, 1917); "March Skies" (February 28, 1917); "April Skies" (April 2, 1917); "May Skies" (May 1, 1917); "June Skies" (June 1, 1917); "July Skies" (July 2, 1917); "August Skies" (July 31, 1917); "September Skies" (August 31, 1917); "October Skies" (October 2, 1917); "November Skies" (November 5, 1917); "December Skies" (December 1, 1917); "January Skies" (January 2, 1918); "February Skies" (February 1, 1918); "March Skies" (March 1, 1918); "April Skies" (April 1, 1918); "May Skies" (May 2, 1918); rpt. *CE3*.

HPL's most extensive and detailed astronomy columns, the articles averaged 1,750 words in length. As with his other articles, they somewhat mechanically cover the major celestial phenomena of the coming month, but as time passes they are enlivened with explanations of the classical names for the stars and constellations, original bits of poetry by HPL himself (usually presented anonymously), and other diversions. Their greatest significance, however, may be biographical, indicating that HPL had begun to emerge from his five-year-long hermitry several months before he joined amateur journalism in April 1914. The series came to an end because "the request of [the paper's] editor for me to make my articles 'so simple that a child might understand them' caused me to withdraw from the field" (HPL to Alfred Galpin, May 27, 1918; ms., JHL).

"Providence in 2000 A.D." Poem (70 lines); probably written in early 1912. First published in the [Providence] *Evening Bulletin* (March 4, 1912).

HPL's first published poem is a satire in which a man in the future returns to Providence and finds all the place names changed to reflect the foreign immigrants in the city. The poem was inspired by a petition by the Italian residents of the city to rename Atwell's Avenue (the chief thoroughfare in the Italian district, Federal Hill) to Columbus Avenue.

[Providence] *Tribune*, Astronomy Articles for. Series of 20 astronomy articles (August 1, 1906–June 1, 1908).

The articles appeared variously in the *Morning Tribune* [MT], *Evening Tribune* [ET], and *Sunday Tribune* [ST], as follows: "In the August Sky" (MT, August 1, 1906; ET, August 1, 1906); "The September Heavens" (MT, September 1, 1906; ET, September 1, 1906); "Astronomy in October" (MT, October 1, 1906; ET, October 1, 1906); "The Skies of November" (MT, November 1, 1906; ET, November 1, 1906); "The Heavens for December" (MT, December 1, 1906; ET, December 1, 1906); "The Heavens in January" (MT, January 1, 1907; ET, January 1, 1907); "The Heavens in February" (MT, February 1, 1907); "The Heavens in March" (MT, March 2, 1907; ET, March 2, 1907); "April Skies" (ET, April 1, 1907); "The Heavens in May" (MT, May 1, 1907; ET, May 1, 1907); "The Heavens in June" (MT, 1 June 1907); "Astronomy in August" (MT, August 1, 1907; ET, August 1, 1907); "The Heavens for September" (ST, September 1, 1907); "The Skies of October" (MT, October 1, 1907; ET, October 1, 1907); "The Heavens in November" (MT, November 1, 1907; ET, November 1, 1907); "Heavens for December" (ST, December 1, 1907); "The Heavens in January" (ET, January 1, 1908; MT, January 2, 1908); "February Skies" (ET, February 1, 1908); "The Heavens in the Month of March" (MT, March 2, 1908; ET, March 3, 1908); "Solar Eclipse Feature of June Heavens" (MT, June 1, 1908; ET, June 1, 1908); rpt. *CE3*.

The articles are somewhat mechanical accounts of celestial phenomena for the coming month, made interesting by the fact that all except those for August and September 1906, June 1907, and June 1908 feature hand-drawn star charts by HPL, the first (and virtually the last) time that any artwork of his was published in his lifetime. (In the article for March 1908, only the illustration appeared in ET, under the title "The Evening Sky in March.") The articles end abruptly because a nervous breakdown caused HPL to withdraw from high school.

Pseudonyms, Lovecraft's. HPL used pseudonyms frequently, but almost exclusively during his years in amateur journalism and mostly for poems. In part, the pseudonyms were a means of disguising the fact that HPL was contributing more than one item to a given issue of a paper; in other cases (e.g., the religious poem "Wisdom"), HPL may have been wishing to conceal his identity in a work whose subject matter would have been considered anomalous for readers who knew his work. Some pseudonyms (e.g., Henry Paget-Lowe, Ward Phillips) did not well conceal his identity. His first pseudonym was "Isaac Bickerstaffe," used in late 1914; and this Augustan *nom de plume* paved the way for numerous other pseudonyms derivative or suggestive of eighteenth-century poetry. HPL never used pseudonyms for his major works of weird fiction. Below is an alphabetical list of HPL's pseudonyms and the works under which they appeared in his lifetime (listed chronologically), followed by brief explanations of their use or origin.

"Lawrence Appleton" was used for the poems "Hylas and Myrrha: A Tale" (*Tryout*, May 1919) and "Myrrha and Strephon" (*Tryout*, July 1919). The name reflects the college where Alfred Galpin studied (Lawrence College in Appleton, Wis.), as these poems deal whimsically with Galpin's schoolboy romances.

For the use of Winifred Virginia Jackson's pseudonym "Elizabeth Berkeley" for HPL's poems "The Unknown" (*Conservative*, December 1916) and "The Peace Advocate" (*Tryout*, May 1917), see entry for Jackson.

"Isaac Bickerstaffe, Jr." was used for HPL's satirical attacks on the astrologer J. F. Hartmann in the [Providence] *Evening News:* "Astrology and the Future" (October 13, 1914), "Delavan's Comet and Astrology" (October 26, 1914), [letter to the editor] (December 21, 1914). For the name see Astrology, Articles on.

"Jeremy Bishop" was used for the poem "Medusa: A Portrait" (*Tryout*, December 1921).

"Alexander Ferguson Blair" was used for "North and South Britons" (*Tryout*, May 1919), a poem urging unity between England and Scotland, hence the Scottish-sounding pseudonym.

"El Imparcial" ("the impartial one") was used for the essays "What Is Amateur Journalism?" (*Lake Breeze*, March 1915), "Consolidation's Autopsy" (*Lake Breeze*, April 1915), "New Department Proposed: Instruction for the Recruit" (*Lake Breeze*, June 1915), "Little Journeys to the Homes of Prominent Amateurs" (*United Amateur*, October 1915 and July 1917), "Among the New-Comers" (*United Amateur*, May 1916), and "Winifred Virginia Jordan: Associate Editor" (*Silver Clarion*, April 1919), all on amateur subjects. Of the two "Little Journeys" articles, the first is a biography of Andrew Francis Lockhart (who had previously written a "Little Journeys" biography of HPL) and the second is a biography of Eleanor J. Barnhart.

"John J. Jones" was used for the self-parodic poem "The Dead Bookworm" (*United Amateur*, September 1919).

"Humphry Littlewit" was used for the story "A Reminiscence of Dr. Samuel Johnson" (*United Amateur*, November 1917), the poem-cycle "Perverted Poesie or Modern Metre" (*O-Wash-Ta-Nong*, December 1937; including the poems "The Introduction," "Unda; or, The Bride of the Sea," "The Peace Advocate," and "A Summer Sunset and Evening"), and possibly for the unlocated newspaper publication of the satiric poem "Waste Paper" (the manuscript has the Littlewit pseudonym affixed to it). The name is suggestive of eighteenth-century satire (cf. the line in "He": "look, ye puling lack-wit!").

"Archibald Maynwaring" was used for the poems "The Pensive Swain" (*Tryout*, October 1919), "To the Eighth of November" (*Tryout*, November 1919), and "Wisdom" (*Silver Clarion*, November 1919). The name is probably derived from Arthur Mainwaring, one of the translators of Sir Samuel Garth's edition of Ovid's *Metamorphoses* (1717), which HPL read as a boy (see *SL* 1.7).

"Michael Ormonde O'Reilly" was used for the juvenile poem "To Pan" (*Tryout*, April 1919; as "Pan").

"Henry [or H.] Paget-Lowe" was used for the poems "January" (*Silver Clarion*, January 1920), "On Religion" (*Tryout*, August 1920), "On a Grecian Colonnade in a Park" (*Tryout*, September 1920), and "October" (*Tryout*, October 1920), and the collaborative story "Poetry and the Gods" (*United Amateur*, September 1920), with Anna Helen Crofts.

"Ward Phillips" was used for the essay "Ward Phillips Replies" (*Conservative*, July 1918; containing the poem "Grace"), the poems "Astrophobos" (*United Amateur*, January 1918), "The Eidolon" (*Tryout*, October 1918), "Ambition" (*United Co-operative*, December 1918), "In Memoriam: J. E. T. D." (*Tryout*, March 1919), "The City" (*Vagrant*, October 1919), "Bells" (*Tryout*, December 1919), "The House" (*Philosopher*, December 1920), "Sir Thomas

Tryout" (*Tryout,* December 1921), and "To Mr. Hoag, on His Ninetieth Birthday" (*Tryout,* February 1921), and a letter to the Bureau of Critics published in the *National Amateur* (January 1919) as by "Ned Softly and Ward Phillips." The name seems used chiefly for HPL's weird poetry. Phillips is also a character in "Through the Gates of the Silver Key" (1932–33).

"Richard Raleigh" was used for the poem "To a Youth" (*Tryout,* February 1921). In a ms. of the poem (JHL), HPL notes: "How is this for an Elizabethan pseudonym?" HPL refers to the celebrated Elizabethan courtier Sir Walter Ralegh (1554?–1618), formerly spelled "Raleigh."

"Ames Dorrance Rowley" was used for the poems "Laeta; a Lament" (*Tryout,* February 1918), "The Volunteer" (*Tryout,* April 1918), "To Maj.-Gen. Omar Bundy, U.S.A." (*Tryout,* January 1919), and "To the Old Pagan Religion" (*Tryout,* April 1919; as "The Last Pagan Speaks"). The name is a parody of the amateur poet James Laurence Crowley. Only one of the poems ("Laeta; a Lament") is itself satirical, and does not appear to be a parody of any poem by Crowley.

"Edward Softly" was used for the poems "Damon and Delia, a Pastoral" (*Tryout,* August 1918), "To Delia, Avoiding Damon" (*Tryout,* September 1918), "Ode to Selene or Diana" (*Tryout,* April 1919; as "To Selene"), "Tryout's Lament for the Vanished Spider" (*Tryout,* January 1920), "The Dream" (*Tryout,* September 1920), "Christmas" (*Tryout,* November 1920), and "Chloris and Damon" (*Tryout,* June 1923). The name is probably meant to augment the satirical intent of the several poems here that spoof romantic love poetry. See also "Ward Phillips" above.

"Lewis Theobald, Jun.," HPL's most frequently used pseudonym, was used for the two stories cowritten with Winifred Virginia Jackson, "The Crawling Chaos" (*United Co-operative,* April 1921) and "The Green Meadow" (*Vagrant,* [Spring 1927]), the essays "The Convention" (*Tryout,* July 1930 [as by "Theobald"]) "Some Causes of Self-Immolation," and the poems "Unda; or, The Bride of the Sea" (*Providence Amateur,* February 1916; as "The Bride of the Sea"), "Ye Ballade of Patrick von Flynn" (*Conservative,* April 1916), "Inspiration" (*Conservative,* October 1916), "Brotherhood" (*Tryout,* December 1916), "The Rutted Road" (*Tryout,* January 1917), "The Nymph's Reply to the Modern Business Man" (*Tryout,* February 1917), "Pacifist War Song" (*Tryout,* March 1917) "Sonnet on Myself" (*Tryout,* July 1918), "Damon—a Monody" (*United Amateur,* May 1919 [as "Theobaldus Senectissimus"]), "Monody on the Late King Alcohol" (*Tryout,* August 1919), "To Mistress Sophia Simple, Queen of the Cinema" (*United Amateur,* November 1919), "To Phillis" (*Tryout,* January 1920), "Cindy: Scrub-Lady in a State Street Skyscraper" (*Tryout,* June 1920), "The Poet's Rash Excuse" (*Tryout,* July 1920), "Ex-Poet's Reply" (*Epgephi,* September 1920), "To Alfred Galpin, Esq." (*Tryout,* December 1920), "On the Return of Maurice Winter Moe, Esq., to the Pedagogical Profession" (*Wolverine,* June 1921), "To Mr. Galpin, upon His 20th Birthday" (*Tryout,* December 1921), "On a Poet's Ninety-first Birthday" (*Tryout,* March 1922), "To Rheinhart Kleiner, Esq., upon His Town Fables and Elegies" (*Tryout,* April 1923), "To Damon" (*Tryout,* August 1923), "To Endymion" (*Tryout,* September 1923), "To J. E. Hoag, Esq.: On His Ninety-second Birthday" (*Tryout,* November 1923), and "The Wood" (*Tryout,* January 1929). A brief biography of Theobald appeared in "News Notes" (*United Amateur,* March 1918); it is unsigned, but is presumably by the Official Editor of the UAPA at the time, Verna McGeoch. The name is derived from Lewis Theobald (1688–1744), the Shakespearean scholar whom Alexander Pope made the "hero" of the first version of his satirical poem, *The Dunciad* (1728). (See R. Boerem, "The First Lewis Theobald," in *Discovering H. P. Lovecraft,* ed. Darrell Schweitzer [1987].) HPL's use of the name cannot be entirely systematized, but it appears that he used it most frequently for poems written to friends (Alfred Galpin, Rheinhart Kleiner, Maurice W. Moe, Jonathan E. Hoag, Frank Belknap Long), or other personal poems. HPL pronounced it in the eighteenth-century manner, as a dissyllable (TIB-uld), and frequently referred to himself in correspondence as "Grandpa Theobald."

For "Albert Frederick Willie," used for the poem "Nathicana" (*Vagrant,* [Spring 1927]), see the entry on Alfred Galpin.

For "Zoilus" see "The Vivisector."

"Augustus T. Swift" was formerly thought to be a pseudonym of HPL's for two letters (one of which contains lavish praise of the pulp writer Francis Stevens) published in the *Argosy* (November 15, 1919, and May 22, 1920); but recent research has ascertained that Swift was a real individual living in Providence. See S. T. Joshi, ed., *H. P. Lovecraft in the Argosy* (Necronomicon Press, 1994). Some have mistaken "Perrin Holmes Lowrey" to be a pseudonym of HPL's because of the initials of his name, but he is an actual person—an amateur journalist of HPL's day. HPL's sonnet "St. Toad's" appeared in *WT* (Canadian; September 1945) as by "J. H. Brownlow," but this is not a pseudonymn.

See Willametta Keffer, "Howard P(seudonym) Lovecraft: The Many Names of HPL," *Fossil* No. 158 (July 1958): 82–84; George T. Wetzel, "The Pseudonymous Lovecraft," *Xenophile* 3, No. 4 (November 1976): 3–5, 73; S. T. Joshi, "The Rationale of Lovecraft's Pseudonyms," *Crypt* No. 80 (Eastertide 1992): 15–24, 29.

"Psychopompos: A Tale in Rhyme." Poem (310 lines); begun in late 1917 but not completed until the summer of 1918. First published in *Vagrant* (October 1919); rpt. *WT* (September 1937).

The title means "Conveyer of souls [i.e., to Hades]," a somewhat peculiar title for a poem about werewolves. The story concerns Sieur and Dame de Blois, who seem merely to be reclusive nobles but are in fact werewolves. When a citizen kills Dame de Blois (in the form of a snake), the Sieur besieges the house of his wife's murderer with a band of other wolves, but he is himself killed.

HPL apparently was influenced by Winifred Virginia Jackson's poem "Insomnia" (*Conservative,* October 1916) in the two quatrains that open the poem. The final two lines as originally written—"For Sieur de Blois (the old wife's tale is through) / Was lost eternally to mortal view"—were changed at the instigation of John Ravenor Bullen of the Transatlantic Circulator, who maintained that "through" as used here was impermissibly colloquial (see *MW* 156). HPL included the work in lists of his fiction.

Pth'thya-l'hi. In "The Shadow over Innsmouth," she is the wife of Obed Marsh and great-great-grandmother of Robert Olmstead. According to HPL's notes, she was born 78,000 B.C. Olmstead meets her in the dream that convinces him to join his forebears and to live forever in Y'ha-nthlei under the ocean.

Purdy, Marjorie. In "Ashes," the secretary of the scientist Arthur Van Allister. Her lover, Malcolm Bruce, thinks she has been reduced to ashes by a formula invented by Van Allister, but in fact she is merely locked in a closet.

Q

"Quest of Iranon, The." Short story (2,800 words); written on February 28, 1921. First published in the *Galleon* (July–August 1935), edited by Lloyd Arthur Eshbach; rpt. *WT* (March 1939); first collected in *BWS;* corrected text in *D;* annotated version in *TD*.

A youthful singer named Iranon comes to the granite city of Teloth, saying that he is seeking his far-off home of Aira, where he was a prince. The men of Teloth, who have no beauty in their lives, do not look kindly on Iranon and force him to work with a cobbler. He meets a boy named Romnod, who similarly yearns for "the warm groves and the distant lands of beauty and song." Romnod thinks that nearby Oonai, the city of lutes and dancing, might be Iranon's Aira. Iranon doubts it, but goes there with Romnod. It is indeed not Aira, but the two of them find welcome there for a time. Iranon wins praises for his singing and lyre-playing, and Romnod learns the coarser pleasures of wine. Years pass; Iranon seems to grow no older, as he continues to hope one day to find Aira. Romnod eventually dies of drink, and Iranon leaves the town and continues his quest. He comes to "the squalid cot of an antique shepherd" and asks him about Aira. The shepherd looks at Iranon curiously and states that he had heard of the name Aira, but that it was merely an imaginary name invented by a beggar's boy he had known long ago. This boy, "given to strange dreams," provoked laughter by thinking himself a king's son. At twilight an old, old man is seen walking calmly into the quicksand. "That night something of youth and beauty died in the elder world."

"The Quest of Iranon" is among the best of HPL's Dunsanian imitations, although there is perhaps a hint of social snobbery at the end (Iranon kills himself because he discovers he is of low birth). HPL wished to use it in his own *Conservative* (whose last issue had appeared in July 1919), but the next issue did not appear until March 1923, and HPL had by then evidently decided against using it there. It was rejected by *WT* and does not appear to have been submitted elsewhere until HPL sent it to the *Galleon.*

See Brian Humphreys, "Who or What Was Iranon?" *LS* No. 25 (Fall 1991): 10–13; Donald R. Burleson, "A Textual Oddity in 'The Quest of Iranon,'" *LS* No. 34 (Spring 1996): 24–26.

Quinn, Seabury [Grandin] (1889–1969). American writer and editor; prolific author of tales about psychic detective Jules de Grandin in *WT.* HPL enjoyed his early tale, "The Phantom Farmhouse" (*WT,* October 1923), but felt other tales to be formula-ridden hackwork, as evinced in a delightful parody of Quinn's work (see *SL* 4.162–63). HPL first met Quinn at Wilfred B. Talman's apartment in New York City on July 6, 1931 (see *SL* 3.382); they met again in early January 1936, during HPL's last New York visit. Quinn is parodied as "Teaberry Quince" in "The Battle That Ended the Century" (1934). His best Jules de Grandin stories were collected in *The Phantom-Fighter* (Arkham House, 1966); another collection is *Is the Devil a Gentleman?* (Mirage Press, 1970).

R

"Rats in the Walls, The." Short story (7,940 words); written late August or early September 1923. First published in *WT* (March 1924); rpt. *WT* (June 1930); first collected in *O*; corrected text in *DH;* annotated version in *An1* and *CC*.

A Virginian of British ancestry, a man named Delapore (his first name is not given), decides to spend his latter years in refurbishing and occupying his ancestral estate in southern England, Exham Priory, whose foundations extend to a period even before the Roman conquest of the first century C.E. Delapore spares no expense in the restoration and proudly moves into his estate on July 16, 1923. He has reverted to the ancestral spelling of his name, de la Poer, despite the fact that the family has a very unsavory reputation with the local population for murder, kidnapping, witchcraft, and other anomalies extending to the time of the first Baron Exham in 1261. Associated with the house or the family is the "dramatic epic of the rats—the lean, filthy, ravenous army which had swept all before it and devoured fowl, cats, dogs, hogs, sheep, and even two hapless human beings before its fury was spent."

All this seems merely conventional ghostly legendry, and de la Poer pays no attention to it. But shortly after his occupancy of Exham Priory, odd things begin to happen; in particular, he and his several cats seem to detect the scurrying of rats in the walls of the structure, even though such a thing is absurd in light of the centuries-long desertion of the place. The scurrying seems to descend to the basement of the edifice, and one night de la Poer and his friend, Capt. Edward Norrys, spend a night there to see if they can discern the mystery. De la Poer wakes to hear the scurrying of the rats continuing *"still downward,* far underneath this deepest of sub-cellars," but Norrys hears nothing. When they come upon a trapdoor leading to a cavern beneath the basement, they decide to call in scientific specialists to investigate the matter. As the explorers descend into the nighted crypt, they come upon an awesome and horrific sight—an enormous expanse of bones: "Like a foamy sea they stretched, some fallen apart, but others wholly or partly articulated as skeletons; these latter invariably in postures of daemoniac frenzy, either fighting off some menace or clutching some other forms with cannibal intent." When de la Poer finds that some bones have rings bearing his own coat of arms, he realizes the truth—his family has been the leaders of an ancient cannibalistic witch-cult that had its origins in primitive times—and he experiences a spectacular evolutionary reversal: speaking successively in archaic English, Middle English, Latin, Gaelic, and primitive ape-cries, he is found crouching over the half-eaten form of Capt. Norrys.

In a late letter HPL states that the story was "suggested by a very commonplace incident—the cracking of wall-paper late at night, and the chain of imaginings resulting from it" (*SL* 5.181), but this specific image does not occur in the story. HPL recorded the kernel of the idea in his commonplace book: "Wall paper cracks off in sinister shape—man dies of fright" (#107). And yet, an earlier entry (#79) is also suggestive: "Horrible secret in crypt of ancient castle—discovered by dweller." HPL first submitted the tale to *Argosy All-Story Weekly,* a Munsey magazine whose managing editor, Robert H. Davis, rejected it as being (in HPL's words) "too horrible for the tender sensibilities of a delicately nurtured publick" (*SL* 1.259).

The name *de la Poe*r has been seen to be an allusion to Edgar Allan Poe; but, as John Kipling Hitz points out, the name is a slight alteration of an actual name, Le Poer, which Poe and his erstwhile fiancée Sarah Helen (Power) Whitman believed to be in both their ancestries. HPL would have known this from reading Caroline Tinknor's biography of Whitman, *Poe's Helen* (1916), which he owned.

Although the English atmosphere is depicted deftly in the tale, HPL appears to commit some errors. The town nearest to Exham Priory is given as Anchester, but there is no such town in England. HPL must have been thinking either of Ancaster in Lincolnshire or (more likely) Alchester in the southern county of Oxfordshire. Perhaps this is a deliberate alteration; but then, what do we make of the statement that "Anchester had been the camp of the Third Augustan Legion"? Neither Alchester nor Ancaster were the sites of legionary fortresses in Roman Britain; what is more, the Third Augustan Legion was never in England, and it was the Second Augustan Legion that was stationed at Isca Silurum (Caerleon-on-Usk) in what is now Wales.

Certain surface features of the tale—and perhaps one essential kernel of the plot—were taken from other works. As Steven J. Mariconda has pointed out, HPL's account of the "epic of the rats" appears to be derived from a chapter in S. Baring-Gould's *Curious Myths of the Middle Ages* (1869). The Gaelic parts of de la Poer's concluding cries were lifted directly from Fiona Macleod's "The Sin-Eater" (1895), which HPL read in Joseph Lewis French's anthology, *Best Psychic Stories* (1920). (This borrowing would have a curious sequel. According to a now discredited historical theory, Gaelic was thought to have been spoken in the north of England rather than the South, where Cymric was spoken. When the tale was reprinted in *WT* for June 1930, Robert E. Howard noticed the discrepancy and sent a letter to the editor, Farnsworth Wright, pointing it out; Wright passed the letter on to HPL, thereby initiating an intense six-year correspondence between the two writers.)

The idea of atavism or reversion to type seems to have been derived from a story by Irvin S. Cobb, "The Unbroken Chain," published in *Cosmopolitan* for September 1923 (the issue, as is customary with many magazines, was probably on the stands at least a month before its cover date) and later collected in Cobb's collection *On an Island That Cost $24.00* (1926). HPL admits that Frank Belknap Long gave him the magazine appearance of this story in 1923 (see HPL to J. Vernon Shea, November 8–22, 1933; ms., JHL), and he alludes to it without title in "Supernatural Horror in Literature." This tale deals with a Frenchman who has a small proportion of negroid blood from a slave brought to America in 1819. When he is run down by a train, he cries out in an African language— "*Niama tumba!*"—the words that his black ancestor shouted when he was attacked by a rhinoceros in Africa.

The story was reprinted in HPL's lifetime in Christine Campbell Thomson's *Switch On the Light* (1931). Its appearance (with "The Dunwich Horror") in Herbert A. Wise and Phyllis Fraser's *Great Tales of Terror and the Supernatural* (Modern Library, 1944) was a significant landmark in HPL's literary recognition.

See Barton Levi St. Armand, *The Roots of Horror in the Fiction of H. P. Lovecraft* (Elizabethtown, N.Y.: Dragon Press, 1977); Steven J. Mariconda, "Baring-Gould and the Ghouls: The Influence of *Curious Myths of the Middle Ages* on 'The Rats in the Walls,'" *Crypt* No. 14 (St. John's Eve 1983): 3–7 (rpt. in Mariconda's *On the Emergence of "Cthulhu" and Other Observations* [Necronomicon Press, 1995]); *Crypt* No. 72 (Roodmas 1990) (special issue on "The Rats in the Walls"); Hubert Van Calenbergh, "The Roots of Horror in *The Golden Bough,*" *LS* No. 26 (Spring 1992): 21–23; Paul Montelone, "'The Rats in the Walls': A Study in Pessimism," *LS* No. 32 (Spring 1995): 18–26; John Kipling Hitz, "Lovecraft and the Whitman Memoir," *LS* No. 37 (Fall 1997): 15–17; Mollie L. Burleson, "H. P. Lovecraft and Charles Dickens: The Rats in Their Walls," *LS* No. 38 (Spring 1998): 34–35; John Kipling Hitz, "Some Notes on 'The Rats in the Walls,'" *LS* No. 40 (Fall 1998): 29–33.

"Regner Lodbrog's Epicedium." Poem (68 lines in 7 stanzas); written in late 1914. First published in the *Acolyte* (Summer 1944).

The work is an English translation of a Latin translation of an eighth-century Runic poem printed in Hugh Blair's *A Critical Dissertation on the Poems of Ossian* (1763), dealing with the military exploits of Regner Lodbrog. HPL relied heavily on an English paraphrase supplied by Blair of the final six stanzas; this is why the first stanza contains more deliberate gaps than the others. HPL quotes some lines of the Latin version as an epigraph to "The Teuton's Battle-Song" (*United Amateur*, February 1916). HPL misconstrued Blair's remarks on Wormius (Ole Wurm, 1588–1654) and assumed that he dated to the thirteenth century; he is so mentioned when HPL attributes to him the Latin translation of the *Necronomicon* (see "History of the *Necronomicon*").

See S. T. Joshi, "Lovecraft, Regner Lodbrog, and Olaus Wormius," *Crypt* No. 89 (Eastertide 1995): 3–7.

Reid, Dr. In "Pickman's Model," a physician who, as a student of comparative pathology, ceased his acquaintance with the artist Richard Upton Pickman, claiming (in Pickman's indignant words) that the artist was "a sort of monster bound down the toboggan of reverse evolution."

"Reminiscence of Dr. Samuel Johnson, A." Short story (2,060 words); probably written in the summer or fall of 1917. First published in the *United Amateur* (September 1917) as by "Humphry Littlewit, Esq." First collected in *Writings in the United Amateur* (1976); corrected text in *MW*.

The narrator, Littlewit, is entering his 228th year, having been born on August 20, 1690. He provides some familiar and not-so-familiar "reminiscences" of Johnson and of his literary circle—Boswell, Goldsmith, Gibbon, and others—all written in a meticulous re-creation of eighteenth-century English. Littlewit is the author of a periodical paper, *The Londoner,* like Johnson's *Rambler, Idler,* and *Adventurer,* and—like HPL—he has a reputation for revising the poetry of others. He undertakes a revision of a poetic lampoon that Boswell directs toward him (this lampoon is actually found in the *Life of Johnson*). Much of the other information in the sketch is derived from Boswell's biography or from Johnson's own works.

Renshaw, Anne (Vyne) Tillery, amateur journalist from Mississippi, instructor, and associate of HPL. Renshaw was a well-known figure in amateur journalism in the 1910s, publishing many poems (whose radicalism HPL chided in "Metrical Regularity" [*Conservative,* July 1915] and "The Vers Libre Epidemic" [*Conservative,* January 1917]) and editing *The Pinfeather* (for which HPL wrote "To the Members of the Pin-Feathers . . .," November 1914), *Ole Miss'* (for which HPL wrote the essay "Systematic Instruction in the United" and the poem "A Mississippi Autumn," both in the December 1915 issue), *The Symphony* (which published HPL's poem "The Smile" [July 1916] and about which HPL wrote in the essay "Symphony and Stress" [*Conservative,* October 1915]), and other papers. HPL was assistant editor for *The Credential,* a paper designed to publish the work of new amateurs, edited by Renshaw; only one issue (April 1920) is known to have been published. In late 1916 HPL, Renshaw, and Mrs. J. G. Smith (about whom nothing is known) teamed up to form the Symphony Literary Service, apparently a professional revision service; this appears to be the first time HPL engaged in such an enterprise, but the service does not seem to have lasted for very long. In 1919 HPL supported Renshaw's successful candidacy for Official Editor of the UAPA ("For Official Editor—Anne Tillery Renshaw," *Conservative,* July 1919). HPL met Renshaw for the first time in Boston on August 17, 1921. At that time she was teaching at the Curry School of Expression; some time previously she had been head of the English department at Research University in Washington, D.C. On April 11, 1925, Renshaw, back in Washington, drove HPL, George Kirk, and Edward L. Sechrist around the city on a sightseeing tour. Some evidence suggests that HPL may have been doing further work for Renshaw in a revisory capacity during the late 1920s. Little is heard of her until early 1936, when Renshaw, now running her own school of speech, proposed to HPL the revision of a manual on speech and grammar, entitled *Well-Bred Speech.* HPL undertook an exhaustive revision of Renshaw's very crude draft, writing entire chapters (including those on "Words Frequently Mispronounced," "Bromides [i.e., clichés] Must Go," and a substantial concluding chapter, "What Shall I Read?"). Because HPL was so slow in getting the book to her (partly because of increasingly bad health, partly because of R. H. Barlow's month-long stay with him that summer), Renshaw had to rush the book into print and omit much of HPL's work. The volume appeared late in the year as *Well Bred Speech: A Brief, Intensive Aid for English Students* (Washington, D.C.: Standard Press, [1936]). She paid HPL only $100 for his work. HPL's chapters and other revisions survive at JHL. The final chapter was published under the title "Suggestions for a Reading Guide" (in *DB;* rpt. *CE2*). Renshaw published another book early the next year—*Salvaging Self Esteem: A Program for Self-Improvement* (Washington, D.C.: Renshaw School of Speech, [1937])—which HPL owned. In her early amateur journalist days, Renshaw wrote a brief article on HPL, "Our Friend, the Conservative," *Ole Miss'* No. 2 (December 1915): 2–3.

"Revelation." Poem (56 lines in 7 stanzas); probably written in early 1919. First published in *Tryout* (March 1919); rpt. *National Enquirer* (April 24, 1919).

The narrator finds himself in a pleasant valley, but as he looks upward to the skies, he finds himself "Ever wiser, ever sadder"; looking back downward, he finds only "terror in the brooklet's ride" as his realm has become a "lost, accursed land."

Rhode Island Journal of Astronomy, The. Juvenile periodical written by HPL, 1903–9. Copies at JHL.

The hectographed paper survives in 69 issues: 1, No. 1 (August 2, 1903); 1, No. 2 (August 9, 1903); 1, No. 3 (August 16, 1903); 1, No. 4 (August 23, 1903); 1, No. 5 (August 30, 1903); 1, No. 6 (September 6, 1903); 1, No. 7 (September 13, 1903); 1, No. 8 (September 20, 1903); 1, No. 9 (September 27, 1903); 1, No. 10 (October 4, 1903); 1, No. 11 (October 11, 1903); 1, No. 12 (October 18, 1903); 1, No. 13 (October 25, 1903); 1, No. 14 (November 1, 1903); 1, No. 15 (November 8, 1903); 1, No. 16 (November 15, 1903); 1, No. 17 (November 22, 1903); 1, No. 18 (November 29, 1903); 1, No. 19 (December 6, 1903); 1, No. 20 (December 13, 1903); 1, No. 21 (December 20, 1903); 1, No. 22 (December 27, 1903); 1, No. 23 (January 3, 1904); 1, No. 24 (January 10, 1904); 1, No 25 (January 17, 1904); 1, No. 26 (January 24, 1904); 1, No. 27 (January 31, 1904); 3, No. 1 (April 16, 1905); [Extra] (April 17, 1905); 3, No. 2 (April 23, 1905); 3, No. 3 (April 30, 1905); 3, No. 4 (May 7, 1905); 3, No. 5 (May 14, 1905); 3, No. 6 (May 21, 1905); 3, No. 7 (May 28, 1905); 3, No. 8 (June 4, 1905); 3, No. 9 (June 11, 1905); 3, No. 10 (June 18, 1905); 3, No. 11 (June 25, 1905); 3, No. 12 (July 2, 1905); 3, No. 13 (July 9, 1905); 3, No. 14 (July 16, 1905); 3, No. 15 (July 23, 1905); 4 [sic], No. 1 (new series) (July 30, 1905); 3, No. 2 (August 6, 1905); 3, No. 3 (August 13, 1905); 3, No. 5 (August 27, 1905); 3, No. 6 (September 3, 1905); 3, No. 7 (September 10, 1905); 3, No. 8 (September 17, 1905); 3, No. 9 (October 8, 1905); 3, No. 10 (October 22, 1905); 3, No. 11 (November 12, 1905); 3, No. 6 [sic] (January 1906); 3, No. 7 (February 1906); 3, No. 8 (March 1906); 3, No. 9 (April 1906); 3, No. 10 (May 1906); 3, No. 11 (June 1906); 4, No. 1 (Special Anniversary Number) (August 1906); 4, No. 2 (September 1906); 4, No. 3 (October 1906); 4, No. 4

(November 1906); 4, No. 5 (December 1906); 4, No. 6 (January 1907); 4, No. 9 (April 1907); 6, No. 6 (January 1909); 6, No. 7 (February 1909).

The paper was HPL's most ambitious and longest-running juvenile periodical. An average issue would contain several different columns, features, and charts, along with news notes, advertisements (for works by HPL, for items from his collection, and for outside merchants or friends), and fillers. Numerous serials appeared in the paper; the issue for September 20, 1903 lists the "original & complete MS." of these: "The Telescope" (12 pp.); "The Moon" (12 pp.); "On Venus" (10 pp.); "Atlas Wld." (7 maps); "Practical Geom[etry]" (34 pp.); "Astronomy" (60 pp.); "Solar System" (27 pp.). The issue for November 1, 1903 notes that HPL has now begun to use the telescope at Ladd Observatory of Brown University; HPL elsewhere states that Prof. Winslow Upton, professor of astronomy at Brown, was a family friend and allowed HPL access to the observatory (*SL* 1.38). Several early drafts of HPL's columns for the *Pawtuxet Valley Gleaner* and [Providence] *Tribune* first appeared here.

Ricci, Angelo. A thief (of Italian ancestry) who meets a bad end when, in "The Terrible Old Man," he attempts to rob an old sea captain of his reputed hoard of Spanish gold and silver.

Rice, Professor Warren. In "The Dunwich Horror," a professor at Miskatonic University who, with Henry Armitage and Francis Morgan, leads the party that exterminates Wilbur Whateley's monstrous twin brother.

Rimel, Duane W[eldon] (1915–1996), author of weird and fantasy tales and correspondent of HPL (1934–37). In his letters HPL wrote expansively to Rimel about numerous subjects, offering constant assistance in matters of literary technique. In a letter dated June 17, 1934, HPL includes a segment called "Notes on Writing a Story," one of several different versions of the essay "Notes on Writing Weird Fiction" (1933). HPL read many of his early stories and revised some of them, including "The Tree on the Hill" (1934; *Polaris,* September 1940) and "The Disinterment" (1935; *WT,* January 1937), and perhaps also "The Jewels of Charlotte" (*Unusual Stories,* May–June 1935). Rimel published many other stories in fanzines and semi-pro magazines. His poem cycle "Dreams of Yith" (*Fantasy Fan,* July and September 1934) was revised by HPL and perhaps by Clark Ashton Smith. In his so-called death diary, HPL mentions revising Rimel's story "From the Sea" in January 1937, but the story apparently is unpublished and does not survive. Rimel briefly spearheaded the HPL fan movement in the 1940s, luring Francis T. Laney back into fandom and coediting *The Acolyte* (1942–46). He went on to write westerns and soft-core pornography under pseudonyms. See his memoir, "H. P. Lovecraft as I Knew Him" (*Crypt* No. 18 [Yuletide 1983]: 9–11). Much of his weird short fiction and poetry has now been reprinted in *The Forbidden Room* (Moshassuck Press, 1988), *The Many Worlds of Duane Rimel* (1988), *The Second Book of Rimel* (1989), and *To Yith and Beyond* (Moshassuck Press, 1990).

Robbins, Maria. In "The Shunned House," a woman from Newport, R.I., hired by Mercy Dexter in 1769 to be a servant at the house. Although her health declines markedly, she stays until 1783, when the Harris family moved out of the house.

Robinson, Buck. In "Herbert West—Reanimator," a semi-professional boxer (nicknamed "The Harlem Smoke") who is killed by "Kid" O'Brien in an informal bout in Bolton, Mass. He is taken to the office of Dr. Herbert West, who hopes to revive him from the dead, but West believes he has failed, since the solution he injected into Robinson (an African American) was "prepared from experience with white specimens only." Later West learns otherwise.

Rogers, George. In "The Horror in the Museum," the curator and chief artist of a wax museum in London who has a penchant for teratological monstrosities and who goes mad after he captures a strange "deity." His latest creation in wax—a depiction of himself mutilated by the deity—proves to be no wax effigy at all.

Romero, Juan. In "Transition of Juan Romero," a Mexican peon who is actually a descendant of the Aztecs. When he and the narrator explore the vast cavern uncovered in the Norton Mine, where they are employed as miners, he witnesses something frightening in the great abyss, and the next day is found dead in his bunk.

Romnod. In "The Quest of Iranon," the boy from Teloth who helps Iranon seek his homeland, Aira. They come to Oonai, "the city of lutes and dancing," where they stay, and there Romnod indulges in strong drink, from which he eventually dies.

Ropes, ———. In *At the Mountains of Madness,* a student and a member of the Miskatonic Antarctic Expedition of 1930–31.

Roulet, Etienne. In "The Shunned House," a Huguenot who flees from France to East Greenwich, R I., in 1686. Roulet is somehow connected with Jacques Roulet of Caude, who in 1598 is accused of lycanthropy. The land on which the Shunned House was built had been leased to Roulet and his wife in 1697.

Rufus, L[ucius] Caelius. In "The Very Old Folk," a provincial quaestor in the Roman province of Hispania Citerior (Spain), who accompanies a cohort of the Roman army to investigate reports of peculiar events in the hills above Tarraco. In the dream inspiring this story, HPL himself was Rufus.

Russell, John, British amateur journalist living in Florida and infrequent associate of HPL. When HPL wrote a letter to the *Argosy* criticizing romance writer Fred Jackson (published in the September 1913 issue), Russell was one of many to protest—but his protest (published in the November 1913 issue) was in verse, leading HPL to respond with the *Ad Criticos* poems. After a year of sporadic exchanges, the editor of the *Argosy* asked the two writers to reconcile, and they did so in an item published as "The Critics' Farewell" in the October 1914 issue, containing HPL's poem "The End of the Jackson War" and Russell's "Our Apology to E. M. W." HPL must have got in touch with Russell personally around this time; he urged Russell to join amateur journalism, but Russell did not do so immediately. Russell's poem "Florida" and HPL's poem "New England" were published together in the Providence *Evening News* (December 18, 1914); Russell's poem was reprinted from the *Tampa Times*. HPL's brief article "An Impartial Spectator" (*Conservative*, October 1915) consists of paragraphs prefacing and following Russell's poem "Metrical Regularity, or, Broken Metre." In April 1925, Russell spent a few days in HPL's company in New York. Thereafter he disappears from the record. No correspondence between HPL and Russell survives.

S

Sandusky, Albert A. (d. 1934?). Amateur journalist and associate of HPL. Sandusky, a resident of Cambridge, Mass., operated the Lincoln Press, and in this capacity he printed the two issues of the *Providence Amateur* (June 1915 and February 1916) for HPL, as well as several issues of HPL's *Conservative* (July 1915, October 1915, January 1916, April 1916, and possibly July 1916). HPL first met Sandusky on a visit to Boston on March 10–11, 1923, to attend a meeting of the Hub Club (an amateur group associated with the NAPA), of which Sandusky was a member. HPL was taken with Sandusky's piquant use of contemporary slang, and his poem "The Feast (Hub Journalist Club, March 10, 1923)," published in the *Hub Club Quill* (May 1923), is dedicated to "Wisecrack Sandusky, B.I., M.B.O. (Bachelor of Intelligence, Massachusetts Brotherhood of Owls)." HPL met Sandusky again in Boston in August 1923, and Sandusky visited HPL in New York in June 1925. No correspondence by HPL to Sandusky has survived.

Sargent, Joe. In "The Shadow over Innsmouth," he drives the motor coach that takes Robert Olmstead between Arkham, Newburyport, and Innsmouth.

Sargent, Moses and Abigail. In "The Thing on the Doorstep," servants of Edward and Asenath Derby who, after being dismissed by Edward, appear to exact some kind of blackmail from him.

Sawyer, Asaph. The vindictive scoundrel in "In the Vault" whose corpse was mutilated by George Birch in order to make it fit a coffin originally intended for a shorter man and who exacts vengeance on Birch even in death.

Sawyer, Earl. In "The Dunwich Horror," a neighbor of the Whateleys who, when selling cattle to that family, detects a horrible stench in their abandoned toolhouse. Later he tends Wilbur Whateley's cattle while Wilbur is visiting the library of Miskatonic University, and still later he is among the party that exterminates Wilbur's twin brother. His "common-law wife" is Mamie Bishop. His relationship to **Sally Sawyer,** housekeeper of Seth Bishop's farm, and her son **Chauncey** is unspecified.

Schmidt, ———. In "The Temple," a seaman on the German submarine U-29 who becomes violently insane and is executed by the commander, Graf von Altberg-Ehrenstein.

Schwartz, Julius (1915–2004), American agent and editor. As editor of *Fantasy Magazine,* Schwartz commissioned HPL (along with C. L. Moore, A. Merritt, Robert E. Howard, and Frank Belknap Long) to write the weird version of "The Challenge from Beyond" for the September 1935 issue (also a science fiction version with other writers). He later became an agent. At a party in New York, probably in the fall of 1935, HPL agreed to let Schwartz market his material; Schwartz sold *At the Mountains of Madness* to *Astounding* for $350 (less 10% commission). In late 1936 he contemplated marketing HPL's tales in England, but if he did so he was unsuccessful. He became an important figure in the comic industry in the 1950s. Schwartz has now published his memoirs, *Man of Two Worlds* (2000).

See Will Murray, "Julius Schwartz on Lovecraft" (interview), *Crypt* No. 76 (Hallowmas 1990): 14–18.

Scientific Gazette, The. Juvenile periodical written by HPL, 1899–1909. Copies at JHL.

The hectographed paper was HPL's first venture in scientific writing, initially inspired by his interest in chemistry beginning in 1898 but later expanding to cover a wider range of scientific topics. Thirty-two issues survive: 1, No. 1 (March 4, 1899); New Issue 1, No. 1 (May 12, 1902); 3, No. 1 (August 16, 1903); 3, No. 2 (August 23, 1903); 3, No. 3 (August 30, 1903); 3, No. 4 (September 6, 1903); 3, No. 5 (September 13, 1903); 3, No. 6 (September 30, 1903); 3, Odd Number 1 (September 22, 1903); 3, Odd Number 2 (September 23, 1903); 3, No. 10 [sic] (September 27, 1903); 3, No. 11 [sic] (October 4, 1903); 3, No. 11 [sic] odd (October 8, 1903); 3, No. 9 (October 11, 1903); 3, No. 10 (October 18, 1903); 3, No. 4 odd (October 20, 1903); 3, No. 11 (October 25, 1903); 3, No. 12 (November 1, 1903); 3, No. 13 (November 8, 1903); 3, No. 14 (November 15, 1903); 3, No. 15 (November 22, 1903); 3, No. 16 (November 29, 1903); 3, No. 17 (December 6, 1903); 3, No. 18 (December 13, 1903); 3, No. 19 (December 20, 1903); 3, No. 20 (December 27, 1903); 3, No. 21 (January 3, 1904); 3, No. 22 (January 10, 1904); 3, No. 23 (January 17, 1904); 3, No. 24 (January 24, 1904); 3, No. 25 (January 31, 1904); 10, No. 11 (January 1909).

The first issue consists of two sentences: "There was a great explosion in the Providence Laboratory this afternoon. While experimenting some potassium blew up causing great damage to everyone." HPL notes that at this time the magazine was a daily but that it "soon degenerated into a weekly" (*SL* 1.37). We are clearly missing any subsequent issues of Volume 1 and all issues of Volume 2. There may not have been very many of these, as HPL notes in the issue of May 12, 1902: "The Scientific Gazette, so long discontinued, has been resumed." The price is now raised from 1¢ to 2¢. HPL states (*Rhode Island Journal of Astronomy,* July 30, 1905) that the paper was revived in May 1904 as a monthly, but no issues survive; the September 16, 1905, issue of the *Rhode Island Journal of Astronomy* announces that the *Scientific Gazette* is now discontinued. In the September 1906 issue of the *Rhode Island Journal* HPL states that his boyhood friend Arthur Fredlund had taken over as editor of the *Scientific Gazette,* but no issues produced under Fredlund's editorship are extant. HPL's fleeting revival of his juvenile paper when he was eighteen years old (and some months after he withdrew from high school without a diploma because of a nervous breakdown) is a poignant indication of the sense of hopelessness he felt at this setback to his intellectual and emotional maturation.

Searight, Richard F[ranklyn] (1902–1975). Pulp writer from Michigan and correspondent of HPL. With Norman E. Hammerstrom, Searight wrote "The Brain in the Jar" (*WT,* November 1924), but it was not until the 1930s that he decided to resume the writing of weird and science fiction. At the suggestion of *WT* editor Farnsworth Wright, whom he visited in the summer of 1933, Searight wrote to HPL asking about the possibility of revising some of his tales. HPL declined, feeling that the "occasional shortcomings" of Searight's tales "are matters of subject-matter rather than of technique" (letter to Searight, August 31, 1933), but he continued to advise Searight in literary matters. In early 1934 Searight wrote "The Sealed Casket" (*WT,* March 1935), for which he created the Eltdown Shards, which HPL cited in "The Shadow out of Time" and "The Challenge from Beyond." HPL had no hand in revising the tale, and he altered only one word of the epigraph (purporting to be from the Eltdown Shards) that was intended to preface the story but was not published in the *WT* version. (HPL quoted the epigraph in a letter to Clark Ashton Smith [c. March 1935; *SL* 5.112], leading some to believe that he wrote it.) Searight published a few pieces in *Wonder Stories* and other pulps but never succeeded in making a full-time career of writing. His historical novel *Wild Empire,* written in the late 1930s and early 1940s, was published in 1994. Necronomicon Press has issued two collections of his tales: *The Brain in the Jar and Others* (1992) and *The Sealed Casket and Others* (1996). HPL's *Letters to Richard F. Searight* also appeared in 1992 from Necronomicon Press. All three volumes have sensitive and informative introductions by Searight's son, Franklyn Searight (b. 1935).

Sechrist, Edward Lloyd (1873–1953), beekeeper, amateur journalist residing in Washington, D.C., and occasional correspondent of HPL. Sechrist, a member of the UAPA, visited HPL in Providence in early 1924 (see *SL* 1.292) then visited HPL in New York on November 3, 1924. He accompanied HPL during much of the latter's trip to Washington on April 11, 1925, and met HPL again in Washington on May 6, 1929. HPL noted (letter to Lillian D. Clark, [May 6, 1929]; ms., JHL) that his poem "The Outpost" (1929) made use of the tales about Zimbabwe told to him by Sechrist, who had actually been to the ruins of the African city. Two late letters published in *SL* (April 15, 1936, and February 14, 1937) mistakenly addressed to "Arthur F. Sechrist" (HPL's salutation is to "Ar-Eph-Ess" or RFS) are in fact to Richard F. Searight.

"Secret Cave, or John Lees Adventure, The." Juvenile story (525 words); written c. 1898–99. First published in *SR*; corrected text in *Juvenilia: 1897–1905* (1985) and *MW.*

Mrs. Lee instructs her ten-year-old son John and two-year-old daughter Alice to be "good children" while both parents are "going off for the day"; but immediately upon their departure John and Alice go down to the cellar and begin "to rummage among the rubbish." When Alice leans against a wall and it suddenly gives way behind her, a passage is discovered. John and Alice enter the passage, coming successively upon a large empty box; a small, very heavy box that is not opened; and a boat with oars. The passage comes to an abrupt end; John pulls away "the obstacle" and finds a torrent of water rushing in. John is a good swimmer, but little Alice is not, and she drowns. John manages to struggle into the boat, clinging to the body of his sister and the small box. Suddenly he realizes that "he could shut off the water"; he does so, although how he does it—and why he did not think of it earlier—is never explained. Finally he reaches the cellar. Later it is discovered that the box contains a solid gold chunk worth $10,000—"enough to pay for any thing but the death of his sister."

"Shadow out of Time, The." Novelette (25,600 words); written November 10, 1934 to February 22, 1935. First published in *Astounding Stories* (June 1936); first collected in *O;* reprinted in *DH;* corrected and annotated text (based on recently discovered AMS): Hippocampus Press, 2001; annotated version in *DWH.*

Nathaniel Wingate Peaslee, a professor of political economy at Miskatonic University, experiences a sudden nervous breakdown on May 14, 1908, while teaching a class. Awaking in the hospital after a collapse, he appears to have suffered amnesia so severe that it has affected even his vocal and motor faculties. Gradually he relearns the use of his body and, indeed, develops tremendous mental capacity, seemingly far beyond that of a normal human being. His wife, sensing that something is gravely wrong, refuses to have anything to do with him and later obtains a divorce; only one of his three children, Wingate, continues to associate with him. Peaslee spends the next five years conducting prodigious research at various libraries around the world and also undertakes expeditions to various mysterious realms. Finally, on September 27, 1913, he suddenly snaps back into his old life: when he awakes after a spell of unconsciousness, he believes he is still teaching the economics course in 1908.

Peaslee is now plagued with dreams of increasing strangeness. He dreams that his mind has been placed in the body of an entity shaped like a ten-foot-high rugose cone, while that entity's mind occupies his own body. These creatures are called the Great Race "because [they] alone had conquered the secret of time": they have perfected a technique of mind-exchange with almost any other life-form throughout the universe and at any point in time—past, present, or future. The Great Race had established a colony on this planet in Australia 150,000,000 years ago. Their minds had previously occupied the bodies of another race but had left them because of some impending cataclysm; later they would migrate to other bodies after the cone-shaped beings were destroyed. They had compiled a voluminous library consisting of the accounts of all the other captive minds throughout the universe. Peaslee writes an account of his time for the Great Race's archives.

Peaslee believes that his dreams of the Great Race are merely the product of his esoteric study during his amnesia; but then an Australian explorer, having read some of Peaslee's articles on his dreams in a psychological journal, writes to him to let him know that some archeological remains very similar to the ones he has described as the city of the Great Race have been recently discovered. Peaslee accompanies the explorer, Robert B. F. Mackenzie, on an expedition to the Great Sandy Desert and is stunned to find that his dreams may have a real source. One night he leaves the camp to conduct a solitary exploration. He winds through the now underground corridors of the Great Race's city, increasingly unnerved at the familiarity of the sites he is traversing. He knows that the only way to discern whether his dreams are only dreams or some monstrous reality is to find the account he dreamed he had written for the archives of the Great Race. After a laborious descent he comes to the place and does indeed find his own record. Reflecting afterward, he writes: "No eye had seen, no hand had touched that book since the advent of man to this planet. And yet, when I flashed my torch upon it in that frightful megalithic abyss, I saw that the queerly pigmented letters on the brittle, aeon-browned cellulose pages were not indeed any nameless hieroglyphs of earth's youth. They were, instead, the letters of our familiar alphabet, spelling out the words of the English language in my own handwriting."

The basic mind-exchange scenario of the tale derives from at least three sources. First is H. B. Drake's *The Shadowy Thing* (1928; first published in England in 1925 as *The Remedy*), which also influenced "The Thing on the Doorstep." Second, there is Henri Béraud's obscure novel *Lazarus* (1925), which HPL owned and which he read in 1928 (HPL to August Derleth, [February 1928]; ms., SHSW). The novel presents a man, Jean Mourin, who remains in a hospital for sixteen years (for the period 1906–22) while suffering a long amnesia. During this time he develops a personality (named Gervais by the hospital staff) very different from that of his usual self. Every now and then this alternate personality returns; once Mourin thinks he sees Gervais when he looks in the mirror, and later he thinks Gervais is stalking him. Mourin even undertakes a study of split personalities, as Peaslee does, in an attempt to come to grips with the situation.

The third dominant influence is the film *Berkeley Square* (1933), which enraptured HPL by its portrayal of a man whose mind somehow drifts back into the body of his ancestor in the eighteenth century. This source in particular may have been critical, for it seems to have supplied HPL with suggestions on how he might embody his long-held belief (expressed in "Notes on Writing Weird Fiction") that "*Conflict with time* seems to me the most potent and fruitful theme in all human expression." HPL first saw *Berkeley Square* in November 1933. Initially he was much taken with the fidelity with which the eighteenth-century atmosphere was captured; but on seeing the film again, he began to detect some flaws in conception. *Berkeley Square* is based on a play of that title by John L. Balderston (1929). It tells the story of Peter Standish, a man in the early twentieth century who is so fascinated with the eighteenth century—and in particular his own ancestor and namesake—that he somehow transports himself literally into the past and into the body of his ancestor. HPL detected two problems with the execution of the idea: (1) Where was the mind or personality of the eighteenth-century Peter Standish when the twentieth-century Peter was occupying his body? (2) How could the eighteenth-century Peter's diary, written in part while the twentieth-century Peter was occupying his body, not take cognizance of the fact (*SL* 4.362–64)? In his story HPL seems to have striven to obviate these difficulties.

Other, smaller features in "The Shadow out of Time" may also have literary sources. Peaslee's alienation from his family may echo Walter de la Mare's novel *The Return* (1910), in which again an eighteenth-century personality seems to fasten itself upon the body of a twentieth-century individual, causing his wife to cease all relations with him. Leonard Cline's *The Dark Chamber* (1927), in which a man attempts to recapture his entire past, is perhaps the source for the vast archives of the Great Race. Cline's protagonist, Richard Pride, keeps an immense warehouse full of documents about his own life, and toward the end of the novel the narrator frantically traverses this warehouse before finding Pride killed by his own dog.

Two other "influences" can be noted if only to be dismissed. It has frequently been assumed that "The Shadow out of Time" is simply an extrapolation upon Wells's *The Time Machine.* HPL read the novel in 1925, but there is little in it that has a direct bearing on his story. Olaf Stapledon's *Last and First Men* (1930) has been suggested as an influence on the enormous stretches of time reflected in the story, but HPL did not read this work until August 1935, months after the tale's completion (see HPL to August Derleth, August 7, 1935; ms., SHSW).

Perhaps a significant literary influence can be found in HPL's own works. The story could be thought of as an exhaustive expansion of the notion of "possession" by an extraterrestrial being as found in "Beyond the Wall of Sleep" (1919). Minor allusions to other older stories appear, since many were being published only for the first time at the time HPL was writing "The Shadow out of Time."

The story's amnesia motif makes for a provocative autobiographical connection. Peaslee's amnesia dates from 1908 to 1913, the exact time when HPL himself, having had to withdraw from high school, descended into hermitry. The inability of the alien inhabiting Peaslee's body to control its facial muscles may correlate to the facial tics that HPL suffered at that time.

HPL experienced considerable difficulty in writing the story. The core of the plot had been conceived as early as 1930, emerging from a discussion between HPL and Clark Ashton Smith regarding the plausibility of stories involving time travel. HPL noted: "The weakness of most tales with this theme is that they do not provide for the recording, in history, of those inexplicable events in the past which were caused by the backward time-voyagings of persons of the present & future" (*SL* 3.217). At that time he already envisioned the cataclysmic ending: "One baffling thing that could be introduced is to have a modern man discover, among documents exhumed from some prehistoric buried city, a mouldering papyrus or parchment *written in English, & in his own handwriting.*"

By March 1932 HPL had devised the basic idea of mind-exchange over time, as outlined in another letter to Smith:

I have a sort of time idea of very simple nature floating around in the back of my head, but don't know when I shall ever get around to using it. The notion is that of a race in primal Lomar perhaps even before the founding of Olathoë & in the heyday of Hyperborean Commoriom—who gained a knowledge of all arts & sciences by sending thoughtstreams ahead to drain the minds of men in future ages—angling in time, as it were. Now

& then they get hold of a really competent man of learning, & annex all his thoughts. Usually they only keep their victims tranced for a short time, but once in a while, when they need some special piece of continuous information, one of their number sacrifices himself for the race & actually changes bodies with the first thoroughly satisfactory victim he finds. The victim's brain then goes back to 100,000 B.C.—into the hypnotist's body to live in Lomar for the rest of his life, while the hypnotist from dead aeons animates the modern clay of his victims. (*SL* 4.25–26)

This passage is quoted at length to show both that HPL made significant alterations in the finished story—the mind of the Great Race rarely remains in a captive body for the rest of its life but only for a period of years, after which a return switch is effected—and that the conception of mind-exchange over time had been devised *before* HPL saw *Berkeley Square,* the only other work that may conceivably have influenced this point.

HPL began writing of the story in late 1934. He announces in November: "I developed that story *mistily and allusively* in 16 pages, but it was no go. Thin and unconvincing, with the climactic revelation wholly unjustified by the hash of visions preceding it" (*SL* 5.71). It is difficult to imagine what this sixteen-page version could have been like. The disquisition about the Great Race must have been radically compressed, and this is what clearly dissatisfied HPL about this version. He came to realize that this passage, far from being an irrelevant digression, was actually the heart of the story. What then occurred is a little unclear: Is the second draft the version we now have? In late December he speaks of a "second version" that "fails to satisfy me" (*SL* 5.86) and is uncertain whether to finish it as it is or to destroy it and start afresh. He may have done the latter, for long after finishing the story he declares that the final version was "itself the 3d complete version of the same story" (*SL* 5.346).

HPL was highly dissatisfied with the story and was disinclined to type it. In a highly unusual maneuver (HPL never circulated his drafts) he sent the manuscript to August Derleth and then expressed irritation that Derleth apparently made no attempt to read the crabbed text. Then, while visiting R. H. Barlow in Florida in the summer of 1935, HPL asked Derleth to send him the manuscript, as Barlow wished to read it. In fact, Barlow surreptitiously typed the story. When HPL sent the typescript for circulation among his correspondents, the first recipient, Donald Wandrei, instead took the story to F. Orlin Tremaine of *Astounding* after he learned of Julius Schwartz's sale of *At the Mountains of Madness* to the magazine. Tremaine accepted it forthwith, apparently without reading it.

The manuscript of the story—formerly in the possession of Barlow, to whom HPL had given it—surfaced in 1994. Consultation of the text reveals that, in spite of HPL's assertions to the contrary, the story was significantly adulterated in its appearance in *Astounding Stories,* specifically in paragraphing. Other errors appear to be the result of Barlow's inability to read HPL's handwriting.

See Robert M. Price, "The Mischief out of Time," *Crypt* No. 4 (Eastertide 1982): 27, 30; Darrell Schweitzer, "Lovecraft's Favorite Movie," *LS* Nos. 19/20 (Fall 1989): 23–25, 27; Will Murray, "Buddai," *Crypt* No. 75 (Michaelmas 1990): 29–33; S. T. Joshi, "The Genesis of 'The Shadow out of Time,'" *LS* No. 33 (Fall 1995): 24–29; Paul Montelone, "The Vanity of Existence in 'The Shadow out of Time,'" *LS* No. 34 (Spring 1996): 27–35.

"Shadow over Innsmouth, The." Novelette (22,150 words); written November–December 3, 1931. First published as a book (Everett, Pa.: Visionary Publishing Co., 1936); rpt. (abridged) *WT* (January 1942); first collected in *O;* corrected text in *DH;* annotated version as a separate booklet (Necronomicon Press, 1994; rev. ed. 1997) and in *CC.*

The narrator, Robert Olmstead (never mentioned by name in the story, but identified in the surviving notes), a native of Ohio, celebrates his coming of age in 1927 by undertaking a tour of New England—"sightseeing, antiquarian, and genealogical"—and, finding that the train fare from Newburyport to Arkham (whence his family derives) is higher than he would like, is grudgingly told by a ticket agent of a bus that makes the trip by way of a seedy coastal town called Innsmouth. The place does not appear on most maps, and many odd rumors are whispered about it. Innsmouth was a flourishing seaport until 1846, when an epidemic of some sort killed over half its citizens. People believe it may have had something to do with the voyages of Captain Obed Marsh, who sailed extensively in China and the South Seas and somehow acquired vast sums in gold and jewels. Now the Marsh refinery is just about the only business of importance in Innsmouth aside from fishing off the shore near Devil's Reef, where fish are always unusually abundant. All the townspeople seem to have repulsive deformities or traits—collectively termed "the Innsmouth look"—and are studiously avoided by the neighboring communities.

This account piques Olmstead's interest as an antiquarian, and he decides to spend at least a day in Innsmouth, planning to catch a bus in the morning and leaving for Arkham in the evening. He goes to the Newburyport Historical Society and is fascinated by a tiara that came from Innsmouth: "It was as if the workmanship were that of another planet." Going to Innsmouth on a seedy bus run by Joe Sargent, whose hairlessness, fishy odor, and never-blinking eyes provoke his loathing, Olmstead begins exploration, aided by directions and a map supplied by a normal-looking young man who works in a grocery store. All around he sees signs of both physical and moral decay from a once distinguished level. The atmosphere begins to oppress him, and he thinks about leaving the town early; but then he catches sight of a nonagenarian named Zadok Allen who, he has been told, is a fount of knowledge about the history of Innsmouth. Olmstead has a chat with Zadok, loosening his tongue with bootleg whiskey.

Zadok tells him a wild story about alien creatures, half fish and half frog, whom Obed Marsh had encountered in the South Seas. Zadok maintains that Obed struck up an agreement with these creatures: they would provide him with bountiful gold and fish in exchange for human sacrifices. This arrangement works for a while, until the fish-frogs seek to mate with humans. This provokes a violent uproar in the town in 1846: many citizens die and the remainder are forced to take the Oath of Dagon, professing loyalty to the hybrid entities. There is, however, a compensating benefit of a sort. The offspring of the fish-frogs and humans acquire a kind of immortality: they undergo a physical change (acquiring "the Innsmouth look"), gaining many of the properties of the aliens, and then they take to the sea and live in vast underwater cities for millennia.

Scarcely knowing what to make of this bizarre tale and alarmed at Zadok's maniacal plea that he leave the town at once because they have been seen talking, Olmstead attempts to catch the evening bus out of Innsmouth. But the bus has suffered inexplicable engine trouble and cannot be repaired until the next day; he will have to stay at the seedy Gilman House, the only hotel in town. Reluctantly checking in, he feels ever-growing intimations of horror and menace as he hears anomalous voices outside his room and other strange noises. He finally realizes his peril when the doorknob is tried from the outside. He attempts to leave the hotel and escape town but is almost overwhelmed at both the number and the loathsomeness of his hybrid pursuers.

Olmstead does manage to escape, but his tale is not over. After a much-needed rest, he continues to pursue genealogical research and finds appalling evidence that he may be directly related to the Marsh family. He learns of a cousin locked in a madhouse in Canton and an uncle who committed suicide because he learned something nameless about himself. Strange dreams of swimming underwater begin to afflict him, and gradually he breaks down. Then one morning he discerns that he has acquired "the Innsmouth look." He considers suicide, but "certain dreams deterred me." Later he comes to his decision: "I shall plan my cousin's escape from that Canton madhouse, and together we shall go to marvel-shadowed Innsmouth. We shall swim out to that brooding reef in the sea and dive down through black abysses to Cyclopean and many-columned Y'ha-nthlei, and in that lair of the Deep Ones we shall dwell amidst wonder and glory for ever."

The writing of the story came at a time when HPL's spirits were at a low ebb because of the nearly simultaneous rejection, in the summer of 1931, of *At the Mountains of Madness* by *WT* and of a collection of his stories by Putnam's. He reports that his revisiting, in the fall of 1931, of the decaying seaport of Newburyport, Mass. (which he had first seen in 1923), led him to conduct a sort of "laboratory experimentation" (*SL* 3.435) to see which style or manner was best suited to the theme. Four drafts (whether complete or not is not clear) were written and discarded (HPL to Donald Wandrei, [November 27, 1931]; *Mysteries of Time and Spirit,* p. 291), and finally HPL simply wrote the story in his accustomed manner. He was, however, profoundly dissatisfied with it. A week after finishing it, he wrote to Derleth: "I don't think the experimenting came to very much. The result, 68 pages long, has all the defects I deplore—especially in point of style, where hackneyed phrases & rhythms have crept in despite all precautions. Use of any other style was like working in a foreign language—hence I was left high & dry. . . . No—I don't intend to offer 'The Shadow over Innsmouth' for publication, for it would stand no chance of acceptance" (HPL to August Derleth, December 10, 1931; ms., SHSW).

Will Murray has conjectured that the story may have been written at least in part with *Strange Tales* in mind. *Strange Tales* paid better than *WT,* but it sought stories with more of an "action" slant; hence the inclusion of Olmstead's pursuit by the Innsmouth entities. Although HPL prepared a typescript of the story and circulated it among his colleagues, he did not submit it to *Strange Tales* or anywhere else. August Derleth submitted the story without HPL's knowledge to *WT* in early 1933; but Farnsworth Wright rejected it: "I have read Lovecraft's story, THE SHADOW OVER INNSMOUTH, and must confess that it fascinates me. But I don't know just what I can do with it. It is hard to break a story of this kind into two parts, and it is too long to run complete in one part" (Farnsworth

Wright to August Derleth, January 17, 1933; ms., SHSW). HPL eventually found out about this surreptitious submission, for by 1934 he is speaking of its rejection by Wright (HPL to F. Lee Baldwin, August 21, 1934; ms., JHL).

At length HPL agreed to let William L. Crawford publish the story as a book (although previously Crawford had conceived of various other plans for the tale—submitting it to *Astounding Stories;* publishing it in one of his semi-professional magazines, *Unusual Stories* or *Marvel Tales;* publishing it as a book together with *At the Mountains of Madness*). The book was published in November 1936 (although the copyright page gives the date of publication as April) and contained so many errors that an errata sheet had to be prepared. Numerous extant copies bear corrections in pencil by HPL. It features four interior illustrations and a dust jacket illustration by Frank Utpatel. About 400 copies were printed; 200 of these were bound, the others later being destroyed. It is the only book of HPL's fiction published and distributed in his lifetime.

The story proves to be a cautionary tale on the ill effects of miscegenation, or the sexual union of different races, and as such can be considered a vast expansion and subtilization of the plot of "Facts Concerning the Late Arthur Jermyn and His Family" (1920).

The name Innsmouth had been coined for "Celephaïs" (1920), then clearly located in England. HPL revived the name for two sonnets ("The Port" and "The Bells") of *Fungi from Yuggoth* (1929–30), where the setting is not entirely clear, although a New England locale is likely.

There seem to be three dominant literary influences on the tale. The use of hybrid fishlike entities derives from at least two works for which HPL always retained a fondness: Irvin S. Cobb's "Fishhead" (which HPL read in the *Cavalier* in 1913 and praised in a letter to the editor, and which was also reprinted in Harré's *Beware After Dark!* [1929], where HPL surely reread it) and Robert W. Chambers's "The Harbor-Master," a short story later included as the first five chapters of the episodic novel *In Search of the Unknown* (1904). (August Derleth had given HPL a copy of the book in the fall of 1930 [*SL* 3.187].) But in both stories there is only a *single* case of hybridism, not that of an entire community or civilization. This latter feature may have been partially derived from Algernon Blackwood's "Ancient Sorceries" (in *John Silence—Physician Extraordinary* [1908]), in which the inhabitants of an entire small town in France all appear to practice sorcery and turn into cats at night. The character Zadok Allen seems loosely based upon the figure of Humphrey Lathrop, an elderly doctor in Herbert Gorman's *The Place Called Dagon* (1927), which HPL read in March 1928 (HPL to August Derleth, March 2, [1928]; ms., SHSW). Like Zadok, Lathrop is the repository for the secret history of the Massachusetts town in which he resides (Leominster, in the north-central part of Massachusetts) and, like Zadok, he is partial to spirits. Zadok, however, has exactly the life-span (1831–1927) of HPL's aged amateur colleague Jonathan E. Hoag.

Olmstead's character and mannerisms reveal several autobiographical touches, especially in regard to HPL's habits as a frugal antiquarian traveler. Olmstead always "seek[s] the cheapest possible route," and this is usually—for Olmstead as for HPL—by bus. His reading up on Innsmouth in the library, and his systematic exploration of the town by way of the map and instructions given to him by the grocery youth, parallel HPL's own thorough researches into the history and topography of the places he wished to visit and his frequent trips to libraries, chambers of commerce, and elsewhere for maps, guidebooks, and historical background. Even the ascetic meal Olmstead eats at a restaurant—"A bowl of vegetable soup with crackers was enough for me"—echoes HPL's parsimonious diet both at home and on his travels.

Olmstead's spectacular conversion at the end—where he not only becomes reconciled to his fate as a nameless hybrid but actually welcomes it—is the most controversial point of the tale. Does this mean that HPL, as in *At the Mountains of Madness,* wishes to transform the Deep Ones from objects of horror to objects of sympathy or identification? Or are we to imagine Olmstead's change of heart as an augmentation of the horror? It would appear that the latter is intended. There is no gradual "reformation" of the Deep Ones as there is of the Old Ones in the earlier novel: our revulsion at their physical hideousness is not mollified or tempered by any subsequent appreciation of their intelligence, courage, or nobility. Olmstead's transformation is the climax of the story and the pinnacle of its horrific scenario: it shows that not merely his physical body but his mind has been ineluctably corrupted. In a way, the ending parallels the conclusion of "The Temple," where the narrator confidently vows with a tone of triumph to enter the sunken city. Olmstead's final utterance, incidentally, seems to be a parody of the 23rd Psalm ("Surely goodness and mercy shall follow me all the days of my life: and I will dwell in the house of the Lord for ever").

See William L. Crawford, "Lovecraft's First Book," in *The Shuttered Room and Other Pieces* (Arkham House, 1959); Dirk W. Mosig, "Innsmouth and the Lovecraft Oeuvre: A Holistic Approach," *Nyctalops* 2, No. 7 (March 1978): 3, 5; T. G. L. Cockcroft, "Some Notes on 'The Shadow over Innsmouth,'" *LS* No. 3 (Fall 1980): 3–4; Bert Atsma, "The Scales of Horror," *Crypt* No. 18 (Yuletide 1983): 16–18; Will Murray, "Lovecraft and *Strange Tales,*" *Crypt* No. 74 (Lammas 1990): 3–11; Sam Gafford, "'The Shadow over Innsmouth': Lovecraft's Melting Pot," *LS* No. 24 (Spring 1991): 6–13; Bennett Lovett-Graff, "Shadows over Lovecraft: Reactionary Fantasy and Immigrant Eugenics," *Extrapolation* 38, No. 3 (Fall 1997): 175–92.

Shea, J[oseph] Vernon (1912–1981), correspondent of HPL (1931–37). Shea, residing in Pittsburgh, engaged HPL in numerous involved (and at times heated) discussions on politics (especially concerning Hitler and the Nazis) and society. Shea's lifelong interest in films also seemed to rub off a bit on HPL, who discussed with Shea numerous films he saw in the 1930s, including *Berkeley Square.* Shea wrote some fiction at this time (HPL was much impressed with a short story called "The Tin Roof"; see *SL* 4.93–94), but it was not published. Shea published a few weird and science fiction stories in magazines in the 1940s and 1950s, and still later wrote some tales imitating HPL: "The Haunter of the Graveyard" (in *Tales of the Cthulhu Mythos,* ed. August Derleth [1969]) and "Dead Giveaway" (*Outré,* 1976). Shea compiled two nonweird anthologies, *Strange Desires* (1954) and *Strange Barriers* (1955). He wrote a poignant memoir, "H. P. Lovecraft: The House and the Shadows" (*Fantasy & Science Fiction,*

May 1966; rpt. Necronomicon Press, 1982). See his collection, *In Search of Lovecraft* (Necronomicon Press, 1991).

Shepherd, Wilson (b. 1917), weird fiction editor and publisher in Oakman, Alabama, and associate of HPL (1932–37). HPL first heard of Shepherd indirectly from R. H. Barlow, who protested that Shepherd was trying to bamboozle him in regard to the exchange of some pulp magazines. HPL's (unintentionally comical) piece, "Correspondence between R. H. Barlow and Wilson Shepherd" (1932; first published in *LS* No. 13 [Fall 1986]: 68–71), attempts to unsnarl the misunderstanding. In 1936 HPL heard directly from Shepherd, who was now assisting Donald A. Wollheim in editing the *Phantagraph.* The two editors also conceived of a semi-professional magazine, *Fanciful Tales,* which was issued in Fall 1936 and contained a severely misprinted version of HPL's "The Nameless City." Shepherd was also attempting to write poetry. HPL slightly touched up an apparently unpublished poem called "Death" (see HPL to Shepherd, August 11, 1936; ms., JHL) and more exhaustively revised a poem called "Wanderer's Return" (see HPL to Shepherd, September 5, 1936), published in the *Literary Quarterly* (Winter 1937). In acknowledgment, Wollheim and Shepherd printed HPL's sonnet "Background" (*Fungi from Yuggoth* 30) as a broadside for his forty-sixth birthday (it purports to be Volume 47, No. 1 of *The Lovecrafter*). After HPL's death Shepherd printed *A History of the Necronomicon* under the imprint of the Rebel Press (1938).

Sherman, ———. In *At the Mountains of Madness,* the cache operator on the Miskatonic Antarctic Expedition of 1930–31, stationed at the supply cache at McMurdo Sound.

Shiel, M[atthew] P[hipps] (1865–1947). British weird writer. HPL discovered Shiel in 1923, when W. Paul Cook lent him *The Pale Ape and Other Pulses* (1911), containing "The House of Sounds" (originally published as "Vaila" in *Shapes in the Fire* [1896]), which HPL deemed one of the ten best weird tales in literature. HPL also enjoyed "Xélucha" (also in *Shapes in the Fire*) and the "last man" novel *The Purple Cloud* (1901; rev. 1929), whose opening pages (describing a trip to the Arctic) may have influenced HPL's *At the Mountains of Madness* (1930). Shiel's *Xélucha and Others* (1975) and *Prince Zaleski and Cummings King Monk* (1977) contain most of his best short weird work.

See A. Reynolds Morse, *The Works of M. P. Shiel: A Study in Bibliography* (Los Angeles: Fantasy Publishing Co., 1948; rev. ed. 1980 [with John D. Squires]); A. Reynolds Morse, ed., *Shiel in Diverse Hands: A Collection of Essays* (Cleveland: Reynolds Morse Foundation, 1983).

"Shunned House, The." Novelette (10,840 words); written in mid-October 1924. First published as a booklet (Athol, Mass.: W. Paul Cook, 1928 [printed but not bound or distributed]); rpt. *WT* (October 1937); first collected in *O;* corrected text in *MM;* annotated version in *An2, PZ,* and *DWH.*

On Benefit Street in Providence, there is a peculiar house about which rumors have long been whispered. This house, occupied by several generations of the Harris family, is never considered "haunted" by the local citizens but merely "unlucky": people simply seem to have an uncanny habit of dying there, or at least of being afflicted with anemia or consumption. Neighboring houses are free of any such taint. It had lain deserted—because of the impossibility of renting it—since the Civil War. The narrator had known of this house since boyhood, when some of his childhood friends would fearfully explore it, sometimes even boldly entering through the unlocked front door "in quest of shudders." As he grows older, he discovers that his uncle, Elihu Whipple, had done considerable research on the house and its tenants, and he finds his seemingly dry genealogical record full of sinister suggestion. He comes to suspect that some nameless object or entity is causing the deaths by somehow sucking the vitality out of the house's occupants; perhaps it has some connection with a strange thing in the cellar, "a vague, shifting deposit of mould or nitre . . . [that] bore an uncanny resemblance to a doubled-up human figure."

After telling, at some length, the history of the house since 1763, the narrator finds himself puzzled on several fronts; in particular, he cannot account for why some of the occupants, just prior to their deaths, would cry out in a coarse and idiomatic form of French, a language they did not know. As he explores town records, he seems at last to have come upon the "French element." A sinister figure named Etienne Roulet had come from France to East Greenwich, R.I., in 1686; he was a Huguenot and fled France after the revocation of the Edict of Nantes, moving to Providence ten years later in spite of much opposition from the town fathers. What particularly intrigues the narrator is his possible connection with an even more dubious figure, Jacques Roulet of Caude, who in 1598 was accused of lycanthropy.

Finally the narrator and his uncle decide to "test—and if possible destroy—the horror of the house." They come one evening in 1919, armed with both a Crookes tube (a device invented by Sir William Crookes that emits electrons between two electrodes) and a flame-thrower. The two men take turns resting; both experience hideous and disturbing dreams. When the narrator wakes up from his dream, he finds that some nameless entity has utterly engulfed his uncle, "who with blackening and decaying features leered and gibbered at me, and reached out dripping claws to rend me in the fury which this horror had brought." Realizing that his uncle is past help, he aims the Crookes tube at him. A further demoniac sight appears to him: the object seems to liquefy and adopt various temporary forms ("He was at once a devil and a multitude, a charnel-house and a pageant"); then the features of the Harris line seem to mingle with his uncle's. The narrator flees down College Hill to the modern downtown business district; when he returns, hours later, the nebulous entity is gone. Later that day he brings six carboys of sulfuric acid to the house, digs up the earth where the doubled-up anthropomorphic shape lies, and pours the acid down the hole—realizing only then that the shape was merely the "titan *elbow*" of some huge and hideous monster.

The story is based upon an actual house in Providence, at 135 Benefit Street; but the writing of the story was triggered by HPL's seeing a similar house in Elizabeth, N.J., in early October 1924. HPL describes the house as follows (HPL to Lillian D. Clark, November 4–6, 1924; ms., JHL): ". . . on the northeast corner of Bridge St. & Elizabeth Ave. is a terrible old house—a hellish place where night-black deeds must have been done in the early seventeen-hundreds—with a blackish unpainted surface, unnaturally steep roof, & an outside flight of steps leading to the second story, suffocatingly embowered in a tangle of ivy so dense that one cannot but imagine it accursed or corpse-fed. It reminded me of the Babbitt house in Benefit St., which as you recall made me write those lines entitled 'The House' in 1920." (HPL refers to his poem "The House," published in the *Philosopher* for December 1920.) This house in Elizabeth is no longer standing. HPL's aunt Lillian had resided in the Providence house in 1919–20 as a companion for Mrs. C. H. Babbitt, and HPL may well have seen its interior at that time. This house, built around 1763, has a basement, two stories, and attic built on the rising hill, with shuttered doors in the basement leading directly out into the sidewalk. In contrast to HPL's comment in the story, it has never been unoccupied. Otherwise, much of the history of the house, as told in the story, is real. The figure of Elihu Whipple appears to be modeled upon that of HPL's own uncle, Franklin Chase Clark.

Other details of Providence history are also authentic: the straightening of Benefit Street after the removal of the graves of the oldest settlers to the North Burial Ground; the great floods of 1815; even the random mention of the fact that "As lately as 1892 an Exeter community exhumed a dead body and ceremoniously burnt its heart in order to prevent certain alleged visitations injurious to the public health and peace." This last point has recently been studied by Faye Ringel Hazel, who notes that several articles on this subject appeared in the *Providence Journal* in March 1892, and goes on to examine the vampire legendry of Exeter (in Washington County, south of Providence) and the neighboring area.

The most interesting elaboration upon history in the story is the figure of Etienne Roulet. This figure is mythical, but Jacques Roulet of Caude is real. HPL's brief mention of him is taken almost verbatim from the account in John Fiske's *Myths and Myth-Makers* (1872), which he owned and which was a significant source of his early views on the anthropology of religion. Part of Fiske's account of Roulet is a direct quotation from S. Baring-Gould's *A Book of Were-wolves* (1865); but HPL had not read this book at this time (he would do so only a decade or so later), so his information on Jacques Roulet must have come from Fiske.

The story shifts from the supernatural to quasi-science-fiction by asserting that the existence of the vampire and its effects may be accounted for by appealing to advanced scientific conceptions: "Such a thing was surely not a physical or biochemical impossibility in the light of a newer science which includes the theories of relativity and intra-atomic action." HPL refers to Einstein's theory of relativity (about which, only a year and a half earlier, he had expressed considerable bafflement and perturbation [see *SL* 1.231] because of its defiance of nineteenth-century conceptions of physics) and to the quantum theory. That the entity is killed not by driving a stake through its heart but by sulfuric acid is telling. The "titan elbow" seems an adaptation of the ending of "Under the Pyramids," where what appeared to be a five-headed hippopotamus proves to be the paw of an immense monster.

W. Paul Cook wished to print the story as a chapbook (with a preface by Frank Belknap Long), but his financial and physical collapse in 1928 prevented the binding and distribution of the book, although 300 copies had been printed.

In 1934 R. H. Barlow secured about 265 of those copies and over the next year bound and distributed fewer then ten; he also distributed some copies of the unbound sheets. The remaining copies (about 150) eventually ended up in the hands of August Derleth of Arkham House, who in 1959 distributed 50 unbound copies and in 1961 about 100 copies bound in black cloth. A forgery of this edition, probably emerging in England, was issued in 1965.

See Faye Ringel Hazel, "Some Strange New England Mortuary Practices: Lovecraft Was Right," *LS* No. 29 (Fall 1993): 13–18.

Silva, Manuel. In "The Terrible Old Man," a thief (of Portuguese ancestry) who meets a bad end when he attempts to rob an old sea captain of his reputed hoard of Spanish gold and silver.

"Silver Key, The." Short story (5,000 words); probably written in early November 1926. First published in *WT* (January 1929); first collected in *O;* corrected text in *MM;* annotated version in *DWH.*

Randolph Carter—revived from "The Unnamable" (1923)—is now thirty; he has "lost the key of the gate of dreams" and therefore seeks to reconcile himself to the real world, which he now finds prosy and aesthetically unrewarding. He tries all manner of literary and physical novelties until one day he finds the key—or, at any rate, a key of silver in his attic. Driving his car along "the old remembered way," he goes back to the rural New England region of his childhood and, in some magical and wisely unexplained manner, finds himself transformed into a nine-year-old boy. Sitting down to dinner with his aunt Martha, Uncle Chris, and the hired man Benijah Corey, Carter finds perfect content as a boy who has sloughed off the tedious complications of adult life for the eternal wonder of childhood.

The story is a lightly fictionalized exposition of HPL's own social, ethical, and aesthetic philosophy. It is not even so much a story as a parable or philosophical diatribe. He attacks literary realism ("He did not dissent when they told him that the animal pain of a stuck pig or dyspeptic ploughman in real life is a greater thing than the peerless beauty of Narath with its hundred carven gates and domes of chalcedony"), conventional religion ("It wearied Carter to see how solemnly people tried to make earthly reality out of old myths which every step of their boasted science confuted"), and bohemians ("their lives were dragged malodorously out in pain, ugliness, and disproportion, yet filled with a ludicrous pride at having escaped from something no more unsound than that which still held them"). The structural framework of the story at this point—Carter samples in succession a variety of aesthetic, religious, and personal experiences in an attempt to lend meaning or interest to his life—may have been derived from J. K. Huysmans' *A Rebours* (1884), in the prologue to which Des Esseintes undertakes exactly such an intellectual journey.

The story is also, as Kenneth W. Faig, Jr. has determined, a fictionalized account of HPL's visit, in October 1926, to the western Rhode Island town of Foster, the home of his maternal ancestors. Details of topography, character names (Benijah Corey is probably an adaptation of two names: Benejah Place, the owner of the farm across the road from the house where HPL stayed, and Emma [Corey] Phillips, the widow of Walter Herbert Phillips, whose grave HPL probably saw), and other similarities make this conclusion unshakable. In some ways, "The Silver Key" is a retelling of "The Tomb," in which Jervas Dudley discovers in his attic a physical key that allows him to unlock the secrets of the past.

In regard to the other Randolph Carter stories, "The Silver Key" portrays Carter's life from his childhood to the age of fifty-four, at which point he doubles back on his own timeline and reverts to boyhood. *The Dream-Quest of Unknown Kadath* is the "first" Randolph Carter tale, for Carter is presumably in his twenties at the time of its events. After he has lost the key of the gate of dreams at thirty, Carter undertakes his experiments in sampling literary realism, religion, bohemianism, and so on; finding all these things unsatisfying, he turns to darker mysteries, involving himself in occultism and more. It is at this time (his age is unspecified) that he encounters Harley Warren and has the experience described in "The Statement of Randolph Carter"; shortly thereafter, returning to Arkham, he appears to experience the events of "The Unnamable," although they are alluded to very obliquely. Even these dallyings into the weird Carter fails to find rewarding, until at age fifty-four he finds the silver key. It was only at E. Hoffmann Price's suggestion that HPL undertook a further account of Carter's adventures in "Through the Gates of the Silver Key" (1932–33).

WT rejected the story upon its initial submittal, which apparently did not occur until the summer of 1927. In the summer of 1928, however, Wright asked to see the tale again and this time accepted it for $70. Following its appearance in January 1929, Wright reported to HPL that readers "violently disliked" the story (HPL to August Derleth, [1929]; ms., SHSW). Wright, however, did not print any of these hostile letters in the magazine's letter column.

See Kenneth W. Faig, Jr., "'The Silver Key' and Lovecraft's Childhood," *Crypt* No. 81 (St. John's Eve 1992): 11–47.

Simes. In "The Disinterment," the butler of Marshall Andrews who is later killed by the narrator, a patient whom Andrews had been treating.

"Simple Speller's Tale, The." Poem (56 lines); probably written in early 1915. First published in the *Conservative* (April 1915).

An attack on simplified spelling. Its final couplet ("Yet why on us your angry hand or wrath use? / We do but ape Professor B——— M———!") alludes to the American critic Brander Matthews, a vigorous proponent of simplified spelling. See also HPL's essay "The Simple Spelling Mania" (*United Co-operative,* December 1918).

Single, ———. The narrator of "The Tree on the Hill" who discovers and photographs a strange tree in a landscape lit by three suns.

Slater (Slaader), Joe. In "Beyond the Wall of Sleep," the vagabond hunter from the Catskill Mountain region, who is committed to the state psychopathic institution because of his peculiar behavior and supposed murder of **Peter Slader,** his neighbor. He is the victim of mind exchange with an unknown "cosmic entity." In "The Shadow out of Time," he is alluded to as an amnesia victim, like Nathaniel Wingate Peaslee, who undergoes mind exchange with a member of an alien race.

Slauenwite, Dr. Thomas (1885–1932). In "Winged Death," a physician who discovers an insect whose bite is fatal and that supposedly takes on its victim's soul or personality. He uses the insect to kill a colleague, Dr. Henry Moore, but later finds that he is pursued by an insect that appears to exhibit Moore's personality. When he himself dies, his own soul enters the body of the insect, and he tells of his plight by dipping his insect body in ink and writing his message on the ceiling.

Sleght, Adriaen. In "The Diary of Alonzo Typer," a man of Dutch ancestry who marries Trintje van der Heyl (daughter of Dirck van der Heyl) and thereby establishes a genealogical link with the narrator of the story.

Smith, Charles W. (1852–1948), amateur journalist and friend of HPL. Smith, residing at 408 Groveland Street in Haverhill, Mass., edited the *Tryout* (a NAPA paper) for more than three decades (1914–1946); it contained many poems by HPL, along with prose articles as well as the first appearances of some of HPL's fiction ("The Cats of Ulthar" [November 1920]; "The Terrible Old Man" [July 1921]; "The Tree" [October 1921]; "In the Vault" [November 1925]). HPL came in touch with Smith by correspondence as early as 1917, when Smith urged HPL to join the NAPA, which HPL did. HPL visited Smith in Haverhill on June 9, 1921, being charmed by Smith's naïveté and devotion to the "boy printer" ideal of the NAPA (Smith had a printing press in a shed behind his house). HPL wrote of his visit in the essay "The Haverhill Convention" (*Tryout,* July 1921; rpt. as "'408 Groveland Street,'" *Boys' Herald,* January 1943). He visited Smith again on August 25, 1921. Smith supplied the central suggestion for "In the Vault"; in gratitude HPL dedicated the story to him. Smith's return to Haverhill from a trip is commemorated in HPL's poem "The Return" (*Tryout,* December 1926). On August 30, 1927, HPL visited Smith again, recording the visit in a rather dry and compressed travelogue, "The Trip of Theobald" (*Tryout,* September 1927). HPL met Smith for the last time on August 24, 1934, in Lawrence, Mass. In 1932 HPL and Smith jointly published a booklet of poems by Eugene B. Kuntz, *Thoughts and Pictures;* the title page states that it was "Cooperatively published by H. P. Loveracft and C. W. Smith"—representative of the typographical errors (which HPL called "tryoutisms") that riddled the *Tryout* and other of Smith's publications. Smith was for a time the owner of the C. W. Smith Box Co.; his writings were published in *Youth's Companion* and other magazines.

Smith, Clark Ashton (1893–1961), poet, fantaisiste, artist, sculptor, and correspondent of HPL (1922–37). Born in Long Valley, Calif., and residing for most of his life in the small town of Auburn in the Sierra foothills, Smith read precociously as a child and began writing fantastic tales and poems at an early age. In 1911 he came in touch with George Sterling, the reigning poet of San Francisco, who found tremendous promise in Smith's poetry. With Sterling's aid Smith published *The Star-Treader and Other Poems* (1912) at the age of nineteen, causing a sensation on the West Coast and eliciting comparisons to Keats, Shelley, and Swinburne. Other volumes of poetry followed: *Odes and Sonnets* (published in 1918 by the prestigious Book Club of California), *Ebony and Crystal* (1922), and *Sandal-*

wood (1925). In the summer of 1922 some of HPL's associates gave HPL copies of these volumes; HPL was so taken with them that he wrote a "fan" letter to Smith on August 12, 1922. Thereupon ensued a voluminous correspondence that lasted until HPL's death, although the two men never met. HPL persuaded *WT* editor Edwin Baird to rescind the magazine's "no poetry" policy and accept Smith's verse. In late 1926 Smith put Donald Wandrei in touch with HPL, thereby initiating an association that would last to the end of HPL's life.

Possibly from HPL's example, Smith resumed the writing of fiction in the mid- to late 1920s, first producing "The Abominations of Yondo" (1925) and then, in the fall of 1929, "The Last Incantation," the first of more than 100 stories he would write in the next six years. HPL was greatly taken with "The Tale of Satampra Zeiros" (written November 16, 1929; published *WT,* November 1931), and he borrowed Smith's invented god Tsathoggua for both "The Mound" (1929–30) and "The Whisperer in Darkness" (1930); as the latter story appeared in *WT* in August 1931, HPL's mention of the entity achieved print first, so that Smith appeared to have borrowed from HPL. Smith also invented *The Book of Eibon* as an analogue to HPL's *Necronomicon.* "The Epiphany of Death" (written January 25, 1930; *Fantasy Fan,* July 1934) is dedicated to HPL. Most of Smith's tales fall into various cycles: Zothique (a continent of the far future); Hyperborea (a continent in mankind's early history); Averoigne (a province in medieval France); Atlantis; Xiccarph (a planet); Mars. Smith's stories emphasize fantasy more than horror, although "The Vaults of Yoh-Vombis" (*WT,* June–July 1932) is a powerful horror tale set on Mars. More representative is "The City of the Singing Flame" (*Wonder Stories,* January 1931), an exotic science fiction/fantasy hybrid. Relatively few of Smith's tales bear any direct influence from HPL: he admitted that "The Statement of Randolph Carter" inspired "The Epiphany of Death," and "Pickman's Model" inspired "The Hunters from Beyond" (*Strange Tales,* October 1932). However, both Smith and HPL influenced each other's fiction by discussing, in correspondence, various plot ideas and offering suggestions for revision.

Smith was frustrated at the lack of recognition of both his scintillating poetry (some of the finest formal poetry written by any American writer of the twentieth century) and his weird fiction. In 1933 he self-published *The Double Shadow and Other Fantasies,* consisting of six stories rejected by *WT.* Smith appeared widely in science fiction and weird fiction pulp magazines—*WT, Wonder Stories, Astounding Stories,* and others—and was more willing than HPL to revise his tales for the sake of a sale, as he had two aging parents, both in poor health, to look after. By 1935 his enthusiasm for writing fiction began to wane, and he turned to the carving of weird sculptures; several of them were inspired by HPL's invented gods and monsters (a photograph of some of them was used as the dust jacket illustration for HPL's *Beyond the Wall of Sleep* [1943]). HPL expressed great enthusiasm for these carvings, as well as for Smith's paintings and drawings, hundreds of which he had seen in the collection of Samuel Loveman and also on loan from Smith.

Upon HPL's death, Smith wrote the poignant elegy "To Howard Phillips Lovecraft" (*WT,* July 1937). A later poem, "H.P.L." (1959), is less effective. Arkham House published most of Smith's story collections—*Out of Space and*

Time (1942), *Lost Worlds* (1944), *Genius Loci* (1948), *The Abominations of Yondo* (1960), *Tales of Science and Sorcery* (1964), *Other Dimensions* (1970)—as well as Smith's later poetry collections, *The Dark Chateau* (1951) and *Spells and Philtres* (1958), and his *Poems in Prose* (1965). Smith had assembled his immense *Selected Poems* in 1944–49, but it was not published by Arkham House until 1971. His relatively few essays were collected in *Planets and Dimensions* (1973). His *Letters to H. P. Lovecraft* appeared from Necronomicon Press in 1987; his *Selected Letters* from Arkham House in 2003. HPL's letters to Smith were sold piecemeal by Smith's literary executor; some are in public institutions, but most are in private hands.

See Donald S. Fryer, "Klarkash-Ton & Ech Pi El: Or the Alleged Influence of H. P. Lovecraft on Clark Ashton Smith," *Mirage* 1, No. 6 (Winter 1963–64): 30–33; *Nyctalops* (August 1972: Special Clark Ashton Smith Issue); Donald Sidney-Fryer, *The Last of the Great Romantic Poets* (Silver Scarab Press, 1973); Donald Sidney-Fryer, *Emperor of Dreams: A Clark Ashton Smith Bibliography* (Donald M. Grant, 1978); Steve Behrends, "CAS & Divers Hands: Ideas of Lovecraft and Others in Smith's Fiction," *Crypt* No. 26 (Hallowmas 1984): 30–31; Steve Behrends, *Clark Ashton Smith* (1990).

Smith, Eleazar. In *The Case of Charles Dexter Ward,* a tavern companion of Ezra Weeden who assists his friend in collecting information regarding Joseph Curwen and participates in the 1771 raid on his farmhouse that results in his apparent death.

Smith, Preserved. In "The Shunned House," a man who is hired by Mercy Dexter to be a servant at the house. He complains that something "sucked his breath" at night and departs abruptly.

"Some Causes of Self-Immolation." Essay (4,290 words); written on December 13, 1931. First published in *Marginalia;* rpt. *MW* and *CE5.*

This curious essay on psychology, written as by "L. Theobald, Jun., N.G., A.S.S.," begins with a potted history of theories of human behavior from the Greeks through Descartes and Hobbes to Schopenhauer, Nietzsche, and modern psychologists and philosophers. It identifies eleven "instincts" (nutrition, flight, repulsion, etc.) and their corresponding emotions (hunger, fear, disgust, etc.). (The list is taken from William McDougall's *Introduction to Social Psychology* [1908].) HPL then adds one of his own, symmetry. Various motives for human behavior are then discussed. That HPL may have written the essay as a parody of psychological obscurantism is indicated by its subtitle ("Motives for Voluntary Self-Subjugation to Unpleasant Conditions by Human Beings") and by the fact that L. Theobald, Jun. is cited as "Professor of Satanism of Applied Irreverence in Philistine University, Chorazin, Nebraska; Mencken Lecturer on Theology in Holy Roller College, Hoke's Four Corners, Tennessee."

"Some Dutch Footprints in New England." Essay (1,420 words); probably written in July 1933. First published in *De Halve Maen* (October 18, 1933); rpt. *MW* and *CE4.*

Written at the behest of Wilfred B. Talman, editor of *De Halve Maen* (*The Half Moon,* published by the Holland Society of New York), the essay somewhat routinely discusses traces of Dutch architecture and folkways in Rhode Island. In his memoir in *The Normal Lovecraft* (1973), Talman admits that he engaged in a lengthy debate over stylistic niceties in the essay as a kind of revenge for what Talman felt was HPL's heavy-handed revision of "Two Black Bottles" (1926).

"Some Notes on Interplanetary Fiction." Essay (2,360 words); originally written in July 1934 for publication in one of W. L. Crawford's magazines. First published in the *Californian* (Winter 1935); rpt. *MW* and *CE2.*

Incorporating passages from "Notes on Writing Weird Fiction," the essay laments the generally low quality of pulp science fiction but looks to such writers as H. G. Wells and Olaf Stapledon to raise the aesthetic level of the field. HPL urges writers to regard with great seriousness the colossal emotional impact of being off the earth and in general recommends an approach that eschews conventional characters and settings, the taking for granted of marvels, and a slipshod style. HPL's tenets surely were unknown by the next generation of "Golden Age" science fiction writers, but their work appears to embody many of his principles.

"Some Repetitions on the Times." Essay (6,270 words); written on February 22, 1933. First published in *LS* (Spring 1986); rpt. *MW* and *CE5.*

An essay fervently urging the new president, Franklin Delano Roosevelt (two weeks prior to his inauguration), to take immediate and radical action to relieve economic hardship caused by the depression, specifically by adoption of old age pensions, unemployment insurance, and an artificial reducing of working hours so that all able-bodied persons can find work. In the political realm, the franchise should be restricted to those who can pass certain examinations (stressing knowledge of "civics") so that capable leaders can be elected to deal with the immensely complex political and economic issues created by a technological society.

This is one of HPL's strongest later essays; it is curious, therefore, that he made no effort to secure its publication, even in an amateur paper, or even to type it to circulate among his colleagues. Many of the central points of the essay are, however, found in HPL's later letters.

Sophonisba. In "Medusa's Coil," a servant—a "very old Zulu woman"; a "witch-woman"—in the household of Denis de Russy and Marceline Bedard. She recognizes the strange heritage of Marceline and worships her as a goddess.

Sorcier, Charles Le. In "The Alchemist," the son of Michel Mauvais and an alchemist who exacts vengeance on the Comtes de C——— for six hundred years for the killing of his father at the hands of Henri, Comte de C———, in the thirteenth century.

Sprague, Tom. In "The Horror in the Burying-Ground," the enemy of Henry Thorndike, the village undertaker, and brother of Thorndike's sweetheart, **Sophie.** Thorndike injects Sprague with a chemical that simulates death, but in the course of embalming Sprague, he accidentally injects himself with the chemical.

St. John, ———. In "The Hound," the narrator's partner in the search for decadent thrills. Like some of HPL's early characters (e.g., Harley Warren, Herbert West), he is the leader of various occult expeditions or activities, the narrators (typically somewhat autobiographical characters) being passive followers. St. John is killed by the ghoul from whose tomb the two stole an exotic amulet for their charnel museum.

Stanfield, Kenton J. The narrator of "In the Walls of Eryx," whose diary of his entrapment in an invisible maze on Venus constitutes most of the story. His initials are those of the story's coauthor, Kenneth J. Sterling.

Starrett, [Charles] Vincent (1886–1974), American bookman, journalist, and brief correspondent of HPL. Starrett was put in touch with HPL by Frank Belknap Long. Starrett was passing through New York in the spring of 1927, and Long gave him two of HPL's stories to read. Starrett was a well-known journalist (he wrote a weekly column on books for the *Chicago Tribune* from 1942 until his death) and the American advocate of Arthur Machen (he wrote the short treatise *Arthur Machen: A Novelist of Ecstasy and Sin* [1918] and edited two collections of Machen's miscellaneous work, *The Shining Pyramid* [1923] and *The Glorious Mystery* [1927]). Starrett was impressed with HPL's tales and wrote to him about them. Starrett also found much merit in HPL's "Supernatural Horror in Literature" as published in the *Recluse* in the summer of 1927. The correspondence ceased by the end of the year. Starrett also published a few weird tales, some in *WT;* they are collected in *The Quick and the Dead* (Arkham House, 1965). After HPL's death Starrett took note of several of HPL's volumes in his *Tribune* column, reviewing *Beyond the Wall of Sleep* (January 2, 1944), *Marginalia* (March 4, 1945), *Something about Cats* (December 18, 1949), and *The Shuttered Room* (January 10, 1960); the first two of these are reprinted in his *Books and Bipeds* (1947). In the first of these reviews he made the memorable, if not entirely accurate, comment: "he was his own most fantastic creation—a Roderick Usher or C. Auguste Dupin born a century too late."

See Peter Ruber, *The Last Bookman: The Life and Times of Vincent Starrett* (1968).

"Statement of Randolph Carter, The." Short story (2,500 words); written in late December 1919. First published in the *Vagrant* (May 1920); rpt. *WT* (February 1925) and *WT* (August 1937); first collected in *O;* corrected text in *MM;* annotated version in *CC.*

Randolph Carter tells a police investigation what happened one night when he and Harley Warren entered an ancient cemetery and only Carter returned. Warren, a learned mystic, had been intrigued by an ancient book that led him to wonder *"why certain corpses never decay, but rest firm and fat in their tombs for a thousand years."* So Warren and Carter walk along the Gainesville pike toward Big Cypress Swamp and approach a particular tomb in an old cemetery, equipped with spades, lanterns, and other paraphernalia—including a portable telephone set with an extremely long cord. After opening the tomb, they see stone steps leading down. Warren refuses to let Carter go down with him because of his "frail nerves," but promises to stay in touch by means of the telephone set. Carter protests, but Warren is adamant and proceeds down into the crypt. After a time Warren begins making increasingly frantic utterances through the telephone—"*God! If you could see what I am seeing! . . . Carter, it's terrible—monstrous—unbelievable!*" Carter anxiously asks Warren what he sees, but Warren does not specify. Finally Warren cries: "*Beat it! For God's sake, put back the slab and beat it, Carter!*" Carter tells Warren he is coming down to help him, but Warren says it is no use. Finally, after a long silence, with Carter crying, "Warren, are you there?", another voice—"deep; hollow; gelatinous; remote; unearthly; inhuman; disembodied"—is heard: "*YOU FOOL, WARREN IS DEAD!*"

HPL stated the story was a nearly literal transcript of a dream he had, probably in early December 1919, in which he and Samuel Loveman make a fateful trip to an ancient cemetery and Loveman suffers some horrible but mysterious fate after he descends alone into a crypt. HPL's account of the dream, in a letter to the Gallomo (December 11, 1919), is strikingly similar in many points of language and plot to the finished story; he must have kept a copy of the letter and later rewritten it. But there are also some interesting differences between the two accounts. In the dream the setting is clearly in New England; in the story the setting is unspecified, but the mention of Big Cypress Swamp and the Gainesville pike (spelled "Gainsville" in the surviving typescript) leads one to suspect a setting in Florida, near the city of Gainesville. (In later stories Warren is said to be a man from the South.) In the dream, HPL had no true idea of the purpose of the cemetery visit; in the story, HPL must have felt that some hint of motivation had to be provided, so he introduced the point about undecaying corpses. Warren's exhaustive collection of esoteric books was probably inspired by Loveman's impressive collection of first editions.

The name Randolph Carter is of some interest. HPL knew that Carter was a Rhode Island family of long standing (John Carter was the founder of Providence's first newspaper in 1762); but he also knew that this family itself had come to Rhode Island from Virginia. In a 1929 letter HPL remarks: "This transposition of a Virginia line to New England always affected my fancy strongly— hence my frequently recurrent fictional character 'Randolph Carter'" (*SL* 2.353). Carter is HPL's most frequently used recurring character, appearing in "The Unnamable" (1923), *The Dream-Quest of Unknown Kadath* (1926–27), "The Silver Key" (1926), and "Through the Gates of the Silver Key" (1932).

The book that impels Warren to explore the cemetery has been thought by some to be the *Necronomicon,* but this is unlikely. Carter declares that he had read every book in Warren's library in the languages known to him; this must mean that Carter is at least versed in the common languages (Latin, Greek, French, German, English), and he even mentions that some books were in Arabic. But of the "fiend-inspired book" Carter declares that it was "written in characters whose like I never saw elsewhere," which suggests that the book was *not* in Arabic or any other common language; later Carter states that the book came from

India. Since, according to HPL's later testimony, the *Necronomicon* exists only in Arabic, Greek, Latin, and English, Warren's book cannot be that volume.

See Robert M. Price, "You Fool! Loveman Is Dead!" *Crypt* No. 98 (Eastertide 1998): 16–21.

Sterling, Kenneth J. (1920–1995), science fiction fan and late correspondent of HPL (1935–37). In early 1935 Sterling's family moved to Providence, where he attended Classical High School. A fan of the science fiction pulps and a member of the Science Fiction League, Sterling boldly called on HPL at 66 College Street in March 1935 and introduced himself. HPL was much impressed with Sterling's precocity and continued the association. In January 1936, Sterling produced a draft of the story "In the Walls of Eryx" (for details on the composition of what would prove to be HPL's last acknowledged collaborative tale, see entry on that story). It was rejected by various science fiction and weird magazines but finally landed with *WT,* appearing in October 1939. Sterling wrote little other fiction, but the title of one story—"The Bipeds of Bjhulhu" (*Wonder Stories,* February 1936)—is presumably a tribute to HPL's Cthulhu. Sterling began attendance at Harvard in the fall of 1936, graduated from there in 1940, received a medical degree at Johns Hopkins and later became a clinical professor of medicine at the Columbia University College of Physicians and Surgeons. He wrote a brief memoir of HPL, "Lovecraft and Science" (in *Marginalia;* in *LR*), then a much more substantial one, "Caverns Measureless to Man" (*Science-Fantasy Correspondent,* 1975; in *LR*), in which he urged that HPL be "remembered as a scholar and thinker as well as an author."

See obituary, *New York Times* (January 27, 1995).

Stof, Oll. In "Collapsing Cosmoses," the President of the Great Council Chamber of the "intra-dimensional city of Kastor-Ya," who urges the commander Hak Ni to take steps to combat the interstellar menace approaching the planet.

"Strange High House in the Mist, The." Short story (3,800 words); written on November 9, 1926. First published in *WT* (October 1931); first collected in *O;* corrected text in *D;* annotated version in *DWH.*

North of Kingsport "the crags climb lofty and curious, terrace on terrace, till the northernmost hangs in the sky like a grey frozen wind-cloud." On that cliff is an ancient house inhabited by some individual whom none of the townsfolk—not even the Terrible Old Man—has ever seen. One day a tourist, the "philosopher" Thomas Olney, decides to visit that house and its secret inhabitant; for he has always longed for the strange and the wondrous. He arduously scales the cliff, but upon reaching the house finds that there is no door on this side, only "a couple of small lattice windows with dingy bull's-eye panes leaded in seventeenth-century fashion"; the house's only door is on the *other* side, flush with the sheer cliff. Then Olney hears a soft voice, and a "great black-bearded face" protrudes from a window and invites him in. Olney climbs through the window and has a colloquy with the occupant, listening to "rumours of old times and far places." Then a knock is heard—at the door that faces the cliff. Eventually the host opens the door, and he and Olney find the room occupied by all manner of wondrous presences—"Trident-bearing Neptune," "hoary Nodens," and oth-ers—and when Olney returns to Kingsport the next day, the Terrible Old Man vows that the man who went up that cliff is not the same one who came down. No longer does Olney's soul long for wonder and mystery; instead, he is content to lead his prosy bourgeois life with his wife and children. But people in Kings-port, looking up at the house on the cliff, say that "at evening the little low win-dows are brighter than formerly."

HPL admitted that he had no specific locale in mind when writing this tale: he states that memories of the "titan cliffs of Magnolia" (*SL* 2.164) in part prompted the setting but that there is no house on the cliff as in the story; a headland near Gloucester called "Mother Ann" (*SL* 3.433) also inspired the set-ting. HPL may have had in mind a passage in Dunsany's *Chronicles of Rodri-guez* about the home of a wizard on the top of a crag.

In regard to the strange transformation of Thomas Olney, which is at the heart of the tale, the Terrible Old Man provides a hint: "somewhere under that grey peaked roof, or amidst inconceivable reaches of that sinister white mist, there lingered still the lost spirit of him who was Thomas Olney." The body has returned to the normal round of things, but the spirit has remained with the oc-cupant of the strange high house in the mist; the encounter with Neptune and Nodens has been an apotheosis, and Olney realizes that it is in this realm of nebulous wonder that he truly belongs. His body is now an empty shell, without soul and without imagination: "His good wife waxes stouter and his children older and prosier and more useful, and he never fails to smile correctly with pride when the occasion calls for it." This tale could be read as a sort of mirror-image of "Celephaïs": whereas Kuranes had to die in the real world in order for his spirit to attain his fantasy realm, Olney's body survives intact but his spirit stays behind.

HPL had submitted the story to *WT* in July 1927 but it was rejected. In 1929, he let W. Paul Cook have it for the second number of *The Recluse* (it had even been typeset), but when it became clear in the spring of 1931 that the issue would never appear, HPL resubmitted the story to *WT*, which accepted it and paid Lovecraft $55.

See Donald R. Burleson, "Strange High Houses: Lovecraft and Melville," *Crypt* No. 80 (Eastertide 1992): 25–26, 29; S. T. Joshi, "Lovecraft and Dun-sany's *Chronicles of Rodriguez*," *Crypt* No. 82 (Hallowmas 1992): 3–6; Cecelia Drewer, "Symbolism of Style in 'The Strange High House in the Mist,'" *LS* No. 31 (Fall 1994): 17–21; Nicholaus Clements, "'The Strange High House in the Mist': Glowing Eyes and the Prohibition of the Impossible," *LS* No. 40 (Fall 1998): 11–15.

Strauch, Carl Ferdinand (1908–1989), literary scholar and brief correspondent of HPL (1931–33). Strauch received a B.A. from Muhlenberg College in Allen-town, Pa., and was put in touch with HPL by his friend Harry K. Brobst, who at the time also lived in Allentown. Strauch visited HPL in Providence in Septem-ber 1932, not long after he published a book of poetry, *Twenty-nine Poems* (1932). He conveyed to HPL much of the "hex" legendry of the Pennsylvania Dutch region. HPL reports in a letter to Robert Bloch ([c. late June 1933]) that

Strauch was working on a "realistic novel," but this evidently came to nothing. Although cordial, the correspondence came to an abrupt end in the summer of 1933: it appears that Strauch was discouraged at the sharp criticism that HPL, Brobst, and E. Hoffmann Price delivered upon a story of Strauch's during a session in Providence in August 1933. Strauch went on to receive a Ph.D. from Yale (1946) and to become a leading scholar on Ralph Waldo Emerson. He was on the editorial board of the *Collected Works of Ralph Waldo Emerson* (Harvard University Press, 1971f.) and wrote *Characteristics of Emerson, Transcendental Poet* (1975) and other monographs, as well as many articles in scholarly journals. He taught at Lehigh University from 1934 to 1974.

"Street, The." Short story (2,250 words); written in late 1919. First published in the *Wolverine* (December 1920); rpt. *National Amateur* (January 1922); first collected in *The Lovecraft Collectors Library,* Volume 2 (1953); corrected text in *D.*

The narrator wishes to tell of The Street, which was built by "men of strength and honour . . . good, valiant men of our blood who had come from the Blessed Isles across the sea." These were grave men in conical hats who had "bonneted wives and sober children" and enough courage to "subdue the forest and till the fields." Two wars came; after the first, there were no more Indians, and after the second "they furled the Old Flag and put up a new Banner of Stripes and Stars." After this, however, there are "strange puffings and shrieks" from the river, and "the air was not quite so pure as before"; but "the spirit of the place had not changed." But now come "days of evil," a time when "many who had known The Street of old knew it no more; and many knew it, who had not known it before." The houses fall into decay, the trees are all gone, and "cheap, ugly new buildings" go up. Another war comes, but by this time "only fear and hatred and ignorance" brood over The Street because of all the "swarthy and sinister" people who now dwell in it. There are now such unheard-of places as Petrovitch's Bakery, the Rifkin School of Modern Economics, and the Liberty Café. There develops a rumour that the houses "contained the leaders of a vast band of terrorists, who on a designated day are to initiate an "orgy of slaughter for the extermination of America and of all the fine old traditions which The Street had loved"; this revolution is to occur, picturesquely, on the fourth of July. But a miracle occurs: without warning, the houses for some reason implode upon themselves, and the threat is gone.

HPL supplies the genesis of this manifestly racist story in a letter: "The Boston police mutiny of last year is what prompted that attempt—the magnitude and significance of such an act appalled me. Last fall it was grimly impressive to see Boston without bluecoats, and to watch the musket-bearing State Guardsmen patrolling the streets as though military occupation were in force. They went in pairs, determined-looking and khaki-clad, as if symbols of the strife that lies ahead in civilisation's struggle with the monster of unrest and bolshevism" (HPL to Frank Belknap Long, November 11, 1920 [AHT]). The Boston police had gone on strike on September 8, 1919, and remained on strike well into October. The story was probably written shortly after the strike concluded.

"The Street" restates the anti-immigrant message of such early poems as "New England Fallen" (1912?) and "On a New-England Village Seen by

Moonlight" (1913). There may be an influence from Dunsany, as the stories in *Tales of War* (1918) have somewhat the same allegorical flavor (but without the racism).

Stubbs, Ermengarde. In "Sweet Ermengarde," the daughter of **Hiram Stubbs,** a bootlegger in Hogton, Vt., whose hand in marriage is sought by two swains, 'Squire Hardman and Jack Manly. After a variety of adventures, she chooses the 'Squire.

Sully, Helen V. (1904–1997), friend of Clark Ashton Smith (daughter of Genevieve Sully, a married woman with whom Smith carried on a longtime affair) and correspondent of HPL (1933–37). She visited HPL in Providence in early July 1933; HPL also took her to Newport, R.I.; Newburyport, Mass.; and elsewhere. HPL told her an impromptu ghost story one night in the churchyard of St. John's Episcopal Church, frightening her so badly that she ran from the cemetery (see her memoir, "Memories of Lovecraft: II" [1971; rpt. *LR*]). After Providence, she went to New York, where HPL's associates were captivated by her (Frank Belknap Long and Donald Wandrei threatened to fight a duel over her). She began corresponding with HPL after her return to California. Some of HPL's replies suggest that Sully was despondent, perhaps even suicidal. He attempted to cheer her up by telling her his own situation was much worse but that he nevertheless found enough interest in life to continue. HPL's biographer L. Sprague de Camp interpreted these remarks as displaying HPL's own depressive and suicidal tendencies at the time, but such an interpretation seems wide of the mark.

"Supernatural Horror in Literature." Essay (28,230 words); written November 1925–May 1927 (revised in the fall of 1933, August 1934). First published in *The Recluse* (1927); revised version serialized (incomplete) in the *Fantasy Fan* (October 1933–February 1935); first complete publication of revised text in *O;* first separate publication: Ben Abramson, 1945; corrected text in *D;* rpt. *CE2;* critical edition (by S. T. Joshi): Hippocampus Press, 2000.

This is HPL's most significant literary essay and one of the finest historical analyses of horror literature. W. Paul Cook had commissioned HPL to write "an article . . . on the element of terror & weirdness in literature" (HPL to Lillian D. Clark, November 11–14, 1925; ms., JHL) for his now-legendary one-shot amateur magazine, *The Recluse.* HPL simultaneously refreshed himself on the classics of weird fiction and began writing parts of the text; most of it was completed before HPL left Brooklyn for Providence in April 1926, but HPL continued to discover new authors and works (e.g., Walter de la Mare in June 1926) and made numerous additions both to the final typescript and, as late as May 1927, to the proofs. *The Recluse* appeared in August, with HPL's essay occupying nearly half the issue. It comprises ten chapters: I. Introduction; II. The Dawn of the Horror-Tale; III. The Early Gothic Novel; IV. The Apex of Gothic Romance; V. The Aftermath of Gothic Fiction; VI. Spectral Literature on the Continent; VII. Edgar Allan Poe; VIII. The Weird Tradition in America; IX. The Weird Tradition in the British Isles; X. The Modern Masters.

Almost immediately upon completing his essay, HPL began taking notes for works to mention in a putative revised edition. These notes (largely a list of works), entitled "Books to mention in new edition of weird article," are found at the back of his commonplace book. The chance to revise the text did not come until the fall of 1933, when Charles D. Hornig offered to serialize the text in the *Fantasy Fan*. HPL revised the essay all at once, sending a marked-up copy of *The Recluse* to Hornig; but the magazine folded with the serialization only having progressed to the middle of Chapter VIII. Although numerous faint prospects for the continuation of the serialization in other fan magazines emerged over the next two years, the essay was never republished in full until after HPL's death. In August 1934 HPL's discovery of William Hope Hodgson impelled him to write the essay "The Weird Work of William Hope Hodgson," which was to be inserted into Chapter X. In April 1935 HPL read Gustav Meyrink's novel *The Golem* and found that his description (based upon the early silent film version) was inaccurate, so he revised the passage accordingly.

The value of the essay is manifold. It is one of the first to provide a coherent historical analysis of the entire range of weird fiction from antiquity to HPL's day. Dorothy Scarborough's *The Supernatural in Modern English Fiction* (1917) is a thematic study, and Edith Birkhead's *The Tale of Terror* (1921)— upon which HPL relied for much of the information in the first five chapters of his treatise—restricts its attention to the Gothic novels of the late eighteenth and early nineteenth centuries. HPL's discussions of Edgar Allan Poe, Nathaniel Hawthorne, Ambrose Bierce, and Hodgson are particularly acute. His identification of the four "modern masters" of weird fiction—Arthur Machen, Lord Dunsany, Algernon Blackwood, and M. R. James—has been vindicated by subsequent research; the only likely addition to this list is HPL himself.

The work is also of great importance regarding HPL's own theory and practice of weird fiction. The Introduction enunciates HPL's mature reflections on the nature and purpose of weird fiction (refined from such earlier texts as *In Defence of Dagon* [1921]) as "a malign and particular suspension or defeat of those fixed laws of Nature which are our only safeguard against the assaults of chaos and the daemons of unplumbed space"—something HPL restated once more in "Notes on Writing Weird Fiction." Throughout the text there are clues as to works that inspired HPL's own earlier and later works, from Maupassant's "The Horla" to M. R. James's "Count Magnus."

It appears that *The Recluse* was sent to the following authors and critics (see HPL to August Derleth, [January 6, 1928; ms, SHSW]), most of whom are mentioned in the article: Algernon Blackwood, Irvin S. Cobb, A. Conan Doyle, Lord Dunsany, Mary E. Wilkins Freeman, Charlotte Perkins Gilman, M. R. James, Rudyard Kipling, Arthur Machen, Carl Van Vechten, and H. G. Wells. (M. P. Shiel was an intended recipient, but could not be reached.) James discusses the essay (he calls HPL's style "most offensive") in a letter dated January 12, 1928.

See Fred Lewis Pattee, [Review], *American Literature* 18 (May 1946): 175–77; E. F. Bleiler, "Introduction to the Dover Edition" of *Supernatural Horror in Literature* (1973); Jack Adrian, "An M. R. James Letter," *Ghosts and Scholars* 8 (1986): 28–33.

Surama. In "The Last Test," the clinical assistant to Dr. Alfred Clarendon, whom Clarendon brought back with him from a trip to North Africa. He is actually an evil Atlantean mage who is developing a powerful disease to overwhelm humankind.

Suydam, Robert. In "The Horror at Red Hook," a wealthy man of ancient Dutch ancestry who lives in Flatbush and engages in cabbalistic activities. He is the literary precursor to Joseph Curwen in *The Case of Charles Dexter Ward.*

Swanson, Carl, would-be magazine publisher and brief correspondent of HPL. In early 1932 Swanson, residing in Washburn, N.D., conceived the idea of a semi-professional magazine, the *Galaxy,* that would use both original stories and reprints from *WT.* Swanson wrote to HPL, asking for contributions; HPL sent him "The Nameless City" and "Beyond the Wall of Sleep," both rejected by *WT* and still professionally unpublished. Swanson accepted them. HPL also wished to send Swanson some *WT* stories for which he owned second serial rights and asked Farnsworth Wright about the matter; but Wright, believing Swanson's magazine a potentially serious rival, informed HPL that he would not allow Swanson to reprint those stories (published in *WT* down to April 1926) for which *WT* owned second serial rights and would not look with favor upon the resale of other stories for which HPL owned second serial rights. HPL responded heatedly to this attempt to limit the sale of his work (see *SL* 4.27), although other writers (like Frank Belknap Long) who contributed more regularly to *WT* were sufficiently cowed by Wright's threats not to send anything to Swanson. Swanson, however, never managed to secure sufficient capital to begin his magazine; later in 1932 he considered publishing the magazine in mimeograph, but even this never occurred. He disappeared from the pulp fiction field shortly thereafter.

"Sweet Ermengarde; or, The Heart of a Country Girl." Short story (2,740 words); date of writing unknown (probably 1919–21); as by "Percy Simple." First published in *BWS;* corrected text in *MW.*

Ermengarde Stubbs is the "beauteous blonde daughter" of Hiram Stubbs, a "poor but honest farmer-bootlegger of Hogton, Vt." She admits to being sixteen years old, and "branded as mendacious all reports to the effect that she was thirty." She is pursued by two lovers who wish to marry her: 'Squire Hardman, who is "very rich and elderly" and, moreover, has a mortgage on Ermengarde's home, and Jack Manly, a childhood friend who is too bashful to declare his love and unfortunately has no money. Jack, however, manages to find the gumption to propose, and Ermengarde accepts with alacrity. Hardman in fury demands Ermangarde's hand from her father lest he foreclose on the mortgage (he has, incidentally, found that the Stubbses' land has gold buried in it). Jack, learning of the matter, vows to go to the city and make his fortune and save the farm.

Hardman, however, takes no chances and has two disreputable accomplices kidnap Ermengarde and hide her in a hovel under the charge of Mother Maria, "a hideous old hag." But as Hardman ponders the matter, he wonders why he is even bothering with the girl, when all he really wants is the farm and its buried gold. He lets Ermengarde go and continues to threaten to foreclose. Meanwhile a band of hunters strays on the Stubbses' property and one of them, Algernon Reginald Jones, finds the gold; not revealing it to his companions or to the Stubbses, Algernon feigns snakebite and goes to the farm, where he instantly falls in love with Ermengarde and wins her over with his sophisticated city ways. She elopes with Algernon a week later, but on the train to the city a piece of paper falls from Algernon's pocket; picking it up, she finds to her horror that it is a love letter from another woman. She pushes Algernon out the window.

Unfortunately, Ermengarde fails to take Algernon's wallet, so she has no money when she reaches the city. She spends a week on park benches and in bread-lines; she tries to look up Jack Manly, but cannot find him. One day she finds a purse; finding that it has not much money in it, she decides to return it to its owner, a Mrs. Van Itty. This aristocrat, amazed at the honesty of the "forlorn waif," takes Ermengarde under her wing. Later Mrs. Van Itty hires a new chauffeur, and Ermengarde is startled to find that it is Algernon! "He had survived— this much was almost immediately evident." It turns out that he had married the woman who wrote the love letter, but that she had deserted him and run off with the milkman. Humbled, Algernon asks Ermengarde's forgiveness.

Ermengarde, now ensconced as a replacement for the daughter Mrs. Van Itty lost many years ago, returns to the old farmstead and is about to buy off the mortgage from Hardman when Jack suddenly returns, bringing a wife, "the fair Bridget Goldstein," in tow. All this time Mrs. Van Itty, sitting in the car, eyes Ermengarde's mother Hannah and finally shrieks: "You—you—Hannah Smith—I know you now! Twenty-eight years ago you were my baby Maude's nurse and stole her from the cradle!!" Then she realizes that Ermengarde is in fact her long-lost daughter. But Ermengarde is now doing some pondering: "How could she get away with the sixteen-year-old stuff if she had been stolen twenty-eight years ago?" She, knowing of the gold on the Stubbses' farm, repudiates Mrs. Van Itty and compels 'Squire Hardman to foreclose on the mortgage and marry her lest she prosecute him for last year's kidnapping. "And the poor dub did."

This is the only work of fiction by HPL that cannot be dated with precision. The manuscript is written on stationery from the Edwin E. Phillips Refrigeration Company, which was a going concern around 1910 or so, but since the story alludes to the passage of the 18th Amendment it must clearly date to 1919 or later. Since Phillips (HPL's uncle) died on November 14, 1918, perhaps the stationery came into HPL's possession shortly thereafter; but it is by no means certain that he wrote the story at that time.

Of possible relevance is a P.S. to HPL's letter in the *Argosy* for March 1914: "I have a design of writing a novel for the entertainment of those readers who complain that they cannot secure enough of Fred Jackson's work. It is to be entitled: 'The Primal Passion, or The Heart of 'Rastus Washington.'" It is possible that Jackson is a subsidiary (or even primary) target for attack here. Several of Jackson's novels have exactly the sort of implausibility of plot and sentimentality of action that is parodied in "Sweet Ermengarde." With "A Reminiscence of Dr. Samuel Johnson" and "Ibid," it forms a trilogy of HPL's comic gems.

Sylvester, Margaret (b. 1918), correspondent of HPL (1934–37). She had written to HPL in care of *WT,* asking him to explain the origin and meaning of the term *Walpurgisnacht.* She later married and became Margaret Ronan, writing the preface to a school edition of HPL's tales, *The Shadow over Innsmouth and Other Stories of Horror* (Scholastic Books, 1971).

T

Talman, Wilfred Blanch (1904–1986), friend and correspondent of HPL (1925–37). Talman, while attending Brown University, subsidized the publication of a volume of his poetry, *Cloisonné and Other Verses* (1925), which he sent to HPL in July 1925. (No copy of this volume has been located.) The two met in New York a month later, and Talman became an irregular member of the Kalem Club. In the summer of 1926 Talman sent HPL a draft of "Two Black Bottles," which HPL exhaustively revised (chiefly in regard to the Dutch dialect in the tale); it appeared in *WT* (August 1927). Talman chafed at the extent of HPL's revision of the tale, but nonetheless expressed his gratitude by designing HPL's bookplate in the summer of 1927. He published a few other stories and poems in *WT*, these not revised by HPL. Talman visited HPL in Providence in September 1927. HPL in return visited Talman's estate in Spring Valley, N.Y., on May 24, 1928; Talman then drove HPL to Tarrytown, where HPL took a bus to Sleepy Hollow. The two met again when HPL came to New York in April 1929, at which time Talman offered to try to get HPL a job with a New York newspaper. HPL declined, of course. At a gathering at Talman's apartment in Brooklyn on July 6, 1931, HPL met Seabury Quinn for the first time. For a time Talman was a reporter for the *New York Times;* later, around 1930, he became editor of the *Texaco Star,* a trade paper operated by the Texaco oil company. Talman suggested that HPL write a series of travel articles for the paper, but HPL did not feel that the plan was practicable, given the idiosyncratic nature of his travel writing. Talman, a pronounced genealogist, encouraged HPL to research his own genealogy, even as he diligently pursued his own New York Dutch roots. For a time he also edited *De Halve Maen* (*The Half Moon*), the magazine of the Holland Society of New York, and commissioned HPL to write "Some Dutch Footprints in New England," which appeared in the issue of October 18, 1933. In late 1936, on his own initiative, Talman approached William Morrow & Co. about the possibility of a novel by HPL; Morrow seemed interested, but HPL had nothing to offer, and by that time was too ill to write one afresh. Long after HPL's death Talman wrote a memoir, included in the booklet *The Normal Lovecraft* (1973; rpt. *LR*), as well as a historical treatise, *Tappan: 300 Years, 1686–1986* (Tappantown Historical Society, 1989).

Tchernevsky, Count Feodor. In "The Ghost-Eater," a Russian nobleman who comes to visit Vasili Oukranikov in his house in the woods and is killed by Oukranikov (who has transformed himself into a werewolf).

"Temple, The." Short story (5,430 words); written sometime after "The Cats of Ulthar" (June 15, 1920) but before "Celephaïs" (early November). First published in *WT* (September 1925); rpt. *WT* (February 1936); first collected in *O;* corrected text in *D;* annotated version in *TD*.

   A German submarine commanded by a Prussian nobleman, Karl Heinrich, Graf von Altberg-Ehrenstein, sinks a British freighter; later a dead seaman from the freighter is found clinging to the railing of the submarine, and in his pocket is found a "very odd bit of ivory carved to represent a youth's head crowned with laurel." The German crew sleep poorly, have bad dreams, and some think that dead bodies are drifting past the portholes. Some crewmen actually go mad, claiming that a curse has fallen upon them; Altberg-Ehrenstein executes them to restore discipline. Some days later an explosion in the engine room cripples the submarine, and still later a general mutiny breaks out, with some sailors further damaging the ship; the commander again executes the culprits. Finally only Altberg-Ehrenstein and Lieutenant Klenze are left alive. The ship sinks lower and lower toward the bottom of the ocean. Klenze then goes mad, shouting: "*He* is calling! *He* is calling! I hear him! We must go!" He voluntarily leaves the ship and plunges into the ocean. As the ship finally reaches the ocean floor, the commander sees a remarkable sight: an entire city at the bottom of the ocean, with various buildings, temples, and villas, mostly built of marble. "Confronted at last with the Atlantis I had formerly deemed largely a myth," Altberg-Ehrenstein notices one especially large temple carved from the solid rock; later he sees that a head sculpted on it is exactly like the figurine taken from the dead British sailor. The commander, finishing his written account of his adventure on August 20, 1917, prepares to explore the temple after he sees an anomalous phosphorescence emerging from far within the temple. "So I will carefully don my diving suit and walk boldly up the steps into that primal shrine; that silent secret of unfathomed waters and uncounted years."

   This is the first of HPL's stories not to have been first published in an amateur journal; possibly its length was a factor, as most amateur journals could not accommodate so long a tale. Like "Dagon," it uses World War I as a vivid backdrop, although HPL mars the story by crude satire on the protagonist's militarist and chauvinist sentiments. There also seems to be an excess of supernaturalism, with many bizarre occurrences that do not seem to unify into a coherent whole. But the story is significant in postulating (like "Dagon") an entire civilization antedating humanity and possibly responsible for many of the intellectual and aesthetic achievements of humanity. In a letter HPL remarks that "the flame that the Graf von Altberg-Ehrenstein beheld was a witch-fire lit by spirits many millennia old" (*SL* 1.287), but no reader could ever make this deduction based solely on the textual evidence. In a late letter (*SL* 5.267–69) he discusses the ancient sources for the myth of Atlantis (in which, of course, he did not believe).

Terrible Old Man, The. In "The Terrible Old Man," the aged and eccentric former sea captain in Kingsport who is rumored by the townsfolk to be fabulously wealthy. A band of robbers who attempt to despoil the feeble old man of his supposed treasure are mysteriously and viciously despatched. He is also briefly mentioned in "The Strange High House in the Mist."

"Terrible Old Man, The." Short story (1,160 words); written on January 28, 1920. First published in the *Tryout* (July 1921); rpt. *WT* (August 1926); first collected in *O;* corrected text in *DH.*

Three thieves—Angelo Ricci, Joe Czanek, and Manuel Silva—plan to rob the home of the Terrible Old Man, who is said to be both fabulously wealthy and very feeble. The Terrible Old Man dwells in Kingsport, a city somewhere in New England. In the "far-off days of his unremembered youth" he was a sea-captain, and seems to have a vast collection of ancient Spanish gold and silver pieces. He has now become very eccentric, appearing to spend hours speaking to an array of bottles in each of which a small piece of lead is suspended from a string. On the night of the planned robbery, Ricci and Silva enter the Terrible Old Man's house while Czanek waits outside. Screams are heard from the house, but there is no sign of the two robbers. Czanek wonders whether his colleagues were forced to kill the old man and make a laborious search through his house for the treasure. But then the Terrible Old Man appears at the doorway, "leaning quietly on his knotted cane and smiling hideously." Later three unidentifiable bodies are found washed in by the tide.

The tale is reminiscent of many stories in Lord Dunsany's *The Book of Wonder* (1912), several of which similarly deal with attempted robberies that usually end badly for the perpetrators. Probably the closest analogy is with "The Probable Adventure of the Three Literary Men." The three thieves represent the three major non-Anglo-Saxon ethnic groups in Rhode Island (Italian, Polish, and Portuguese).

The location of Kingsport is unspecified; only later, in "The Festival" (1923), did HPL identify it with the town of Marblehead and situate it in Massachusetts.

See Donald R. Burleson, "'The Terrible Old Man': A Deconstruction," *LS* No. 15 (Fall 1987): 65–70; Carl Buchanan, "'The Terrible Old Man': A Myth of the Devouring Father," *LS* No. 29 (Fall 1993): 19–31.

Theunis, Constantin. In "The Tree on the Hill," a scholar who suffers a seizure after examining a strange photograph through a special viewing apparatus he has invented.

"Thing on the Doorstep, The." Novelette (10,830 words); written August 21–24, 1933. First published in *WT* (January 1937); first collected in *O;* corrected text in *DH;* annotated version in *An2* and *TD.*

The narrator, Daniel Upton, tells of his young friend Edward Derby, who since boyhood has displayed a remarkable aesthetic sensitivity toward the weird, in spite—or perhaps because—of the overprotective coddling of his parents. Derby attends Miskatonic University and becomes a moderately recognized *fantaisiste* and poet. He frequently visits Upton, using a characteristic knock—three raps followed by two more after an interval—to announce himself. When he is thirty-eight he meets Asenath Waite, a young woman at Miskatonic, about whom strange things are whispered: she has anomalous hypnotic powers, creating the momentary impression in her subjects that they are in her body looking across at themselves. Even stranger things are whispered of her father, Ephraim Waite, who died under very peculiar circumstances. Over his father's opposition, Derby marries Asenath—who is one of the Innsmouth Waites—and settles in a home in Arkham. They seem to undertake very recondite and perhaps dangerous occult experiments. Moreover, people observe curious changes in both of them: whereas Asenath is extremely strong-willed and determined, Edward is flabby and weak-willed; but on occasion he is seen driving Asenath's car (even though he did not previously know how to drive) with a resolute and almost demonic expression, and conversely Asenath is seen from a window looking unwontedly meek and defeated. One day Upton receives a call from Maine: Derby is there in a crazed state, and Upton has to fetch him because Derby has suddenly lost the ability to drive. On the trip back Derby tells Upton a wild tale of Asenath forcing his mind from his body and going on to suggest that Asenath is really Ephraim, who forced out the mind of his daughter and placed it in his own dying body. Abruptly Derby's ramblings come to an end, as if "shut off with an almost mechanical click." Derby takes the wheel from Upton and tells him to pay no attention to what he may just have said.

Some months later Derby visits Upton again. He is in a tremendously excited state, claiming that Asenath has gone away and that he will seek a divorce. Around Christmas of that year Derby breaks down entirely. He cries out: "My brain! My brain! God, Dan—it's tugging—from beyond—knocking—clawing— that she-devil—even now—Ephraim. . . ." He is placed in a mental hospital and shows no signs of recovery until one day he suddenly seems to be better; but, to Upton's disappointment and even latent horror, Derby is now in that curiously "energised" state such as he had been during the ride back from Maine. Upton is in an utter turmoil of confusion when one evening he receives a phone call. He cannot make out what the caller is saying—it sounds like "glub . . . glub"—but a little later someone knocks at his door, using Derby's familiar three-and-two signal. This creature—a "foul, stunted parody" of a human being—is wearing one of Derby's old coats, which is clearly too big for it. It hands Upton a sheet of paper that explains the whole story: Derby had killed Asenath to escape her influence and her plans to switch bodies with him permanently; but death did not extinguish Asenath/Ephraim's mind, for it emerged from the body, thrust itself into the body of Derby, and hurled his mind into Asenath's corpse, buried in the cellar of their home. Now, with a final burst of determination, Derby (in the body of Asenath) has climbed out of the shallow grave and is now delivering this message to Upton, since he was unable to communicate with him on the phone. Upton

264   "Thing on the Doorstep, The"

promptly goes to the madhouse and shoots the thing in Edward Derby's body; this account is his confession and attempt at exculpation.

The story was written as part of HPL's campaign, in the summer and fall of 1933, to rejuvenate his writing (and his entire literary outlook) by a renewed reading of the classics of weird fiction. The autograph manuscript was typed by a "delinquent revision client" (*SL* 4.310). This might be Hazel Heald, although it cannot be the same person who typed "The Dreams in the Witch House" for HPL: firstly, the typewriter faces on the existing typescripts are very different; secondly, the typescript for this story is extremely inaccurate, to such a degree that HPL's chapter divisions have been overlooked, resulting in only five chapters instead of seven. These errors were not corrected until *DH* (1984 ed.).

The story appears to have two significant literary influences. One is H. B. Drake's *The Shadowy Thing* (1928; first published in England in 1925 as *The Remedy*), a novel about a man who displays anomalous powers of hypnosis and mind-transference. An entry in HPL's commonplace book (#158) records the plot-germ: "Man has terrible wizard friend who gains influence over him. Kills him in defence of his soul—walls body up in ancient cellar—BUT—the dead wizard (who has said strange things about soul lingering in body) *changes bodies with him . . .* leaving him a conscious corpse in cellar." This is not exactly a description of the plot of *The Shadowy Thing,* but rather an imaginative extrapolation based upon it. In Drake's novel, Avery Booth exhibits powers that seem akin to hypnosis, to such a degree that he can oust the mind or personality from another person's body and occupy it. He does so on several occasions, and in the final episode he appears to have come back from the dead (he had been killed in a battle in World War I) and occupied the body of a friend and soldier who had himself been horribly mangled in battle. HPL has amended this plot by introducing the notion of *mind-exchange:* whereas Drake does not clarify what happens to the ousted mind when it is taken over by the mind of Booth, HPL envisages an exact transference whereby the ousted mind occupies the body of its possessor. The notion of mind-exchange between persons of different genders may have been derived from the other presumed literary influence, Barry Pain's *An Exchange of Souls* (1911), which HPL owned. Here a scientist persuades his wife to undergo an experiment whereby their "souls" or personalities are exchanged by means of a machine he has built; but in the course of the experiment the man's body dies and the machine is damaged. The rest of the novel is involved in the ultimately unsuccessful attempt by the woman (now endowed with her husband's personality but lacking much of his scientific knowledge) to repair the machine. "The Shadow out of Time" (1934–35) takes the notion a step further, describing the exchange of minds between a human being and an alien creature.

Some features of Edward Derby's life supply a twisted version of HPL's own childhood. But there are some anomalies in the portrayal of the youthful Edward Derby that need to be addressed. Upton refers to Derby as "the most phenomenal child scholar I have ever known." It is unlikely, given his characteristic modesty, that HPL would have made such a statement about a character modeled upon himself. Derby may be instead an amalgam of several of HPL's associates. Consider this remark about Alfred Galpin: "He is intellectually *exactly like me* save in degree. In degree he is immensely my superior" (*SL* 1.128); elsewhere he refers to Galpin—who was only seventeen when HPL first knew him in 1918—as "the most brilliant, accurate, steel-cold intellect I have ever encountered" (*SL* 1.256). Galpin never wrote "verse of a sombre, fantastic, almost morbid cast" as Derby did as a boy, nor published a volume of poetry when he was eighteen. But Clark Ashton Smith created a sensation as a boy prodigy when he published *The Star-Treader and Other Poems* in 1912, when he was nineteen. And Smith was a close colleague of George Sterling, who— like Justin Geoffrey in the tale—died in 1926 (Sterling by suicide, Geoffrey of unknown causes). HPL's mention that Derby's "attempts to grow a moustache were discernible only with difficulty" recalls his frequent censures of the thin moustache Frank Belknap Long attempted for years to cultivate in the 1920s.

But if Derby's youth and young manhood are an amalgam of HPL and some of his closest friends, his marriage to Asenath Waite clearly brings certain aspects of HPL's marriage to Sonia Greene to mind. Sonia was clearly the more strong-willed member of the couple; it was certainly from her initiative that the marriage took place at all and that HPL uprooted himself from Providence to come to live in New York. The objections of Derby's father to Asenath—and specifically to Derby's wish to marry her—may dimly echo objections of HPL's aunts to his marriage to Sonia. (Such objections can only be inferred from the tenor of some of HPL's letters to his aunts.)

In one sense the story is a reprise of *The Case of Charles Dexter Ward:* the attempt by Asenath (in Derby's body) to pass herself off as Edward in the madhouse is precisely analogous to Joseph Curwen's attempts to maintain that he is Charles Dexter Ward.

One glancing note in the story that has caused considerable misunderstanding is Upton's remark about Asenath: "Her crowning rage . . . was that she was not a man; since she believed a male brain had certain unique and far-reaching cosmic powers." This sentiment is clearly expressed as Asenath's (who, let us recall, is only Ephraim in another body), and need not be attributed to HPL. A decade earlier HPL had indeed uttered some silly remarks on women's intelligence: "Females are in Truth much given to affected Baby Lisping . . . They are by Nature literal, prosaic, and commonplace, given to dull realistick Details and practical Things, and incapable alike of vigorous artistick Creation and genuine, first-hand appreciation" (*SL* 1.238). But by the 1930s he had come to a more sensible position: "I do not regard the rise of woman as a bad sign. Rather do I fancy that her traditional subordination was itself an artificial and undesirable condition based on Oriental influences. . . . The feminine mind does not cover the same territory as the masculine, but is probably little if any inferior in total quality" (*SL* 5.64).

HPL was so dissatisfied with the story upon its completion that he refused to submit it anywhere. At last, in the summer of 1936, when Julius Schwartz proposed to HPL to market some of his tales in England, HPL reluctantly submitted the story, along with "The Haunter of the Dark," to Farnsworth Wright of *WT,* who promptly accepted both.

See S. T. Joshi, "Autobiography in Lovecraft," *LS* No. 1 (Fall 1979): 7–19 (esp. 12–15); Donald R. Burleson, "The Thing: On the Doorstep," *LS* No. 33 (Fall 1995): 14–18.

Thorfinnssen, Georg. In *At the Mountains of Madness,* the captain of the barque *Miskatonic,* one of the supply ships for the Miskatonic Antarctic Expedition of 1930–31.

Thorndike, Henry. In "The Horror in the Burying-Ground," the village undertaker who invents a chemical that can simulate death in a person who remains alive and conscious. He accidentally injects himself with his chemical and is buried alive.

Thornton, ———. In "The Rats in the Walls," a "psychic investigator" brought in by Delapore to investigate the crypt beneath Exham Priory.

"Through the Gates of the Silver Key." Novelette (14,550 words); written in collaboration with E. Hoffmann Price, October 1932–April 1933. First published in *WT* (July 1934); first collected in *O;* corrected text in *MM;* annotated version in *DWH.*

Several individuals gather in New Orleans—Etienne Laurent de Marigny, Ward Phillips, the lawyer Ernest B. Aspinwall, and a strange individual named the Swami Chandraputra—to discuss the disposition of the estate of Randolph Carter. The Swami opposes any action, because he maintains that Carter is still alive. He proceeds to tell a fabulous story of what happened to Carter after his return to boyhood (as noted in "The Silver Key").

Carter passed through a succession of "Gates" into some realm "outside time and the dimensions we know," led by a "Guide," 'Umr at-Tawil, the Prolonged of Life. This guide eventually led Carter to the thrones of the Ancient Ones, from whom he learned that there are "archetypes" for every entity in the universe and that each person's entire ancestry is nothing more than a facet of the single archetype; Carter learned that he himself is a facet of the "SUPREME ARCHETYPE." Then, somehow, Carter found himself in the body of a fantastically alien being, Zkauba the Wizard, on the planet Yaddith. He managed to return to earth but must go about in concealment because of his alien form.

When the hard-nosed lawyer Aspinwall scoffs at the Swami's story, a final revelation is made: the Swami is Randolph Carter, still in the monstrous shape of Zkauba. Aspinwall, having removed Carter's mask, dies immediately of apoplexy. Carter then disappears through a large clock in the room.

The story is based on a draft, entitled "The Lord of Illusion," written by Price. Price had become so enamored of "The Silver Key" that, during HPL's visit with him in New Orleans in June 1932, he "suggested a sequel to account for Randolph Carter's doings after his disappearance" (Price, "The Man Who Was Lovecraft," in *Cats,* p. 281). Sending "The Lord of Illusion" to HPL in late August, he expressed hope that HPL might revise it and allow it to be published as an acknowledged collaboration.

"The Lord of Illusion" (first printed in *Crypt* No. 10 [1982]: 46–56) tells the story of how Randolph Carter, after finding the silver key, enters a strange cavern in the hills behind his family home in Massachusetts and encounters a strange man who announces himself as "'Umr at-Tawil, your guide," who leads Carter to some other-dimensional realm where he meets the Ancient Ones. These entities explain the nature of the universe to Carter: just as a circle is produced from the intersection of a cone with a plane, so our three-dimensional world is produced from the intersection of a plane with a figure of a higher dimension; analogously, time is an illusion, being merely the result of this sort of "cutting" of infinity. It transpires that all Carters who have ever lived are part of a single archetype, so that if Carter could manipulate his "section-plane" (the plane that determines his situation in time), he could be any Carter he wished to be, from antiquity to the distant future. In a purported surprise ending, Carter reveals himself as an old man among a group of individuals who had assembled to divide up Carter's estate.

HPL, upon reading the draft, stated that extensive changes would need to be made in the story to bring it in line with the original tale. In the letter in which he evaluates Price's work, he specifies several faults that must be rectified: (1) the style must be made more similar to that of "The Silver Key" (Price's version, devoid of his usual action and swordplay, is generally flat, stilted, and pompous); (2) various points of the plot must be reconciled with that of "The Silver Key"; (3) the transition from the mundane world to the hyperspace realm must be vastly subtilized; and (4) the atmosphere of lecture-room didacticism in the Ancient Ones' discussions with Carter must be eliminated.

Price has remarked that "I estimated that [HPL] had left unchanged fewer than fifty of my original words" ("The Man Who Was Lovecraft," p. 282), a comment that has led many to believe that the finished version of "Through the Gates of the Silver Key" is radically different from Price's original; but, as we have seen, HPL adhered to the basic framework of Price's tale as best he could. The quotations from the *Necronomicon* are largely Price's, although somewhat amended by HPL.

Price submitted the story to *WT* on June 19, 1933, both praising the story and minimizing his own role in it. Wright's response was not unexpected: "I have carefully read THROUGH THE GATES OF THE SILVER KEY and am almost overwhelmed by the colossal scope of the story. It is cyclopean in its daring and titanic in its execution. . . . But I am afraid to offer it to our readers. Many there would be . . . who would go into raptures of esthetic delight while reading the story; just as certainly there would be a great many—probably a clear majority—of our readers who would be unable to wade through it. These would find the descriptions and discussions of polydimensional space poison to their enjoyment of the tale. . . . I assure you that never have I turned down a story with more regret than in this case" (Farnsworth Wright to HPL, August 17, 1933; ms., JHL). But by mid-November 1933 Wright was asking to see the story again, and he accepted it a week later. It in fact elicited a hostile response from the young Henry Kuttner, published in the letter column of *WT* (September 1934).

See Norm Gayford, "Randolph Carter: An Anti-Hero's Quest," *LS* No. 16 (Spring 1988): 3–11; No. 17 (Fall 1988): 5–13.

Thurber, ———. The narrator of "Pickman's Model." At first, he is one of Richard Upton Pickman's staunchest supporters. Following Pickman's disappearance, he refuses to venture into the subway system or the cellars of Boston after viewing a photograph of the subject of one of Pickman's paintings.

Thurston, Francis Weyland. "The Call of Cthulhu" is Thurston's written dissertation of his piecing together various accounts of the Cthulhu cult from the research of his uncle, George Gammell Angell (in "The Horror in Clay"); his uncle's encounter with police inspector John Raymond Legrasse ("The Tale of Inspector Legrasse"); and the diary of Gustav Johansen, the Norwegian sailor who encounters Cthulhu firsthand ("The Madness from the Sea"). His name is cited in full in the subtitle of the story; in earlier editions, this subtitle was frequently omitted.

"'Till A' the Seas.'" Short story (3,300 words); written in collaboration with R. H. Barlow, January 1935. First published in the *Californian* (Summer 1935); first collected in *HM* (1970 ed.); corrected text in *HM*.

Humanity finds himself in dire straits as the earth gradually approaches closer and closer to the sun. Drought ravages the planet "for unnumbered aeons," and towns, cities, and entire countries are deserted as the few struggling remnants of mankind seek the final traces of water near the poles. At length all the oceans dry up. Finally humanity is reduced to hundreds, then tens. A young man named Ull is compelled to leave his dwelling when his companion, an old woman named Mladdna, finally dies. In search of both water and companionship, he seeks out a colony that he has heard dwells over the mountains; but when he reaches the huts of the colony, he realizes that everyone is dead. Then, in the middle of the town, he sees a well. Groping for the chain and bucket in the well, Ull slips and falls into it, dying. He is the last man on earth.

Barlow's typescript, with HPL's revisions in pen, survives, so that the exact degree of the latter's authorship can be ascertained (see the article by Joshi, in which the text is reproduced with HPL's words placed in brackets). HPL has made no significant structural changes, merely making cosmetic changes in style and diction; but he has written the bulk of the concluding section, especially the purportedly cosmic reflections when the last man on earth finally meets his ironic death. The title is from Robert Burns's "A Red, Red Rose" (1796): "Till a' the seas gang dry, my dear. . . ."

See S. T. Joshi, "Lovecraft's Contribution to 'Till A' the Seas,'" *Crypt* No. 17 (Hallowmas 1983): 33–39.

Tillinghast, Crawford. In "From Beyond," the mad scientist who invents a machine that reveals creatures and worlds perceptible to the five senses. He dies, ostensibly of "apoplexy," after demonstrating his machine to his unnamed colleague. (In HPL's original draft of the story, the character was named Henry Annesley.)

Tillinghast, Dutee. In *The Case of Charles Dexter Ward,* a ship-captain who is in the employ of Joseph Curwen in eighteenth-century Providence. Evidently under some terrible compulsion, he is forced to permit Curwen to marry his only daughter, **Eliza,** so that Curwen can repair his reputation in Providence society. Eliza and Curwen have a daughter, **Ann.** After Curwen's apparent death, Eliza resumes her maiden name; Ann Tillinghast later marries Welcome Potter, Charles Dexter Ward's great-great-grandfather.

Tilton, Anna. In "The Shadow over Innsmouth," the curator of the Newbury-port Historical Society who shows Robert Olmstead the strange marine-motif jewelry associated with Innsmouth, which he later recognizes among jewelry that belonged to his great-grandmother.

T'la-yub. In "The Mound," a noblewoman in Panfilo de Zamacona's "affection-group" who attempts to escape the underworld realm with Zamacona but fails hideously: captured by the mound denizens, she is tortured in the amphitheatre and becomes a half-dematerialized corpse-slave who is stationed as a guard at the entrance of the mound. It is her occasional appearance aboveground that leads to rumors of a ghost haunting the mound.

"To a Dreamer." Poem (24 lines in quatrains); written on April 25, 1920. First published in the *Coyote* (January 1921); rpt. *WT* (November 1924).

The narrator scans the features of a nameless dreamer and wonders where his "dream-steps" have led him. The poem contains the first mentions of such terms (used later in HPL's stories) as the "peaks of Thok" and the "vaults of Zin"; the "vale of Pnath" is also mentioned, although Pnath had first been coined in "The Doom That Came to Sarnath" (1919). HPL notes in a letter to Frank Belknap Long (June 4, 1921; AHT) that the poem was founded on an idea occurring among Baudelaire's notes and jottings (presumably from *Baudelaire: His Prose and Poetry*, ed. T. R. Smith [Modern Library, 1919], which HPL owned and which was the source of the epigraph in "Hypnos").

"To a Sophisticated Young Gentleman, Presented by His Grandfather with a Volume of Contemporary Literature." Poem (82 lines); written on December 15, 1928. First published in *SL* 2.255–57.

The poem was written to accompany a copy of Marcel Proust's *Swann's Way*, which HPL presented to Frank Belknap Long for Christmas. In the course of the poem HPL delivers telling blows on the freakishness and extravagance of much modern literature and the culture that produced it. In the first published appearance (a letter to James F. Morton, [January 1929]), the poem bears a variant title: "An Epistle to Francis, Ld. Belknap. . . ."

"To Charlie of the Comics." Poem (32 lines in 4 stanzas); probably written in late September 1915. First published in the *Providence Amateur* (February 1916).

A poem on Charlie Chaplin. It was written in response to Rheinhart Kleiner's poem "To Mary of the Movies" (*Piper,* September 1915), about Mary Pickford. HPL professed enjoyment of Chaplin's films, many of which he saw (see *SL* 1.18, 50–51). For another poem on films, see the satire "To Mistress Sophia Simple, Queen of the Cinema" (written August 1917; first published in the *United Amateur,* November 1919), a reply to Kleiner's "To a Movie Star," published in the same issue of the *United Amateur.*

"To Clark Ashton Smith, Esq., upon His Phantastick Tales, Verses, Pictures, and Sculptures." Poem (sonnet); written in December 1936. First published in *WT* (April 1938) (as "To Clark Ashton Smith").

A tribute to HPL's longtime colleague, the poem bears at least one variant title ("To Klarkash-Ton, Lord of Averoigne") alluding to the fictitious region in medieval France invented by Smith in some of his tales. In "The Whisperer in Darkness" and other tales, HPL alludes to Smith (as he does repeatedly in his letters to him) as Klarkash-Ton.

"To Mr. Finlay, upon His Drawing for Mr. Bloch's Tale, 'The Faceless God.'" Poem (sonnet); written on November 30, 1936. First published in the *Phantagraph* (May 1937); rpt. *WT* (July 1937).

HPL composed the poem while writing a letter to Finlay, who had lamented the decline of the tradition of dedicatory poems. "The Faceless God" had appeared in *WT* (May 1936), and Finlay's illustration is generally considered the finest ever published in the magazine.

"To Zara." Poem (42 lines); written on August 31, 1922. First published in *SL* 1.164–65 (in a letter to Maurice W. Moe, [September] 1922).

The poem is a hoax: it is purportedly written by Poe (in one ms. HPL dates it to 1829) and is an imitation/parody of Poe's numerous and extravagant poems to women (this one is dedicated to "Miss Sarah Longhurst"). HPL wrote it as a joke on Alfred Galpin, who generally regarded HPL's poetry with disdain. HPL and Frank Belknap Long claimed that they had found the poem in the possession of an ancient Maine man who had known Poe. Galpin, although not believing this story, thought the poem was copied from the work of some obscure nineteenth-century poet, perhaps Arthur O'Shaughnessy.

Tobey, William. In "The Lurking Fear," he and George Bennett accompany the narrator to the Martense mansion in search of the entity that haunts it. They spend the night, but Tobey and Bennett mysteriously disappear.

Toldridge, Elizabeth [Anne] (1861–1940), poet and correspondent of HPL (1928–37). Toldridge published two collections of verse, *The Soul of Love* (New York: Broadway Publishing Co., 1910) and *Mother's Love Songs* (Boston: R. G. Badger, 1911), long before she ever came in touch with HPL. She was also widely published in amateur and semi-professional magazines and anthologies. She got in touch with HPL in 1928, some years after HPL had served as a judge for a poetry contest (otherwise unknown) in which Toldridge had participated. She was disabled in some unknown manner and was unable to leave her apartment in Washington, D.C. HPL visited her there on May 6, 1929; in 1936 R. H. Barlow visited her while traveling from Florida to Providence. Her discussions of poetry with HPL may have been instrumental in HPL's shift away from archaistic verse in theory and practice.

"Tomb, The." Short story (4,190 words); written in June 1917. First published in the *Vagrant* (March 1922); rpt. *WT* (January 1926); first collected in *O;* corrected text in *D;* annotated version in *TD.*

Jervas Dudley tells of his lonely and secluded life. He discovers, in a wooded hollow near his home, a tomb that houses the remains of a family, the Hydes, that dwelt in a mansion nearby. This mansion had been struck by lightning and burned to the ground, although only one member of the family had perished in the flame. The tomb exercises an unholy fascination upon Dudley, and he haunts it for hours at a time. It is locked, but the door is "fastened *ajar* in a queerly sinister way by means of heavy iron chains and padlocks, according to a gruesome fashion of half a century ago." Dudley resolves to enter this tomb at any cost, but he is too young and weak to break open the lock (he is only ten years old at this time). Gradually he begins to display various odd traits, in particular a knowledge of very ancient things that he could not possibly have learned from books. One night, as he is lying on a bower outside the tomb, he seems to hear voices from within: "Every shade of New England dialect, from the uncouth syllables of the Puritan colonists to the precise rhetoric of fifty years ago, seemed represented in that shadowy colloquy. . . ." He does not say what the colloquy was about, but upon returning home he goes directly to a rotting chest in the attic and finds a key to unlock the tomb.

Dudley spends much time in the tomb. But now another peculiar change takes place in him: hitherto a sequestered recluse, he begins to show signs of "ribald revelry" as he returns from the tomb. In one instance he declaims a drinking song of Georgian cast. He also develops a fear of thunderstorms. Dudley's parents, worried about his increasingly odd behavior, now hire a "spy" to follow his actions. On one occasion Dudley thinks that this spy has seen him coming out of the tomb, but the spy tells his parents that Dudley had spent the night on the bower outside the tomb. Dudley, now convinced that he is under some sort of supernatural protection, frequents the tomb without fear or circumspection. One night, as thunder is in the air, he goes to the tomb and sees the mansion as it was in its heyday. A party is under way, and guests in powdered wigs are brought in by carriage. But a peal of thunder interrupts the "swinish revelry" and a fire breaks out. Dudley flees, but finds himself being restrained by two men. They maintain that Dudley had spent the entire night outside the tomb and point to the rusted and unopened lock as evidence. Dudley is put away in a madhouse. A servant, "for whom I bore a fondness in infancy," goes to the tomb, breaks it open, and finds a porcelain miniature with the initials "J. H."; the picture could be of Dudley's twin. "On a slab in an alcove he found an old but empty coffin whose tarnished plate bears the single word '*Jervas*'. In that coffin and in that vault they have promised me I shall be buried."

HPL noted that the genesis of the story occurred in June 1917, when he was walking with his aunt Lillian Clark through Swan Point Cemetery and came upon a tombstone dating to 1711. "Why could I not talk with him, and enter more intimately into the life of my chosen age? What had left his body, that it could no longer converse with me? I looked long at that grave, and the night after I returned home I began my first story of the new series—'The Tomb'" (HPL to the Gallomo, [January] 1920). The tombstone is evidently one in the Clark plot—one Simon Smith (d. March 4, 1711), apparently a distant ancestor of Mrs. Clark.

William Fulwiler points out that the use of the name Hyde is a nod to Stevenson's *The Strange Case of Dr. Jekyll and Mr. Hyde,* suggesting that both works involve a double. There may also be an influence from Poe's "Ligeia."

The so-called "Drinking Song from 'The Tomb'" was written separately, perhaps years before the story itself. The manuscript of the poem survives at JHL as part of an unfinished letter to an unknown correspondent. There the song is titled "Gaudeamus," and HPL evidently wrote it as a response to another poem (apparently by an amateur journalist) of the same title, which HPL considered inferior. Will Murray has conjectured that the song may have been inspired by a similar song contained in Thomas Morton's *New English Canaan or New Canaan* (1637), but a likelier source may be a song in Richard Brinsley Sheridan's *School for Scandal* (1777).

See William Fulwiler, "'The Tomb' and 'Dagon': A Double Dissection," *Crypt* No. 38 (Eastertide 1986): 8–14; Will Murray, "A Probable Source for the Drinking Song from 'The Tomb,'" *LS* No. 15 (Fall 1987): 77–80.

Torres, Dr. In "Cool Air," a physician in Valencia, Spain, who was the colleague of Dr. Muñoz in their quest to defeat death.

"Transition of Juan Romero, The." Short story (2,710 words); written on September 16, 1919. First published in *Marginalia;* corrected text in *D.*

The narrator, an Englishman who because of nameless "calamities" has migrated from his native land (after spending many years in India) to work as a common laborer in America, tells the story of an incident occurring in 1894 at the Norton Mine (presumably somewhere in the Southwest). The narrator becomes friendly with a Mexican peon named Juan Romero, who exhibits a strange fascination for the Hindu ring he owns. One day dynamite is used to blast a cavity for further mining; but the result is the opening up of an immeasurable cavern that cannot be sounded. That night a storm gathers, but beyond the roar of the wind and rain there is another sound, which the frightened Romero can only deem *"el ritmo de la tierra*—THAT THROB DOWN IN THE GROUND!" The narrator also hears it—some huge rhythmical pounding in the newly opened abyss. Possessed by some fatality, they both descend down ladders into the cavern; Romero then dashes off ahead of the narrator, only to plunge into a further abyss, screaming hideously. The narrator cautiously peers over the edge, sees something—*"but God! I dare not tell you what I saw!"*—and flees back to the camp. That morning he and Romero are both found in their bunks, Romero dead. Other miners swear that neither of them left their cabin that night. The narrator later discovers that his Hindu ring is missing.

There is some suggestion that Romero is not in fact Mexican but is descended from the Aztecs, a suggestion enhanced by his crying the name *"Huitzilopotchli"* as he descends into the abyss. The narrator remarks of this word: "Later I definitely placed that word in the works of a great historian—and shuddered when the association came to me." HPL explicitly footnotes Prescott's *Conquest of Mexico,* which contains a vivid passage on the Aztec god and the sacrifices practiced in his name.

HPL, clearly unsatisfied with this story, refused to allow it to be published in his lifetime, even in the amateur press. He disavowed it relatively early in life, and it fails to appear on most lists of his stories; he does not even seem to have shown it to anyone until 1932, when R. H. Barlow persuaded HPL to send him the manuscript so that he could prepare a typescript of it. Aside from the revisions "The Curse of Yig" and "The Mound," it is HPL's only tale set in the Southwest.

"Trap, The." Short story (8,570 words); written in collaboration with Henry S. Whitehead, probably in the summer of 1931. First published in *Strange Tales* (March 1932); first collected in *Uncollected Prose and Poetry II* (1980); corrected text in *HM*.

Robert Grandison, one of the pupils at the Connecticut academy where Gerald Canevin teaches, comes upon an anomalous mirror in Canevin's house that sucks hapless individuals into a strange realm where colors are altered and where objects, both animate and inanimate, have a sort of intangible, dreamlike existence. The mirror had been devised by a seventeenth-century Danish glassblower named Axel Holm who yearned for immortality and found it, after a fashion, in his mirror-world, since "'life' in the sense of form and consciousness would go on virtually forever" so long as the mirror itself was not destroyed. Grandison manages to bring his plight to Canevin's attention, and Canevin contrives to release Grandison from his "trap."

HPL and Whitehead probably worked on the tale, or at least discussed it, during HPL's three-week visit to Whitehead's home in Dunedin, Fla., in May–June 1931. He says in one letter that he "revised & totally recast" the tale (HPL to August Derleth, December 23, 1931; ms., SHSW) and in another that he "suppl[ied] the central part myself" (HPL to R. H. Barlow, February 25, 1932; ms., JHL). Judging purely from the prose style, it can be conjectured that the latter three-fourths of the story is HPL's. Nevertheless, HPL clearly did not wish to share a byline with Whitehead for the story, maintaining that his help was simply a courtesy. The story appears in the second of Whitehead's two posthumously published collections of tales, *West India Lights* (1946); HPL's contribution to the story only came to light in the late 1970s.

Trask, Dr. In "The Rats in the Walls," the anthropologist who attempts to classify the human and subhuman bones found beneath Exham Priory.

Travels, Lovecraft's. In 1915 HPL wrote: "I have never been outside the three states of Rhode Island, Massachusetts, and Connecticut!" (*SL* 1.10). HPL was born in Providence, R.I., but shortly thereafter his parents returned to their home in Dorchester, Mass.; they also visited Dudley, Mass. (in the south-central part of the state) in the summer of 1892 and resided (according to HPL's unverified testimony) with Louise Imogen Guiney in Auburndale in the winter of 1892–93; then, upon the illness of HPL's father, they returned to Providence. HPL (and, presumably, his mother) went to Foster, R.I., in 1896, visiting ancestral sites (*SL* 3.409), perhaps as a way of relieving the gloom attending the death of HPL's grandmother earlier that year. HPL also spent the summer of 1899 with his mother in Westminster, Mass., in the north-central part of the state (*SL* 2.348). The trip to Connecticut may have been the visit of 1901 that HPL mentions on several occasions (e.g. *SL* 1.298), although he never specifies the locale of the visit. HPL also visited his cousin Phillips Gamwell on numerous occasions in Cambridge in the 1910–16 period.

But HPL's hermitry ended in 1919–20, when developing ties to amateur writers impelled him to take trips of increasing breadth; not coincidentally, the illness of his mother and her removal from 454 Angell Street also freed HPL to roam farther than he had done previously. Among his several trips to the Boston area at this time, the most memorable was a trip to the Copley Plaza in Boston in October 1919 to hear Lord Dunsany lecture (*SL* 1.91–93). He traveled to Boston several more times in 1921, as well as visiting C. W. "Tryout" Smith and Myrta Alice Little in Haverhill, Mass. (June 1921); he wrote of the visit in "The Haverhill Convention" (*Tryout*, July 1921; rpt. *CE*1). The NAPA convention in Boston saw HPL in attendance; it was on this occasion that he first met his future wife, Sonia H. Greene. He wrote of the gathering in an unpublished essay, "The Convention Banquet" (ms., JHL). At Sonia's urging, HPL made a six-day trip to New York in April 1922. He went with Sonia to Gloucester and Magnolia, Mass., in late June and early July, then returned to New York in late July prior to heading the farthest west he would ever venture—Cleveland, Ohio—in August to visit Alfred Galpin and Samuel Loveman. He returned to New York, staying there until late September. In mid-September his visit with Rheinhart Kleiner to the Dutch Reformed Church in Brooklyn led to the writing of "The Hound" (1922). Late in 1922 HPL made his ecstatic first visit to the colonial haven of Marblehead, Mass., later the site for "The Festival" (1923). Further trips to New England—chiefly Salem, Marblehead, and Newburyport, Mass. (April), and Portsmouth, N.H. (August), and areas in western Rhode Island with James F. Morton (September) and C. M. Eddy (November)—occupied much of 1923.

HPL's most momentous voyage was his two-year stay in Brooklyn (March 1924–April 1926). Initially thrilled at being in the vibrant metropolis, HPL later came to hate the place for its gigantism, its general absence of colonial landmarks, and its legions of "foreigners" who teemed at every street corner. HPL sought as best he could to explore nearby antiquarian landmarks: Elizabeth, N.J. (October 1924, June and August 1925), Philadelphia (seen briefly during his honeymoon and explored more exhaustively in November 1924), Washington, D.C. (April 1925), Paterson, N.J. (August 1925), Yonkers and Tarrytown, N.Y. (September 1925), Jamaica, Mineola, Hempstead, and Garden City, Long Island (September 1925). These visits provided much-needed respite from the clangor of the metropolis and from his unproductive life of poverty in Brooklyn.

HPL returned ecstatically to Providence in April 1926, but as early as September he was back in New York (evidently at Sonia's bidding), staying for two weeks and briefly visiting Philadelphia. In October he revisited the ancestral sites in Foster, with Annie E. P. Gamwell. In the summer of 1927, HPL initiated what would become an annual and ever-widening series of jaunts up and down the eastern seaboard in quest of antiquarian havens. In July, he went with Donald Wandrei to Boston, Salem, Marblehead, and Athol, Mass., and Newport, R.I. The next month he visited Worcester, Amherst, and Deerfield, Mass., detouring briefly into Vermont (described in "Vermont—A First Impression" [1927]); Portland, Me; Portsmouth, N.H.; and Newburyport and Haverhill, Mass. (described in a compressed travelogue, "The Trip of Theobald," *Tryout*, September 1927).

In 1928 HPL's travels began unexpectedly early, as in April he was summoned to Brooklyn by Sonia, who was setting up a hat shop and requested HPL's assistance. He took the occasion to go on an expedition by car with Frank Belknap Long up the Hudson River and (on a later trip with Long) to Stamford and Ridgefield, Conn. In May he visited James F. Morton at his museum in Paterson, N.J., and visited Wilfred B. Talman in Spring Valley (Rockland Co.), N.Y., returning via Tarrytown and Sleepy Hollow. Then Vrest Orton invited HPL to visit him in Brattleboro, Vt., and HPL spent two weeks there in June. Later that month he proceeded to Wilbraham, Mass., where he visited Edith Miniter; the impressions he derived from that visit were incorporated into the topography of "The Dunwich Horror" (1928). In July he headed south, passing through New York and going on to Philadelphia, Baltimore, Washington, D.C., Annapolis, Alexandria, George Washington's residence at Mt. Vernon, and the Endless Caverns in New Market, Va. This series of travels was described in one of his finest travelogues, "Observations on Several Parts of America" (1928).

HPL's travels of 1929 began at the very start of the year, as Samuel Loveman came to Providence and went with HPL to Boston, Salem, and Marblehead. In April HPL came to New York and then spent several weeks in Vrest Orton's home in Yonkers. In May he headed south, visiting Washington and exhaustively exploring Richmond, Williamsburg, Jamestown, Yorktown, Fredericksburg, and Falmouth, Va. Later he spent a few more days in Washington, returned to New York, and was driven by the Longs to West Shokan, N.Y., the residence of Bernard Austin Dwyer. HPL explored the abundant Dutch colonial remains of the nearby towns of Kingston, Hurley, and New Paltz. HPL wrote of these travels in "Travels in the Provinces of America" (1929). In August he took a trip to the Fairbanks house (1636) in Dedham, Mass., writing of the visit in the essay, "An Account of a Trip to the Fairbanks House" (1929; first published CE4). Later that month the Longs took HPL on a visit to New Bedford and Cape Cod. It was on this occasion that HPL, for the first and last only time, flew in an airplane (a $3 ride over Buzzard's Bay). Late in August HPL and his aunt Annie Gamwell revisited sites in Foster.

In late April 1930 HPL headed directly from Providence to Charleston, S. C., whose colonial remains entranced him. It came to be his second favorite town, after Providence, and he wrote of it in "An Account of Charleston" (1930). In May HPL returned north through Richmond, New York City, and Kingston, N.Y., returning home in mid-June. The next month he attended the NAPA convention in Boston, and in August the Longs took him again to Cape Cod. Then, in late August, he took a cheap excursion to Quebec, whose colonial relics impelled him to write *A Description of the Town of Quebeck* (1930–31), his single longest literary work.

HPL's travels of 1931 reached the widest extent they would ever achieve. In May he left for New York, spent much time in Charleston, visited Savannah, Ga., and spent two weeks in St. Augustine, Fla. He also visited Henry S. Whitehead in Dunedin, briefly visited Miami, and then spent several days in Key West. He returned north via St. Augustine, Charleston, Richmond, Fredericksburg, Philadelphia, and New York. The Longs took him for a weekend to the beach resort of Asbury Park, N.J., and he spent a week with Talman in Brooklyn. He returned home in mid-July. In October he went with W. Paul Cook to Boston, Newburyport, and Haverhill; in November to Boston, Salem, Marblehead, Newburyport (which inspired the writing of "The Shadow over Innsmouth"), and Portsmouth. He wrote no travelogue of these visits, but they are chronicled extensively in his letters.

In May 1932 HPL left Providence for New York, then went south to Knoxville, Chattanooga, and Memphis, Tennessee, and Vicksburg and Natchez, Mississippi. He then proceeded to New Orleans, spending time with E. Hoffmann Price. HPL subsequently explored Mobile and Montgomery, Ala., and Atlanta, returning north via Fredericksburg, Annapolis, Philadelphia, and New York. He was called home abruptly in early July by the illness of his aunt Lillian, who died on July 3. In late August HPL visited Cook in Boston; they went to Newburyport to see a solar eclipse, after which HPL spent several days in Quebec. HPL revisited Salem and Marblehead in October. Toward the end of the year HPL initiated a new tradition of spending New Year's Day in New York City, visiting his many friends there; on these occasions he usually stayed with the Longs.

HPL visited Hartford, Conn., in March 1933, seeing his ex-wife Sonia for the last time. Following his move to 66 College Street in May, HPL visited sites in Narragansett County, R.I., in a car driven by E. Hoffmann Price. The Longs came through Providence in late July and took HPL to Cape Cod, and he later visited Newport in the company of James F. Morton. HPL's third trip to Quebec occurred in September; he also spent one day in Montreal. He again visited New York for New Year's celebrations.

In mid-March 1934 HPL's young friend R. H. Barlow invited HPL for an extended stay at his home in De Land, Fla. HPL accepted the offer, heading south the next month, spending time in New York and Charleston, and reaching De Land on May 2. He stayed until mid-June, after which he visited St. Augustine, Charleston, Richmond, Fredericksburg, Washington, Philadelphia, and New York; the Longs then took him to Asbury Park and Ocean Grove, N.J. In August HPL went with Cook and Edward H. Cole to Boston, Salem, and Marblehead. Later that month HPL visited Nantucket for the first time, being enchanted by the antiquities there and writing of his visit in "The Unknown City in the Ocean" (*Perspective Review,* Winter 1934). HPL again spent New Year's in New York City.

HPL returned to Boston and Marblehead with Cole in May 1935. The next month HPL returned to Barlow's Florida home, staying from June 9 to August 18. HPL then visited St. Augustine, Charleston, Richmond, Washington, Philadelphia, and New York, reaching home on September 14. It would prove the last of HPL's extensive summer travels, although he did visit various sites (including Cape Cod) with Cole in September, and New Haven, Conn., and Boston (with Samuel Loveman) in October. The end of the year saw HPL's last New Year's visit to New York City.

Most of 1936 was full of illness (both for HPL and for his aunt Annie), poverty, and grueling revision work, so HPL did little traveling. In July HPL managed to get to Newport; and when Maurice W. Moe and his son Robert visited later that month, they took HPL to Pawtuxet and other sites in Rhode Island. HPL visited an area called Squantum Woods, on the east shore of Narragansett

Bay, in October, and later that month visited the Neutaconkanut woods three miles northwest of his home; but thereafter he became too ill to travel.

HPL's travel writings—whether in letters or in formal travelogues—are some of his most engaging documents. Aside from the meticulousness with which he records the history and topography of his chosen sites, the thrill he experienced at visiting antiquarian havens from Quebec to Key West is infectiously transmitted to the reader. It is possible, with HPL's travelogues of Charleston, Quebec, and other locales in hand, to follow his footsteps exactly. On one occasion HPL wrote out a detailed itinerary from memory of the antiquarian sites in Newport for his aunt Annie (letter dated September 1927; ms., JHL). The impressions HPL derived from his travels enter extensively into his fiction from as early as "The Festival" to such important tales as "The Silver Key," "The Colour out of Space," "The Dunwich Horror," "The Whisperer in Darkness," and "The Shadow over Innsmouth"; these tales (as well as those set in his native Providence—"The Shunned House," "The Call of Cthulhu," *The Case of Charles Dexter Ward*, and "The Haunter of the Dark") establish HPL as a significant New England regionalist as well as a master of the horror tale.

"Travels in the Provinces of America." Essay (19,800 words); probably written in the fall of 1929. First published in *MW* and *CE4*.

The second of HPL's great travelogues (after "Observations on Several Parts of America" [1928]), covering his travels of the spring and summer of 1929. It covers HPL's visits to Yonkers (Vrest Orton) and New Rochelle, N.Y.; Richmond, Williamsburg, Jamestown, Yorktown, and Fredericksburg, Va.; Washington, D.C.; Philadelphia; West Shokan (Bernard Austin Dwyer), Kingston, Hurley, and New Paltz, N.Y.; Athol (W. Paul Cook) and Barre, Mass.

"Tree, The." Short story (1,640 words); written in the first half of 1920. First published in *Tryout* (October 1921); rpt. *WT* (August 1938); first collected in *BWS;* corrected text in *D;* annotated version in *DWH.*

The "Tyrant of Syracuse" proposes a contest between the two great sculptors, Kalos and Musides, to carve a statue of Tyché. The two artists are the closest of friends, but their lives are very different: whereas Musides "revelled by night amidst the urban gaieties of Tegea," Kalos remains home in quiet contemplation. They begin working on their respective statues, but Kalos gradually takes ill and, despite Musides' constant nursing, eventually dies. Musides wins the contest by default, but both he and his lovely statue are weirdly destroyed when a strange olive tree growing out of Kalos' tomb suddenly falls upon Musides' residence.

It is evident that Musides, for all his supposed devotion to his friend, has poisoned Kalos and suffers supernatural revenge. HPL says as much in a discussion of the story in *In Defence of Dagon* (*MW* 156). Although generally considered a "Dunsanian" tale, the story had been conceived no later than 1918, a year before HPL ever read Dunsany. He outlines the plot in a letter to Alfred Galpin (August 1918), saying that it had by that time been "long conceived but never elaborated into literary form"; he postponed writing the story because he evidently felt that

Galpin's own tale "Marsh-Mad" (*Philosopher*, December 1920) had preempted him by utilizing the "living tree" idea.

This early plot synopsis did not suggest that the tale was set in ancient Greece, as it manifestly is. HPL's knowledge of Greek history and literature was put to good use. The names of the artists—Kalos ("handsome" or "fair") and Musides ("son of the Muse[s]")—are both apt although not actual Greek names. Tyché means "chance" (or sometimes "fate"), and actual cults of Tyché were established in Greece sometime after 371 B.C.E. Other allusions in the story establish that the events must take place in the period 353–344 B.C.E., when Dionysius II was Tyrant of Syracuse.

See S. T. Joshi, "'The Tree' and Ancient History," *Nyctalops* 4, No. 1 (April 1991): 68–71.

"Tree on the Hill, The." Short story (4,280 words); written in collaboration with Duane W. Rimel, May 1934. First published in *Polaris* (September 1940); first collected in *HM*.

Near the town of Hampden, Idaho, the narrator, named Single, stumbles upon a strange landscape whose central feature is a peculiar tree with round leaves. He manages to photograph the site and brings the developed photographs to his friend Constantine Theunis, a writer of esoteric books. Theunis, usually languid and bored, is startled by the photographs, as he realizes that the landscape must be from a planet that has three suns. Theunis then remembers that Rudolf Yergler's *Chronicle of Nath* mentions some such landscape. The passage in question speaks of a "shadow that should not be on Earth," and it bodes ill for humanity unless a "Gem" can be found to drive the shadow back into the cosmic realm from which it came. Theunis knows where the Gem is housed, and he manages to borrow it. Some weeks later Single is asked to come to a hospital where Theunis is placed, suffering from some seizure. Theunis tells Single that he has saved the world, but he must destroy the photographs and any sketches that Theunis may have made; but before doing so, Single sees a sketch that suggests that the peculiar tree is in reality the gnarled, twisted hand of some hideous entity.

Clearly HPL revised the tale from a draft by Rimel. HPL says in a letter: "I read your 'Tree on the Hill' with great interest, & believe it truly captures the essence of the weird. I like it exceedingly despite a certain cumbrousness & tendency toward anticlimax in the later parts. I've made a few emendations which you may find helpful, & have tried a bit of strengthening toward the end. Hope you'll like what I've done" (HPL to Duane W. Rimel, May 13, 1934; ms., JHL). Of the three sections of the story, the final one—as well as the citation from the mythical *Chronicle of Nath* in the second section—is certainly by HPL. Some have believed that much of the rest of the second section is also HPL's, but this is an open question that must be decided merely from internal evidence, as no manuscript survives. The title *Chronicle of Nath* is probably Rimel's invention, as he mentions it in several of his stories.

See Donald R. Burleson, "Lovecraftian Branches in Rimel's 'Tree,'" *Crypt* No. 17 (Hallowmas 1983): 3–4; Peter Cannon, "Who Wrote 'The Tree on the Hill?'" *Crypt* No. 17 (Hallowmas 1983): 5; William Fulwiler, "Some Comments on 'The Tree on the Hill,'" *Crypt* No. 17 (Hallowmas 1983): 6; S. T. Joshi, "On

'The Tree on the Hill,'" *Crypt* No. 17 (Hallowmas 1983): 6–9; Steven Mariconda, "Lovecraft's Role in 'The Tree on the Hill,'" *Crypt* No. 17 (Hallowmas 1983): 10–12, 24; Will Murray, "Examining 'The Tree on the Hill,'" *Crypt* No. 17 (Hallowmas 1983): 13–14; Robert M. Price, "A 'New' Lovecraft Revision," *Crypt* No. 17 (Hallowmas 1983): 15–19; David E. Schultz, "Regarding Lovecraft's Hand in 'The Tree on the Hill,'" *Crypt* No. 17 (Hallowmas 1983): 19–21.

Tremaine, F[rederick] Orlin (1899–1956), American author and editor. Tremaine was editor of *Astounding Stories* (1933–37); he accepted HPL's *At the Mountains of Madness* (sold by Julius Schwartz) and "The Shadow out of Time" (sold by Donald Wandrei), apparently without reading them; but he permitted both tales to be severely abridged and edited by copyeditors, although HPL complained vociferously only about the former (it was on this occasion that HPL referred to Tremaine as "that god-damn'd dung of a hyaena": HPL to R. H. Barlow, June 4, 1936; ms., JHL). Tremaine later edited *Comet Stories* (1940) and became editor at Bartholomew House, which published the first paperback editions of HPL, *The Weird Shadow over Innsmouth* (1944) and *The Dunwich Horror* (1945).

See Will Murray, "The Man Who Edited Lovecraft," *Crypt* No. 48 (St. John's Eve 1987): 3–5.

Trever, Alfred. In "Old Bugs," the son of **Eleanor (Wing) Trever,** who enters a tavern in search of liquor but is repulsed by the actions of a crazed drunkard, Old Bugs, who he realizes is the former lover of his mother.

"Two Black Bottles." Short story (4,870 words); written in collaboration with Wilfred Blanch Talman, June–October 1926. First published in *WT* (August 1927); first collected in *HM* (1970 ed.); corrected text in *HM.*

The first-person narrator, a man named Hoffman, comes to examine the estate of his uncle, Dominie Johannes Vanderhoof, who has just died. Vanderhoof was the pastor of the small town of Daalbergen in the Ramapo Mountains (located in northern New Jersey and extending into New York State), and strange tales were told of him. He had fallen under the influence of an aged sexton, Abel Foster, and had taken to delivering fiery and daemoniac sermons to an ever-dwindling congregation. Hoffman, investigating the matter, finds Foster in the church, drunk and frightened. Foster tells a strange tale of the first pastor of the church, Dominie Guilliam Slott, who in the early eighteenth century had amassed a collection of esoteric volumes and appeared to practice some form of demonology. Foster reads these books himself and follows in Slott's footsteps—to the point that, when Vanderhoof dies, he takes his soul from his body and puts it in a little black bottle. But Vanderhoof, now caught between heaven and hell, rests uneasily in his grave, and there are indications that he is trying to emerge from it. Hoffman, scarcely knowing what to make of this wild story, now sees the cross on Vanderhoof's grave tilting perceptibly. Then seeing two black bottles on the table near Foster, he reaches for one of them, and in a scuffle with Foster one of them breaks. Foster shrieks: "I'm done fer! That one in there was mine! *Dominie Slott took it out two hundred years ago!"* Foster's body crumbles rapidly into dust.

Judging from HPL's letters to Talman, it seems clear that HPL has not only written some of the tale—especially the parts in dialect—but also made significant suggestions regarding its structure. Talman had evidently sent HPL both a draft and a synopsis—or, perhaps, a draft of only the beginning and a synopsis of the rest. HPL recommended a simplification of the structure so that all the events are seen through the eyes of Hoffman. In terms of the diction, HPL writes: "As for what I've done to the MS.—I am sure you'll find nothing to interfere with your sense of creation. My changes are in virtually every case merely verbal, and all in the interest of finish and fluency of style" (*SL* 2.61). In his 1973 memoir Talman reveals some irritation at HPL's revisions: "He did some minor gratuitous editing, particularly of dialog . . . After re-reading it in print, I wish Lovecraft hadn't changed the dialog, for his use of dialect was stilted" (*The Normal Lovecraft* [Gerry de la Ree, 1973], p. 8). This may have led Talman to downplay HPL's role in the work, for there are many passages beyond the dialect parts that clearly reveal his hand.

Two-Gun Bob. In "The Battle That Ended the Century," one of two antagonists who engage in a boxing match in the year 2001. The character (nicknamed "the Terror of the Plains") is a parody of HPL's friend Robert E. Howard, of Cross Plains, Tex.

T'yog. In "Out of the Æons," the millennia-old petrified mummy housed in the Cabot Museum of Archaeology in Boston. The curator of the museum, Richard H. Johnson, thinks that the mummy is that of a man spoken of in Von Junzt's *Black Book*. This man, T'yog, attempted to scale Mount Yaddith-Gho on the continent of Mu 175,000 years ago to free the people from the tyranny of the god Ghatanothoa, but was turned to stone (with his brain still living) by the god.

Typer, Alonzo Hasbrouck. In "The Diary of Alonzo Typer," an occult explorer from Kingston, N.Y., who investigates the spectral van der Heyl house near Attica. Typer is in fact related to the van der Heyls and has been summoned to the home for some unknown purpose.

U

Ull. In "'Till A' the Seas,'" a young man who, in the distant future, becomes the last surviving member of the human race. After tending to Mladdna, an old woman, until she dies, he seeks out what he believes to be another colony of human beings beyond the mountains, but finds it full of decaying skeletons. He dies shortly thereafter by falling into a well.

"Under the Pyramids." Novelette (10,950 words); ghostwritten for Harry Houdini in February 1924. First published (as "Imprisoned with the Pharaohs") in *WT* (May–June–July 1924); rpt. *WT* (June–July 1939); first collected in *Marginalia;* corrected text in *D;* annotated version in *TD.*

   The escape artist Harry Houdini narrates in the first person an account of a peculiar adventure he experienced in Egypt. Some Arabs—led by a man who uses the name Abdul Reis el Drogman—bring Houdini to witness a boxing match on the top of the Great Pyramid; but after the fight is over the Arabs seize him and cast him, bound tightly by rope, down a spectacularly deep chasm in the Temple of the Sphinx. After awaking, he struggles not merely to escape from the temple but to answer an "idle question" that had haunted him throughout his stay in Egypt: *"what huge and loathsome abnormality was the Sphinx originally carven to represent?"* As he seeks an exit, Houdini encounters an immense underground cavern—"Bases of columns whose middles were higher than human sight . . . mere bases of things that must each dwarf the Eiffel Tower to insignificance"—peopled with hideous hybrid entities. Houdini ponders the curiously morbid temperament of the ancient Egyptians, in particular their notions of the spirit or *ka,* which can return to its body or other bodies after it had "wandered about the upper and lower worlds in a horrible way." There are "blood-congealing legends" of what "decadent priestcraft" fashioned on occasion—"*composite mummies* made by the artificial union of human trunks and limbs with the heads of animals in imitation of the elder gods." Considering all this,

Houdini is dumbfounded to come upon *living embodiments* of such entities: *"their crazy torches began to cast shadows on the surface of those stupendous columns. . . . Hippopotami should not have human hands and carry torches . . . men should not have the heads of crocodiles. . . ."* But an even greater horror is revealed by Houdini's discovery of the answer to that "idle question" he had asked himself earlier. The composite creatures appear to be laying down huge amounts of food as offerings to some strange entity that appears fleetingly out of an aperture in the underground cavern: "It was as large, perhaps, as a good-sized hippopotamus, but very curiously shaped. It seemed to have no neck, but five separate shaggy heads springing in a row from a roughly cylindrical trunk . . . Out of these heads darted curious rigid tentacles which seized ravenously on the *excessively great* quantities of unmentionable food placed before the aperture." What could it possibly be? "The five-headed monster that emerged . . . that five-headed monster as large as a hippopotamus . . . the five-headed monster—*and that of which it is the merest fore paw. . . ."*

HPL recounts at length in letters how he came to write the tale. *WT* was struggling financially, and the owner, J. C. Henneberger, felt that Houdini's affiliation with the magazine might attract readers. Houdini was the reputed author of a column ("Ask Houdini") that ran in a few issues, as well as of two short stories probably ghostwritten by others. In mid-February Henneberger commissioned HPL to write "Under the Pyramids." Houdini was claiming that he had actually been bound and gagged by Arabs and dropped down a shaft in the pyramid called Campbell's Tomb; but as HPL began exploring the historical and geographical background of the account, he came to the conclusion that it was complete fiction, and so he received permission from Henneberger to elaborate the account with his own imaginative additions. Henneberger had planned to publish the story as by "Houdini and H. P. Lovecraft," but was disconcerted that HPL had written the account in the first person; he thought readers would be confused by a first-person story with a joint byline, so HPL's name was omitted. (His role in the story was acknowledged in an editor's note accompanying the 1939 reprint of the story.) HPL received $100 for the tale, paid in advance. He wrote the tale hastily in the last week of February, but then left the typescript in the train station in Providence while leaving to go to New York to marry Sonia H. Greene. (The ad HPL placed in the lost-and-found section of the *Providence Journal* supplies his original title to the story.) Accordingly, he and Sonia spent much of their honeymoon preparing a new typescript of the story from HPL's autograph manuscript, which fortunately he had brought with him.

The tale is surprisingly effective and suspenseful, with a genuinely surprising ending for those reading it for the first time. HPL's Egyptian research was probably derived from several volumes in his library, notably *The Tomb of Perneb* (1916), a volume issued by the Metropolitan Museum of Art. He had seen many Egyptian antiquities firsthand at the museum in 1922. Some of the imagery of the story probably also derives from Théophile Gautier's nonsupernatural tale of Egyptian horror, "One of Cleopatra's Nights"; HPL owned Lafcadio Hearn's translation of *One of Cleopatra's Nights and Other Fantastic Romances* (1882). The writing is somewhat florid, but deliberately so; and there must be a certain tart satire in the fact that Houdini—one of the strongest men of his day—faints three times in the course of his adventure.

"Unknown, The." Poem (12 lines in quatrains); probably written in the fall of 1916. First published in the *Conservative* (October 1916) (as by "Elizabeth Berkeley").

A weird vignette in which the narrator finds something horrifying in the face of the moon. HPL notes in a letter to the Gallomo (September 12, 1923; AHT) that the poem was published under Winifred Virginia Jackson's pseudonym "in an effort to mystify the [amateur] public by having widely dissimilar work from the same nominal hand." HPL also published "The Peace Advocate" (*Tryout*, May 1917) under this pseudonym.

See Donald R. Burleson, "Lovecraft's 'The Unknown': A Sort of Runic Rhyme," *LS* No. 26 (Spring 1992): 19–21.

"Unnamable, The." Short story (2,970 words); written September 1923. First published in *WT* (July 1925); first collected in *BWS;* corrected text in *D;* annotated version in *DWH.*

In an old burying ground in Arkham, the first-person narrator, "Carter," and his friend Joel Manton discuss Carter's horror tales. Manton enunciates his objections to the weird—as contrary to probability, as not based on "realism," and as extravagant and unrelated to life. In particular, he scoffs at the idea of something being termed "unnamable"; but later that evening the two men encounter just such an entity in the burying ground.

Although Carter's first name is never mentioned, one assumes that he is Randolph Carter of "The Statement of Randolph Carter" (1919). But because of the uncertainty of his identity, "The Unnamable" has frequently not been considered part of the sequence of stories involving Carter. Only the most glancing reference to the incident related in this story appears in "The Silver Key" (1926): "Then he went back to Arkham, . . . and had experiences in the dark, amidst the hoary willows, and tottering gambrel roofs, which made him seal forever certain pages in the diary of a wild-minded ancestor."

In part, the tale is a satire on the stolid bourgeois unresponsiveness to the weird tale. Carter's observation that "it is the province of the artist . . . to arouse strong emotion by action, ecstasy, and astonishment" signals HPL's absorption of the literary theory of Arthur Machen (whom he was first reading at this time), specifically the treatise *Hieroglyphics: A Note upon Ecstasy in Literature* (1902). The tale might have been directly inspired by the opening of Machen's episodic novel *The Three Impostors* (1895), in which two characters debate as to the proper function of literature, one of them (analogous to Manton) remarking that "one has no business to make use of the wonderful, the improbable, the odd coincidence in literature . . . that it was wrong to do so, because as a matter of fact the wonderful and the improbable don't happen. . . ." In HPL's story, the satire becomes more pointed because the character of Manton is clearly based upon HPL's friend Maurice W. Moe (Manton is "principal of the East High School," just as Moe was an instructor at the West Division High School in Milwaukee).

Carter points out that Manton actually "believ[ed] in the supernatural much more fully than I"—an allusion to Manton's (and Moe's) religious beliefs. The story also explores the sense of the lurking horror of New England history and topography. It is set in Arkham, but the actual inspiration for the setting—a "dilapidated seventeenth-century tomb" and, nearby, a "giant willow in the centre of the cemetery, whose trunk has nearly engulfed an ancient, illegible slab"—is the Charter Street Burying Ground in Salem, where just such a tree-engulfed slab can be found. Later in the story HPL records various "old-wives' superstitions," some of which are taken from Cotton Mather's *Magnalia Christi Americana* (1702), of which he owned an ancestral copy.

Upton, Daniel. The narrator of "The Thing on the Doorstep" and a close friend of Edward Derby. He shoots Derby to liberate him from the decaying corpse of Asenath Waite, into which Derby's personality had been cast following his murder of Asenath.

Utpatel, Frank (1905–1980), artist and late correspondent of HPL (1936–37). Utpatel, a Wisconsinite, was a friend of August Derleth, and in 1932 Derleth asked Utpatel to prepare some illustrations to HPL's "The Shadow over Innsmouth," even though that tale had not been accepted for publication. The whereabouts of these illustrations are unknown; but HPL, remembering them, urged William L. Crawford of the Visionary Press to commission Utpatel to make illustrations for the upcoming book publication of *The Shadow over Innsmouth* (1936). Utpatel prepared four illustrations, one of which appeared on the dust jacket. HPL professed to like them, even though the bearded Zadok Allen was portrayed as clean-shaven. In later years Utpatel became a distinguished fantasy illustrator, doing much work for Arkham House; he took many years to draw illustrations for HPL's *Collected Poems* (Arkham House, 1963) but produced some of his best work there. He also drew the dust jacket for *DB* and for Frank Belknap Long's *Howard Phillips Lovecraft: Dreamer on the Nightside* (Arkham House, 1975).

V

Van Allister, Prof. Arthur. In "Ashes," a scientist who discovers a chemical compound that can reduce any substance to mere ashes. He later dies when thrown into a large vat of his own formula by his assistant, Malcolm Bruce.

van der Heyl, Claes (d. 1591). In "The Diary of Alonzo Typer," a member of a strange Dutch family who lived in Holland in the later sixteenth century and kept a diary between 1560 and 1580 telling of his strange delvings into the supernatural. His descendant, **Hendrik,** came to New-Netherland (i.e., New York state) in 1638 in search of a nameless "Thing." **Dirck,** now settled in Albany, N.Y., built a house near Attica around 1760. He married a woman from Salem, Mass., and was the father of **Joris** (b. 1773), "that frightful hybrid," and of **Trintje,** who would later marry Adriaen Sleght.

Vanderhoof, Johannes. In "Two Black Bottles," the recently deceased pastor ("dominie") and uncle of the narrator, Hoffman. Vanderhoof's soul is entrapped in a little black bottle by his sexton, Abel Foster.

Van Itty, Mrs. In "Sweet Ermengarde," a wealthy society woman who adopts Ermengarde Stubbs and later discovers that she is her long-lost daughter.

Van Keulen, Dr. Cornelius. In "Winged Death," a coroner's physician who discovers the dead body of Dr. Thomas Slauenwite in a hotel room in Bloemfontein, South Africa, as well as Slauenwite's strange diary.

Verhaeren, M. In "Facts Concerning the Late Arthur Jermyn and His Family," a Belgian agent at a trading post in the Congo who sends Arthur Jermyn a box containing a curious specimen he has found among the N'bangus—a specimen that impels Jermyn to kill himself.

286   "Vermont—A First Impression"

"Vermont—A First Impression." Essay (1,630 words); probably written in the fall of 1927. First published in *Driftwind* (March 1928); rpt. *MW* and *CE4*.

A brief account of HPL's first visit to New Hampshire in the summer of 1927. It speaks in glowing terms of the beauty of the countryside as well as of the city of Brattleboro, and concludes with a paean to "Vermont's gentle poet," Arthur Goodenough. Several paragraphs of the essay were incorporated, with significant revision, into "The Whisperer in Darkness" (1930).

"Very Old Folk, The." Short story (2,500 words); written on November 3, 1927. First published (in this form) in *Scienti-Snaps* (Summer 1940); corrected text in *MW*.

In the Roman province of Hispania Citerior (Spain), the proconsul, P. Scribonius Libo, summons a provincial quaestor named L. Caelius Rufus to the small town of Pompelo because of strange rumors in the hills above the town. There, a shadowy group of hill-dwellers, perhaps not fully human, named the Very Old Folk customarily kidnap a few villagers on the day before the Kalends of Maius (May Eve) and the Kalends of November (Halloween). But this year, it is the day before the Kalends of November and no villager has been taken. This very lack of activity is suspicious, and Rufus is concerned that something far graver is afoot. He argues with the military tribune Sextus Asellius and with the legatus Cn. Balbutius, urging that the Roman army take strong action to suppress the Very Old Folk once and for all; after much debate, Rufus wins Libo to his side and prevails. As a cohort of Roman soldiers ascends the hills, the atmosphere becomes increasingly sinister; then some of the horses *scream,* the stars are blotted out of the night sky, a cold wind sweeps down upon the cohort, and the stoic Libo, facing some nameless horror, intones ponderously: *"Malitia vetus—malitia vetus est . . . venit . . . tandem venit"* ("The old evil—it is the old evil . . . it comes . . . it comes at last").

The "story" is in fact an account, in a letter to Donald Wandrei, of a remarkably vivid and long-lasting dream that HPL had on Halloween night, inspired by the time of the year and by his reading of James Rhoades's translation of Virgil's *Aeneid* (1921). HPL recounted the dream (with slight variations in each account) to at least two other correspondents: Bernard Austin Dwyer (see *SL* 2.189–97) and Frank Belknap Long. HPL frequently mentioned that he hoped to use the kernel of the dream in a story, but he never did so; in 1929, Long received HPL's permission to borrow the text of his dream-account for his novel, *The Horror from the Hills* (*WT,* January and February–March 1931; Arkham House, 1963), where it comprises the central section of chapter 5. HPL states that the events of the dream "must have been in the late republic"; i.e., prior to the commencement of Augustus' reign as emperor of Rome (27 B.C.E.).

"Vivisector, The." Column appearing in five installments in the *Wolverine* (March, June, November 1921; March 1922; Spring 1923), all as by "Zoilus"; rpt. *CE1*.

Much confusion has existed as to which of the columns—if any—were written by HPL; but examination of correspondence by Horace L. Lawson (editor of the *Wolverine*) to HPL (at JHL) clarifies the matter. These documents testify that HPL wrote the columns for March and June 1921, March 1922, and Spring 1923. Lawson in fact regarded HPL as the "editor" of the column. The column for November 1921 was written by Alfred Galpin and is a review of the previous issues of the *Wolverine;* included is a lengthy discussion of HPL's "Facts Concerning the Late Arthur Jermyn and His Family." The first column discusses a variety of amateur journals; the second focuses on Galpin's *Philosopher* (December 1920), and HPL characteristically disparages his own contributions to that paper, "Polaris" and "The House"; the columns for March 1922 and Spring 1923 are friendly analyses of the poetry of Lillian Middleton and Rheinhart Kleiner, respectively. The pseudonym "Zoilus" used in all the columns refers to the fourth-century B.C.E. Greek critic who severely criticized the Homeric poems, so that his name came to refer to any unduly censorious critic; but the articles themselves are on the whole genial and complimentary.

"Volunteer, The." Poem (48 lines in 6 stanzas); written in mid- to late January 1918. First published in the [Providence] *Evening News* (February 1, 1918); rpt. *National Enquirer* (February 7, 1918); rpt. *Tryout* (April 1918); rpt. *Appleton* [Wis.] *Post* (date unknown); *St. Petersburg* [Fla.] *Evening Independent* (date unknown); *Trench and Camp* (military paper at San Antonio, Tex.) (date unknown).

The most reprinted poem in HPL's lifetime; a response to "Only a Volunteer" by Sgt. Hayes P. Miller (*National Enquirer,* January 17, 1918), which had suggested that all the sympathy and recognition went to American conscript soldiers rather than to volunteers. The last three appearances were cited in a note in the *United Amateur* (May 1918) and have not been located; the appearance in the *Appleton Post* was presumably arranged by Maurice W. Moe, that in the *St. Petersburg Evening Independent* probably by John Russell.

W

Waite, Asenath. In "The Thing on the Doorstep," the domineering woman who, at the age of twenty-three, marries the thirty-eight-year-old Edward Derby. Derby's father does not approve of her because of the crowd to which she belongs, but he is unable to prevent their marriage. Asenath—whose family comes from Innsmouth—exchanges personalities with Derby, at first only intermittently. Derby kills her to thwart her attempt to effect a permanent exchange, but her will is so strong that she still manages to accomplish the exchange even after her death. But the personality that overtakes Derby is actually not Asenath at all, but her father **Ephraim,** who as his own death was approaching overtook his own weak-willed daughter's body.

There are very few female characters in HPL's fiction. None is as fully developed as Asenath, but even she is revealed to be no woman at all, but actually her father Ephraim. Derby's resistance to Asenath's strong will may evoke his own feelings to some of the dominating females in his own life, most notably his mother and his wife. The names Asenath and Ephraim are perhaps meant to parody a passage in Genesis, where Asenath is the wife of Joseph (41:45) and gives birth to Ephraim (46:20); HPL reverses the genealogy and makes Ephraim the father of Asenath.

Walakea. In "The Shadow over Innsmouth," the chief of a band of Kanakas dwelling on an island in the South Seas, whose inhabitants mate with loathsome sea-creatures and derive great bounties of fish and gold as a result. Walakea has no hybrid blood in him, as he is of a royal line that intermarries only with royal lines on other islands.

Walter, Dorothy C[harlotte] (1889–1967), friend of HPL. In early 1934, at the urging of her friend W. Paul Cook, Walter wrote to HPL urging him to visit her at her temporary residence in Providence (Walter was a native of Vermont). But on the day of the planned visit, HPL found the weather so cold that he could not venture outdoors without risk of serious illness, so he telephoned Walter and apologized effusively. He visited a few days later, an incident recounted in Walter's "Three Hours with H. P. Lovecraft" (in *SR;* rpt. *LR*). Walter also wrote a sensitive piece on HPL's relation to his native city, "Lovecraft and Benefit Street" (*Ghost,* Spring 1943; rpt. *LR*).

Wandrei, Donald [Albert] (1908–1987), weird poet and short story writer living chiefly in St. Paul, Minn., and correspondent of HPL (1926–37). Wandrei had been corresponding with Clark Ashton Smith since 1924; in late 1926 Smith asked Wandrei to return some of HPL's manuscripts directly to HPL after reading them. Wandrei did so, thereby initiating an association that lasted till HPL's death. The two writers exchanged manuscripts, and HPL offered advice to Wandrei on some of his but did no revision. Wandrei had already written "The Chuckler," a pseudo-sequel to HPL's "The Statement of Randolph Carter," although it remained unpublished until it appeared in *Fantasy Magazine* (September 1934). Wandrei had an extensive library of weird fiction and lent HPL several key volumes, notably F. Marion Crawford's *Wandering Ghosts* (1911) and Charles Fort's *The Book of the Damned* (1919). HPL was instrumental in securing the acceptance of Wandrei's "The Twilight of Time" for *WT* (it appeared in the October 1927 issue under the title "The Red Brain"); Wandrei returned the favor when visiting the *WT* offices in the summer of 1927, urging Farnsworth Wright to accept HPL's "The Call of Cthulhu," which Wright had earlier rejected. Wandrei's trip was part of a long hitchhiking expedition from St. Paul to Providence, with an extensive stop in New York to meet HPL's friends (especially Samuel Loveman). Wandrei arrived in Providence on July 12, staying till July 29. Part of this time Frank Belknap Long and James F. Morton were also present. Some months later HPL put Wandrei in touch with August Derleth, initiating a lifelong relationship. HPL advised Wandrei to let W. Paul Cook publish his first volume of poetry, *Ecstasy and Other Poems* (1928). A second volume, *Dark Odyssey* (1931), was published in St. Paul.

After 1929 the correspondence became more sporadic. For a time Wandrei worked in the advertising department of E. P. Dutton in New York, but he gave up the job and returned to St. Paul to write. Wandrei published numerous horror tales in *WT;* HPL had a high regard for many of them, finding in them a cosmic quality lacking in much work of its kind (see *SL* 3.196). In 1931–32 Wandrei wrote the weird novel *Dead Titans, Waken!*, partially inspired by HPL's work; HPL admired it but suggested numerous revisions in style and proportioning. The novel was not published in this form, but appeared years later in a revised edition as *The Web of Easter Island* (1948). In 1932 Wandrei completed a mainstream novel, *Invisible Sun;* HPL also expressed approbation of this work (even though it contained much explicit sexual content), but it too remained unpublished. (This novel and *Dead Titans, Waken!* have now been published in one volume [Fedogan & Bremer, 2001].) In September 1932 Wandrei visited HPL again in Providence; he met HPL also occasionally during the latter's year-end visits to New York in the 1930s. By this time he was doing much writing for the science fiction pulps, with such tales as "Colossus" (*Astounding Stories,* January

1934) and "Infinity Zero" (*Astounding Stories,* October 1936), as well as stories for the mystery pulps, many involving the detective Ivy Frost. He also appeared occasionally in high-paying mainstream markets; for example, "The Eye and the Finger" (*Esquire,* December 1936). A horror tale, "The Tree-Men of M'Bwa" (*WT,* February 1932), is regarded by some as Lovecraftian. HPL thought Wandrei's later work had succumbed to pulp standards—a criticism that Wandrei found highly discouraging when he read it in HPL's letters years later.

After HPL's death August Derleth and Donald Wandrei founded Arkham House to publish HPL's work in hard covers. Wandrei was particularly insistent that HPL's letters be published, and he spent years editing HPL's *Selected Letters* (1965–76), even though his enlistment in the army in 1942 curtailed his literary career and his other work for Arkham House. Wandrei's literary career never resumed thereafter, largely because he needed to tend to his increasingly ailing mother and sister; he became a virtual recluse in his home in St. Paul. Arkham House published two collections of his weird tales, *The Eye and the Finger* (1944) and *Strange Harvest* (1965), and his poetry, *Poems for Midnight* (1964). Wandrei prepared texts of the last two volumes of HPL's *Selected Letters,* and, although his name does not appear as editor, it seems that his texts were largely used as the basis of the selections. After Derleth's death in 1971, Wandrei became embroiled in a bitter dispute with Derleth's successors at Arkham House and ultimately severed his relations with the firm. Following his death, his work was gathered in more thematically coherent editions: *Collected Poems* (Necronomicon Press, 1988); *Colossus* (Fedogan & Bremer, 1989), his collected science fiction tales; *Don't Dream* (Fedogan & Bremer, 1997), his collected horror and fantasy tales; and *Frost* (Fedogan & Bremer, 2000), a collection of his detective tales (others are forthcoming). The joint HPL-Wandrei correspondence has been published as *Mysteries of Time and Spirit* (Night Shade Books, 2002).

See *Studies in Weird Fiction* No. 3 (Fall 1988) (special Wandrei issue, with articles by Dennis Rickard, S. T. Joshi, Marc A. Michaud, Steve Behrends, and T. E. D. Klein); Richard L. Tierney, "Introduction" to Wandrei's *Colossus* (1989); D. H. Olson, "Afterword: Of Donald Wandrei, August Derleth and H. P. Lovecraft," in Wandrei's *Don't Dream* (1997).

Wandrei, Howard [Elmer] (1909–1956), artist and late associate of HPL (1933–37). Howard, Donald Wandrei's younger brother, had a turbulent youth, being arrested for burglary at the age of eighteen and spending three years in a reformatory. By this time, however, he had developed into a brilliant and distinctive pictorial artist, chiefly in pen-and-ink work. He illustrated Donald's book of poetry, *Dark Odyssey* (1931), and then did some illustrations for the weird and science fiction pulps. He also took to writing, publishing numerous detective, horror, and science fiction tales in the pulp magazines. HPL met Wandrei for the first time in New York on December 27, 1933, and they corresponded sporadically thereafter. HPL had a high regard for Wandrei's artwork ("he certainly has a vastly greater talent than anyone else in the gang. I was astonished at [the paintings'] sheer genius & maturity": HPL to Annie E. P. Gamwell, [December 28, 1933; ms., JHL]); later, when he read some of Wandrei's stories, he was also impressed ("I'm hang'd if I don't think the kid is, all apart

from his pictorial genius, getting to be a better *writer* than big bwuvver!": HPL
to R. H. Barlow, April 20, 1935; ms., JHL). Wandrei's weird tales have now
been collected in *Time Burial* (Fedogan & Bremer, 1995); some of his detective
tales are contained in *The Last Pin* (Fedogan & Bremer, 1996) and *The Eerie
Mr. Murphy* (Fedogan & Bremer, 2001). Other volumes are forthcoming.

Ward, Charles Dexter (1902–1928). In *The Case of Charles Dexter Ward,* the
great-great-great-grandson of Joseph Curwen. Ward's discovery of a colonial
portrait of Curwen (who is an exact double of Ward) spurs his search, beginning
in 1919, for more information about a man so despised and feared that nearly all
information about him had disappeared from the public record. Ward's quest
takes him to Europe to investigate Curwen's correspondents overseas. He unearths Curwen's papers and is able to resurrect Curwen from his "essential Saltes." But Curwen kills Ward and attempts unsuccessfully to adopt his identity.
Ward is not quite an autobiographical character, but his celebrated homecoming
from Europe parallels HPL's own joyous return to Providence shortly before the
novel was written.

Ward, Theodore Howland. In *The Case of Charles Dexter Ward,* the father of
Charles Dexter Ward. Although initially encouraging his son in the latter's discovery of various papers relating to his long-lost ancestor, Joseph Curwen, Ward
is increasingly disturbed by his son's strange behavior and asks the family doctor, Marinus Willett, to see if anything can be done to restore his son's mental
health. (Ward's wife—never named—is still more disturbed, and on Willett's
advice she is sent for a rest in Atlantic City.) Ward accompanies Willett on an
exploration of the abandoned Pawtuxet bungalow of Curwen and Ward, but the
noxious odors emerging from an underground chamber cause him to faint, so
that Willett is forced to conduct the investigation alone.

Warren, Harley. In "The Statement of Randolph Carter," the South Carolina
mystic (so identified only in "Through the Gates of the Silver Key") whose studies take him and Carter to an ancient cemetery (apparently in Florida, although
this is never explicitly stated in the story). When Warren ventures underground,
leaving Carter behind, he dies mysteriously, his death being announced from
below ground by the hideous voice of an unknown entity. In the dream that inspired the story, it was HPL's friend Samuel Loveman who went underground,
leaving HPL behind.

"Waste Paper: A Poem of Profound Insignificance." Poem (134 lines);
probably written in late 1922 or early 1923. First publication unknown; rpt.
Books at Brown 26 (1978): 48–52.
   A devastating parody of T. S. Eliot's *The Waste Land,* which, when it appeared in the *Dial* (November 1922), was billed a "poem of profound significance." It is a pendant to HPL's condemnation of Eliot's poem in the editorial
"Rudis Indigestaque Moles" (*Conservative,* March 1923), in which he declares
The Waste Land to be "a practically meaningless collection of phrases, learned
allusions, quotations, slang, and scraps in general." HPL's poem (the only one of

his poems aside from "Plaster-All" [1922] written in free verse) is similarly composed of quotations (from Pope's *Odyssey,* popular songs, etc.), self-referential allusions ("We called ourselves the Blackstone Military Band"), puns (including the pungent conclusion: "Nobody home / In the shantih," parodying Eliot's concluding "Shantih shantih shantih"), and the like. The epigraph is HPL's Greek translation of his nihilistic utterance, "All is laughter, all is dust, all is nothing" (rendered into Latin as the epigraph to the "Aletheia Phrikodes" section of "The Poe-et's Nightmare"). HPL claimed (*SL* 4.159) the poem was published in "the newspaper" (probably the [Providence] *Evening Bulletin*), but exhaustive searches in this and other Providence papers have yielded nothing.

See Barton L. St. Armand and John H. Stanley, "H. P. Lovecraft's *Waste Paper:* A Facsimile and Transcript of the Original Draft," *Books at Brown* 26 (1978): 31–47.

Webb, William Channing. In "The Call of Cthulhu," Professor of Anthropology at Princeton University. In 1860, he encounters the Cthulhu Cult in Greenland.

Weeden, Ezra. In *The Case of Charles Dexter Ward,* the second mate of the *Enterprise* who had hoped to marry Eliza Tillinghast, but who is pushed aside by the wealthy and influential Joseph Curwen. The envious Weeden undertakes an investigation of Curwen's mysterious affairs, enlisting support for a raid on Curwen's bungalow in Pawtuxet in 1771. A descendant, **Hazard Weeden,** of 598 Angell Street (HPL's own residence from 1904 to 1924), expresses shock when unidentified persons desecrate the grave of his ancestor in the North Burial Ground.

Weir, John J. (1922–1977), late correspondent of HPL (1936–37). Weir came in touch with HPL in December 1936 when he asked him for a contribution for his fan magazine, *Fantasmagoria.* HPL sent him the poem "Astrophobos," which appeared in the magazine's first issue (March 1937). Weir accepted other works by HPL (including "The Tree"), but no more issues appeared, as Weir seems to have lost his interest in weird fiction shortly after HPL's death.

Weird Tales. Pulp magazine (1923–54) in which many of HPL's stories appeared.

WT was founded in 1923 by J. C. Henneberger, who with J. M. Lansinger founded Rural Publications, Inc., in 1922 to publish a variety of popular magazines (including the successful *College Humor*). Henneberger had received promises from leading popular writers of the period—among them Hamlin Garland and Ben Hecht—that they would contribute "unconventional" stories to the new magazine; but as it happened, they did not contribute, and the only significant names to appear in the magazine (whose first issue was dated March 1923) were Vincent Starrett and such veterans of the *Argosy* and *All-Story* as Don Mark Lemon and Harold Ward. Accordingly, *WT* was, more than many other pulp magazines, open to the contributions of beginning writers.

HPL read and purchased it from its first issue, and was encouraged by numerous colleagues—Everett McNeil, James F. Morton, Clark Ashton Smith—to submit to the magazine. He did so in May 1923, sending in five stories ("Dagon," "The Statement of Randolph Carter," "The Cats of Ulthar," "Facts Concerning the Late Arthur Jermyn and His Family," and "The Hound"). Edwin Baird, the magazine's first editor, liked them all, but wished them to be double-spaced (the single-spaced typescripts survive at JHL). HPL grudgingly retyped the stories. His first published contribution to the magazine, however, was his snide cover letter accompanying the stories, published in the September 1923 issue. HPL quickly became a fixture in the magazine, appearing in most of the issues edited by Baird. The summit of his early involvement occurred in February 1924, when Henneberger commissioned him to ghostwrite "Under the Pyramids" for Harry Houdini, paying HPL $100 in advance.

Around this time HPL was offered the editorship of the magazine, but he declined. HPL has been criticized for so doing, since it would have given him a stable income at a time when, newly married, he needed one. But the job would have required his moving to Chicago, a prospect HPL did not fancy; moreover, the magazine was deeply in debt, and it might well have folded, leaving HPL stranded in Chicago and far from his wife in New York and family in Providence. In any event, Baird was dismissed in the spring of 1924 and Farnsworth Wright was appointed as interim editor, becoming the permanent editor in the fall. Wright was more idiosyncratic in his editorial criteria than Baird and was careful to offer readers what he thought they wanted; he rejected several tales by HPL ("The Shunned House," *At the Mountains of Madness,* "The Shadow over Innsmouth") because he thought them too long, not sufficiently "action"-packed, and (as with the initial rejections of "The Call of Cthulhu" and "Through the Gates of the Silver Key," later accepted) too exotically imaginative for the average reader. Wright was also concerned about the gruesomeness of some of HPL's tales (e.g., "In the Vault," "Cool Air"), even though in other senses they seemed just the sort of relatively conventional stories that Wright would have wanted. But he had been alarmed at the near-banning of *WT* in Indiana as a result of its publication of the HPL-Eddy story "The Loved Dead" (*WT,* May–June–July 1924), and from that time forward he was extremely careful not to accept stories that were too grisly. HPL was irritated and even wounded by these rejections, thinking that they reflected upon his own abilities as a creative artist. Wright, however, customarily rejected many stories with the understanding that writers would revise them and resubmit them; but HPL never did so, and those tales that were accepted after an initial rejection were accepted only because Wright asked to see them again.

Toward the end of his life HPL thought that the unconscious desire to write material suitable for *WT* had made his work too obvious and explanatory. In speaking of the rejection of a collection of his stories by Putnam's in 1931, HPL noted: "That ass Wright got me into the habit of obvious writing with his never-ending complaints against the indefiniteness of my early stuff" (*SL* 3.395–96). HPL is probably correct in this assessment. HPL was so disgusted with Wright's rejections that he himself submitted only one story ("In the Vault") to *WT* in almost five and a half years (Spring 1931–Summer 1936), although in this period others such as August Derleth submitted HPL's stories without his knowledge or permission.

HPL might have had more leverage with Wright if he could have developed a second pulp market to offset *WT. Amazing Stories* had taken "The Colour out of Space" in 1927, but it paid him only ⅕ of a cent per word for the story. (*WT* generally paid HPL 1 to 1½ cents per word, the latter being its highest rate.) He submitted several stories to *Strange Tales* (1931–33), edited by Harry Bates, but all were rejected as the magazine wanted "action" stories quite unlike HPL's average product. Carl Swanson's *Galaxy*, contemplated in 1932, never got off the ground. HPL's two late sales to *Astounding Stories* may have contributed to Wright's quick acceptance of "The Thing on the Doorstep" and "The Haunter of the Dark" in July 1936, although they were just the sort he would have liked in any case.

After HPL's death Wright accepted many HPL stories and poems that he had formerly rejected, when they were submitted by August Derleth. This policy continued with *WT*'s third and final editor, Dorothy McIlwraith, who took over in 1940. It was, however, her decision to abridge some of HPL's longer works ("The Mound" [November 1940]; *The Case of Charles Dexter Ward* [May and July 1941]; "The Shadow over Innsmouth" [January 1942]), although these had appeared or were about to appear in collections of HPL's tales published by Arkham House.

For a complete list of HPL's contributions to *WT,* see S. T. Joshi, "Lovecraft in *Weird Tales," New Lovecraft Collector* 10 (Spring 1995): 3–4. *H. P. Lovecraft in "The Eyrie,"* ed. S. T. Joshi and Marc A. Michaud (Necronomicon Press, 1979), contains letters by or about HPL in the letter column of *WT.*

See Robert Weinberg, *The Weird Tales Story* (West Linn, Ore.: FAX Collector's Editions, 1977); *Science Fiction, Fantasy, and Weird Fiction Magazines,* ed. Marshall B. Tymn and Mike Ashley (Greenwood Press, 1985); Frank H. Parnell and Mike Ashley, *Monthly Terrors* (Greenwood Press, 1985) (contains complete issue-by-issue index to *WT*).

Weiss, Henry George (1898–1946), Canadian-born poet and essayist who wrote weird and science fiction tales under the pseudonym Francis Flagg. Weiss corresponded with HPL sporadically during the period 1930–37; at this time he had communist leanings and may have contributed to HPL's gradual shift toward socialism. He wrote an HPL-influenced story, "The Distortion out of Space" (*WT,* August 1934); also a poem, "To Howard Phillips Lovecraft" (*WT,* March 1938; rpt. *Marginalia*). See also *The Night People* (1947), a science fiction novel.

West, Herbert. In "Herbert West—Reanimator," the medical student who hopes to learn the secret of reanimating the dead. The story follows his exploits through his college days and post-graduate work, to service during World War I and his own medical practice, as he comes closer and closer, but never fully succeeding, in his attempts at reanimation. Ultimately, the specimens he reanimates band together and destroy him.

"What Belongs in Verse." Essay (730 words); probably written in early 1935. First published in *Perspective Review* (Spring 1935); rpt. *MW* and *CE2.*

This important essay reflects HPL's later views on poetry, in which he is shown to have modified his earlier rigidly classicist stance; he now maintains that good poetry must be a matter of images and symbols rather than plain statement.

"What the Moon Brings." Prose poem (740 words); written on June 5, 1922. First published in the *National Amateur* (May 1923); first collected in *BWS;* corrected text in *MW.*

The narrator professes at the outset, "I hate the moon—I am afraid of it" because he once saw the moon shining on an old garden near a shallow stream. Various strange sights greet the narrator's eye, including dead faces in the river. Then the waters ebb, and the narrator sees an appalling sight: the vast basalt crown of a "shocking eikon" whose forehead was beginning to appear from under the waves, and whose feet must be an incalculable distance below. The narrator flees in terror.

The vignette suffers from vagueness and from a certain hysterical tone that makes the entire work seem flamboyant and unmotivated.

Whateley, Wilbur (1913–1928). In "The Dunwich Horror," the more human of the twin offspring of Lavinia Whateley and Yog-Sothoth. Old Whateley indoctrinates the precocious but abnormally mature boy in esoteric study. He is slain by a watchdog when trying to steal a copy of the *Necronomicon* from the library of Miskatonic University. **Lavinia Whateley (c. 1878–1926)** is the deformed albino mother of Wilbur and his alien fraternal twin. **Old Whateley** is the aged wizard who is Lavinia's father and Wilbur's grandfather. The relationship of these three characters is somewhat of a parody of that of HPL, his mother (no albino, but noted for her queer behavior), and his maternal grandfather, Whipple V. Phillips, who was HPL's surrogate father until he died. When their respective grandfathers died, Wilbur and HPL were both about fourteen years of age. Other members of the Whateley family include: **Curtis Whateley,** son of Zechariah Whateley, who looks through a telescope and sees Wilbur's monstrous twin brother; **Mrs. Whateley,** Old Whateley's wife, who died under mysterious circumstances when Lavinia was twelve; **Squire Sawyer Whateley,** chairman of the local draft board who in 1917 had difficulty finding enough young Dunwich men fit to send to a development camp; **Zebulon Whateley,** "of a branch that hovered about half way between soundness and decadence," who receives a frantic telephone call from George Corey's wife about the ravages of Wilbur's twin brother; and **Zechariah Whateley,** who brings Old Whateley some cows that the latter had purchased from his son Curtis.

Wheeler, Arthur. In "The Man of Stone," a sculptor who is turned to stone by Daniel Morris when Morris suspects him of making designs on his wife.

Wheeler, Henry. In "The Dunwich Horror," one of the party that exterminates Wilbur Whateley's monstrous twin brother.

Whipple, Dr. Elihu. In "The Shunned House," a physician, antiquarian, and uncle of the story's narrator. He shares his research of the history of the Shunned House with his nephew, and the two eventually attempt to determine the source of the house's notoriety. In so doing, they encounter the monstrous entity that inhabits the house and which overwhelms the elderly doctor.

"Whisperer in Darkness, The." Novelette (26,700 words); written February 24–September 26, 1930. First published in *WT* (August 1931); first collected in *O;* corrected text in *DH;* annotated version in *CC.*

The Vermont floods of November 3, 1927, cause great destruction in the rural parts of the state and also engender reports of strange bodies—not recognizably human or animal—floating down the flood-choked rivers. Albert N. Wilmarth, a professor of literature at Miskatonic University with an interest in folklore, dismisses these accounts as standard myth-making; but then he hears from a reclusive but evidently learned individual in Vermont, Henry Wentworth Akeley, who not only confirms the reports but also maintains there is an entire colony of extraterrestrials dwelling in the region, whose purpose is to mine a metal they cannot find on their own planet (which may be the recently discovered ninth planet of the solar system, called Yuggoth in various occult writings) and also, by means of a complicated mechanical device, to remove the brains of human beings from their bodies and to take them on fantastic cosmic voyagings. Wilmarth is skeptical of Akeley's tale, but the latter sends him photographs of a hideous black stone with inexplicable hieroglyphs on it along with a phonograph recording he made of some sort of ritual in the woods near his home—a ritual in which both humans and (judging from the bizarre buzzing voice) some utterly nonhuman creatures participated. As their correspondence continues, Wilmarth slowly becomes convinced of the truth of Akeley's claims—and is both wholly convinced and increasingly alarmed as some of their letters go unaccountably astray and Akeley finds himself embroiled in a battle with guns and dogs as the aliens besiege his house.

Then, in a startling reversal, Akeley sends him a reassuring letter stating that he has come to terms with the aliens: he had misinterpreted their motives and now believes that they are merely trying to establish a workable rapport with human beings for mutual benefit. He is reconciled to the prospect of his brain being removed and taken to Yuggoth and beyond, for he will thereby acquire cosmic knowledge made available only to a handful of human beings since the beginning of civilization. He urges Wilmarth to visit him to discuss the matter, reminding him to bring all the papers and other materials he had sent so that they can be consulted if necessary. Wilmarth agrees, taking a spectral journey into the heart of the Vermont backwoods and meeting with Akeley, who has suffered some inexplicable malady: he can only speak in a whisper, and he is wrapped from head to foot with a blanket except for his face and hands. He tells Wilmarth wondrous tales of traveling faster than the speed of light and of the strange machines in the room used to transport brains through the cosmos. Numbed with astonishment, Wilmarth retires to bed, but hears a disturbing colloquy in Akeley's room with several of the buzzing voices and other, human voices. But what makes him flee from the place is a very simple thing he sees as he sneaks down to Akeley's room late at night: "For the things in the chair, perfect to the last, subtle detail of microscopic resemblance—or identity—were the face and hands of Henry Wentworth Akeley."

Without the necessity of stating it, HPL makes clear the true state of affairs: the last, reassuring letter by "Akeley" was in fact a forgery by the alien entities, written as a means of getting Wilmarth to come up to Vermont with all the evidence of his relations with Akeley; the speaker in the chair was not Akeley— whose brain had been removed from his body and placed in one of the machines—but one of the aliens, perhaps Nyarlathotep himself, whom they worship. The attempted "rapport" that the aliens claim to desire with human beings is a sham, and they in fact wish to enslave the human race; hence Wilmarth must write his account to warn the world of this lurking menace.

There are numerous autobiographical details in the story. HPL knew of the Vermont floods of 1927, as they were extensively reported in newspapers across the East Coast. More generally, the Vermont background of the tale is clearly derived from HPL's visits to the state in 1927 and 1928; whole passages of the essay "Vermont—A First Impression" (1927) appear in the text but subtly altered so as to emphasize both the terror and the fascination of the rustic landscape. Wilmarth's ride into Vermont in a Ford car duplicates the ride HPL took to Vrest Orton's farm in 1928: "We were met [in Brattleboro] with a Ford, owned by a neighbour, & hurried out of all earthly reality amongst the vivid hills & mystic winding roads of a land unchanged for a century" (HPL to Lillian D. Clark, [June 12, 1928]; ms., JHL). Henry Wentworth Akeley is based in part on the rustic Bert G. Akley whom HPL met on this trip. Akeley's secluded farmhouse seems to be based on both the Orton residence in Brattleboro and Arthur Goodenough's home farther north. There is a mention of "The Pendrifter" (the columnist for the *Brattleboro Reformer*) early in the story, and the later mention of "Lee's Swamp" is a nod to the Lee boys who were Orton's neighbors.

Steven J. Mariconda has discussed in detail the particularly difficult genesis of the tale. As the manuscript states, it was "provisionally finished" in Charleston, South Carolina, on May 7, 1930, but underwent significant revision thereafter. HPL first took it to New York, where he read it to Frank Belknap Long. In his 1944 memoir, Long speaks of the matter; although parts of his account clearly are erroneous, there is perhaps a kernel of truth in his recollection of one point: "Howard's voice becoming suddenly sepulchral: 'And from the box a tortured voice spoke: "Go while there is still time—"'" ("Some Random Memories of H. P. L.," *Marginalia*, p. 336). HPL then went to Kingston to visit Bernard Austin Dwyer and read him the story as well. In a letter HPL states: "My 'Whisperer in Darkness' has retrogressed to the constructional stage as a result of some extremely sound & penetrating criticism on Dwyer's part. I shall not try to tinker with it during the residue of this trip, but shall make it the first item of work on my programme after I get home—which will no doubt be in less than a week now. There will be considerable condensation throughout, & a great deal of subtilisation at the end" (HPL to August Derleth, June 7, 1930; ms., SHSW). It appears that at least one point on which Dwyer suggested revision is this warning to Wilmarth (presumably by Akeley's brain from one of the canisters), which is so obvious that it would dilute the purported "surprise" ending of the story (if indeed the story in this version ended as it did). It also appears that Dwyer recommended that Wilmarth be made to seem less gullible, but HPL did not much succeed in this area. Although he apparently inserted random details to heighten Wilmarth's skepticism, especially in regard to the obviously forged final letter by "Akeley," Wilmarth still seems very naive in proceeding blithely to Vermont despite all the documentary evidence he has received from Akeley.

It cannot be said that the discovery of Pluto inspired the writing of the tale. C. W. Tombaugh had discovered the planet on February 18, 1930, after ten months of searching, but it was first announced on the front page of the *New York Times* only on March 14, to coincide with the 147th anniversary of the discovery of Uranus and the seventy-fifth anniversary of the birth of Percival Lowell, who had himself searched for a trans-Neptunian planet. HPL was tremendously captivated by the discovery: the day after its announcement he writes, "Whatcha thinka the NEW PLANET? HOT STUFF!!! It is probably Yuggoth" (HPL to James F. Morton, [March 15, 1930]; AHT).

One point of controversy is the possibility that the false Akeley is not merely one of the fungi but is in fact Nyarlathotep himself. The evidence comes chiefly from the phonograph recording of the ritual in the woods made by Akeley, in which one of the fungi at one point declares, "To Nyarlathotep, Mighty Messenger, must all things be told. And He shall put on the semblance of men, the waxen mask and the robe that hides, and come down from the world of Seven Suns to mock. . . ." This seems a clear allusion to Nyarlathotep disguised with Akeley's face and hands; but if so, it means that at this time he actually *is,* in bodily form, one of the fungi—especially if, as seems likely, Nyarlathotep is one of the two buzzing voices Wilmarth overhears at the end (the one who "held an unmistakable note of authority"). There are, however, problems with this identification. Nyarlathotep has been regarded by some critics as a shapeshifter, but only because he appears in various stories in widely different forms—as an Egyptian pharaoh in the prose poem of 1920 and *The Dream-Quest of Unknown Kadath,* here as an extraterrestrial entity, as the "Black Man" in "The Dreams in the Witch House" (1932), and so on; his "avatar" appears as a winged entity in "The Haunter of the Dark" (1935). But if Nyarlathotep were a true shapeshifter, why would he don the face and hands of Akeley instead of merely reshaping himself as Akeley?

The story was readily accepted by Farnsworth Wright, who paid HPL $350 for it—the largest amount he ever received for a single work of fiction. Wright planned to run it as a two-part serial, but early in 1931 *WT* was forced into bimonthly publication for about half a year, so that the story appeared complete in the August 1931 issue.

See Fritz Leiber, "The Whisperer Re-examined," *Haunted* 2, No. 2 (December 1964): 22–25 (rpt. *The Book of Fritz Leiber* [New York: DAW, 1974]); Alan S. Wheelock, "Dark Mountain: H. P. Lovecraft and the 'Vermont Horror,'" *Vermont History* 45 (1977): 221–28; Donald R. Burleson, "Humour Beneath Horror: Some Sources for 'The Dunwich Horror' and 'The Whisperer in Darkness,'" *LS* No. 2 (Spring 1980): 5–15; Darrell Schweitzer, "About 'The Whisperer in Darkness,'" *LS* No. 32 (Spring 1995): 8–11; Steven J. Mariconda, "Tightening the Coil: The Revision of 'The Whisperer in Darkness,'" *LS* No. 32 (Spring 1995): 12–17; Robert M. Price, "The Pseudo-Akeley: A Tale of Two Brothers," *Crypt* No. 97 (Hallowmas 1997): 3–5.

White, Ann. In "The Shunned House," a woman from North Kingstown, R.I., who is hired by Mercy Dexter to be a servant at the house around 1770. She begins spreading rumors about the sinister abode and is later dismissed.

White, Lee McBride, Jr. (1915–1989), correspondent of HPL (1932–37). White spent most of his youth in Birmingham, Ala.; he appears to have contacted HPL through *WT.* His chief interest was not in the weird but in Metaphysical poetry, specifically John Donne. White attended Howard College (now Samford University) in Birmingham, graduating in 1937; he worked on school publications there, sending some of them to HPL. After HPL's death White did graduate work at Harvard and Columbia, returned to Alabama and became a journalist, served in the air force during World War II, and later worked for the Communications Workers of America. He edited *The American Revolution in Notes, Quotes, and Anecdotes* (1975) for the U.S. Bicentennial.

"White Ship, The." Short story (2,550 words); probably written in October 1919. First published in the *United Amateur* (November 1919); rpt. *WT* (March 1927); first collected in *BWS;* corrected text in *D;* annotated version in *TD.*

Basil Elton, "keeper of the North Point light," one day "walk[s] out over the waters . . . on a bridge of moonbeams" to a White Ship that has come from the South, captained by an aged bearded man. They sail to various fantastic realms: the Land of Zar, "where dwell all the dreams and thoughts of beauty that come to men once and then are forgotten"; the Land of Thalarion, "the City of a Thousand Wonders, wherein reside all those mysteries that man has striven in vain to fathom"; Xura, "the Land of Pleasures Unattained"; and finally Sona-Nyl, in which "there is neither time nor space, neither suffering nor death." Although Elton spends "many aeons" there in evident contentment, he gradually finds himself yearning for the realm of Cathuria, the Land of Hope, beyond the basalt pillars of the West, which he believes to be an even more wondrous realm than Sona-Nyl. The captain warns him against pursuing Cathuria, but Elton is adamant and compels the captain to launch his ship once more. But they discover that beyond the basalt pillars of the West is only a "monstrous cataract, wherein the oceans of the world drop down to abysmal nothingness." As their ship is destroyed, Elton finds himself on the platform of his lighthouse. The White Ship comes to him no more.

The plot of the story clearly derives from Dunsany's "Idle Days on the Yann" (in *A Dreamer's Tales,* 1910), but there the resemblance ends, for Dunsany's tale tells only of a dream-voyage by a man who boards a ship, the *Bird of the River,* and encounters one magical land after another; there is no significant philosophical content in these realms, and their principal function is merely an evocation of fantastic beauty. HPL's tale is meant to be interpreted allegorically or symbolically and as such enunciates several central tenets of his philosophical thought, principally the folly of abandoning the Epicurean goal of *ataraxia,* tranquillity (interpreted as the absence of pain), embodied in the land of Sona-Nyl. By forsaking it Basil Elton brings upon his head a justified doom—not death, but sadness and discontent.

After the story's first publication, Alfred Galpin, chairman of the Department of Public Criticism of the UAPA, gave it a warm reception (see "Department of Public Criticism," *United Amateur,* March 1920). See also Dirk W. Mosig, "'The White Ship': A Psychic Odyssey," *Whispers* (November 1974) (rpt. *FDOC*); Paul Montelone, "'The White Ship': A Schopenhauerian Odyssey," *LS* No. 36 (Spring 1997): 2–14.

Whitehead, Henry S[t. Clair] (1882–1932), American author of weird tales and friend of HPL (1931–32). HPL reports ("In Memoriam: Henry St. Clair Whitehead") that Whitehead, a New Jersey native, graduated from Harvard in 1904; this is false, although Whitehead did study at Harvard and Columbia. HPL also notes that he later received a Ph.D.; this also appears to be false, although Whitehead earned an M.A. from Ewing College in Illinois. He also became an Anglican priest. From 1921 to 1929 Whitehead served as Acting Archdeacon in the Virgin Islands, thereby absorbing a fund of native lore (especially regarding zombies, jumbees, and other legendary entities) for his weird tales. Whitehead published voluminously in *WT, Strange Tales, Adventure,* and other pulps; his tales, although on the whole unadventurous in conception, are written with elegance and occasional emotive power. They were posthumously collected in two volumes published by Arkham House: *Jumbee and Other Uncanny Tales* (1944) and *West India Lights* (1946).

HPL visited Whitehead in Dunedin, Fla., from May 21 to June 10, 1931. Among HPL's activities then was an impromptu narration of the plot of "The Cats of Ulthar" to a boys' club organized by Whitehead. At this time or a few months later, HPL assisted Whitehead on the revision of his story, "The Trap"; as revised, the story is perhaps one-half to three-fourths by HPL, but it was published only under Whitehead's byline in *Strange Tales* (March 1932). Later that year HPL apparently allowed Whitehead to use a plot-germ from his commonplace book (entry #133, about a man with a miniature Siamese twin); Whitehead wrote up the idea as "Cassius" (*Strange Tales,* November 1931), but HPL later admitted that his development of the idea would have been very different from Whitehead's (see *SL* 5.33–35). In the spring and summer of 1932 HPL appears to have assisted Whitehead on another story, apparently titled "The Bruise." This story (about a man who experiences strange visions after receiving a blow to the head) had been rejected by *Strange Tales* as too tame, and HPL devised an elaborate plot involving the man's access to hereditary memory, so that he sees in his mind his distant ancestor's experience of the destruction of the Pacific continent of Mu 20,000 years ago. HPL was unsure whether Whitehead had managed to finish the story prior to his death on November 23, 1932. A story in *West India Lights* entitled "Bothon" (published simultaneously in *Amazing Stories,* August 1946) is the story in question. From internal evidence, there appears to be no prose by HPL in the tale, but it may well have been based upon what seems to be a detailed synopsis by HPL. A. Langley Searles has conjectured that August Derleth in fact wrote the story from HPL's synopsis and published it under Whitehead's byline.

In 1932 R. H. Barlow planned a very limited edition of Whitehead's letters, to be entitled *Caneviniana,* but never progressed beyond the setting of a few pages in type. HPL's letters to Whitehead were apparently destroyed (see Barlow's introduction to *Jumbee*). No letters by Whitehead to HPL survive. HPL's "In Memoriam: Henry St. Clair Whitehead" was a brief obituary that appeared in *WT* (March 1933). HPL notes that editor Farnsworth Wright used only about a quarter of what HPL had written (see HPL to R. H. Barlow, April 9, 1933; ms., JHL); however, the full version of this essay is probably similar to a lengthy letter by HPL to E. Hoffmann Price, December 7, 1932 (ms., JHL; printed in part in *SL* 4.116–17), written a few weeks after Whitehead's death.

See R. Alain Everts, *Henry St. Clair Whitehead* (Strange Co., 1975); A. Langley Searles, "Fantasy and Outré Themes in the Short Fiction of Edward Lucas White and Henry S. Whitehead," in *American Supernatural Fiction*, ed. Douglas Robillard (New York: Garland, 1996), pp. 59–76.

Wilcox, Henry Anthony. In "The Call of Cthulhu," the young artist who fashions, following a dream, a strange bas-relief resembling idols worshipped by members of the Cthulhu Cult.

Willett, Dr. Marinus Bicknell. In *The Case of Charles Dexter Ward*, the Ward family's doctor. When Ward realizes his error in revivifying Joseph Curwen, he enlists Bicknell's help to destroy Curwen, but too late to save his own life. HPL had conceived his novel as a work of detective fiction, and Willett is his detective. Willett solves the mystery of Curwen's resurrection and destroys him.

Williams, ———. In "The Descendant," a young man who presents to Lord Northam a copy of the *Necronomicon*. He had "known of the dreaded volume since his sixteenth year."

Williamson, James. In "The Shadow over Innsmouth," the uncle of Robert Olmstead, brother of **Douglas** (who commited suicide when he learned the family secret), and father of **Lawrence** (who is confined to a sanitarium). When he shows Olmstead various family artifacts, Olmstead cannot help but conclude that he, like his cousin Lawrence, is of tainted Innsmouth ancestry.

Willis, John. In "The Mound," a government marshal who went into the mound region of Oklahoma in 1892 and came back with bizarre tales of supernatural entities in the area.

Wilmarth, Albert N. In "The Whisperer in Darkness," a professor of literature at Miskatonic University whose interest in folklore impels him to investigate reports about alien creatures observed in the Vermont River following the floods of 1927.

Wilson, Dr. In "The Shadow out of Time," the doctor who attends Nathaniel Wingate Peaslee following the abrupt cessation of his "amnesia" on September 27, 1913.

"Winged Death." Novelette (10,070 words); ghostwritten for Hazel Heald, probably in the summer of 1932. First published in *WT* (March 1934); first collected in *Marginalia;* corrected text in *HM*.

A scientist, Thomas Slauenwite, discovers a rare insect in South Africa whose bite is fatal unless treated with a certain drug; the natives call the insect the "devil-fly" because after killing its victim it purportedly takes over the deceased's soul or personality. Slauenwite kills a rival scientist, Henry Moore, with this insect, but is later haunted by an insect that seems uncannily to bear tokens of Moore's personality. Slauenwite is killed (by heart failure induced by fright, not by the bite of an insect), his soul enters the body of the insect, and he writes a message on the ceiling of his room by dipping his insect body in ink and walking across the ceiling. His diary is found in his hotel room by puzzled policemen and medical examiners.

HPL discusses the story in a letter that probably dates to summer 1932: "Something odd befell a client of mine the other day—involving a story-element which *I* had intended & introduced under the impression that it was strictly original with me. The tale was sent to Handsome Harry [Bates], & he rejected it on the ground that the element in question (the act of an insect dipping itself in ink & writing on a white surface with its own body) formed the crux of another tale which he *had* accepted. Hell's bells!—& I thought I'd hit on an idea of absolute novelty & uniqueness!" (HPL to August Derleth, [August 1932]; ms., SHSW). The interesting thing about this is that the tale had thus been submitted to *Strange Tales,* edited by Harry Bates. It is plausible that the earlier Heald tales were written with this better-paying market in view (the magazine folded after the January 1933 issue). After its appearance in *WT,* HPL wrote: "'Winged Death' is nothing to run a temperature over. . . . My share in it is something like 90 to 95%" (*SL* 4.403).

"Wisdom." Poem (49 lines); probably written in the fall of 1919. First published in the *Silver Clarion* (November 1919); rpt. *National Enquirer* (December 4, 1919).

The poem's subtitle declares: "The 28th or 'Gold-Miner's Chapter of Job, paraphrased from a literal translation of the original Hebrew text, supplied by Dr. S. Hall Young." If this seems an odd poem for the atheist HPL to write, we should remember that the *Silver Clarion,* an amateur paper edited by John Milton Samples, was, in HPL's words, "an able and consistent exponent of that literary mildness and wholesomeness which in the professional world are exemplified by *The Youth's Companion* and the better grade of religious publications" (HPL, "Comment," *Silver Clarion,* June 1918).

Wolejko, Anastasia. In "The Dreams in the Witch House," a "clod-like laundry worker" in Arkham whose two-year-old child, **Ladislas Wolejko,** vanishes and is later killed by Brown Jenkin.

Wollheim, Donald A[llen] (1914–1990), science fiction fan and editor, and correspondent of HPL (1935–37). In 1935 Wollheim took over a magazine previously edited by Wilson Shepherd and renamed it *The Phantagraph;* he asked HPL to contribute, and HPL sent several poems as well as the essays "Robert Ervin Howard: 1906–1936" (August 1936) and "The Weird Work of William Hope Hodgson" (February 1937). A letter to Duane W. Rimel (September 28,

1935) appeared anonymously as "What's the Trouble with Weird Fiction?" (February 1937). Wollheim also coedited, with Shepherd, one issue of *Fanciful Tales* (Fall 1936), containing HPL's "The Nameless City," which was marred by numerous typographical errors. Wollheim continued to publish HPL's work in *The Phantagraph* after his death. Wollheim later became a distinguished science fiction and fantasy editor (*The Portable Novels of Science* [1945]; *Avon Fantasy Reader* [1947–52; 18 volumes]; *Terror in the Modern Vein* [1955]) and author of numerous science fiction tales for young adults.

Wooley, Natalie H[artley], poet and correspondent of HPL (1933–37). Wooley published poetry widely in amateur journals in the 1930s. She was, with Maurice W. Moe, John Adams, and HPL, a member of a round-robin correspondence circle, the Coryciani, mainly devoted to the criticism of poetry.

World War I. HPL joined amateur journalism in April 1914, just four months before the outbreak of World War I. He wasted little time in writing of the conflict. In the first issue of the *Conservative* (April 1915), he wrote the controversial essay "The Crime of the Century," which asserted that the war was a shameful battle of "blood brothers"—the British and the Germans, the two great branches of the Teutonic race—and that it might lead to "the self-decimation of the one mighty branch of humanity on which the future welfare of the world depends." HPL vigorously condemned American neutrality during the first three years of the war, claiming that the nation ought to align itself to its natural ally, England (see "Old England and the 'Hyphen,'" *Conservative,* October 1916). HPL also took note of a side issue of the war—the Irish rebellion of 1916. He discusses it in the letters to the Irish-American John T. Dunn and also in the satirical poem "Ye Ballade of Patrick von Flynn" (*Conservative,* April 1916).

But HPL felt more inclined to express his views of the war in verse. He wrote numerous poems on various aspects of the war, including a condemnation of the sinking of the *Lusitania* ("The Crime of Crimes," *Interesting Items,* July 1915); tributes to England ("An American to Mother England," *Poesy,* July 1916; "The Rose of England," *Scot,* October 1916; "Britannia Victura," *Inspiration,* April 1917; "An American to the British Flag," *Little Budget of Knowledge and Nonsense,* November 1917; "Ad Britannos—1918," *Tryout,* April 1918); paeans to the uniting of America and England to battle the Germans in 1917 ("Iterum Conjunctae," *Tryout,* May 1917; "The Link," *Tryout,* July 1918); attacks on Germany ("1914," *Interesting Items,* March 1915; "Germania—1918," *Tryout,* November 1918); a patriotic ode ("Ode for July Fourth, 1917," *United Amateur,* July 1917); attacks on pacifism ("The Beauties of Peace," [Providence] *Evening News,* June 27, 1916; "Pacifist War Song—1917," *Tryout,* March 1917; "The Peace Advocate," *Tryout,* May 1917); a tribute to the American poet Alan Seeger, who died in battle ("To Alan Seeger," *Tryout,* July 1918); and poems on volunteers and conscripts, respectively ("The Volunteer," [Providence] *Evening News,* February 1, 1918; "The Conscript" [unpublished in HPL's lifetime]). But HPL's finest war poem is the moving ode "On a Battlefield in Picardy," *National Enquirer,* May 30, 1918 (rpt. *Voice from the Mountains,* July 1918, as "On a Battlefield in France").

HPL's most dramatic action during the war was to enlist in the R.I. National Guard in early May 1917, a short time before President Wilson's signing of the draft bill on May 18, 1917 (see *SL* 1.45–49). Although he passed his initial physical examination, he was prevented from joining the National Guard by his mother, who had HPL's physician declare him physically unfit to serve. (HPL would not have gone overseas had he remained a member of the National Guard; probably he would have been stationed at Fort Standish in Boston.) In December HPL registered for the draft, as he was legally obliged to do; he was declared "totally and permanently unfit" (see *SL* 1.52).

After the war HPL participated in the "Red Scare" in the brief but intemperate article "Bolshevism" (*Conservative*, July 1919); he also expressed cynical doubts as to the efficacy of the League of Nations in "The League" (*Conservative*, July 1919). But the end of the war, and the nation's subsequent lack of foreign threats, allowed HPL to develop his political theories at greater leisure (see "Nietzscheism and Realism," *Rainbow*, October 1921). HPL's writings on the war cannot be said to be notably acute, but they at least refute the notion that he was an "eccentric recluse" who had no interest in the political, social, and cultural events of his time.

World War I enters fleetingly but provocatively into HPL's fiction. "Dagon" (1917) was written a few months after American entry into the war and is set in the war-torn Pacific. "The Temple" (1920) purports to be the account of a German commander of a U-boat. The fifth segment of "Herbert West—Reanimator" (1921–22) is set in Flanders, as West and the narrator are, in 1915, among "the many Americans to precede the [U.S.] government itself into the gigantic struggle." Thurber, the narrator of "Pickman's Model" (1926), adduces his war experience as testimony to his physical and mental toughness; an electrical repairman in "Cool Air" (1926) is terrified at the sight of Dr. Muñoz, even though he "had been through the terrors of the Great War without having incurred any fright so thorough." In "The Silver Key" (1926) Randolph Carter is said to have "served from the first in the Foreign Legion of France." Because he has doubled back upon his own time-line, Carter, in 1897, pales at the mention of the French town of Belloy-en-Santerre, where he was almost mortally wounded in 1916. (The town is where the poet Alan Seeger was killed.) Most intriguingly, Peaslee in "The Shadow out of Time" (1934–35), after being a captive mind of the Great Race and learning the secrets of the universe both past and future, finds that "The war gave me strange impressions of *remembering* some of its far-off *consequences*—as if I knew how it was coming out and could look *back* upon it in the light of future information."

Wright, Farnsworth (1888–1940), editor of *WT*. Wright took editorship of the magazine in early 1924, replacing Edwin Baird. He had served in World War I and was music critic for the *Chicago Herald and Examiner,* continuing in this capacity for a time even while editing *WT*. By early 1921 he had contracted Parkinson's disease, and by around 1930 he was incapable of signing his letters; ultimately it would prove fatal. Wright was compelled to balance the interests of the magazine's readers (most of whom were relatively unsophisticated and ill-educated) with the search for quality; HPL tended to feel that he was unduly influenced by the readers who wrote to the magazine's letter column, "The Eyrie." Wright published a vast amount of rubbish in *WT* but managed to keep *WT* afloat through the Depression, when many other pulp magazines (notably the rival *Strange Tales* [1931–33]) failed.

Wright did not get off on the right foot with HPL by rejecting "The Shunned House" when it was submitted to him in 1925; it was HPL's first rejection by the magazine, as Edwin Baird previously had accepted everything HPL had submitted. Thereafter Wright tended to accept HPL's more conventional tales and to reject his more aesthetically challenging ones. He was also greatly concerned about censorship: the May–June–July 1924 issue had almost been banned in Indiana because of the gruesomeness of the HPL–Eddy story "The Loved Dead," and Wright (according to HPL) was in terror of a repeat of such an incident; accordingly, he rejected HPL's "In the Vault" and "Cool Air" on the grounds that they were too grisly. Wright also rejected several of HPL's Dunsanian fantasies. Wright appeared to wish HPL to be more explicit in the matter of the causes of his supernatural phenomena; HPL felt that this repeated plea had a deleterious effect on his later work by making it too obvious and explanatory.

In late 1926 Wright proposed a collection of HPL's stories, to be part of a series of books issued by *WT*. In a long letter to Wright (December 22, 1927; AHT), HPL outlined a proposed table of contents for the book (which he wished to call *The Outsider and Other Stories* because "I consider the touch of cosmic *outsideness*—of dim, shadowy *non-terrestrial* hints—to be the characteristic feature of my writing"): the "*indispensable* nucleus" would be "The Outsider," "Arthur Jermyn," "The Rats in the Walls," "The Picture in the House," "Pickman's Model," "The Music of Erich Zann," "Dagon," "The Statement of Randolph Carter," and "The Cats of Ulthar"; to be augmented by one of the following—"The Call of Cthulhu," "The Horror at Red Hook," or "The Colour out of Space." But the Popular Fiction Publishing Company's first book, *The Moon Terror* by A. G. Birch and others, sold so poorly that plans to issue further volumes were dropped.

In 1931 Wright gravely offended HPL by rejecting *At the Mountains of Madness*, which HPL considered his most ambitious work. Although HPL felt the short novel was suited for serialization by simply dividing after Chapter 6, Wright felt that it was "'too long,' 'not easily divisible into parts,' 'not convincing'—& so on" (*SL* 3.395). For the next five and a half years HPL submitted only one story to *WT*, even though Wright repeated asked him to do so and reprinted several earlier tales. (August Derleth submitted "The Shadow over Innsmouth" in 1933 and "The Dreams in the Witch House" in 1934 without HPL's knowledge or permission; the former was rejected, the latter accepted.) In 1932 Wright further angered HPL by urging him not to deal with Carl Swanson, who was attempting to form a magazine, *Galaxy*, that Wright regarded as a potential rival to *WT*. HPL grudgingly submitted "The Thing on the Doorstep" and "The Haunter of the Dark" to Wright in the autumn of 1936; they were promptly accepted. After HPL's death Wright published many of HPL's stories that he had previously rejected. He edited *WT* until his death, when Dorothy McIlwraith took the helm.

See E. Hoffmann Price, "Farnsworth Wright," *Ghost* (July 1944); rpt. *Anubis* No. 3 (1968); rpt. *Etchings and Odysseys* No. 3 (1983); in Price's *The Book of the Dead* (Arkham House, 2001).

Y

"Year Off, A." Poem (44 lines in quatrains); written on July 24, 1925. First published in *BWS*.

HPL imagines voyaging to various exotic lands, but then decides that his imaginative journey was sufficient and that he need not actually travel anywhere. The poem was written for a Blue Pencil Club meeting in which amateurs were asked to prepare literary contributions on a stated theme.

Z

Zamacona y Nuñez, Panfilo de. In "The Mound," a member of Coronado's expedition who leaves the party and goes on to explore the mound region of Oklahoma, hoping to find Xinaián, a legendary underground realm of great wealth. An Indian guide leads him there, but he is soon enslaved by the inhabitants; his later attempt to escape from them is unsuccessful. His narrative of his adventures, discovered by the narrator, constitutes the body of the story.

Zann, Erich. In "The Music of Erich Zann," the mute, possessed composer and cellist who is the subject of the story. His garret room does not overlook the streets of Paris, but "the blackness of space illimitable," the apparent inspiration for his weird music.

Zimmer, ———. In "The Temple," a seaman on the German submarine U-29 who apparently commits suicide to escape the horrors he thinks are besetting his vessel.

General Bibliography

PRIMARY SOURCES

The Ancient Track: Complete Poetical Works. Edited by S. T. Joshi. San Francisco: Night Shade Books, 2001.

The Annotated H. P. Lovecraft. Edited by S. T. Joshi. New York: Dell, 1997.

The Annotated Supernatural Horror in Literature. Edited by S. T. Joshi. New York: Hippocampus Press, 2000.

At the Mountains of Madness and Other Novels. Selected by August Derleth; Texts Edited by S. T. Joshi. Sauk City, Wis.: Arkham House, 1985.

Beyond the Wall of Sleep. Collected by August Derleth and Donald Wandrei. Sauk City, Wis.: Arkham House, 1943.

The Call of Cthulhu and Other Weird Stories. Edited by S. T. Joshi. New York: Penguin, 1999.

Collected Essays. Edited by S. T. Joshi. New York: Hippocampus Press, 2004–06. 5 vols.

Commonplace Book. Edited and annotated by David E. Schultz. West Warwick, R.I.: Necronomicon Press, 1987. 2 vols.

Dagon and Other Macabre Tales. Selected by August Derleth; Texts Edited by S. T. Joshi. Sauk City, Wis.: Arkham House, 1986.

The Dreams in the Witch House and Other Weird Stories. Edited by S. T. Joshi. New York: Penguin, 2004.

The Dunwich Horror and Others. Selected by August Derleth; Texts Edited by S. T. Joshi. Sauk City, Wis.: Arkham House, 1984.

From the Pest Zone: The New York Stories. Edited by S. T. Joshi and David E. Schultz. New York: Hippocampus Press, 2002.

The Horror in the Museum and Other Revisions. Edited by S. T. Joshi. Sauk City, Wis.: Arkham House, 1989.

Letters from New York. Edited by S. T. Joshi and David E. Schultz. San Francisco: Night Shade Books, 2004.

Letters to Alfred Galpin. Edited by S. T. Joshi and David E. Schultz. New York: Hippocampus Press, 2003.

Lord of a Visible World: An Autobiography in Letters. Edited by S. T. Joshi and David E. Schultz. Athens, Ohio: Ohio University Press, 2000.
Lovecraft at Last (with Willis Conover). Arlington, Va.: Carrollton-Clark, 1975; rpt. New York: Cooper Square Press, 2002.
Marginalia. Edited by August Derleth and Donald Wandrei. Sauk City, Wis.: Arkham House, 1944.
Miscellaneous Writings. Edited by S. T. Joshi. Sauk City, Wis.: Arkham House, 1995.
More Annotated H. P. Lovecraft. Edited by S. T. Joshi and Peter Cannon. New York: Dell, 1999.
Mysteries of Time and Spirit: Letters of H. P.Lovecraft and Donald Wandrei. Edited by S. T. Joshi and David E. Schultz. San Francisco: Night Shade Books, 2002.
The Outsider and Others. Collected by August Derleth and Donald Wandrei. Sauk City, Wis.: Arkham House, 1939.
Selected Letters. Edited by August Derleth, Donald Wandrei, and James Turner. Sauk City, Wis.: Arkham House, 1965–76. 5 vols.
The Shadow out of Time. Edited by S. T. Joshi and David E. Schultz. New York: Hippocampus Press, 2001.
The Shadow over Innsmouth. Edited by S. T. Joshi and David E. Schultz. West Warwick, R.I.: Necronomicon Press, 1994 (rev. 1997).
The Shuttered Room and Other Pieces. Edited by August Derleth. Sauk City, Wis.: Arkham House, 1959.
Something about Cats and Other Pieces. Edited by August Derleth. Sauk City, Wis.: Arkham House, 1949.
Tales of H. P. Lovecraft. Edited by Joyce Carol Oates. Hopewell, N.J.: Ecco Press, 1997.
The Thing on the Doorstep and Other Weird Stories. Edited by S. T. Joshi. New York: Penguin, 2001.
To Quebec and the Stars. Edited by L. Sprague de Camp. West Kingston, R.I.: Donald M. Grant, 1976.
Uncollected Letters. Edited by S. T. Joshi. West Warwick, R.I.: Necronomicon Press, 1986.
Uncollected Prose and Poetry. Edited by S. T. Joshi and Marc A. Michaud. West Warwick, R.I.: Necronomicon Press, 1978–82. 3 vols.

SECONDARY SOURCES

Airaksinen, Timo. *The Philosophy of H. P. Lovecraft: The Route to Horror.* New York: Peter Lang, 1999.
Books at Brown 38–39 (1991–92). Special H. P. Lovecraft issue.
Burleson, Donald R. *H. P. Lovecraft: A Critical Study.* Westport, Conn.: Greenwood Press, 1983.
———. *Lovecraft: Disturbing the Universe.* Lexington: University Press of Kentucky, 1990.
Cannon, Peter. *H. P. Lovecraft.* Boston: Twayne, 1989.
———. *"Sunset Terrace Imagery in Lovecraft" and Other Essays.* West Warwick, R.I.: Necronomicon Press, 1990.
———, ed. *Lovecraft Remembered.* Sauk City, Wis.: Arkham House, 1998.
Connors, Scott, ed. *A Century Less a Dream: Selected Criticism on H. P. Lovecraft.* Holicong, Pa.: Wildside Press, 2002.
Cook, W. Paul. *In Memoriam: Howard Phillips Lovecraft: Recollections, Appreciations, Estimates.* North Montpelier, VT: Driftwind Press, 1941. West Warwick, R.I.: Necronomicon Press, 1977 (rpt. 1991).

Davis, Sonia H. *The Private Life of H. P. Lovecraft.* Edited by S. T. Joshi. West Warwick, R.I.: Necronomicon Press, 1985 (rev. 1992).

de Camp, L. Sprague. *Lovecraft: A Biography.* Garden City, N.Y.: Doubleday, 1975.

Derleth, August. *H. P. L.: A Memoir.* New York: Ben Abramson, 1945.

Everts, R. Alain. *The Death of a Gentleman: The Last Days of Howard Phillips Lovecraft.* Madison, Wis.: The Strange Co., 1987.

Faig, Kenneth W., Jr. *H. P. Lovecraft: His Life, His Work.* West Warwick, R.I.: Necronomicon Press, 1979.

———. *The Parents of Howard Phillips Lovecraft.* West Warwick, R.I.: Necronomicon
Press, 1990.

Frierson, Meade, and Penny Frierson, eds. *HPL.* Birmingham, Ala.: Meade and Penny
Frierson, 1972.

Jarocha-Ernst, Chris. *A Cthulhu Mythos Bibliography & Concordance.* Seattle: Armitage
House, 1999.

Joshi, S. T. *H. P. Lovecraft: A Life.* West Warwick, R.I.: Necronomicon Press, 1996.

———. *H. P. Lovecraft: The Decline of the West.* Mercer Island, Wash: Starmont House,
1990.

———. *H. P. Lovecraft and Lovecraft Criticism: An Annotated Bibliography.* Kent,
Ohio: Kent State University Press, 1981; rpt. Holicong, Pa.: Wildside Press, 2003.

———. *An Index to the Fiction and Poetry of H. P. Lovecraft.* West Warwick, R.I.: Necronomicon Press, 1992.

———. *Primal Sources: Essays on H. P. Lovecraft.* New York: Hippocampus Press,
2003.

———. *Selected Papers on Lovecraft.* West Warwick, R.I.: Necronomicon Press, 1989.

———. *A Subtler Magick: The Writings and Philosophy of H. P. Lovecraft.* San Berna-
dino, Calif.: Borgo Press, 1996.

———, ed. *Caverns Measureless to Man: 18 Memoirs of H. P. Lovecraft.* West Warwick, R.I.: Necronomicon Press, 1996.

———, ed. *H. P. Lovecraft: Four Decades of Criticism.* Athens: Ohio University Press,
1980.

Joshi, S. T., and Marc A. Michaud. *Lovecraft's Library: A Catalogue.* West Warwick,
R.I.: Necronomicon Press, 1980. Rev. ed. New York: Hippocampus Press, 2002.

Koki, Arthur S. "H. P. Lovecraft: An Introduction to His Life and Writings." M.A. thesis:
Columbia University, 1962.

Lévy, Maurice. *Lovecraft: A Study in the Fantastic.* Translated by S. T. Joshi. Detroit:
Wayne State University Press, 1988.

Long, Frank Belknap. *Howard Phillips Lovecraft: Dreamer on the Nightside.* Sauk City,
Wis.: Arkham House, 1975.

Mariconda, Steven J. *"On the Emergence of Cthulhu" and Other Observations.* West
Warwick, R.I.: Necronomicon Press, 1995.

Migliore, Andrew, and John Strysik. *The Lurker in the Lobby: A Guide to the Cinema of
H. P. Lovecraft.* Seattle: Armitage House, 2000.

Mosig, Dirk W. *Mosig at Last: A Psychologist Looks at H. P. Lovecraft.* West Warwick,
R.I.: Necronomicon Press, 1997.

Price, Robert M. *H. P. Lovecraft and the Cthulhu Mythos.* Mercer Island, Wash: Starmont House, 1990.

St. Armand, Barton L. *H. P. Lovecraft: New England Decadent.* Albuquerque, N.M.:
Silver Scarab Press, 1979.

———. *The Roots of Horror in the Fiction of H. P. Lovecraft.* Elizabethtown, N.Y.:
Dragon Press, 1977.

Schultz, David E., and S. T. Joshi, ed. *An Epicure in the Terrible: A Centennial Anthology of Essays in Honor of H. P. Lovecraft.* Rutherford, N.J.: Fairleigh Dickinson University Press, 1991.

Schweitzer, Darrell, ed. *Discovering H. P. Lovecraft.* Mercer Island, Wash: Starmont House, 1987.

Shreffler, Philip A. *The H. P. Lovecraft Companion.* Westport, Conn.: Greenwood Press, 1977.

Talman, Wilfred B., et al. *The Normal Lovecraft.* Saddle River, N.J.: Gerry de la Ree, 1973.

Wetzel, George T., ed. *Howard Phillips Lovecraft: Memoirs, Critiques, and Bibliographies.* North Tonawanda, N.Y.: SSR Publications, 1955.

Index

Numbers in italics indicate main entries.

A Rebours (Huysmans) 118, 244
"Abominations of Yondo, The" (Smith) 247
Abraham, Margaret 3, 97
"Account of a Trip to the Fairbanks House, An" 275
"Account of Charleston, An" *1*, 139, 275
Acids 134
Ackerman, Forrest J. *1–2*, 90, 126
Acolyte 6, 15, 16, 113, 224, 227
"Ad Britannos—1918" 303
Ad Criticos 2, 228
"Adept's Gambit" (Leiber) 143
Adrian, Jack 256
Adventure 300
Aeneid (Virgil) 286
"Aeneid, The" 133
"Æpyornis Island" (Wells) 11
Aftermath 168
Age of Fable, The (Bulfinch) 133, 134
Akeley, George Goodenough 2
Akeley, Henry Wentworth *2*, 190, 195, 296–98
Akley, Bert G. 2, 195, 297
Akron Beacon Journal 138
"Alchemist, The" *2–3*, 27, 132, 164, 249
"Aletheia Phrikodes" 208, 292
Alfredo; a Tragedy 3, 97, 169
Alhazred, Abdul 28, 92, 111, 118, 181, 182, 186–87
Allen, Zadok *3*, 112, 237, 239, 284
Allgood, Sarah 153, 155
"Allowable Rhyme, The" 138
All-Story 292
Alos *3*
Alouette, L' 172
Altberg-Ehrenstein, Karl Heinrich, Graf von *3*, 231, 261
"Amateur Affairs" (Bradofsky) 24
Amateur Correspondent 45, 93, 190, 213
"Amateur Criticism" 124
Amateur Journalism *3–5*
"Amateur Journalism: Its Possible Needs and Betterment" 180
"Amateur Journalism and the English Teacher" (Moe) 169
"Amateur Press Club, The" 124
"Amateur Standards" 124
Amazing Stories 41, 43, 127, 143, 202, 294, 300
"Ambition" 216
American Amateur 148
American Book-Prices Current 143
American Mercury 122, 169, 195
"American to Mother England, An" 70, 303
"American to the British Flag, An" 303
American Weekly 167

"Americanism" *5*
"Amissa Minerva" *5*, 210
"Among the New-Comers" 216
"Ancient Sorceries" (Blackwood) 239
"Ancient Track, The" *5*, 78, 210
Ancient Track: Complete Poetical Works, The x, 210–11
Anderson, James 118, 205
Anderson, Sherwood 90
Andrews, Marshall *6*, 68, 183
Angarola, Anthony 204
Angell, George Gammell *6*, 27, 29, 39, 131, 143, 268
Angell, Thomas *6*
Anger, William Frederick *6*
"Anglo-Saxondom" 124
"Annals of the Jinns" (Barlow) 15
Annals of the Providence Observatory 134
Annesley, Henry 94, 268
Antarctic Atlas 134
Apollonius Rhodius 134
Appleton, Lawrence 215
Appleton Post 287
"Aquarium, The" (Jacobi) 130
Arabian Nights 13, 132, 154
"Argonauts, The" 133–34
Argosy 2, 4, 57, 58, 127, 144, 167, 209, 218, 228–29, 258, 292
Argosy All-Story Weekly 223
Arkham *6–7*, 22, 50, 67, 94, 206, 283–84
Arkham Advertiser 6
Arkham Gazette 6
Armitage, Henry *7*, 39, 79–80, 171, 227
Arney, Lance 167
Arruda, Capt. Manuel *7*, 33–34
Art of Fusion Melting Pudling & Casting 134
"Arthur Jermyn." *See* "Facts Concerning the Late Arthur Jermyn and His Family"
Asbury, Herbert *7*
Asellius, Sex[tus] *7*, 286
"Ashes" (Lovecraft-Eddy) *8*, 25, 84, 219, 285
Asheville Gazette-News 176, 178–79
Ashley, Mike 21, 294
"Ask Houdini" (Houdini) 116, 282
Aspinwall, Ernest B. *8*, 266
Astounding Stories 9, 12, 17, 48, 106, 127, 151, 231, 233, 236, 239, 247, 279, 289, 290, 294
Astrology, Articles on *8*

"Astrology and the European War" (Hartmann) 8, 105
"Astrology and the Future" 8, 216
Astronomy/The Monthly Almanack 9, 134
Astronomy with the Naked Eye (Serviss) 19
"Astrophobos" *9*, 216, 292
"At Providence in 1918" (Kleiner) 138
At the Mountains of Madness 6, *9–13*, 31, 48, 51, 53, 58, 70, 75, 82, 99, 106, 116, 137, 141, 173, 182, 187, 200, 207, 228, 231, 236, 238, 239, 240, 241, 266, 279, 293, 305
Atal *13*, 71, 196
Atlantis 261, 262
Atsma, Bert 12, 48, 240
Atwood, Professor *13*
Austin, John Osborne 40
Autobiographical Memoir (Long) 152
"Automatic Executioner, The" (Danziger) 62, 86
"Ave atque Vale" 112
"Ave atque Vale!" (Cole) 41
Aylesbury *13*, 94
"Azathoth" *13*, 74
Azathoth and Other Horrors (Derby) 64
Azif, Al (Alhazred) 186

Babbit, Mrs. C. H. 243
Babson, Eunice *14*
"Background" 87, 241
Bacon's Essays 5, 164, 197
Badger 30
Baird, Edwin *14*, 44, 109, 115, 145, 247, 293, 305
Baker, Albert A. 186
Balbutius, Cn[aeus] *14*, 286
Balderston, John L. 234
Baldwin, F[ranklin] Lee 7, *14–15*, 50, 146
"Ballade of Patrick von Flynn; or, The Hibernio-German-American England-Hater, Ye" *15*, 210, 217, 303
Baring-Gould, S. 223, 243
Barlow, Robert H[ayward] 1, 12, *15–16*, 17–18, 23, 24, 25, 30–31, 34, 35, 41, 44, 46, 49, 62, 66, 95, 98, 107, 123, 139, 143, 146, 148, 151, 170, 171, 173, 189, 199, 208, 226, 236, 241, 244, 268, 270, 272, 276, 300–301
Barnhart, Eleanor J. 216
Barnum & Bailey circus 131

Barry, Denys *17*, 170, 185
Barzai the Wise 13, *17*, 71, 196
Bates, Harry [Hiram Gilmore] III *17*, 294, 302
Batta *17*, 98
"Battle That Ended the Century, The" (Lovecraft-Barlow) 1, 15, *17–18*, 81, 120, 126, 139, 221, 280
Baudelaire, Charles 269
Bayboro *18*
Beardson, W. E. 174
"Beast in the Cave, The" *18*, 132, 182
Beaumont, Francis 3
"Beauties of Peace, The" 303
"Beauty in Crystal" 43
Beckford, William 13, 74, 186–87
Bedard, Marceline. *See* de Russy, Marceline (Bedard)
Beebe, Evanore 168, 175
Before Adam (London) 19
Behrends, Steve 248, 290
Bell, Ian 112
"Bells, The" 127, 216
Bennett, George *19*, 159, 270
Benson, Gordon R., Jr. 140, 171
Béraud, Henri 234
"Berenice" (Poe) 199, 207
Bergier, Jacques 177
Berkeley, Elizabeth. *See* Jackson, Winifred Virginia
Berkeley Square 234, 236, 240
Best Psychic Stories (French) 223
Best Short Stories . . ., The (O'Brien) 192
Best Supernatural Stories 65
Beware After Dark! (Harré) 30, 103, 104, 239
"Beyond the Wall" (Bierce) 19
"Beyond the Wall of Sleep" 17, *19*, 92, 112, 121, 182, 235, 245, 257
Beyond the Wall of Sleep 247, 250
"Beyond Zimbabwe" (Lovecraft-Barlow) 24
Bickerstaffe, Isaac, Jr. 8, 105, 215, 216
Bierce, Ambrose [Gwinnett] *19–20*, 36, 52, 53, 62, 80, 118, 156, 207, 256
Biglow Papers (Lowell) 206
"Biographical Notice" 192
"Bipeds of Bjhulhu, The" (Sterling) 252
Birch, A. G. 305
Birch, George *20*, 58, 92, 125, 184, 230
Birkhead, Edith 256
"Birthday Lines to Margfred Galbraham" 97

"Birthday of the Infanta, The" (Wilde) 198
Bishop, Jeremy 216
Bishop, Mamie *20*, 231
Bishop, Seth 20
Bishop, Silas 20
Bishop, Zealia Brown Reed *20*, 52, 55–56, 146, 151, 157, 165–66, 173–74
"Black, Dead Thing, The." *See* "Second Night Out"
"Black Noon" (Eddy) 84
Black Rites (Luveh-Keraph) 22
"Black Stone, The" (Howard) 119
"Black Thirst" (Moore) 171
Blackmore, L. D. 75
Blackstone Military Band 176, 292
Blackwood, Algernon [Henry] *20–21*, 80, 102, 112, 131, 167, 189, 190, 239
Blair, Alexander Ferguson 216
Blair, Hugh 224
Blake, Richard *21*, 61, 171
Blake, Robert *21*, 105–6, 184
Blanchard, Isaac 202
Blandot *21*, 176
Blarney Stone 209
Bleiler, E. F. 256
Blish, James *21–22*, 95, 187
Bloch, Robert 21, *22*, 52, 93, 106, 146, 205, 208, 253, 270
Blue Book 127
Blue Pencil Club 5, 35, 178, 213, 306
Boerem, R. 96, 208, 218
"Boiling Point, The" 1, 90
Bolingbroke, Henry St. John, Viscount 118, 138
"Bolshevism" *22*, 304
Bolton *22–23*
Bonner, Marion F. *23*
Bonnet 41, 129
"Book, The" (sonnet) 91
"Book, The" (story fragment) *23*, 182
Book of Eibon, The 247
Book of Forbidden Things 68
Book of Iod, The (Kuttner) 140
Book of the Damned, The (Fort) 289
Book of Were-wolves, A (Baring-Gould) 243
Book of Wonder, The (Dunsany) 35, 36, 181–82, 262
Books and Bipeds (Starrett) 250
Books at Brown 145, 291
"Books to mention in new edition of weird article" 256

"Bookstall, The" 138
Bor, Dam *23,* 41
Borel, Pierre 23, 33
Borelli, Giovanni 23
Borellus *23–24,* 32, 33
Boswell, James 225
"Bothon" (Whitehead) 300
"Bouts Rimés" (Lovecraft-Barlow) 15, *24*
Bowen, Hannah *24*
Boyle, Dr. E. M. *24*
Boys' Herald 5, 246
Boy's World 150
Bradofsky, Hyman 5, *24,* 189, 208
"Brain in the Jar, The" (Searight-Hammerstrom) 232
Braithwaite, William Stanley 130
Brandon, Ruth 117
Brandt, C. A. 43
Brattleboro Reformer 101, 195, 297
Brennan, Joseph Payne 83
Briden, William *24*
Bridge, The (Crane) 48
"Brief Autobiography of an Inconsequential Scribbler, The" 5
Brief Course in Astronomy, A 135
Brief Course in Inorganic Chemistry, A 135
Brinton, William *24*
"Britannia Victura" 303
Brobst, Harry K[ern] *24–25,* 213, 253–54
Brooklynite 178, 213
"Brotherhood" 217
Brown, David J. 199
Brown, Luther *25*
Brown, Susan Jenkins 48
Brown, Walter *25*
Brown brothers (John, Joseph, Nicholas, Moses) 32
Brown University 6, 16, 25, 27, 29, 39, 98, 99, 194, 227, 260
Brownlow, J. H. 218
Bruce, Malcolm 8, *25,* 285
"Bruise, The." *See* "Bothon"
"Brumalian Wish, A" 188
Bryant, Roger 24
Buchanan, Carl 178, 199, 262
Bulfinch, Thomas 133, 134
Bullen, John Ravenor *25,* 124, 193, 218
"Bureau of Critics" *25–26,* 157
"Bureau of Critics Comment on Verse, Typography, Prose" 25

Burleson, Donald R. 5, 13, 43, 55, 80, 81, 96, 107, 168, 178, 187, 221, 253, 262, 265, 278, 283, 298
Burleson, Mollie L. 199, 224
Burns, Robert 268
Bush, David Van *26,* 83, 146
Butman, Robert 139
By Daylight Only (Thomson) 205
"By Post from Providence" 138–39
"By the North Sea" (Swinburne) 78
Byfield, Bruce 144
Byrd, Richard E. 9, 10

C———, Antoine, Comte de 2, *27*
"C.S.A.: 1861–1865" 133
Cabala of Saboth, The 22
Cabell, James Branch 194
Californian 15, 16, 24, 48, 112, 113, 138, 139, 149, 168, 170, 174, 189, 208, 213, 249, 268
"Call of Cthulhu, The" 6, 24, *27–30,* 35, 39, 51, 58, 80, 103, 104, 131, 143, 161, 167, 168, 172, 268, 277, 289, 292, 293, 301, 305
Campbell, Ada P. 4, 63
Campbell, George *30,* 37
Campbell, Paul J[onas] *30*
Campbell, Ramsey 54
Can Such Things Be? (Bierce) 19
"Canal, The" 96
Cancer of Superstition, The (Lovecraft-Eddy) 84, 117
Canevin, Gerald *30–31,* 101, 273
Caneviniana (Whitehead) 16, 300
Cannon, Peter 12, 30, 75, 81, 150, 152, 174, 207, 278
Carnacki, the Ghost-Finder (Hodgson) 112
Carroll, ——— *31*
Carter, Christopher *31,* 48, 244
Carter, Lin 22, 53
Carter, Martha 31, 244
Carter, Randolph W. 8, 13, *31,* 38, 48, 66, 70–74, 78, 140, 163, 190, 203, 244–45, 250–51, 266, 283, 291, 304
Case of Charles Dexter Ward, The x, 7, 23, *31–34,* 39, 56, 63, 79, 81, 94, 107, 120, 131, 137, 160, 195, 248, 257, 265, 268, 277, 291, 292, 294, 301
Casey *34–35*
"Cassius" (Whitehead) 300
Castro 28, 29, *35*
"Cats, The" 210

"Cats and Dogs" 35
"Cats of Ulthar, The" 13, 35, 74, 77, 139, 167, 189, 246, 261, 293, 300, 305
Cats of Ulthar, The 16, 85
Cave, Hugh B[arnett] 36
"Caverns Measureless to Man" (Sterling) 45, 126, 252
"Celephaïs" 36, 48, 59, 74, 77, 127, 140, 261
Celestial Objects for All 135
Centaur, The (Blackwood) 21
Cerasini, Marc A. 12, 120, 166
Chain Lightning 150
"Chairman of the Bureau of Critics Reports on Poetry" 25
"Challenge from Beyond, The" (Moore-Merritt-Lovecraft-Howard-Long) 30, 37–38, 151, 167, 171, 231, 232
Chambers, Robert W[illiam] 38, 52, 53, 74, 239
Chandraputra, Swami 31, 38, 266
Chaplin, Charlie 138, 269
Characteristics of Emerson, Transcendental Poet (Strauch) 254
Charging Buffalo 38
Charleston 1, 139
"Charm of Fine Woodwork, The" 43
Checkley, Dr. 33
Chemistry 134
Chemistry III 134
Chemistry IV 134
Chemistry, Magic & Electricity 134
Chicago Herald and Examiner 304
Chicago Tribune 250
"Chloris and Damon" 217
Choynski, Paul 38
"Christmas" 217
Chronicle of Nath (Yergler) 278
Chronicles of Rodriguez, The (Dunsany) 108, 253
"Chuckler, The" (Wandrei) 289
"Cindy: Scrub Lady in a State Street Skyscraper" 138, 217
Cisco, Michael 23
"City, The" 38–39, 207, 210, 216
"City of the Singing Flame, The" (Smith) 247
Clapham-Lee, Major Sir Eric Moreland, D.S.O. 39
Clarendon, Dr. Alfred Schuyler 39, 58, 132, 141–42, 257
Clarendon, Georgina 39, 58, 141–42
"Clarendon's Last Test." See "Last

Test, The"
Clark, Dr. Franklin Chase, M.D. 39, 40, 243
Clark, Lillian D[elora Phillips] 33, 39, 40, 47, 67, 98, 146, 203, 243, 271, 276
Clay, Ed 40
Clay, Walker 40
Clements, Nicholaus 144, 253
Cleveland Sun 70
Cline, Leonard 235
Cloisonné and Other Verses (Talman) 260
Clore, Dan 96, 182, 188
"Clouds" 56
Club of the Seven Dreamers, The 40
Coates, Walter J[ohn] 40–41, 104, 164
Cobb, Irvin S. 58, 224, 239, 256
Cockcroft, T. G. L. 167, 240
Cole, Edward H[arold] 26, 41, 145, 169, 276
Cole, E[dward] Sherman 41
Cole, Helene Hoffman 41
Cole, Ira A[lbert] 41, 138, 145, 169
Coleman, Stuart 176
Coleridge, Samuel Taylor 133
"Collapsing Cosmoses" (Lovecraft-Barlow) 15, 23, 41, 188, 252
Collected Ghost Stories of M. R. James, The (James) 131
Collected Poems 213, 284
College Humor 109, 292
Collins, Tom 152
"Colossus" (Wandrei) 289
Colour Line, The (Smith) 134
"Colour out of Space, The" 6, 14, 22, 41–43, 84, 99, 116, 143, 182–83, 189, 192, 207, 277, 294, 305
Colour out of Space, The 152
Comet Stories 279
"Comment" 302
"Commercial Blurbs" 43, 143
Commonplace Book 11, 28, 33, 36, 43–44, 54, 80, 121, 148, 182, 223, 264, 300
Comptons 44
"Concerning the Conservative" 127
"Confession of Unfaith, A" 30, 44, 123
Conger, Alice 147
Conjure Wife (Leiber) 143
Connoisseur and Other Stories, The (de la Mare) 63
Connors, Scott 207
Conover, Willis 44–45, 93, 146

Conquest of Mexico (Prescott) 272
"Conscript, The" 303
Conservative 4, 15, 22, 25, 41, *45–46,*
50, 85, 97, 123, 124, 127, 128, 129,
130, 138, 150, 157, 176, 188, 193, 218,
220, 225, 229, 230, 245, 283, 291, 303,
304
"'Conservatism' Gone Mad" (Morton)
172
"Consolidation's Autopsy" 216
"Continuity" 85, 95
"Convention, The" 217
"Convention Banquet, The" 274
"Conversation of Eiros and Charmion,
The" (Poe) 167
Cook, W[illiam] Paul 3, 25, 40, 45, *46,*
101, 109, 145, 148, 151, 157, 158, 168,
175, 188, 192–93, 195, 241, 243–44,
255, 276, 277, 288, 289
"Cool Air" *46–48,* 111, 137, 161, 175,
207, 272, 293, 305
Corey, Benijah *48,* 244
Corey, George 25, *48,* 295
Corey, Wesley 48
Cornelius, B. 109
Coronado, Francisco Vasquez 173, 307
"Coronation of Mr. Thomas Shap, The"
(Dunsany) 36
"Correspondence between R. H. Barlow
and Wilson Shepherd" 241
Coryciani 170
Cosmopolitan 224
"Count Magnus" (James) 34, 131, 256
Cox, Michael 131
Coyote 269
Crafton Revision Service 172
Crane, Charles 195
Crane, [Harold] Hart *48,* 142, 157, 158
Crawford, F. Marion 289
Crawford, William L. *48–49,* 239, 240,
249, 284
"Crawling Chaos, The" (Lovecraft-
Jackson) *49–50,* 129, 182, 217
Credential 4, 225
Creeps by Night (Hammett) 103, 106,
178
Crime of Crimes, The 4, 104, 209, 303
"Crime of the Century, The" *50,* 303
"'Critics' Farewell, The" (Lovecraft-
Russell) 229
"Critics Submit First Report" 25
*Critical Dissertation on the Poems of
Ossian, A* (Blair) 224

Crofts, Anna Helen *50,* 208–9, 216
Crookes, Sir William 242
Crossman, Willis Tete. *See* Cook,
W[illiam] Paul
Crowley, James Laurence 217
Cthulhu 27–30, 116, 131
Cthulhu (Howard) 119
Cthulhu Mythos xi, *50–55,* 65, 86, 142,
143, 197
"Cthulhu Mythos: Wondrous and Terri-
ble, The" (Leiber) 144
*Cthulhu Mythos Bibliography & Concor-
dance, A* (Jarocha-Ernst) xi
Cultes des Goules (d'Erlette) 22
Curious Myths of the Middle Ages (Bar-
ing-Gould) 223
Curse of the Wise Woman, The (Dun-
sany) 78, 170
"Curse of Yig, The" (Lovecraft-Bishop)
20, 44, *55–56,* 61, 102, 183, 273
Curwen, Joseph 7, 31–32, 34, *56,* 81,
120, 195, 248, 257, 265, 268, 291, 292,
301
"Cycle of Verse, A" *56*
Czanek, Joe *56, 262*

Daas, Edward F. 4, *57*
Daemon of the Valley *57,* 99, 167
"Dagon" 29, 46, 50, *57–58,* 183, 208,
261, 293, 304, 305
Dalton, James *58,* 141–42
"Damned Thing, The" (Bierce) 20, 80
"Damon—a Monody" 97, 217
"Damon and Delia, a Pastoral" 97, 217
Dance of the Machines, The (O'Brien)
192
Danforth, ——— 10, *58,* 82, 99
Danziger, Gustav Adolphe. *See* de Cas-
tro, Adolphe
Dark Chamber, The (Cline) 235
Dark Odyssey (Wandrei) 289, 290
Darrow, Jack 126
Davenport, Eli *58*
Davis, Dr. *58,* 125
Davis, [Francis] Graeme *59*
Davis, Dr. Nathaniel 61
Davis, Robert H. 223
Davis, Sonia H[aft Greene Lovecraft] 5,
36, *59–61,* 67, 85, 113, 114, 130, 145,
153, 154, 155, 158, 160, 188, 265, 274,
275, 276, 282, 293
Davis, Walker and Audrey 44, 55, *61*
Day, F. H. 102

Day the Earth Stood Still, The 17
"Dead Bookworm, The" 210, 216
"Dead Giveaway" (Shea) 240
Dead Titans, Waken! (Wandrei) 289
"Deaf, Dumb, and Blind" (Lovecraft-
    Eddy) 18, 21, *61–62*, 84, 91, 171
Dealings of Daniel Kesserich, The
    (Leiber) 143
"Death" (Hoag) 112
"Death" (Shepherd) 241
[Death Diary] *62*
Death of a Gentleman, The (Everts) 62
"Death Waters" (Long) 150
de Camp, Catherine Crook 120
de Camp, L. Sprague 66, 67, 74, 77, 120,
    144, 151–52, 255
de Castro, Adolphe 20, 29, 35, *62–63*,
    85–86, 123, 141–42, 146, 151, 157, 170
Decline of the West, The (Spengler) 11
Dee, John 51, 151, 187
"Defense of Astrology, A" (Hartmann)
    8, 105
"Defence Remains Open!, The" 123
"Defence Reopens!, The" 123
de la Mare, Walter [John] 33, *63*, 235,
    255
de la Poer, Gilbert 63
de la Poer, Walter 63
Delapore, ——— *63*, 189–90, 222–23,
    266
Delapore, Alfred 63, 189
Delapore, Randolph 63
de la Ree, Gerry 61, 93
"Delavan's Comet and Astrology" 8,
    105, 216
Delrio, Antoine 115
"Demons of the Upper Air" (Leiber) 143
Dendle, Peter 94
"Department of Public Criticism" 4, 25,
    63–64, 70, 158
Derby, Asenath (Waite). *See* Waite,
    Asenath
Derby, Edward Pickman 14, *64*, 154,
    230, 263–65, 284, 288
Derleth, August [William] 12, 16, 34, 35,
    50, 52–54, 55, 61, 62, *64–65*, 69, 76,
    84, 90, 91, 99, 103, 104, 112, 119–20,
    125, 139, 146, 147, 148, 154, 162, 166,
    170, 174, 179, 188, 198, 236, 238, 239,
    244, 284, 289, 290, 293, 294, 300, 305
d'Erlette, Comte 22
de Russy, Antoine 65, 163, 165–66,
    184–85

de Russy, Denis *65–66*, 163, 165–66,
    184, 249
de Russy, Marceline (Bedard) 65, *66*,
    163, 165–66, 184, 249
Descartes, René 248
"Descendant, The" *66*, 190, 301
Description of the Town of Quebeck, A
    66–67, 275
"Despair" *67*, 207, 210
Desrochers, ——— *67*
Detective Tales 14, 109, 115
"De Triumpho Naturae" 134, 209
De Vermis Mysteriis (Prinn) 22
Dexter, Mercy *67*, 228, 248, 299
[Diary: 1925] 28, *67*
"Diary of Alonzo Typer, The" *67–68*,
    159, 246, 280, 285
"Dignity of Journalism, The" 5, 70
DiGregorio, Michael 174
"Dim-Remembered Story, A" (Barlow)
    15
"Disinterment, The" (Lovecraft-Rimel)
    6, *68–69*, 183, 227, 245
"Distortion out of Space, The" (Weiss)
    294
Dixie Booster 212
"Does Vulcan Exist?" *69*
Dombrowski, Mr. and Mrs. *69*
Donne, John 299
"Doom That Came to Sarnath, The" 17,
    48, *69–70*, 77, 269
Doorways to Poetry (Moe) 170
Doré, Gustave 204
Double Shadow and Other Fantasies,
    The (Smith) 247
Douglas, Capt. J. B. *70*
Dow, Johnny *70*
Dowdell, William J. 4, *70*, 212
Dowdell's Bearcat 5, 70, 156
Dowe, Jennie E. T. 168
Doyle, Sir Arthur Conan 118, 132, 256
"Dr. Eugene B. Kunz" 140
Dr. Grimshaw's Secret (Hawthorne) 107
"Dr. Whitlock's Price" (Long) 150
Dracula (Stoker) 168
Dragon Fly 16
Drake, H. B. 234, 264
"Dream, The" 217
Dreamer's Tales, A (Dunsany) 77, 299
Dream-Quest of Unknown Kadath, The
    x, 13, 31, 36, *70–75*, 77–78, 107, 137,
    140, 196, 203, 204, 205, 245, 251, 298
"Dreams in the Witch House, The" 6, 38,

64, 67, 69, *75–77*, 87, 101, 107, 127,
128, 140, 143, 162, 164, 264, 298, 302,
305
"Dreams of Yith" (Rimel) 227
Dreiser, Theodore 195
Drewer, Cecelia 253
Driftwind 40, 41, 164, 286
"Drinking Song from 'The Tomb'" 272
Drogman, Abdul Reis el *77*
Dryden, John 209
Dudley, Jervas *77*, 111, 120, 270–71
Dunciad, The (Pope) 218
Dunn, John T[homas] 15, *77*, 145, 303
Dunsany, Lord 35, 52, 66, 60–70, 74, 75,
77–78, 90, 108, 131, 152, 170, 181–82,
191, 196, 197, 205, 207, 211, 220, 253,
255, 256, 262, 274, 277, 299, 304
Dunwich 5, *78*, 94
"Dunwich Horror, The" 5, 6, 7, 13, 20,
25, 39, 44, 46, 48, 50, 62, 78, *79–81*,
91, 105, 112, 116, 117, 120, 161, 168,
171, 175, 187, 192, 195, 224, 227,
230–31, 275, 277, 295
Dvorak, Lucile 137, 138
"Dweller in Martian Depths, The"
(Smith) 1
Dwellers in the Mirage, The (Merritt)
167
Dwight, Frederick N. *81*
Dwight, Walter C. *81*
Dwyer, Bernard Austin 47, *81*, 87, 138,
183, 275, 277, 286, 297
Dyer, Faye (Eddy) 84
Dyer, William 9–10, 11, 58, *82*, 99
Dziemianowicz, Stefan 30, 102, 144

Early Long, The (Long) 152
Early Rhode Island 134
"East and West Harvard Conservatism"
26, *83*
"East India Brick Row, The" *83*, 95
East Side Historical Club 176
East Side News 176
Ebony and Crystal (Smith) 246
Eckhardt, Jason C. 10, 12, 35, 206–7
Ecstasy and Other Poems (Wandrei) 289
Eddy, Clifford M[artin], Jr. 8, 18, 61–62,
83–84, 91, 100, 101, 117, 118, 125,
156, 274, 293, 304
Eddy, Grace 84
Eddy, Muriel E[lizabeth] (Gammons) *84*,
100, 108–9
Eddy, Ruth 84

"Edith Miniter" 168, 175
"Editorial" (*Conservative*) *85*
"Editorial" (*United Amateur*) *85*
Edkins, Ernest A[rthur] *85*, 146
Education of Uncle Paul, The (Black-
wood) 21
Egyptian Myths 134
"Eidolon, The" *85*, 207, 210, 216
Einstein, Albert 243
"Elder Pharos, The" 91
"Elder Thing, The" (Lumley) 159
"Electric Executioner, The" (Lovecraft-
de Castro) 62, *85–86*, 91, 183
"Elegy on Franklin Chase Clark, M.D."
39
"Elegy on Phillips Gamwell, Esq." 99
Eliot, ———— *86*
Eliot, Matt *86*
Eliot, T. S. 124, 210, 291–92
Elliot, Hugh 94
Elton, Basil *87*, 299
Elwood, Frank 76, *87*
Emerson, Ralph Waldo 254
Encyclopaedia Britannica 115, 182
"End of the Jackson War, The" 229
"Epiphany of Death, The" (Smith) 247
Erford, F. Roy 164
Eshbach, Lloyd Arthur *87*, 220
Esquire 290
"Ethel: Cashier in a Broad Street Buffet"
(Kleiner) 138
Etidorhpa (Lloyd) 74
Eurus 129
Evans, William H. 16
Evening in Spring (Derleth) 64
"Evening Star" 95
Everts, R. Alain 46, 61, 62, 130, 153,
301
"Evil Clergyman, The" 81, *87–88*, 183
Ewers, Hanns Heinz 106
"Ex Oblivione" *88*, 148, 183
Exchange of Souls, An (Pain) 264
"Expectancy" 96
Explosives 134
"Extracts from H. P. Lovecraft's Letters
to G. W. Macauley" 161
"Eye Above the Mantel, The" (Long)
150
"Eye and the Finger, The" (Wandrei)
290
"Eyes of the God" (Barlow) 15
"Eyrie, The" 304
"Ex-Poet's Reply" 217

"Faceless God, The" (Bloch) 270
"Facts Concerning the Late Arthur Jermyn and His Family" 89–90, 160, 178, 239, 285, 287, 293, 305
"Facts in the Case of M. Valdemar" (Poe) 47, 207
Faig, Kenneth W., Jr. 15, 16, 91, 99, 108, 153, 155, 203, 204, 244, 245
Fantaisiste's Mirror 202
"Falco Ossifracus: By Mr. Goodguile" (Miniter) 168
"Fall of Astrology, The" 8, 105
"Fall of the House of Usher, The" (Poe) 106, 207
"Falsity of Astrology, The" 8, 105
Famous Monsters of Filmland 1
Fanciful Tales 181, 182, 241, 303
Fantasmagoria 292
Fantasy Commentator 15
Fantasy Fan 1, 6, 14, 15, 19, 45, 48, 90–91, 94, 113, 159, 182, 196, 202, 211, 227, 247, 255–56
Fantasy Magazine 15, 37, 120, 124, 182, 197, 231, 289
"Farewell to the Master" (Bates) 17
Farnese, Harold S. 53, 91
Farr, Fred 91
"Feast, The" 230
Feldon, Arthur 86, 91, 183
"Felis: A Prose Poem" (Long) 150
Fenham 21, 91, 102, 156
Fenner, Matthew 92, 125
Fenton, Dr. 92
"Festival" 92
"Festival, The" 87, 92–93, 137, 183, 187, 274, 277
"Few Memories, A" (Morton) 173
"Final Words" 123
"Finale" 30
Finlay, Virgil [Warden] 45, 93, 210, 270
"Fire of Asshurbanipal, The" (Howard) 119
"Fishhead" (Cobb) 58, 239
Fiske, John 123, 243
Flagg, Francis. See Weiss, Henry George
Fletcher, John 3
"Florida" (Russell) 229
"For Official Editor—Anne Tillery Renshaw" 70, 225
"For What Does the United Stand?" 5, 93–94
Fort, Charles 289
Fossil 5

Foster, Abel 94, 279, 285
Four Acrostic Sonnets on Edgar Allan Poe 123, 170
"Four O'Clock" (Greene) 59
"'408 Groveland Street'" 246
Foxfield 94
"Fragment on Whitman" 123
"Fragments from the Journal of a Solitary Man" (Hawthorne) 107, 198
Frankenstein (Shelley) 111, 198
Fraser, Phyllis 81, 224
Fredlund, Arthur 232
Freeman, Mary E. Wilkins 256
French, Joseph Lewis 223
"From Beyond" 91, 94, 183–84, 268
"From the Sea" (Rimel) 227
Frome, Nils [Helmer] 95
Frozen Pirate, The (Russell) 132
Frye family 95
Fulwiler, William 58, 197, 199, 271, 272, 278
Fungi from Yuggoth 6, 16, 23, 44, 45, 85, 87, 91, 95–96, 127, 165, 170, 203, 210, 239, 241
Further Criticism of Poetry 4–5

Gafford, Sam 112, 240
Galaxy 182, 257, 294, 305
Galleon 87, 182, 220, 221
Gallomo 21, 98, 145, 169, 251, 283
Galpin, Alfred 3, 5, 45, 50, 59, 63, 64, 90, 97–98, 145, 157, 169, 186, 188, 193, 210, 211, 215, 218, 264–65, 270, 274, 277–78, 287, 300
Galpin, Alfred (Old Bugs) 98, 193, 279
Gamba 98
Gamwell, Annie E[meline] Phillips 6, 16, 29, 98–99, 127, 145, 146, 203, 274, 275, 277
Gamwell, Edward F[rancis] 98, 99
Gamwell, Marion Roby 98, 99
Gamwell, Phillips 98, 144, 273
Gangs of New York, The (Asbury) 7
Gardner family 99
Gardner, Merwin 42, 99
Gardner, Nabby 42, 99
Gardner, Nahum 41–42, 99, 182
Gardner, Thaddeus 42, 99
Gardner, Zenas 42, 99
Garland, Hamlin 109, 292
Garrett, Michael 30
Garth, Sir Samuel 216
"Gaudeamus" 272

Gautier, Théophile 282
Gayford, Norm 267
Gedney, ——— 10, *99*
"Gems from 'In a Minor Key'" 127
Genie *99*, 167
Gentleman from Angell Street, The
   (Eddy) 84, 108
"Germania—1918" 303
Gernsback, Hugo 43, 126
Gerritsen, Cornelia 34, *100*, 114
Ghost 46, 64, 289
"Ghost-Eater, The" (Lovecraft-Eddy) 84,
   100, 101, 184, 196, 261
Ghost Stories 94, 125, 166
Gibbon, Edward 225
Gibson, Walter 116
Gidlow, Elsa 124, 158
Gifford, Jonathan *100–101*
Gilman, Charlotte Perkins 256
Gilman, Walter 38, 67, 75–76, 87, *101*,
   128, 162, 164
Glendale 100, *101, 196*
Gll'-Hthaa-Ynn *101*
Goblin Tower, The (Long) 15, 151
Gods of Pegāna, The (Dunsany) 52, 78,
   191, 196
Gods of the Mountain, The (Dunsany) 70
Goldsmith, Oliver 225
Golem, The (Meyrink) 256
"Gone—but Whither?" 132
Good Anaesthetic, A 134
Goodenough, Arthur [Henry] *101*, 116,
   286, 297
Gorgo 113
Gorman, Herbert 3, 239
"Grace" 124, 216
Grandison, Robert *101*, 273
"Graveyard Rats, The" (Kuttner) 140
"Great God Pan, The" (Machen) 80, 161
Great Meadow Country Clubhouse 176
"Great Stone Face, The" (Hawthorne)
   107
*Great Tales of Terror and the Supernatu-
   ral* (Wise-Fraser) 81, 224
"Green Meadow, The" (Lovecraft-
   Jackson) 49, *101–2*, 129, 184, 217
Greene, Florence 59, 60
Greene, Nathanael 203
Greene, Sonia H. *See* Davis, Sonia H.
Grenander, M. E. 20
Gresham, Mr. *102*
"Grewsome Tales." *See* "Herbert West—
   Reanimator"

Grey Eagle, Chief *102*
Griffin, Jane Whittington 120
"Gryphus in Asinum Mutatus" 210
Gubar, Susan 171
Guiney, Louise Imogen *102*, 153, 154,
   273

"H. Lovecraft's Attempted Journey . . ."
   133, 209
"H. P. L." (Smith) 247
H. P. L.: A Memoir (Derleth) 65, 69
"H.P.L.: A Remembrance" (Munn) 175
"H. P. L. in Red Hook" (Long) 151
"H. P. Lovecraft: A Biographical Sketch"
   (Baldwin) 15
"H. P. Lovecraft: A Pupil's View"
   (Bishop) 20
"H. P. Lovecraft as I Knew Him" (Rimel)
   227
*H. P. Lovecraft: Notes toward a Biogra-
   phy* (Derleth) 65
"H. P. Lovecraft, Outsider" (Derleth) 54,
   65
"H. P. Lovecraft: The House and the
   Shadows" (Shea) 240
"H. P. Lovecraft: The Making of a Liter-
   ary Reputation, 1937–1971" (Derleth)
   65
"H. P. Lovecraft the Man" (Price) 213
Haines, Mark *103*
Hall, Desmond 18
Hall, James B. 178
"Hallowe'en in a Suburb" *103*
Halsey, Allan *103*, 110
Halsey, Thomas Lloyd 33
Halve Maen, De 248, 249, 260
Hamilton, Edmond 41, 126
Hamlet, Alice 77
Hammerstrom, Norman E. 232
Hammett, [Samuel] Dashiell *103*, 106,
   178
"Harbor-Master, The" (Chambers) 38,
   239
"Harbour Whistles" 87, 96
Hardman, 'Squire *103*, 255, 257–58
Harkins, Edwin D. 70
Harré, T[homas] Everett 30, *103–4*, 239
Harris, Abigail 104
Harris, Archer 104
Harris, Arthur *104*
Harris, Carrington 104
Harris, Dutee 104
Harris, Elkanah 104

Harris, Peleg 104
Harris, Phoebe (Hetfield) 104
Harris, Rathbone 104
Harris, Rhoby (Dexter) 67, 104
Harris, Ruth 104
Harris, Welcome 104
Harris, William 24, *104*
Harris, William, Jr., 104
Harris, Woodburn *104*, 146
Harrison, James A. 40
Hart, Bertrand K[elton] 29, *104–5*, 168
Hart, Lawrence 16
Hart, Mara Kirk 138
Hart, Philomela 105
Hart Crane: A Conversation (Loveman) 158
Hartmann, J[oachim] F[riedrich] 8, *105*, 216
Hartwell, Dr. *105*
Hasting, Consul. *See* Galpin, Alfred
Hastur 52, 53
Hathaway, Abbie E. 133
Haughton, Ida C. 210
"Haunted House, The" 132, 148
"Haunter of the Dark, The" 21, 22, 44, 93, *105–7*, 184, 188, 277, 294, 298, 305
"Haunter of the Graveyard, The" (Shea) 240
"Haverhill Convention, The" 246, 274
Hawthorne, Julian 28
Hawthorne, Nathaniel *107*, 187, 198, 207, 256
Hayden, Ben *107*
Hazel, Faye Ringel 243, 244
"He" *107–8*, 184
Heald, Hazel 76, *108–9*, 115–16, 146, 162–63, 196–97, 264, 301–2
Hearn, Lafcadio 282
Heaton, ——— *109*
Hecht, Ben 109, 292
"Helene Hoffman Cole: 1893–1919: The Club's Tribute" 41, 129
"Helene Hoffman Cole—Litterateur" 41
Henley, Samuel 186
Henneberger, J[acob] C[lark] 14, *109–10*, 116–17, 282, 292–93
"Herbert West—Reanimator" 6, 22, 39, 103, *110–11*, 119, 143, 160, 184, 192, 228, 294, 304
"Heritage or Modernism: Common Sense in Art Forms" 149, 170
Hermaphrodite, The (Loveman) 157

Hermaphrodite and Other Poems, The (Loveman) 158
"Hermit, The" 133
Herrero, Esteban 111
Herrero, Mrs. 46, *111*
Herron, Don 120
Hesperia 179–80
Hess, Clara 42, 154
Hieroglyphics: A Note upon Ecstasy in Literature (Machen) 162, 283
Hill, Emma Jane Lovecraft 153
Hiram *111*
Historic Guide to Cambridge, An (Gamwell) 99
Historical Account of Last Year's War with SPAIN, An 134
History of Dartmouth College (Richardson) 195
"History of the *Necronomicon*" 51, *111–12*, 186, 224, 241
Hitz, John Kipling 223, 224
Hoadley, Abijah *112*
Hoag, Jonathan E[than] 3, *112*, 129, 218, 239
"Hoard of the Wizard-Beast, The" (Lovecraft-Barlow) 15
Hobbes, Thomas 248
Hodge Podge 140
Hodgson, William Hope 21, *112*, 139, 256
Hoffman, Charles 120
Hoffman, Helene E. *See* Cole, Helene Hoffman
Holm, Axel *112–13*, 273
Holmes, Oliver Wendell 39, 102
Holt, Ebenezer *113*
Home Brew 110, 111, 119, 159, 160
"Homecoming" 44, 91
"Homes and Shrines of Poe" *113*, 208
Hopkins, Stephen 32
"Horla, The" (Maupassant) 28, 80, 256
Hornig, Charles D[erwin] 90, *113*, 256
"Horror at Martin's Beach, The" (Lovecraft-Greene) 59, *113*, 195
"Horror at Red Hook, The" 7, 34, 100, *114–15*, 162, 212, 257, 305
Horror from the Hills, The (Long) 151, 286
"Horror in the Burying-Ground, The" (Lovecraft-Heald) 70, 109, *115–16*, 212, 249–50, 266
"Horror in the Museum, The" (Lovecraft-Heald) 109, *116*, 132, 194, 228

"Horseman in the Sky, A" (Bierce) 36
Horton, Thomas 48
Houdini, Harry (pseud. of Ehrich Weiss)
  60, 77, 84, 109, *116–17*, 281–83, 293
Houghton, Dr. *117*
"Hound, The" 114, *117–18*, 138, 156,
  184, 186, 207, 250, 274, 293
Hound of the Baskervilles, The (Doyle)
  118
"Hounds of Tindalos, The" (Long) 151
"House, The" 97, *119*, 207, 210, 216,
  243, 287
"House of Sounds, The" (Shiel) 241
House of the Seven Gables, The (Haw-
  thorne) 107
House on the Borderland, The (Hodgson)
  112
Houtain, George Julian 111, *119*, 160,
  188
"How Our State Police Have Spurred
  Their Way to Fame" (Van de Water)
  19
Howard, Dr. I. M. 119
Howard, Robert E[rvin] 38, 52, 90, *119–
  20*, 146, 147, 167, 171, 212, 223, 231,
  280
"Howard P. Lovecraft's Fiction" (Cook)
  46
"Howard Phillips Lovecraft" (Eddy) 84
"Howard Phillips Lovecraft" (Kleiner)
  138
"Howard Phillips Lovecraft" (Loveman)
  158
"Howard Phillips Lovecraft: The Sage of
  Providence" (Moe) 170
"Howard Phillips Lovecraft as His Wife
  Remembers Him" (Davis) 61
*Howard Phillips Lovecraft: Dreamer on
  the Nightside* (Long) 151, 284
Hub Club 230
Hub Club Quill 230
Humphreys, Brian 189, 221
"Hunters from Beyond, The" (Smith) 247
Hutchins family *120*
Hutchinson, Edward *120*
Huxley, Thomas Henry 206
Huysmans, Joris-Karl 118, 244
Hyde *120*
"Hylas and Myrrha: A Tale" 97, 215
"Hypnos" *120–21*, 157, 184, 269

"Ibid" *122–23*, 149, 161, 169–70, 258
"Idealism and Materialism—A Reflec-
  tion" *123*
"Idiosyncrasies of HPL" (Edkins) 85
"Idle Days on the Yann" (Dunsany) 35,
  70, 299
"Iliad, The" 133
Imagery Aids (Moe) 170
Imagination 1
Imparcial, El 216
"Impartial Spectator, An" 229
"Imprisoned with the Pharaohs." *See*
  "Under the Pyramids"
"In a Major Key" *123*, 127, 128, 172
In a Minor Key 123, 127, 128, 172
"In a Sequester'd Providence Churchyard
  Where Once Poe Walk'd" 45, *123*,
  208
In Defence of Dagon 88, *123–24*, 256,
  277
"In Memoriam: Henry St. Clair White-
  head" 300, 301
In Memoriam: Howard Phillips Lovecraft
  (Cook) 46
"In Memoriam: J. E. T. D." 168, 216
"In Memoriam: Robert Ervin Howard"
  120, *124*
In Search of the Unknown (Chambers)
  38, 239
In the Confessional and the Following
  (Danziger) 62, 86
"In the Editor's Study" 45, *124–25*, 157
In the Midst of Life (Bierce) 19
"In the Vault" 17, 20, 58, 92, *125*, 184,
  205, 230, 246, 293, 305
"In the Walls of Eryx" (Lovecraft-
  Sterling) 1, 81, *126–27*, 168, 250, 252
"Incantation from Red Hook, The" 115
Incantations (Smith) 16
Incredible Adventures (Blackwood) 21
*Index to the Fiction and Poetry of H., P.
  Lovecraft, An* (Joshi) xi
Indick, Ben P. 12, 152
Innsmouth 78, *127*
"Insomnia" (Jackson) 130, 218
"Inspiration" 217
"Instructions in Case of Decease" 16, 98
Interesting Items 104
"Interview with E. Hoffman Price, An"
  (Anger-Smith) 6
"Interview with Harry K. Brobst, An" 25
"Introducing Mr. Chester Pierce Munroe"
  176
Introduction to Social Psychology
  (McDougall) 248

Invictus 30
"Invisible Monster, The." *See* "Horror at Martin's Beach, The"
Invisible Sun (Wandrei) 289
Iranon *127*, 220
Iron Working 134
Isaacson, Charles D[avid] 46, 123, *127*, 128, 172, 210
"Isaacsonio-Mortoniad, The" *127–28*, 172, 210
"Iterum Conjunctae" 303
Iwanicki, Father *128*

Jack *129*
Jackson, Fred 2, 144, 258
Jackson, Henry *129*
Jackson, Horace 130
Jackson, Winifred Virginia 13, 45, 49, 50, 101–2, *129–30*, 145, 167, 188, 215, 217, 218, 283
Jacobi, Carl *130*
James, M[ontague] R[hodes] 34, *130–31*, 190, 256
"January" 216
Jarocha-Ernst, Chris xi, 55
Jermyn, Arthur 89, *131*, 178, 285
Jermyn, Nevil 131
Jermyn, Sir Philip 131
Jermyn, Sir Robert 89, 131
Jermyn, Sir Wade 89, 90, 131
"Jewels of Charlotte, The" (Rimel) 227
Jimbo: A Fantasy (Blackwood) 21
Johansen, Gustav 28, *131*, 268
"John Oldham: 1653–1683" (Kleiner) 138
"John Oldham: A Defence" 138
John Silence—Physician Extraordinary (Blackwood) 21
"John, the Detective" 132, 180
Johnson, Dr. Richard H. *131–32*
Johnson, Samuel 225
Jones, Algernon Reginald *132*, 258
Jones, Dr. *132*, 141–42
Jones, John J. 216
Jones, Stephen 116, *132*
Jordan, Steven J. 16
Jordan, Winifred Virginia. *See* Jackson, Winifred Virginia
Joshi, S. T. xi, 12, 16, 21, 22, 23, 34, 38, 45, 55, 66, 75, 77, 78, 90, 94, 108, 140, 144, 147, 152, 174, 207, 211, 212, 218, 224, 236, 253, 255, 265, 268, 278, 290, 294

Joyce, James 194
Jumbee and Other Uncanny Tales (Whitehead) 30, 300, 301
Junior Literature: Book Two (Leonard-Moffett) 193
Junzt, Friedrich Wilhelm von 119–20, 280
Jurgen (Cabell) 194
Juvenile works: Fiction *132–33*
Juvenile works: Poetry *133–34*
Juvenile works: Science *134–34*
Juvenilia: 1897–1905 133, 179, 180, 233

Kalem Club *136–37*, 138, 143, 146, 150, 157, 164–65, 172, 195, 260
Kalos *137*, 178, 277, 278
Kay, James 176
Keffer, Willametta 218
Keil, Paul Livingston 194
Keller, David H. 154
Ketterer, David 22
Kimball, Gertrude Selwyn 33
King Argimenes and the Unknown Warrior (Dunsany) 35
King in Yellow, The (Chambers) 38, 52, 74
Kingsport *137*, 183, 194, 252–53, 262
Kipling, Rudyard 49, 256
Kirk, George Willard 20, 47, 67, 136, *137–38*, 146, 165, 225
Kleicomolo 41, 138, 145, 169
"Kleicomolo, The" (Kleiner) 138, 145
Klein, T. E. D. 78, 290
Kleiner, Rheinhart 3, 5, 26, 41, 43, 45, 59, 63, 67, 85, 112, 114, 118, 124, 136, 137, *138–39*, 145, 169, 210, 218, 269, 274, 287
Klenze, Lieutenant *139*, 261
Knockout Bernie 17, 81, *139*
Koenig, H[erman] C[harles] 1, 112, *139*
Kranon *139*
Kuntz, Eugene B[asil] *139–40*, 246
Kuranes 36, 71, 72, *140*
Kuttner, Henry 53, 123, *140*, 171, 267

Lactantius 33, 93
Ladd Observatory 227
"Laeta; a Lament" 210, 217
"Lair of the Star-Spawn" (Derleth-Schorer) 64
Lake, —— 9, 10, 31, 99, *141*, 173
"Lament for H.P.L." (Galpin) 98
Laney, Francis T. 16, 53, 227

Lang, Andrew 154
Langland, Joseph 178
Lansinger, J. M. 109, 292
Larson, Randall 22
Last and First Men (Stapledon) 235
"Last Incantation, The" (Smith) 247
"Last Pagan Speaks, The." *See* "To the
    Old Pagan Religion"
"Last Test, The" (Lovecraft-de Castro)
    39, 58, 62, 86, 132, *141–42,* 257
Lawson, Horace L. 286–87
Lawton, Captain George E. *142*
Lazare, Edward *142–43*
Lazarus (Béraud) 234
"League, The" 124, 304
Leaves 13, 16, 23, 35, 41, 66, 123
Leavitt, Robert *143*
Leeds, Arthur 43, 136, *143,* 146, 165
Legrasse, John Raymond 6, 27, 28, *143,*
    268
Leiber, Fritz [Reuter] 76–77, 139, *143–
    44,* 146, 298
Leinster, Murray 37
Lemon, Don Mark 292
Leonard, Sterling 193
Letters, Lovecraft's *144–47*
Letters to H. P. Lovecraft (Smith) 146,
    248
Letters to Henry Kuttner 140
Letters to Richard F. Searight 232
Letters to Robert Bloch 6, 22
*Letters to Samuel Loveman and Vincent
    Starrett* 158
Lewis, Thomas S. W. 48
Liberal 30, 44
Libo, P[ublius] Scribonius 14, *147,* 286
Liddeason, Eli *148*
"Life and Death" 88, *148*
"Life for Humanity's Sake" *148*
Life of Johnson (Boswell) 225
"Ligeia" (Poe) 271
Lillibridge, Edwin M. *148*
"Lines on Graudation from the R.I. Hos-
    pital's School of Nurses" 77
Lingerer 59
"Link, The" 303
Lippi, Giuseppe 75
"List of certain basic underlying horrors
    effectively used in weird fiction, A"
    190
"List of primary ideas motivating possi-
    ble weird tales" 190
"Listeners, The" (de la Mare) 63

"Literary Copernicus, A" (Leiber) 144
"Literary Persons Meet in Guilford" 101
Literary Quarterly 241
Little, Myrta Alice *149,* 188, 274
"Little Glass Bottle, The" 132, *149*
"Little Journeys to the Homes of Promi-
    nent Amateurs" 150, 216
"Little Journeys to the Homes of Promi-
    nent Amateurs" (Lockhart) 150
Littlewit, Humphry 216, 225
"Living Heritage: Roman Architecture in
    Today's America, A" *149*
Lloyd, John Uri 74
Lock and Key Library, The (Hawthorne)
    28
Lockhart, Andrew F[rancis] 85, *150,* 216
London, Jack 19
[London] *Evening Standard* 178
Long, Frank Belknap, Jr. 5, 11, 13, 15,
    17, 18, 20, 38, 51, 64, 67, 104, 110,
    114, 136, 139, 145, 146, *150–52,* 153,
    157, 161, 166, 167, 171, 173, 174, 187,
    188, 218, 224, 231, 243, 250, 255, 257,
    265, 269, 270, 275, 284, 286, 289, 297
"Looking Backward" 4, 85, *152*
Lord, Glenn 120
"Lord Dunsany and His Work" 78, *152*
"Lord of Illusion, The" (Price) 213, 266–
    67
Loucks, Donovan K. 93
Love, Dr. 47, 175
Lovecraft family *153*
Lovecraft, George 153, 155
Lovecraft, Joseph S. 153
Lovecraft, Mary Fulford 153
Lovecraft, Sarah Susan Phillips 40, 67,
    84, 98, 102, 145, 149, *153–55,* 203,
    204, 273–74, 295
Lovecraft, Thomas 153
Lovecraft, Winfield Scott 153–54, *155,*
    201, 273
Lovecraft: A Biography (de Camp) 151–
    52
"Lovecraft—an Appreciation" (Goode-
    nough) 101
"Lovecraft and Benefit Street" (Walter)
    289
"Lovecraft and Science" (Sterling) 252
"Lovecraft as a Conversationalist"
    (Loveman) 158
"Lovecraft as an Illustrator" (Baldwin)
    15
"Lovecraft as I Knew Him" (Davis) 61

Lovecraft at Last (Lovecraft-Conover) 45

"Lovecraft, My Childhood Friend" (Munro) 176

"Lovecraft Offers Verse Criticism" 25

Lovecraft Studies ix, 43, 241, 249

Lovecrafter 241

"Lovecraft's First Book" (Crawford) 49

"Loved Dead, The" (Lovecraft-Eddy) 18, 47, 84, 91, 102, 125, *156,* 184, 293, 305

Loveman, Samuel 5, 20, 45, 48, 59, 62, 67, 112, 114, 118, 121, 137, 142, 145, *156–57,* 172, 188, 191, 251, 274, 275, 276, 289, 291

Lovett-Graff, Bennett 90, 160, 240

Lowell, James Russell 206–7

Lowell, Percival 200, 298

Lowndes, Robert A[ugustine] W[ard] *158*

Lowrey, Perrin Holmes 218

Lubbock, S. G. 131

"Lucubrations Lovecraftian" 5, 15, *158*

Lumley, Brian 54

Lumley, William 67–68, 126, *158–59*

Lurker at the Lobby, The (Migliore-Strysik) xi

Lurker at the Threshold, The (Derleth) 65, 84

"Lurking Fear, The" 19, 100–101, 112, 119, *159–60,* 163, 175, 184, 270

Luveh-Keraph 22

Lyman, Dr. *160*

Mabbott, T. O. 208, 210

Macauley, George W[illiam] *161*

MacDonald, George 74

Machen, Arthur [Llewellyn Jones] 28–29, 42, 47, 52, 66, 78, 80, 93, 131, 150, *161–62,* 167, 190, 207, 250, 256, 283

Mackenzie, Robert B. F. 24, *162,* 234

Macleod, Fiona (pseud. of William Sharp) 223

MacLoughlin, E. Dorothy 119

Magazine of Fun 110

Magician among the Spirits, A (Houdini) 117

Magnalia Christi Americana (Mather) 23, 33, 93, 284

Mainwaring, Arthur 216

Malkowski, Dr. *162*

Malone, Thomas F. 34, 114–15, *162*

Man from Genoa, A (Long) 151

"Man of Stone, The" (Lovecraft-Heald) 107, 109, 129, *162–63,* 171, 295

Man of Two Worlds (Schwartz) 231

"Man Who Came at Midnight, The" (Eddy) 84

"Man Who Was Lovecraft, The" (Price) 213, 266, 267

Manly, Jack *163,* 255, 257–58

Manning, James 32

Manton, Joel *163,* 169, 283

Manual of Roman Antiquities, A 134

"Map of the Principal Parts of Arkham, Massachusetts" 6

Marble Faun, The (Hawthorne) 107

Marcia *163,* 208–9

Marginalia 250, 272

Mariani, Paul 48

Mariconda, Steven J. 5, 12, 30, 43, 48, 55, 107, 118, 121, 223, 224, 279, 297, 298

Marigny, Etienne-Laurent de *163,* 266

Marsh, Barnabas (Old Man) 3, *163*

Marsh, Frank 65–66, *163,* 165–66

Marsh, Obed 86, 163, 194, 219, 237

Marsh, Onesiphorus 163

"Marsh-Mad: A Nightmare" (Galpin) 97, 278

Marten, Robert D. 6, 7, 22, 111, 206, 207

Martense, Gerrit 159, 163

Martense, Jan 100–101, 159, *163–64*

Marvel Tales 36, 48, 69, 239

Mason, Keziah 75–76, 101, 128, *164*

"Masque of the Red Death, The" (Poe) 199, 207

"Materialist Today, The" 40, *164*

Mather, Cotton 23, 33, 93, 284

Mathews, Martha Helen 202

"Matter of Uniteds, A" 5, *164*

Matthews, Brander 245

Maupassant, Guy de 28, 80

Mauran, William Lippitt 33

Mauvais, Michel 2, 27, *164,* 249

Maxwell, Victoria Clarissa 99

"May Skies" 208

Mayfair 100, 196

Maynwaring, Archibald 216

Mazurewicz, Joe 128, *164*

McColl, Gavin T. 69

McCrosson, Diana Ross 63

McDonald, Philip B. 124

McDougall, William 248

McGavack, Henry Clapham 45

McGeoch, Verna 218

McGrath, Patrick 157
McIlwraith, Dorothy 305
McKeag, Ernest Lionel 179
McNamara, M. Eileen 34, 154
McNeil, [Henry] Everett 136, 143, 146, *164–65*, 292
McNeill, Dr. 55, *165*
McTighe, ——— *165*
McWilliams, Carey 20
"Medusa's Coil" (Lovecraft-Bishop) 20, 65–66, 163, *165–66*, 184–85, 216, 249
Mellon, Mary Louise Lovecraft 153
"Memoir of Lovecraft, A" (Kleiner) 138
"Memories of a Friendship" (Galpin) 98
"Memories of Lovecraft: I" (Davis) 61
"Memories of Lovecraft: II" (Sully) 255
"Memory" 57, 99, *167*
Menes 35, *167*
Merritt, A[braham] 16, 29, 37, *167,* 171, 231
Merritt, John 31, 33
"Messenger, The" 29, 95, 105, *168,* 210
Metamorphoses (Ovid) 133, 210, 216
"Metrical Regularity" 225
"Metrical Regularity, or, Broken Metre" (Russell) 229
Mevana *168*
Meyrink, Gustav 256
Michaud, Marc A. 290, 294
Middleton, Lilian 287
Migliore, Andrew xi
Miller, Sgt. Hayes P. 287
Miller, William 21–22, 95
Miller, Wesley P. *168*
"Million Years After, A" (Roof) 11
Mills, Roswell George 124
Mind Power Plus 26, 83
Miniter, Edith [May Dowe] 78, 80, *168– 69,* 174–75, 193, 275
Minnesota Quarterly 130
"Mirage" 91
"Miscellaneous Impressions of H.P.L." (Bonner) 23
"Mississippi Autumn, A" 209
"Mive" (Jacobi) 130
Mladdna *169,* 268, 281
"Modern Mythological Fiction" (But- man) 139
Modern Science and Materialism (Elliot) 94
Modern Tales of Horror (Hammett) 103
Moe, Donald 169
Moe, Maurice W[inter] 3, 5, 41, 97, 98, 122–23, 138, 144, 145, 149, 163, *169– 70,* 188, 192, 193, 211, 218, 270, 276, 283–84, 287
Moe, Robert 169, 170, 276
Moffett, Harold Y. 193
Moitoret, Anthony F. 70
Monadnock Monthly 46
Monk and the Hangman's Daughter, The (Voss-Bierce-de Castro) 20, 62
"Monody on the Late King Alcohol" 212, 217
"Monster-God of Mamurth, The" (Hamil- ton) 126
Montelone, Paul 88, 199, 224, 236, 300
"Moon-Bog, The" 17, *170–71,* 185
"Moon Pool, The" (Merritt) 29, 167
Moon Terror, The (Birch et al.) 305
Moore, C[atherine] L[ucile] 16, 37, 134, 140, 146, 167, *171,* 231
Moore, Dr. Henry Sargent *171,* 246, 302
Mooser, Clare 16
"More *Chain Lightning*" 150
More Seven Club Tales (Austin) 40
Morehouse, Dr. Arlo *171*
Morgan, Dr. Francis *171,* 227
Morris, Daniel ("Mad Dan") 162, *171,* 295
Morris, Rose 162, 171
Morris, Roy, Jr. 20
"Mors Omnibus Communis" (Lovecraft- Greene) 59
Morse, A. Reynolds 241
Morse, Richard Ely *172*
Morton, James Ferdinand, Jr. 5, 29, 46, 50, 59, 112, 114, 127, 128, 136, 145, 146, 165, *172–73,* 210, 274, 275, 276, 289, 292
Morton, Thomas 272
Mosig, Dirk W. 39, 54, 107, 199, 208, 240, 300
Moskowitz, Sam 43, 95, 112, 167
"Mother Earth" 56
"Mouches Fantastiques, Les" 124
Moulton, ——— *173*
"Mound, The" (Lovecraft-Bishop) 20, 38, 40, 44, 52, 101, 102, 109, 142, 166, *173–74,* 185, 269, 273, 294, 301, 307
"Mrs. Miniter—Estimates and Recollec- tions" 68, *174–75*
"MS. Found in a Bottle" (Poe) 149
Muffin Man 168
Müller, ——— *175*

Munn, H[arold] Warner 78, 80, *175*
Muñoz, Dr. 46–47, 111, *175,* 272, 304
Munro, Harold W. 176
Munroe, Arthur 159, 160, *175*
Munroe, Chester Pierce 160, *175–76,*
179
Munroe, Harold Bateman 160, *176*
"Murders in the Rue Morgue, The" (Poe)
18
Murray, Margaret A. 93
Murray, Will 6, 7, 12, 13, 17, 43, 48, 54,
55, 58, 69, 77, 81, 94, 191, 205, 206,
236, 238, 240, 272, 279
"Music of Erich Zann, The" 21, 103,
176–78, 185, 305, 307
Musides 137, *178,* 277, 278
Mwanu *178*
"My Correspondence with Lovecraft"
(Leiber) 144
"My Favourite Character" *178*
My Opinion as to the lunar canals 134
"Myrrha and Strephon" 97, 215
"Mysteries of the Heavens Revealed by
Astronomy" 176, *178–79*
Mysteries of the Worm (Prinn) 22
"Mysterious Ship, The" 132, *179*
"Mystery of Murdon Grange, The" *179–
80*
"Mystery of the Grave-Yard, The" 132,
180
Mystery Stories 30
Mythology for the Young 134
Myths and Myth-Makers (Fiske) 123,
243

"Nameless City, The" 17, *181–82,* 185,
186, 241, 257, 303
Nameless Cults (Junzt) 119, 196
*Narrative of Arthur Gordon Pym of Nan-
tucket, The* (Poe) 12, 207
Narrators, Unidentified *182–86*
"Nathicana" 98, *186,* 207, 218
National Amateur 4–5, 103, 119, 120,
123, 137, 157, 176, 191, 206, 211, 212,
213, 217, 254, 295
National Amateur Press Association xi,
4–5, 24, 46, 59, 59, 70, 130, 172, 212,
246, 274, 275
National Enquirer 56, 193, 212, 226,
287, 302
Necronomicon (Alhazred) 7, 9, 22, 28,
51, 79, 80, 92, 111–12, 118, 119, 139,
151, 182, *186–88,* 190, 224, 247, 251,
267
"Nemesis" 97, *188,* 207, 210
"New Department Proposed: Instruction
for the Recruit" 216
"New England" 229
"New-England Fallen" 209, 254
New English Canaan or New Cannan
(Morton) 272
New Member 161
New Way, The (de Castro) 62
New York Evening Post 108
New York Times 62, 151, 252, 260, 298
New York Tribune 19
"News Notes" 169, *188,* 218
Ni, Hak 41, *188,* 252
Nietzsche, Friedrich 97, 188, 248
"Nietzsche as a Practical Prophet" (Gal-
pin) 97
"Nietzscheism and Realism" 59, *188,*
304
"Night-Gaunts" 203
Night Land, The (Hodgson) 112
"Night Ocean, The" (Lovecraft-Barlow)
16, 185, *189*
"Nightmare Lake, The" *189,* 207
Night's Black Agents (Leiber) 143
"1914" 104, 303
Nith *189*
"Noble Eavesdropper, The" 132
Normal Lovecraft, The (Talman et al.)
249, 261
Norrys, Capt. Edward 63, *189–90,* 222–
23
"North and South Britons" 216
Northam, Lord 66, *190*
Not at Night! (Asbury) 7
Not at Night Omnibus (Thomson) 205
"Note on Howard P. Lovecraft's Verse,
A" (Kleiner) 138, 210
Notes & Commonplace Book, The 16,
43, 190
Notes on Weird Fiction 44, *190,* 249
"Notes on Writing a Story" 227
"Notes on Writing Weird Fiction" *190,*
227, 234, 256
"Novel of the Black Seal" (Machen) 28–
29, 161
"Novel of the White Powder" (Machen)
47, 161, 207
Noyes, ——— *190*
Nyarlathotep 2, 49, 53, 71, 73, 185, 191,
297, 298
"Nyarlathotep" 49, 95, 157, 185, *190–91*

"Nymph's Reply to the Modern Business Man, The" 217

O. Henry Memorial Award Prize Stories (Williams) 192
Oakes, David A. 13
O'Brien, Edward J[oseph Harrington] *192*
O'Brien, Fitz-James 80
O'Brien, "Kid" *192, 228*
"Observations on Several Parts of America" 169, *192–93*, 275, 277
Occult Review 163
"Ocean Leech, The" (Long) 150
"Oceanus" 56
"October" 216
"Ode for July Fourth, 1917" 303
"Ode to Selene or Diana" 133, 217
Odes and Sonnets (Smith) 137, 246
Odyssey (Homer) 133, 292
"Of Gold and Sawdust" (Loveman) 158
"Ol' Black Sarah" (Dwyer) 81
Old Bugs. *See* Galpin, Alfred (Old Bugs)
"Old Bugs" 98, *193*, 212, 279
"Old Christmas" *193*
"Old England and the 'Hyphen'" *193–94*, 303
Old World Footprints (Symmes) 151
Ole Miss' 209, 225, 226
Olmstead, Robert 3, 186, *194*, 219, 230, 237–40, 269, 301
Olney, Thomas *194*, 252–53
Olson, D. H. 290
Olympian 41, 173
"Omnipresent Philistine, The" *194*
"On a Battlefield in Picardy" 303
"On a Grecian Colonnade in a Park" 216
"On a Modern Lothario" 209
"On a New-England Village Seen by Moonlight" 254–55
"On a Poet's Ninety-second Birthday" 217
"On Collaboration" (Lovecraft-Kleiner) 138
On Lovecraft and Life (Barlow) 16
"On Receiving a Picture of Swans" 209
"On Receiving a Portraiture of Mrs. Berkeley, ye Poetess" 129
"On Religion" 216
"On the Cowboys of the West" 41
"On the Creation of Niggers" 209
"On the Death of a Rhyming Critic" 210
"On the Return of Maurice Winter Moe, Esq. . . ." 169, 217
"On the Ruin of Rome" 133
"On the Vanity of Human Ambition" 133
Once Around the Bloch (Bloch) 22
Onderdonk, Matthew H. 54
"One of Cleopatra's Nights" (Gautier) 282
O'Neail, N. J. 52
"Only a Volunteer" (Miller) 287
"Ooze" (Rud) 80
Orabona *194*
Oracle 194
O'Reilly, Michael Ormonde 216
Orne, Benjamin *195*
Orne, Eliza 195
Orne, Capt. James P. *195*
Orne, Simon/Jedediah *195*
Orton, [Kenneth] Vrest [Teachout] 136, 192, *195*, 275, 277, 297
O'Shaughnessy, Arthur 270
Osborn, Joe *195*
"Other Gods, The" 17, 75, 77, 91, 121, *196*, 197
Oukranikov, Vasili 100, *196*, 261
"Our Apology to E. M. W." (Russell) 229
"Our Friend, the Conservative" (Renshaw) 226
Our Natupski Neighbors (Miniter) 168
"Out of the Æons" (Lovecraft-Heald) 38, 109, 131, 163, *196–97*, 280
"Outpost, The" 95, *197*, 210, 232
"Outsider, The" 69, 107, 185, *197–99*, 207, 305
Outsider and Other Stories, The 305
Outsider and Others, The 65, 99
"Oval Portrait, The" (Poe) 205
Ovid 133, 210, 216
"Ovid's Metamorphoses" 133
O-Wash-Ta-Nong 122, 161, 170
Owens, J. C. 207
Owings, Mark 188

Pabodie, Frank H. 9, *200*
"Pacifist War Song" 217, 303
Page, Brett 117
Paget-Lowe, Henry 50, 208, 216
Pain, Barry 264
Pale Ape and Other Pulses, The (Shiel) 241
"Pan." *See* "To Pan"
Parente, Audrey 36

Parker, Rowland 78
Parnell, Frank H. 294
"Pastorale" (Crane) 48
Pattee, Fred Lewis 256
Pawtuxet Valley Gleaner, Astronomy articles for *200–201*, 227
Peabody, E. Lapham *201*
"Peace Advocate, The" 130, 215, 283, 303
Peaslee, Alice (Keezar) 201, 233
Peaslee, Hannah 201
Peaslee, Nathaniel Wingate 24, 39, 82, 162, *201–2*, 233–35, 245, 301, 304
Peaslee, Robert K. 201
Peaslee, Wingate 201, *202*, 233
"Pendrifter, The" (Crane) 195, 297
"Pensive Swain, The" 216
"Personality in Clocks" 43
Perspective Review 276, 294
"Perverted Poesie or Modern Metre" 161, 216
Petaja, Emil *202*
Pfaff, Richard William 131
Phantagraph 88, 93, 103, 112, 120, 122, 139, 241, 270, 302–3
Phantastique/Science Fiction Critic 22, 95
"Phantom Farmhouse, The" (Quinn) 221
Phillips, Asaph 202
Phillips, Edwin E[verett] 154, *202, 203*, 258
Phillips, Emeline Estella 203
Phillips, Emma (Corey) 244
Phillips, Esther 202
Phillips family *202–3*
Phillips, George 202
Phillips, Henry Byron 202
Phillips, James 203
Phillips, James Wheaton 154, *203*
Phillips, Jeremiah 202, 203
Phillips, Michael 202
Phillips, Robie Alzada 40, 98, 99, 153, 202, *203*
Phillips, Robie (Rathbun) 202, 203
Phillips, Walter Herbert 244
Phillips, Ward 88, 179, 186, *203,* 216–17, 266
Phillips, Whipple Van Buren 8, 40, 98, 99, 145, 153, 154, 200, 202, *203–4,* 295
Philosopher 97, 119, 211, 243, 287
Pickford, Mary 138, 269
Pickman, Richard Upton 71–72, *204,* 224–25, 267

"Pickman's Model" 74, 86, 125, 133, *204–5,* 224–25, 247, 267, 304
"Picture, The" 133, *205*
"Picture in the House, The" 6, 107, 111, 113, 123, 185, 192, *206–7,* 305
Pierce, Ammi 41–42, 183, *207*
Pierce, Mehitabel 148
Pigafetta, Filippo 113
"Pigeon-Flyers, The" 165
Pine Cones 19, 67
Pinfeather 225
Piper 138
Pippin 169
Place, Benejah 244
Place Called Dagon, The (Gorman) 3, 239
Place of Hawks (Derleth) 64
Plainsman 41
"Plan of Foxfield—for possible fictional use" 94
Planet 134
Planeteer 21
Planets and Dimensions (Smith) 247
"Plaster-All" 48, 292
"Plea for Lovecraft, A" (Cook) 46
Poe, Edgar Allan 12, 18, 40, 47, 52, 62, 85, 90, 104, 106, 113, 118, 123, 140, 149, 167, 190, 198–99, 205, *207–8,* 211, 223, 256, 270, 271
"Poe-et's Nightmare, The" *208,* 210, 292
"Poem of Ulysses, The" 133
Poemata Minora, Volume 2 133, 134
Poems (Loveman) 156
Poems for a Competition (Barlow) 16
Poe's Helen (Tinknor) 223
Poetical Works of Jonathan E. Hoag, The (Hoag) 112, 172
"Poetry and the Gods" (Lovecraft-Crofts) 50, 163, *208–9,* 216
Poetry, Lovecraft's *209–11*
"Poetry of John Ravenor Bullen, The" 25
"Poets of Amateur Journalism" (White) 157
"Poet's Rash Excuse, The" 217
"Polaris" 3, 17, 97, 169, 185, *211–12,* 287
Polaris 227, 278
Pope, Alexander 133, 209, 218, 292
Popkins, George 84
Potter, Welcome 268
"Port, The" 127
Portrait of Ambrose Bierce (de Castro) 20, 62, 151

Powell, Chris 63
"Power of Wine: A Satire, The" *212*
Pratt, Dr. *212*
Prescott, William H. 272
"President's Message" (*National Amateur*) *212*
"President's Message" (*United Amateur*) *212*
Price, E[dgar] Hoffmann 6, 115, 124, 126, 146, 163, *212–13*, 254, 305
Price, Robert M. 11–12, 22, 24, 30, 43, 54, 55, 65, 78, 81, 115, 120, 140, 178, 187, 188, 196, 199, 208, 236, 245, 252, 266–67, 276, 279, 298, 301
"Primavera" 210, *213*
Primitive Culture (Tylor) 115
Prinn, Ludvig 22
Private Life of H. P. Lovecraft, The (Davis) 61
"Probable Adventure of the Three Literary Men, The" (Dunsany) 182, 262
"Professional Incubus, The" *213*
"Proposed Author's Union, The" 124
"Providence" *213*
Providence Amateur 4, 77, 138, 230, 269
Providence Amateur Press Club 4, 41, 77, 145
Providence Astronomical Society 176
Providence Detective Agency 176
[Providence] *Evening Bulletin* 209, 213, 214, 292
[Providence] *Evening News* 8, 39, 99, 105, 208, 212, 213–14, 216, 229, 287
[Providence] *Evening News,* Astronomy articles for *213–14*
[Providence] *Evening Tribune* 214
Providence in Colonial Times (Kimball) 33
"Providence in 2000 A.D." 209, *214*
Providence Journal 29, 69, 83, 96, 104, 168, 200, 243, 282
[Providence] *Morning Tribune* 215
Providence Observatory . . . 134
[Providence] *Sunday Tribune* 214
[Providence] *Tribune,* Astronomy articles for 200, *214–15,* 227
Pryor, John Clinton 158
Pseudonyms, Lovecraft's *215–18*
"Pseudo-United, The" 164
"Psychopompos: A Tale in Rhyme" 130, 210, *218*
Pth'thya-l'hi 194, *219*
Purdy, Marjorie 8, *219*

Purple Cloud, The (Shiel) 10

"Quest of Iranon, The" 77, 87, 127, *220–21, 228*
Quinn, Seabury [Grandin] 212, *221,* 260

Railroad Review 134
Rainbow 36, 59, 97, 188, 304
Ralegh, Sir Walter 217
Raleigh, Richard 217
Ramsey, Shawn 140
"Random Memories of H.P.L." (Long) 151
"Rats in the Walls, The" 24, 63, 119, 160, 189–90, 207, *222–24,* 266, 273, 305
Reader and Collector 139
"Real Colonial Heritage, A" 43
"Recapture" 16, 95
Recluse 40, 46, 235, 250, 253, 255–56
"Recollections of H. P. Lovecraft" (Orton) 195
"Red Brain, The" (Wandrei) 30, 289
"Regner Lodbrog's Epicedium" 187, *224*
Regnum Congo (Pigafetta) 113, 206
Reid, Dr. *224–25*
"Remarkable Document, A" 124
"Reminiscence of Dr. Samuel Johnson, A" 149, 216, *225,* 258
Renshaw, Anne (Vyne) Tillery 26, 45, 137, 145, *225–26*
"Reply to *The Lingerer,* A" 59
"Report of Bureau of Critics" 25
"Return, The" 246
Return, The (de la Mare) 33, 63
"Return of Hastur, The" (Derleth) 52, 65
"Return of the Undead, The" (Leeds) 143
"Revelation" *226*
"Revolutionary Mythology" 124
Reynolds, B. M. 106
Rhan-Tegoth 116
Rhoades, James 286
Rhode Island Journal of Astronomy 99, 134, 176, 201, *226–27,* 232
Ricci, Angelo *227,* 262
Rice, Professor Warren 171, *227*
Richardson, Leon Burr 195
Rickard, Dennis 290
Riddle and Other Stories, The (de la Mare) 63
Rime of the Ancient Mariner, The (Coleridge) 133

Rimel, Duane W[eldon] 14, 30, 68–69, 146, 202, *227*, 278–79, 302
Robbins, Maria *228*
"Robert Ervin Howard: 1906–1936" 120, 124, 302
Robinson, Buck 110, 192, *228*
Roerich, Nicholai 11
Rogers, George 116, 132, 194, *228*
Romero, Juan 186, *228, 272*
Romnod 127, 220, *228*
Ronan, Margaret. *See* Sylvester, Margaret
Roof, Katharine Metcalf 11
Roosevelt, Franklin Delano 249
Ropes, —— *228*
"Rose of England, The" 303
Roulet, Etienne *228*, 242, 243
Roulet, Jacques 228, 242, 243
Rowley, Ames Dorrance 179, 217
Ruber, Peter 250
Rud, Anthony M. 80
"Rudis Indigestaque Moles" 124, 291
Rufus, L[ucius] Caelius *228, 286*
"Rursus Adsumus" 124
Russell, John *228–29*, 287
Russell, W. Clark 132
"Rutted Road, The" 210, 217

"Sacrifice to Science, A" (Danziger) 62, 142
"Sage of College Street, The" (Price) 213
"Salem Horror, The" (Kuttner) 140
Salvaging Self Esteem (Renshaw) 226
Samples, John Milton 302
Sampson, Robert 30
Sandalwood (Smith) 246–47
Sandusky, Albert A. 45, 169, *230*
Sargent, Joe *230*, 237
Sargent, Moses and Abigail *230*
"Satan's Servants" (Bloch) 22
Saturday Review 195
Saturnalia and Other Poems 2, 24, 127
Saturnian 156–57
Sawyer, Asaph 125, *230*
Sawyer, Chauncey 231
Sawyer, Earl *230–31*
Sawyer, Sally 231
Scarborough, Dorothy 256
Schmidt, —— *231*
School for Scandal, The (Sheridan) 272
Schopenhauer, Arthur 188, 246
Schorer, Mark 64
Schultz, David E. 22, 54, 55, 77, 91, 96,

123, 140, 147, 156, 279
Schwartz, Julius 12, 37, 182, *231*, 236, 265
Schweitzer, Darrell 78, 236, 298
Science-Fantasy Correspondent 44–45, 93, 123, 208, 252
"Science Library, The" 134
"Science of Astrology, The" (Hartmann) 8, 105
"Science versus Charlatanry" 8, 105
Science vs. Charlatanry: Essays on Astrology (Lovecraft-Hartmann) 8
Scientific Gazette 134, *231–32*
Scienti-Snaps 286
Scot 69
Scott, Winfield Townley 61, 96, 168, 210, 211
Scott-Elliott, W. 29
Sea Gull 15
"Sealed Casket, The" (Searight) 232
Searight, Franklyn 232
Searight, Richard F[ranklyn] 146, *232*
Searles, A. Langley 300, 301
Sechrist, Edward Lloyd 197, 225, *232*
"Second Night Out" (Long) 151
"Secret Cave, or John Lees Adventure, The" 132, *233*
"Secret of the Grave, The" 132
Seeger, Alan 303, 304
Selected Letters 65, 147, 290
Selected Letters (Howard) 119
Selected Poems (Smith) 248
"Senenaio-Phantasma" (Galpin) 97, 188
Selley, April 34
Septimius Felton (Hawthorne) 107
Serviss, Garrett P. 19
Setiya, K. 205
"Shadow from the Steeple, The" (Bloch) 22
"Shadow Kingdom, The" (Howard) 119
"Shadow out of Time, The" 6, 9, 15, 24, 38, 39, 44, 48, 64, 82, 106, 112, 119, 162, 168, 201, 202, 232, *233–36*, 245, 264, 279, 301, 304
"Shadow over Innsmouth, The" 3, 6, 34, 38, 48, 58, 64, 86, 112, 127, 128, 137, 160, 163, 186, 194, 195, 201, 219, 230, 237–40, 269, 276, 277, 284, 288, 293, 294, 305
Shadow over Innsmouth, The 48–49, 284
Shadow over Innsmouth and Other Stories of Horror, The 259
Shadowy Thing, The (Drake) 234, 264

"Shambleau" (Moore) 171
"Shambler from the Stars, The" (Bloch) 22, 106
Shea, J[oseph] Vernon 198, *240–41*
Shearer, Ronald 77
Shelley, Mary 111, 198
Shepherd, Mrs. 25
Shepherd, Wilson 111, 146, 182, *241,* 302, 303
Sheridan, Richard Brinsley 272
Sherman, ——— *241*
Shiel, M[atthew] P[hipps] 10, *241,* 256
Short Story, The (Hall-Langland) 178
"Shunned House, The" 14, 24, 39, 40, 46, 67, 104, 107, 115, 119, 148, 186, 228, *241–44,* 248, 277, 293, 295–96, 299, 305
Shunned House, The 15, 46, 151
"Shuttered Room, The" (Derleth) 54
Shuttered Room and Other Pieces, The 250
"Side Glances" (Baldwin) 14
"Sideshow, The" (Hart) 104–5, 168
Sidney-Fryer, Donald 248
"Sign of the Dragon" (Eddy) 83
"Silence—a Fable" (Poe) 167
Silva, Manuel *244, 262*
Silver Clarion 5, 112, 129, 302
"Silver Key, The" 8, 31, 48, 77, 137, 186, 190, 192, 203, 213, *244–45,* 251, 266–67, 277, 283, 304
Silverman, Kenneth 117
Sime, Sidney 204
Simes 68, *245*
Simple, Percy 257
"Simple Speller's Tale, The" *245*
"Simple Spelling Mania, The" 245
"Sin-Eater, The" (Macleod) 223
Single, ——— *245, 278*
"Sir Thomas Tryout" 216–17
"Skull-Face" (Howard) 52
Slader, Peter 245
Slater (Slaader), Joe 19, 182, *245*
Slauenwite, Dr. Thomas 17, 98, 168, 171, *246,* 285, 302
"Slaying of the Monster, The" (Lovecraft-Barlow) 15
"Sleepy Hollow To-day" 193
Sleght, Adriaen *246*
"Smile, The" 225
Smisor, George T. 16, 189
Smith, Charles W. 84, 125, 152, *246,* 274

Smith, Clark Ashton 1, 16, 20, 24, 43, 51–52, 64, 87, 90, 91, 95, 98, 118, 137, 145, 146, 156, 160, 188, 210, 227, 232, 235, *246–48,* 255, 265, 269–70, 289, 292
Smith, E. E. "Doc" 37, 41
Smith, Eleazar *248*
Smith, Mrs. J. G. 225
Smith, Louis C. 6
Smith, Preserved *248*
Smith, R. Dixon 130
Smith, Simeon 271
Smith, T. R. 269
Smith, William Benjamin 134
Softly, Edward 217
"Some Causes of Self-Immolation" 217, *248*
"Some Current Amateur Verse" 25
Some Current Motives and Practices 5, 24
"Some Dutch Footprints in New England" *248–49,* 260
"Some Lovecraft Sidelights" (Baldwin) 15
"Some Notes on a Nonentity" 78
"Some Notes on Interplanetary Fiction" 48, *249*
"Some Repetitions on the Times" *249*
"Something about Cats." *See* "Cats and Dogs"
Something about Cats and Other Pieces 250
"Sonnet on Myself" 217
"Sonnet Study" 170
Sophonisba 165, *249*
Sorcier, Charles Le 2, 27, 164, *249*
"Space-Eaters, The" (Long) 51, 151, 187
Spengler, Oswald 11
Sphinx, The (Loveman) 158
"Spider, The" (Ewers) 106
Spindrift 179, 180
Spink, Helm C. 26
Sprague, Sophie 115, 249
Sprague, Tom 70, 115, 212, *249–50*
Squires, John D. 241
Squires, Richard D. 153, 155
St. Armand, Barton L. 24, 34, 224, 292
St. John, ——— 117–18, 184, *250*
St. Petersburg Evening Independent 287
"St. Toad's" 218
Stanfield, Kenton, J. 81, 126, 168, *250*
Stanley, John H. 292
Stapledon, Olaf 235, 249

Star-Treader and Other Poems, The
    (Smith) 98, 246, 265
Starrett, [Charles] Vincent *250*, 292
"Statement of Randolph Carter, The" 31,
    62, 157, 187, 191, 245, 247, *250–52,*
    283, 289, 291, 293, 305
Static Electricity 134
Sterling, George 156, 246, 265
Sterling, Kenneth J. 1, 45, 126–27, 250,
    252
Stevens, Francis 217
Stevenson, Robert Louis 271
Stof, Oll 41, *252*
Stoker, Bram 168
Story of Atlantis and the Lost Lemuria,
    The (Scott-Elliott) 29
Strange Case of Dr. Jekyll and Mr. Hyde,
    The (Stevenson) 271
Strange Eons (Blohc) 22
"Strange High House in the Mist, The"
    77, 137, 194, 212, *252–53*, 262
Strange Tales 17, 238, 247, 273, 294,
    300, 302
"Stranger from Kurdistan, The" (Price)
    115, 212
Strauch, Carl Ferdinand 24, *253–54*
"Street, The" *254–55*
Strysik, John xi, 178
Stubbs, Ermengarde 103, 132, 163, *255,*
    257–58, 285
Stubbs, Hiram 103, 255, 257–58
"Suicide, The" (Edkins) 85
"Suggestions for a Reading Guide" 226
"Suggestions for writing weird story . . ."
    190
Sullivan, Jack 131
Sully, Genevieve 255
Sully, Helen V. *255*
"Supernatural Horror in Literature" 20,
    21, 28, 33, 38, 45, 46, 63, 64, 70, 78,
    91, 106, 107, 113, 131, 156, 187, 189,
    202, 205, 207–8, 250, *255–56*
Supernatural Horror in Literature as
    Revised in 1936 45
Supernatural in Modern English Fiction,
    The (Scarborough) 256
Supramundane Stories 95, 190
Surama 39, 141–42, *257*
Suydam, Robert 34, 100, 114, 162, *257*
Swanson, Carl 182, *257*, 294, 305
Sweet Christmas Time (Little) 149
"Sweet Ermengarde; or, The Heart of a
    Country Girl" 103, 132, 149, 163, 255,

257–58, 285
Swift, Augustus T. 218
Swinburne, Algernon Charles 78, 188
Switch On the Light (Thomson) 224
Sylvester, Margaret *259*
Symmes, Mrs. William B. 151
"Symphonic Ideal, The" 124
Symphony 225
"Symphony and Stress" 225
Symphony Literary Service 26, 145, 225
"Systematic Instruction in the United"
    225

"Tale of Satampra Zeiros, The" (Smith)
    51–52, 247
Tale of Terror, The (Birkhead) 256
Tales of Magic and Mystery 46, 47
Tales of Soldiers and Civilians (Bierce)
    19, 36
Tales of Terror 18
Tales of the Cthulhu Mythos (Derleth) 65
Tales of the Folio Club (Poe) 40
Tales of War (Dunsany) 255
"Tales of the Werewolf Clan" (Munn)
    175
Talman, Wilfred Blanch 5, 136, 146,
    221, 249, *260–61*, 275, 279–80
Tarkington, Booth 124
"Task for Amateur Journalists, A" 161
Tchernevsky, Count Feodor 100, *261*
"Temperance Song" 212
"Temple, The" 3, 139, 175, 231, 240,
    261–62, 304, 307
Terrible Old Man, The 252, 253, *262*
"Terrible Old Man, The" 56, 137, 227,
    244, 246, *262*
Terror, The (Machen) 78
"Terror from the Depths, The" (Leiber)
    143
Tesla, Nicola 191
"Teuton's Battle-Song, The" 224
Texaco Star 260
Theobald, Lewis 218
Theobald, Lewis, Jun. 49, 101, 129, 179,
    217–18, 248
Theunis, Constantin *262*, 278
Thing in the Woods, The (Williams) 80
"Thing on the Doorstep, The" 6, 14, 44,
    64, 88, 93, 127, 137, 154, 230, 234,
    262–65, 284, 288, 294, 305
Thompson, C. Hall 54, 65
Thomson, Christine Campbell 7, 205,
    224

Thorfinnssen, Georg 266
Thorndike, Henry 115, 212, 249, 266
Thornton, —— 266
Thoughts and Pictures (Kuntz) 139–40, 246
Three Heroines of New England Romance (Guiney et al.) 102
"Three Hours with H. P. Lovecraft" (Walter) 289
Three Impostors, The (Machen) 28, 161, 283
"Through the Gates of the Silver Key" (Lovecraft-Price) 6, 8, 31, 38, 137, 163, 186, 203, 213, 217, 245, 251, 266–67, 291, 293
Thurber, —— 204–5, 267, 304
Thurston, Francis Wayland 27–28, 29, 131, 268
Tierney, Richard L. 53, 54
"'Till A' the Seas'" (Lovecraft-Barlow) 15, 268, 281
Tillinghast, Ann 32, 268
Tillinghast, Crawford 94, 183–84, 268
Tillinghast, Dutee 268
Tillinghast, Eliza 32, 56, 268, 292
Tilton, Anna 269
Time and the Gods (Dunsany) 52, 78, 191
Time Machine, The (Wells) 235
"Tin Roof, The" (Shea) 240
Tinknor, Caroline 223
T'la-yub 269
"To a Dreamer" 269
"To a Movie Star" (Kleiner) 138, 269
"To a Sophisticated Young Gentleman, Presented by His Grandfather with a Volume of Contemporary Literature" 269
"To a Youth" 97, 217
"To Alan Seeger" 303
"To Alfred Galpin, Esq." 97, 217
"To Arkham and the Stars" (Leiber) 143–44
"To Arthur Goodenough, Esq." 101
"To Charlie of the Comics" 138, 269
"To Clark Ashton Smith, Esq., upon His Phantastick Tales, Verses, Pictures, and Sculptures" 269–70
"To Damon" 217
"To Delia, Avoiding Damon" 97, 217
"To Endymion" 150, 217
"To General Villa" 209
"To George Kirk, Esq. . . ." 137

"To George Willard Kirk, Gent. . . ." 137
"To Howard Phillips Lovecraft" (Smith) 247
"To Howard Phillips Lovecraft" (Weiss) 294
"To J. E. Hoag, Esq. . . ." 217
"To Klarkash-Ton, Lord of Averoigne." See "To Clark Ashton Smith, Esq. . . ."
"To M. W. M." 169
"To Maj.-Gen. Omar Bundy, U.S.A." 217
"To Mary of the Movies" (Kleiner) 138, 269
"To Mistress Sophia Simple, Queen of the Cinema" 138, 217, 269
"To Mr. Finlay, upon His Drawing for Mr. Bloch's Tale, 'The Faceless God'" 93, 270
"To Mr. Galpin . . ." 97, 217
"To Mr. Hoag, on His Ninetieth Birthday" 217
"To Mr. Lockhart, on His Poetry" 150
"To Mr. Theobald" (Loveman) 157
"To Pan" 133, 216
"To Phillis" 217
To Quebec and the Stars 66
"To Rheinhart Kleiner, Esq., upon His Town Fables and Elegies" 217
"To Samuel Loveman, Esquire . . ." 70, 156
"To Satan" (Loveman) 157
"To Selene." See "Ode to Selene or Diana"
"To the American Flag" (Hoag) 112
"To the Eighth of November" 97, 216
"To the Members of the Pinfeathers . . ." 225
"To the Old Pagan Religion" 133, 217
"To the United Amateur Press Association from the Providence Amateur Press Club" 77
"To Zara" 270
Tobey, William 17, 159, 270
Toldridge, Elizabeth [Anne] 18, 95, 270
Toledo Amateur 5
"Tomb, The" 58, 77, 111, 120, 211, 245, 270–72
"Tomb from Beyond, The" (Jacobi) 130
Tomb of Perneb, The 282
Tombaugh, C. W. 298
Torres, Dr. 272
Transatlantic Circulator 25, 124, 193, 218
"Transition of Juan Romero, The" 186,

228, *272–73*
"Trap, The" (Lovecraft-Whitehead) 17, 30–31, 101, 112–13, *273*, 300
Trask, Dr. *273*
Travels, Lovecraft's *273–77*
"Travels in the Provinces of America" 86, 169, 275, *277*
"Tree, The" 77, 97, 137, 170, 178, 246, *277–78*, 292
"Tree-Men of M'Bwa, The" (Wandrei) 290
"Tree on the Hill, The" (Lovecraft-Rimel) 227, 245, 262, *278–79*
Tremaine, F[rederick] Orlin 12, *279*
Trench and Camp 287
Trever, Alfred 98, 193, *279*
Trever, Eleanor (Wing) 193, 279
"Tribute from the Past, A" (Cole) 41
"Trimmings" 129
"Trip of Theobald, The" 246, 274
"True Home of Literature, A" 43
Tryout 35, 56, 59, 77, 84, 85, 101, 125, 130, 138, 150, 152, 168, 175, 193, 212, 226, 246, 262, 277, 283, 287
"Tryout's Lament for the Vanished Spider" 217
Tsathoggua 52, 247
Tucker, Bob 126
Tupper, George Washington 168
Turner, James 152
"20 Webster Street" (Houtain) 119
Twenty-nine Poems (Strauch) 253
Twenty-one Letters of Ambrose Bierce (Bierce-Loveman) 20, 137, 156
"Twilight of Time, The." *See* "Red Brain, The"
"Two Black Bottles" (Lovecraft-Talman) 94, 103, 249, 260, *279–80*, 285
"Two Comments" 54
Two-Gun Bob 17, *280*
Tylor, Edward Burnett 115
Tymn, Marshall 294
T'yog 196–97, *280*
Typer, Alonzo Hasbrouck 67–68, *280*

Ull 268, *281*
Ulysses (Joyce) 194
Unaussprechlichen Kulten (Junzt) 120
"Unbroken Chain, The" (Cobb) 224
"Unda; or, The Bride of the Sea" 217
"Under the Pyramids" (Lovecraft-Houdini) 60, 77, 109, 116–17, 243, *281–83*, 293

"United, 1917–1918, The" 124
United Amateur 2, 4, 5, 9, 25, 41, 50, 60, 63, 85, 88, 93, 129, 138, 145, 148, 150, 157, 169, 188, 190–91, 208, 212, 218, 224, 225, 269, 287, 299
United Co-operative 4, 5, 49, 129, 138, 158, 167, 245
United Amateur Press Association xi, 4–5, 25, 26, 46, 57, 59, 60, 70, 84, 85, 94, 97, 149, 150, 161, 164, 188, 212, 232
United Amateur Press Association: Exponent of Amateur Journalism 4
United Official Quarterly 138, 150
"Unknown, The" 130, 215, *283*
"Unknown City in the Ocean, The" 276
"Unnamable, The" 6, 31, 107, 162, 163, 169, 244, 245, 251, *283–84*
Unterecker, John 48
Unusual Stories 48, 227, 239
Upham, Ronald 176
Upton, Daniel 64, 263–64, *284*
Upton, Winslow 227
Utpatel, Frank 239, *284*
Utter, Virgil S. 140, 171

Vagrant 18, 38, 46, 57, 99, 101, 186, 188, 208, 218, 250, 270
"Valley of Unrest, The" (Poe) 167
Van Allister, Prof. Arthur 8, 25, 219, *285*
Van Calenbergh, Hubert 12, 224
Van de Water, F. F. 19
van der Heyl, Claes *285*
van der Heyl, Dirck 246, 285
van der Heyl, Hendrik 285
van der Heyl, Joris 285
van der Heyl, Trintje 246, 285
Vanderhoof, Johannes 94, 103, 279, *285*
Van Itty, Mrs. 258, *285*
Van Keulen, Dr. Cornelius *285*
Van Vechten, Carl 256
Vathek (Beckford) 13, 74, 187
Vaughan, Ralph E. 96, 212
"Vaults of Yoh-Vombis, The" (Smith) 247
Verhaeren, M. *285*
"Vermont—A First Impression" 274, *286*, 297
Verne, Jules 132, 150
"Vers Libre Epidemic, The" 124, 225
"Very Old Folk, The" 7, 14, 147, 228, *286*
View from a Hill, A (Barlow) 16
Vilaseca, David 34

Vincent, Harl 37
Virgil 286
"Vivisector, The" 218, *286–87*
"Volunteer, The" *287, 303*
Voss, Richard 20, 62
Voyages of Capt. Ross, R.N., The 10, 134

Waite, Asenath 14, 64, 230, 263–65, 284, *288*
Waite, Ephraim 263, 288
Walakea *288*
"Walks with H. P. Lovecraft" (Eddy) 84
Walter, Dorothy C[harlotte] *288–89*
"Wanderer's Return" (Lovecraft-Shepherd) 241
Wandering Ghosts (Crawford) 289
Wandrei, Donald [Albert] 16, 18, 30, 34, 37, 52, 64–65, 99, 146, 147, 173, 205, 247, 255, 279, 286, *289–90*
Wandrei, Howard [Elmer] *290–91*
Ward, Charles Dexter 32, 33, 34, 56, 81, 120, 160, 195, 265, *291, 301*
Ward, Harold 292
Ward, Richard 34, 131
Ward, Theodore Howland *291*
"Ward Phillips Replies" 124, 216
Warren, Harley 245, 250–51, *291*
Waste Land, The (Eliot) 124, 210, 291
"Waste Paper: A Poem of Profound Insignficance" 210, 216, *291–92*
Watchers out of Time and Others, The (Derleth) 65
Waugh, Robert H. 96, 199, 207
Wayland, Francis 29
Web of Easter Island, The (Wandrei) 289
Webb, William Channing *292*
Weber, Brom 158
Weeden, Ezra 32, 56, 248, *292*
Weeden, Hazard 292
Weinbaum, Stanley G. 37
Weinberg, Robert 294
Weinstein, Lee 38
Weir, John J. *292*
"Weird Story Plots" 190
"Weird Tale in English Since 1890, The" (Derleth) 64
Weird Tales 5, 6, 7, 11, 12, 14, 20, 22, 24, 27, 30, 31, 34, 35, 36, 43, 46, 47, 51, 55, 57, 61, 62, 64, 67, 68, 69, 75, 76, 79, 81, 84, 85, 87, 89, 90, 92, 93, 94, 96, 100, 105, 106, 107, 109–10, 113, 114, 115, 116, 117, 119, 120, 123,

124, 125, 126, 127, 130, 140, 141, 142, 143, 150, 151, 156, 159, 164, 165, 166, 170, 173, 174, 175, 176, 181, 182, 188, 196, 197, 202, 204, 206, 208, 211, 212, 213, 218, 220, 221, 222, 223, 227, 232, 237, 238, 241, 244, 245, 247, 250, 252, 253, 257, 260, 261, 262, 265, 266, 267, 269, 270, 277, 279, 281, 282, 283, 286, 289, 290, *292–94*, 296, 298, 299, 300, 301, 302, 304–5
"Weird Work of William Hope Hodgson, The" 112, 139, 302
"Weird Writer Is In Our Midst, A" (Orton) 195
Weiss, Ehrich. *See* Houdini, Harry
Weiss, Henry George *294*
Well-Bred Speech (Renshaw) 225–26
Wells, H. G. 11, 150, 235, 249, 256
"Wendigo, The" (Blackwood) 20, 80
"Werewolf of Ponkert, The" (Munn) 175
West, Herbert 39, 103, 110–11, 143, 184, 228, 250, *294*, 304
West India Lights (Whitehead) 273, 300
Wetzel, George T. 16, 54, 130, 148, 198, 218
"What Amateurdom and I Have Done for Each Other" 5, 63
"What Belongs in Verse" *294–95*
"What Is Amateur Journalism?" 216
"What the Moon Brings" 186, *295*
"What Was It?" (O'Brien) 80
Whateley, Curtis 295
Whateley, Lavinia 79, 295
Whateley, Mrs. 295
Whateley, Old 62, 79, 117, 295
Whateley, Squire Sawyer 295
Whateley, Wilbur 7, 25, 48, 62, 79, 91, 171, 195, 227, 230–31, *295*
Whateley, Zebulon 295
Whateley, Zechariah 295
"What's the Matter with Weird Fiction?" 303
Wheeler, Arthur 107, 129, 162, *295*
Wheeler, Henry *295*
Wheelock, Alan S. 298
"When Sonia Sizzled" (de la Ree) 61
Whipple, Dr. Elihu 39, 186, 242, 243, *295–96*
"Whisperer in Darkness, The" x, 2, 25, 52, 53, 58, 81, 96, 101, 116, 161, 190, 195, 247, 270, 277, 286, *296–98*, 301
"'Whisperer' Re-examined, The" (Leiber) 144

White, Ann *299*
White, Lee McBride, Jr. *299*
White, Michael Oscar 157
"White Ape, The." *See* "Facts Concerning the Late Arthur Jermyn and His Family"
"White Elephant, The" (Lovecraft-Barlow) 24
"White People, The" (Machen) 42, 162
"White Ship, The" 74, 77, 87, *299–300*
White Fire (Bullen) 25
Whitehead, Henry S[t. Clair] 16, 17, 30–31, 146, 273, 275, *300–301*
Whitman, Sarah Helen (Power) 223
Whitman, Walt 123, 127, 128
Whittier, John Greenleaf 13
"Wicked Clergyman, The." *See* "Evil Clergyman, The"
Wilcox, Henry Anthony 6, 27, 29, 104, *301*
Wild Empire (Searight) 232
Wilde, Oscar 124, 198
Wilkes's Explorations 10, 134
Willett, Dr. Marinus Bicknell 32, 34, 39, 56, 81, 120, 195, 291, *301*
"William Wilson" (Poe) 198
Williams, ——— 66, 190, *301*
Williams, Blanche Colton 192
Williams, Harper 80
Williams, Roger 6
Williamson, Douglas 301
Williamson, James 194, *301*
Williamson, Lawrence 301
Willie, Albert Frederick 98, 218
Willis, John *301*
"Willows, The" (Blackwood) 20, 21, 102
Wilmarth, Albert N. 2, 190, 296–98, *301*
Wilson, Alison Morley 65
Wilson, Colin 198
Wilson, Dr. *301*
Wilson, Woodrow 304
"Wind That Is In the Grass, The" (Barlow) 16
Winesburg, Ohio (Anderson) 90
Wing, Eleanor. *See* Trever, Eleanor (Wing)
"Winged Death" (Lovecraft-Heald) 17, 98, 109, 168, 171, 246, 285, *301–2*
"Winifred Virginia Jackson: A 'Different' Poetess" 129
"Winifred Virginia Jordan: Associate Editor" 129, 216
Winskill, Benjamin 179

Winter Garden (Morse) 172
Wise, Herbert A. 81, 224
"Wisdom" 215, 216, *302*
Witch-Cult in Western Europe, The (Murray) 93
"Within the Circle" (Baldwin) 14
"Within the Gates" 5
Wolejko, Anastasia *302*
Wolejko, Ladislas 302
Wolf, Howard 138
Wollheim, Donald A[llen] 146, 182, 241, *302–3*
Wolverine 89, 90, 181, 254, 286–87
"Wood, The" 21, 210, 218
Wonder Stories 1, 113, 126, 127, 130, 162, 232, 247, 252
Wooley, Natalie H[artley] *303*
"Work of Frank Belknap Long, Jun., The" 150
World War I *303–4*
Wormius, Olaus 187, 224
"Worms of the Earth" (Howard) 119
Wright, Farnsworth 12, 24, 30, 46, 51, 54, 76, 92, 109, 119, 123, 125, 126, 146, 174, 212, 223, 238–29, 245, 257, 265, 267, 289, 293, 298, 301, *304–5*
Writer's Digest 143

Xélucha" (Shiel) 241

"Year Off, A" *306*
Yergler, Rudolf 278
Yesley, ——— 43, 143
Yog-Sothoth 51, 79, 295
Young, S. Hall 302
Youth's Companion 246, 302
Yuggoth 96
Yurregarth and Yannimaid (Farnese) 91

Zachrau, Thekla 54
Zamacona y Nuñez, Panfilo de 38, 101, 173–74, 185, 269, *307*
Zanger, Jules 12
Zann, Erich 176–78, 185, *307*
Zenith 119
Zimmer, ——— *307*
Zoilus 90, 218, 286–8

About the Authors

S. T. JOSHI is a widely published freelance author and editor. He has compiled bibliographies of H. P. Lovecraft (1981), Lord Dunsany (1993), Ramsey Campbell (1995), and Ambrose Bierce (1999), and is the author of several critical and biographical studies, including *The Weird Tale* (1990), *Lord Dunsany: Master of the Anglo-Irish Imagination* (1995), *H. P. Lovecraft: A Life* (1996), and *The Modern Weird Tale* (2001). He has prepared editions of Lovecraft's collected fiction, poetry, and essays, and other annotated editions, including *The Call of Cthulhu and Other Weird Stories* (1999), *The Thing on the Doorstep and Other Weird Stories* (2001), and *The Dreams in the Witch House and Other Weird Stories* (2004). He has also edited Bierce's *Collected Fables* (2000), *The Unabridged Devil's Dictionary* (2000), and *A Much Misunderstood Man: Selected Letters* (2003), as well as *Documents of American Prejudice* (1999) and *Atheism: A Reader* (2000).

DAVID E. SCHULTZ is a technical editor for an environmental engineering firm in Milwaukee. He edited a critical edition of H. P. Lovecraft's *Commonplace Book* (1987), and with S. T. Joshi has edited several works by and about Ambrose Bierce, including *A Sole Survivor: Bits of Autobiography* (1998); *The Unabridged Devil's Dictionary; The Fall of the Republic and Other Political Satires* (2000); *A Much Misunderstood Man: Selected Letters* (2003), and the Bierce bibliography, and works of H. P. Lovecraft, including *Lord of a Visible World: An Autobiography in Letters* (2000), *The Shadow out of Time* (2001; annotated), *Mysteries of Time and Spirit: The Letters of H. P. Lovecraft and Donald Wandrei* (2002), and *Letters from New York* (2004). With Joshi, he is editing Bierce's collected fiction and other volumes of Lovecraft's letters.

Printed in the United Kingdom by
Lightning Source UK Ltd., Milton Keynes
139068UK00001B/133/A